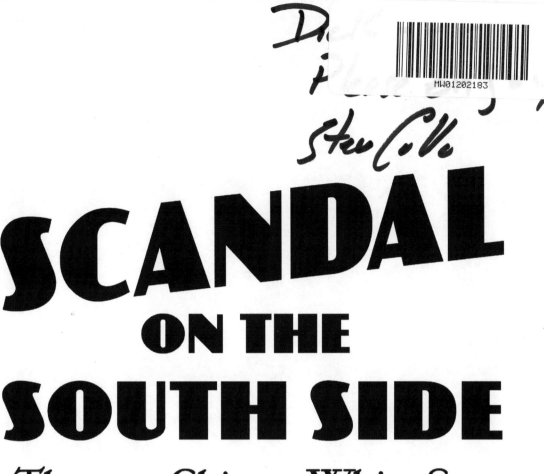

SCANDAL
ON THE
SOUTH SIDE

The 1919 Chicago White Sox

Edited by Jacob Pomrenke

Associate Editors: Rick Huhn, Bill Nowlin, Len Levin

Society for American Baseball Research, Inc.

Phoenix, AZ

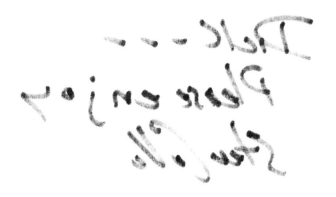

Scandal on the South Side: The 1919 Chicago White Sox
Edited by Jacob Pomrenke
Associate editors Rick Huhn, Bill Nowlin, Len Levin

ISBN 978-1-933599-95-3
(Ebook ISBN 978-1-933599-94-6)

Cover and book design: Gilly Rosenthol, Rosenthol Design

Cover photo: National Baseball Hall of Fame Library, Cooperstown, New York

Society for American Baseball Research
Cronkite School at ASU
555 N. Central Ave. #416
Phoenix, AZ 85004
Phone: (602) 496-1460

Web: www.sabr.org
Facebook: Society for American Baseball Research
Twitter: @SABR

TABLE OF CONTENTS

INTRODUCTION

ON THE WESTERN EDGE OF Canada's Yukon Territory, at the confluence of the Yukon and Klondike Rivers just across the border from Alaska, is an old mining town called Dawson City, population 1,300. At the turn of the twentieth century, Dawson City became the bustling center of the Klondike Gold Rush and drew the likes of writer Jack London and others searching for fame and fortune. But the golden dream quickly died for thousands of prospectors, and the town returned to its sleepy roots, the end of the line for the Klondike Highway and any travelers who happened to be heading north on it.

Dawson City also happened to be the end of the line for hundreds of silent films that were shown to residents in the town's recreation hall during the 1910s and '20s. These films were sometimes full-length features, but many were newsreels of current events, comedy shorts, or human-interest stories shown before the main event. The nitrate film reels were too expensive—and too dangerous, since they were highly explosive—to ship back south when folks in Dawson City were finished watching them, so it was easier to dispose of them. Instead of dumping the tin canisters in the Yukon River, the most common disposal method at the time, town leaders decided to bury them under an abandoned swimming pool that was used as an ice-hockey rink.

The films remained there, preserved pristinely in the permafrost, for a half-century until 1978, when construction workers razed the ice rink and discovered the buried treasure underneath. The find made international headlines. It took many years before the highly flammable reels could be safely moved across the country, transferred to modern formats, and made available to researchers. Some of them still have never been seen.

In January 2014 a Chicago filmmaker, Bill Morrison, visiting the Library and Archives Canada found one of these old Dawson City film reels with the curious label "1919 World Series." What he discovered was remarkable: never-before-seen newsreel footage featuring nearly five minutes of game action from that notorious World Series in which Shoeless Joe Jackson, Buck Weaver, Eddie Cicotte, and other members of the Chicago White Sox were banned for intentionally throwing games to the Cincinnati Reds—an event that has gone down in history as the Black Sox Scandal.

This rare newsreel, which was originally filmed by the British Canadian Pathé News service, is not the first footage ever seen from the 1919 World Series. But it's by far the most extensive and highest quality of film available from that fateful fall classic. The film shows some of the most disputed and discussed plays from Games One and Three, along with aerial views of Redland (later Crosley) Field in Cincinnati, and candid shots of players from both teams.

And now we can watch it on YouTube, over and over again.

The Dawson City film is one of many exciting discoveries related to the 1919 World Series and the Black Sox Scandal that have come to light in recent years. As Gene Carney—the late founding chairman of SABR's Black Sox Scandal Research Committee, whose members produced the book you're about to read—liked to say, "The Black Sox Scandal is a cold case, not a closed case." Thanks to these amazing finds, we're learning more and more about the 1919 World Series all the time.

In his classic history of the 1919 World Series, *Eight Men Out*, Eliot Asinof told a dramatic story of undereducated and underpaid ballplayers, disgruntled by their low pay and poor treatment by White Sox management, who fell prey to the wiles of double-crossing big-city gamblers offering them bribes to lose the World Series. Asinof's story does contain elements of truth: Eight White Sox players, including Shoeless Joe Jackson, perhaps the greatest pure hitter of his generation, *did* throw the World Series. And they *did* receive bribes of $5,000 or more to do the deed that got them kicked out of baseball. But the devil is in the details, and it's in those details where much of the popular narrative about the Black Sox Scandal falls apart under close scrutiny—specifically, any notion that the banished players were undereducated or underpaid, or that they were unwittingly seduced by gamblers, or that the Big Fix brought about a loss of innocence in baseball that nearly destroyed, in F. Scott Fitzgerald's famous phrase, "the faith of fifty million" fans until Babe Ruth came along to rescue the national pastime with his prodigious home runs. All of that is simply untrue.

We can say this with some certainty now because we have access to so much new information that Eliot Asinof and many other writers never had. In the late 1950s, when Asinof began his research for what turned into *Eight Men Out*, he searched high and low for the transcripts and testimony from the Black Sox grand-jury proceedings and criminal trial. He never found them. We know where to find a copy of them now: at the Chicago History Museum, which in 2007 acquired a "treasure trove" of documents related to the scandal that included hundreds of legal files that had eluded researchers for decades before.

We also have accurate salary information about major-league players in 1919 for the first time, thanks to a massive collection of organizational contract cards acquired in 2002 by the National Baseball Hall of Fame Library in Cooperstown, New York. We have access to hundreds of articles about gamblers and underworld figures involved in the scandal who were almost impossible to track down before.

Some of this information was both uncovered and included by the late Gene Carney in his seminal 2006 book *Burying the Black Sox: How Baseball's Cover-Up of the 1919 World Series Fix Almost Succeeded*. He broke new ground on the story of Shoeless Joe Jackson's civil lawsuit against the White Sox after his suspension from baseball and he cast serious doubt on what baseball officials knew about the World Series fix, when they knew it, and what they did about it. Carney's tremendous generosity in sharing his research also helped inspire another generation of Black Sox sleuths to pick up the cold—not closed—case after he died in 2009. Additional insight into the case was provided by author and retired prosecutor William F. Lamb in *Black Sox in the Courtroom: The Grand Jury, Criminal Trial and Civil Litigation*, published in 2013. (Lamb is a contributing author to this book.)

All of these new pieces fit somewhere in the big Black Sox puzzle, providing definitive answers to some old mysteries and raising other questions in their place. The book you're reading now, published by the Society for American Baseball Research, will integrate all of that new information about the scandal for the first time.

However, the Black Sox Scandal isn't the only story worth telling about the 1919 Chicago White Sox. The team included three future Hall of Famers (Eddie Collins, Ray Schalk, and Red Faber), a 20-year-old spitballer who would go on to win 300 games in the minor leagues (Frank Shellenback), a rookie manager (Kid Gleason) who had a colorful playing career as a pitcher and second baseman for two decades, and even a batboy (Eddie Bennett) who later became a celebrity with the "Murderers' Row" New York Yankees in the 1920s.

All of their stories are included in this book, too, which has full-life biographies of each of the 31 players who made an appearance for the White Sox in 1919, plus team executives like owner Charles Comiskey, Harry Grabiner, and Tip O'Neill. We've also included a comprehensive recap of the White Sox' pennant-winning season, which culminated in Shoeless Joe Jackson's dramatic walk-off single to clinch the American League championship in September at Comiskey Park. The year 1919 was a notorious one in Chicago, and baseball fans in the Windy City could not escape the real world during that hot, violent postwar summer of race riots, the anti-communist "Red Scare," and the lingering flu epidemic, all of which had an effect on the White Sox's season. Those stories are also in this book.

In addition, we'll also clear up some of the misconceptions about the 1919 White Sox team that have been passed down through history. After reading this book, you'll know the real story behind Charles Comiskey's reputation as a greedy miser who forced his players to play in dirty, unlaundered uniforms. You'll learn about the $10,000 bonus allegedly promised to star pitcher Eddie Cicotte if he won 30 games that season. You'll learn new details about the complicated Black Sox legal proceedings, their "disappearing" confessions, and the reasons behind their acquittal in a Chicago courtroom. And you'll learn how uneducated and underpaid the White Sox really were, as compared to other players around the American League.

This book isn't a rewriting of *Eight Men Out*, but it is the complete story of everyone associated with the 1919 Chicago White Sox, told in full for the first time. We'll help bring you up to date on what we collectively know about the Black Sox Scandal and the infamous team at the center of it all. We won't take sides on whether certain players were guilty or whether they were punished fairly. We just present the best available information to you—and as you can tell by now, there's a lot of new information out there. With this book, we hope to challenge your assumptions and help you gain a better understanding of what historians Harold Seymour and Dorothy Seymour called "baseball's darkest hour"—the fixing of the 1919 World Series by key members of the Chicago White Sox.

Jacob Pomrenke
Phoenix, Arizona
February 1, 2015

PROLOGUE: OFFSEASON, 1918-19

By Jacob Pomrenke

IT'S ACCEPTED WISDOM TODAY that the Chicago White Sox, in the final years of the Deadball Era, were on their way to becoming one of the greatest teams in baseball history. Led by Shoeless Joe Jackson, Eddie Collins, and Ray Schalk in the field and Eddie Cicotte, Lefty Williams, and Red Faber on the mound, the White Sox captured a World Series championship in 1917 and were in serious contention to win two more titles in 1919 and 1920. If not for the corruption of the eight Black Sox players who were later banned from Organized Baseball for fixing the 1919 World Series, there's no telling how good they might have been for years to come.

But few observers shared that opinion about the White Sox entering the 1919 season. Coming off a disastrous sixth-place finish in a year shortened by World War I, and with a surprising managerial change in the offseason, South Side fans weren't sure what to expect when their team took the field on Opening Day. You could say the same about baseball itself: Now that the Great War was finally over, no one quite knew what to expect.

Baseball in 1919 was at a crossroads—between the pitching-dominated Deadball Era that was about to end and the glamorous, home-run-happy era that was to epitomize the Roaring Twenties. Babe Ruth was already a star with the Boston Red Sox, but he was known as the best left-handed pitcher in the American League and not for his hitting exploits yet to come. Earlier in the decade, the major leagues had survived the threat of the upstart Federal League, which had folded due to financial troubles after challenging the American League and National League for supremacy. Nearly every major-league team was playing its games in new concrete-and-steel stadiums built within the last decade. Few ballparks were more celebrated than Charles Comiskey's "baseball palace of the world" at the corner of 35th Street and Shields Avenue in Chicago. The White Sox would call Comiskey Park home for 80 years.

Baseball then was still a rough-and-tumble game, played by "shysters, con men, drunks, and outright thieves … [and] midwestern farm boys who came out of cow pasture Sunday leagues," as author Bill James put it in his *Historical Baseball Abstract*. Gambling was rampant within baseball, and the two pastimes enjoyed an intimate, mutually beneficial relationship. Thousands of fans participated in popular daily or weekly "baseball pools," similar to modern fantasy football leagues and basketball tournament brackets. Ballplayers also mixed freely with underworld figures at saloons, casinos, and pool halls in every city, offering insider tips and sometimes even placing bets on their own games. At some ballparks, notably Fenway Park and Braves Field in Boston, bettors congregated in certain sections of the grandstands to conveniently make wagers on the game taking place on the field. Baseball's powers-that-be looked the other way because profits were strong and attendance was high.

But America's involvement in World War I had disrupted the entire sport in 1918. Attendance at Comiskey Park dropped by more than 70 percent from the White Sox' championship season of a year before. In July, the US government issued a mandatory "work or fight" order that affected most major-league players, who were forced to decide between enlisting in the military or taking a job deemed essential to the war effort. With their teams' rosters depleted, baseball owners abruptly ended the season in early September and a lackluster World Series was played between the Boston Red Sox and Chicago Cubs. Like many fall classics played during the Deadball Era, the 1918 World Series was troubled by rumors of game-fixing, although any evidence to prove that the Series had been tampered with was thin. The White Sox ended the disappointing season on an eight-game losing streak, finishing with a 57-67 record, 17 games behind the champion Red Sox.

Baseball owners were so rattled by the low attendance and lack of enthusiasm for baseball in 1918 that they decided to shorten the 1919 season to 140 games from the normal 154. Almost every team had lost money because of the war; the Yankees and White Sox each claimed a net loss of more than $45,000 in 1918 and, in a rare gesture, White Sox owner Charles Comiskey chose to cut his own salary to $5,000, lower than even those of a handful of his own players. In another attempt to cut costs, National League owners in January 1919 approved an $11,000-per-month player salary cap, which worked out to a team payroll of less than $58,000 in a 140-game season, according to baseball historian Bob Hoie. American League clubs refused to go along with the plan, and even some NL clubs completely ignored it, so the plan was quickly forgotten. The White Sox team payroll on Opening Day 1919 turned out to be $88,461, just under those of the Yankees and the defending champion Red Sox as the highest among all major-league clubs; the Cincinnati Reds were at $76,870, which would have ranked them only sixth highest in the American League.

The owners' decision to shorten the schedule also had the effect of cutting most players' salaries, since players were paid only for the time they were in season, from Opening Day to the final scheduled game. For instance, Joe Jackson's $1,000-per-month contract, which normally earned him $6,000 from the White Sox, came out to only $5,250 in 1919. (Comiskey made it up to him, according to Hoie's research, with a $750 bonus if he were a "member of the Chicago club in good standing" after the season, thereby bringing his compensation back to the usual $6,000.) Chick Gandil, on the other hand, was paid only $3,500 on his $666.66-per-month contract instead of his usual $4,000 because of the shortened season. He received no bonus, at least not from Comiskey.

The "work or fight" order was the major story in baseball in 1918. With the war looming over their

White Sox team photo (National Baseball Hall of Fame Library, Cooperstown, N.Y.)

heads all summer, ballplayers who chose to enlist in the military—like future Hall of Famers Ty Cobb and Christy Mathewson—were celebrated for their service to the country. But any able-bodied professional athlete who chose to take a war-essential job rather than enlist, even if his draft status allowed him to do so when he had a family to support, came under heavy criticism from the press and the public.

No one in baseball found himself under more scrutiny in 1918 than the White Sox' star left fielder, Joe Jackson. Just after the season began, he learned that his draft board in Greenville, South Carolina, had changed his status to 1-A. He had been initially spared from military service because he was married. Instead of waiting for the Army to call his number, Jackson controversially quit the team in May and took a job at a Delaware shipyard, where he and White Sox teammate Lefty Williams (who had left the Sox shortly after Jackson) led the company's baseball team to an industrial-league championship.

Just one day after Jackson left the White Sox, Army Gen. Enoch Crowder began an investigation into the disproportionate number of professional athletes who had suddenly taken "bomb-proof" jobs in the shipyards. Jackson was by no means the only player with a cushy job where his most strenuous duties involved swinging a baseball bat, but he was singled out as a symbol of the "unpatriotic" draft-dodgers who were avoiding combat in Europe. In contrast, Jackson's teammate Eddie Collins joined the Marine Corps in August 1918, three months before the war ended, and he was widely praised for his service—even though he spent most of his time at a military base in Pennsylvania, a few long fly balls away from where Jackson and Williams were stationed.

Comiskey publicly vowed never to let Jackson or the other "paint and putty league" ballplayers—Williams, outfielder Happy Felsch, and backup catcher Byrd Lynn—play for the White Sox again. Rumors circulated during the offseason that Comiskey intended to trade away one or both of his top outfielders, Jackson and Felsch. At the American League's annual meeting in December, one month after the armistice was signed

to end World War I, Comiskey supported a resolution to blacklist any shipyard players from rejoining the majors. But his stance softened when he realized he would have to rebuild his championship team all over again, and with a nudge from new manager Kid Gleason (who reportedly agreed to take the job only if Comiskey re-signed all of his old players), he soon sent contract offers to Jackson and the others. Still, no one knew how Shoeless Joe would be treated by the fans once the 1919 season began.

The division between enlisted soldiers and shipyard workers wasn't the only fault line in the White Sox clubhouse. Even while the White Sox were winning the World Series in 1917, they were a team riddled with dissension.

One clique was led by the second baseman Eddie Collins, a college-educated aristocrat from New York whose nickname "Cocky" was well earned. The two rough-and-tumble Californians who flanked him in the infield, first baseman Chick Gandil and shortstop Swede Risberg, hated Collins so much that they reportedly refused to throw the ball his way during practice. Another group on the team consisted of quiet Southerners like Joe Jackson and Lefty Williams, who generally kept to themselves. Collins later said, "There were frequent arguments and open hostility. All the things you think—and are taught to believe—are vital to the success of any athletic organization were missing from (the White Sox), and yet it was the greatest collection of players ever assembled, I would say."

All of the White Sox starters from their 1917 World Series team had returned to the fold, including pitchers Eddie Cicotte, Lefty Williams, and Red Faber, plus future Hall of Famers Eddie Collins at second base and Ray Schalk behind the plate. Joe Jackson and Happy Felsch anchored the outfield and powered the middle of Chicago's potent lineup, while Buck Weaver, Swede Risberg, and Chick Gandil rounded out the AL's best infield.

The faces on the field were familiar, but the manager leading them was new—sort of. On New Year's Eve,

December 31, 1918, owner Charles Comiskey made a surprise announcement that he had dismissed Pants Rowland as manager after four seasons. Rowland had managed the White Sox since 1915 and had steadily improved their place in the standings each year, from third place to second place to a World Series championship. He could hardly be blamed for the sixth-place effort during the tumultuous 1918 campaign. But Comiskey—who had never retained a White Sox manager for longer than four seasons—sensed his veteran team needed a new man in charge.

Rowland's replacement was the White Sox' longtime coach, William "Kid" Gleason, who had spent more than three decades in baseball but had never managed in the major leagues. The 52-year-old Gleason had been a star pitcher and second baseman around the turn of the twentieth century. As a White Sox assistant coach since 1912 under Rowland and previous manager Nixey Callahan, Gleason had played a key role in developing the team's young infielders like Weaver, Risberg, and Fred McMullin. The new boss was well liked and respected throughout the game.

But like Joe Jackson, Gleason had also quit the White Sox in 1918, sitting out the entire season in what was widely believed to be a financial dispute with Comiskey. On the day Gleason was hired as manager, Comiskey responded to newspaper reports that he had failed to pay Gleason a promised bonus after the White Sox won the 1917 World Series: "Nothing was ever at any time mentioned as to a bonus, and he received everything due him from the White Sox." (The same accusation against Comiskey was later repeated by some of the banished Black Sox players when they filed lawsuits seeking back pay owed to them.) There is no record of how Comiskey and Gleason finally settled the grievance.

In any case, Comiskey put aside his personal problems with Gleason and hired a manager he felt could get the most out of his veteran ballclub. James Crusinberry of the *Chicago Tribune* praised the move, writing on January 1, "No one was ever shrewder in a game of ball.... There isn't a ballplayer in the game today or any of those who played with the Kid in the old days who will not declare him as fair and square a man on and off the ball field as ever lived."

As the White Sox headed to spring training in Mineral Wells, Texas, no one was quite sure how Gleason's team would fare in the pennant race. The White Sox' lack of pitching depth behind Eddie Cicotte and Lefty Williams was cited as a major concern by *Chicago Tribune* reporter Irving Sanborn, who predicted on April 20, "Unless he has a lot of luck developing new pitchers … (Gleason) is going to have a hard time keeping his team in the first division of the American League." Veteran Red Faber, who had won three games in the 1917 World Series, was hampered by arm and ankle injuries, and he had come down with the flu virus and could not shake it. A global influenza epidemic had killed more than 600,000 Americans in the winter of 1918-19 alone. Faber's condition was noticeably weak during spring training and it took him all year to fully recover.

The White Sox had plenty of unproven candidates to take Faber's place in the pitching rotation. But only

Eddie Collins and Kid Gleason, circa 1921 (Bain Collection, Library of Congress, Prints and Photographs Division)

WHITE SOX AT COMISKEY
PARK, 1919

St. Louis	May 1, 2, 3, 4
Detroit	May 5, 6, 7
Boston	May 14, 15, 16
Philadelphia	May 17, 18, 19, 20
New York	May 21, 22, 23, 24
Washington	May 25, 26, 27
Cleveland	May 30, 30, 31, June 1
Cleveland	June 23, 24, 25
Detroit	July 4, 4, 5, 6
Philadelphia	July 9, 10, 11
Boston	July 12, 13, 14, 15
Washington	July 16, 17, 18, 19
New York	July 20, 21, 22
St. Louis	July 24, 25, 26, 27
Boston	Aug. 14, 15, 16
Philadelphia	Aug. 17, 18, 19
Washington	Aug. 20, 21, 22
New York	Aug. 23, 24, 25
Cleveland	Sept. 5, 6, 7
St. Louis	Sept. 24, 25
Detroit	Sept. 26, 27, 28

1919 White Sox team schedule on the back of a season pass
(Courtesy of Mike Nola / BlackBetsy.com)

Dickey Kerr, a 25-year-old left-hander from Missouri, would emerge from the pack of rookies to contribute to Chicago's success in 1919. Kid Gleason had to rely heavily on his stars Cicotte and Williams to carry the load, and they were up to the challenge, recording 52 of the team's 88 wins during the regular season. Even Gleason was a bit surprised at how dependable his top two pitchers turned out to be.

The batting lineup didn't have much depth, either—only Fred McMullin and Shano Collins received significant playing time among the reserves—and if not for the normal aches and pains and slumps over the course of a long season, Gleason would have been happy penciling in the same eight starters every day in this order:

Nemo Leibold, RF

Eddie Collins, 2B
Buck Weaver, 3B
Joe Jackson, LF
Happy Felsch, CF
Chick Gandil, 1B
Swede Risberg, SS
Ray Schalk, C

For a franchise long saddled with the nickname "Hitless Wonders," these White Sox had a powerful offensive attack. They would go on to lead the American League in hits, runs scored, and stolen bases. Jackson batted .351, fourth highest in the AL, and finished among the league leaders in slugging, on-base percentage, RBIs, and total bases.

As the White Sox took the field for Opening Day on April 23, 1919, against the St. Louis Browns at Sportsman's Park, it quickly became apparent to the rest of the American League that all the preseason fears about their chances were premature. Chicago's 13-4 win behind Lefty Williams's complete-game effort and Joe Jackson's three hits showed that the Sox were back in championship form. Manager Kid Gleason never stopped worrying about his over-reliance on Williams and Eddie Cicotte and continued to look for pitching help wherever he could find it, but for now, the season's outlook appeared extremely bright.

SOURCES

"Bombproof Jobs of Ball Players Due For Probing," *Chicago Tribune*, May 16, 1918.

"Commy Tells His Side of the Felsch Story," *Chicago Tribune*, January 1, 1919.

Crusinberry, Jim. "Kid Gleason Appointed Manager of the White Sox," *Chicago Tribune*, January 1, 1919.

Deveney, Sean. *The Original Curse: Did the Cubs Throw the 1918 World Series to Babe Ruth's Red Sox and Incite the Black Sox Scandal* (New York: McGraw-Hill, 2009).

Hoie, Bob. "1919 Baseball Salaries and the Mythically Underpaid Chicago White Sox." *Base Ball: A Journal of the Early Game* (Jefferson, North Carolina: McFarland & Co., Spring 2012).

Huhn, Rick. *Eddie Collins: A Baseball Biography* (Jefferson, North Carolina: McFarland & Co., 2008).

James, Bill. *The New Bill James Historical Baseball Abstract* (New York: Free Press, 2001).

Leeke, Jim. "The Delaware River Shipbuilding League, 1918," *The National Pastime: From Swampoodle to South Philly* (Phoenix, Arizona: Society for American Baseball Research, 2013).

Sanborn, Irving. "Baseball Races Start on Wednesday," *Chicago Tribune*, April 20, 1919.

JOE BENZ

By William F. Lamb

UNTIL AGE AND ARM MISERIES precipitated his release in May 1919, right-hander Joe Benz was a valuable member of the Chicago White Sox pitching corps. During the preceding eight seasons, Benz had alternated between the starting rotation, spot-starter duty, and long relief, never posting an ERA higher than 2.90. Usually overshadowed by mound mates like Ed Walsh, Red Faber, and Eddie Cicotte, Joe found his moment in the spotlight in May 1914, when he pitched a no-hitter, the fifth in White Sox history. Apart from that and a solid major-league career, he achieved another distinction of sorts: Joe Benz was, by all accounts, a genuinely decent man.

The future White Sox hurler was born Joseph Louis Benz in New Alsace, Indiana, on January 21, 1886, the second of four children born to Michael Benz (d. 1941) and his wife, Mary, née Wilhelm (d. 1929).[1] The Benz family was of German Catholic stock, Joe's grandfather, also named Michael, having emigrated from the Grand Duchy of Baden in 1849. Upon arriving in New Alsace, Michael the patriarch established the meat-butchering business that would sustain the Benz clan for the next three generations. In 1892 Joe's father and two uncles relocated to Batesville, Indiana, where they opened Benz Brothers, on-premise butchers and purveyors of livestock products. The enterprise quickly prospered, affording employment to many in the extended Benz family, including young Joe.[2]

A strapping youth — baseball references usually list him at 6-feet-1, 194 pounds — Benz began playing baseball for the Batesville Reserves and other local nines at about the age of 14. By 1904 Joe had switched from the outfield to the mound, overpowering area competition with a fastball that earned him the moniker Blitzen (German for lightning) Benz. He also developed a serviceable curve, a knuckler, and the pitch that would become his big-league meal ticket: a quick-breaking spitball.

The date of Benz's entry into the professional ranks is difficult to pinpoint. One account has him signing a $125-a-month contract with a White Sox scout in 1908.[3] Yet local newspapers are replete with accounts of Joe pitching for Batesville that season.[4] Those same sources establish that he began the 1909 season with the Clarksburg (West Virginia) Bees of the Class D Pennsylvania-West Virginia League.[5] But an early-season arm injury, the first of the throwing ailments that would plague Benz's career, prompted his release. He returned home to recuperate and was soon in the outfield for the Batesville nine.[6] Thereafter, dominant pitching performances, including a 9-0 no-hitter over Aurora on June 20 and a 20-inning, 20-strikeout complete game in a 1-1 tie against the Indianapolis TTs on July 11, 1909, demonstrated that Joe's pitching arm was again sound, and revived professional interest in him. Benz resumed his pro career in Newark, Ohio, where he posted a 10-7 record for the Newks of the Class D Ohio State League. He also played 12 games in the outfield but managed only a .202 batting average.[7] By late season 1909, Benz had been promoted to the Des Moines Boosters of the Class A Western League, where, in sparing work, he made a mark sufficient to gain a roster spot for the 1910 season.[8]

Benz began that season with Des Moines but pitched erratically in the early going. After an ineffective relief outing against Topeka, Boosters manager George Davis traced the problem to a flaw in Joe's spitball grip that, if corrected would "make a valuable pitcher out of Benz."[9] But after several more lackluster appearances, Benz was sold to the Green Bay Bays of the Class C Wisconsin-Illinois League.[10] He started strongly in Green Bay but had to be shut down with arm trouble shortly after pitching a July 19 double-header shutout against Racine, winning each contest

2-0 while fanning 19. A one-hit blanking of Fond du Lac in early September, however, signaled a late-season return to form.[11] Notwithstanding the demotion to Green Bay, Des Moines retained interest in Benz, including him on the reserve list submitted to Western League offices at the close of the 1910 season.[12] Pitching for a woeful last-place Boosters team in 1911, Benz managed a respectable 10-10 log in 33 games before his contract was purchased by the White Sox.[13]

Benz made his major-league debut on August 16, 1911, relieving Doc White in an 8-1 loss to Detroit and making a favorable first impression. Sportswriter I.E. Sanborn informed readers, "Benz looked remarkably like a pitcher during the three innings that he worked. He mixed a spitter with good speed and perfect control, and apparently was cool and confident."[14] Benz notched his first win three weeks later, pitching 8⅓ sterling innings against the St. Louis Browns, again in relief of White. By campaign's end, Joe's record stood at 3-2, with a 2.26 ERA in 12 games. But the late-inning unsteadiness that would dog him throughout his White Sox career was early in evidence. Manager Hugh Duffy went quick to the hook with Benz, allowing him to complete only one of his six starts. Still, Benz had forged a promising beginning in Chicago, his prospects enhanced by a solid relief outing during the annual postseason series against the hated Cubs.[15]

Another career-long Benz characteristic manifested itself the following spring: early arrival at training camp in midseason condition. In between workouts one day, Benz assisted fellow staff contender George Mogridge's hotel pool rescue of floundering nonswimmer Rube Peters, another young White Sox hurler. Once Peters was safe, Joe supposedly turned to Mogridge and kidded, "Why did you pull him out? Don't you know that he's after our jobs?"[16] Early in the regular season, Benz solidified his spot on the White Sox staff, hurling a five-hit shutout of Cleveland. Promptly elevated to the starting rotation by new manager Nixey Callahan, Benz pitched well but frequently in bad luck. His 13-17 record included seven one-run losses, often the result of poor play by White Sox infielders—perhaps an occupational hazard for

a spitball pitcher.[17] At season's end, Callahan told Chicago sports scribes that Benz had been "a lot better pitcher than his record shows"[18] and slotted him for a start against the Cubs in the upcoming city series. But Callahan's faith in Benz went only so far; he permitted Benz to finish only six of 31 starts during the 1912 campaign.

Joe spent the offseason in Batesville working in the family shop, a matter that, once discovered by the Chicago sports press, earned Benz the enduring nickname Butcher Boy. Reporting to spring training early and in his customary fit condition, Benz got off to a good start in 1913. Early-season work included four strikeouts of Joe Jackson in a 13-3 win over Cleveland, and a three-hit shutout of New York. But in June arm trouble reappeared. A diagnosis of torn ligaments put Joe on the sidelines for several weeks and reduced his overall season stats to 7-10 in only 151 innings. Yet, some modest postseason consolation was afforded Benz by a three-hit, 11-inning shutout of the Cubs before 27,000 fans attending the City Series. This performance apparently spurred Joe to a last-minute decision to accompany his teammates on a world exhibition tour. Organized by White Sox owner Charles A. Comiskey and New York Giants manager John McGraw, the trip would emulate the storied 1887-1888 world tour of Al Spalding's White Stockings and become a memorable part of Joe Benz's life.

Joe Benz (Bain Collection, Library of Congress, Prints and Photographs Division)

Residents of Batesville flocked to nearby Cincinnati to see their hero start the tour's opening game. But alas, Joe was shelled, losing 11-2.[19] Playing their way to the West Coast, the teams embarked from Seattle in November 1913, and within hours Joe and the rest of the company were below decks, suffering the effects of the rough seas that their voyage would often encounter on the Pacific. Those following the tour's progress in Chicago newspapers were subsequently regaled with satiric dispatches by Ring Lardner and others, recounting the misadventures of "Sir Joseph Benz of Batesville Manor," the bumpkin abroad who slept through stops at exotic ports of call, became seasick while riding a camel, and was mistaken by tourists for the Sphinx.[20] The good-natured Benz took the caricatures in stride, and if his mind was somewhat distracted during the tour, it was not without cause. For just before the team's ship departed Manila, Joe had cabled a proposal of marriage to sweetheart Alice Leddy back in Chicago. Alice promptly accepted, but the nuptials had to await completion of a five-continent trip highlighted by an audience with Pope Pius IX in Rome and a command game performance for King George V of Great Britain, who reportedly enjoyed the exhibition immensely.[21] The tour arrived in New York on March 8, 1914, but Benz skipped homecoming festivities and headed straight for Chicago. Two days later, family, friends, and various White Sox teammates attended the wedding of Joe and Alice at Our Lady of Mercy Chapel of Corpus Christi Church. Immediately thereafter, the newlyweds departed for the White Sox training camp in Paso Robles, California.[22] Meanwhile, St. Louis Church in Batesville accepted delivery of a magnificent organ donated to the parish by Joe upon his return from overseas.[23]

During that spring Benz rejected overtures from the upstart Federal League; he would remain a member of the White Sox his entire major-league career. Joe began the 1914 season strongly, posting a 1-0 victory over Cleveland in his first start. Some seven weeks later, on May 31, the Naps were the victims of Benz's masterpiece, a 6-1 no-hitter. Joe kept it going in his next outing, holding the Senators hitless until Eddie Ainsmith was credited with a disputed ninth-inning

single. Among those in attendance who thought that the hit should have been scored an error was American League President Ban Johnson, who had, but chose not to exercise, the authority to change the scorer's ruling.[24] Thus, Benz had to content himself with a one-hit, 1-0 decision over nemesis Walter Johnson, the pitching master whom Benz regularly volunteered to face but rarely beat.[25]

Benz was the workhorse of the 1914 White Sox staff, leading the team in appearances (48) and innings pitched (283⅓) while posting a 2.26 ERA. But poor support and habitual hard luck reduced Benz's log to 15-19 for the sixth-place White Sox. Ill fortune followed Joe in the offseason, as well. He was stricken by a serious case of typhoid fever and did not fully recover until the next spring. Benz's belated 1915 debut, a three-hit win over the Browns, was promising, but he was not his previous self. Used more cautiously, he posted a 15-11 record with a 2.11 ERA over 238⅓ innings as the White Sox surged into the first division.

By 1916 the respect that Joe had accumulated around the American League was reflected in a preseason column penned by Browns veteran Jimmy Austin, who placed Benz among the "Six Hardest Pitchers I Ever Faced."[26] But age and recurring arm trouble were beginning to take their toll. No longer a rotation mainstay, Benz was used in spots, with starts often reserved for the Athletics and Senators, Joe's perennial patsies. By season's close he had logged only 142 innings, going 9-5 with a career-low 2.03 earned-run average. Joe spent the winter in Chicago, where his new Buick quickly became a familiar sight on the city streets.[27] He also attended organizing sessions of a new players union but was outspoken in opposition to strike talk.[28] As the 1917 season approached, there was far more consequential strife on the horizon but Joe, like fellow White Sox hurler Eddie Cicotte, was already beyond World War I draft age. Used only sporadically that year, Benz closed a 7-3 season with a complete-game six-hit win over the Washington Senators. Joe was included on the postseason roster of the pennant-winning White Sox but saw no action in the 1917 World Series conquest of the Giants. His only appearance against New York came in a post-Series soldiers' benefit game played on Long Island. Still, Joe reveled in being a member of the new baseball champions, a joy only heightened by the arrival of Joseph Louis Benz, Jr., born at home in Chicago on November 10, 1917.

Despite being set back by a severe winter cold that worsened into pneumonia, Benz maintained his practice of being an early arrival in training camp for the 1918 season. Hampered by a hand injury and ineffective in his initial outings, Joe startled his teammates by announcing that he was abandoning his now unreliable spitter.[29] Second thoughts quickly set in and days later Benz threw a spitball-aided complete game at the Browns. The last highlight of Benz's big- league career came in late July, when he whitewashed Johnson and the Senators, winning 1-0 without striking out a single batter in 13 innings. Benz finished the 1918 season at 8-8, with a 2.63 ERA in 154 innings. With World War I shortening the season, Joe returned to an offseason job in a Chicago steel mill. And like a multitude of other idled MLB players, he hooked up with local semipro teams, pitching into the late fall. The following season, Benz broke camp with the White Sox but made only a single 1919 appearance, a two-inning relief stint. He was released by the Sox in mid-May after refusing assignment to Kansas City of the American Association.[30] His final major-league mark was 77-75, with 17 shutouts and a lifetime 2.43 ERA in 1,359⅔ innings — a record Benz would always take justifiable pride in.

The end of his major-league career did not sever Benz's connection to baseball. For the remainder of the year he pitched on weekends for various Chicago area semipro teams. In the meantime the White Sox, sparked by the play of soon-to-be-banished Eddie Cicotte, Joe Jackson, Buck Weaver, Lefty Williams, et al, captured the American League flag. While the games of the infamous 1919 World Series were in progress, Benz served as the featured attraction at the Auditorium Theater, where ticketless White Sox fans could follow game action on an electronic scoreboard.[31] Thereafter, Benz spent several more summers pitching

in the Chicago semipro ranks. The years after he hung up the glove entirely were largely happy ones, the arrival of daughter Rita in 1922 making the Benz family complete. Benz lived a modest but comfortable life, supporting the family as a tavern owner, stationary engineer, surveyor, and church custodian. In January 1927 he was briefly back in the news, one of the many former White Sox players summoned to Commissioner Kenesaw M. Landis's inquiry into Swede Risberg's claim that the White Sox had bribed the Tigers during the 1917 pennant chase. Benz branded the allegation "absolutely, a lie."[32] Ultimately, Landis came to the same conclusion, taking no action in the matter. During the 1930s Benz periodically suited up for old-timers' games at Comiskey Park and during World War II was active in support of the war effort, once helping to sell $721,000 in War Bonds between games of a White Sox-Yankees doubleheader.[33] Notoriety of a different sort attached to a 1939 court appearance during which his position as custodian of St Killian's Church obliged him to testify against a young man accused of theft from the poorbox. Although it had been 20 years since Benz had pitched for the Sox, Judge Joseph Hermes immediately recognized him and fondly reminisced about seeing Joe and his mates play — before dispatching the miscreant to jail for six months.[34]

For the remainder of his life, Joe operated a neighborhood tavern near Comiskey Park and was frequently in attendance at Chicago sports banquets, usually seated with old friends Red Faber and Ray Schalk. In January 1954 Benz was the guest of honor at the annual dinner of the Pitch and Hit Club, and the butt of genial gibes by featured speaker Lefty Gomez.[35] In February 1957 Joe and old White Sox pals were together again at the yearly winter fete of the Chicago Old Timers, a local baseball organization of which Benz was a vice president. Two months later he was felled by a stroke. Benz died in Chicago on April 22, 1957. He was 71 and was survived by his wife, children, and brother Mike.[36] A good pitcher and a kindly man, Joe Benz's passing was noted sadly by the baseball world.[37] He rests with family in Chicago's Holy Sepulchre Cemetery.

NOTES

1 The Benz siblings were Michael Jr. (1884-1964), Martha (1890-1907), and Leo (c. 1892-1952). Joe's parents also raised orphaned cousins Hugo and Matilda Benz.

2 As per Minnie S. Wycoff, *Builders of a City* (Batesville, Indiana: Batesville Area Historical Society, 2003), a posthumously published local history kindly provided to the writer by genealogist Denean Williams of the Batesville Memorial Public Library. Information on the Benz family was also gleaned from the "Memory Lane" column of *Granny* (Elizabeth Ollier), published in the *Batesville Herald Tribune*, May 1, 1952.

3 *Batesville Herald Tribune*, June 14, 1997.

4 A capsule summary of notable games Benz pitched for the hometown nine in 1908 was published in the *Batesville Herald Tribune*, July 12, 1951.

5 *Batesville Tribune*, March 24 and April 14, 1909, and reiterated in the *Washington Post*, September 30, 1917. In his Clarksburg debut, Joe held the opposition hitless, striking out eight, before a fifth-inning muscle pull in his upper arm necessitated his removal from the game, as per the *Batesville Tribune*, April 21, 1909.

6 As reflected in the box score published in the *Batesville Tribune*, June 2, 1909. The 1909 Batesville team photo also features Joe and his older brother Mike, an infielder.

7 See baseball-reference.com/minors/team.cgi?id=26877 for Joe Benz's record with Newark.

8 Baseball-Reference.com has no record of Benz pitching for Des Moines in 1909 but his membership on that team is noted in the *Batesville Tribune*, October 6, 1909, and confirmed in various 1910 preseason reviews of Boosters prospects. See, e.g., *Des Moines News*, March 30, 1910, *Des Moines Register & Leader*, April 1, 1910.

9 *Des Moines News*, April 30, 1910.

10 As reported in the Des Moines papers, May 18, 1910. Said the *Evening Tribune:* "There is no question but that Benz has a lot of pitching ability in him but thus far he has not been able to get going in the Western League." Strangely, Baseball-Reference.com has no 1910 data whatever for Benz. From the reportage of the 1910 Des Moines press, the writer calculates Benz's Boosters pitching record as 0-1, with one save, in six appearances.

11 Based upon game accounts and box scores published in the *Green Bay Gazette* and the *Green Bay Semi-Weekly Gazette*, the Joe Benz Green Bay pitching log appears to be 20 games (19 starts, 1 relief appearance), 177⅓ innings pitched, and a 9-8 won/lost record, with 103 hits allowed, 111 strikeouts, 23 walks, 17 complete games, and 0 saves. The writer is indebted to historian David Williams of Madison for helping research Benz's tenure with Green Bay.

12 *Des Moines Register & Leader/Des Moines Daily Capital*, October 6, 1910.

13 The oft-told tale that Benz's acquisition by the White Sox was occasioned by correspondence between Joe's father and White Sox owner Comiskey is apocryphal. But a January 1910 letter from Comiskey to Joe himself (thanking him for New Year's good wishes and reminding Joe that he was under contract to Des Moines team owner John F. Higgins) is contained in the slim collection of Joe Benz papers on file at the Chicago History Museum.

14 *Chicago Tribune*, August 17, 1911.

15 Pitching once again in relief of Doc White, Benz's two scoreless frames "won him lasting laurels and the respect of everybody," according to the *Chicago Tribune*, October 15, 1911.

16 *Chicago Tribune*, February 26, 1912.

17 As a major leaguer, Benz pitched to contact, averaging less than 4 strikeouts per 9 innings during his career. In 1912 Benz compounded his infield problems by being an unsteady fielder himself, recording 10 errors of his own that season.

18 *Chicago Tribune*, October 2, 1912. Burgeoning regard for Benz is also reflected in the United Press Syndicate circulation of a first-person column under a Joe Benz byline that season. See the oddly titled "My Batting Jinx," *Los Angeles Times*, August 12, 1912, and elsewhere.

19 The October 19, 1913 *Chicago Tribune* account of the game was subheadlined, "Joe Benz Slaughtered."

20 See the *Chicago Tribune*, January 26-February 22, 1914, passim.

21 See generally, G.W. Axelson, *Commy: The Life Story of Charles A. Comiskey* (Chicago: Reilly & Lee, 1919), 156-185. See also *Chicago Tribune*, March 29, 2000. Benz pitched in the game attended by the King, the last contest of the tour and played before a crowd reported at 35,000.

22 Months before his own marriage, Joe was in attendance when cousin Charlotte Benz was wed to fellow WhiteSox hurler Reb Russell, Joe's boarding-house roommate.

23 As recalled by Joe's nephew, Hugh J. Benz of Batesville, email to the writer, March 31, 2011.

24 *Washington Post*, June 12, 1914.

25 Johnson held a 10-2 advantage in decisions involving the two pitchers.

26 *Boston Globe*, March 21, 1916. The others were Walter Johnson, Joe Wood, George Dauss, Guy Morton, and Jim Scott.

27 A friend driving the Buick was stopped by a Chicago cop who recognized Benz's vehicle on sight and detained the driver until Joe could be found to vouch for the friend's permission to use the car, as reported in the *Chicago Tribune*, January 17, 1917.

28 Said Benz: "I have been well treated by the magnates and I believe it is up to every ball player to look out for his own interests," as per the *Chicago Tribune*, January 14, 1917.

29 *Atlanta Constitution*, June 24, 1918.

30 *Chicago Tribune*, May 17, 1919. In addition to being separated from family, Joe was disinclined to pitch in the American Association, a league that had just outlawed the spitball.

31 As advertised daily in the *Chicago Tribune* and elsewhere.

32 *Chicago Tribune*, January 5, 1927.

33 *Chicago Tribune*, July 20, 1944.

34 *Chicago Tribune*, January 17, 1939.

35 *Chicago Tribune*, January 29, 1954.

36 Alice Leddy Benz died in 1972, age 86. Joe Jr. (1917-2006) and Rita (1922-2010), a nun also known as Sister Mary Borgia, never married and died childless.

37 *Chicago Daily News* sportswriter John P. Carmichael remembered Joe Benz as "one of the fine characters of baseball … a gentleman of the old school who liked to relive the days of his youth just for kicks," in *The Sporting News*, May 1, 1957.

EDDIE CICOTTE

By Jim Sandoval

THOUGH HE DIDN'T INVENT the pitch, Eddie "Knuckles" Cicotte was perhaps the first major-league pitcher to master the knuckleball. According to one description, Cicotte gripped the knuckler by holding the ball "on the three fingers of a closed hand, with his thumb and forefinger to guide it, throwing it with an overhand motion, and sending it from his hand as one would snap a whip. The ball acts like a 'spitter,' but is a new-fangled thing."[1]

Cicotte once estimated that 75 percent of the pitches he threw were knuckleballs. The rest of the time the right-hander relied on a fadeaway, slider, screwball, spitter, emery ball, shine ball, and a pitch he called the "sailor," a rising fastball that "would sail much in the same manner of a flat stone thrown by a small boy."[2] Whether he was sailing or sinking the ball, shining it or darkening it, the 5-foot-9, 175-pound Cicotte had more pitches than a traveling salesman. "Perhaps no pitcher in the world has such a varied assortment of wares in his repertory as Cicotte," *The Sporting News* observed in 1918. "He throws with effect practically every kind of ball known to pitching science."[3]

But the most famous pitch Cicotte ever threw was the one that nailed Cincinnati Reds leadoff man Morrie Rath squarely in the back to lead off the 1919 World Series, a pitch that signaled to the gamblers that the fix was on. After confessing to his role in the scandal one year later, Cicotte was banned from the game for life, a punishment that perhaps denied the 209-game-winner a spot in the Hall of Fame.

Edgar Victor Cicotte (pronounced SEE-cot)[4] was born on June 19, 1884, in Springwells, Michigan, a former township in the Detroit metropolitan area, into a family of French heritage. He was the son of Ambrose and Archangel (Drouillard) Cicotte. Eddie's brother, Alva, was the grandfather of Al Cicotte, who

pitched in the major leagues for five seasons from 1957 to 1962. By the time Eddie was 16 years old, his father had died, forcing his mother to support her large family as a dressmaker. Leaving school early, Eddie took up work as a boxmaker to help pay the family bills.

Cicotte began his baseball career, according to some sources, as early as 1903, playing semipro ball in the Upper Peninsula of Michigan. In 1904 he pitched for Calumet (Michigan) and Sault Ste. Marie (Ontario) in the Northern Copper League, posting a record of 38-4 with 11 shutouts.[5] Based on that dominating performance, Cicotte earned a tryout with the Detroit Tigers in the spring of 1905. The Tigers determined that he wasn't ready for the majors, and optioned him to Augusta (Georgia) of the South Atlantic League, where he compiled a record of 15 wins against 9 losses, and brawled with his young teammate Ty Cobb after a Cobb stunt cost Cicotte a shutout. As a joke Cobb had taken popcorn with him to his position in center field and as a result committed an error that led to a run.[6] This incident notwithstanding, among his teammates Cicotte was known as an easygoing prankster who enjoyed a good laugh.

Near the end of the season Detroit brought Cicotte up and he made his major-league debut on September 3, 1905, allowing one run in relief and getting tagged with the loss in a 10-inning game. Two days later Cicotte earned his first major-league win, a completegame victory over the Chicago White Sox. He finished the year 1-1 with a 3.50 ERA, but would not return to the major leagues for another three seasons.

Cicotte began 1906 with Indianapolis of the American Association, where he posted a 1-4 record in 72 innings before landing with Des Moines of the Western League. Cicotte blossomed with his new team, registering an 18-9 record. The following season he pitched for Lincoln, also of the Western League, going 21-14. Impressed by the young hurler's arsenal of pitches, the Boston Red Sox purchased Cicotte's contract for $2,500 at the end of the 1907 season.

During his five-year stint with the Red Sox, Cicotte lost nearly as many games as he won, and frequently found himself in trouble with Red Sox owner John I. Taylor, who accused the pitcher of underachieving. "He was suspended without pay so much of the time that it was like having no job," the *Chicago Tribune*'s Sam Weller wrote of Cicotte's Boston career.[7] On a club that consistently failed to meet expectations, Cicotte often became the scapegoat, and in 1911 Taylor tried to secure waivers on his inconsistent pitcher, only to pull back when another team made a claim. "[Taylor] wouldn't like the way I was working, or perhaps the opposition had made one or two hits," Cicotte later charged. "Taylor never liked me; I never liked him, and it was seldom that I went through a game without having him comment upon it."[8]

After Cicotte started the 1912 season with a 1-3 record and a 5.67 ERA in six starts, the Red Sox, though no longer owned by Taylor, had finally seen enough. On July 22 the team sold Cicotte's contract to the Chicago White Sox, where the 28-year-old right-hander began to mature into one of the game's best pitchers. With Boston, Cicotte had won 52 games and lost 46. Over the next 8½ seasons with the White Sox, he won 156 games against 101 losses.

The biggest reason for this improvement was Cicotte's gradual mastery of his expansive pitching repertoire. As his command over his knuckleball improved, Cicotte's walk rate dramatically decreased; from 1912 to 1920 he ranked among the league's 10 best in fewest walks per nine innings seven times, leading the league in 1918 and 1919, when he walked 89 in 572⅔ innings.

Cicotte also fully exploited the era's liberal regulations regarding the doctoring of the ball. In this area, his most infamous pitch was the shine ball, in which he rubbed one side of the ball against the pocket of his right trouser leg, which had been filled with talcum powder.

Flustered opponents protested to American League President Ban Johnson that the pitch should be outlawed, but Johnson ruled the pitch legal in 1917, and it would remain so until February 1920. Thanks to the knuckleball, the shine ball, the emery ball (ruled illegal by Johnson in early 1915), and other trick pitches, Cicotte struck out a fair number of batters, placing in the top 10 in strikeouts per nine innings three times, even though his fastball probably couldn't break a plane of glass. Asked to explain his success, Cicotte chalked it up to "head work," adding, "It involves an ability to adapt pitching to certain conditions when they arise and perhaps use altogether different methods in the very next inning."[9]

In 1913 Cicotte enjoyed his first standout season in the major leagues, posting an 18-11 record to go along with a 1.58 ERA, second best in the American League.

Eddie Cicotte, circa 1919 (Bain Collection, Library of Congress, Prints and Photographs Division)

That offseason, Pittsburgh of the newly formed Federal League attempted to sign Cicotte, but White Sox owner Charles Comiskey was able to secure the pitcher's loyalty through a three-year contract. In the first year of his contract, Eddie managed only an 11-16 record, although his 2.04 ERA was fifth best in the league. After a mediocre 13-12 campaign in 1915, Cicotte finally hit his stride in 1916, when he split time between the starting rotation and bullpen, posted a 1.78 ERA, won 15 out of 22 decisions, and had what today would be five saves. (The statistic hadn't been invented yet.)

The following year, 1917, Cicotte moved back to the starting rotation and enjoyed the best season of his career, as the White Sox captured their first pennant in 11 seasons. Cicotte led the way, ranking first in the league in wins (28), ERA (1.53), and innings pitched (346⅔). Eddie also tossed seven shutouts, including a no-hitter against the St. Louis Browns on April 14, the first of six no-hitters pitched in the major leagues that season. In that year's World Series, Cicotte contributed one win to Chicago's six-game triumph over the New York Giants. He was, according to Grantland Rice, "the most feared pitcher of the series."[10]

After Cicotte's breakthrough season, Comiskey offered his star pitcher a $5,000 contract, with a $2,000 signing bonus, making him one of the highest compensated pitchers in baseball.[11] But Cicotte failed to produce an encore suitable to his dominant 1917 campaign, as he wrenched his ankle in early May, and limped his way through the season to a mediocre 2.77 ERA and 19 losses, tied for the most in the league. It was not a performance to inspire Comiskey to hand out a raise, and when the 1919 season began, financial troubles were weighing heavily on Cicotte. According to the 1920 Census, Cicotte was the head of household for a family of 12, including his wife, Rose; their three children; his wife's parents; Eddie's brother and wife; and a brother-in-law and his wife and child. To make room for his large family, Cicotte took out a $4,000 mortgage on a Michigan farm.[12]

Cicotte regained his 1917 form, pitching the White Sox to their second pennant in three years. Once again, Eddie led the American League in victories (29) and

innings pitched (306⅔, tied with Jim Shaw). His 29-7 record was good enough to lead the league in winning percentage (.806), and his 1.82 ERA ranked second. In early September, first baseman Chick Gandil and infielder Fred McMullin approached Cicotte about throwing the World Series. After thinking it over, Eddie agreed to the scheme, telling Gandil privately, "I would not do anything like that for less than $10,000." Three days before the Series began, Cicotte demanded to have the money in hand before the team left for Cincinnati. That night, he found $10,000 under his pillow.[13]

Contrary to conventional wisdom, Cicotte's abysmal performance in the 1919 World Series was not a complete surprise to informed observers. Throughout September, reports surfaced that the overworked Cicotte was suffering from a sore shoulder. Prior to the first game of the Series, Christy Mathewson noted, Cicotte "has had less than a week [actually two days] to rest up for his first start…. And that may not prove to be enough. If he blows up for a single inning it may cost the White Sox the championship, for I think the first battle is going to have a very strong bearing on the outcome, especially if the Reds win it."[14]

With at least six of his other teammates in on the fix, Cicotte led the way in blowing the first game, surrendering seven hits and six runs in 3⅔ innings of work, and fueling Cincinnati's winning rally by throwing slowly to second base on what should have been an inning-ending double-play ball. The performance was so bad that it generated renewed speculation that Cicotte was suffering from a "dead arm."

For his second start, in Game Four, with the White Sox trailing two games to one, Eddie pitched more effectively, holding the Reds to just five hits and two unearned runs, both coming in the fifth inning on two Cicotte errors, including one inexplicable play in which he muffed an attempt to cut off a throw from the outfield, allowing the ball to go to the backstop and letting a Cincinnati runner—who had already stopped at third—score. The miscues were enough to ensure that the White Sox lost the game, 2-0. Afterward, Chicago manager Kid Gleason declared,

"They shouldn't have scored on Cicotte in 40 innings.... There wasn't any occasion for Cicotte to intercept that throw. He did it to prevent Kopf from going to second. But Kopf had no more intention of going to second than I have of jumping in the lake."[15]

Though Eddie had received his $10,000 before the start of the Series, many of his fellow conspirators had not received the money promised them by the gamblers, so before Cicotte's third start, in Game Seven of the best-of-nine Series, the players decided to play the game to win. Accordingly, Cicotte put forth his best effort of the Series, allowing just one run on seven hits in a 4-1 Chicago victory. Lefty Williams threw the following game, however, giving Cincinnati the world championship. In the wake of Chicago's defeat, Mathewson publicly tossed aside rumors that the Series had been fixed, saying, "No pitcher could guarantee to toss a game.... Even if a pitcher should let the other side get two or three runs before he was yanked, he could not guarantee that the other side wouldn't come up the next inning and make four or five. That wipes out any single pitcher and leaves the proposition of fixing on a club. This can't be done."[16]

Despite the persistent rumors that swirled around the club that offseason, Cicotte re-signed with Chicago for 1920, and put forth another excellent season, posting a 21-10 record with a 3.26 ERA. That summer Babe Ruth electrified the sport with his 54 home runs for the New York Yankees, but Cicotte grabbed a few headlines of his own after he stymied Ruth in several encounters. Asked to explain his success, the crafty Cicotte allowed that he mixed up his pitches and relied heavily on the spitball, because the pitch was "hard to hit for a long clout."[17]

Before the season, the spitball and other doctored pitches, including Cicotte's famous shine ball, had been banned from baseball. Although a number of established spitball pitchers were given a one-year exemption from the rule, Cicotte was not one of them.

On September 27, 1920, the *Philadelphia North American* ran a story in which Billy Maharg, one of the gamblers in on the Series fix the previous fall, testified to his role in the affair, and specifically named Cicotte as the man who initiated the plot. The next day, Eddie met with White Sox counsel Alfred Austrian and admitted to his role in the scandal. He also implicated seven of his teammates.[18] Afterward, he went to the Cook County Courthouse and repeated his story for a grand jury charged with investigating corruption in baseball. The grand jury responded to Cicotte's testimony by indicting all eight of the "Black Sox" players for throwing the 1919 World Series.

In front of the grand jury, Cicotte testified that he began to have second thoughts during the Series. After losing Game One, he was "sick all night" in the hotel and told roommate Happy Felsch, "Happy, it will never be done again." He also said that he tried his best to win Game Four, claiming "I didn't care whether I got shot out there the next minute. I was going to win the ball game and the series." But he never offered to return the gamblers' money. "I couldn't very well do that," he admitted.[19]

Though he and the other seven accused players were acquitted of conspiracy charges the following year, Eddie Cicotte's major-league baseball career ended with his confession. For the next three years he played with several of his banned teammates for outlaw teams in Illinois, Wisconsin, and Minnesota, but by 1924 Cicotte had moved on with his life.[20] He worked as a Michigan game warden and managed a service station before finding a job with the Ford Motor Company, where he remained until his retirement in 1944.

During the last 25 years of his life, Cicotte raised strawberries on a 5½-acre farm near Farmington, Michigan. In an interview with Detroit sportswriter Joe Falls in 1965 he said he lived his life quietly, answering letters from youngsters who sometimes asked about the scandal. He agreed that he had made mistakes, but insisted that he had tried to make up for it by living as clean a life as he could. "I admit I did wrong," he said, "but I've paid for it the past 45 years."[21] Falls seemed to agree, noting that as he prepared to leave Cicotte's home, he looked at Eddie's socks. They were white.

Eddie Cicotte died on May 5, 1969, at Henry Ford Hospital in Detroit. His death certificate listed his occupation as baseball player, Chicago White Sox. He was buried in Park View Cemetery in Livonia, Michigan.

SOURCES

Asinof, Eliot, *Eight Men Out* (New York: Henry Holt and Company, 1987).

Falls, Joe, Interview with Eddie Cicotte. *Detroit Free Press*, December 4, 1965.

Lardner, Ring, *Chicago Examiner*. July 21, 1912.

MacFarlane, Paul, ed., *Daguerreotypes. The Sporting News*, 1981.

Stump, Al, *Cobb* (New York: Algonquin Books, 1996).

findagrave.com.

Obituary, *The Sporting News*. May 24, 1969.

Michigan Death Certificate.

Obituary, *New York Times*. May 9, 1969.

1880 Wayne County, Michigan, Federal Census.

1920 Wayne County, Michigan, Federal Census.

1930 Wayne County, Michigan, Federal Census.

ancestry.com.

The Sporting News, February 23, 1933, 8.

retrosheet.org.

Contract card, National Baseball Library, Hall of Fame.

Washington Post, August 24, 1906; August 24, 1907; March 8, 1908; April 15, 1917.

New York Times, April 15, 1917.

Sporting Life, February 21, 1914.

Kermisch, Al, "From a Researcher's Notebook." *Baseball Research Journal #23* (Cleveland: SABR, 1994.)

Chicago Daily Tribune, August 27, 1906.

baseball-reference.com.

NOTES

1   *Washington Post*, March 8, 1908.

2   Ty Cobb, *Memoirs of Twenty Years in Baseball* (New York: Dover Publications, 2009), 65, 68.

3   *The Sporting News*, May 2, 1918.

4   The proper pronunciation of Eddie Cicotte's name was cleared up during the Black Sox criminal trial in 1921: After multiple attorneys butchered his name in court, Cicotte reportedly told Judge Hugo Friend, "Would you please have it entered in the court record that my name is … pronounced See-kott, with the accent on the See?" See (Chillicothe, Missouri) *Daily Constitution*, August 22, 1921.

5   *Indianapolis News*, February 22, 1906.

6   Associated Press, July 18, 1961.

7   *Chicago Tribune*, July 11, 1912.

8   *Milwaukee Sentinel*, December 28, 1912.

9   Eddie Cicotte, "The Secrets of Successful Pitching," *Baseball Magazine*, July 1918. Accessed online at LA84.org.

10   Grantland Rice, "The Battle of the Leagues," *Collier's*, October 13, 1917.

11   Bob Hoie, "1919 Baseball Salaries and the Mythically Underpaid Chicago White Sox," *Base Ball: A Journal of the Early Game*. (Jefferson, North Carolina: McFarland & Co., Spring 2012), 29. Cicotte also agreed to a "substantial" off-contract performance bonus, which he didn't earn in 1918. But after rebounding to a stellar 29-7 season in 1919, Comiskey paid him an additional $3,000 that, according to Hoie, was "likely a carryover from the 1918 agreement." Hoie writes that in terms of total compensation, Cicotte was the second highest paid pitcher in baseball in 1918-20 behind Walter Johnson.

12   Bill Lamb, *Black Sox in the Courtroom: The Grand Jury, Criminal Trial and Civil Litigation*. (Jefferson, North Carolina: McFarland & Co., 2013), 50-51.

13   Ibid.

14   *Boston Globe*, October 1, 1919.

15   *Chicago Tribune*, October 5, 1919.

16   Christy Mathewson, *New York Times*, October 16, 1919.

17   *Chicago Tribune*, August 4, 1920.

18   Lamb, 49-50. According to the notes taken by Assistant State's Attorney Hartley Replogle, who was present in Austrian's office for the meeting, Cicotte initially named Fred McMullin, Chick Gandil, Buck Weaver, Lefty Williams, Joe Jackson, and Happy Felsch as "the men who were in the deal." Cicotte apparently did not mention Swede Risberg's name in Austrian's office. But in his grand-jury testimony later that day, he did name Risberg as being present at two September players' meetings discussing the fix, one at the Ansonia Hotel in New York and one at the Warner Hotel in Chicago.

19   Lamb, 51.

20   Jacob Pomrenke, "The Black Sox: After the Fall." The National
     Pastime Museum, April 4, 2013. Accessed online at thenational-
     pastimemuseum.com/article/black-sox-after-fall.

21   Joe Falls interview with Cicotte, *Detroit Free Press*,
     December 4, 1965.

EDDIE COLLINS

By Paul Mittermeyer

AN EXCELLENT PLACE-hitter, slick fielder, and brainy baserunner, Eddie Collins epitomized the style of play that made the Deadball Era unique. At the plate, the 5-foot-9, 175-pound left-handed batter possessed a sharp batting eye, and aimed to hit outside pitches to the opposite field and trick deliveries back through the box. Once on base, Collins was a master at stealing, even though his foot speed wasn't particularly noteworthy. A believer in the principle that a runner steals off the pitcher and not the catcher, Collins practiced the art of studying pitchers — how they held the ball for certain pitches, how they looked off runners, all the pitcher's moves. He focused especially on the feet and hips of the pitcher, rather than just his hands, and thus was able to take large leads off first base and get excellent jumps.

An Ivy League graduate, Collins was one of the smartest players of his day, and he knew it. Saddled with the nickname "Cocky" from early in his career, Collins drew the resentment of teammates for his self-confidence and good breeding that at times seemed as though it belonged more in a ballroom than a baseball clubhouse. Perhaps for this reason, contradiction and complexity became a recurring theme throughout his 25-year major-league career. He made his major-league debut under an alias and later served as captain of the most infamous team in baseball history, the 1919 Chicago White Sox. He won an award recognizing him as the most valuable player in the league, only to be sold off to another club in the subsequent offseason. Despite his upper-class origins and education, Collins abided by a litany of superstitions, although he insisted he was "not superstitious, just thought it unlucky not to get base hits."[1]

Edward Trowbridge Collins was born on May 2, 1887, in Millerton, New York, the son of railroad freight agent John Rossman Collins and Mary Meade (Trowbridge) Collins. When Eddie was 8 months old, the Collins family moved to Tarrytown, New York, in the Hudson Valley 30 miles north of New York City. Young Collins registered at the Irving School in Tarrytown for the fourth grade in 1895. By legend, he played ball there that afternoon, and continued smashing hits for Irving through the spring of 1903, when he graduated from the prep school. That fall he entered Columbia University. Though a slight 135 pounds, the precocious 16-year-old quarterbacked the freshman football team and later one season on the varsity before the school dropped football entirely — "At that time," Collins recalled, "I liked football better than I liked baseball"[2] — and was the starting shortstop for the college nine.

Shortly after beginning his amateur athletic career at Columbia, Collins began picking up paying gigs on the side. In 1904 he pitched for the Tarrytown Terrors for $1 per game. He also performed for a Red Hook (New York) squad, drawing closer to $5 a contest. In the summer of 1906, Eddie played for a succession of semipro clubs — in Plattsburgh, Rutland, and Rockville — before his professional career was discovered, thus invalidating his senior year of eligibility at Columbia. The summer was not to be a total loss, however. While honeymooning, Andy Coakley, a pitcher with the Philadelphia Athletics, happened to see Collins playing for Rutland. Coakley sent word of the youngster to Connie Mack, who dispatched backup catcher Jimmy Byrnes to develop an in-depth scouting report.[3] When Byrnes confirmed the pitcher's observations, Mack signed Collins to a 1907 contract, but not before Collins obtained a written promise that Mack would not send him to the minor leagues without his consent. John McGraw, manager of the New York Giants, had been aware of the budding prospect but declined to offer him a trial.

At Connie Mack's suggestion, Collins made his major-league debut under the alias of Eddie T. Sullivan on September 17, 1906, at Chicago's South Side Park. "I put on a uniform that did not fit me too well," he recalled later. "Gosh, I weighed about only 140 pounds. I was self-conscious among all those big fellows—men like [Rube] Waddell, whom I had read so much about."[4] He played that first game at shortstop behind the future Hall of Famer Waddell, who completely subdued Eddie in batting practice. Nonetheless, "Sullivan" managed to reach Chicago's Big Ed Walsh for a bunt single in his first at-bat. Six fielding chances were executed flawlessly that day, though Eddie's tenure at short was not to last.

Having played six games with the Athletics, Collins was back in class at Columbia shortly after the Mackmen completed their Western tour. On March 26, 1907, the day of Columbia's opening game, Collins ran out to take the field at shortstop before being informed that the University Committee on Athletics at Columbia had ruled him ineligible for the 1907 season—not because of his time with the Athletics, which wasn't revealed publicly until years later, but because he had been paid to play with semipro teams in Plattsburgh and Rockville. Still, Eddie's game smarts earned him the unprecedented position of undergraduate assistant coach for the Lions' 1907 squad. By this time, the baseball bug had a firm hold on Collins and the youngster postponed his plans for a legal career to rejoin the Athletics after graduation in 1907, appearing in 14 games for Philadelphia that summer.

Collins became a regular player in the majors in 1908. That first full season, he split time at five positions: shortstop, second base, and all three outfield spots, hitting .273 in 102 games. He converted to second base full-time in 1909, pushing Danny Murphy to right field, and from there his remarkable career took wing. It was no small coincidence that when Collins became the starting second baseman, the team also took off. Eddie played every game in 1909, hitting .347 as the club rose to second, chasing the pennant-winning Tigers to the wire. The young second sacker finished second in the circuit in hits, walks, steals, and batting average, and placed third in the league in runs, total bases, and slugging. He led all second basemen in putouts, assists, double plays, and fielding average.

In 1910 the club broke through, winning the first of four pennants in a five-year stretch by a convincing 14½ games. Eddie led the American League in steals, was third in hits and RBIs, and fourth in batting, while leading in most fielding categories. Philadelphia dusted the Cubs in five games to give Connie Mack his first World Series title. Collins was the star of the Series, batting .429 and hitting safely in each contest. His play in Game Two, when he had three hits, stole two bases, and made several outstanding defensive plays, confirmed his status as one of the American League's top stars.[5] A month after the championship was secured, Eddie married Mabel Doane, whose father was a close friend of Connie Mack's; Mack himself had introduced them. Collins and Mack had a standing bet as to who would get married first, which Mack won by a week. The Collinses remained married for more than 30 years until Mabel's death in 1943.

In 1911 the A's, with the "$100,000 Infield" of Home Run Baker, Jack Barry, Collins, and Stuffy McInnis now intact, repeated as world champs, besting Detroit by 13½ games, and downing John McGraw's Giants in six. After finishing fourth in hitting (.365) during the year and leading the league's second basemen in putouts, Collins had a modest Series, batting .286 with three errors. Still, the A's had successfully defended their championship and, Collins, just 24, had experienced little but success in his few years of prep, collegiate, and professional play.

Collins's plainly evident self-confidence could rub people the wrong way. As educated and ostensibly sophisticated as he was, cockiness could lead to actions that in hindsight at least were not entirely smart. During the Athletics' championship run, some of his teammates groused about Collins's loyalties and priorities. Collins, like other baseball stars such as Ty Cobb and Christy Mathewson, was often commissioned by newspapers and magazines to write articles on the inner workings of the game. Some A's players argued that other teams were able to correct the weaknesses

Collins had pointed out in his articles, thereby hurting Philadelphia's chances at winning the pennant. In 1912 Collins led the league in runs and posted a .348 average with 63 stolen bases, but the dissension in the clubhouse was at least in part attributable to the gifted second baseman, and the A's finished out of first place. The anti-Collins faction in the A's clubhouse was led

Eddie Collins, circa 1922 (Bain Collection, Library of Congress, Prints and Photographs Division)

by backup catcher Ira Thomas, whom Mack named his field captain in 1914 spring training.

The bright, confident, and successful Collins was given to a litany of less than "rational" practices and observances. At the plate he kept his gum on his hat button until two strikes, then would remove it and commence chewing. He loathed black cats, and would walk or drive out of his way to avoid crossing paths with one. If he saw a load of barrels, he believed he'd make one or two hits that day. Finding a hairpin meant a single, two hairpins a double. Scraps of paper littering the dugout steps drove him crazy. He would refrain from

changing game socks during a winning streak, and as player-manager for the White Sox is said to have fired a clubhouse man for acting in violation of this practice. He believed it lucky to have someone spit on his hat before a game. Each winter Collins soaked his bats in oil, dried them out, and rubbed them down with a bone. This practice became the stuff of lore, as it has even been said that he buried his bats in cow dung piles to "keep 'em alive." On the more practical side, he would wear heavier shoes as spring approached so that his feet would feel lighter when the season opened.

Known as a gentleman off the field, the brainy star gave grudging quarter at best between the foul lines. Hard-nosed play around the bag invited like responses and incurred the enmity of some. One such encounter in 1912 would have long-term consequences. An unflinching tag by Eddie broke the nose of Washington first baseman Chick Gandil. Chick's teammate Clyde Milan witnessed the play and noted that "for the rest of his playing career, Gandil was out to get even. He went into the bag against Collins 200 times I guess, and always got the worst of it."[6]

In 1913 the A's returned to form, winning their third World Series, in five games over the Giants, as Collins hit .421, with five runs, three RBIs, and three steals. His standout autumn followed a regular campaign that featured 55 steals, 73 RBIs, and a robust .345 average. In 1914 the A's repeated as American League champs, and Collins was honored as the Chalmers Award winner, given to the league's most valuable player. Unfortunately, the bat that drove in 85 runs and registered a .344 clip was utterly absent in the Series. Philadelphia was stunned in four straight by the "Miracle Braves," with Collins batting .214.

In the aftermath of the upset, his team's harmony fractured by overtures from the Federal League, Connie Mack began to clean house in Philadelphia. On December 8, 1914, Collins was sold to the Chicago White Sox for a reported $50,000. As part of the deal, the White Sox agreed to pay Collins a salary of $15,000 per year, plus a signing bonus of $10,000.[7] By 1919 his salary was still more than double that of any of his Chicago teammates.[8]

The White Sox had spent the first half of the 1910s languishing between fourth place and sixth place. Collins's tenure in Chicago lasted 12 years. For all 12 seasons, he was a genuine star. For the last two-plus years, he was player-manager. During Collins's first year in Chicago, the great Cleveland outfielder Joe Jackson joined the club via trade with 45 games remaining in the campaign. Though by skill they were peers, there was little evidence of friendship or social interaction between the two stars. The educated and savvy Collins may have intimidated his illiterate teammate.

A sub-.500 team in 1914, the White Sox steadily rose in the standings. The 1915 club finished third, besting the .600 mark with 93 wins. Collins was second in the league in batting, led in walks, was third in steals, and was fifth in total bases while leading second basemen in both assists and fielding average. In 1916 the White Sox chased the Red Sox all summer, finishing a mere two games back. Collins led the league's second basemen in double plays and fielding average, while on the offensive side of the ledger he was second in triples, third in walks, and fourth in steals. In 1917 the White Sox won the pennant by a convincing nine games, with 100 wins for a .649 percentage. Though Collins's average dipped to .289, he led second basemen in putouts, and was second in the circuit in steals and walks.

In that year's fall classic, Collins enjoyed his third great World Series, with a .409 average, and scored the first run in the sixth and final game by outthinking the Giants defense. Though immortalized as the "Heinie Zimmerman boner," it was actually catcher Bill Rariden, first baseman Walter Holke, and pitcher Rube Benton who were the real goats. In a rundown between third base and home plate, Rariden allowed Collins to slip past him, and Holke and Benton neglected to cover home. With a foot pursuit his only option, the lumbering Zimmerman failed to catch Collins as he slid across the plate with what proved to be the Series-winning run. "In a World's Series game, when you see a base uncovered you run for it," Collins later recalled. "Believe me, I didn't waste any time on that play.... At least two, possibly three other

men could have covered the plate on that play. Why they didn't I'll never know."[9]

Like many other players, Collins's 1918 campaign was cut short by US involvement in the Great War. On August 19, 1918, Collins joined the Marine Corps, missing the final 16 games of the season. His decision to enlist in the military was greeted with patriotic fanfare—unlike his teammates Joe Jackson, Lefty Williams, and Byrd Lynn, who were harshly criticized for taking war-essential jobs in the shipyards. Collins's actual service wasn't much different from theirs, consisting mainly of drills and guard duty at the Philadelphia Naval Yard, but he received a Good Conduct Medal and was honorably discharged on February 6, 1919, in time for spring training.

As the great White Sox team coalesced, it became ever more socially segmented. When Chick Gandil had arrived before the 1917 season, the calcification of some of these divisions was pretty much assured. There was resentment, right or wrong, of owner Comiskey's penny-pinching ways, and Gandil's pre-existing bitterness towards Collins helped to focus some of the discontent on the captain. Collins came to represent management, and his status as one of Commy's favorites further poisoned the atmosphere. Of all the performers in this ill-fated cast, Collins was sharp enough to have sensed the malignant potential. Perhaps his privileged status, his seemingly unbroken record of personal success, and the team's burgeoning success combined to help dull such sensitivity.

One might expect that if Collins were so aware and adept at the multidimensions of leadership, he might have sensed and tried to mitigate intrasquad tensions. The superficial machismo of clubhouse camaraderie should not have been too significant a hurdle for a well-bred, broadly experienced, established star. The distinct cliques among the 1919 White Sox might have been immutable, but few were better equipped than Collins to initiate the select one-to-one rapprochements that might have modulated such tensions.

The 1919 White Sox finished with a record of 88-52 for a .629 percentage, besting Cleveland by 3½ games.

Collins hit .319 and drove in 80 runs while leading second basemen in putouts and finishing second in double plays. The 1919 White Sox were the greatest he ever saw because, in part, they won despite widening dissension: "(The club) was torn by discord and hatred during much of the '19 season," Collins later said. "From the moment I arrived at training camp from service, I could see that something was amiss. We may have had our troubles in other years, but in 1919 we were a club that pulled apart rather than together. There were frequent arguments and open hostility. All the things you think—and are taught to believe—are vital to the success of any athletic organization were missing from it, and yet it was the greatest collection of players ever assembled, I would say."[10]

Over the years Collins was inconsistent when discussing what he knew about his teammates' plot to throw World Series games, as well as when he knew it. After the scandal was first exposed in the fall of 1920, Collins was quoted in *Collyer's Eye*, a small gamblers' newspaper, as saying, "there wasn't a single doubt in my mind" as early as the first inning of Game One that the games were being thrown. Collins added, "If the gamblers didn't have (Buck) Weaver and (Eddie) Cicotte in their pocket then I don't know a thing about baseball"—and that he told "all this" to owner Charles Comiskey (which Comiskey always denied).[11] Years later, Collins changed his story considerably. "I was to be a witness to the greatest tragedy in baseball's history—and I didn't know it at the time," he told Jim Leonard of *The Sporting News* in 1950.[12]

After the scandal gutted the club, Collins still starred. He was one of the few bright lights for the decimated White Sox in the early 1920s. He filled in as player-manager for 27 games during the 1924 season, and assumed the role full-time for the 1925 and 1926 campaigns. The club finished fifth in each of his full years at the helm. Injuries cut into his playing time in both of these seasons. Deposed as White Sox manager on November 11, 1926, Collins was released as a player two days later. He signed with Philadelphia six weeks later, and emerged as a solid pinch-hitter in 1927. From 1928 through 1930 he mostly coached, finally playing his last game at age 43 on August 5, 1930.

Collins concluded his career with a .333 batting average, 1,821 runs scored, 3,315 hits, and 741 steals, figures that assured his induction into the Hall of Fame in 1939, as one of the original 13 players honored by the baseball writers upon the museum's opening. Also in 1939, Eddie Collins Jr. made his debut with the Athletics, where he would spend three seasons as a light-hitting outfielder. Collins's other son, the Rev. Paul Collins, officiated his father's marriage to his second wife, Emily Jane Hall, in 1945.

Collins coached full-time for Philadelphia in 1931 and 1932 before joining the Boston Red Sox as vice president and general manager when fellow Irving schooler Tom Yawkey purchased the team in early 1933. Collins remained with the Red Sox for the rest of his life, and in one notable scouting trip to California signed two future Hall of Famers, Bobby Doerr and Ted Williams. But his most notable act as general manager may have been his failure to pursue and sign Jackie Robinson after Robinson and two other Negro League players tried out for the Red Sox. Facing pressure from local press and politicians, Collins and Yawkey had offered the sham tryout only reluctantly, and their failure to take Robinson and the other black prospects seriously resulted in the Red Sox becoming the last team to integrate instead of the first.

Due to deteriorating health, Collins turned over the general manager's reins to Joe Cronin after the 1947 season but remained as vice president. A cerebral hemorrhage in August 1950 left Eddie partially paralyzed and visually impaired. Devoutly religious throughout his life, he succumbed to complications from cardiovascular disease on Easter Sunday evening, March 25, 1951, at age 63. He was buried in Linwood Cemetery in Weston, Massachusetts, and was survived by his wife and two sons.

SOURCES

Asinof, Eliot. *Eight Men Out* (New York: Henry Holt, 1988).

The Baseball Encyclopedia, Eighth Edition (New York: Macmillan Publishing, 1990).

Bryant, Howard. *Shut Out: A Story of Race and Baseball in Boston.* (New York: Routledge, 2002).

Eddie Collins player file, National Baseball Hall of Fame Library, Cooperstown, New York.

Huhn, Rick. *Eddie Collins: A Baseball Biography* (Jefferson, North Carolina: McFarland & Co., 2008).

Ritter, Lawrence. *The Glory of Their Times* (New York: Collier Books, 1971).

Verral, Charles S. *The Mighty Men of Baseball* (New York: Aladdin Books, 1955).

NOTES

1   Undated article in Eddie Collins player file, National Baseball Hall of Fame Library, Cooperstown, New York.

2   *The Sporting News*, October 11, 1950.

3   *Philadelphia Inquirer*, October 8, 1930.

4   *The Sporting News*, August 16, 1950.

5   Rick Huhn, *Eddie Collins: A Baseball Biography* (Jefferson, North Carolina: McFarland & Co., 2008), 74-75.

6   *Washington Post*, March 27, 1951.

7   *St. Louis Post-Dispatch*, February 22, 1929. AL President Ban Johnson claimed that he promised Collins an additional $5,000 for considering the White Sox' offer, and that Collins insisted he make good on the promise after signing. "I signed my personal check for $5,000," Johnson said.

8   According to historian Bob Hoie, based on his research of American League contract cards housed at the Baseball Hall of Fame, Buck Weaver's $7,250 salary was the second highest to Collins among all White Sox players in 1919. See Bob Hoie, "1919 Baseball Salaries and the Mythically Underpaid Chicago White Sox," *Base Ball: A Journal of the Early Game* (Jefferson, North Carolina: McFarland & Co., Spring 2012).

9   *The Sporting News*, October 25, 1950.

10 *The Sporting News*, August 30, 1969.

11 *Collyer's Eye*, October 30, 1920. For analysis of Collins's statements about the fix, see Rick Huhn's *Eddie Collins*, 179-83.

12 *The Sporting News*, October 25, 1950.

SHANO COLLINS

By Andy Sturgill

THE NAMES OF BASEBALL'S most famous lineups are familiar: Murderers' Row, the Big Red Machine, the Black Sox. The people who make up those lineups are familiar, too: Ruth, Rose, Shoeless Joe.

However, even baseball's most prominent teams include men more or less forgotten to history. Of the nine men in the starting lineup for the American League champion Chicago White Sox in Game One of the 1919 World Series, only one did not end up either banished from baseball for life or elected to the Hall of Fame. His name is Shano Collins.

John Francis Collins was born on December 4, 1885, in Charlestown, a Boston neighborhood with a heavy Irish-American population. The Collins family fit in with the profile of the neighborhood: All four of his grandparents were born in Ireland. Shano's father, Joseph, was born in Rhode Island and his mother, Mary, was born in Massachusetts. Shano was the third of five children, along with Joseph, Mary, William, and Henry. Joseph Collins the elder provided for his family as a salesman, while Mary worked as a housekeeper.[1]

Shano's connection to baseball began at a young age. He sold peanuts at Boston's Walpole Street Grounds, home to the city's National League club.[2] Collins excelled as a semipro pitcher, then signed with Haverhill of the Class B New England League in 1907. He played one season at Haverhill,[3] where he was a teammate of future Hall of Famer Sliding Billy Hamilton, then apparently dropped out of Organized Baseball for a year before he was purchased by Springfield of the Connecticut State League in 1909. There, his .322 batting average in 88 games caught the eyes of Lou Barbour and Bob Connery, former players with connections to Chicago White Sox owner Charles Comiskey.[4]

An arm injury eventually forced Collins off the mound;[5] he played mostly shortstop and second base in the minors before moving to the outfield and occasionally playing first base in the major leagues.

As for Collins's nickname, most sources agree that "Shano" (sometimes spelled "Shauno" because it was pronounced that way) came about as a clubhouse corruption of Sean, the Gaelic equivalent of John and a nod to his Irish heritage.[6]

Collins made his major-league debut with the White Sox on April 21, 1910, a 4-1 loss to the Browns in St. Louis. That season the 24-year old played in 97 games for the White Sox, hitting .197 in 315 at-bats. Collins played about two-thirds of his games in the outfield and the balance at first base, where he substituted for Chick Gandil.

In 1911 the White Sox finished nine games better than in the previous season, tying Boston for fourth place in the American League. Collins improved marginally along with his team. Playing first base consistently in place of Gandil, who had been sold to Montreal of the Eastern League, Collins raised his batting average by 65 points to .262 and his slugging percentage over 100 points to .403. He hit a career-high four home runs, good for eighth in the league.

Throughout the decade, the 6-foot-tall, 185-pound Collins established himself as a solid if unspectacular major-league player. He was a strong defensive outfielder, possessing the versatility to play all three outfield positions as well as first base, and was a good teammate. Collins also showed hints of solid offensive production, placing third in the AL with 34 doubles in 1914 and fourth with 85 RBIs a year later.

Under first-year manager Pants Rowland, and with newly acquired stars like Shoeless Joe Jackson and Eddie Collins, the White Sox finished third in 1915. A second-place finish followed in 1916, and in 1917

Chicago captured the pennant with a 100-54 mark. In the team's pennant clincher, on September 21 against Boston, Collins came through with the game-winning hit in Chicago's 2-1 victory.

After platooning with Nemo Leibold throughout the regular season, Collins led off and played right field in all six games of the 1917 World Series against the New York Giants. He had a rough day in the White Sox' 2-0 loss in Game Three, making two errors in right field and going 0-for-4 at the plate. Collins hit .286 and scored two runs The White Sox downed the Giants in six games.

Two years later, the White Sox found themselves back in the World Series, this time against the Cincinnati Reds. To increase revenue, which had fallen off after World War I, the Series was a best-of-nine contest, which the Reds captured five games to three. Collins was the first batter of the Series, leading off Game One at Cincinnati's Redland Field (later renamed Crosley Field), and played in four of the eight games, hitting .250 (4-for-16) with a double and two runs scored.

No evidence exists to suggest that Collins was a part of the plot to throw the World Series to the Reds or had any knowledge of the plot. Despite their talent, the White Sox were a fractured lot, with the gentlemanly, sophisticated crowd embodied by the Columbia University-educated Eddie Collins and the rough-and-tumble crowd led by first baseman Chick Gandil. Shano fit in more with the Eddie Collins crowd, and was never offered a role in the fixing of the World Series.

Collins spent most of the 1920 season at first base in place of Gandil, who abruptly retired from baseball before the season began. In that first year of the live-ball era, Collins put together one of his best offensive seasons, hitting over .300 for the only time in his career. The White Sox remained in the pennant race the entire season, right up until the 1919 conspirators were suspended during the season's final week as the scandal came to light. Chicago finished two games behind pennant-winning Cleveland.

In March 1921 Collins was traded to his hometown Red Sox along with his platoon partner, Nemo Leibold, in exchange for Harry Hooper, the aging former star outfielder for Boston. The Red Sox of the early 1920s were a dreadful squad, and finished last in the American League in three of Collins's five years with the team. The best record the Red Sox posted during that span was 75-79 in 1921, before Boston had finished selling off its best players to the New York Yankees.

Collins was a part of a scary moment in July 1921, when he was hit above the left ear and knocked unconscious by a pitch from Detroit's Jim Middleton. The concerned crowd kept silent for several moments, memories of Ray Chapman's fatal beaning a year earlier still fresh in their minds. Adding insult to the injury, the game was wiped out by rain in the fifth inning.[7] Collins recovered and again showed his versatility, playing first base and all three outfield positions, and hitting .286 in 141 games.[8]

Collins remained with the Red Sox until 1925, when at the age of 39 he was released in June after having played in only two games. He signed with the Pittsfield

Shano Collins, circa 1917 (Bain Collection, Library of Congress, Prints and Photographs Division)

(Massachusetts) Hillies of the Eastern League, played more than 100 games in the outfield and also took over as manager. For the next two seasons he was the player-manager of Des Moines of the Western League, and managed Pittsfield again in 1928 and '29.[9]

In the winter of 1926-27, Collins was called to testify before Commissioner Kenesaw Mountain Landis about allegations that the White Sox had paid the Detroit Tigers to throw a late-season series in 1917 when Chicago was fighting for a pennant.[10] Numerous White Sox players, along with manager Pants Rowland, denied the allegation, which had been made by exiled Black Sox infielder Swede Risberg. Landis exonerated the White Sox, deciding that the money was not paid to the Tigers for throwing the series to Chicago, but for beating their top rivals, the Red Sox, later in the season.[11]

Collins began 1930 as manager of Nashua of the New England League, but when the league folded he moved back to Des Moines for the remainder of the season. Collins took Des Moines from last place to third place by the end of the season.[12]

In 1931 Collins returned to the major leagues as the manager of the Red Sox. Owner Bob Quinn had attempted to fill a managerial vacancy by hiring Joe McCarthy of the New York Yankees, but he was unable to lure McCarthy away from tThe Bronx. Quinn cited Collins's success as a minor-league manager when he announced the hire. Quinn said, "I have not signed him for any year or term of years but have promised him the job as long as I live if he hustles and runs the club to my satisfaction. I am tired of engaging managers and have high hopes that I have solved this managerial problem for the remainder of my baseball career."[13]

Unfortunately for Collins, this stability never materialized and he lasted just parts of two seasons as the Red Sox manager. He resigned in the middle of the 1932 season after compiling a record of 73-134. Under Collins and his successor, Marty McManus, the Red Sox went 43-111 in 1932.

Collins was called out of retirement briefly to manage Pittsfield again in 1942. But his career in uniform was otherwise over. He remained involved with baseball, scouting for the Detroit Tigers and participating in wartime exhibition games in the Boston area.[14]

Tragedy fell upon Collins and his family in the spring of 1945. His son, Marine Private Robert D. Collins, was killed in action on March 11 at Iwo Jima.[15] Robert, who had played baseball in high school before attending Providence College and Yale, was 20 years old.[16]

On September 10, 1955, Collins died suddenly at his home in Newton, Massachusetts, at the age of 69. He was buried at St. Mary's Cemetery in nearby Needham. He was survived by his wife, Elizabeth, three daughters, a son, four sisters, and a brother. One of his grandsons, Bob Gallagher, played for four seasons as an outfielder for the Red Sox, Mets, and Astros in the 1970s.

ACKNOWLEDGEMENTS

Special thanks to Michael Lynch and Bill Nowlin for their assistance.

SOURCES

In addition to the sources listed in the notes, the author also consulted Ancestry.com and Baseball-Reference.com.

NOTES

1   1900 US Census.

2   Bill Nowlin, *Red Sox Threads: Odds & Ends From Red Sox History* (Burlington, Massachusetts: Rounder Books, 2008), 178-79.

3   "Shano Collins," *The Sporting News*, September 21, 1955, 26.

4   Ernest J. Lanigan, "Shauno' Collins Broke Into Pro Ball 22 Years Ago," *Hartford Courant*, January 8, 1928.

5   "Collins Is Named Sox Manager, Does Not Sign Contract," *Lewiston* (Maine) *Daily Sun*, December 2, 1930, 19.

6   Mike Shatzkin, ed., *The Ballplayers* (New York: Arbor House, 1990), 213.

7   Michael Lynch, *Harry Frazee, Ban Johnson, and the Feud That Nearly Destroyed the American League* (Jefferson, North Carolina: McFarland, 2008), 154.

8   Collins played in 464 games for the Red Sox in his career, and as of 2014 had the most career at-bats (1,599) for the Red Sox of any native Bostonian. Nowlin, *Red Sox Threads*.

9   "Shano Collins," *The Sporting News*, September 21, 1955, 26; "Six Red Sox Rookies to Work With Hillies," *Boston Globe*, April 7, 1929; "Hillies Drill at Fenway Park," *Boston Globe*, April 9, 1929, 14.

10   Don Maxwell, "26 Deny Charges of 'Thrown' Games," *Chicago Tribune*, January 6, 1927, 15.

11   "Landis Exonerates 21 Ball Players," *Chicago Tribune*, January 12, 1927, 21.

12   "Collins Is Named Sox Manager."

13   "Collins Is Named Sox Manager."

14   "Shano Collins," *The Sporting News*, September 21, 1955, 26.

15   *The Sporting News*, April 12, 1945, 15.

16   "Shauno Collins' Son, Ex-Newton Athlete, Killed on Iwo Jima," *Boston Globe*, April 6, 1945, 15.

DAVE DANFORTH

By Steve Steinberg

DAVE DANFORTH (1890-1970) IS one of the most controversial figures in the history of the national pastime. Over the course of a career that stretched from 1911 to 1932, he kept puzzling hitters and overcoming suspicion that he used illegal pitches. The mystery of what he threw and how he pitched has never been resolved. St. Louis sports editor J. Roy Stockton wrote, "It is doubtful if ever a professional athlete has encountered circumstances so discouraging as those which Dave Danforth has had to hurdle in the course of his baseball career."[1]

A star relief pitcher on the 1917 world champion Chicago White Sox, Danforth saw his career hit rock bottom in 1919, and he was traded by the White Sox just a few weeks before the infamous World Series. He would resurrect his career, but was unable to do so in 1919. He also had a remarkable knack for being involved in a number of significant baseball events, a Forrest Gump of the game.

David Charles Danforth was born in the small farming community of Granger, Texas, on March 7, 1890, the fifth of six children of Charles and Henrietta Danforth. His father, who studied medicine in St. Louis and New Orleans and got his medical degree at Tulane, died when Dave was only 2 years old.[2] Neither Dave nor any of his three brothers had sons to carry on the family name.[3]

From his early days, Danforth was a pitcher. He pitched in high school and at Baylor University, which he attended for two years. His second year, 1910-11, he had a perfect 10-0 mark—including a no-hitter—and led the school to the Texas Collegiate Championship.

Danforth was a tall, slender southpaw (listed at 6 feet, 167 pounds) who caught the eye of one of Connie Mack's informal scouts, Hyman Pearlstone, a grocer and banker from Palestine, Texas. Pearlstone promised the youngster a $500 signing bonus if he joined the Philadelphia Athletics, which Danforth did, on August 1, 1911.

The rookie pitcher soon proved crucial to the A's pennant march. The team's starting pitchers were worn down and benefited greatly from backup from the Texas youngster. The following week, Danforth relieved Chief Bender, Eddie Plank, Jack Coombs, and Harry Krause. He finished the season with a 4-1 record, with 12 of his 14 appearances in relief. Mack declared that he had found another Waddell: "Never seen a kid who had more prospects of being a corker."[4]

Danforth was not eligible for the World Series, but as was not unusual with Mack's sharing club, he was awarded a full winner's share of $3,654.58, at the age of 21.

In May 1912 Mack decided to farm him out. The A's were loaded with young pitchers, and Mack wanted Danforth to get plenty of work, so he sent the lefty to Jack Dunn's Baltimore Orioles. Years later, Mack said he let Danforth go because he didn't have a curveball.[5]

Danforth became one of the anchors of the 1912-13 Orioles.[6] At the same time, he was thinking long-term, about life after baseball. In 1913 he entered the University of Maryland Dental School. Dunn provided him with a private room for his studies at spring training, and the dental school's dean allowed Danforth to miss many of his classes and get lecture notes from a classmate.

Danforth tossed a shutout on Opening Day 1914, and the O's starter the next day—making his professional debut—also threw a shutout: George Herman Ruth. That season, Dunn's Orioles were on the front line of a war with the upstart Federal League, whose Terrapins team quickly devastated the attendance and thus the finances of the Orioles. By midseason, Dunn had to generate cash to stay afloat and started selling players, including Ruth to the Boston Red Sox. A month later, on August 8, he sold Danforth to the Louisville Colonels of the American Association for $3,000.[7]

Before Danforth joined his new team, he married 19-year-old Margaret Oliphant, a Baltimore girl. That fall, he returned to his studies and graduated the following spring. He also became the manager of the University of Maryland baseball team.

In 1915, Danforth took his game to another level. He began experimenting with different pitches. His most effective pitch was one for which he became famous, as the father of the "shine ball." Danforth explained how he stumbled upon the pitch, with two slightly varying accounts. The dusty field in hot and dry Louisville was regularly sprayed with oil, to keep the dirt from swirling. But the oily ball was hard to grip. According to one version, he would rub the oily ball on his pants leg. Under the other story, he would put rosin on his pants leg and rub the ball on it.[8]

In both accounts, in attempting to remove the oil, he made one side of the ball smoother and darker; hence "the shine." The result of the contrasting surfaces of the ball was similar to many trick pitches: a ball with an unpredictable flight, one it was hard to make contact with. Danforth became harder to hit as the season went on. After striking out 15 men on September 8, he tossed a two-hit shutout and struck out 18 Kansas City batters four days later. In doing so, he broke Marty O'Toole's American Association record of 17.[9] Just three days after that, Danforth beat St. Paul 1-0 and struck out 15 Saints.[10] Later that month the Chicago White Sox drafted him. Dave Danforth was coming back to the majors.

Often the inventor of something is not the one who maximizes its use, whether in baseball or another endeavor. Elmer Stricklett (career record of 35-51) was one of the pitchers credited with introducing the spitball in the majors, yet his teammate and disciple, the White Sox' Ed Walsh, rode it to fame. In Chicago Danforth showed the shine ball to a journeyman pitcher by the name of Eddie Cicotte. Up until 1915,

Eddie had a record of 91-81; after that 13-12 season, he fashioned a 105-55 mark and became one of the game's best pitchers.

F.C. Lane, the editor of *Baseball* magazine, said that Lefty Williams, Cicotte's teammate, told him that Danforth did indeed teach the shine ball to Cicotte.[11] During that 1916 spring training, Danforth befriended another pitcher who would later ride the shine ball to fame: Hod Eller.[12]

Danforth's reputation was preceding him, and he was reputed to throw more trick pitches than just the shine ball. Tigers manager Hughie Jennings accused him of throwing the emery ball, and Tigers star Ty Cobb would point an accusing finger at Danforth for years.[13] The *Sporting News* spoke of his "new-fangled mystery ball," a fastball "that did everything but talk."[14] One newspaper said that he used his large and powerful fingers — with the help of a rough fingernail — to loosen the cover of the ball and throw a "wrinkle ball."[15] Danforth was not forthcoming about anything. He denied any changes to his pitching and said he threw just as he had in 1911.[16] With all the controversy swirling around him, teammate Eddie Collins dubbed him "Dauntless Dave."[17]

Danforth also became known for a controversial pickoff move that many felt was a balk. His move to first base remained contentious for the rest of his career.[18] His 1916 season was fairly ordinary, with a 6-5 record and a 3.27 earned-run average. His White Sox were improving dramatically. New manager Clarence "Pants" Rowland led them to 93 wins in 1915 and 89 in 1916, when they fell just two games short of the pennant.

The 1917 White Sox won the pennant and beat the New York Giants in the World Series. One of the tools Rowland employed was the relief pitcher, and Dave Danforth was his man. He appeared in 50 games (only nine starts) and had nine saves (as computed retroactively), both league-leading numbers. Controversy continued to swirl around him. In August Cleveland manager Lee Fohl declared that if the

White Sox won the pennant, they would do so by "unfair tactics," referring to Danforth's pitching.[19]

The suspicions and charges went beyond Danforth to the White Sox pitching staff as a whole. Damon Runyon wrote, "There is a firm belief among many managers and players in the American League that the success of the White Sox pitchers has been due to trickery—to 'monkeying' with the baseball … using vaseline and other substances." Runyon went further, writing that some players have said that baseballs at White Sox home games were being tampered with by use of a nail file.[20]

On August 14 the first pitch Danforth threw in relief hit Cleveland star outfielder Tris Speaker in the temple and knocked him unconscious. The team doctor said that had the pitch hit an inch lower, "it might have been all up with Spoke."[21] Speaker later criticized two White Sox hurlers. "The game will go to the dogs unless a stop is put to the doctoring of the ball by [Eddie] Cicotte and Danforth.… If the Sox win, that is what will give them the pennant."[22]

The White Sox won four games from the Tigers in early September 1917 that would be the focus of a major controversy almost a decade later. In late 1926 banned Black Sox player Swede Risberg charged that the Tigers deliberately lost those games and that he helped gather the payoff money from most of the White Sox players. (The Tigers committed nine errors in those games.) When confronted with the undeniable evidence that they did pay the money, the Chicago players said the money was paid to the Tigers as a token of thanks for their beating the Boston Red Sox three times later that month. The only action Commissioner Kenesaw M. Landis took was to ban the paying of such "thank you" money from that point forward.

However, the White Sox' explanation seemed odd since they had a commanding lead of 8½ games over Boston when the Tigers met the Red Sox. Also interesting was the fact that only a handful of members of the White Sox did not contribute to the Detroit payoff pool: manager Rowland, coach Kid Gleason,

Eddie Murphy, and Dave Danforth.[23] "I didn't pay a dime toward a pool," Danforth declared.[24] Danforth appeared in only one game of the 1917 World Series against the New York Giants. He gave up a single, triple, and home run in a Game Four White Sox loss. The White Sox then won the fifth and sixth games, the latter remembered for Heinie Zimmerman's chase of Eddie Collins across home plate, as Red Faber closed out the Series for the champion White Sox.

Spring training of 1918 was marked by controversy when the respected black trainer of the White Sox, William "Doc" Buckner, was released. The *Chicago Defender*, the city's black paper, demanded to know the reason and wondered if Rowland really was running the team "or are some of those southern crackers on the team running it?"[25] Chicago sportswriter I.E. Sanborn suggested Dave Danforth was involved. More than five years later, respected Detroit sportswriter H.G. Salsinger elaborated. That spring, Danforth had "borrowed" Buckner's sharp scalpel to whittle a piece of wood. When Buckner called Danforth down for taking his tool, Salsinger wrote, Danforth went after Buckner with a baseball bat. Buckner would return to the White Sox in 1920, after Danforth had left the team.[26]

Neither Danforth nor the White Sox came close to replicating their season in 1918. His record went from 11-6 to 6-15, with only two saves and a jump of nearly 0.80 in his earned-run average. The Sox won less than half of their games and fell to sixth place. Yet some things were not changing. Washington manager Clark Griffith (a master of nicking the ball with his spikes when he had pitched two decades earlier) charged Danforth with defacing the ball.[27]

The 1918 major-league season ended a month early, as young men from all walks of life were being drafted and sent to Europe to fight for the Allies. Danforth was not called up. Not only was he married, but he was supporting his widowed mother (who was living with his family), and his first child, Dorothy, was born in 1917. After the shortened 1918 season ended, he joined the Baltimore Dry Docks, a powerful semipro baseball team.

In 1919 the White Sox tried many veteran pitchers, including Joe Benz, Big Bill James, Grover Lowdermilk, and Erskine Mayer, to round out their staff. "One by one," wrote *The Sporting News*, "pitching experiments that have been tried and found to be excess baggage are cut away by the club.... The Kid's [Gleason's] big gamble this year has been Dave Danforth."[28] With Red Faber's "off" season, Chicago finally settled on rookie Dickie Kerr as their third starter, behind Cicotte and Williams.

While the White Sox bounced back in 1919, Danforth did not. He won only one game, and his earned-run average ballooned to 7.78. His July 12 performance epitomized his season. He relieved Dickie Kerr in the third inning of a game against the Red Sox. Babe Ruth hit the first pitch he threw out of the park, Ruth's first Comiskey Park home run.[29] By the time the game was over, Danforth had given up nine earned runs. Four days later, he gave up six earned runs in relief.

On August 26 the White Sox traded Danforth to Columbus of the American Association (which league he had pitched in both in 1914 and 1915) in exchange for pitcher Roy Wilkinson. Wilkinson had won 17 games with a 2.08 earned-run average for Columbus. He would win only 12 games in the majors, and had a 4-20 record for the 1921 White Sox.[30] Danforth threatened to bring an action to the National Commission against the White Sox for a World Series share and eventually did receive a partial share.[31] One is left to wonder what role, if any, he would have played in the Black Sox scandal.

Danforth refused to report to Columbus and instead again joined the Baltimore Dry Docks.[32] They played a best-of-seven series against the powerful Baltimore Orioles of the International League in September. After Columbus general manager Joe Tinker grudgingly gave permission for Danforth to pitch, he led the Dry Docks to the series win with three victories.[33] He won the seventh game, 5-0, on one day's rest, with 15 strikeouts. The Orioles grumbled about his unfair pitches, and one Baltimore paper called him "the Paraffin Kid."[34] The Dry Docks went on to win the national Shipyard Championship, a tourney in which Danforth tossed a 1-0 gem.[35]

In 1920 Danforth joined Columbus and fashioned a 13-12 record with a 2.57 earned-run average; he led the league in strikeouts with 188. Once again his season was not without controversy. In early July he was suspended for "loading up" with a spitter, and he was suspended again a couple of months later.[36] When he returned from his suspension, Dave one-hit Milwaukee. Pants Rowland took over as Columbus manager in 1921. He had been a big booster of Danforth's. Back in 1919, he said the pitcher had got a raw deal, having been released so close to the World Series.[37] While the Senators were a very bad team in 1921—they won only 66 games—Danforth won 25 of them to tie for the league lead in wins. He also led the American Association in strikeouts, earned-run average, and complete games.[38] Again, his work was marked by accusations of illegal pitches; the *Columbus Dispatch* called him "the icicle of the swirling vortex."[39] But

Dave Danforth, circa 1916 (Courtesy of Michael Aronstein / TCMA Ltd.)

Danforth's spectacular season would propel him to the major leagues for the third time.

After the season Rowland began evaluating a number of offers for Danforth. In mid-December, the St. Louis Browns stunned the baseball world when they acquired him in exchange for 11 men, in what one paper called "probably the most unique deal ever recorded in baseball."[40] White Sox manager Kid Gleason, who had dealt a struggling Dave away in 1919, declared, "Anybody who gambles on a left-hander ought to be put in an insane asylum.… The three most dangerous things in the world are a four-flush, an unloaded shotgun, and a left-handed pitcher."[41] Pants Rowland was far more supportive. He told the Browns, "I am not peddling you a lemon. Danforth will make you a pennant contender next year."[42]

The Browns were an offensive powerhouse that was one good pitcher away from contending for the American League pennant. A newspaper in Mobile, Alabama, where the Browns were training, declared, "If he [Danforth] flashes, it means the flag."[43] That spring Danforth explained that he modeled himself on the great left-hander Eddie Plank. Plank fidgeted and delayed so much on the mound that he had opposing batters seeing red. "Get the batter nervous, and you have him down," Danforth told the *St. Louis Times*.[44] His reputation had batters so worked up that they were diverting their focus from something more important: hitting the ball.

Accusations dogged Danforth from the start of the '22 season. His nemesis, Ty Cobb, protested his delivery in an early-season series and declared that he would expose the pitcher.[45] Matters finally came to a head on July 27, 1922. In a game against the Yankees, Danforth threw a pitch that sailed, and he was ejected for throwing a ball with loaded seams, though he had just entered the game. An automatic ten-game suspension followed.

Browns manager Lee Fohl was coming to the conclusion that the pitcher they had paid so dearly for was not "clean." In early August they put him on waivers, and not a single team claimed him. Veteran St. Louis

sportswriter John Wray was moved to write, "Dave was either unanimously voted of little value, or a tacit agreement to 'railroad' him for the good of the game had taken effect."[46] The next day the usually taciturn Danforth made a lengthy statement to the *Post-Dispatch*. He said that he had never loaded the seams of a ball or applied a foreign substance to it.

The Browns sent him to Tulsa of the Western League (with an option to recall him), and his six victories helped them win the pennant. On August 26 he struck out 15 men, breaking Dan Tipple's league record of 14, set earlier that year. His shutout then helped Tulsa beat the Mobile Bears of the Southern Association for the Class A championship. The St. Louis Browns were not as fortunate. They lost the pennant by just one game to the Yankees. Had Danforth stayed with them during the stretch run, they would have had a good chance to finish in first place.

The stories of just what Danforth did to the ball swirled around him, and they were all across the board. He was said to have a nail on his left thumb that was so sharp that he could slit the seams, or so rough that he could make an abrasion on the ball. He was reputed to sleep with his pitching hand soaking in a tray of pickle brine, to make his skin as abrasive as emery paper and let him roughen up the ball. He was also accused of using his large and powerful hands to loosen the cover of the ball.[47]

A couple of weeks after the season, the Browns recalled Danforth for 1923. Lee Fohl did not want him back. He told a reporter that Danforth had been given more chances to go straight (or throw straight) than he deserved.[48] But owner Phil Ball had overruled his manager.

A pall was cast over the Browns' 1923 season when George Sisler was forced to sit out the year with a serious eye injury. Danforth became a mainstay of the Browns' pitching staff, but controversy still shadowed him. On August 1, in a game against the Athletics, Danforth was ejected by umpire George Moriarty for throwing a ball with rough spots on it. He and Danforth had a long-running feud, the source of which remains unknown.[49] Once again, an automatic ten-game suspension followed.

Yet it wasn't just Moriarty who questioned Danforth's pitches. When this latest controversy broke, *St. Louis Times* sports editor Sid Keener wrote, "I have talked with almost every umpire in the American League on the charge against Danforth. The report from them is unanimous—that Dave applies a foreign substance or otherwise tampers with the ball."[50]

Danforth's teammates rallied to his side. George Sisler, who would become his manager in 1924 and 1925, told *Baseball* magazine, "I have never known Dave Danforth to use any illegal delivery.... Danforth is a high grade fellow in every way and he deserves the right to work at his profession without being molested."[51]

His teammates even put together a petition to send to league President Ban Johnson. But the team's soft-spoken manager would not sign it. Fohl met with Sid Keener and showed him some balls that he said Danforth had tampered with. Keener went public with this evidence a few weeks later.[52]

Keener weighed in on the controversy. "I know the character of Lee Fohl. He would give a friend the last dime he had in the world.... If Lee wouldn't sign [the petition] there must be some black smoke in the air."[53] A few days later, Fohl was fired by a furious owner. Phil Ball felt he had gone to great lengths and cost to secure Danforth, only to be undercut by a manager who refused to use the talent he was given. A close confidant of Phil Ball, American League President Johnson did not agree with Ball in this matter. Johnson said that Danforth had a "mania" for doctoring the ball and was "incurable" as an illegal pitcher.[54]

On August 16, with both Johnson and Commissioner Landis in the St. Louis stands, Danforth returned to the mound, against the league-leading Yankees. He understood that his career would end if he resorted to trick pitches. With Billy Evans behind the plate, Danforth decided to remove any suspicion by asking for a new baseball whenever the ball became discolored or marked up in any way. An incredible 58 balls were

put in play, and still he was effective. He threw a three-hitter, but Herb Pennock and the Yankees came out on top, 3-1.

Danforth lost the game, but he won over a lot of hearts on that day. Sid Keener saluted him, writing, "It was a game that only a steel heart and a concrete spine could have pitched. Considering all events in the case I have never seen its equal on the ball field."[55] It was this performance that prompted J. Roy Stockton to write the quote at the top of this chapter.

Danforth finished the 1923 season with the most wins (16), innings pitched, complete games, and strikeouts in his major-league career. In 1924 he posted numbers close to those of '23. The clamor over his delivery subsided but did not disappear. Ban Johnson said that if Danforth was using his "sandpapered" hand on the ball, he should discontinue doing so at once.[56] When Danforth shut out the Yankees on June 8—one of only two career shutouts—Yankees manager Miller Huggins complained that Danforth's thumbnail was loosening the cover and that he was throwing the spitter.[57] When he three-hit the Tigers on July 6, he had to do it with Ty Cobb constantly heckling and accusing him of pitching illegally.

Danforth's final season in the major leagues was 1925. His record was a pedestrian 7-9, and he led the league in home runs allowed, with 19. On May 6 he gave up a home run to his nemesis, Ty Cobb, one of five Cobb hit in two consecutive games in St. Louis.

Approaching the age of 36, Danforth seemed to be near the end of his baseball life. Yet he was about to embark on another minor-league career, one that would include remarkable team and personal achievements. Danforth joined the Milwaukee Brewers of the American Association in 1926, and his 17 wins helped fuel the Brewers' 21-game winning streak, a new league record. He won the 10th and 20th games of that streak. Early in the 1927 season, after Danforth pitched poorly in a few games, the Brewers sold him to New Orleans. His 16-4 record and sparkling 2.24 earned-run average helped lead the Pelicans to the Southern Association pennant. His manager, Larry

Gilbert, said, "I never learned what he did—if he did anything. I know he wanted the batters to think so."[58]

In 1928 and 1929, neither Danforth nor the Pelicans could replicate their 1927 performances. At the age of 40, he played for both Dallas and Buffalo in 1930. With the latter, he found himself in the spotlight, quite literally. On July 3 he pitched the International League's first night baseball game with permanent lighting (what were called "arc lights," 24,000 watts of them) against Montreal, a month after the first such minor-league game was played.[59] Years later, Danforth's player-manager on the Bisons, Jimmy Cooney, said that Danforth had a little black bag that he kept locked at all times.[60]

Danforth won 12 of 20 decisions for Buffalo in 1930, and none was bigger than when he set an International League record by striking out 20 Rochester Red Wings on September 20.[61] His pro career ended in 1932, when the 42-year-old pitcher had a young teammate by the name of Billy Werber. In 2001 the 93-year-old former major-league star immediately recalled Danforth. He told the author, "Danforth, he was a lefty. A gentlemanly type ... a quiet fellow. Never had a hell of a lot to say.... Dave didn't have the disposition to do anything illegal with the ball."[62]

In retirement, Danforth drew on his degree of almost 20 years earlier and began to practice dentistry in his hometown of Baltimore. He would do so until 1960, when he turned 70. He also taught "operative dentistry" at the University of Maryland twice a week for a number of years. Danforth coached the Loyola College baseball team in 1937 and 1938.[63] "I haven't gotten as far in it [dentistry] as I did in baseball, nor does it appeal to me as baseball did," he later admitted.[64]

Danforth enjoyed golf, fishing, and gardening. He suffered from Alzheimer's disease at the end of his life and died at the age of 80 on September 19, 1970, in Baltimore.

Dave Danforth's scientific approach to pitching was years ahead of its time. In a 1926 *Baseball* magazine article entitled "Why Pitching Is in Its Infancy," he said, "Pitching twenty or thirty years from now will be much more complex than it is today.... No Major League club manager, scout, or anyone else, has any clear idea of just what the human hand can do with a baseball." He noted that physics and math experts had not determined just what could be done with a baseball. The magazine wrote that Danforth's "enquiring mind" and "restless spirit of investigation" had led to his constant experimentation with pitches and deliveries.[65] Years earlier, St. Louis sportswriter J. Roy Stockton wrote about his growing fame as a trick pitcher. Stockton noted that Danforth was inquisitive—always warming up in the bullpen, trying out new pitches and perfecting them.[66]

Danforth often said that there was no secret to his pitching, "just psychology and a good fastball." He added, "There's no rule against rubbing a ball with your hands. Often I did it deliberately a long time for psychological effect."[67] At times, he explained, his large hands and long fingers enabled him to get an especially good grip on the ball.[68]

But there was also Dave's frank admission: "I will admit that in my time I have used every delivery that I ever heard of. If I had known of any others I should have used them."[69] He was also often quick to note, "I never pitched an illegal ball in my life. Sure I invented the shine ball and used it until the pitch was ruled out with other freak pitching in 1920. I have nothing to hide."[70]

The respected Hall of Fame umpire Billy Evans was one of the few arbiters of the game who felt Danforth was not tampering with the ball. "Danforth doesn't have to cheat," wrote Evans, because his strong grip enabled him to get a natural "hop" on the ball and make it sail.[71] In early July 1922, Evans commented on Danforth's "heart," for having the fortitude to keep coming back in the face of constant accusations.[72]

Danforth's former manager, Pants Rowland, said the same thing, but in a more colorful way: "He does it by his grip. For hours he kneads his knuckles and keeps clenching and unclenching his hands to get that grip. He takes those gripping machines with him just as [classical pianist Ignacy] Paderewski plays the piano all the while at practice, and [classical pianist Dirk] Schaefer tickles the ivories to keep his eye and stroke, so does Dave keep working on that grip."[73]

Danforth's career was marred by ongoing accusations about his pitching. He bemoaned the "continual nagging" by umpires.[74] One sportswriter noted that he had had been "persecuted rather than prosecuted."[75] Yet Danforth really brought on that suspicion, as part of his "mind games" with batters. He also put umpires in a difficult position. Sportswriter Fred Turbyville provided some perspective from the men in blue. He wrote that umpires hated rows, and whenever Dave Danforth pitched, there were rows. "David was a crucifix for umpires."[76]

New York sportswriter Tom Meany may have provided insight into Dave's pitching style and approach. "It seemed that Danforth was not only a pitcher but a practical psychologist as well. Nobody ever saw the left hand which was supposed to be so ruinous to the surface of a baseball.… Batters who are always seeking to detect some sign of chicanery on a pitcher's part sometimes become so engrossed in looking for illegal pitches that they forget to hit the legal ones."[77]

Ironically, 1919 was the low point in Dave Danforth's baseball career. He could not weave his pitching magic and sow doubt in the minds of batters because he was so ineffective that season. "You never heard a squawk on my bad days," he was known to say.[78] The 1919 season was a long "bad day" for Danforth and ultimately was for his former White Sox team, too.

NOTES

1   *St. Louis Post-Dispatch*, August 19, 1923.

2   In the 1880 census, Charles is listed as a farmer. Henrietta and her parents were born in Germany, as listed in the 1890 Census. His father and his parents were American-born.

3   Email from Lajuna Danforth Carabasi, Danforth's niece, to the author, dated April 5, 2011.

4   *Washington Post*, August 10, 1911; *Charlotte Observer*, September 6, 1911.

5   *Philadelphia Evening Ledger*, August 31, 1917; *Lexington Herald*, October 18, 1917. Mack may have had an option to

recall him, but in late August, when he acquired Jimmy Walsh and Eddie Murphy from the Orioles, he may have had to cut Danforth loose.

6   He won 28 games; Bob Shawkey won 26.

7   Hall of Fame contract card. Red Sox scout and former Red Sox manager Patsy Donovan said that he was sent to Baltimore to scout Danforth and to decide whether the Red Sox should purchase him. Instead, Donovan was so impressed by Ruth and Ernie Shore that he told Boston owner Joe Lannin to buy them instead. Arthur Daley, "Remember Patsy Donovan," *Baseball Digest*, May 1949.

8   Danforth obituary, *New York Times*, September 22, 1970. Danforth said he got the idea by watching a bootblack shine shoes with a rag.

9   O'Toole was with St. Paul and set the mark against Milwaukee on July 10, 1911.

10 Some accounts say that Danforth struck out 16 in that game. The current American Association record of 20 was set by Maurice "Mickey" McDermott on May 24, 1949.

11 *Hartford Courant*, September 2, 1923. Eddie Collins confirmed this. (*Los Angeles Times*, January 17, 1927.) In the late Teens, there was much debate over the shine ball, with many suggesting it didn't really exist, that Eddie Cicotte simply led people to believe he was doing something with the ball.

12 *New York Times*, September 28, 1919. Eller did not make the 1916 White Sox after spring training. Coincidentally, he would be one of the aces of the 1919 world champion Cincinnati Reds.

13 *The Sporting News*, April 20, 1916. In a syndicated newspaper series on his career, Cobb said Danforth would slit the ball with a razor, load it with paraffin (which was invisible), which he would later scrape away to raise the seams. *New York Evening Journal*, January 23, 1924.

14 *The Sporting News*, April 20, 1916.

15 *Baltimore Sun*, December 20, 1915.

16 *Daily Morning Oregonian* (Portland), April 27, 1917.

17 Danforth's other nicknames include "Daring Dave" and "Dashing Dave."

18 Danforth was called for a balk 13 times in his major-league career, with seven of them in 1922-1923.

19 *Wilkes-Barre Times-Leader*, August 14, 1917.

20 *New York American*, August 31, 1917.

21 Charles Alexander, *Spoke*, 121. Dave was not known as a "headhunter." He hit only three batsmen in 1916, and the same number in 1917. Carl Mays hit 9 and 14, respectively, those years. The resultant concussion and blurred vision kept Speaker out of the next seven games. Other than 1923, Dave never hit more than five batters (1918). His 12 hit batsmen would have led the National League in 1923, but Howard Ehmke and Walter Johnson hit 20 men in the American League.

22 *New York Tribune*, August 26, 1917.

23 Danforth pitched briefly in three of the games. In two, he snuffed out rallies and was pulled for pinch hitters in the bottom of the first inning in which he appeared. In the third game, he was not as effective.

24 *Boston Daily Globe*, January 2, 1927. Men considered above reproach, such as Eddie Collins and Ray Schalk, did contribute.

25 *Chicago Defender*, March 23, 1918.

26 *Washington Post*, September 19, 1923. Salsinger brought this up after Danforth was the center of another controversy, one that had cost his manager his job.

27 *Washington Post*, May 17, 1918. Three years later, Griffith would offer $50,000 in an unsuccessful attempt to acquire Danforth. *Washington Post*, December 9, 1921.

28 *The Sporting News*, July 24, 1919. There was only one brief mention of Danforth having a physical ailment in 1919, a "bad neck" early in the season. *Chicago Daily Journal*, May 13, 1919.

29 It was Ruth's 11th home run of 1919 and the 31st of his career.

30 The *Chicago Daily Journal* noted that the White Sox also included cash in the deal, a reflection of how far Danforth's stock had fallen. August 26, 1919.

31 *New York Tribune*, September 15, 1919. Historian Gene Carney told the author in an email dated October 22, 2003, that it was a one-quarter share, A November 7, 1919, letter from Charles Comiskey to Garry Hermann also notes that Danforth received a one-quarter share; this file is contained in the American League's Black Sox Scandal records at the Baseball Hall of Fame. The *Baltimore Evening Sun* (October 2, 1919) said that Danforth, Wilkinson, and pitcher Erskine Mayer would split a share equally. The *Chicago Daily Journal* (October 10, 1919) wrote that Danforth and Mayer would each get a one-half share.

32 Danforth's Hall of Fame contract card shows that he was suspended for this action and later reinstated, when the 1920 season approached. The International League champion did not play the American Association champion in the Little World Series that year. Instead, the AA's St. Paul Saints met the Pacific Coast League champion, and the Orioles were available to play the Dry Docks.

33 Newspaper clipping, Danforth family scrapbook. Orioles owner Jack Dunn was close to Joe Tinker, which probably explains the latter's granting Dave clearance to play.

34 *Baltimore Evening Sun*, September 26, 1919. There were no restrictions on pitches in the series—Dunn wanted the Dry Docks to be at "best strength." Newspaper clipping, Danforth family scrapbook.

35 Jimmy Keenan, "Lefty Russell," SABR BioProject, sabr.org/bioproject. Red Sox youngster Waite Hoyt also pitched a key win.

36 *Kansas City Times*, July 2, 1920; *Columbus Dispatch*, September 14, 1920. Each infraction resulted in an automatic ten-day suspension. The spitball had been banned in the league back in 1918.

37 Newspaper clipping, Danforth family scrapbook. Rowland had been fired as White Sox manager after the 1918 season.

38 Danforth's league-leading figures for 1920 (strikeouts) and 1921 are from *The Encyclopedia of Minor League Baseball*, Third Edition, edited by Lloyd Johnson and Miles Wolff.

39 *Columbus Dispatch*, June 2, 1921.

40 Newspaper clipping, Dave Danforth scrapbook. Six men were named; two would be named in 1922, two more in 1923, and one in 1924. They included men with major league experience who were not on the Browns roster, men the Browns still had "strings" on.

41 *Columbus Dispatch*, January 1, 1922.

42 *St. Louis Times*, December 15, 1921. Umpire Billy Evans also assured the Browns that Danforth's delivery was clean. *Columbus Dispatch*, January 13, 1922.

43 *Mobile Register*, March 19, 1922.

44 *St. Louis Times*, March 4, 1922, and March 15, 1922. Apparently Danforth sought out Plank, his old Philadelphia teammate, when he returned to the major leagues in 1916. *Wilkes-Barre Times-Leader*, June 19, 1922.

45 *Kansas City Star*, April 26, 1922; *New York Globe and Commercial Advertiser*, April 28, 1922.

46 *St. Louis Post-Dispatch*, August 12, 1922.

47 Basenfelder manuscript and an undated *Sporting News* article, conveyed by historian Norman Macht, said that Danforth did so. Danforth's son-in-law, Jim Thompson, told the author that Dave did indeed soak his hand in brine, but not overnight. Danforth's daughter, Jean Danforth Thompson, said to the author that he used the fluid that is used on violin bows on his hand. Phone conversations with the author, January 6, 2002.

48 Martin J. Haley, *St. Louis Globe-Democrat*, October 20, 1922.

49 Danforth's former manager, Connie Mack, made the initial complaint. Moriarty and Danforth had been teammates on the 1916 Chicago White Sox. Before that, Moriarty had been a teammate of Ty Cobb's for many years.

50 *St. Louis Times*, August 3, 1923.

51 "Why Dave Danforth Has Been a Storm Center," *Baseball Magazine*, July 1924.

52 *St. Louis Times*, August 22, 1923. All were new balls that had a rough spot of about two inches square. Keener included diagrams of the balls in his column.

53 *St. Louis Times*, August 3, 1923.

54 *St. Louis Globe-Democrat*, August 15, 1923; *New York Times*, August 15, 1923.

55 *St. Louis Times*, August 17, 1923.

56 June 3, 1924 letter, American League Archives, National Baseball Hall of Fame Library.

57 *New York Telegram and Evening Mail*, June 9, 1924; St. *Louis Post-Dispatch*, June 13, 1924.

58 *Atlanta Constitution*, March 13, 1937.

59 On May 2, 1930, a Western League game in Des Moines (played at night against Wichita) drew 12,000 fans for a team that was averaging 600. minorleaguebaseball.com/milb/history/timeline.jsp.

60 *Buffalo Evening News*, August 1, 1964.

61 Danforth broke the record of 17 set by Lefty Grove of Baltimore and Leroy Herrmann of Reading. The current International League record of 22 was set by Bob Veale on August 10, 1962. *New York Times*, September 2, 1934. Veale set his record with the Columbus Jets, against the Buffalo Bisons.

62 Billy Werber (1908-2009) telephone interview with the author, July 11, 2001.

63 *Hartford Courant*, May 2, 1937, and March 16, 1938.

64 Undated Danforth letter in Danforth family scrapbook. Another clip in the scrapbook notes he had returned to the Baltimore College of Dental Surgery for postgraduate review back in 1927.

65 "Why Pitching Is in Its Infancy," *Baseball* magazine, February 1926.

66 J. Roy Stockton, *St. Louis Post-Dispatch*, undated 1917 newspaper clipping, Danforth family scrapbook.

67 *Chicago Daily Tribune*, March 24, 1944.

68 *Philadelphia Inquirer*, December 25, 1921.

69 "Why Dave Danforth Has Been a Storm Center," *Baseball* magazine, July 1924.

70 Don Basenfelder manuscript, *Sporting News* files.

71 *New York Globe and Commercial Advertiser*, December 15, 1921. In one of his columns, Evans listed all the things Dave had been accused of doing and then declared, "None of these things were ever proved." Newspaper clipping, Danforth family scrapbook.

72 *San Jose Evening News*, July 7, 1922.

73 *Charlotte Observer*, February 24, 1922.

74 *St. Louis Post-Dispatch*, August 13, 1922.

75 John Wray, *St. Louis Post-Dispatch*, August 18, 1923.

76 Fred Turbyville, undated *Evening Star* newspaper clipping in Danforth family scrapbook. Detroit sportswriter H.G. Salsinger supported this line of thinking when he wrote, "Umpires felt like resigning whenever Danforth warmed up, for it meant another tough afternoon for them." *Detroit News*, April 19, 1923.

77 Tom Meany, *Baseball's Greatest Teams*, 197.

78 *Chicago Daily Tribune*, March 24, 1944.

RED FABER

By Brian Cooper

URBAN "RED" FABER, ONE OF the last pitchers to legally throw a spitball, persevered through illness and injury, a world war, and the Black Sox Scandal to win a place in the National Baseball Hall of Fame.

The right-hander played his entire 20-year major-league career with the White Sox, one of the league's strongest teams before the scandal and a perennial also-ran afterward. Faber won 254 games—a total that Ray Schalk, Faber's longtime batterymate and friend, contended might have reached 300 had the team not been decimated after its misdeeds came to light in 1920.[1]

He learned the spitball, the pitch that brought him major-league success, in the minor leagues, after an arm injury jeopardized his career. "I never resorted to the spitter until I was obliged to," Faber later said. "I nearly ruined my arm throwing curves."[2] Wetting the tips of the first two fingers on his right hand, Faber threw the spitter from a variety of arm angles, befuddling batters with the pitch's late-breaking downward movement. "A batter cannot guess with Faber," Goose Goslin remarked. "His only chance is to close the eyes and hope bat meets ball."[3] To get the consistency required to throw his spitter, Faber was known to chew a combination of slippery elm and tobacco, though he preferred the latter. "And I don't chew [tobacco] because I like it, either," explained Faber, a lifelong smoker. "In fact, I never chew except when I am pitching."[4]

Urban Clarence Faber (some references incorrectly list his middle name as Charles) was born on his parents' farm near Cascade, a tiny community in northeast Iowa, on September 6, 1888. The second of four children born to Nicholas and Margaret Grief Faber, he was of Luxembourg descent. German was the primary language spoken in the Faber home and

at the Catholic elementary school the Faber children attended. In 1893 the family moved into Cascade, where Nicholas operated a tavern and then opened the Hotel Faber. With his real-estate holdings and successful hotel, Nicholas Faber became one of Cascade's most affluent citizens. The Fabers could afford to send the children to out-of-town prep schools and colleges, and for several years before World War I they lived off of Nicholas's investment income.[5]

The red-haired Faber apparently had a sporadic and unspectacular high-school baseball career. He attended prep academies associated with colleges in two Mississippi River communities—Sacred Heart, in Prairie du Chien, Wisconsin, and then St. Joseph's in Dubuque, Iowa. In 1909, when he was 20 and studying at a Dubuque business school, he joined the college varsity of his prep alma mater, St. Joseph's. The institution, now Loras College, has no record of Faber taking any college classes there; however, there is ample documentation of his dominance over college batters in 1909, when St. Joseph's went undefeated in its half-dozen games.[6] The highlight was Faber's 22-strikeout performance against St. Ambrose College, which mustered only three hits.

Faber's performance for St. Joseph's and semipro clubs caught the attention of Clarence "Pants" Rowland, former owner of Dubuque's minor-league team and an acquaintance of Chicago White Sox owner Charles Comiskey. (Rowland was between baseball jobs at the time, managing a hotel bar in Dubuque.) Rowland encouraged Faber to sign with the Dubuque Miners, who were struggling in the Class B Three-I (Illinois-Indiana-Iowa) League. Joining the team with two months left in the 1909 season, Faber went 7-6. In August 1910, during his first full season as a professional, Faber (18-19) threw a perfect game against Davenport; only one ball reached the outfield. The Pittsburgh Pirates bought his contract the next day.

Faber made the Pirates' 1911 Opening Day roster, but manager Fred Clarke never used him and in mid-May sent him to Minneapolis of the American Association. Within days of his arrival in Minnesota, Faber entered a distance-throwing contest and injured his pitching arm. During his short stay in Minneapolis, Faber had a career-changing experience: Teammate Harry Peaster taught him the finer points of the spitball, which at the time was a legal pitch.[7]

Within weeks the sore-armed Faber was shipped to Pueblo of the Western League. The young Iowan worked on his spitter over the next 2½ seasons, first in Pueblo and then for two years with Des Moines of the Western League. In 1913, his second year in Des Moines, Faber solidified an "iron man" reputation, sometimes pitching on consecutive days and once, during an Iowa heat wave, pitching all 18 innings of a tie game ended by darkness. In the closing weeks of the 1913 season, White Sox owner Comiskey bought Faber's contract for 1914.

Faber's offseason was abbreviated. In October 1913, at the urging of Rowland, Comiskey belatedly added Faber to the White Sox roster for the around-the-world exhibition tour with the New York Giants. The rookie-to-be performed adequately on the domestic leg of the tour, but Comiskey planned to drop Faber from the squad before departure for Japan, Australia, the Mideast and Western Europe.[8] However, Faber caught another break: Just hours before the teams embarked on their Pacific crossing, Giants pitcher Christy Mathewson, the most popular American athlete of the day, quit the tour because he feared becoming seasick on the journey. Comiskey and Giants manager John McGraw made an agreement: Faber was loaned to the Giants to take Mathewson's place.[9]

Mathewson must have felt vindicated in his decision to remain stateside: A powerful storm nearly wrecked the teams' ship as it crossed the Pacific, and all the passengers experienced bouts of seasickness. None suffered more than Matty's replacement, Faber, who was too ill to leave the ship for a day or two after its arrival in Japan. Eventually, Faber took regular turns pitching against his future team. In the finale, in London, with King George V in attendance, Faber pitched tenaciously for 11 innings but took the loss. On the voyage back to the United States, McGraw tried to buy Faber's contract. Comiskey refused.[10]

After a no-decision start and a handful of relief assignments, the 6-foot-2, 180-pound rookie forged into the national spotlight in June 1914. On June 1 Faber pitched 12⅓ innings in a 2-1 loss to Detroit. Six days later, he earned his first major-league victory with a three-hit shutout of the New York Yankees. Ten days after that, Faber came within three outs of no-hitting defending World Series champion Philadelphia; an infielder's slow work on a bouncer allowed the only hit. He cooled off in the second half of the season — a sore elbow sidelined him for a month — and finished 10-9 with a 2.68 ERA.

Before the 1915 season, Comiskey surprised the baseball world by selecting Pants Rowland, who lacked any major-league playing or managing experience, as the White Sox manager. Faber responded to the new skipper, posting a 24-14 record with a 2.55 ERA. Though the spitball was a big part of his repertoire, Faber also relied on his fastball and curve. He said that just the awareness that he might unleash a spitter at any time was enough to keep most batters guessing.[11] His forte was getting hitters to swing early in the count and beat the ball into the ground. That skill was best demonstrated on May 12, 1915, in Comiskey Park,

Red Faber, circa 1917 (Bain Collection, Library of Congress, Prints and Photographs Division)

when Faber required a record-low 67 pitches to defeat Washington.[12] Faber pitched less in 1916 due to injury, but he improved to 17-9 with a 2.02 ERA for a team that lost the pennant by two games.

Faber's competitive fire and pleasant personality made him popular with White Sox fans and management—though later in his career, as his losses due to teammates' miscues mounted, he became crankier and a manager briefly benched him.

Comiskey, who owned a Wisconsin game preserve, named a moose after his young pitcher. In September 1916 the moose escaped; it startled a couple of local youths, one of whom happened to be carrying a rifle. When word of the incident reached the Chicago newspapers, headline writers had some fun. One headed an article, "Shoots Red Faber, Pride of Comiskey! Moose, not pitcher."[13]

Faber was a battler. In a single at-bat, he decked Ty Cobb on three consecutive knockdown pitches. He also earned opponents' respect. Babe Ruth, who once described Faber as "the nicest man in the world,"[14] shook hands and posed for pictures with the spitballer at Red Faber Day at Comiskey Park in 1929.

In 1917 Faber posted a career-best 1.92 ERA, winning 16 games for the White Sox en route to their first pennant in 11 seasons. In the World Series, against New York, Faber tied a Series record with three victories. He won Game Two, lost Game Four, won Game Five in relief, and then closed out the host Giants with a complete-game victory in Game Six. His pitching performance overshadowed his baserunning blunder in Game Two, when he tried to steal third while it was occupied by teammate Buck Weaver.

With World War I raging as the 1918 season opened, it appeared likely that major leaguers would be drafted into military service. As a 29-year-old bachelor, Faber was virtually certain to be conscripted. He won his first four decisions, enlisted in the Navy, and lost his farewell game. Though he told reporters that he wanted assignment to a submarine[15]—apparently he forgot his seasickness during the world tour—Faber served

his entire tour at Great Lakes Naval Base, near Chicago. A chief yeoman, he supervised recreation programs and pitched for the base team for the duration of the war.

Back in a baseball uniform for 1919, Faber (11-9) struggled with the flu—he was weak and underweight—and with arm and ankle injuries. After a layoff of several weeks, he struggled in his only appearance during the final month of the regular season and remained on the bench throughout the tainted 1919 World Series. White Sox catcher and fellow Hall of Famer Ray Schalk long contended that the Black Sox Scandal would have been impossible had Faber been healthy; the conspirators would not have had enough pitching to succeed.[16]

After the 1920 season, the 32-year-old Iowan married 22-year-old Milwaukee native Irene Margaret Walsh, of Chicago. They met by accident—literally. He was a bystander who came to her assistance after she was hurt in an auto collision. The couple had no children, and she experienced ongoing health problems that reportedly included dependency on painkillers. A Faber relative described their marriage as unhappy.[17] There were whispers that she became romantically involved with White Sox outfielder Johnny Mostil, and that his 1927 suicide attempt occurred after Faber confronted him about the affair. (More likely Mostil became despondent when he learned that his longtime girlfriend had thrown him over for his teammate Bill Barrett, whom she subsequently married.) In any case, the Fabers remained married until March 1943, when Irene died of a cerebral hemorrhage at age 44.

The advent of the lively-ball era coincided with the best three-season stretch of Faber's career (1920-22), when he went a combined 69-45 and led the league in ERA in 1921 and 1922. He was among the 17 "grandfathered" pitchers permitted to throw the otherwise banned spitball for the rest of his career. In 1921, when the White Sox were a shambles after the Black Sox indictments, Faber's 25 wins (against 15 losses) represented 40 percent of all the team's victories. He followed that with his third consecutive 20-win season (21-17). But after 1923, when he went 14-11, it was clear that Faber's days of dominance were behind him; age, injury, and White Sox ineptitude took their toll. He suffered his first losing season (9-11) in 1924, when he got a late start after elbow surgery.

As early as the mid-1920s, sportswriters started predicting Faber's retirement. But he remained generally effective, and kept returning, season after season. He explained his longevity by noting that the spitball exerted less stress on his arm.[18] Faber showed occasional flashes of his old form. He registered his third and final career one-hitter in 1929.

In 1932 new manager Lew Fonseca took Faber out of the starting rotation, and his record tumbled to 2-11. By 1933, his 20th season in the majors, Faber (3-4) was the American League's oldest player—he turned 45 that fall—and its last "legal" spitballer. (A grandfathered National League spitballer, Burleigh Grimes, crossed over and pitched 18 innings for the 1934 Yankees.) In the postseason City Series against the Cubs, Faber got the Game Two start at the last minute. He responded with his best performance in years, a five-hit shutout. Though no one knew it at the time, it was Faber's last appearance against major-league competition.

After a combined 5-15 record the previous two seasons, Faber was upset with his 1934 contract offer from the White Sox, who wanted to cut his pay by one-third, to $5,000. He secured his release and hoped to join another major-league team, but there were no takers. He closed his career with a 254-213 record.

In retirement Faber tried his hand at selling cars and real estate—his low level of success was attributed to his high level of honesty—before acquiring a bowling alley in suburban Chicago. Early in the 1946 season, Ted Lyons became the White Sox manager and hired Faber as pitching coach; they lasted three seasons.

In April 1947 the 58-year-old Faber married 29-year-old divorcee Frances Knudtzon. They became parents the next year with the arrival of their only child, Urban C. Faber, II, nicknamed Pepper. In the mid-1950s, the Cook County (Chicago) Highway Department hired

Faber; he worked on a survey crew until he was nearly 80.[19]

In the late 1950s Pepper Faber's Little League team, the Rebels, might have been the only Little League squad in the nation to have *two* ex-major leaguers as assistant coaches—Pepper's father and Nick Etten, who had played first base for the Yankees, Phillies, and Athletics. Urban tossed batting practice and helped manager Ted Cushing wherever needed and without interfering. "If a first-base umpire is needed, Red takes the job," columnist and neighbor Bill Gleason wrote, "and the opposing manager knows all decisions will be fair."[20] In 1963, when he was 14, Pepper Faber suffered a broken neck and nearly died in a swimming accident. Though he survived, health problems continue to dog Urban II.

Exactly 50 years after his rookie season, in 1964, Red Faber was inducted into the National Baseball Hall of Fame. His acceptance speech lasted 100 words:

"Mr. Commissioner, ladies and gentlemen. It's a great honor to me to be named to the Hall of Fame. It's very hard for me to even imagine that I would ever be elected to it. But now that I am, and about to join all those celebrities that I used to know and play against and with, why, I hardly know what to say. I know there are all baseball fans here. They must be or they wouldn't have come this far to see an event like this. And I'm happy to greet you all in our behalf. Thank you."[21]

In retirement, Faber was among the founders of Baseball Anonymous, an organization created to help former ballplayers (and athletes from other sports) who were down on their luck. Growing to nearly 700 members (at $2 per year) in its first year, Baseball Anonymous performed many good deeds; most were handled quietly, but in 1958, when Faber was the group's general chairman, Baseball Anonymous arranged a Comiskey Park ceremony to honor former White Sox pitching great Ed Walsh, who was 77 years old and struggling physically and financially.[22] The group also staged benefits for other former players who had fallen upon hard times. Faber was a regular at Hot Stove

League banquets and old-timer's games in Chicago and Milwaukee.

Faber, who took up the habit of smoking at age 8, suffered two heart attacks within a two-year period in the mid-1960s. He experienced increasing heart and respiratory problems in later years. He died at home on September 25, 1976, at the age of 88. He was survived by his wife, Frances, who died in 1992, and their son. Red Faber's grave marker in Chicago's Acacia Park Cemetery cites his Navy service but makes no mention of his baseball glory.

Note: An expanded version of this biography was published by Brian Cooper as *Red Faber: A Biography of the Hall of Fame Spitball Pitcher* (Jefferson, North Carolina: McFarland & Co., 2006).

SOURCES

Associated Press

Baseball Magazine

Cascade (Iowa) *Pioneer*

Chicago American

Chicago Tribune

Elfers, James E., *The Tour to End All Tours* (Lincoln, Nebraska: University of Nebraska Press, 2003)

Farrell, James T., *My Baseball Diary* (New York: A.S. Barnes and Company and The Copp Clark Company, Ltd., 1957. Board of Trustees, Southern Illinois University, 1998)

Iowa Historical Society

Lindberg, Richard C., *The White Sox Encyclopedia* (Philadelphia: Temple University Press, 1997)

Loras College, Dubuque, Iowa

New York Times

Retrosheet.org

St. Louis Star

Society for American Baseball Research; various publications

Sporting Life

The Sporting News

Dubuque (Iowa) *Telegraph Herald*

United States National Archives

Washington Post

NOTES

1   *The Sporting News*, October 16, 1976.

2   *Baseball Magazine*, September 1922.

3   *St. Louis Star*, May 15, 1931.

4   *Baseball Magazine*, September 1922.

5   1910 Census, US Department of Commerce and Labor, and Dubuque city directories. Nicholas Faber's occupation is listed on census records as "own income."

6   "Retrorsum," Columbia (now Loras) College, 1923.

7   *The Sporting News*, October 16, 1976.

8   James E. Elfers, *The Tour to End All Tours*, 82.

9   Elfers, 28; Lee Allen, "Cooperstown Corner," May 30, 1964.

10 Elfers, 28.

11 *The Sporting News*, October 16, 1976.

12 *Sporting Life*, May 22, 1915.

13 *Chicago Tribune*, September 27, 1916.

14 *Palimpsest*, Iowa Historical Society, Vol. 36, No. 4, 1955.

15 *Cascade* (Iowa) *Pioneer*, June 13, 1918.

16 Associated Press, February 5, 1964.

17 Mary Ione Theisen, a niece, interview with author, June 18, 2003.

18 *Christian Science Monitor*, August 3, 1964.

19 *The Sporting News*, October 16, 1976.

20 *Chicago American*, June 13, 1958

21 Associated Press, July 29, 1964.

22 *The Sporting News*, July 2, 1958.

SEASON TIMELINE: APRIL 1919

White Sox record: 6-1 (.857)
Runs scored: 47 | Runs allowed: 29

AL standings
April 30, 1919

Team	W	L	PCT	GB
CHW	6	1	.857	—
BOS	4	1	.800	1
CLE	3	1	.750	1½
NYY	2	2	.500	2½
PHA	2	3	.400	3
WSH	2	4	.333	3½
DET	1	4	.200	4
SLB	1	5	.167	4½

PLAYER OF THE MONTH

	G	PA	AB	R	H	2B	3B	HR	RBI	SB	BB	SO	BA	OBP	SLG	OPS
Joe Jackson	7	34	30	5	16	4	0	2	6	1	2	0	.533	.588	.867	1.455

After hitting a career-low .301 in 1917 and controversially leaving the White Sox for a Delaware shipyard during the war-shortened 1918 season, the 32-year-old Joe Jackson quickly showed he was back in form for 1919. Beginning with a 3-for-5 performance on Opening Day, he had multiple hits in six of the seven April games, and at least one extra-base hit in five games.

PITCHER OF THE MONTH

	W	L	ERA	G	GS	CG	SHO	IP	H	R	ER	BB	SO	WHIP
Eddie Cicotte	2	0	0.50	2	2	2	0	18	12	3	1	2	5	0.778

The superstitious Eddie Cicotte was averse to pitching on Opening Day, so Lefty Williams took that honor instead. But Cicotte shined in his two April starts, tossing matching six-hit complete games against the St. Louis Browns, a 5-2 win on April 24, and the Detroit Tigers, a 3-1 win on April 29.

DAY BY DAY

Wednesday, April 23
Sportsman's Park, St. Louis
"White Sox Bombard Browns in Year's First Battle, 13-4" — *Chicago Tribune*

White Sox (1-0)   003   510   013—13 21 1
Browns (0-1)   201   000   100—4 10 2
WP: Lefty Williams (1-0). LP: Tom Rogers (0-1).
Lefty Williams: 9 IP, 10 H, 4 R, 2 ER, 1 BB, 6 K.
Buck Weaver: 4-6, 3B, SB, 3 R, 5 RBI. Eddie Collins: 2-4, HR, SB, 3 RBI.

Thursday, April 24
Sportsman's Park, St. Louis
"Sox Cop Again in Shivering S'Louis" — *Chicago Tribune*

White Sox (2-0)	004	010	000 — 5 10 1
Browns (0-2)	200	000	000 — 2 6 1

WP: Eddie Cicotte (1-0). LP: Allan Sothoron (0-1).
Eddie Cicotte: 9 IP, 6 H, 2 R, 0 ER, 1 BB, 1 K.
Buck Weaver: 3-5, 2 R, SB, RBI. Swede Risberg: 3-3, R, SB.

Friday, April 25
Sportsman's Park, St. Louis
"Lack of a Starter Slows Up Sox Machine, 7 to 2" — *Chicago Tribune*

White Sox (2-1)	200	000	000 — 2 6 1
Browns (1-2)	240	010	00x — 7 10 2

WP: Bert Gallia (1-0). LP: Dave Danforth (0-1).
Dave Danforth: 1 IP, 3 H, 5 R, 5 ER, 3 BB, 0 K.
Joe Jackson: 2-3, 2B, HR, 2 RBI.

Saturday, April 26
Sportsman's Park, St. Louis
"Gleason Tribe's Six Run Attack Wins 9-4 Battle" — *Chicago Tribune*

White Sox (3-1)	300	006	000 — 9 13 0
Browns (1-3)	103	000	000 — 4 8 2

WP: Red Faber (1-0). LP: Dave Davenport (0-1).
Red Faber: 6⅔ IP, 4 H, 0 R, 0 ER, 4 BB, 4 K.
Chick Gandil: 4-5, 2 2B, R, 3 RBI. Eddie Collins: 2-4, 3 SB, R, 2 RBI.

Sunday, April 27
Navin Field, Detroit
"Sox Win Duel of Crashing Bats Before 25,000 Detroiters, 6-4" — *Chicago Tribune*

White Sox (4-1)	010	021	101 — 6 13 5
Tigers (1-2)	010	100	101 — 4 8 1

WP: Lefty Williams (2-0). LP: Hooks Dauss (0-1).
Lefty Williams: 9 IP, 8 H, 4 R, 2 ER, 0 BB, 2 K.
Buck Weaver: 2-4, 2B, 2 R, SB. Ray Schalk: 3-4, SB, 2 RBI. Joe Jackson: 1-3, HR.

Monday, April 28
Postponed, rain
"Sox Get Peevish When Weather Keeps 'Em Idle" — *Chicago Tribune*

Tuesday, April 29
Navin Field, Detroit
"Just Like 1917! Sox Outslug Ravenous Tigers; Lead League" — *Chicago Tribune*

White Sox (5-1)	000	210	000 — 3 11 0
Tigers (1-3)	000	000	001 — 1 6 2

WP: Eddie Cicotte (2-0). LP: Howard Ehmke (1-1).
Eddie Cicotte: 9 IP, 6 H, 1 R, 1 ER, 1 BB, 4 K.
Joe Jackson: 3-5, R, SB. Nemo Leibold: 2-4, 2B, SB. Buck Weaver: 1-4, SB, 2 RBI.

Wednesday, April 30
Navin Field, Detroit
"White Sox Finish Tigers And Series, 9 to 7; At Home Today" — *Chicago Tribune*

White Sox (6-1)	102	014	001 — 9 8 2
Tigers (1-4)	200	001	013 — 7 12 6

WP: Dickey Kerr (1-0). LP: Eric Erickson (0-1).
Dickey Kerr: 9 IP, 12 H, 7 R, 7 ER, 4 BB, 6 K.
Eddie Collins: 1-5, 2 R, 2B, SB. Joe Jackson: 2-4, 2B, R. Happy Felsch: 2-5, 2B.

APRIL HIGHLIGHTS

Preseason Dope: Even the hometown writers weren't optimistic that the White Sox had enough pitching depth to win in 1919. Irving Sanborn of the *Chicago Tribune* wrote on April 20, "Gleason has the machine that won the world's championship of 1917 practically intact … [but] unless he has a lot of luck in developing new pitchers, Gleason is going to have a hard time keeping his team in the first division.… Cicotte and Williams cannot do it all alone." Syndicated columnist Hugh Fullerton, the country's leading "dopester," picked the White Sox to finish third in the AL standings and the Cincinnati Reds to finish fourth in the NL.

World Series Preview: The White Sox tuned up for the regular season with two exhibitions on April 19 and 20 against the Cincinnati Reds at Redland Field (later called Crosley Field). Dickey Kerr, in his first action of any kind against another major-league team, beat the Reds 3-1 in 10 innings on Saturday, while Chick Gandil's go-ahead double in the ninth inning helped the Sox beat Cincinnati 5-3 on Sunday. Months later, in October, the rookie Kerr surprisingly defeated the Reds twice in the World Series — with one of those victories coming via a walkoff single by Gandil in Game Six.

Opening Day: The White Sox offense came out blazing in a 13-4 season-opening win at St. Louis on April 23. The frustrations of the war-shortened 1918 season were quickly forgotten as Kid Gleason celebrated his first win as White Sox manager. Every player in the Sox lineup reached base, led by Buck Weaver (4-6, 3 R, 5 RBI) and pitcher Lefty Williams (3-5, 3B, 3 R). The White Sox compiled a season-high 21 hits.

Dickey's Debut: The Sox suffered their only loss of the month on April 25, a 7-2 beating by the Browns at Sportsman's Park. Starter Dave Danforth lasted just one inning before he was replaced by 25-year-old left-hander Dickey Kerr, making his first regular-season appearance in the majors. Kerr allowed just two runs over seven innings in relief, a role he excelled in all season. Decades before the age of bullpen specialization, Kid Gleason called on Kerr to serve as the White Sox' top relief ace—he went 7-1 with a 1.78 ERA in 22 relief appearances in 1919.

South Side Hitmen: By the end of April, the White Sox had outscored every team in baseball, thanks in part to that Opening Day blowout of St. Louis. They terrorized American League pitchers all season, leading the AL in batting (.287), hits (1,343), runs (668), and stolen bases (150). Their offense was well-balanced, with Nemo Leibold and Eddie Collins reaching base more than 40 percent of the time in front of sluggers Joe Jackson and Happy Felsch, who each hit a team-high seven homers. Five of their eight starters scored more than 60 runs apiece and five starters drove in more than 60 runs.

Note: All game-by-game statistics listed in this book were found at Baseball-Reference.com and Retrosheet.org. Because RBIs were not considered an official statistic until the 1920 season, there may be some discrepancies between a player's game-by-game totals and his official season statistics. In some cases, game-by-game RBI totals may be omitted from the season timelines in this book when accurate information could not be verified.

HAPPY FELSCH

By James R. Nitz

THE BLACK SOX SCANDAL shocked the sporting public and led to fundamental changes in the governance of professional baseball. Central to this astonishing fix were eight Chicago White Sox ballplayers, including star center-fielder Oscar "Happy" Felsch.

An unpretentious Milwaukee native, the "Pride of Teutonia Avenue" only left his hometown to play ball. Felsch, one of 12 children of German immigrants, rose to the pinnacle of the baseball world only to be consigned forever to the sport's hell.

White Sox left fielder Shoeless Joe Jackson and third baseman George "Buck" Weaver have garnered the most attention of the "Eight Men Out," becoming mythologized in books and movies. Happy Felsch was just a common Milwaukeean caught up in momentous events of the turbulent 1910s and '20s. More than 40 years later, his account of those events would be the primary source for Eliot Asinof's book *Eight Men Out* and the movie that molded present-day understanding of the fix.

Oscar Emil Felsch, who grew up to be arguably the best baseball player ever produced by Milwaukee's north side, was born in 1891 in a German working-class neighborhood. His birth certificate does not exist because there are no Felsch family public-health records from that era.[1] Many baseball historical resources list Felsch's birth date as August 22, 1891, or unspecified dates in 1893 or 1894. However, his 1943 application for a Social Security number and his 1964 death certificate both state that he was born on April 7, 1891, to Berlin natives Charles and Marie Felsch (nee Tietz or Tiegs).[2] Charles was a north side carpenter.[3]

In the census of 1900, young Oscar was one of 10 living Felsch children and one of seven still residing in a mortgaged 26th Street frame house. He did not read or write in 1900 but eventually could after receiving a sixth-grade education. This lack of further formal education proved to haunt Felsch when he had to deal with shrewd baseball executives, underhanded gamblers, lawyers, and college-educated teammates.[4] The teenage Oscar went to work as a $10-a-week factory laborer and shoe worker, giving all but 25 cents of his pay to his father.[5]

Felsch's rise from the Milwaukee sandlots was due in no small part to his ballplaying dad and brothers. Reputed to be a first baseman of great ability, Charles had three more sons who played on area teams. As typical members of the aspiring working class, the boys hoped to develop their reputations in prominent local leagues in order to gain notice from pro scouts.[6] Following the example of many other second-generation German children, the youthful Oscar turned away from individual sports like gymnastics and wrestling and gravitated toward the popular American team game of baseball. A member of the *Turnverein* (or Turners, a German gymnastics movement that emphasized physical education), the powerfully built wrestling champion eventually gave up grappling for baseball.

The broad-shouldered Felsch, listed at heights between 5-feet-9 and 5-feet-11 and weights of 160 to 190 pounds over his playing career, first appeared on the local baseball scene in 1911.[7] Now employed as a shingler, the right-handed throwing and hitting shortstop-third baseman spent his spare time performing for Sisson and Sewell, a semipro club sponsored by a local clothing store. Their Sunday contests allowed Felsch to display his developing skills. The *Milwaukee Sentinel* noticed the budding star's four hits and seven successful fielding chances on August 6, declaring, "Felch [*sic*] played a swell game at third."[8]

In 1912 Oscar played with four semipro teams throughout Wisconsin. The star Sewell shortstop left in mid-

June to sign with Manitowoc of the higher-level Lake Shore League, then later played with Grand Rapids (now Wisconsin Rapids). Felsch then manned third base behind pitcher Stoney McGlynn, a former St. Louis Cardinal and Milwaukee Brewer. Larger crowds in Lake Shore League towns like Racine and Sheboygan gave an athlete of Felsch's caliber the opportunity for more lucrative paydays.[9] By late August, the Grand Rapids team had disbanded and Felsch signed on with Stevens Point for the rest of the season.

Felsch's easygoing nature and wonderful smile made the family nickname "Happy" a perfect fit. Newspapers adopted the sobriquet as early as 1912. At times he even preferred practices to games just for the sheer joy of hitting, fielding, and running.[10] In 1913 Felsch continually appeared in the dailies as he advanced to minor-league ball with the Milwaukee Creams of the Class C Wisconsin-Illinois League. The youthful shortstop made a powerful first impression on Opening Day at Athletic Park (later called Borchert Field) as he went 5-for-5 with a grand slam in the first inning, drove in seven runs, and made two errors. The Creams defeated Appleton, 12-5, in the April 30 game, played immediately after the American Association Brewers contest.[11]

Felsch continued his impressive hitting, including a three-homer game in Oshkosh, and sensational but error-prone fielding during his abbreviated stay in his hometown. Meager crowds for this farm team of the higher-level Brewers forced the Creams to move on June 28 to Fond du Lac, where they became the Molls. There Felsch continued to spend time at both shortstop and his new position, right field.[12]

By early August, the Brewers called up their phenom. This allowed him to vault to Double-A, the top category of the minors, bypassing the B and A levels. Following are Felsch's impressive Deadball Era statistics with the Cream/Molls, his first professional team: 18 home runs and 16 stolen bases with a .319 batting average in 357 at-bats. The promising youngster's future was in the outfield as he committed only two errors in 34 games there (.971 fielding percentage)

while booting the ball 36 times in 58 games (.868 fielding average) at shortstop.[13]

Felsch did not play often for the pennant-winning Brewers in 1913, as he needed polishing. He finished with a batting average of .183 with two home runs in only 26 games.[14]

In 1914 the muscular Felsch showcased his major-league potential both at the plate and in the outfield. He set home-run distance records in Milwaukee (over 500 feet at Athletic Park, by one account) and Kansas City, and led the American Association in round-trippers with 19. Felsch batted a potent .304 with 41 doubles, 11 triples, and 19 stolen bases for the repeat-champion Brewers. He demonstrated his outfield prowess with great range and a rifle arm.[15]

By early August the Brewers, an independent club, knew they owned a star fit to sell to the highest major-league bidder. The Senators, Cubs, White Sox, Giants, and Reds were scouting the left fielder. On August 8 the White Sox acquired Felsch for $12,000 plus an infielder and an outfielder from their organization. The Brewers were delighted that Chicago allowed their "fence breaker" to remain in Milwaukee for the duration of 1914. Felsch, declared the greatest Brewer ever by their business manager, Lou Nahin, then signed a two-year contract with Chicago at a salary of $2,500 per year.[16]

The 1915 season developed into an eventful one for the White Sox' rookie center fielder. Not only did Felsch make his major-league debut on April 14 in St. Louis with a single and a stolen base, but he also got married.[17]

The 1915 White Sox started their steady ascent toward the top of the American League by rising from sixth place to third with a 93-61 record. This was due to the addition of energetic 33-year-old manager Clarence "Pants" Rowland and five new position players, including future Hall of Fame second baseman Eddie Collins, Shoeless Joe Jackson, and Felsch. The newcomer in center finished with a .248 batting average, 3 home runs, and 16 stolen bases in 121 games as a semi-regular. Felsch's numbers could have been stronger except for a nagging leg injury he suffered early in the season.[18]

After the conclusion of the hotly contested Chicago City Series between the White Sox and Cubs, the handsome, square-jawed 24-year-old major leaguer returned to Milwaukee, where he married Marie Wagner, described on the marriage certificate as a 22-year-old north side homemaker, on October 27.[19]

Felsch spent what should have been his honeymoon getting his first experience with the judicial system. On October 29 the newlywed was asked to testify in pitcher Cy Slapnicka's lawsuit against the Brewers for back pay. After the case was postponed until December, Felsch, Slapnicka, and the Philadelphia Phillies' Fred Luderus, also from Milwaukee, embarked for Little Chute, Wisconsin, for a Sunday exhibition contest.[20]

The coming 1916 baseball season surely brought hope to Felsch and the White Sox. The promising club advanced to second place, overcoming a slow start to finish only two games behind the Red Sox. Charles Comiskey, the White Sox owner, was spending money to make money. Adding a pitcher of the caliber of Claude "Lefty" Williams to a staff that already included stars Eddie Cicotte, Red Faber, and Reb Russell helped the White Sox break their attendance record with 679,923 fans, 140,462 more than in 1915.[21]

Comiskey Park loyalists enjoyed watching Felsch belt seven home runs, out of a team total of 17. He led the Deadball Era White Sox and tied for third in the American League. Suddenly the sophomore from the sandlots of Milwaukee was in the upper echelon of AL hitters as he batted an even .300 and finished sixth in the league with a slugging average of .427. Under the tutelage of coach William "Kid" Gleason, the sure-handed Hap, an honorable mention member on *Baseball Magazine's* AL All-America Baseball Club, topped all AL outfielders with a fielding percentage of .981.[22]

For Happy Felsch it would never get better than 1917. In only his fifth season of professional baseball, he had become a national hero, thanks to a remarkable regular season and an exceptional World Series. The White Sox center fielder was in a class with future Hall of Fame outfielders Tris Speaker and Ty Cobb thanks to his 1917 statistics: .308 batting average (fifth in American League); 102 RBIs (tied for second with Ty Cobb, first White Sox player ever with 100 RBIs); 440 putouts (first among AL outfielders); and six home runs (tied for fourth in AL).

Comiskey had picked up shortstop Swede Risberg and first baseman Chick Gandil to round out the starting lineup. Although both players were welcome additions on the diamond, they helped form divisive cliques in the clubhouse. Gandil also retained his connections to gamblers. Felsch fraternized with the boisterous, card-playing Risberg/Gandil group that was often in conflict with the higher-educated Ray Schalk/Eddie Collins faction. The seeds of discord that led to the 1919 scandal were sown.[23]

Climaxing this year of destiny was the 1917 World Series. Game One, played at Comiskey Park on Saturday, October 6, was decided by a "loud and vicious clout from the trusty bludgeon of Felsch." "Milwaukee's famous beef and brawn" hit a long home run to deep left field, giving the White Sox a 2-0 lead in a game they eventually won 2-1 over the New York Giants. The center fielder also made a sensational one-handed cutoff play of a Giant double, preventing a round-tripper.

Felsch, who drove his new Packard from Milwaukee to Chicago the day before, was rewarded with two $50 Liberty Bonds, including one from entertainer Al Jolson. He also accepted a new suit, hat, shoes, and other clothing articles from Chicago merchants. Milwaukeeans, thrilled over Felsch's success, presented him with a baseball-shaped diamond stickpin before Game One and jokingly threatened to take it away if he did not hit a home run. Felsch proceeded to earn the pin and much adulation by slugging the only Sox homer in that fall classic. A thousand Milwaukee fans, including Felsch's father and a brother, were at Comiskey Park that day. Back home, 20,000 more flocked to local electric scoreboards in theaters or to tickers and blackboards in restaurants and businesses.

Fans were just as loud as if they were at the game and remained in a frenzy for 15 minutes after the home run.[24]

In Game Two, Chicago continued its winning ways as the "pride of the Cream city" contributed to the 7-2 victory with a hit-and-run single and several outstanding fielding plays. In Milwaukee, Felsch fans went wild again as 35-cent tickets to the electric-scoreboard venues were scalped for $1. That Sunday evening the White Sox and Giants left for New York, arriving on Monday afternoon. Game Three, scheduled for Tuesday at the Polo Grounds, was rained out. Off-the-field news included a flattering invitation for Felsch, Eddie Cicotte, and outfielder John Collins to appear in New York vaudeville. The three did not say whether they accepted.[25]

The Giants recovered to tie the Series at two games each with back-to-back shutouts of the hard-hitting White Sox. Comiskey Park hosted Game Five on Saturday, October 13. Chicago came back from a 5-2 deficit to win 8-5 with Felsch going 3-for-5. The teams traveled again to New York where, on Monday in Game Six, the White Sox captured the Series with a 4-2 victory.[26]

The White Sox were the toast of the Windy City as they returned to thousands of exultant fans, orators, and two big brass bands. The ballplayer that "made Milwaukee famous" was welcomed back with numerous parties, receptions, banquets, and dances throughout his proud hometown. Friends, local clubs, and city officials helped to arrange the celebrations that honored the man New York sportswriters believed made the difference in the Series, with both his bat and his glove. The smiling ballplayer enjoyed the attention, but insisted that he not speak in front of throngs of his clamoring fans.

In addition to his World Series check of $3,669 (almost matching his salary of $3,750), the popular star received presents including a gold watch, a set of silverware, and $100 worth of shares in American Aircraft. The papers glorified Felsch by claiming that he made $10,000 a year and accepted enough complimentary drinks to start his own brewery. After all the honors

and gifts were bestowed upon Felsch, "the greatest citizen the north side has ever produced," he left for the solitude of a three-week fishing and hunting trip in the northern woods.[27]

Major-league baseball, the White Sox, and Felsch experienced tough times in the intensified war year of 1918. The season was shortened so that baseball could comply with the "work or fight" edict of May 18. This decreed that any male between 21 and 31 years old in a nonessential job must enlist, secure a war-related job, or be reclassified with a lower draft number. Players who did not enlist hurried to take exempt jobs in shipyards, steel mills, war-production factories, and farms. Many of them, now subject to criticism as slackers, then played ball in industrial leagues.[28]

The defending champion White Sox got off to a rocky start as the train taking them to spring training derailed March 18 in Texas. No one was hurt. Then Felsch missed the beginning of camp because of a sudden illness. The season continued downhill as the White Sox lost many key players to the war effort. The club finished in sixth place with a 57-67 record before only 195,081 Comiskey Park customers. This was a significant decline from the 684,521 who watched the 100-54 pennant winners of 1917.[29]

The glory of 1917 must have seemed like a distant memory to Happy Felsch as he struggled both on and off the field in 1918. The star outfielder left the White Sox for 12 days in May as he visited a seriously injured brother in a Texas Army camp. Alarming his family and manager Rowland, the distraught Felsch remained incommunicado during the entire trip.[30] The "mighty Happy" departed for good on July 1, leaving Rowland with a punchless, spiritless shell of a team. Surprising the defending champs with his sudden resignation, Felsch announced that he was taking a war-effort job at the Milwaukee Gas Company for $125 a month plus earnings from weekend semipro ball. This paled in comparison to the $3,750 contract he walked away from. In an effort to boost attendance, the Kosciuskos of the Lake Shore League quickly signed the former World Series star.[31]

Normally a modest man, Felsch kept quiet about the dispute until July 18. That day, the Milwaukee *Sentinel* reported the disgruntled star's desire to return to the American League with any team other than the White Sox.[32] *The Sporting News* reported that Felsch had left because of disputes with Comiskey over pay, abstinence from drinking, and the Texas journey, plus a personal conflict with Eddie Collins.[33]

"Milwaukee's most famous diamond gladiator" was welcomed home by his many local admirers. The Koskys now played before packed houses both on the road as well as at Milwaukee's South Side Park and Athletic Park. As expected, Felsch hit very well and showed his versatility by handling all three outfield positions, first base, and catcher. Not only did he remain a Kosky through early October but he also participated in several "All-Star" games in Milwaukee and Chicago. These contests included major leaguers Braggo Roth, Dickey Kerr, Jack Quinn, Fred Luderus, and others.[34]

After the 1918 season, Comiskey replaced manager Rowland with popular longtime White Sox coach Kid Gleason, stating that Pants had lost control of the team. Even though the war ended on November 11, heading off the expected shutdown of the 1919 season, 1918 had a profound impact on the White Sox. The club was torn by dissension over wage disparities and disputes between players who enlisted in the military versus those who took exempt war-effort jobs.[35] Owners and the press resented athletes who avoided military service by working for companies with baseball teams. A disgusted Comiskey, alluding to Felsch, Joe Jackson, and Lefty Williams, went so far as to say, "There is no room on my club for players who wish to evade the army draft by entering the employ of ship owners."[36]

Comiskey conveniently set aside his anger in order to rebuild his remarkable team. With Gleason serving as a capable conciliator, the White Sox promptly brought back stateside war workers Felsch, Jackson, and Williams. Felsch quickly regained his form in 1919, leading the American League with 32 outfield assists and 14 double plays.[37] Four of the assists came

on August 14, tying a major-league record. Accepting 12 chances on June 23 let the gifted ball hawk tie another American League record. The assist and double-play figures were still major-league records as of 2014. His 15 outfield double plays are still a major-league season record.[38]

Felsch batted a solid .275 for the top run-producing team in the majors and slugged seven home runs, tying Jackson for the club lead. His 24 homers that decade were more than any other White Sox player hit.

Many of these statistics could have been more impressive had the owners not shortened the 1919 campaign. Anticipating lower attendance as the public recovered from the war, the baseball moguls cut the regular season from 154 to 140 games. In addition, American League rosters were reduced from 25 to 21, and salaries were depressed in anticipation of lower gate receipts. These concerns proved to be unfounded as war-weary fans flocked back to the national pastime. Attendance rose to 627,186 from 195,081 for the AL champion White Sox and to 6.5 million from 3 million in the majors. In an effort to recoup some revenue lost to the ill-advised shortened season, the owners extended the World Series between the Cincinnati Reds and the Sox from seven to nine games.[39]

Felsch's banishment from Organized Baseball was a result of the 1919 fall classic, his second and last. Some of the White Sox, playing in an atmosphere poisoned by unchecked wagering and lower-than-market salaries, were eager to cash in. Owners and league executives generally ignored betting as they encouraged any interest in their sport. Baseball was revered as upright and patriotic. Charles Comiskey stated in an authorized 1919 biography, "To me baseball is as honorable as any other business.... It has to be or it could not last a season out. Crookedness and baseball do not mix." At the very same time, his own players were mixing the two.[40]

In this era long before free agency, many players received wages far below their market value. Bound to their teams by the reserve clause, they could sign for what the owners offered or go home. Black Sox Felsch,

Jackson, and fix organizer Gandil were rightly upset that their three salaries combined were less than the $15,000 made by college-educated Eddie Collins. The eight Black Sox averaged $4,300 in 1919.[41] Certainly, Felsch's $3,750 annual 1917-19 contracts (plus the potential for $5,000 in World Series pay) compared favorably with the average blue-collar pay range of $1,000 to $2,400, cited by Steven Reiss in his 1999 book, *Touching Base: Professional Baseball and American Culture in the Progressive Era*.[42]

It is still unclear exactly how the Series was fixed and who the principals were. However, many of the favored White Sox did play poorly, whether it was because they took money from gamblers, feared retribution from gangsters, or endured an ordinary slump. Felsch himself was full of contradictions, both in his on-field performance as well as in interviews in later years.

At the plate Felsch produced only a .192 batting average with one extra-base hit, a double, in the eight-game Series loss.[43] The hard hitter made satisfactory contact but was robbed several times by superb Cincinnati fielding. In hindsight, some sportswriters looked at his sudden inability to advance runners, as well as several questionable running and fielding misplays, as possible proof of Felsch's involvement in a fix. After botching catches in Games Five and Six, the normally sure-handed center fielder was demoted to right field for Game Seven.[44] The *Milwaukee Sentinel* believed that the hometown hero hit in bad luck and was just "outshone" by Cincinnati's Edd Roush. The paper did not hint at a fix, but stated that the White Sox were down and lethargic. After Felsch hit his two-bagger, the *Sentinel* exclaimed, "Felsch was also on the job, much to everyone's surprise, and walloped a double."[45]

After dropping the World Series, the defeated Sox returned home with promised losers' shares of $3,254 and without their normal triumphant attitude and the $5,207 winners' portions, up to then the largest in baseball history. Comiskey, responding to what he called "nasty rumors," even publicly offered a $20,000 reward to anyone with evidence of a fix, but added, "I believe my boys fought the battles of the recent World Series on the level, as they have always done." Later

he announced that he was withholding the losers' shares from eight of his players "pending further investigations." Despite his protestations of ignorance, Comiskey chose the correct eight.

The *Sentinel* sarcastically reported, "Felsch is back home and will amuse himself on the bowling alleys this winter. If he makes as many strikes as he did in the world's series he ought to be good for a couple of 300-scores."[46]

Rumors of a fix were flying even before the first game. Many sportswriters heard them, but they never appeared in print. The day after the Series ended, one of the most prominent writers, Hugh Fullerton, urged his readers to "forget the suspicious and evil-minded yarns that may be circulated." However, he added, "There are seven men on the [White Sox] team who will not be there when the gong sounds next Spring...." Later Fullerton wrote that he had been

Happy Felsch, circa 1920 (Bain Collection, Library of Congress, Prints and Photographs Division)

present when manager Gleason told Comiskey that the rumors were fact.[47]

The offseason proved disturbing for Happy Felsch. In November he and other Black Sox were the subjects of a private investigation. Comiskey hired detectives to check if his players were making suspiciously large purchases or lifestyle changes.[48] Operative number 11 of Hunter's Secret Service conducted the Felsch surveillance only to uncover contradictory information. After culling tips from many north side taverns, the investigator discovered that Felsch had recently moved from his father's home on North 26th Street back to his in-laws' neighborhood on Teutonia Avenue. While the slugger was on a duck-hunting trip, number 11 gained access to the Felsch apartment under the pretense of renting a furnished room. The eight-room, no-bath living quarters above a grocery were crowded as the Felsch family lived with Marie's parents, sister, and the sister's two small children. The private eye believed the neighborhood to be poor. He found Hap's recent purchase of a new $1,800 Hupmobile — a solid automobile bought by those rising from the working class — inconsistent with living in a cramped $22-a-month apartment.[49]

After the secret investigation, Comiskey was left with no choice but to mail the $3,254 checks. He could find no evidence that anyone but Gandil went on a spending spree.[50]

Felsch then received an unexpectedly generous contract from the White Sox. Comiskey's top assistant, Harry Grabiner, made a special trip to Teutonia Avenue in late 1919 to ink the center fielder to a 1920 contract that included a surprising $3,000 raise. Felsch, taken aback by Comiskey's sudden largesse, signed even as Grabiner reminded him that he could not play with anyone but the White Sox. In addition, Grabiner mentioned the swirling scandal rumors and called for Felsch's silence, both with the press and with American League inquisitors.[51] It was apparent that Comiskey desired his stars back and was finally willing to invest in salaries commensurate with their talents in order to purchase their silence. Further investigations could result in ruinous player punishments.[52]

Felsch's finest year on the diamond was to be his last. He established career highs of 14 home runs (first on the White Sox and fourth in the AL behind Babe Ruth's unbelievable 54), 188 hits, 88 runs, 40 doubles, 15 triples, 115 RBIs, and a .338 batting average.[53] Batters in 1920 enjoyed a livelier ball, the new requirement that umpires keep only fresh, unmarred spheres in play, and the outlawing of trick pitches (except for the grandfathered spitball pitchers).[54] The 29-year-old, now in his prime, was considered one of the American League's top players, pacing the circuit's outfielders with 10 double plays.[55]

After the defending American League champs trained in Waco, Texas, they arrived at Milwaukee's Athletic Park for several preseason exhibitions with the Brewers. Felsch, the hometown idol, responded to a rousing ovation from the 5,000 fans on April 10 with a 2-for-4 day.[56] The White Sox proceeded to stay in the 1920 pennant race until the events of a turbulent September caused them to succumb to the Cleveland Indians.

September of 1920 proved to be the final month of Happy Felsch's brilliant career. On the 7th a grand jury was impaneled in Chicago to investigate the possible fix of an August 31 Cubs-Phillies game. After the hearings began on September 22, the focus quickly shifted to the tainted 1919 World Series. On Monday, September 26, Felsch suited up for the last time in an 8-1 win over the Detroit Tigers. Two days later, Cicotte and Jackson, counseled by Comiskey's attorney, confessed to the grand jury. Immediately after the indictments, Comiskey suspended the seven implicated players. The Sox were only a half-game behind the Indians.[57]

By now, the fix story was front-page national news. Reporter Harry Reutlinger of the *Chicago Evening American* was looking to secure his scandal facts firsthand from one of the players. He was advised to visit Felsch, who was uneducated but considered affable enough to talk. Armed with a bottle of scotch, Reutlinger quickly got Felsch, who was in a bathrobe soaking his swollen big toe, to open up.[58] In a September 30, 1920, article, Felsch verified Cicotte's confession:

"Well, the beans are all spilled and I think that I am through with baseball. I got my $5,000 and I suppose the others got theirs too. If you say anything about me, don't make it appear that I'm trying to put up an alibi. I'm not. I'm as guilty as the rest of them. We were in it alike. I don't know what I'm going to do now.... I'm going to hell, I guess.... I wish that I hadn't gone into it. I guess we all do.... I never knew where my $5,000 came from. It was left in my locker at the clubhouse and there was always a good deal of mystery about the way it was dealt out. That was one of the reasons why we never knew who double crossed us on the split of the $100,000. It was to have been an even split. But we never got it.... But when they let me in on the idea too many men were involved. I didn't like to be a squealer and I knew that if I stayed out of the deal and said nothing about it they would go ahead without me and I'd be that much money out without accomplishing anything. I'm not saying this to pass the buck to the others. I suppose that if I had refused to enter the plot and had stood my ground I might have stopped the whole deal. We all share the blame equally. I'm not saying that I double crossed the gamblers, but I had nothing to do with the loss of the world's series. The breaks just came so that I was not given a chance to do anything toward throwing the game. The records show that I played a pretty good game. I know I missed one terrible fly but, you can believe me or not, I was trying to catch that ball.... I got $5,000. I could have got just about that much by being on the level if the Sox had won the series. And now I'm out of baseball—the only profession I know anything about, and a lot of gamblers have gotten rich. The joke seems to be on us."[59]

Some historians view this acknowledgment of bad intentions as an attempt to placate shadowy gamblers.[60] Felsch did admit to receiving the $5,000, but not to contributing to the Series loss.

Felsch's last big-league campaign was much less gratifying than his statistics might indicate. He told Reutlinger, "It's been hell for me" in dealing with his injured toe and the grand-jury investigation. In addition, the White Sox clubhouse was more divided than ever as some of the "Clean Sox" believed that the Black Sox were accepting money to throw 1920 regular-season games. Felsch denied this in the *Evening American* interview, but the adverse impact of gamblers on the White Sox could not be disputed.[61]

The indicted man the *Milwaukee Sentinel* considered "the best ball player ever produced in Milwaukee" was the object of considerable consternation from his loyal local fans. Some recalled that three days before the 1919 World Series, Felsch instructed his Milwaukee friends to bet on the White Sox. Even after losing three games to the Reds, he still advised his father-in-law to continue wagering on Chicago.[62]

As 1920 ended, Felsch, Swede Risberg, Buck Weaver, and utility infielder Fred McMullin hired an attorney, Thomas Nash, as they began their fight for reinstatement. Felsch returned to Wisconsin to fish and ponder his future.[63] Meanwhile, the owners set the tone for baseball's future by hiring their first commissioner, stern federal Judge Kenesaw Mountain Landis.

Two strikingly different versions of justice were meted out to Happy Felsch and the Black Sox in 1921. Acquitted in court, the players were nevertheless banned forever from Organized Baseball by the newly omnipotent Landis.

Attorney Nash desired a speedy, open trial for his clients and asked Felsch to travel to Chicago on January 31 to file a $10,000 bond to guarantee his appearance.[64] Arraignment took place on February 14; due to poorly worded indictments and missing evidence, the initial case was dismissed. At this point, just before spring training, Comiskey hoped to get his talented players back. However, Landis—in his endeavor to clean up baseball and rescue its public image—declared the eight players ineligible. The commissioner knew that his decisions to protect the game would not always favor an individual owner's interest.[65] The decimated 1921 Sox proceeded to finish a dismal seventh.

Through the work of American League President Ban Johnson, enough fresh evidence was secured to support new indictments. Jury trial proceedings began in Chicago on June 27. Judge Hugo Friend decreed that the players could only be convicted for conspiring to defraud the public and injuring the businesses of Comiskey and the American League because there was no law against fixing baseball games. This made the trial of little historical use in determining the truth.[66]

Felsch's interview with Reutlinger was disallowed as evidence. Judge Friend said there was so little evidence against Felsch and Weaver that he doubted he could let a guilty jury verdict stand. The trial took place from July 18 to August 2 before packed galleries that supported the encouraged players as slandered heroes rather than wrongdoers.[67] Even the accused Felsch appeared jovial as he surprisingly exclaimed, "Hope you win the pennant, boys!" to the Clean Sox clique visiting the courtroom.[68] At the end of the trial, the state asked for five-year jail sentences and $2,000 fines. After less than three hours of deliberation, the jury acquitted the players as no state law prohibited throwing games. The Black Sox and the jurors celebrated together at a restaurant.[69]

The following day, August 3, the party ended as Judge Landis, in his relentless effort to redeem baseball's credibility, gave this famous edict:

> "Regardless of the verdict of juries, no player that throws a ball game; no player that undertakes or promises to throw a ball game; no player that sits in a conference with a bunch of crooked players and gamblers where the ways and means of throwing games are planned and discussed and does not promptly tell his club about it, will ever play professional baseball."[70]

The press portrayed the devastated Comiskey as a tragic victim and the Black Sox as aberrant, evil men who betrayed baseball's purity. In reality, the fix was the culmination of many years of whitewashed baseball corruption.[71] It can be claimed that Comiskey self-inflicted his enormous losses with his tight-fisted treatment of players.

Felsch, now 30, was a free and innocent man in the eyes of the law; however, he was forever exiled from the game he loved so much and played so well. Landis's autocracy held a long reach as he threatened to blacklist anyone who competed with or against the Black Sox. The ban forced the former stars to go vast distances to play baseball.[72]

In attempts to make money in 1921, Felsch and the seven others formed barnstorming teams in Chicago, northern Indiana, and Wisconsin. Their efforts generally went for naught as ballpark operators and opposing teams were afraid of the consequences of any association with the contaminated Black Sox.[73]

Felsch endured the death of his father on July 28, adding more unwanted stress during the trial. The 68-year-old carpenter died at home from a cerebral hemorrhage.[74] His son was allowed to return to Milwaukee for the funeral; however, Judge Friend demanded Happy's appearance in court on Monday morning, August 1. Another defense attorney, Ray Cannon, successfully objected, stating that Felsch should be permitted to attend his father's burial on Monday afternoon.[75]

Even though his professional career was prematurely over, the tenacious Felsch refused to give up on the diamond or in the legal system in 1922. With a new son, Oscar Ray, born in July, the north-sider set out with the "Ex-Major Leaguers." This team, which booked nearly 20 games, could boast of athletes including attorney/pitcher Cannon (a former semipro teammate of Felsch) and Black Sox Weaver, Risberg, Cicotte, and Williams. Playing in mostly small towns, the club drew enthusiastic gatherings reaching 3,000 to witness the big-name stars.[76]

At the same time, Felsch and Risberg sued the White Sox for $100,000 each, declaring that they were ousted from baseball through a conspiracy. Felsch also sought $1,120 in back pay from 1920 and $1,500 for the remainder of a promised 1917 pennant bonus.[77] In July Comiskey moved to dismiss the suits for lack of evidence and because of the players' conspiracy to throw games. He claimed that he paid them in full up until the September 1920 suspensions and denied the 1917 bonus claim.78

The legal proceedings dragged into 1923, when Felsch sued for another $100,000 in damages. He claimed that his "name and reputation has been permanently impaired and destroyed" and that he had "been barred from playing base ball with any professional base ball team in any of the leagues of organized base ball of the United States." Again, Comiskey requested dismissal of the suits. On June 16 Judge John Gregory dismissed the original $100,000 conspiracy complaint. After much judicial tussling, it was not until 1924 that the case finally went to trial.79

During the protracted battle over his baseball career, Felsch opened a grocery in 1923. Marie and Oscar lived on site for about a year as they attempted to proceed with the stark reality of their new lives.80

In 1924 Milwaukee's most famous grocer became an accused perjurer and outlaw ballplayer. That January in Milwaukee, Joe Jackson's suit against Comiskey commenced. Jackson accepted Ray Cannon's offer of representation in an action similar to Felsch's and Risberg's. After turning down a White Sox settlement offer of $2,500, Cannon proceeded in this first Black Sox civil trial. He promised Jackson that Felsch and Risberg would "go the limit for you" in their testimony.81

The trial, well-publicized and heavily attended, provided three weeks of emotional drama. While on the witness stand, a nervous and flustered Felsch denied his signatures on, and knowledge of, his 1920 White Sox contract and related correspondence, mistakenly thinking he was protecting himself. Cannon was taken aback by Felsch's naïveté, saying, "If it's your signature, Happy, say so." Even he could not rescue the ballplayer from perjury charges. "The pride of Milwaukee's baseball history" was led away to jail in front of an impassive Comiskey and an astonished courtroom. Felsch, who normally "had been a magnet of friendship wherever he happened to move," stoically looked straight ahead as he departed. Several hours of jail time ensued until friends posted $2,000 cash bond. The bewildered slugger, whose 16 signature denials

abruptly suspended the trial, faced arraignment with a potential penalty of two years in a state prison. A handwriting expert confirmed that the 1920 inscriptions matched those that Felsch provided in court and said, "Felsch must be mistaken when he denies it." Comiskey said he was sorry for his former star "for he was a great baseball player."82

Judge Gregory called the perjury "malicious and vindictive." Felsch said he misunderstood the questions and did not intend to perjure himself. The case went to the jury at the end of this tumultuous third week. While the jury was deliberating, Gregory sent Jackson to jail for perjury under $5,000 bond. Gregory overturned the verdict of $16,711 (most of his 1921 and 1922 pay) in favor of Jackson. The sudden, unexplained reappearance of the stolen 1920 confessions caused Gregory to say Jackson's testimony of game-fixing innocence "reeks with perjury." Eventually, Jackson, frustrated by his inability to clear his name, settled with Comiskey out of court for a fraction of the verdict, eliminating any appeals. The district attorney dropped the Jackson perjury charges due to insufficient evidence.83

Felsch discovered that playing ball — albeit an outlaw version in south-central Wisconsin — was more fitting and profitable than selling groceries. He was again enjoying what he did best with the Twin City (Sauk City and Prairie du Sac) Red Sox. This small-town club competed with black, Native American, House of David, and other Wisconsin teams unconcerned with the threat of blacklisting by Landis. In addition, Felsch played against fellow Black Sox Weaver (Reedsburg) and Risberg (Minnesota). Thanks to their slugger's star power and .365 batting average, the 33-20 Red Sox drew crowds as large as 5,000.84

Felsch concluded his skirmishes with the legal system in 1925 and discovered more lucrative, yet distant, playing opportunities. In early February, his perjury case encountered delays, as the district attorney was reluctant to try it.85 Then Felsch's civil suit against the Sox was settled out of court. This occurred only minutes before the trial was to have finally begun. All of his claims netted Felsch only $1,166 plus interest and costs for a total of about $1,500. The club, claiming that

Comiskey was in poor health, did not want to endure another three-week ordeal.[86] With criminal accusations hanging over his client's head, Cannon must have been apprehensive about proceeding with another trial. On May 18 Felsch pleaded guilty to false-swearing, charges that were pending for more than 15 months. Judge Gregory dropped the perjury count and sentenced Felsch to one year of probation.[87]

Now the 33-year-old was free to play ball. In June he joined Risberg in Scobey, Montana.[88] Thus began many years of semipro baseball for Felsch in Montana, Saskatchewan, and Manitoba. Out of the reach of Commissioner Landis, the two Black Sox played before crowded ballparks in Canada and North and South Dakota. Scobey fans adored Felsch for his prodigious home runs, willingness to perform at any position, and jocular personality.[89] The pair were each paid a healthy $600 a month plus expenses as they guided their club to a 30-3 record in an environment of heavy gambling and drinking. They often endured opponents' taunts — and responded with brawling — about their descent from the big leagues to a "cow pasture."[90]

Felsch returned home to Teutonia Avenue for the winters.[91] Montana baseball lured him back to Scobey for 1926. There he toiled in relative obscurity as the local newspapers gave the fallen star very little ink. In 1927 many small Montana towns, including Scobey, dropped semipro ball in favor of less expensive amateur teams consisting of local players.[92]

Felsch then elected to play for Regina, Saskatchewan. The opportunity to manage the Balmorals and receive greater publicity in a larger community was very appealing. Utilizing their star's famed name in advertisements, "Hap Felsch's Regina Balmorals" began the season on May 25. First baseman Felsch led the way with clutch doubles in the first two games. Competing against other independent semipros from Manitoba, Saskatchewan, Alberta, and North Dakota (including Risberg's Lignite team), the "Felschmen" were most often victorious. Their manager frequently displayed his awesome home-run power and fielding flexibility (first and third base and pitcher).[93]

Back home, Felsch's name was in the papers for a new litigious reason. Late in 1926 Risberg charged 20 ballplayers, including Felsch, with fixing games during the 1917 and 1919 seasons. These allegedly thrown games were intended to alter the final American League standings and the resulting first-, second-, and third-place money. After two days of contentious hearings, Judge Landis exonerated the accused in what some observers described as a quick and convenient whitewash.[94]

In the summer of 1928, the 37-year-old Felsch returned to Montana. Plentywood, Scobey's rival, secured Felsch's services as the semipros competed again in small Montana towns. The acclaimed center fielder joined Plentywood in mid-May for a preseason exhibition tour from Minneapolis back home.[95] On Opening Day, May 27, the team lived up to its name, the Plentywood All-Stars, as they crushed Scobey, 20-4. In five at-bats, Felsch hit a double, two triples, and a home run.[96] Plentywood played black, House of David, Canadian, Dakota, Minnesota, Iowa, and other eastern Montana clubs. The *Sioux City Journal* reported that Felsch was one of the greatest throwers ever after he unleashed a peg about 10 feet above the ground from center field into the catcher's mitt. The one-hopper bounced directly over home plate as "Happy Felsch's All-Stars" swept an August doubleheader.[97]

Felsch's last itinerant years were 1929 and 1930 in Virden, Manitoba. This semipro club also performed against Canadian, Dakota, black, and House of David opponents. In an effort to win more games, Virden signed Felsch in early July, well into the 1929 season. The center fielder supplied power and his famous name to this wheat/railroad town with 1,500 residents.[98] Once second baseman Swede Risberg joined the club, the local paper could not contain its glee, stating, "Hap Felsch and his merry men are just about the smoothest all-around combination that has invaded Wesley diamond for a long, long time. Hap has slowed some, but his gardening last night left nothing to be desired."[99] This popular team was closely identified with its star, acquiring the nicknames "Hap Felsch's Virden All-Stars" and "the Felsch troupe."[100]

In 1930 Felsch started out as a headliner with the American-Canadian Clown team. These barnstormers, with their star playing second base, competed against Virden on May 24. By June 6, the Manitoba town reacquired its ex-big leaguer. Felsch finished the 1930 season, his last on the road, with Virden. The potent club employed its center fielder's name in its advertisements and his bat and glove in its many victories.[101] One ad exclaimed, "See the great Hap Felsch spear the fast ones off the top of the fence."[102]

In 1931 Felsch stayed out of the public eye. He was still listed in city directories as a ballplayer but his diamond career was essentially over.

A slower Felsch, now 40, returned for one last chance at baseball glory on the Milwaukee sandlots in 1932. Shortly after the Brewers prohibited Felsch's "contaminated" presence at an all-star game at Borchert Field, Triangle Billiards, an amateur club, gained his services. The newspapers claimed that the team had secured Judge Landis's permission before adding the former White Sox hero to their roster. Triangle drew much press and a capacity crowd of 15,000 on May 15 to see Felsch patrol center field. Fans exulted in the legend's return as he exhibited his great skills and familiar gestures of pulling his nose and hat while squinting at the pitcher.

While on the Triangle bench, Felsch entertained several admiring children and smoked cigarettes, displaying his famous grin. One newspaper noted his quiet way, observing that maybe he was thinking that this was "a hell of a place" to be for so illustrious a ballplayer.[103] Even though he was considerably past his prime, Felsch continued to play in the area for several more years, shifting to first base as his weight climbed to 200 pounds.[104]

The Felsch family moved around Milwaukee's north side an extraordinary number of times in Happy's post-baseball years. These were often efforts to obtain a new saloon location. During the Prohibition year of 1932, the family opened a new soft-drink parlor and lived at the site.[105] In 1933 the family moved again and lived near their latest tavern as Prohibition ended. The

business shifted north in 1936. By 1938, the family had again relocated their tavern and residence further northward.[106]

The notable former big leaguer did his best to remain cordial with his patrons. The *Milwaukee Journal* reported:

"In the mid-thirties Felsch's tavern on W. Center St. became a gathering place for sand lot players and managers. Happy served free peanuts and kept the bowls on the bar full. The crunch of shells underfoot mingled with baseball talk that often lasted far into the night. Occasionally, a customer would try to draw Felsch into a comparison of the top players of the 1930's with those he had served with in the majors. Happy refused to comment. He seldom became angry when questioned — even about the Black Sox scandal — but found that silence was most effective in ending a distasteful subject."[107]

The 1940s began with Oscar and Marie operating the Barn Grove Tavern. By 1943, Happy had left the saloon business, relocated closer to town, and worked as an assembler and watchman. The family moved again in 1947, only several blocks north of Borchert Field, the site of Felsch's successes more than 30 years earlier.

By 1949, Happy had begun his final career as a crane operator. In 1952 he and Marie, parents of three and eventual grandparents of 11, ended their somewhat nomadic existence as they entered their final home on the second floor of a flat at 2460 N. 49th Street. At this location, *Eight Men Out* author Eliot Asinof and sportswriter Westbrook Pegler conducted their pivotal interviews with Felsch.

In 1962 Felsch, over 70 years old, retired as a crane operator for the George Meyer Company. His family adoringly remembered him as "always in a good mood." Card playing, bowling, hunting, fishing, smoking, and coffee drinking were his favorite pastimes when he was not listening to the Milwaukee Braves on the radio.[108]

Judge Terence Evans recalled playing ball as a child in Garfield Park (now Rose Park) at Fifth and Burleigh. During this time in the late 1940s and early 1950s,

Felsch would often observe Evans and his friends on the diamond. The children called him "Happy" and would converse with the local legend frequently. Evans did notice that Felsch, in poor physical condition, held one arm in a peculiar fashion, as if he had suffered a slight stroke.[109]

The north side's finest ballplayer succumbed to a coronary blood clot due to arteriosclerosis on August 17, 1964, at Milwaukee's St. Francis Hospital. The 73-year-old suffered from varicose veins and a leg abscess for years, but was not seriously ill until six months before his death. Diabetes, a liver ailment, and a pancreatic tumor also complicated his health.

Felsch was survived by his wife, son, and two daughters. The funeral was held on August 20 at the Franzen, Jung and Kaufmann Funeral Home, with entombment in "The Gardens of the Last Supper" at Wisconsin Memorial Park in the northwestern suburb of Brookfield.[110]

If not for the Black Sox scandal, Happy Felsch might be remembered as one of the best all-around center fielders in baseball history. His superb skills induced reporters and managers of his era to compare him favorably with future Hall of Famers. Philadelphia Athletics manager Connie Mack referred to Happy as "the greatest all around fielder in the country today, not barring Tris Speaker and Ty Cobb."[111] Cobb himself proclaimed, "Hap Felsch was a wonder."[112] None other than Babe Ruth ranked the pride of Milwaukee as the best center fielder of his era, asserting, "I would rate Hap Felsch of the old White Sox and Tris Speaker far superior to Cobb on the defense. Felsch was a greater ball hawk than Speaker, and what an arm he had!"[113]

Happy Felsch gave his side of the story in several interviews. Thanks to groundbreaking conversations with Felsch, writers including Asinof, Pegler, and Reutlinger were able to shed some light on the Black Sox scandal. Most of the other fix participants were either too ashamed or fearful of gangster retribution to speak on the record. Major-league baseball preferred to keep the embarrassment of 1919 out of the public

eye. Even in 1959, Commissioner Ford Frick persuaded a major television network to cancel a dramatization of the Black Sox scandal, stating that it would be bad for baseball and, therefore, bad for America.[114]

The amiable Felsch, however, did speak his piece in the last years of his life. Asinof was so appreciative of the center fielder's openness that he dedicated his book, *Bleeding Between the Lines*, to the memory of Felsch.[115] In this 1979 work, Asinof recounts his interview of Felsch for *Eight Men Out*, his 1963 chronicle of the scandal. The former minor leaguer first started his detailed research in 1960 when only four of the eight Black Sox were still alive. Cicotte, Gandil, and Risberg either refused or stonewalled Asinof's inquiries.[116] Felsch became his primary source.[117]

During his research, Asinof visited Milwaukee in an attempt to interview the ailing Felsch. Even after receiving repeated phone calls and a letter, the protective Marie continued to turn down the author. Asinof finally mustered enough courage to visit their home only after a man he met in a bar, who had been acquainted with Felsch, described him as a "real good guy" that everybody liked.

Marie relented when the polite yet persistent Asinof appeared at her door with a bottle of scotch to share with Happy, as Reutlinger did in 1920. She led him to the dark upstairs sitting room, asked for kindness in his questioning, and allowed the two men to spend the afternoon in conversation. Asinof detected hurt, guilt, and remorse in Felsch's voice as he said, "I shoulda knew better. I just didn't have the sense I was born with. It matters. It still matters."[118]

With his heavily bandaged foot resting on an ottoman, the ruddy-faced Felsch opened up to Asinof. He was pleased to talk baseball and recounted his early days as Milwaukee's baseball prodigy. The 70-year-old vividly recalled his underprivileged childhood, saying, "Seems like all I ever wanted was to hit a new ball with a new bat."

Asinof described Felsch as a fine storyteller who was humble and amusing. He did express great contempt for the penny-pinching Comiskey and his fawning sportswriters. Regarding the scandal, he told Asinof, "It was a crazy time. I don't know how it happened, but it did, all right." He went on to say, "God damn, I was dumb, all right. Old Gandil was smart and the rest of us was dumb." Felsch also recollected the times he was pressured by menacing gamblers into committing misplays in local leagues, the 1919 World Series, and the 1920 season.[119]

For his series of Black Sox articles in 1956, writer Westbrook Pegler also called on Felsch at his home, expecting to be refused. Instead, he was warmly received. After telling Pegler that an abscessed varicose vein near his right ankle kept him from sleeping more than four hours a night, Felsch recounted his careers as a tavern owner and crane operator. He explained how argumentative drinkers and a tire-slashing incident prompted the family to finally sell a business as public as a saloon. After quickly spending too much of the tavern's proceeds, Happy told Pegler, "I gotta cut that out" and began the crane job. The former star went on to assert that Buck Weaver, who played very well in the 1919 Series, was unfairly banned. Felsch did not admit to any guilt and stated that his Series statistics were poor due to fine plays by the Reds.[120]

Asinof, in a 1999 interview, was convinced that Felsch was willing to talk more openly in the 1960s as his illnesses and impending death made him unafraid of vengeful gamblers. During the three-hour interview in the stale, dingy sickroom, Asinof found the uneducated retiree to be charming and articulate. Felsch actually wanted the author to stay longer as the conversation appeared to be liberating for him.[121] Pegler and Reutlinger did not experience this advantageous passing of time. Felsch could finally be forthright about the disastrous influence gambling had upon the Black Sox, baseball, and his own life.

NOTES

1   Telephone interview with Milwaukee historian John Gurda, November 5, 1999.

2   Felsch's *Application for Social Security Account Number*, December 3, 1943; Wisconsin Original Certificate of Death #'64 024373; and 1900 and 1930 United States Censuses.

3   1891 Milwaukee City Directory.

4   1900 US Census; *The Sporting News*, August 29, 1964; Steven A. Reiss, *Touching Base: Professional Baseball and American Culture in the Progressive Era* (Urbana and Chicago: University of Illinois Press, 1999), 176; Richard Lindberg, *The White Sox Encyclopedia* (Philadelphia: Temple University Press, 1997), 149.

5   1907-1909 Milwaukee City Directories; Eliot Asinof, *Eight Men Out* (New York: Henry Holt, 1963), 53-4.

6   Reiss, 177; *Milwaukee Journal*, October 7, 1917; *Milwaukee Journal*, August 18, 1964.

7   Lindberg, 149; Joseph L. Reichler, ed., *The Baseball Encyclopedia* (New York: Macmillan, 1985), 906; "Felsch Eager ..."; David Neft and Richard Cohen, *The Sports Encyclopedia: Baseball* (New York: St. Martin's Press), 97.

8   1911 Milwaukee City Directory; *Milwaukee Sentinel*, July 17, August 7, and September 17, 1911; *Milwaukee Journal*, April 8 and June 11, 1911.

9   *Milwaukee Sentinel*, June 12 and July 8 and 21, 1912; *Manitowoc* (Wisconsin) *Daily Herald*, June 15 and 17 and July 1 and 8, 1912.

10 Asinof, 53; *Milwaukee Sentinel*, June 12, 1912; "Felsch Eager ..." and "Hap Felsch, Idol of Sox, Wanted to Be Wrestler," unidentified 1917 newspaper articles from the National Baseball Hall of Fame Felsch Clippings File.

11 *Milwaukee Sentinel*, April 30 and May 1, 1913.

12 *Milwaukee Sentinel*, June 26-30, 1913; *Milwaukee Journal*, August 9, 1914; Lloyd Johnson and Miles Wolff, eds., *The Encyclopedia of Minor League Baseball, 2nd Edition* (Durham, North Carolina: Baseball America, 1997), 189.

13 *Milwaukee Journal*, August 9, 1914.

14 *Milwaukee Journal*, August 7-11, 17-19, 1913; Marshall D. Wright, *The American Association* (Jefferson, North Carolina: McFarland, 1997), 67-68.

15 Wright, 73-74; *Milwaukee Journal*, August 9, 1914.

16 Asinof, 54; *Milwaukee Journal*, August 7-9, 1914, and February 24, 1941.

17 *Milwaukee Sentinel*, April 15, 1915.

18 Lindberg, 21-22; "Felsch Eager ..."

19 1915 Milwaukee City Directory; Eliot Asinof, *Bleeding Between the Lines* (New York: Holt, Rinehart and Winston: 1979), 79; Milwaukee County Marriage Records, 1915, vol. 256, 320; *Milwaukee Journal* and *Milwaukee Sentinel*, October 1915; telephone interviews with Milwaukee historians John Gurda and Harry Anderson, November 5, 1999.

20 *Milwaukee Journal*, October 29, 1915; *Milwaukee Sentinel*, October 29, 1915.

21 Warren Brown, *The Chicago White Sox* (New York: G.P. Putnam's Sons, 1952), 68; Lindberg, 23.

22 Asinof, *Eight Men Out*, 180; Robert C. Cottrell, *Blackball, the Black Sox, and the Babe: Baseball's Crucial 1920 Season* (Jefferson, North Carolina: McFarland, 2002), 51; John Thorn, Pete Palmer, and Michael Gershman, eds., *Total Baseball, Seventh Edition* (Kingston, New York: Total Sports Publishing, 2001), 762 and 2117.

23 G.W. Axelson, *Commy: The Life Story of Charles A. Comiskey* (Chicago: The Reilly & Lee Co., 1919), 204-205; Frommer, 70, 76-77; Lindberg, *The White Sox Encyclopedia*, 434; Joseph P. Murphy, Jr., "Pants Rowland: The Busher from Dubuque," *Baseball Research Journal #24*, 118-119; 1924 Joe Jackson Milwaukee trial transcripts, #64442 Circuit Court Bill of Exceptions, Volume 3, 1566-1588.

24 *Milwaukee Journal*, October 7, 10, and 25, 1917.

25 *Milwaukee Journal*, October 8 and 10, 1917.

26 Thorn, *Third Edition*, 355.

27 *Milwaukee Journal*, October 14, 16, 17, 18, 23, 24, and 25, 1917; *Milwaukee Sentinel*, October 21 and 24, 1917; and Felsch/Sox 1917-1919 contract, Chicago White Sox Hall of Fame, Comiskey Park, Chicago.

28 Koppett, 128-129.

29 *Milwaukee Sentinel*, March 18 and 19, 1918; Frommer, 80-83.

30 *Milwaukee Sentinel*, May 10-21, 1918.

31 *Milwaukee Sentinel*, July 2-3, 1918; Felsch/Sox 1917-1919 contract.

32 *Milwaukee Sentinel*, July 2-4, 14, 18, 1918.

33 Cottrell, 82, 83, 287; *The Sporting News*, January 9, 1919.

34 *Milwaukee Sentinel*, July 5 to October 14, 1918.

35 Brown, 82-83, Daniel E. Ginsburg, *The Fix Is In: A History of Baseball Gambling and Game Fixing Scandals* (Jefferson, North Carolina: McFarland, 1995), 110; Koppett, 129 Murphy, 119.

36 Neft, 97; W.A. Phelon, "Closing Events of 1918 Baseball Season," *Baseball Magazine*, October 1918, 483, 500, 501; Harold and Dorothy Seymour, *Baseball: The Golden Age* (New York: Oxford University Press: 1971), 250-251.

37 Lindberg, *Sox: The Complete Record . . .*, 62; "The Return of the Prodigals," *The Sporting News*, January 2 and 23, 1919.

38 Baseball-almanac.com/rb_ofas.shtml; Baseball-almanac.com/rb_ofdp.shtml.

39 Frommer, 85-91, Seymour, 255; Stein, 131 and 142-143.

40 Eliot Asinof, *1919: America's Loss of Innocence*, (New York: Donald I. Fine, 1990), 301 and 325; Ginsburg, 91-93 and 100 Edward G. White, *Creating the National Pastime: Baseball Transforms Itself*, 1903-1953 (Princeton, New Jersey: Princeton University Press, 1996), 86.

41 Bob Hoie, "1919 Baseball Salaries and the Mythically Underpaid Chicago White Sox," *Base Ball: A Journal of the Early Game* (Jefferson, North Carolina: McFarland & Co.), Spring 2012.

42 Asinof, *Eight Men Out*, 54; Frommer, 86; Reiss, 43, 52, 93, 171-172; Stein, 158.

43 Reichler, 906.

44 Brown, 87-105; Stein, 164-186.

45 *Milwaukee Sentinel*, October 3-18, 1919.

46 Asinof, *Eight Men Out*, 129-131; Stein, 194; *Milwaukee Sentinel*, October 11 and 13, 1919.

47 Asinof, *Eight Men Out*, 123-124.

48 Reiss, 94.

49 Telephone interview with Steve Christie of the Hupmobile Club, Inc., November 10, 1999; Ed Linn and Bill Veeck, *The Hustler's Handbook* (Durham, North Carolina: Baseball America, 1996), 225; 1924 Jackson trial transcripts.

50 Asinof, *Eight Men Out*, 131.

51 1924 Jackson trial transcripts.

52 Reiss, 94.

53 Thorn, *Third Edition*, 831 and 1965.

54 Koppett, 139.

55 Axelson, 203-204; Bill James, *The New Bill James Historical Baseball Abstract* (New York: The Free Press, 2001), 765; Lindberg, *Sox: The Complete Record ...*, 64.

56 Frommer, 125; *Milwaukee Sentinel*, October 11, 1920.

57 Asinof, *Eight Men Out*, 168, 169, and 175; Gropman, 185; Koppett, 140-145; *Milwaukee Sentinel*, September 27-28, 1920; Seymour, 303.

58 Asinof, *Eight Men Out*, 188-193.

59 *Chicago Evening American*, September 30, 1920.

60 Victor Luhrs, *The Great Baseball Mystery: The 1919 World Series* (South Brunswick, New Jersey: A.S. Barnes, 1966), 184 and 250; Seymour, 333.

61 Eliot Asinof, *Bleeding*, 92-94; Asinof, *Eight Men Out*, 144-148, 160, and 190-191; *Chicago Evening American*, September 30, 1920.

62 *Milwaukee Sentinel*, September 28 and 30, 1920.

63 *Milwaukee Sentinel*, October 4, 1920.

64 *Milwaukee Sentinel*, February 1, 1921.

65 Ginsburg, 142-3; David Pietrusza, *Judge and Jury: The Life and Times of Judge Kenesaw Mountain Landis* (South Bend, Indiana: Diamond Communications, 1998), 176-7, and 186; White, 104.

66 Ginsburg, 142-4; *Milwaukee Journal*, July 19, 1921; Rader, 105.

67 Asinof, *Eight Men Out*, 240; Ginsburg, 142-4.

68 Asinof, *Eight Men Out*, 242.

69 *Milwaukee Journal*, July 29, 1921; Rader, 105; Stein, 270-1.

70 Seymour, 330.

71 Asinof, *Eight Men Out*, 202; Koppett, 101-2.

72 Seymour, 330.

73 Cottrell, 253; *Milwaukee Sentinel*, August 7, 1921; Stein, 265.

74 Milwaukee County Death Records, 1921, vol. 458, 140.

75 *Milwaukee Sentinel*, July 31, 1921.

76 Milwaukee County Birth Records, 1922, vol. 811, 130; *Milwaukee Journal*, October 3, 1988; *Milwaukee Sentinel*, June 23, and 25, 1922; 1922 Milwaukee City Directory.

77 Felsch vs. American League Baseball Club of Chicago causes of action (Milwaukee County Circuit Court, June 21, 1922); and *Milwaukee Sentinel*, June 21, 1922.

78 Felsch vs. American League Baseball Club of Chicago answer (Milwaukee County Circuit Court, July 28, 1922); *Milwaukee Sentinel*, July 28, 1922.

79 Felsch vs. American League Baseball Club of Chicago amended complaint and answer (Milwaukee County Circuit Court, April 2, 1923); *Milwaukee Journal*, May 18, 1939; *Milwaukee Sentinel*, June 16, 1923.

80 1923 Milwaukee City Directory.

81 Ray Cannon, Letter to Joe Jackson, January 11, 1924, 1924 Joe Jackson Milwaukee trial papers, Milwaukee County Historical Society, Milwaukee, Wisconsin.

82 Anderson interview; Gurda interview; *Milwaukee Sentinel*, February 11-14, 1924.

83 Asinof, *Eight Men Out*, 289-292; Ginsburg, 155; Gropman, 220-7 and 302; *Milwaukee Sentinel*, February 14, 15, and 21, 1924 *Milwaukee Journal*, March 13, 1966.

84 *Milwaukee Journal Sentinel*, June 21, 1998; Stephen J. Rundio III, *From Black Sox to Sauk Sox 1924* (Cleveland: Society for American Baseball Research, 1997), 1-8.

85 *Milwaukee Journal*, February 5, 1925; Ray Cannon, Letter to Joe Jackson, August 11, 1924, 1924 Joe Jackson Milwaukee trial papers, Milwaukee County Historical Society, Milwaukee, Wisconsin.

86 *Milwaukee Journal*, February 9, 1925; *Milwaukee Sentinel*, February 10, 1925.

87 *Milwaukee Sentinel*, May 19, 1925.

88 *Plentywood* (Montana) *Herald*, June 19, 1925.

89 *Daniels County* (Montana) *Leader*, August 20, 1925.

90 Gary Lucht, "Scobey's Touring Pros: Wheat, Baseball and Illicit Booze," *Montana the Magazine of Western History*, Summer 1970, 88-93.

91 1923-1927 Milwaukee City Directories.

92 *Plentywood Herald*, June 4, 1926, and April 22, 1927.

93 *Regina* (Saskatchewan) *Morning Leader*, May 18 to August 23, 1927.

94 Pietrusza, 296-302.

95 *Plentywood Herald*, May 18, 1928.

96 *Plentywood Herald*, June 1, 1928.

97 *Plentywood Herald*, June 8 to August 16, 1928.

98 *Virden* (Manitoba) *Empire-Advance*, May 14 to July 23, 1929.

99 *Virden Empire-Advance*, July 23, 1929.

100 *Virden Empire-Advance*, August 6, 1929.

101 *Virden Empire-Advance*, May 6 to August 19, 1930.

102 *Virden Empire-Advance*, July 8, 1930.

103 *Milwaukee Journal*, May 8, 15, 16, 21, and 22, 1932; *Milwaukee Sentinel*, May 21 and 23, 1932; *Virden Empire-Advance*, May 25, 1932.

104 *Milwaukee Journal*, August 18, 1964; *New York World Telegram*, July 27, 1937.

105 1932 Milwaukee City Directory.

106 1933-1939 Milwaukee City Directories.

107 *Milwaukee Journal*, August 18, 1964.

108 Asinof, *Bleeding*, 89; Asinof, *Eight Men Out*, 284; *Milwaukee Journal*, August 18, 1964; *Milwaukee Sentinel*, September 25, 1956; personal interviews with Felsch's son and daughter-in-law, Oscar R. and Ruth Felsch and Felsch's granddaughters, Kathy Repka and Laura Laurishke, February 9, 2001; 1940-1965 Milwaukee City Directories; 1943-1957 Milwaukee Phone Books.

109 *Milwaukee Journal Sentinel*, November 18, 2001; telephone interview with U.S. Circuit Court of Appeals Judge Terence T. Evans, May 11, 1999.

110 Wisconsin Original Certificate of Death #'64 024373; *Milwaukee Journal*, August 18, 1964.

111 *Milwaukee Leader*, August 12, 1916; Charles Einstein, ed., *The Third Fireside Book of Baseball* (New York: Simon and Schuster, 1968), 133.

112 Stein, 312.

113 Allison Danzig and Joe Reichler, *The History of Baseball* (Englewood Cliffs, New Jersey: Prentice-Hall, 1959), 175.

114 Asinof, *1919*, 345; Paul Green, "The Later Lives of the Banished Sox," *Sports Collectors Digest*, April 22, 1988, 196-7.

115 Asinof, *Bleeding*, dedication page.

116 Asinof, *Bleeding*, 58-64 and 85-92.

117 Ginsburg, 160-1.

118 Asinof, *Bleeding*, 79, 89, 90, and 113.

119 Asinof, *Bleeding*, 113-118.

120 *Milwaukee Sentinel*, September 25, 1956.

121 Telephone interview with Eliot Asinof, November 5, 1999.

CHICK GANDIL

By Daniel Ginsburg

PRIOR TO HIS INFAMOUS involvement in the 1919 Black Sox scandal, Chick Gandil was one of the most highly regarded first basemen in the American League, both for his play on the field and his solid work ethic. In 1916 a Cleveland newspaper described Gandil as "a most likeable player, and one of excellent habits."[1] From 1912 to 1915 the right-handed Gandil starred for the Washington Senators, leading the club in runs batted in three times and batting .293. In the field Gandil paced American League first sackers in fielding percentage four times and in assists three times.

He continued his strong work with the Chicago White Sox from 1917 to 1919, helping the club to two American League pennants before forever tarnishing his legacy by helping to fix the 1919 World Series. Yet Gandil may have been the only banished player who gained more than he lost from the fix. After the 1919 World Series, the first baseman retired from major-league baseball, reportedly taking $35,000 in cash with him.

Arnold Gandil was born on January 19, 1888, in St. Paul, Minnesota, the only child of Christian and Louise Bechel Gandil. The family relocated to Berkeley, California, where Gandil was raised. As a youngster he loved baseball, splitting his time between pitcher, catcher, and the outfield. By all accounts he was a problem child, and after two years at Oakland High School[2] (where he also played quarterback on the football team), Gandil left home to make it on his own.

After playing some semipro ball in Los Angeles, Fresno, and Amarillo, Texas, Gandil made his debut in Organized Baseball in 1906.[3] He played a handful of games with Los Angeles and Fresno of the Pacific Coast League that year, but did not stick. In 1907 he had a one-game tryout with Portland of the PCL but spent most of the season in Humboldt, Arizona, as

the catcher for a semipro team sponsored by the local copper smelter.[4]

The Humboldt club experienced financial problems, however, and Gandil moved on to a team in Cananea, Mexico, 40 miles from the US border. It was with Cananea that Gandil became a first baseman. In addition to his employment as a baseball player, Gandil worked as a boilermaker in the rugged copper mines. He also did a bit of professional boxing, reportedly receiving $150 per bout.[5] The year before Gandil's arrival, the mine in which he worked had been the site of one of history's most famous labor battles, with the Mexican Army and Arizona Rangers bloodily suppressing a workers' uprising at the behest of the American-owned mining company—an incident that many historians consider the first battle of the Mexican Revolution.[6]

Gandil spent the 1908 season with Shreveport (Louisiana) in the Texas League, batting a solid .269. Off the field, he wed Laurel Kelly, a 17-year-old Mississippi native who went by Faye.[7] They had one daughter, Idella, and were married for 62 years.

After the season Chick was drafted by the St. Louis Browns, but failed to make the club the following year. The Browns ordered him back to Shreveport, but Gandil refused to report, instead joining the Fresno team in the outlaw California State League. Faced with being blacklisted by Organized Baseball, Gandil joined Sacramento of the Pacific Coast League for the 1909 season. He was soon arrested for absconding with $225 from the Fresno team coffers,[8] but had good success in Sacramento, batting .282. Late in the year he was sold to the Chicago White Sox, but wasn't required to report until the following season.

Gandil's rookie season, 1910, was by far the worst of his career. As a part-time performer with the White Sox, he appeared in 77 games, hitting an anemic .193.

Reportedly, he had trouble hitting major-league curve-balls.[9] In mid-September, he and infielder Charlie French were sold by the White Sox to Montreal of the Eastern League, a deal that caused Gandil's first dispute with owner Charles Comiskey. Since the deal was made within 10 days of the end of the minor-league season, Gandil and French appealed to receive their full major-league pay for the season. But the National Commission ruled against them because they had refused to report to Montreal.[10]

Gandil spent the offseason back in Shreveport as a policeman[11] and then reported to Montreal in the spring. He responded with a solid season, batting .304. In December 1911 Chicago Cubs owner Charles Murphy worked out a deal to acquire Gandil for $5,000 and two players, but two other National League teams blocked the transaction.[12] So Gandil returned to Montreal.

Gandil got off to a solid start in 1912, batting .309 in 29 games, after which he was traded to the Washington Senators. This time, the big first sacker was ready for the major leagues, and in 117 games with Washington he hit .305 and led American League first basemen in fielding percentage.

Gandil was highly regarded by Washington. In 1914 Senators manager Clark Griffith wrote, "He proved to be 'The Missing Link' needed to round out my infield. We won seventeen straight games after he joined the club, which shows that we must have been strengthened a good bit somewhere. I class Gandil ahead of McInnes [sic] as he has a greater range in scooping up throws to the bag and is just as good a batsman."[13]

Gandil continued to perform well with Washington both at bat and in the field. In 1913 he hit for a career-high average of .318. He was also tough and durable, averaging 143 games during his three full seasons with Washington, despite knee problems that haunted him throughout his career. When asked by a reporter after the 1912 season what his greatest asset was, he replied "plenty of grit."[14] He reportedly used the heaviest

lumber in the American League, as his bats weighed between 53 and 56 ounces.

Gandil was sold to Cleveland before the 1916 season for a reported price of $7,500. One of the main reasons for the sale was supposedly the fact that Gandil was a chain smoker, occasionally lighting up between innings, which annoyed Griffith.[15] In any event, the Indians also picked up Tris Speaker for that season, and things were looking bright in Cleveland. Although the Indians only climbed from seventh place to sixth, the team won 20 more games than the previous season, reaching the .500 mark. Gandil was unspectacular, batting only .259.

In February 1917 Gandil was sold to his original major-league team, the Chicago White Sox. A headline in the *Chicago Tribune* prophetically announced: "GET YOUR SEAT FOR '17 SERIES! WHITE SOX PURCHASE GANDIL." Manager Pants Rowland pushed White Sox owner Charles Comiskey to make the deal, and *Tribune* writer John Alcock described Gandil as "the ideal type of athlete—a fighter on the field, a player who never quits under the most discouraging circumstances, and so game that he is one of the most dangerous batters in the league when a hit means a ball game."[16]

Gandil appeared in 149 games for the 1917 world champion White Sox, batting .273 with little power. He then hit .261 in the World Series win over the New York Giants, leading the team with five RBIs. Exempt from the draft because he had a wife and daughter, Gandil had a similar year in the war-shortened 1918 season, batting .271 in 114 games, as the White Sox slumped to sixth place.

After World War I ended, baseball owners, fearing a continued slump in attendance, cut back on costs wherever possible and shortened the season to 140 games. Gandil signed a contract for $666.67 per month, the same salary he had been making since 1914. But with the shortened schedule in place, his annual salary now worked out to $3,500 instead of $4,000.[17]

Chick Gandil with the Washington Senators, circa 1913 (National Photo Company Collection, Library of Congress, Prints and Photographs Division)

No one knows the full story of the Black Sox scandal—few of the participants were willing to talk, and the whole plot was confused and poorly managed. But by all accounts Gandil, furious with Comiskey's miserly ways, was one of the ringleaders. Most accounts agree that it was Gandil who approached gambler Sport Sullivan with the idea of fixing the Series, and that he also served as the players' liaison with a second gambling syndicate that included Bill Burns (a former teammate of Gandil's) and Abe Attell.[18] Chick was also the go-between for all payments, and reportedly kept the lion's share of the money. Though none of the other fixers took home more than $10,000 from the gamblers, Gandil reportedly pocketed $35,000 in payoffs.

It's interesting to note that Gandil had a reasonably good Series. Although he hit only .233, that was the fourth best average among White Sox regulars. He was second on the team with five RBIs, and he had one game-winning hit. However, he made several suspicious plays in the field, and all but one of his seven hits came in games the fixers were trying to win, or in which they were already losing comfortably.

Rumors of a Series fix began to circulate, with Gandil's name prominently mentioned.

The next spring Gandil demanded a raise to $10,000 per year. When Comiskey balked, Gandil and his wife decided to remain in California. Flush with his financial windfall from the Series, Gandil announced his retirement from the majors, instead spending the season with outlaw teams in St. Anthony, Idaho, and Bakersfield, California.[19] Thus Gandil was far away from the scene as investigations into the 1919 World Series began during the fall of 1920.

After the players' acquittal on conspiracy charges in August 1921, Gandil said, "I guess that'll learn Ban Johnson he can't frame an honest bunch of ball players."[20] However, the players' joy was short-lived, as Commissioner Kenesaw Mountain Landis announced that the eight Black Sox were permanently expelled from baseball.

Gandil, who had retired from the major leagues anyway, continued to play baseball after his expulsion. A month after the trial he was in contact with Joe Gedeon, Swede Risberg, Joe Jackson, and Fred McMullin, attempting to put together a team in Southern California. In the mid-1920s Gandil played with Hal Chase, Buck Weaver, Lefty Williams, and other banished players in the Copper League, which had teams near the US-Mexico border in Arizona, New Mexico, and Texas.[21]

By the early 1930s Gandil and his wife had settled in Berkeley, California, where he worked mostly as a plumber.[22] Around 1956, Gandil and his wife moved to Calistoga, in the Napa Valley. He had carbuncles, and the town's mud baths and mineral springs aided his health.

To the end of his life, Gandil denied any role in fixing the 1919 World Series. In a 1956 *Sports Illustrated* article, he told writer Melvin Durslag that the players had planned to fix the Series, but abandoned the scheme when rumors began to circulate.[23] In an interview with Dwight Chapin, published in the *Los Angeles Times* on August 14, 1969, Gandil again denied that he threw the Series, stating, "I'm going to my grave with a clear conscience."

Chick Gandil died at the age of 82 in Calistoga on December 13, 1970, and was buried in St. Helena Cemetery in the nearby town of the same name. The cause of death was listed as cardiac failure. People in town had no idea of his fame, and his death reached the sports wires only due to the efforts of SABR founding member Tom Hufford.

SOURCES

Cleveland Plain Dealer, June 1, 1919.

Ginsburg, Daniel, *The Fix Is In* (Jefferson, North Carolina: McFarland & Co., 1995).

The files of Tom Shea.

Letter to Joe Gedeon dated September 15, 1921.

Saturday Evening Post, April 30, 1938.

Arizona Daily Star (Tucson), December 16, 1990.

NOTES

1   *Cleveland Press*, March 17, 1916.

2   "'Chic' Gandil, the Man Who Started the Famous 'Seventeen Straight,'" *Baseball Magazine*, August 1914, accessed online at LA84.org. In 1940 Gandil reported that he had completed four years of high school to US Census takers. Regardless of whether he completed two or four years, it's clear that Gandil, like his future White Sox teammate Swede Risberg, had more formal education than is commonly believed.

3   *Los Angeles Herald*, June 20, 1904; *Bisbee Daily Review*, June 27, 1909; *Amarillo Daily News*, January 7, 1913.

4   "'Chic' Gandil, the Man Who Started the Famous 'Seventeen Straight.'"

5   Chick Gandil as told to Melvin Durslag, "This Is My Story of the Black Sox Series," *Sports Illustrated*, September 17, 1956.

6   *New York Times*, June 3, 1906; John Mason Hart, *Revolutionary Mexico: The Coming and Process of the Mexican Revolution* (Berkeley, California: University of California Press, 1997).

7   Ancestry.com, US Censuses 1920-40; *Santa Rosa Press Democrat*, December 14, 1970.

8   *San Francisco Call*, March 25, 1909.

9   *Chicago Tribune*, December 19, 1920.

10   *New York Times*, April 22, 1911.

11   *Chicago Tribune*, September 20, 1910; December 24, 1910.

12   *Chicago Tribune*, December 16, 1911.

13   "'Chic' Gandil, the Man Who Started the Famous 'Seventeen Straight.'"

14   Chick Gandil player file, National Baseball Hall of Fame Library, Cooperstown, New York.

15   *Cleveland Press*, March 17, 1916.

16   *Chicago Tribune*, March 2, 1917.

17   Bob Hoie, "1919 Baseball Salaries and the Mythically Underpaid Chicago White Sox," *Base Ball: A Journal of the Early Game*, Spring 2012, Volume 6, Number 1 (Jefferson, North Carolina: McFarland & Co.).

18   Bill Lamb, *Black Sox in the Courtroom: The Grand Jury, Criminal Trial, and Civil Litigation.* (Jefferson, North Carolina: McFarland & Co., 2013).

19   *Idaho Statesman*, February 23, 1920, and June 11, 1920; *The Oregonian* (Portland), September 29, 1920.

20   *Chicago Tribune*, August 3, 1921.

21   Lynn Bevill, "Outlaw Baseball Players in the Copper League: 1925-27" (master's thesis, Western New Mexico University, 1988), accessed online at BevillsAdvocate.org.

22   United States Censuses, 1930-40, accessed online at Ancestry.com.

23   "This Is My Story of the Black Sox Series."

SHOELESS JOE JACKSON

By David Fleitz

SHOELESS JOE JACKSON WAS A country boy from South Carolina who never learned to read or write much ("It don't take school stuff to help a fella play ball," he once said[1]) but is widely hailed as the greatest natural hitter in the history of the game. A left-handed batter and right-handed thrower, Jackson stood 6-feet-1 and weighed 178 well-built pounds. He belted sharp line drives to all corners of the ballpark, and was fast enough to lead the American League in triples three times. He never won a batting title, but his average of .408 in 1911 still stands as a Cleveland team record and a major-league rookie record.

Unfortunately, after Cleveland traded him to the Chicago White Sox, Jackson's career ended ignominiously because of his involvement in the infamous Black Sox Scandal of 1919. He was expelled from the game in his prime, and for that reason he has never received a plaque in the Baseball Hall of Fame at Cooperstown.

Joseph Jefferson Wofford Jackson was born on July 16, 1888, in rural Pickens County, South Carolina.[2] His father, George, was a laborer who settled in nearby Greenville soon after Joe's birth and found employment at Brandon Mill, a textile factory that paid $1.25 a day. Brandon Mill stood on the west side of Greenville, and there George Jackson and his wife, Martha, set up a household in one of the small, company-owned houses. Joe, the oldest of eight children, began working at the mill at age 6 or 7. He never attended school, but he did learn to play baseball. Brandon Mill sponsored a team that faced squads from other mills and factories, and Joe earned a spot in the lineup when he was 13 years old. He had his father's unusually long arms and he excelled at throwing and hitting a ball. He soon became renowned throughout the Carolinas as an outfielder, pitcher, and

home-run hitter, which were known throughout the mill league as "Saturday Specials."

A local fan named Charlie Ferguson made bats in his spare time, and he chose a four-by-four beam from the north side of a particularly strong hickory tree to make one for young Joe Jackson. It measured 36 inches long and weighed about 48 ounces. Ferguson darkened the bat with tobacco juice; Joe called it "Black Betsy" and eventually took it to the major leagues.

Joe played for factory teams and semipro clubs until 1908, when Greenville obtained a franchise in the Carolina Association, a new Class D league on the lowest level of Organized Baseball. He signed a contract with the Greenville Spinners for $75 a month. Jackson, who was making about $45 a month between working at the mill and playing ball, reportedly told manager Tom Stouch, "I'll play my head off for $75 a month."[3] Although Jackson later learned to trace his own name, he signed his first professional contract with an "X."

The strong, agile 19-year-old quickly became the biggest star in the Carolina Association, leading the league with a .346 average, making phenomenal throws and catches in center field, and serving as mop-up pitcher. A reporter for the *Greenville News* tagged him with his nickname that season, when Joe played a game in his stocking feet because his new baseball shoes were not yet broken in. For the rest of his life he was known as Shoeless Joe Jackson. He didn't like his nickname and later told Atlanta reporter Furman Bisher, "I've read and heard every kind of yarn imaginable on how I got the name.... I never played the outfield barefoot, and that was the only day I ever played in my stockinged feet, but it stuck with me."[4]

He also gained a wife that year, marrying 15-year-old Katie Wynn on July 19, 1908. She had brown hair and brown eyes, and some education, since she could read and white. She remained married to Joe for 43 years, and until the day Joe died she wrote his letters, managed his money, and read his contracts in and out of baseball.

In August 1908 Philadelphia Athletics manager Connie Mack bought Jackson's contract for a reported $900.[5] Joe was reluctant to go north, and Greenville manager Stouch accompanied him on the train ride to Philadelphia. Joe made his first major-league appearance on August 25, and singled in his first trip to the plate. However, Joe was homesick, and three days later he boarded a train back to Greenville. He returned in early September, but Philadelphia, a city of 2 million people, was frightening to the illiterate country boy. Jackson jumped the team once more before the 1908 season ended, finishing his first major-league stint with three hits in 23 at-bats.

Jackson bounced between Philadelphia and the minors for the next two years. He won batting titles at Savannah in 1909 and at New Orleans in 1910, but did not hit well in Philadelphia in a 1909 late-season call-up. Joe admired manager Connie Mack ("a mighty fine man [who] taught me more baseball than any other manager I had"[6]) but he did not get along with his A's teammates, many of whom teased him mercilessly about his illiteracy, which he tried to hide, and lack of polish. Mack reluctantly decided that Joe would never succeed in Philadelphia, and traded him to the Cleveland Naps for outfielder Bris Lord and $6,000 in July 1910. In mid-September, at the conclusion of New Orleans' season, Joe reported to Cleveland.

Cleveland was a smaller city than Philadelphia. Many of Jackson's new teammates were either Southerners or had played in the South, so Joe fit in well. Playing in right field and center field, Joe batted .387 in the final month of the 1910 season and claimed a permanent place in the Cleveland lineup.

In 1911 he made a major leap to stardom, battering American League pitching for 233 hits, 45 doubles, 19 triples, and a .408 batting average. He did not win the batting title (Detroit's Ty Cobb batted .420), but he set Cleveland team records for hits, average, and out-

Joe Jackson posing as a catcher, circa 1919 (Bain Collection, Library of Congress, Prints and Photographs Division)

field assists (32) that still stand (as of 2014). His torrid hitting helped lift the Naps to a third-place finish. Cobb paid tribute to Jackson as the season ended. "Joe is a grand ball player, and one who will get better and better. There is no denying that he is a better ball player his first year in the big league than anyone ever was."[7]

Jackson swung the bat harder than most of his contemporaries, and players swore that his line drives sounded different from anyone else's. Many other players held their hands apart on the bat and punched at the ball, but Joe put his hands together near the bottom of the handle and took a full swing. "I used to draw a line three inches from the plate every time I came to bat," Jackson said many years later. "I drew a right angle line at the end of it, right next to the catcher, and put my left foot on it exactly three inches from home plate."[8] He stood in the box, feet close together, then took one long step into the pitch and ripped at it with his left-handed swing. "I copied my swing after Joe Jackson's," Babe Ruth told Grantland Rice in 1919. "His is the perfectest."[9]

Though the Naps fell from third place to fifth in 1912, Jackson batted .395, with 121 runs scored, 226 hits, and

30 outfield assists. He also set a new American League record with 26 triples, a mark that was tied by Sam Crawford in 1914 but has never been surpassed. However, Joe once again finished second in the batting race to Cobb, who batted .409 for the Tigers. "What a hell of a league this is," Jackson wailed to a reporter. "I hit .387, .408, and .395 the last three years and I ain't won nothing yet!"[10]

Jackson displayed his power on June 4, 1913, when he belted a fastball from the Yankees' Russ Ford; the hit bounced off the roof of the right-field grandstand at the Polo Grounds and into the street beyond. The newspapers claimed that the blast traveled more than 500 feet. Jackson's .373 average that year trailed Cobb once again, but he led the league in hits (197), doubles (39) and slugging (.551), finishing second in the Chalmers Award balloting. His total of walks also increased sharply, from 54 to 80.

Joe turned down offers from the new Federal League in early 1914, though two Cleveland pitchers joined the new circuit and left the Naps shorthanded on the mound. Federal League raids and the sudden decline of Nap Lajoie caused the Naps to drop from contention, and injuries to Jackson and shortstop Ray Chapman doomed them to last place for the first time in their history. Forced by a broken leg to miss 35 games, Joe saw his average dip to .338 with only 61 runs scored and 53 runs batted in, and he posted new career lows in the speed-dependent categories of triples and stolen bases.

Controversy swirled around Jackson during the 1915 season. He had spent the winter months headlining a vaudeville show that drew curious crowds throughout the South. Joe enjoyed the theatrical life so much that he refused to report for spring training, threatening to quit baseball and begin a new career on the stage. Katie Jackson reacted poorly to that idea, and filed for divorce that March (though she and Joe soon reconciled). In May, team owner Charles Somers ordered manager Joe Birmingham to move Jackson to first base to make room for rookie Elmer Smith in the outfield. Joe played 30 games at first, but the experiment ended when Joe left the lineup with a sore arm.

Somers became incensed when Birmingham blamed the position switch for Jackson's injury, and the team owner soon fired Birmingham, appointing coach Lee Fohl to succeed him.

In 1915 Somers, teetering on the edge of bankruptcy, decided that he could not afford to keep his two best players, Jackson and Chapman. He needed to trade one and rebuild the ballclub (which was renamed the Indians after the team sold Lajoie to Philadelphia that spring) around the other. Somers' mind was made up when the newspapers reported that the Federal League had offered Jackson a multiple-year contract at a salary of $10,000 per year. Somers feared that Jackson would bolt for the new circuit, leaving the Indians with nothing in exchange, so the Cleveland owner solicited offers for his cleanup hitter.

Jackson, who at the time was in the second season of a three-year contract for $6,000 a year, was not opposed to a trade. "I think I am in a rut here in Cleveland," he told local sportswriter Henry Edwards, "and would play better somewhere else."[11] Indeed, Jackson's batting average had now declined for four consecutive years. The Washington Senators offered a package of players for Jackson, but Somers rejected the bid to await a better one, which soon came from the Chicago White Sox. Owner Charles Comiskey coveted Jackson, and sent his secretary, Harry Grabiner, to Cleveland with a blank check. "Go to Cleveland," Comiskey ordered, "watch the bidding for Jackson, [and] raise the highest one made by any club until they all drop out."[12]

On August 21, 1915, Grabiner and Somers reached an agreement. Somers signed Joe to a three-year contract extension at his previous salary, then sent him to Chicago for $31,500 in cash and three players (outfielders Bobby Roth and Larry Chappell and pitcher Ed Klepfer) who collectively had cost the White Sox $34,000 to acquire. In terms of the total value of cash and players, this $65,500 transaction was the most expensive deal ever made in baseball up to that time.

Joe's five-year stay in Cleveland ended with some sniping from the sports pages. Henry Edwards of the *Plain Dealer* criticized Jackson on his way out of town.

"While he does not admit it, he was becoming … a purely individual player who sacrificed team work for Joe Jackson.… If he were still the Jackson of 1911, 1912, and 1913, the team would not have let him get away."[13]

Jackson joined a contending team, one that featured four future Hall of Famers (second baseman Eddie Collins, catcher Ray Schalk, and pitchers Red Faber and Ed Walsh). Jackson hit poorly (for him) in the last six weeks of the 1915 season, and some observers believed that Joe's career was on the downslide. However, he rebounded in 1916, batting .341 with a league-leading 21 triples as the White Sox challenged Boston for the league lead. Chicago finished second that season, but roared to the pennant with a 100-win season in 1917 despite a subpar performance by Jackson, who was hobbled all year after he sprained an ankle in spring training. Joe's average dipped to .277 in early September, but he finished with a flurry of hits that lifted his final mark to .301.

With the pennant safely clinched, the White Sox sent Jackson and Buck Weaver to Boston for an all-star game to benefit the family of the popular player-turned-sportswriter Tim Murnane, who had died in February. Before the game, Jackson won a distance-throwing competition by heaving a ball 396 feet, 8 inches, which was said to be a modern record for a big leaguer.[14] The all-stars, with an outfield of Ty Cobb, Tris Speaker, and Jackson, and Walter Johnson on the mound, lost 2-0 to Babe Ruth and the Red Sox.

During the World Series New York Giants manager John McGraw used left-handed starting pitchers in four of the six games in a bid to neutralize the hitting of Collins and Jackson, but Joe batted .304 and saved the first game with a circus catch in left field. Red Faber won three decisions as the White Sox defeated the Giants four games to two for their second World Series championship, and the last one they would win for more than eight decades. Joe celebrated the victory, and the $3,669.32 winning share that went along with it, by purchasing a new Oldsmobile Pacemaker from a dealership in his new home of Savannah, Georgia, where he and Katie had moved to after his trade to the White Sox.

The White Sox were rocked by the entry of the United States into World War I. Several Chicago players enlisted in the military, while others were drafted in the early months of 1918. Joe, as a married man, was granted a deferment by his hometown draft board in Greenville, but after he played 17 games with the White Sox the board reversed its decision and ordered him to report for induction.[15] Instead, Jackson found employment at a Delaware shipyard, where he helped build battleships and played ball in a hastily assembled factory circuit, the Bethlehem Steel League. Jackson was the first prominent player to avoid the draft by opting for war work, for which he was severely criticized in the sporting press, especially in Chicago.

When two of Jackson's close friends, pitcher Lefty Williams and reserve catcher Byrd Lynn, followed him into the shipyards, owner Charles Comiskey swore he would not let any of them return to his team. "There is no room on my club for players who wish to evade the army draft by entering the employ of ship concerns!" he fumed.[16] But after a sixth-place finish and the war's end, he changed his tune. Jackson won the factory league batting title with a .393 average and helped lead the Harlan & Hollingsworth team to the championship among shipyards on the Atlantic coast, but the controversy permanently damaged his relationships with the Chicago sportswriters.

With little leverage, Jackson signed a new one-year contract for $6,000 — the same salary he had been receiving since 1914 — and returned to the White Sox. He was healthy again, and led the club in batting as the White Sox grabbed first place and held it for most of the 1919 season. Joe finished fourth in the league in batting with a .351 mark, his best average since 1913, with 181 hits and 96 runs batted in. Faber, Chicago's leading pitcher, was sidelined late in the season with a sore arm, but Eddie Cicotte (29-7) and Lefty Williams (23-11) picked up the slack and pitched the White Sox into a comfortable lead in the standings. On September 24 Jackson drove home the winning run in the pennant-clinching game against the St. Louis Browns.

The White Sox were considered the most talented team in baseball, but they were also one of the unhappiest. The biggest problem facing the team was the same one that had been festering for several years. Eddie Collins, Red Faber, and Ray Schalk made up one clique, while Chick Gandil, Fred McMullin, Swede Risberg, and Buck Weaver made up an opposing faction. The two groups sniped at each other all season long. "The wonderful (Philadelphia) Athletic teams I played for believed in teamwork and cooperation," Collins said many years later. "I always thought you couldn't win without those virtues until I joined the White Sox."[17] A third group, including Jackson, Happy Felsch, and Lefty Williams, rarely spoke to the college-educated Collins and Faber, less out of animosity than out of a lack of common interests.

Late in the season, first baseman Chick Gandil, the leader of the first group, concocted a plan to fix the coming World Series against the Cincinnati Reds. Jackson, according to his own later admissions, rebuffed Gandil's first offer to throw the Series for $10,000 but he later agreed to participate after Gandil upped the offer to $20,000 — an amount more than three times his annual salary.[18] Jackson had nothing to do with the planning of the fix; unlike Gandil, he had no contacts in the netherworld of gambling and nightlife. Joe's participation consisted solely of trusting Gandil, a stunning amount of faith in a man whom he didn't know very well. It was an incredible lapse of judgment, as well as a failure of character, on Jackson's part.

Jackson, who ultimately received only $5,000, batted .375 against the Reds but failed to drive in a run in the first five games, four of which the White Sox lost (it was a best-of-nine Series that year). Chicago won the sixth and seventh games, but fell behind quickly in the eighth contest. Jackson belted a homer, the only one of the Series, and drove in three runs in Game Eight, but his production came too late. Cincinnati defeated the favored White Sox by a 10-5 score and won its first World Series title. Jackson tied a record with his 12 hits in the Series, but eight of the 12 came

during the four games the White Sox tried to win. In Chicago's first four losses, Jackson went 4-for-16.

Before going home for the winter, Jackson went to Comiskey's office in the ballpark and waited to see the Old Roman. Jackson wanted to tell Comiskey about the fix and possibly to return the money he had received. He stayed for several hours, but Comiskey holed up in his office and Jackson eventually left without talking to the White Sox owner.

In February 1920 team secretary Harry Grabiner traveled to Jackson's home in Savannah and signed him to a substantial raise, a three-year deal for $8,000 per year. Jackson operated a successful poolroom there and a dry-cleaning business that employed more than 20 people. He and Katie used the money he had received for fixing the World Series to pay for his ill sister Gertrude's hospital bills.

Despite the cloud of suspicion that hovered over him and several of his teammates, Jackson gave one of his finest performances in 1920, with a .382 average, a career-best 121 runs batted in, and a league-leading 20 triples. However, amid growing rumors that the White Sox were continuing to throw games in the 1920 season, Jackson felt alienated from most of the other Series conspirators. His evenings on the road consisted of going to the movies or bars with Lefty Williams, his best friend on the team.

With the White Sox fighting for a pennant entering the season's final week, Jackson's season ended abruptly on September 28, a day after a Philadelphia newspaper published allegations by gambler Billy Maharg claiming that eight members of the White Sox had helped him and other gamblers fix the World Series. Later that day, on the advice of White Sox team counsel Alfred Austrian, Cicotte, Jackson, and Williams appeared before a Cook County grand jury investigating the matter and testified about their involvement. Comiskey immediately suspended Jackson and the six other accused players who were still with the team.

Jackson's appearance before the grand jury on September 28 was responsible for one of the most enduring legends in sports. As reported by Charley Owens of the *Chicago Daily News*, a small child is said to have looked at Jackson exiting the court building and begged, "Say it ain't so, Joe." Jackson and many others denied that the incident ever happened. "There wasn't a bit of truth in it," Jackson told reporter Furman Bisher in 1949. "When I came out of the building, this deputy asked me where I was going, and I told him to the South Side…. There was a big crowd hanging around the front of the building, but nobody else said anything to me. It just didn't happen, that's all. Charley Owens just made up a good story and wrote it."[19]

Despite being acquitted by a trial jury, all eight accused players, including the retired Gandil, were eventually expelled from baseball for life by new Commissioner Kenesaw Mountain Landis. The scandal brought a sad and untimely end to Joe Jackson's brilliant baseball career.

Jackson, whose lifetime batting average of .356 is the third highest in the game's history, played semipro and "unorganized" ball, mostly in the South, for many years thereafter. Wherever he went, his cannon arm and effortless swing drew attention. In 1923 he signed with a team from Americus, Georgia, in the outlaw South Georgia League, and helped lead them to a championship. There was some controversy because the league did not want its younger players to be penalized or banned from Organized Baseball for playing with him. However, he batted well over .400, made incredible catches and throws, and drew large crowds throughout the season.

In 1923 Jackson hired a Milwaukee-based attorney, Ray Cannon, and sued the White Sox for back pay he felt was owed to him after his acquittal in the Black Sox trial. Joe believed that Harry Grabiner had taken advantage of his illiteracy in obtaining his signature on a contract that included the hated "reserve clause," which effectively allowed teams to control their players in perpetuity. A jury sided with Jackson and awarded him more than $16,000 in back pay, but Jackson's deposition about his involvement in the World Series scandal clashed so much with his 1920 grand jury

testimony that the judge threw out the verdict and charged Jackson with perjury. Jackson settled with Comiskey for an undisclosed amount and went back home to Georgia.[20]

For the next several years, Jackson played ball in the South, where folks regarded him with kindness and still stood in awe of his ability. He sported a sizable paunch around his midsection, but he could still knock the stuffing out of a baseball until he was nearly 50 years old. He gave a few newspaper interviews in which he made his case for reinstatement, but mostly stayed out the public eye during the last three decades of his life.

"All the big sportswriters seemed to enjoy writing about me as an ignorant cotton-mill boy with nothing but lint where my brains ought to be," Jackson said in 1949. "That was all right with me. I was able to fool a lot of pitchers and managers and club owners I wouldn't have been able to fool if they'd thought I was smarter."[21]

Jackson eventually moved back to his old neighborhood in Greenville, near the Brandon Mill textile factory, where he operated a successful restaurant and a liquor store for many years. He spent a great deal of time teaching baseball to the local youngsters and organizing impromptu games, even as he suffered from diabetes and liver and heart problems in his later years. In September 1951 Cleveland Indians fans honored him by voting him into the team's Hall of Fame and, in the ensuing publicity blitz, Jackson agreed to travel to New York to appear on Ed Sullivan's "Toast of the Town" television show. However, just two weeks before his scheduled appearance, Jackson suffered a heart attack and he died at home, at the age of 63, on December 5, 1951. He was buried in Woodlawn Memorial Park in Greenville.

NOTES

1   Paul Dickson, *Baseball's Greatest Quotations* (New York: Harper Perennial, 1992), 204.

2   Jackson's date of birth has been recorded as 1887, 1888, and 1889 in different places. The family Bible was lost in a fire many years

ago, but although Joe's official birth certificate lists his birth year as 1889, his tombstone lists his year of birth as 1888.

3   F.C. Lane, "The Man Who Might Have Been the Greatest Player in the Game," *Baseball Magazine*, March 1916, 59.

4   Furman Bisher, "This Is the Truth," *Sport Magazine*, October 1949.

5   *Greenville News*, August 17, 1908. Mack paid $1,500 for Jackson and outfielder/pitcher Scotty Barr. The Greenville newspaper reported that Jackson's value was $900, though other sources differ on the breakdown.

6   Bisher, "This Is the Truth."

7   *Cleveland Plain Dealer*, October 4, 1911.

8   Bisher, "This Is the Truth."

9   Peter Golenbock, *Fenway: An Unexpurgated History of the Boston Red Sox* (New York: Putnam Publishing, 1992), 56.

10   Harvey Frommer, *Shoeless Joe and Ragtime Baseball* (Dallas: Taylor Publishing, 1992), 41.

11   *Cleveland Plain Dealer*, August 21, 1915.

12   *The Sporting News*, August 26, 1915.

13   *Cleveland Plain Dealer*, August 21, 1915.

14   However, several minor leaguers had cleared 400 feet in earlier distance-throwing competitions. And in 1881, pitcher Tony Mullane had thrown a ball nearly 417 feet.

15   *Chicago Daily News*, May 3, 1918.

16   *The Sporting News*, June 20, 1918.

17   Bob Broeg, *Superstars of Baseball* (St. Louis: The Sporting News, 1971), 38.

18   This is the explanation Joe Jackson gave in his testimony to the Cook County Grand Jury on September 28, 1920.

19   Bisher, "This Is the Truth."

20   *Chicago Herald-Examiner*, February 16, 1924.

21   Bisher, "This Is the Truth."

BILL JAMES

By Steven G. McPherson

BIG BILL JAMES'S INVOLVE-ment, if any, in the 1919 Black Sox Scandal remains curiously unexplored by most baseball historians. Yet the tall right-handed pitcher from Michigan pops up in three different game-fixing incidents during the Deadball Era.

As a member of the Chicago White Sox for just two months in 1919, James saw little action in the infamous fixed World Series against the Cincinnati Reds. But when the scandal broke a year later, Billy Maharg, one of the gamblers involved, mentioned his name in an explosive interview with a Philadelphia newspaper.[1] Maharg, an old ballplayer and boxer who was also one of James's hunting buddies in the offseason, never accused James of any wrongdoing, but Maharg and Sleepy Bill Burns, another former major leaguer turned oilman, were two of the conspirators who helped organize the World Series fix.

James was also identified as having knowledge of a disputed game late in the 1919 regular season between the Detroit Tigers, his former team, and the Cleveland Indians, managed by Tris Speaker.[2]

While he was with the Tigers in 1917, James reportedly told White Sox first baseman Chick Gandil that he and his teammates would take it easy on them during a four-game series scheduled for Labor Day weekend. At the time, the White Sox were in a fierce fight for the American League pennant with the Boston Red Sox. Chicago swept the series, and about three weeks later, after the White Sox had clinched the pennant, money changed hands.[3]

Although James was still a productive pitcher in 1919 at the age of 32, perhaps the stigma of his proximity to the Black Sox Scandal hurt his chances to continue pitching in the big leagues. After the season he was dispatched prematurely to the minor leagues, never to return to the majors.

Born in Detroit on January 20, 1887, to William P. and Emma James, William Henry James grew up in nearby Ann Arbor, in the shadow of the University of Michigan.[4] He had a brother, Albert, a year younger. Both of his parents emigrated from England around 1881 and were married in 1883, eventually settling in Ann Arbor. According to city directory information and US Census information, James's father worked as a carpenter and contractor. His mother died of a cerebral hemorrhage in July 1905, when Bill was 18.[5]

James appears to have attended Ann Arbor High School for four years before trading in his English, math, and science books for a pool cue, hammer, and baseball glove around 1906 at the age of 19. According to one school publication, he repeated his sophomore year. The school does not list him as a graduate.[6]

Neither James nor his younger brother, Albert, appear to have played baseball for Ann Arbor High School; however, in 1906 a note in the school annual indicates that "several" of the best men were declared ineligible for baseball.[7]

James gained his baseball acumen and experience toiling in the amateur and semipro baseball leagues in and around Ann Arbor, about 50 miles west of Detroit.[8] He was fast, big, and a switch-hitter who could throw hard.

According to city directories, James's day job during those years before professional baseball included working as a clerk in a pool hall and bowling alley operated by Samuel Rottenstein in Ann Arbor. Later, before baseball and then in the offseason, James followed his father into the carpentry business.[9]

James signed with Toledo of the American Association in 1910, but Toledo shipped him to Jackson, Michigan, where he played for the Jackson Convicts of the Class D Southern Michigan Association. (The team's nickname derived from the fact that there was a state prison in Jackson.) Though he lost 19 games, the 6-foot-4 right-hander proved durable and effective, allowing just 222 hits in 288 innings while walking a manageable 83 batters and earning 14 of his team's 51 victories. In September 1910 the Chicago Cubs drafted him from Jackson in the Rule 5 Draft.

Before the 1911 season, the Cleveland Naps acquired James from the Cubs and assigned him to the Toledo Mud Hens. In early June, young James struck out veteran Jack Hayden, who was then playing with Louisville. When teammates and fans ribbed Hayden after his embarrassing at-bat, he retorted, "You can't hit what you can't see."[10] Several news clips during that period suggest that Big Bill was a hard thrower who "threw smoke," and reporters opined that Cleveland might have difficulty finding a catcher who could handle his pitches.

In June Cleveland brought James to the big leagues. On June 12 he made his first start for the Naps, losing a 4-1 decision to Jack Quinn and the New York

Bill James (Courtesy of Michael Aronstein / TCMA Ltd.)

Highlanders. In his major-league debut, James went the distance, allowing four runs (one earned) and five hits, walking four, striking out five, and hitting a batter.[11] He finished his first season in the big leagues with a 2-4 record and a 4.88 ERA in 51⅔ innings.

After starting the 1912 season with Toledo, James was recalled to Cleveland in August and pitched three games for the Naps. He went back to the minors afterward, and finished 13-13 for the second-place Mud Hens. Toledo ownership, apparently unimpressed, released him at season's end.

In 1913 James signed with the Portland Beavers of the Pacific Coast League. He pitched the entire year for league-leading Portland, winning 24 games with a 1.98 ERA in 328 innings, and leading the PCL in strikeouts with 215. The last-place St. Louis Browns, managed by Branch Rickey, quickly snapped him up from Portland in the Rule 5 Draft after the PCL season.

James spent 1914, his first full season in the major leagues, with St. Louis. He logged a 15-14 record with a 2.85 ERA, while striking out 109 batters in 284 innings for the fifth-place Browns. His regular-season performance earned him a spot on an American League all-star team that traveled to Hawaii and Japan after the World Series.

James started the 1915 season with St. Louis, going 6-10 with a 3.59 ERA in 170⅓ innings. He secured his place in history on July 21 in St. Louis, when Babe Ruth slammed what has been called the first "tape measure" home run off him.[12] The 475-foot blast reportedly cleared the right-field stands at Sportsman's Park and crossed Grand Avenue before piercing the front window of an automobile showroom in a 4-2 loss to the Red Sox.

On August 18, 1915, St. Louis shipped James to Detroit for outfielder Baby Doll Jacobson and $15,000.[13] The Tigers were in a tight pennant race with the Red Sox and hoped James would help carry them to the World Series. He pitched well after being traded, starting nine games and going 7-3 with a 2.42 ERA in 67 innings, but Detroit still finished 2½ games back of

Boston. The 28-year-old James closed out the season with an overall record of 13-13 and a respectable 3.26 ERA in 237⅓ innings.

In 1916 James began experiencing arm problems and dropped to 8-12 with a 3.68 ERA in only 151⅔ innings for third-place Detroit. The Tigers finished four games behind rival Boston and two games behind the second-place White Sox.

James rebounded in 1917, posting a 13-10 record with a 2.09 ERA in 198 innings as Detroit dropped to fourth place, 21½ games behind the White Sox. On August 10, 1917, he gave up yet another long, memorable home run to Babe Ruth—an estimated 465-foot shot into the eighth row of the center-field bleachers at Fenway Park in Boston.[14] Though the White Sox won the pennant by nine games over Boston, the integrity of their championship season would, in the ensuing decade, be the subject of much debate. James and the Tigers were right in the middle of it all.

According to White Sox first baseman Chick Gandil, James approached him underneath the grandstand before the opener of a Labor Day series against Detroit at Comiskey Park and said, "Well, you fellows get out there and hustle. The boys won't bear down very hard on you."[15] Gandil countered with an offer to "fix up" James and the Tigers with a reward. "If it goes all right, I will see that you are fixed up for it," Gandil reportedly said.[16] The White Sox swept the four-game series, which they did, to take firm control of the AL pennant race.

After the White Sox clinched the pennant, Gandil and Swede Risberg collected $45 apiece from each of their teammates—including Shoeless Joe Jackson, Eddie Collins, and others—then traveled to Philadelphia, where Detroit was finishing its season. They delivered their "gift" of nearly $1,000 to James, Detroit's bag man, and then returned to New York to prepare for the World Series.[17]

James later claimed the money paid to the Tigers was not a bribe but a reward—a common practice at the time—for beating the hated Boston Red Sox in a late-September series. The biggest flaw in James's version was that by the time the Tigers faced the Red Sox, the White Sox had all but clinched the pennant, enjoying a 9½-game lead with just nine left to play while second-place Boston, in a must-win series, had 12 games remaining.[18]

Additionally, Detroit's play in the Labor Day series against the White Sox reeked of indifference and produced the following commentary from *Detroit Free Press* reporter E.A. Batchelor in his coverage of the games:

Game One on Sunday, September 2, a 7-2 White Sox win: "Hard hitting in the first and third innings, coupled with some very amateurish fielding by the Tigers in these rounds made the first game a romp for the Sox."[19]

Game Two on Sunday, September 2, a 6-5 White Sox win: "Bases on balls and failure to hold men on the sacks.… Three of the Sox's runs were scored by men who had walked and there were six thefts, all due to long leads that George [Cunningham] allowed."[20]

Game One on Monday, September 3, a 7-5 White Sox win: "But Ehmke couldn't get the ball over and between putting men on and letting them run hog wild after they got there, tossed it off.… The wildness of the Detroit hurlers and the base-running of the Sox decided the first joust. Chicago stole seven bases and six of its seven (runs) were scored by men who had walked."[21]

Game Two on Monday, September 3, a 14-8 White Sox win: "No language that a respectable family newspaper would print would do justice to this carnival. It was a grand medley of bad pitching, loose fielding, and hard hitting."[22]

James pitched in both of the Monday games, allowing one run in two innings of Game One and five runs (two earned) on seven hits and two walks in three innings of Game Two, picking up the loss.

The Labor Day series was largely forgotten until 1922, when attorneys for three of the banished Black Sox players, Joe Jackson, Buck Weaver, and Happy Felsch, brought up their payment to the Tigers during their lawsuits against the White Sox for back pay owed to them.

In late 1926 Risberg revived the allegations on the heels of a controversial scandal involving future Hall of Famers Ty Cobb and Tris Speaker, telling a *Chicago Tribune* reporter that that he had information that would implicate "twenty big leaguers who never before have been mentioned in connection with crookedness."[23]

This time, Commissioner Kenesaw Mountain Landis decided to hold a hearing to clear the air once and for all. After hearing uneven testimony from Risberg and Gandil, Landis took the easy way out, siding with Bill James, whose testimony had been corroborated, in part, by about 30 former players. The Landis decision essentially absolved the Tigers and White Sox of any wrongdoing. Landis did, however, put an end to the once-common practice of players "rewarding" opposing teams with performance bonuses.[24]

In the war-shortened 1918 season, James won only six games while losing 11 as his ERA increased to 3.76, his highest since his two-year stint with Cleveland. He allowed more hits (127) than innings pitched (122) while striking out only 42. With the US government's "work or fight" order looming, James left the Tigers on July 27 and joined the Army. He was stationed at Camp Custer, near Battle Creek, Michigan.[25] He served less than a year and, with the war over, returned to sign his Detroit contract in February 1919.

James started the 1919 season with the Tigers, but on May 24, after he had appeared in just two games, the *Detroit Free Press* reported that James and the Tigers had agreed it was time for him to move on.[26] The Tigers sold him to the Red Sox for cash. A *Free Press* article claimed James was "thin skinned" and the "fans' taunts disheartened him." The article also indicated that during his Detroit years James, who hailed from nearby Ann Arbor, had pitched much better on the road than at home.[27]

After twirling 72 innings and posting a 3-5 record and a 4.09 ERA with the Red Sox in 1919, James was placed on waivers and the White Sox picked him up on August 18. Pitching in a pennant race seemed to rejuvenate him, and he pitched well down the stretch, tossing two shutouts while posting a 3-2 record and 2.52 ERA in five starts for the 1919 American League champions.

Chicago's acquisition of James provided the White Sox with a veteran hurler, giving them flexibility and depth. His arrival also gave manager Kid Gleason the opportunity to rest his overworked star pitchers, Eddie Cicotte and Lefty Williams.

James did not see any action in the early games of the 1919 World Series, despite the fact that Cicotte and Williams each had suspiciously poor performances. In the best-of-nine format, the White Sox fell behind four games to one before rallying to win Games Six and Seven. Although scribes from the *Detroit News* wrote that Kid Gleason was leaning toward starting James in Game Seven of the World Series rather than Cicotte on short rest, Cicotte started the game and pitched well for the Sox in a 4-1 win.[28]

The next day, James relieved Lefty Williams in the first inning of Game Eight, with the Reds already leading 3-0. James allowed an inherited runner to score, but held the Reds mostly at bay until he tired in the sixth inning. He was responsible for four runs in 4⅔ innings, allowing eight hits and three walks while striking out two. Cincinnati won the game 10-5 and clinched the World Series. It was James's final appearance in the major leagues.

In February 1920, upon returning from a hunting trip, James learned about his brother Albert's death from pneumonia.[29] Albert and his wife, Nellie, resided in the family home in Ann Arbor with their two children, William and Ellen.[30]

A couple of weeks later, in spite of his strong performance down the stretch the previous season, the White Sox released James to the Minneapolis Millers of the American Association.[31] He pitched well for the

Millers, throwing 299 innings and winning more than 20 games (21-17, 3.22) for the second time in his minor-league career.

As the 1920 season came to a close, gambler Billy Maharg and others began publicly exposing details of the 1919 World Series fix. When Maharg confessed his involvement in what would become known as the Black Sox Scandal, he unwittingly mentioned that he, co-conspirator Sleepy Bill Burns, and James had planned a hunting trip scheduled shortly after the end of the 1919 regular season but had postponed it so that he and Burns could arrange and execute the fix with Chick Gandil.[32]

Maharg exonerated James, saying he was not involved in the planning or the throwing of World Series games, and James's relationship with the two gamblers merited little attention in the press. Perhaps this is because James was no longer playing in the major leagues or because he was never mentioned publicly by any of the disgraced Black Sox. In any case, he was also ignored by prosecutors, both in the legal system and in the court of public opinion.

In 1921, at the age of 33, James married 34-year-old Olga Ponto, also from Ann Arbor.[33] On the field, he pitched only 195 innings for the Millers, finishing 10-16 with a 5.45 ERA.

After gaining his release from Minneapolis, James signed with the Vernon Tigers of the Pacific Coast League, tossing 297 innings with a 21-12 record and a 3.27 ERA in 45 games in 1922. Vernon finished four games behind the pennant-winning San Francisco Seals.

In 1923 James started again with Vernon but pitched poorly (6-7, 4.82) in 25 games before being reassigned to Class A Mobile, where he finished 1-6 with a 3.63 ERA for the Bears of the Southern Association. Vernon finished last (77-122) in the Pacific Coast League while the San Francisco Seals (124-77) again finished first. Before Vernon sent James to Mobile, he defeated the Seals, 3-2. *Los Angeles Times* reporter Harry Williams said this about Big Bill's last significant performance in the PCL: "Bill had the Seals

looking like Whiffengills in the first six rounds" in a game where he scattered eight hits, struck out six, and walked none.[34] But James pitched poorly after his demotion to Mobile and retired after the season ended.

James's professional baseball career spanned 15 years. He posted a 64-71 record with a 3.21 ERA over eight seasons in the major leagues, and a 110-106 minor-league record with a 2.47 ERA, winning 20 or more games three times in seven seasons.

In retirement James mostly stayed away from professional baseball with the exception of his 1927 testimony to Judge Landis about the controversial White Sox-Tigers series from 10 years earlier.

James sold real estate for Burton Real Estate in Los Angeles until the Great Depression wiped out the firm.[35] Later, he worked as a foreman for the Works Progress Administration.[36]

UCLA appointed James as interim head baseball coach when Jack Fournier resigned eight games into the 1936 season. Under James's guidance, the Bruins finished 12-7. James stuck around as an assistant to new coach Marty Krug, a former big leaguer, in 1937.[37]

James suffered from cirrhosis of the liver in his later years and eventually became bedridden. He spent his last days in a Veterans Administration facility in West Los Angeles and died at the age of 55 on May 25, 1942.[38] He was buried at the National Cemetery in Los Angeles. His wife, Olga, died in 1954 in Los Angeles. Olga and Bill were married for 22 years; they had no children.

AUTHOR'S NOTE

In preparing this biography, I relied heavily on two articles by Lowell Blaisdell in *NINE: A Journal of Baseball History and Culture*: "The Cobb-Speaker Scandal: Exonerated but Probably Guilty" (Spring 2005, Vol. 13, No. 2) and "Judge Landis Takes a Different Approach: The 1917 Fixing Scandal between Detroit and the Chicago White Sox" (Spring 2007, Vol. 15, No. 2). Additionally, I relied on the National Baseball Hall of Fame Library materials related to the Black Sox Scandal and the aforementioned two incidents. I would also like to thank SABR members Jacob Pomrenke, Jim Gordon, Bob Timmermann, and Dorothy Mills, as well as Jennifer Barr and Karen Jania at the Bentley Historical Library, University of Michigan, Ann Arbor, for their research help. Last but not least, thanks to Tim Wiles and Fred Berowski at the Baseball Hall of Fame Research Library for their assistance and due diligence.

NOTES

1   James C. Isaminger, "White Sox Were Promised $100,000 Thru Cicotte; Got Only $10,000," *Philadelphia North American*, September 28, 1920.

2   Bill James, "Twenty-Two Men Out," *Bill James Historical Baseball Abstract* (New York: Villard Books, 1985), 136. According to author-historian Bill James, Big Bill James had knowledge of the 1919 incident involving Ty Cobb, Tris Speaker, Smoky Joe Wood, and Dutch Leonard.

3   Lowell Blaisdell, "Judge Landis Takes a Different Approach: The 1917 Fixing Scandal between Detroit and the Chicago White Sox," *Nine: A Journal of Baseball History & Culture, Vol. 15, No. 2 Spring 2007* (Lincoln: University of Nebraska Press, 2007), 33.

4   The James family lived at 1341 Geddes Avenue. The land is now home to student apartments for the University of Michigan.

5   Michigan Death Certificate.

6   *Catalogue of the Ann Arbor High School Academic Year* (Ann Arbor: Board of Education, 1900-1909); *General catalog of officers & graduates, 1856-1909* (Ann Arbor: Board of Education, 1909).

7   *The Omega, Ann Arbor High School Yearbook (1903-1907)*. Volunteers, including the players themselves, coached and managed the school baseball teams. The Omega reported that until 1903 the baseball team had never had the experience or expertise of a paid baseball coach. On that occasion Albert Taft, the brother of the team's captain and a graduate of Grinnell University, coached and managed the team's 13 games.

8   "Tigers Buy James From St. Louis Browns," *Detroit Free Press*, August 19, 1915.

9   1910 US Census.

10 *Sporting Life*, June 24, 1911.

11 "Jack Quinn Puzzled Cleveland Batsmen," *New York Times*, June 13, 1911.

12 Burt Solomon, *The Baseball Timeline*. (New York: Avon Books), 198; Bill Jenkinson, *The Year Babe Ruth Hit 104 Home Runs* (New York: Carroll & Graf Publishers, 2007), 300.

13 "Tigers Buy James from St. Louis Browns."

14 Jenkinson, 300.

15 "What Chick Gandil and Bill James Told Landis," *Chicago Tribune*, January 8, 1927, 20.

16 "Gandil's Affidavit Tells Complete Story of 1917 Series; Swears He Plotted with James and Handled Money," *Chicago Tribune*, January 9, 1927, 19.

17 Blaisdell, 34.

18 Ibid.

19 E.A. Batchelor, "The Tigers Drop Both Games to Chicago," *Detroit Free Press*, September 3, 1917.

20 Ibid.

21 E.A. Batchelor, "The White Sox Beat Tigers Twice More," *Detroit Free Press*, September 4, 1917.

22 Ibid.

23 "Bill James Silent on Ball Quiz," *Los Angeles Times*, January 4, 1927.

24 Offering performance bonuses had the potential, since payoffs were paid from the anticipated proceeds of a pennant winner's World Series check, of making two teams partners in the pennant race, e.g., in this case, the Tigers partnered with the White Sox to defeat the Red Sox, playing hard versus the Red Sox and sloughing off versus the White Sox. Because the conspiracy was successful, both teams essentially shared Chicago's 1917 World Series earnings.

25 Harry Bullion, "Tigers Drop Third Fracas to Mackmen," *Detroit Free Press*, July 28, 1918.

26 "Regrets Will Accompany James' Release by Tigers," *Detroit Free Press*, May 14, 1919.

27 Ibid.

28 Harry Bullion, "Dope Points to Bill James as Sox Hurler on Wednesday," *Detroit Free Press*, October 8, 1919.

29 Michigan Death Certificate.

30 1920 census data, Ann Arbor.

31 "Baseball Brevities," *Chicago Tribune*, February 11, 1920.

32 Isaminger.

33 1930 census data, Los Angeles.

34 Harry A. Williams, "Tables Turned on Seals." *Los Angeles Times*, June 21, 1923.

35 1930 census data, Los Angeles; Los Angeles County land records.

36 California Death Certificate.

37 *Los Angeles Times*, January 27, 1937.

38 James's death certificate lists his home address as 2039 Witner in Venice; however, there is (and was) no such address in Venice or in the greater Los Angeles area; 1940 Federal Census reports indicate he and his wife resided at 539 Westminster Ave. in Venice.

JOE JENKINS

By Jacob Pomrenke

N OCTOBER 1919 JOE JENKINS found himself embroiled in the Black Sox Scandal, the fixing of that year's World Series by eight of his Chicago White Sox teammates. It was the biggest black eye in baseball's history. Yet Jenkins, who didn't make an appearance in the World Series, couldn't even claim bragging rights within his own family for front-page headlines that month. Just ten days after the World Series ended, Joe learned that his brother William, a prominent businessman in Mexico and a US consular agent there, had been kidnapped by revolutionary rebels. The incident set off an international furor between the two countries that stained William Jenkins' reputation for the rest of his life.

William was released safely after a week and Joe was soon released by the White Sox, too. His major-league career consisted of just 40 games between 1914 and 1919; he saw more combat time and gained more acclaim for his service in the World War than he did in the American League. After leaving the White Sox, Joe spent another decade catching in the minor leagues before retiring to California and running the ranch that William had bought for their elderly father.

Joseph Daniel Jenkins was born on October 12, 1890, in Shelbyville, Tennessee, the fifth of the seven children of John and Elizabeth (Biddle) Jenkins who survived to adulthood.[1] John was a vineyard farmer by trade. When Joe was 10, his brother William, 23, penniless, left for Mexico with his wife and never returned. Over the next decade, William found success as an entrepreneur in the textile industry, specifically cotton hosiery, and he became a significant figure in the Puebla region.[2]

By then Joe was excelling in football and baseball at Battle Ground Academy in Franklin, Tennessee.[3] He signed his first professional contract with Rome

(Georgia) of the Southeastern League in 1911. After first trying out as an outfielder, Jenkins settled in as a catcher with Rome, developing a reputation as a better hitter than fielder.[4] In 1913 he was sold to Keokuk (Iowa) of the Central Association, where he hit .283 and stole 14 bases in 121 games.[5]

After the 1913 season Jenkins was drafted by the St. Louis Browns and made his big-league debut on April 30, 1914, going 0-for-4 in a 12-inning tie against the Cleveland Indians. He made an error and allowed a passed ball.[6] Manager Branch Rickey wasn't satisfied with Jenkins' defense or with any of the other catchers on his roster,[7] plugging in seven different players at the position in 1914. Jenkins got into only 19 games and hit .125 in 32 at-bats, and Rickey sent the 24-year-old back down to the minor leagues for more seasoning.

Jenkins spent 1915 with the Atlanta Crackers of the Southern Association, and then hit a robust .319 with 24 doubles and 10 triples for the Houston Buffaloes of the Texas League in 1916. His contract was purchased by the Chicago White Sox, who went on to win the American League pennant in 1917. Jenkins served mostly as the team's bullpen catcher and, with his booming voice and Tennessee drawl, provided his teammates with comic relief as a storyteller in the clubhouse. That suited him just fine, as his daughter Betty Joe Asbury later related: "He was not a hard worker, as everyone knew, but he was likable and friendly."[8]

Jenkins played only one game in the field for the White Sox in 1917 and came to bat just ten times (with one hit). In Game Five of the World Series, he "had one of the busiest days of his career," according to the *Chicago Tribune*. "He warmed up four different fellows for service and had a fifth on the fire when the game was over."[9] But he was voted a full World Series share by the champion Sox.

With war raging in Europe, Jenkins' offseason got busy in a hurry. He was among the first thousand drafted by the US Army in July 1917 and he reported to Camp Gordon, near Atlanta, in November with about 70 other recruits from Tennessee. He was soon promoted to corporal and was fast-tracked to officer training.[10] His baseball skills came in handy as he formed a star battery on the Camp Gordon team with Brooklyn Robins left-hander Sherry Smith. In the spring of 1918, Jenkins shipped overseas to France with the 132nd Infantry Regiment—coincidentally made up of many White Sox fans from the South Side of Chicago, as he explained in a letter to Sox owner Charles Comiskey that was published in the *Chicago Tribune*:

"We have been scrapping for the past ten days on the Meuse, north of Verdun, and believe me the fighting has been hot and sharp. It is becoming more apparent that Germany is through.… I am with the One Hundred and Thirty-second regiment, which is commanded by Col. Davis of Chicago, and most of the men in my platoon are from the south side, and their favorite spot is the left field of the bleachers. Believe me, those south siders can go some.… Give my regards to all the boys and tell them that in this league over here the pitchers all have plenty on everything that they throw."[11]

In addition to the Meuse-Argonne offensive, Jenkins' unit also saw combat at Flanders and St. Mihiel; he

Joe Jenkins, circa 1917 (Bain Collection, Library of Congress, Prints and Photographs Division)

won a commission for bravery and arrived back home as a first lieutenant. He was back with the White Sox for Opening Day in that fateful season of 1919.

A grizzled veteran now at 29, Jenkins cheerfully took up his old role as bullpen catcher behind future Hall of Famer Ray Schalk and reserve Byrd Lynn. "How can you beat out a guy like Schalk?" Jenkins recalled years later. "He was the greatest."[12] Jenkins again didn't play much, and wasn't very good when he did. He worked in only four games behind the plate all season, made three errors in the four games, and hit just .158 in 19 at-bats. But he was present for the World Series, and watched the infamous fix unfold from his seat in the bullpen. Jenkins said it was obvious "something was up."[13]

"We players who weren't involved in the payoff thought things were funny in that first game in Cincinnati," he recalled to the *Fresno Bee* in 1962. "We should have beaten Cincinnati blindfolded. We had everything, the hitters, the pitchers, the power and the speed.… Yes, it was a terrible mess."[14]

In Game One, White Sox ace Eddie Cicotte was shelled 9-1 by the underdog Reds. The next day Lefty Williams, who had exhibited stellar control all season, walked six batters in a 4-2 loss. Both pitchers later testified before a Chicago grand jury that they had accepted bribes from gamblers to throw the Series. In the experimental best-of-nine-games format that was in place from 1919 to 1921, the Sox lost five games to three.

Six other players were implicated in the Black Sox Scandal—outfielders Shoeless Joe Jackson and Happy Felsch, and infielders Chick Gandil, Swede Risberg, Buck Weaver, and Fred McMullin—and all were banned from the game for life by baseball commissioner Kenesaw Mountain Landis. Jenkins and the other "clean Sox" later received a check for $1,500 from team owner Charles Comiskey—about the difference between a winning share and a losing share. He didn't play a single inning in the Series.

But Jenkins' mind soon turned to family matters. On October 19, ten days after the decisive Game Eight in Chicago, Joe's brother William was kidnapped by Zapatista rebels at his mill in Puebla, Mexico. He spent a week in captivity before a $300,000 ransom was paid to the rebels and he was released. Rumors immediately circulated that the *yanqui* William Jenkins had been given as much as half of the ransom money by his captors, and in November the embarrassed administration of President Venustiano Carranza had Jenkins arrested and charged with staging his own kidnapping. The accusation, which Jenkins biographer Andrew Paxman argues was born largely from politicized fear-mongering and xenophobic stereotypes, "took U.S.-Mexican tensions to a new high."[15]

Senator Albert Fall of New Mexico called for a Senate resolution breaking off relations between the two countries, and tensions remained high for some months after Jenkins was released and reluctantly cleared. But as Jenkins bought up the best sugar-producing land in the Matamoros Valley and later as he held a virtual monopoly on the country's movie theaters — by 1960, *Time* magazine would call him "the richest man in Mexico"[16] — the suspicions about how he made his fortune dogged him for the rest of his life. The name William Jenkins continues to be relevant in 21st-century Mexico through the foundation he set up and named for his late wife, Mary Street Jenkins, which funds hospitals, universities, and other philanthropic causes in the Puebla region.[17]

Back in the United States, Joe Jenkins found himself playing in the Pacific Coast League for the 1920 season. The veteran catcher spent 4½ seasons with the Salt Lake Bees and hit a stellar .337 and .350 for them in 1921 and 1923, respectively. Moving to the Coast League was a fortuitous move for Jenkins personally, as he met his wife, Fay Miner, in Los Angeles and married her in 1921. Fay was the daughter of an Iowa coal miner and had recently moved to California with her sister Inez, a bookkeeper.[18] Joe and Fay had three children, Betty Joe, Peggy Jean, and Joseph Jr., who went by Dan.

As Joe continued to make a living in the minor leagues — after leaving Salt Lake in 1924, he played

for teams in Atlanta, Seattle, Newark, Buffalo, and Elmira — the family moved around Southern California in the 1920s. Jenkins returned home every year to play winter ball in Los Angeles and support his beloved Association of Professional Ballplayers in America, which often held charity games to benefit former players in financial distress.[19]

The 1930 season was Jenkins' final one in professional baseball, and at age 39 he ended on a high note, batting .320 for Elmira (New York) in the New York-Pennsylvania League before hanging 'em up. After retirement, in the midst of the Great Depression, he was one of millions of Americans who had trouble finding work, and the family neared bankruptcy without his steady job in baseball. So when his brother William asked him to move to Northern California and help their ailing father and their sister, Mamie, on their struggling fruit ranch, Joe agreed to relocate his family to Hanford.[20]

Joe and Fay stayed in Hanford for 40 years; he spent the time working odd jobs around the ranch ("He didn't do very much. It was really Mamie who ran it," Betty Joe said[21]), coaching softball, spoiling his six grandchildren, and turning into a prodigious golfer. He claimed one year to have spent 313 days on the course at Kings Country Club, playing "at least" 18 holes a day.[22] His connections to baseball were few, though he followed the game for the rest of his life. He continued to support the APBPA and in 1940 was one of the few former players to attend the funeral of Cincinnati Reds catcher Willard Hershberger, baseball's only in-season suicide death, held in nearby Fresno.[23] After the Giants moved to San Francisco in 1958, Jenkins saw a couple of games at Candlestick Park — the first major-league games he had attended since 1920, he later told the *Fresno Bee*.[24]

On June 21, 1974, Jenkins died at the age of 83. He was buried at Belmont Memorial Park in Fresno, California.[25]

ACKNOWLEDGMENTS

Thanks to Bill Francis, Tracy Greer, Sherman Lee, Andrew Paxman, Melissa Scroggins, Bill Secrest, Jr., and Rod Williamson for their help in preparing this biography.

SOURCES

Books

Davids, L. Robert, ed., *Minor League Baseball Stars, Volume III* (Cleveland: Society for American Baseball Research, 1992).

Joseph, Gilbert Michael, and Timothy J. Henderson, *The Mexico Reader: History, Culture, Politics* (Durham, North Carolina: Duke University Press, 2002).

McNeil, William F., *The California Winter League: America's First Integrated Professional Baseball League* (Jefferson, North Carolina: McFarland & Co., 2002).

Paxman, Andrew. *William Jenkins, Business Elites, and the Evolution of the Mexican State: 1910-1960* (Ph.D. dissertation, University of Texas, 2008). Accessed online at http://repositories.lib.utexas.edu/handle/2152/11640 on August 18, 2011.

Newspapers, magazines

Meehan, Tom, "Hanford's Jenkins, Black Sox Innocent, Talks of One Big Smirch on Baseball," *Fresno Bee*, May 13, 1962. From the Gene P. Carney Collection, Shoeless Joe Jackson Museum and Baseball Library, Greenville, South Carolina.

"Ex-Catcher Jenkins Dies At 83," *Fresno Bee*, June 23, 1974.

"Joseph Jenkins," *Hanford Sentinel*, June 24, 1974.

"Meet Mr. Jenkins." *Time*, December 26, 1960. Accessed online at http://www.time.com/time/magazine/article/0,9171,895150,00.html on August 18, 2011.

Other periodicals: *Atlanta Daily Constitution* (1917-1930), *Chicago Daily Tribune* (1914-1920), *Fresno Bee* (1962-1974), *Hanford Sentinel* (1974), *Los Angeles Times* (1917-1940), *New York Times* (1914-1963), *The Sporting News* (1910-1974), *Vancouver Daily Sun* (1917-1930).

Online Sources

"Joe Jenkins," Baseball-Reference.com. Accessed online at http://www.baseball-reference.com/players/j/jenkijo01.shtml on August 18, 2011.

Joe Jenkins player file, National Baseball Hall of Fame Library, Cooperstown, New York.

Ancestry.com.

Personal correspondence

E-mails to the author from Andrew Paxman, September 5, 2011; September 30, 2011; and October 18, 2011. Some material used from notes of Paxman's interview with Betty Joe (Jenkins) Asbury, Fresno, California, May 25, 2005.

NOTES

1   United States Censuses, 1900-1920, available at Ancestry.com.

2   Andrew Paxman, *William Jenkins, Business Elites, and the Evolution of the Mexican State: 1910-1960.* (Ph.D. dissertation, University of Texas, 2008). Accessed online at http://repositories. lib.utexas.edu/handle/2152/11640 on August 18, 2011.

3   Tom Meehan, "Hanford's Jenkins, Black Sox Innocent, Talks of One Big Smirch on Baseball," *Fresno Bee*, May 13, 1962.

4   *The Sporting* News, October 18, 1911; L. Robert Davids, ed. *Minor League Baseball Stars, Vol. III.* (Cleveland: Society for American Baseball Research, 1992).

5   *Minor League Baseball Stars, Vol. III.*

6   *The Sporting News*, May 7, 1914.

7   1914 St. Louis Browns fielding statistics, Baseball-Reference. com. Accessed on January 20, 2013.

8   Andrew Paxman telephone interview with Betty Asbury, May 25, 2005, shared with the author.

9   "World Series Notes," *Chicago Tribune*, October 14, 1917.

10 *Vancouver Daily Sun*, November 16, 1917; "Honor Roll in War Service," *Chicago Tribune*, January 13, 1918.

11 "Jenkins Brings Sox Hun Trophy," *Chicago Tribune*, January 12, 1919.

12 Meehan, "Hanford's Jenkins, Black Sox Innocent, Talks of One Big Smirch on Baseball,"

13 Ibid.

14 Ibid.

15 Paxman, *William Jenkins, Business Elites, and the Evolution of the Mexican State: 1910-1960.*

16 "Meet Mr. Jenkins," *Time*, December 26, 1960. Accessed online at time.com/time/magazine/article/0,9171,895150,00.html on August 18, 2011.

17 Michael Joseph Gilbert and Timothy J. Henderson, *The Mexico Reader: History, Culture, Politics* (Durham, North Carolina: Duke University Press, 2002).

18 United States Census, 1920, available at Ancestry.com.

19 *Los Angeles Times*, June 19, 1932; *Los Angeles Times*, June 27, 1936.

20 Paxman, *William Jenkins, Business Elites, and the Evolution of the Mexican State: 1910-1960.*

21 Andrew Paxman interview with Betty Asbury, May 25, 2005.

22 Meehan, "Hanford's Jenkins, Black Sox Innocent, Talks of One Big Smirch on Baseball."

23 *Los Angeles Times*, August 9, 1940.

24 Meehan, "Hanford's Jenkins, Black Sox Innocent, Talks of One Big Smirch on Baseball."

25 "Ex-Catcher Jenkins Dies At 83," *Fresno Bee*, June 23, 1974.

DICKEY KERR

By Adrian Marcewicz

EXACTLY 90 MINUTES AFTER Chicago White Sox left-hander Dickey[1] Kerr fired a strike past Cincinnati's Morrie Rath to start Game Three of the 1919 World Series, he coaxed the dangerous Heinie Groh to tap an 0-1 pitch harmlessly to third base. Buck Weaver, the White Sox third baseman, fielded the ball effortlessly and threw over to Chick Gandil at first base to end the game, a 3-0 whitewashing of the Reds.

Staring down the barrel of an 0-2 Series deficit, White Sox manager William "Kid" Gleason had turned to Kerr, a 26-year-old rookie, in hopes that he could succeed where Gleason's veteran stars — Eddie Cicotte and Claude "Lefty" Williams — had failed. Undaunted by the pressure, Kerr responded with a three-hitter. Only twice did the Reds get a runner to second base; neither reached third.

It was one of the most dominating pitching performances in the 15-year history of the World Series.[2]

Richard Henry Kerr was born on July 3, 1893, in St. Louis, one of nine children of Richard J. and Anna (Tieman) Kerr.[3] The elder Richard Kerr was a firefighter and later a raftsman on the Mississippi River; Anna a housewife.[4]

Though he was a slight youth, Dickey participated in many sports and was known as a pretty fair amateur boxer.[5] But he showed a special ability on the baseball field. By the age of 14, he was playing on local nines with adults. During one lopsided loss when his team ran out of available pitchers, Kerr was asked to fill in on the mound. He held the opposition scoreless the rest of the way, and his pitching career was born.[6]

At 16, Kerr made his professional debut in 1909 with the Paragould Scouts in the low-level Northeast Arkansas League, playing alongside his brother Robert.[7] He registered a 13-8 mark over two seasons with the Scouts. In 1911 he joined the Cairo (Texas)

Egyptians in the Kentucky-Illinois-Tennessee (or Kitty) League, then spent the 1912 season with the Cleburne (Texas) Railroaders of the South Central League.[8] The teenager played sparingly, but gained invaluable baseball experience.

Kerr's next stop, with Paris, Texas, in the Texas-Oklahoma League, was a memorable one. He met a local girl, Cora Downing (nicknamed Pep), and they married on July 7, 1914, four days after his 21st birthday. The two were inseparable for nearly half a century.

Kerr's baseball career also began to take flight in Paris: He posted a 41-15 record over two seasons there, and followed that up in 1915-16 with two more 20-win seasons with Fort Worth in the Texas League and Memphis in the Southern League. In Memphis his batterymate was Muddy Ruel, who would go on to have a 19-year major-league career.[9]

In 1917, at the age of 22, Kerr signed with the Milwaukee Brewers of the American Association, one of the highest rungs on the minor-league ladder. He pitched 484 innings in two seasons for the Brewers, and led the league in wins, innings pitched, and strikeouts in 1918.[10] Despite having compiled a 147-76 record in 10 minor-league seasons, the little left-hander still had not been given a shot with a major-league club. "Scouts would notice I had a pretty good record for some minor-league club and would look me up, but when they got one look at me they'd turn the other way. 'Too little,' they'd say."[11]

But the 5-foot-7, 155-pound Kerr had caught the eye of a couple of important people. Clarence "Pants" Rowland, the former manager of the White Sox, was a part-owner of the Brewers. When that team shut down because of the "work or fight" order in World War I, Kerr moved on to Fairbanks-Morse, a semipro industrial outfit in Wisconsin. One of his teammates was White Sox third baseman Buck Weaver, who was working as a mechanic in the company's manufacturing plant.[12] Weaver and Rowland recommended Kerr to the White Sox.

The 1919 White Sox had a veteran team with plenty of star power, including Shoeless Joe Jackson and future Hall of Famers Eddie Collins and Ray Schalk. However, pitching depth was a problem. Eddie Cicotte and Lefty Williams were dependable starters, but Red Faber, another future Hall of Famer, was limited all season due to the lingering effects of influenza.

Despite the fact that new manager William "Kid" Gleason himself had had a successful pitching career even though he was of short stature, Gleason was initially wary of Kerr's size. During spring training he confided to reporters that Kerr was "too small for the big league."[13] But Kerr gradually won Gleason

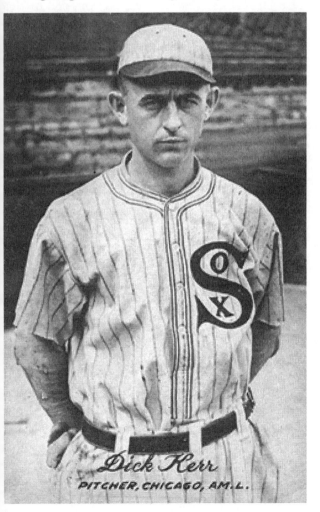

Dickey Kerr baseball card (1921 Exhibit Supply Company W461 baseball card set)

over by pitching well in exhibition games, first in relief and then in spot starting assignments. Five days before the start of the season, Kerr secured his spot on the big-league roster with a complete-game 3-1 win over the Cincinnati Reds.

The Reds would see him again later that season.

Kerr finished his rookie season with a 13-7 record and a 2.88 ERA. More importantly for the Sox, he had developed into the solid third starter Kid Gleason had been looking for back in spring training. Umpire Billy Evans, who worked the 1919 World Series, wrote in his syndicated column that Kerr was "a pretty pert southpaw," one who "may prove to be Gleason's ace in the hole."[14] Gleason was effusive in his praise of his protégé: "Don't overlook that midget [Kerr] — he's a wonder — a better pitcher, in fact, than I had figured. He has a cool head, a fast-breaking curve, a mighty swell fastball, and a good change (of) pace. Kerr has everything a pitcher needs. He might come through this year just as [Red] Faber did in 1917."[15]

Kerr did shine in the World Series against the Reds. His three-hit shutout in Game Three gave the fans (and his "clean" teammates) hope after Cicotte and Williams were defeated in the first two, and his Game Six performance was a study in steadfast determination — he went the distance, allowing 11 hits, a pair of walks and a hit batter, as the White Sox rallied to win 5-4 in 10 innings.

It might not have been obvious to all what was happening in the Series, but those closer to the action — the players and some of the more astute writers — knew what was transpiring. After another set of back-to-back losses by Cicotte and Williams put the Sox in a dire four-games-to-one hole in the best-of-nine series, Gleason penned in his syndicated column, "I'm going to send Dick Kerr to the slab tomorrow. Maybe if he wins, I shall send him back the next day, and if he wins that one I might send him back again!"[16]

As much as he might have liked to, Gleason couldn't send Kerr back out the next day, and the next. Cicotte reversed form in Game Seven and gave Chicago a strong outing, but in Game Eight Lefty Williams—who may or may not have been threatened by anxious gamblers before the game—lasted just 16 pitches as the Reds closed out the series with a 10-5 triumph over the White Sox.

Given the circumstances of October 1919, it was no surprise that when the following spring training rolled around, the Sox were a splintered bunch. Chick Gandil and Eddie Cicotte, two of the fix leaders, were holding out for new contracts, as were Buck Weaver and Swede Risberg. So was Dickey Kerr.

All were eventually re-signed—with the exception of Gandil, who sat out the whole year and never played in the major leagues again—and the White Sox again got out to a strong start in 1920. By September 1, they were in first place with a 77-48 record, a half-game up on the second-place Cleveland Indians.

The two aces, Cicotte and Williams, were among the league leaders in wins again, and a healthy Red Faber had finally returned to form. After a temporary demotion to the bullpen in May, the 26-year-old Kerr emerged as one of the league's top pitchers. In July and August, he went 12-3 with a 2.65 ERA and 10 complete games. One of those losses came in a relief effort just one day after he had beaten the Yankees with a complete game.

Kerr had consistent success against the powerhouse Yankees, who were not yet known as Murderers' Row but won three AL pennants from 1921-23. His career 14-4 record (.778) against the Bronx Bombers is among the all-time best, ahead of Babe Ruth (17-5, .773), Hall of Famer Addie Joss (28-9, .757), and 21st-century star Roy Halladay (18-7, .720).[17]

Kerr also had his share of memorable one-on-one confrontations with Ruth, who joined the Yankees in 1920. On July 19, in the fourth game of a six-game series at the Polo Grounds, Kerr surrendered Ruth's single-season record-breaking 30th home run, a curveball poled to the right-field bleachers that gave the Yankees a 2-1 lead. Ruth added a second homer in the

bottom of the ninth, but Kerr and the White Sox prevailed 8-5.

The White Sox entered the final month of the 1920 season a half-game ahead of Cleveland and one game up on New York, but the pennant race soon become secondary to a Cook County grand jury empaneled to investigate gambling in baseball, specifically the fix rumors surrounding the 1919 World Series.

On September 11 tempers and pent-up frustrations boiled over during Kerr's start against the Boston Red Sox in Chicago. An easy fly ball fell untouched in the outfield between Joe Jackson and Happy Felsch, and a perfect force throw from Kerr was flat-out dropped by Buck Weaver; these miscues helped turn a 1-0 Boston lead into a 6-0 laugher.

Kerr, however, wasn't laughing. At the end of the inning, he reportedly flung his glove across the field in disgust, glowered at Weaver and Swede Risberg, and screamed at them, "If you'd told me you wanted to lose the game, I could have done it a lot easier!"[18] A riot nearly broke out on the White Sox bench, Ray Schalk joining his batterymate in the scrum, and manager Kid Gleason had to break up fistfights between teammates. The White Sox fell, 9-7, unable to overcome six errors.

Despite the obvious internal turmoil on the club, the White Sox remained in the pennant race until the final weekend. Down the stretch Kerr pitched and won three complete games and allowed just four earned runs. Two of those wins, an 8-3 victory over the Yankees and a 10-3 decision over the Indians, came against the White Sox' top contenders for the AL crown.

On September 28, with three games left in the season, Eddie Cicotte and Joe Jackson testified before the grand jury that the World Series had been fixed. Lefty Williams followed them into the courtroom a day later to confess. Eight players were implicated in the fix: Cicotte, Jackson, Williams, Happy Felsch, Swede Risberg, Chick Gandil, Fred McMullin, and Buck Weaver. They were suspended indefinitely by White Sox owner Charles Comiskey.

The "square" members of the team, some of whom suspected the players of also throwing games in 1920,[19] cheered the suspensions and held a celebratory dinner at a downtown Chicago restaurant, then continued their party into the night at Eddie Collins's South Side home. The festivities were still going strong at midnight, and a messenger was sent out to buy cheese, chicken, and other items.[20]

But without the services of their top two pitchers and five members of their starting lineup, the White Sox had no chance to repeat as American League champions. With a makeshift roster, the Sox lost two of three games to the St. Louis Browns—Kerr won the season finale after the Cleveland Indians had already clinched with a victory over the Detroit Tigers.

It was Kerr's 21st victory against just 9 losses, a .700 winning percentage that ranked third in the league. The 1920 White Sox staff set a record with four 20-game winners, a feat that wasn't tied for more than a half-century, when the 1971 Baltimore Orioles turned the trick. Along with Kerr at 21-9, Red Faber went 23-13, Eddie Cicotte went 21-10, and Lefty Williams went 22-14.

After his breakout season at age 26, Kerr staged another holdout in spring training of 1921. And why not? In addition to his 1920 success, the little lefty had shown he was a big-game performer in the World Series as a rookie. And with the absence of Black Sox Cicotte and Williams, both banned, Kerr and Red Faber were the only proven starters on the staff and would be asked to shoulder a much heavier load.

Management wasn't pleased with Kerr's holdout. Owner Charles Comiskey felt he was taking advantage of the team's unprecedented situation: it was so hard-pressed to find able bodies in the wake of the Black Sox Scandal that it would have no choice but to acquiesce to Kerr's demands. Team secretary Harry Grabiner expressed his disappointment: "I give Kerr credit for having more brains than that, after what we agreed to when I signed him at Waco last spring. His terms for this season were fixed then...."[21]

The two sides eventually agreed to terms, and Kerr indicated he was "well pleased with his new contract."[22]

With the exception of Kerr on the mound and future Hall of Famers Ray Schalk at catcher and Eddie Collins at second base, the depleted White Sox took the field for Opening Day 1921 at Detroit with a team full of rookies and castoffs. Kerr lasted just 6⅔ innings, allowing five runs, as the Tigers rallied late behind reliever Suds Sutherland, making his major-league debut, to win 6-5.

Kerr struggled to find any consistency in 1921, with a string of solid performances offset by an outing where he was shelled. Hard-fought pitching duels with Urban Shocker and Walter "Duster" Mails were followed by 17-3 and 16-8 losses. Wins over powerhouses New York and Cleveland were followed by 10-8, 6-1, and 11-10 losses to the Tigers, Browns, and Indians.

One aspect of Kerr's performance that did stay consistent: his mastery of the Yankees. In seven starts against New York, he pitched six complete games, posting a 6-1 record with a 2.70 ERA. Against the rest of the American League, Kerr was 13-16 with a 5.23 ERA. He also fared well against the defending World Series champion Indians, shutting them out twice, one a 5-0 whitewashing on September 29 that effectively ended Cleveland's chances of repeating.[23] That was Kerr's 19th win and it came, appropriately enough, on "Dick Kerr Day" in Chicago. Kerr was honored with a 52-piece silverware set in a mahogany chest.[24]

No one knew it at the time, but the shutout would be Kerr's last big-league victory.

The 1922 offseason began much as it had in previous seasons: with Kerr holding out in a contract dispute. His failure to report to the White Sox' spring-training site in Seguin, Texas, raised concerns with management. For a second straight year, Kerr and Faber were the only major-league-caliber hurlers on the Sox staff.

Team secretary Harry Grabiner was once again dispatched to Texas to speak with Kerr personally. Kerr was optimistic about achieving a speedy resolution—he had sent word to the club that he was keeping in good shape, that he was coaching a high-school team, and "hoped for a quick adjustment on salary differences so that he could report."[25]

Kerr's request for a raise to $7,500 per year was hardly outlandish, given that his 40 wins in 1920-21 were the sixth-highest total in the American League. At issue was his insistence on a three-year contract, while the club wanted to limit the arrangement to one year.[26]

The two sides could not strike a deal. Grabiner refused to discuss negotiations, and Kerr grew testy over the lack of progress, eventually issuing an ultimatum: "If they think I am going to wait until the last day and not report and draw a fine and a suspension they are badly fooled. One week more and I will sign a contract with someone else."[27]

Kerr met with manager Kid Gleason on March 24 in Austin, Texas, in an effort to work things out. A week later, however, the White Sox still hadn't budged off their stance and, true to his word, on April 1 it was reported that the lefty had signed to play with Chicago's semipro City Hall club.[28] It was no April Fool's joke:

"Considerable feeling is being shown by the fans of Chicago over the way Dick Kerr is being treated by Comiskey. The rooters are sore about it.... They seem to think he's justified in holding out the way he has, as he is one of the greatest little pitchers in the American League and is entitled to an increase in pay for the work he has done for the South Side Machine."[29]

By April 9, Kerr still hadn't reported to the City Hall squad, fueling speculation that he'd been rethinking the wisdom of simply walking away from the major leagues. He made the trek to Chicago from his Paris, Texas, home, and the City Hall team (now called the Chicagos) issued a statement on April 15 saying he had signed a contract and would pitch the following day. The White Sox responded with a statement saying the club was no longer pursuing Kerr's services. Promoters of the Chicagos challenged that assertion, claiming Kid Gleason had gone so far as to meet with Kerr at the train depot when he arrived in town, and had even accompanied the hurler during negotiations with the Chicagos' representatives.[30]

Kerr did take the mound for the Chicagos on April 16 against the Firemen at DePaul Field, winning 7-4, but it earned him an indefinite suspension from the White Sox and later a "permanent" one from Commissioner Kenesaw Mountain Landis. If Kerr thought the White Sox were bluffing, he was wrong. They refused to concede to his contract demands, and the 1922 season passed without Kerr making an appearance in the major leagues. So did the 1923 season. Kerr continued pitching for semipro teams in Chicago; Kenosha, Wisconsin; Moberly, Missouri; and other areas, earning "more than I would have with the Chicago [White Sox]."[31]

Eventually the siren song of the major leagues proved too alluring to resist, and Kerr stopped playing semipro ball in order to serve a probationary period and make himself eligible for reinstatement. Landis returned the lefty to baseball's good graces on August 4, 1925. Kerr quickly agreed to contract terms with the White Sox and caught a train to Boston to meet the team.

It took Kerr just a week to declare himself ready for game action. But new White Sox skipper Eddie Collins, his old teammate, opted to wait until the team was back in Chicago to give Kerr his first opportunity to pitch again.

Kerr's return came on August 15 against the Tigers in Comiskey Park. Red Faber allowed three quick runs to Detroit and Kerr relieved him in the third inning. Kerr received a huge ovation from the 20,000 fans on hand,[32] and rewarded the home crowd with two scoreless innings as the White Sox rallied to even the score at 3-3. But he recorded just one out in the fifth inning, allowing two runs, before he was relieved by Sarge Connally. Still, it was a promising debut for a pitcher who had been out of the major leagues for 3 years and 10 months. The White Sox made the day triumphant with a run in the seventh inning and six in the eighth to win, 12-5.

But the good feelings upon Kerr's return did not last. Maybe it was the sheer number of innings Kerr had pitched in 15 years of professional and semiprofessional ball, or maybe age (31) was starting to catch up with him. Whatever the case, Kerr was less than effective in his abbreviated season with the White Sox. He pitched in 12 games (two starts) and finished 0-1 with a 5.15 ERA, and 45 hits and 18 walks allowed in 36⅔ innings. The White Sox released him after the season.

In parts of four seasons in the majors, Kerr ended up with a 53-34 career record and a 3.84 ERA in 811⅓ innings pitched.

After a few seasons in the minor leagues with the San Francisco Seals of the Pacific Coast League and Fort Worth and Waco of the Texas League, Kerr carved out a new career for himself in baseball: as a manager.

He got his first taste of managing in 1927 when he took over the helm at Rice Institute (later Rice University) in Houston. He led the Owls to a 6-14 conference record over parts of two seasons before being replaced by Charley Schwartz.[33] In 1937 he took a job in Wausau, Wisconsin, in the Class D Northern League. The following year, Kerr moved on to Huntington, West Virginia, to coach in the Class D Mountain State League. In 1940 he was hired to manage the Daytona Beach Islanders in the Florida State League, where he would once again be remembered for his sterling character and integrity.

One of the top prospects on the Islanders, a St. Louis Cardinals farm club, was a left-handed pitcher from Donora, Pennsylvania. Stan Musial had been moderately successful with Williamson in the Mountain State League in 1939, posting a 9-2 mark. But some in the Cardinals organization questioned his pitching ability, which was wild to say the least — Musial averaged more than eight walks per nine innings. But he did show promise as a hitter (.352 in 71 at-bats).

Under Kerr's tutelage in 1940, the 19-year-old Musial prospered. He later said Kerr "taught him concentration, control and how to use his legs for more leverage."[34] The result was an 18-5 record with a 2.62 ERA.

Musial also continued his hot hitting as well, batting .311 in 405 at-bats. With just 14 men on the roster, Kerr made sure Musial got plenty of at-bats by using him as an outfielder between starts.

On August 11, 1940, while playing center field against Orlando, Musial chased a sinking liner to left-center. As he reached for the ball, his spikes caught in the turf and he crashed hard on his left (throwing) shoulder. Musial's pitching career was virtually over. He won just two more games that season, and battled shoulder soreness afterward.

The youngster was disappointed, but Kerr's reassurance kept Musial upbeat and focused. He suggested that Musial focus more on hitting to make it to the major leagues. "I became discouraged and was afraid Dickey would tell me to forget about baseball. Then Dickey gave me the big pat on the back I needed — and just at the right time," Musial said later.[35]

Kerr was more than a coach and teacher to Musial; he was a mentor and a father figure, too.

Before the season, Kerr and his wife, Cora, took Stan and his pregnant girlfriend, Lillian, into their home to help the young couple save money before the birth of their first child. In August, just a week before Stan's shoulder injury, it was Dickey Kerr who drove Lil to the hospital, "four or five miles away, in five minutes, against red lights."[36] The Musials named their son Richard in honor of Kerr.

Both Kerr and Musial moved on from Daytona after the 1940 season: Musial climbed the next rung on his way to the major leagues and a Hall of Fame career with the Cardinals, while Kerr left the game for several years before coming back to manage Hutchinson (Kansas) in the Western Association in 1946 and Davenport (Iowa) in the Three-I League in 1947.

Kerr worked as a scout for the Cardinals in the early 1950s before retiring from the sport. He later worked as an office manager for the B&M Electric Company in Houston.

Musial never forgot the kindness Dickey and Cora bestowed upon him. In 1958, he purchased a home in Houston and handed the deed over to the Kerrs. Modesty prevented Kerr and Musial from talking about the gift, but when *Houston Post* sports editor Clark Nealon learned of the gesture, he felt compelled to write about it, saying, "It glowed of too much of the good, the right, and the grateful to keep it out of print."[37]

By the early 1960s, Kerr had been out of organized ball for several years, but the game didn't forget him. On January 10, 1961, he received the inaugural Tris Speaker Memorial Award from the Houston Chapter of the Baseball Writers Association of America. The award was created "to honor players or officials who make outstanding contributions to baseball."[38]

On June 28, 1961, Kerr was honored with a "night" at Busch Stadium (formerly known as Buffalo Stadium) in Houston. He was presented with a large silver tray — inscribed "To Dickie Kerr, a great baseball hero" — by Commissioner Ford Frick. "Baseball owes an eternal debt to Dickie Kerr," Frick said.[39] (Four decades earlier, in his final season with the White Sox, Kerr had a night where he received a 52-piece silverware set. "I've still got every piece of it," Kerr said in Houston.[40])

"There are men who won fame for the asking, but here's a man who took the hard way," Frick said. "He shone for his honor and integrity."[41]

Houston Mayor Lewis W. Cutrer was also on hand for the festivities, presenting Kerr with a key to the city, and a group of fans from nearby Huntsville presented Kerr with a framed resolution passed by the town's Chamber of Commerce urging Organized Baseball to induct Kerr into the Hall of Fame.[42]

Less than a year later, Kerr was diagnosed with cancer. The prognosis was grim and Kerr admitted, "It was hard to take. But then I thought of all the wonderful things that had happened to me, the thrills I've had playing and watching baseball from coast to coast. How could I do anything but accept my fate and spend my last days at home just remembering Ruth, Schalk, Musial and all the rest? Baseball was good to me."[43]

Kerr died on May 4, 1963, a couple of months shy of his and Cora's 49th anniversary. He was buried at Forest Park Lawndale Cemetery in Houston. Stan Musial was in attendance; Ford Frick and White Sox Hall of Famers Ray Schalk and Ted Lyons were among those who sent their condolences.[44]

NOTES

1   Kerr told newspaper writers in 1963 that he spelled his name D-I-C-K-E-Y, but it almost always appeared in print as D-I-C-K-I-E. Joe Coppage, "Kerr Won Fame as Honest Hero of Black Sox," *The Sporting News*, May 18, 1963.

2   There had been one one-hitter and four two-hitters in the previous 88 World Series games.

3   Ancestry.com. Missouri Birth Records, 1851-1910.

4   Ancestry.com, 1900-10 US Censuses; St. Louis City Directories, 1895-1903.

5   *Chicago Herald & Examiner*, October 3, 1919.

6   "The Man Who Was Too Little to Pitch," *Baseball Magazine*, December 1919.

7   *Memphis Commercial Appeal*, February 25, 1937.

8   *St. Louis Post-Dispatch*, September 23, 1919.

9   *Memphis Commercial Appeal*, February 25, 1937.

10   SABR Minor League Database, Baseball-Reference.com.

11   *The Sporting News*, May 18, 1963.

12   *Chicago Tribune*, October 4, 1919.

13   *New York Sun*, October 4, 1919.

14   *New York Times*, September 30, 1919.

15   *Chicago Daily News*, September 30, 1919. Faber won three games (one in relief) and pitched two complete games in the White Sox' 1917 World Series victory over the Giants.

16   *New York American*, October 7, 1919.

17   Mark Simon, "Halladay: King of the Yankee-killers," ESPNNewYork.com, June 14, 2010.

18   Gerry Hern, "The Tipoff on the Black Sox," *Baseball Digest*, June 1949.

19   Bill Veeck with Ed Linn, *The Hustler's Handbook* (New York: G.P. Putnam's Sons, 1965), 284.

20   *Chicago Tribune*, September 29, 1920.

21   *The Sporting News*, January 27, 1921.

22   *Chicago Herald & Examiner*, March 8, 1921.

23 The loss dropped the Indians 2½ games behind the Yankees with three games to play.

24 *Chicago Tribune*, September 30, 1921.

25 *Philadelphia Inquirer*, March 9, 1922.

26 *Kansas City Star*, February 14, 1923.

27 That "someone else" couldn't be another major-league team. There was no free agency due to the reserve clause, which remained in effect until 1975, a dozen years after Kerr's death.

28 *Chicago Herald & Examiner*, April 1, 1922.

29 *The Sporting News*, April 13, 1922.

30 *Chicago Tribune*, April 16, 1922.

31 *Memphis Commercial Appeal*, February 25, 1937.

32 *Chicago Herald & Examiner*, August 16, 1925.

33 "Rice University Baseball History," RiceOwls.com, accessed online at grfx.cstv.com/photos/schools/rice/sports/m-basebl/auto_pdf/07-mg-baseball-history.pdf on October 19, 2013.

34 James N. Giglio, *Musial: From Stash to Stan the Man* (Columbia, Missouri: University of Missouri Press, 2001), 36.

35 *The Sporting News*, May 18, 1963.

36 Ibid.

37 Ibid.

38 *Ocala* (Florida) *Star-Banner*. January 6, 1963.

39 *New York Times*, July 7, 1961.

40 *The Sporting News*, June 14, 1961.

41 *The Sporting News*, July 5, 1961.

42 Despite spending just four years in the major leagues, Kerr actually did receive votes for the Baseball Hall of Fame. He received his first vote in 1937, and garnered as many as 25 votes (10 percent) in 1955, the last year he received consideration.

43 *The Sporting News*, May 18, 1963.

44 *Houston Post*, May 7, 1963.

SEASON TIMELINE: MAY 1919

White Sox record: 18-6 (.750)
Runs scored: 92 | Runs allowed: 60

AL STANDINGS

May 31, 1919

Team	W	L	PCT	GB
CHW	24	7	.774	—
CLE	18	11	.621	5
NYY	15	10	.600	6
SLB	15	13	.536	7
DET	13	16	.448	10
BOS	12	15	.444	10
WSH	8	19	.296	14
PHA	6	20	.231	15½

PLAYER OF THE MONTH

	G	PA	AB	R	H	2B	3B	HR	RBI	SB	BB	SO	BA	OBP	SLG	OPS
Buck Weaver	24	100	93	16	31	10	2	0	6	5	1	2	.333	.354	.484	.840

A career .258 batter entering the season, the switch-hitting Weaver had a breakout year at the plate in 1919. He hit almost as many doubles in May (10) as he had hit in all of 1918 (12), highlighted by a career-high three doubles off Boston's star lefty Babe Ruth in a thrilling 12-inning contest on May 15.

PITCHER OF THE MONTH

	W	L	ERA	G	GS	CG	SHO	IP	H	R	ER	BB	SO	WHIP
Eddie Cicotte	7	1	1.17	8	7	7	3	61⅔	43	10	8	6	22	0.795

Cicotte had a reputation for early-season dominance, and he usually turned it on in the month of May. On May 14, he began a streak of 29⅔ consecutive scoreless innings with a four-hit shutout to beat the defending World Series champion Boston Red Sox, 1-0. Four days later, he shut out the Philadelphia Athletics, 1-0, also on four hits, and on May 23 he scattered nine hits in a 5-0 whitewashing of the New York Yankees.

DAY BY DAY RECAP

Thursday, May 1
Postponed, rain
"Rainy Welcome Forces Delay of White Sox Opener" — *Chicago Tribune*

Friday, May 2
Comiskey Park, Chicago
"Browns Crab White Sox Inaugural By Winning, 11 to 4" — *Chicago Tribune*

Browns (2-5)	150	101	201 — 11	16	0
White Sox (6-2)	010	002	010 — 4	5	3

WP: Bert Gallia (2-0). LP: Lefty Williams (2-1).
Lefty Williams: 1⅔ IP, 5 H, 5 R, 3 ER, 0 BB, 1 K.
Chick Gandil: 1-2, HR, 2 RBI, 2 BB. Joe Jackson: 1-4, 2B, 2 R.

Saturday, May 3
Postponed, rain
"Sox Honor Day Off Due To Rain; Team Hits Well" — *Chicago Tribune*

Sunday, May 4
Comiskey Park, Chicago
"Submarine Sox Trick Both Browns and Rain King, 4-2" — *Chicago Tribune*

Browns (2-6)	000	02—2 3 3
White Sox (7-2)	004	00—4 5 0

WP: Eddie Cicotte (3-0). LP: Allan Sothoron (0-3).
Eddie Cicotte: 5 IP, 3 H, 2 R, 2 ER, 0 BB, 1 K.
Eddie Collins: 2-3, R, 2 SB. Chick Gandil: 1-2, 2B, RBI, SB. Buck Weaver: 1-1, R, RBI, 2 SB, HBP.

Monday, May 5
Scheduled day off

Tuesday, May 6
Comiskey Park, Chicago
"War Heroes See Williams and Sox Tame Tigers, 3 to 1" — *Chicago Tribune*

Tigers (3-7)	000	010	000—1 4 1
White Sox (8-2)	010	002	00x—3 7 0

WP: Lefty Williams (3-1). LP: Bernie Boland (1-2).
Lefty Williams: 9 IP, 4 H, 1 R, 1 ER, 2 BB, 4 K.
Joe Jackson: 2-4, 3B, R, RBI. Happy Felsch: 1-3, 2B, R, SB, SF, RBI.

Wednesday, May 7
Comiskey Park, Chicago
"Faber Comes Into His Own Again, Beating Tigers 9 to 3" — *Chicago Tribune*

Tigers (3-8)	021	000	000—3 9 2
White Sox (9-2)	230	000	31x—9 11 0

WP: Red Faber (2-0). LP: Eric Erickson (0-2).
Red Faber: 9 IP, 9 H, 3 R, 3 ER, 1 BB, 4 K.
Joe Jackson: 2-5, 3B, SB, 2 R, 2 RBI. Happy Felsch: 2-3, 2 2B, SB, R, RBI. Eddie Collins: 1-4, 3B, R, 4 RBI, SB.

Thursday, May 8
Dunn Field, Cleveland
"Indians' Piratical Catches Can't Stop Sox, Who Win, 4-1" — *Chicago Tribune*

White Sox (10-2)	000	101	020—4 10 1

Indians (6-5)   000   100   000 — 1 6 2
WP: Eddie Cicotte (4-0). LP: Stan Coveleski (1-3).
Eddie Cicotte: 9 IP, 6 H, 1 R, 1 ER, 0 BB, 3 K.
Joe Jackson: 2-3, 2 RBI. Happy Felsch: 1-4, 2B, R, RBI. Nemo Leibold: 3-3, 2B, R.

Friday, May 9
Postponed, rain
"Rain in Cleveland Tangles Sox Schedule For Next Week" — *Chicago Tribune*

Saturday, May 10
Dunn Field, Cleveland
"Umpire in Way Costs Sox Runs;
Lose in the 11th" — *Chicago Tribune*

White Sox (10-3)   003   010   001   00 — 5 12 2
Indians (7-5)   003   000   101   01 — 6 8 2
WP: Tom Phillips (1-0). LP: Eddie Cicotte (4-1).
Eddie Cicotte: 2⅔ IP, 4 H, 2 R, 2 ER, 2 BB, 2 K.
Buck Weaver: 3-5, 2B, R, RBI. Swede Risberg: 2-5, 2 SB, R. Joe Jackson: 2-4, 2B, 2 RBI.

Sunday, May 11
Dunn Field, Cleveland
"White Sox Smash Cleveland's New Pitching Idol, 10 to 2" — *Chicago Tribune*

White Sox (11-3)   000   014   203 — 10 17 1
Indians (7-6)   000   000   002 — 2 8 4
WP: Lefty Williams (4-1). LP: George Uhle (2-1).
Lefty Williams: 9 IP, 8 H, 2 R, 2 ER, 1 BB, 5 K.
Swede Risberg: 3-5, 3B, 2 R, 4 RBI. Ray Schalk: 2-3, R, 2 RBI. Eddie Collins: 3-4, 2B, 2 R. Happy Felsch: 2-5, 2B, SB, 2 R, RBI.

Monday, May 12
Comiskey Park, Chicago
"Sox Triumph Over Bert Gallia, Their Brown Jinx, 4 to 3" — *Chicago Tribune*

Browns (3-10)   020   010   000 — 3 9 2
White Sox (12-3)   020   020   00x — 4 7 1
WP: Frank Shellenback (1-0). LP: Bert Gallia (2-2).
Frank Shellenback: 9 IP, 9 H, 3 R, 2 ER, 1 BB, 4 K.
Buck Weaver: 2-4, 2B, R. Joe Jackson: 1-3, SB, RBI. Ray Schalk: 1-3, RBI.

Tuesday, May 13
Comiskey Park, Chicago
"Old Man Horseshoes Helps Browns Lick White Sox, 2-1" — *Chicago Tribune*

Browns (4-10)   110   000   000 — 2 9 3
White Sox (12-4)   001   000   000 — 1 5 2

WP: Dave Davenport (1-1). LP: Charlie Robertson (0-1).
Charlie Robertson: 2 IP, 5 H, 2 R, 2 ER, 0 BB, 1 K.
Chick Gandil: 2-4. Happy Felsch: 1-3, SB. Joe Jackson: 0-2, 2 BB, SB, R.

Wednesday, May 14
Comiskey Park, Chicago
"Double By Joe Jackson Beats the Mighty Red Sox, 1 to 0" — *Chicago Tribune*

Red Sox (7-5)	000	000	000—0 4 2	
White Sox (13-4)	000	001	00x—1 5 2	

WP: Eddie Cicotte (5-1). LP: Carl Mays (2-2).
Eddie Cicotte: 9 IP, 4 H, 0 R, 0 ER, 0 BB, 3 K.
Joe Jackson: 1-4, 2B, RBI. Eddie Collins: 1-4, R.

Thursday, May 15
Comiskey Park, Chicago
"Sox Lose Most Spectacular Game in Years to Boston, 6-5" — *Chicago Tribune*

Red Sox (8-5)	200	200	100	001—6 15 0
White Sox (13-5)	000	130	001	000—5 13 3

WP: Babe Ruth (2-0). LP: Frank Shellenback (1-1).
Frank Shellenback: 3 IP, 3 H, 1 R, 1 ER, 1 BB, 0 K.
Buck Weaver: 3-6, 3 2B, R, RBI. Eddie Collins: 2-6, SB, 2 RBI. Ray Schalk: 2-6, 2 R.

Friday, May 16
Comiskey Park, Chicago
"White Sox Maul Boston Hose Into Submission, 7 to 4" — *Chicago Tribune*

Red Sox (8-6)	300	001	000—4 3 0
White Sox (14-5)	040	010	20x—7 10 1

WP: Red Faber (3-0). LP: Ray Caldwell (2-1).
Red Faber: 9 IP, 3 H, 4 R, 1 ER, 4 BB, 3 K.
Happy Felsch: 2-4, 2 3B, 2 R, RBI. Buck Weaver: 1-4, 2B, R. Eddie Collins: 1-3, 2 RBI.

Saturday, May 17
Comiskey Park, Chicago
"Triple and Fly Beat White Sox in 1 to 0 Scrap" — *Chicago Tribune*

Athletics (4-10)	010	000	000—1 4 0
White Sox (14-6)	000	000	000—0 4 0

WP: Tom Rogers (1-1). LP: Lefty Williams (4-2).
Lefty Williams: 8 IP, 3 H, 1 R, 1 ER, 2 BB, 6 K.
Nemo Leibold: 1-4, 2B. Happy Felsch: 1-4.

Sunday, May 18
Comiskey Park, Chicago
"Crowd of Over 20,000 Sees Sox Shut Out Mackmen, 1 to 0" — *Chicago Tribune*

Athletics (4-11)   000   000   000 — 0 4 2
White Sox (15-6)   100   000   00x — 1 7 0
WP: Eddie Cicotte (6-1). LP: Scott Perry (0-5).
Eddie Cicotte: 9 IP, 4 H, 0 R, 0 ER, 0 BB, 6 K.
Buck Weaver: 2-4, SB, R. Eddie Collins: 1-3. Nemo Leibold: 2-4.

Monday, May 19
Postponed, rain
"Locker 13 Given Mr. Lowdermilk as He Joins Sox" — *Chicago Tribune*

Tuesday, May 20
Comiskey Park, Chicago
"Red Faber and Four Double Plays Subdue Macks, 2 to 1" — *Chicago Tribune*

Athletics (4-12)   100   000   000 — 1 7 1
White Sox (16-6)   100   000   10x — 2 5 3
WP: Red Faber (4-0). LP: Jing Johnson (1-3).
Red Faber: 9 IP, 7 H, 1 R, 1 ER, 1 BB, 0 K.
Buck Weaver: 2-4, 2B, SB. Joe Jackson: 1-2, R, RBI, BB. Eddie Collins: 0-3, BB, R.

Wednesday, May 21
Postponed, rain
"Sox and Yanks to Decide Lead in 3 Games Here" — *Chicago Tribune*

Thursday, May 22
Comiskey Park, Chicago
"Give Jack Quinn Horseshoe, Then Sox Put Kick In It" — *Chicago Tribune*

Yankees (10-6)   000   000   000 — 0 9 3
White Sox (17-6)   100   000   00x — 1 4 0
WP: Lefty Williams (5-2). LP: Jack Quinn (3-1).
Lefty Williams: 9 IP, 9 H, 0 R, 0 ER, 0 BB, 4 K.
Buck Weaver: 1-4, 2B, R. Joe Jackson: 1-3, RBI. Swede Risberg: 1-3, SB.

Friday, May 23
Comiskey Park, Chicago
"Circus Fielding Helps Cicotte Shut Out Yankees, 5 to 0" — *Chicago Tribune*

Yankees (10-7)   000   000   000 — 0 9 2
White Sox (18-6)   200   100   02x — 5 10 0
WP: Eddie Cicotte (7-1). LP: Bob Shawkey (3-3).
Eddie Cicotte: 9 IP, 9 H, 0 R, 0 ER, 3 BB, 3 K.
Joe Jackson: 2-3, 2B, R. Happy Felsch: 1-2, 2 R, 2 BB. Ray Schalk: 2-3, SB, RBI.

Saturday, May 24
Comiskey Park, Chicago
"Bunched Swats Give 2-1 Combat to Huggins' Men" — *Chicago Tribune*

Yankees (11-7)	000	200	000—2 8 2
White Sox (18-7)	001	000	000—1 5 0

WP: Hank Thormahlen (4-0). LP: Red Faber (4-1).
Red Faber: 8 IP, 8 H, 2 R, 2 ER, 0 BB, 2 K.
Eddie Collins: 2-4. Swede Risberg: 2-3, R. Ray Schalk: 1-2, BB.

Sunday, May 25
Comiskey Park, Chicago
"Sox Emerge From Inning of a Lifetime With 6-5 Victory" — *Chicago Tribune*

Senators (8-13)	000	002	030—5 9 1
White Sox (19-7)	002	010	03x—6 13 1

WP: Dickey Kerr (2-0). LP: Walter Johnson (3-4). SV: Dave Danforth (1).
Grover Lowdermilk: 7 IP, 7 H, 4 R, 4 ER, 3 BB, 1 K.
Buck Weaver: 2-4, 3B, R, 2 RBI. Happy Felsch: 2-4, 2 RBI. Nemo Leibold: 2-4, 2 R, RBI. Ray Schalk: 2-3, 2 R.

Monday, May 26
Comiskey Park, Chicago
"Million Dollar Fielding Feats Win 3 to 2 Game For Sox" — *Chicago Tribune*

Senators (8-14)	010	000	100—2 8 1
White Sox (20-7)	111	000	00x—3 6 0

WP: Lefty Williams (6-2). LP: Harry Thompson (0-3).
Lefty Williams: 9 IP, 8 H, 2 R, 2 ER, 2 BB, 4 K.
Chick Gandil: 1-2, 3B, BB, R. Happy Felsch: 1-3, RBI. Ray Schalk: 1-3, RBI.

Tuesday, May 27
Comiskey Park, Chicago
"Happy Felsch Gets Right Mad and Beats Griffs, 4 to 3" — *Chicago Tribune*

Senators (8-15)	002	100	000—3 6 2
White Sox (21-7)	000	121	00x—4 6 2

WP: Eddie Cicotte (8-1). LP: Walter Johnson (3-5).
Eddie Cicotte: 9 IP, 6 H, 3 R, 1 ER, 1 BB, 1 K.
Happy Felsch: 1-2, 2B, BB, R, RBI. Eddie Collins: 1-3, SB, BB, R, RBI. Shano Collins: 1-2, 2B, BB.

Wednesday, May 28
Scheduled day off
"Gleasons Spend Off Day in Skull Practice at South Side Park" — *Chicago Tribune*

Thursday, May 29
Scheduled day off

White Sox defeat Decatur Staleys 7-4 in exhibition game at Decatur, Illinois.

Friday, May 30
Comiskey Park, Chicago
"30,000 Fans See Sox Take Both From Cleveland" — *Chicago Tribune*

Indians (18-9)   100   000   000 — 1 4 1
White Sox (22-7)   102   100   00x — 4 10 0
WP: Red Faber (5-1). LP: Jim Bagby (3-2).
Red Faber: 9 IP, 4 H, 1 R, 1 ER, 2 BB, 3 K.
Happy Felsch: 3-4, 2B, R, RBI. Buck Weaver: 2-4, 2B, 3B, R, RBI. Swede Risberg: 2-4, 2B.

Indians (18-10)   000   000   101 — 2 8 2
White Sox (23-7)   000   200   001 — 3 8 2
WP: Lefty Williams (7-2). LP: George Uhle (2-2).
Lefty Williams: 9 IP, 8 H, 2 R, 1 ER, 0 BB, 4 K.
Swede Risberg: 2-3, 2 RBI. Chick Gandil: 1-4, RBI. Joe Jackson: 1-2, R, BB.

Saturday, May 31
Comiskey Park, Chicago
"Gandil and Speaker Stage Fight as Sox Beat Injuns, 5-2" — *Chicago Tribune*

Indians (18-11)   020   000   000 — 2 7 1
White Sox (24-7)   000   500   00x — 5 5 1
WP: Eddie Cicotte (9-1). LP: Tom Phillips (2-1).
Eddie Cicotte: 9 IP, 7 H, 2 R, 2 ER, 0 BB, 3 K.
Happy Felsch: 1-4, R, RBI. Chick Gandil: 1-3, R, RBI. Eddie Cicotte: 1-3, 2 RBI.

MAY HIGHLIGHTS

Inaugural Ceremonies: The specter of World War I loomed over the White Sox' home opener against the St. Louis Browns on May 2, held one day late because of inclement weather. As the *Chicago Tribune* reported, the pregame ceremony included "the dedication of a spick and span new United States flag." A color guard of US Marines, led by White Sox captain and Marine veteran Eddie Collins, unveiled the flag and the two teams marched it to the flagpole in left field. Then the Marine band played "The Star-Spangled Banner"—which wouldn't be officially named as the national anthem until 1931—and special gifts were presented to the Sox players, including a gold watch for Joe Jackson and a leather travel bag for Ray Schalk.

Faber and the Flu: Weakened by influenza and later an ankle injury, right-hander Red Faber was unable to be a reliable starter for the White Sox in 1919. But given enough rest, the future Hall of Famer was still plenty effective. He went 4-1 with a 1.64 ERA in five May starts, with one coming on 10 days' rest and another on eight days' rest. But after Kid Gleason added him to the regular rotation, Faber went on a long losing streak between May 30 and July 9. He made just one start in September and didn't appear in the World Series against the Reds.

Thieves Raid Sox Clubhouse: Security must not have been too tight at Comiskey Park as the White Sox prepared for a quick road trip to Cleveland. On consecutive nights, May 6 and 7, burglars broke into the team clubhouse. The first night, the thief or thieves pilfered a few items from minor-league recruit Earl Keiser's locker before being frightened away. The next day, according to the *Chicago Tribune*, the thief returned. Missing items included "a number of left-handed fielders' gloves, several sweater jackets, and other things left behind." *Tribune* reporter Irving Sanborn said, "About the only thing they didn't steal was bases."

Clash of the Champions: In a highly anticipated series on May 14-16, the White Sox, champions of 1917, took two of three games from the visiting Boston Red Sox, champions of 1918. In the opener, Eddie Cicotte outdueled Carl Mays to win, 1-0, getting the powerful Babe Ruth to fly out to center with the tying run on base to end the game; Joe Jackson's sixth-inning RBI double scored Eddie Collins for the game's only run. "You will live a long time before you will see another battle of slabmen to equal that between Cicotte and Carl Mays, the celebrated subterranean hurler," wrote Irving Sanborn of the *Chicago Tribune*. "There wasn't a man on either side who would not have broken a leg to win." In the second game, Babe Ruth was wild but effective in 11 innings of relief (13 hits, 8 walks, 0 strikeouts). Buck Weaver's game-tying RBI double in the ninth extended the game but Stuffy McInnis drove in the go-ahead run in the 12th to win it 6-5 for Boston. In the rubber matchup, Red Faber held the Red Sox to three hits (first baseman Chick Gandil registered 19 putouts) and Happy Felsch slammed two triples to give Chicago a 7-4 win. Some of the White Sox played with heavy hearts after learning of the sudden death of baseball funnyman Herman "Germany" Schaefer, 43, who had traveled around the world with the White Sox and New York Giants on their 1913-14 baseball tour. Charles Comiskey lowered the flags at Comiskey Park to half-staff the following day.

"Chicken Feed" at the Ticket Windows: Nearing the end of an unusually long 18-game homestand, White Sox officials expressed some frustrations about fan behavior to the *Chicago Tribune*, which prompted this humorous note on May 25: "To avoid last Sunday's delay at the ticket windows, Secretary [Harry] Grabiner has issued a request that patrons bring some 'chicken feed' with them today. It takes a long time for a ticket seller to extract 85 cents or $1.10 from a $20 bill, and nearly everybody last Sunday had the twenty but not the dime or nickel to pay the war tax. And nearly everybody plans to reach the Sox park at ten minutes to 3 o'clock."

Gandil-Speaker Fight: "An old time fistfight such as probably hasn't occurred on a big league ball field in the last fifteen years or more broke loose at the White Sox park," James Crusinberry wrote in the *Chicago Tribune* about an eighth-inning scuffle between Chick Gandil and Cleveland Indians star Tris Speaker on May 31. "It was a rough and tumble tiger battle with claws, spikes, fists, feet, and possibly even teeth before the two finally were dragged apart." Speaker had slid hard into first base on a routine groundout, and Gandil took exception. After the inning ended, Speaker quickly jumped out of the dugout to go to his position in center field and he exchanged more harsh words with Gandil as they passed each other. Then the fighting began. As Crusinberry wrote, "Baseball fights generally are stopped after about one exchange of blows. This pair were tumbling over the earth from first base halfway to the pitcher's slab, then back toward second, and still nobody stopped them." (In *Eight Men Out*, author Eliot Asinof claimed that the White Sox infielders didn't intervene because "they all wanted [the hated] Gandil to get his lumps," but there is no evidence that this is true. Crusinberry and other observers were simply awestruck at how quickly the fight turned vicious, and the players probably were, too.) The police had to be called in, and both players were restrained and ejected. When order was restored, fans in the bleachers began throwing bottles and trash at Indians left fielder Jack Graney until White Sox manager Kid Gleason went out to calm the irate crowd. Afterward, Indians manager Lee Fohl said the real cause of the fight was Eddie Cicotte's infamous "shine ball," which Cleveland players had been protesting vigorously for several years. "My players simply got mad," Fohl said. "The rules declare there shall be no discoloration of the ball. Cicotte repeatedly discolors it. We appeal to the umpires and they do nothing." Speaker and Gandil, who both sustained facial lacerations and some impressive shiners, were each suspended for five games by American League President Ban Johnson.

NEMO LEIBOLD

By Gregory H. Wolf

ASCRAPPY OUTFIELDER, NEMO Leibold had a 13-year major-league career and played on four World Series teams, winning a championship with the Chicago White Sox in 1917 and another with the Washington Senators in 1924. Later a distinguished manager in the minor leagues from 1928 to 1948, Leibold is best known for passing through the Black Sox Scandal of 1919 with his reputation and honor intact.

Harry Loran Leibold—a German name pronounced LYE-bold—was born February 17, 1892, in Butler, Indiana, to Henry and Etta Leibold. One year later, his family moved to Detroit, where his father worked in factories. Growing up an only child in a family of limited means, Harry, also called "half-pint" because of his small stature, began playing baseball in Detroit's competitive sandlot leagues by the time he was in junior high school. Playing center field on his high-school team, the quick and agile Leibold quit school to work for Edison Electric Co. and earn much-needed pocket money to help his parents.[1] On Sundays he played for Delray, a local semipro team that played in Factory Park in the industrialized southwest part of the city.

In 1910 Leibold traveled to western Michigan to try out for the Kalamazoo Kazoos, in the Class D Southern Michigan League.[2] He made the team, but after three weeks player-manager Charles Wagner sent him home before he had seen action in a game. A disappointed Leibold returned to Detroit and resumed playing for Delray. His fortunes appeared to have changed when Jimmy Barrett, a former big-league outfielder with the Tigers, saw him play. Barrett, who played for the Milwaukee Brewers in the American Association at the time, intended to purchase the Oshkosh Indians in the Class C Wisconsin-Illinois League and offered Leibold a contract with the team; however, the deal to buy the team fell through.[3]

But fate was on Leibold's side. Barrett was named player-manager of the Brewers for the 1911 season and immediately told Brewers owner Otto Borchert about the 5-foot-6 speedster Leibold. Borchert dispatched his right-hand man and expert talent evaluator, Louis M. Nahin, to Detroit, where he signed Leibold to a contract.[4]

Leibold's skills were well suited to baseball in the Deadball Era. He was fast on the basepaths and in the outfield, where he could play all three positions. He was nimble, agile, and quick, and he was a slap hitter and solid bunter. Leibold reported to the Brewers' spring-training site at the University of Illinois in Champaign in 1911. Longtime Milwaukee sportswriter Manning Vaughn recalled how Leibold was greeted with jeers and snide remarks because of his size; however, Vaughn was amazed by Leibold's athleticism and fielding ability, writing, "[Leibold] could throw equally well with either arm."[5] Once he earned a regular job, the natural left-handed-hitting Leibold threw right-handed. As a 19-year-old, Harry struggled in his first year with the Brewers, batting just .177.[6]

Playing for manager Hugh Duffy, a former big-league batting champ later elected to the Baseball Hall of Fame, Leibold blossomed in 1912 for the Brewers. Described as a "midget player" by *Sporting Life*, Leibold raised his batting average to .285, prompting Duffy to predict that he would be as good as Donie Bush, the Detroit Tigers' slick-fielding shortstop and reportedly the shortest player in the major leagues.[7]

Leibold began to attract the attention of major-league scouts. Bob Gilks, a scout for the Cleveland Naps in the American League, was impressed with Leibold's natural fielding instincts and his ability to track fly balls even in the sun. At the end of the season, the Naps drafted Leibold from the Brewers for a reported $2,500.[8]

For the 1913 season, Leibold joined manager Joe Birmingham's Naps (a name honoring the team's star player, Nap Lajoie) and was given the title of "smallest man in the league" by *Sporting Life*.[9] Teammate Jack Lelivelt began calling Leibold "Nemo" based on the popular comic strip "Little Nemo," and the nickname stuck with Leibold for the rest of his playing career. Teaming with Shoeless Joe Jackson and Jack Graney in the outfield, Nemo took over center field by mid-season and finished with a .259 batting average in 286 at-bats. "[Leibold] should be one of the best flychasers in the American League next season," *Sporting Life* predicted.[10]

In 1914 Leibold married Edena (née Loranger), one year younger than he, and together they had five children, Edna, Raymond, Harry, Edwin, and Robert, during the first ten years of their marriage.[11] In the offseason Leibold was reunited with his family in Detroit, where he lived his entire life after moving there with his parents.

After a surprising third-place finish in Leibold's rookie season, the Naps' hope for a championship in 1914 were dashed when, in spring training, Nemo injured

Nemo Leibold, circa 1919 (Bain Collection, Library of Congress, Prints and Photographs Division)

his knee and shortstop Ray Chapman broke his leg, landing both of them in Cleveland's Charity Hospital. Leibold returned to bat .264 in 402 at-bats, but the team fell to last place with a 51-102 record. Naps owner Charles W. Somers, one of the principal founders of the American League in 1901, actively shopped Leibold during the season. Somers was in financial straits in part because of poor attendance, but especially due to the upstart Federal League, which aggressively attempted to sign players and drove up salaries.

Leibold flirted with the Federal League before its inaugural season in 1914 and approached the Pittsburgh Rebels about a job. Reports from the *Milwaukee Sentinel* that Leibold, dissatisfied with his contract with Cleveland, had jumped to the Buffalo Blues of the Federal League for the 1915 season, proved to be inaccurate.[12] Batting .256 in midseason for Cleveland, Leibold lost his job to Billy Southworth and was placed on waivers. On July 7 the Chicago White Sox purchased his contract for a reported $7,500.

Leibold could not dislodge Shano Collins or fellow 23-year-olds Happy Felsch and Eddie Murphy from the White Sox outfield. He played sparingly in 1915, batting .230 in 74 at-bats. With the acquisition of Leibold's former Naps teammate Shoeless Joe Jackson, the White Sox outfield grew even more formidable. Leibold was relegated to the role of fifth outfielder and his playing time was limited to just 82 at-bats in 1916.

Even though Leibold was a backup outfielder in his first 1½ seasons with the White Sox, the *Pittsburgh Press* described him as a future "star" and said that manager Pants Rowland would give him a chance to start in 1917.[13] Leibold earned a starting job in the outfield, but was often replaced by Shano Collins when facing left-handed pitchers. Rooming with future Hall of Famer Eddie Collins on the road and typically batting leadoff, Leibold was a hustling spark-plug for the team. Though he batted just .236 in 428 at-bats, his 74 walks trailed only Eddie Collins on the team. Known for his quick, instinctive jump on balls hit to the outfield, Leibold often played shallow and dared hitters to try to hit over his head. With a 100-54 record, the White Sox cruised to the American League pennant behind Eddie Cicotte's 28 wins and an AL-leading team ERA of 2.16, earning the right to play the New York Giants in the World Series.

The White Sox faced left-handed starting pitchers in every game of the Series; consequently, Shano Collins got the starting nod over Leibold. In a 7-2 victory in Game Two, Leibold pinch-hit for Collins and rapped an RBI single in the fourth inning to score Buck Weaver, and then took over right field. His next action came in the deciding Game Six, when he pinch-hit again for Collins. In his second at-bat in the ninth inning, he hit a single to center field, scoring Weaver for the final run in the 4-2 Series-clinching victory. In right field for the final out, Leibold celebrated with teammates as Red Faber got pinch-hitting Lew McCarty to ground out to second to secure the first White Sox championship since 1906.

Anticipating another pennant in 1918, the White Sox struggled to a sixth-place finish, their roster depleted by the government's "work or fight" order which prevented baseball players from being exempted from wartime service. Leibold was off to the best start in his career, playing in 116 of the team's 124 games during the abbreviated season and batting .250.

In 1919 the White Sox got off to a fast start and won their second pennant in three seasons. Under new manager Kid Gleason, Leibold excelled, platooning in right field with Shano Collins, but seeing most of the playing time and batting .302 in 434 at-bats. His 72 walks led the team and his .404 on-base percentage trailed only Shoeless Joe Jackson among the regulars.

The White Sox were to face the Cincinnati Reds in the best-of-nine World Series. Washington Senators manager and co-owner Clark Griffith predicted that Chicago would win the Series and praised Nemo: "[Leibold is] hard to pitch to and has a good eye. If the balls are bad, he won't take a cut at them. If they are in, he is liable to crack for two or three as he is a single."[14]

Playing against right-handed pitchers in the Series, Leibold went hitless in his first 13 at-bats (with two walks) before lining a single in the deciding Game Eight loss. He finished the Series with just one hit in 18 at-bats.

With rumors of a fixed World Series resonating throughout baseball in 1920, a grand jury was convened in Chicago in September to investigate the allegations. Despite the disruptions, the 1920 White Sox played well and were in first place to begin the last month of the season. "It was a reeling blow to us when the investigations proved the 1919 Series had been fixed," Leibold recalled almost 40 years later. "We could not believe that eight of our teammates let us down."[15]

Leibold thought the White Sox should have won the pennant again in 1920, but that chance was lost when White Sox owner Comiskey suspended seven players—Cicotte, Felsch, Jackson, Fred McMullin, Swede Risberg, Weaver, and Lefty Williams (Chick Gandil sat out the 1920 season in a salary dispute)—on the eve of the season's final series.[16] Those eight players were subsequently banned from baseball by Commissioner Kenesaw Mountain Landis.

Summoned by the grand jury to testify, Leibold revealed that friends from Detroit had contacted him about a rumored fix and wanted an inside scoop, but he never wrote to them. Under oath, Leibold said, "[I told them] I was in a spot where I couldn't advise you either way, so I just didn't answer. That was the only thing I could do."[17] Leibold said he had no knowledge of a fix. "I roomed with Buck [Weaver] throughout the 1919 and 1920 season and I never had any inkling that there was anything wrong," he said.[18] Leibold, who suffered a broken left hand in 1920 that limited his batted average to .220, was never implicated in the scandal.

Along with Shano Collins, Leibold was traded to the Boston Red Sox for right fielder (and future Hall of Famer) Harry Hooper during spring training in 1921. Lauded as "one of the best outfielders in the American League," Leibold was reunited with manager Hugh Duffy and had his best season at the plate, batting a career-high .306 in 467 at-bats and playing center field.[19] Platooning at center with Collins in 1922,

Leibold saw his average fall to .258 for the last-place Red Sox.

Playing sparingly for new Red Sox manager Frank Chance in 1923, Leibold had a stroke of luck when Washington Senators player-manager Donie Bush, to whom he had been compared as a young player, persuaded Clark Griffith to acquire Leibold at the waiver price in late May. Installed as the starting center fielder soon after his arrival, Leibold batted .305, one of five regulars to bat over .300.

Under the leadership of new player-manager Bucky Harris, the Senators got off to a slow start in 1924. Their record on June 16 was 24-26. Then the Senators caught fire, winning 68 of their final 104 games to claim their first pennant. Harris praised Leibold's ability to get on base and start rallies. With a .293 batting average and a .398 on-base percentage (trailing only Goose Goslin), Leibold was part of an outfield *The Sporting News* considered one of the strongest in baseball.[20]

A steady, dependable, and experienced leader on the field, Leibold was thought to be finished as a player when the Senators acquired him. However, Clark Griffith said during the final days of September, "The splendid playing of Leibold has proved one of the season's surprises in the American League."[21]

Facing the powerful New York Giants in the World Series, the Senators took the National League champs to Game Seven. Down 3-1 with one out in the bottom of the eighth inning, Leibold pinch-hit for third baseman Tommy Taylor and responded with the biggest hit of his career: a double to left field, which put him in position to score along with Muddy Ruel on Harris's two-out single to tie the game. "[Leibold's] vitally necessary two-bagger was no surprise," said Harris after the game.[22] In the bottom of the 12th, Earl McNeely scored Ruel with a dramatic game-ending hit to give the Senators and Walter Johnson, who pitched the final four innings in relief, their first title.

Citing Leibold's leadership qualities, Bucky Harris and Clark Griffith thought he would be an excellent coach or manager. They may have even toyed with the idea of naming Leibold a Senators coach for the 1926 season, his last in the major leagues. While the Senators won their second consecutive pennant in 1925 in convincing fashion, the 33-year-old Leibold was hobbled by nagging injuries to his legs and had difficulties playing in the outfield. In 84 at-bats, his lowest total since 1916, he batted .274. In the Senators' seven-game World Series defeat by the Pittsburgh Pirates, Leibold saw action as a pinch-hitter on three occasions (hitting a double and scoring in the Game Five defeat), but did not play in the field.

Leibold was given his unconditional release after the season. He played in 1,268 games in his major-league career and batted .266 in 4,167 at-bats. In four World Series—with his teams winning two—he hit .161 (five hits in 31 at-bats.)

Leibold added a new chapter to his career in 1928. He was named player-manager of the Columbus (Ohio) Senators (no connection to the Washington Senators) in the American Association. Batting a solid .296 from 1928 through 1930, Leibold skippered the Senators in their last three years of independence before they signed an affiliation contract with the St. Louis Cardinals for the 1931 season. Though the Senators finished seventh, sixth, and sixth in the eight-team league during his tenure, Leibold proved to be popular with the fans and a positive influence on his players, most of whom had or would have some experience in the major leagues.

Cardinals general manager Branch Rickey retained Leibold as manager of the team, renamed the Red Birds, in 1931. Leibold was an innovative trainer who stressed physical fitness. At the Red Birds' spring training site in Bradenton, Florida, he was one of the first known managers to employ volleyball to improve players' reflexes and agility.[23] After leading the Red Birds to a winning record and a fourth-place finish in 1931, he was replaced in midseason 1932 by Billy Southworth.

In 1933 Leibold began a professional relationship with the Boston Red Sox that lasted until 1948, during which time he led various Boston minor-league affiliates to six league championships.[24] Acting on the advice of Red Sox general manager Eddie Collins, who knew Leibold well, Bob Quinn hired Leibold to manage the Reading Red Sox of the New York-Penn League in 1933. After two consecutive winning seasons, Leibold moved up to the Syracuse Chiefs of the International League.[25] Chiefs president Jack Corbett cited Leibold's aggressive style of game management which harkened back to the Deadball Era.[26]

After a second-place finish in the regular season, the Chiefs beat the Montreal Royals to secure the inaugural Governor's Cup as league champions in 1935. Fired after the first third of the season in 1936, Leibold served as a team scout before managing the Rocky Mount (North Carolina) Red Sox in the Class B Piedmont League and the Clarksdale (Mississippi) Red Sox in the Class C Cotton States League in 1937 and 1938.

On "Nemo Night" in his honor in 1938, he received gifts including a set of golf clubs and $48 collected from fans in the stands, but more impressive was when the 46-year-old inserted himself in the outfield, shagged fly balls, and hit a double and a single in two at-bats in his team's victory.[27]

After leading the Class A Scranton Red Sox to five consecutive playoff appearances from 1939 to 1943, including two league titles, Leibold was named manager of Boston's top affiliate in the American Association, the Louisville Colonels. Replacing Bill Burwell, Leibold led Louisville to three consecutive league championships in his first three years (1944-46).

In 1946 Leibold was involved in a nationally reported controversy when he had an altercation with umpire Forrest Peters in a game on June 16. Peters claimed Leibold punched and pushed him; Leibold was suspended indefinitely and fined $100 by American Association president H. Roy Hamey. However, when the suspension was lifted after just six days, Peters and his fellow umpire at the game, Milton Steengrafe,

resigned in protest and appealed to W.G. Bramham, president of the National Association, the minor leagues' governing body.

While coaching first base at the league's all-star game on July 17, Leibold was informed that Bramham had suspended him for the remainder of the season, effective immediately. "The decision of Judge Bramham is an injustice to me," Leibold said. "I at least deserve a hearing."[28] He was granted a hearing in Chicago at the end of July and the suspension was reduced to 45 games, making him eligible to coach the Colonels at the end of the season.

After losing the league finals in 1947, the Colonels were mired in last place for most of 1948. Ten days before the end of the season, Leibold surprisingly announced his retirement. The timing of the announcement stirred rumors of a falling-out between Leibold and Red Sox management. Joe Cronin had replaced Leibold's old teammate, Eddie Collins, as Boston's general manager.

"I feel that I have outlived my usefulness to Louisville and Boston," Leibold said. "I have been manager in Louisville for five seasons and that's a long time."[29] Despite his comments, the rumor mill churned out reports that he would take a job with the Philadelphia Phillies or his hometown Detroit Tigers.

Richard Leibold, Nemo Leibold's grandson, told the author that the falling-out may have been more complicated than typically reported. He suggested that Nemo felt he was never able to completely overcome the stigma of the Black Sox Scandal. Nemo told his family he felt a sense of "guilt by association" with anyone involved with the 1919 White Sox, even though he was not implicated in any wrongdoing. According to Richard Leibold (and his deceased father, Robert Leibold), Nemo felt betrayed by the Red Sox, an organization he had served since 1933.[30]

Several months after Leibold resigned from the Colonels, he agreed to a contract with the Detroit Tigers' affiliate in the American Association, the Toledo Mud Hens. But before the 1949 season he abruptly resigned, citing poor health and a desire to remain closer to his wife and family. Leibold never managed or coached again in professional baseball. He scouted for the Tigers in 1950 and 1951 before retiring at the age of 58.[31]

For the remainder of his life, Leibold lived in Detroit. "He never really talked about his baseball career," grandson Richard Leibold said. "He had lots of memorabilia lying around the house and was casual with it. We'd play baseball with balls and bats signed by members of the 1924 Senators."[32]

Leibold drifted away from the game in retirement, and did not maintain close relationships with either the Red Sox or White Sox organizations. "My grandfather enjoyed watching games with us," said his grandson, "and got upset when players didn't play fundamentally sound baseball. He never lost his coaching instincts."

Leibold died of natural causes at the age of 84 on February 4, 1977. He was buried at Holy Sepulchre Cemetery in Southfield, Michigan, near Detroit.

Leibold was a scrappy competitor as a player and manager. Sam Levy of the *Milwaukee Journal* described him as a "rough rider from the old school" because of his no-nonsense style and insistence that players play hard. But he also noted Leibold's fatherly side and compassionate concern for his players' welfare.[33] "Baseball owes me nothing and I owe baseball nothing," Leibold said. "I've always done the best I could."[34]

AUTHOR'S NOTE

The author would like to thank Richard Leibold, grandson of Nemo Leibold, whom he interviewed on April 22, 2013.

SOURCES

Ancestry.com

BaseballLibrary.com

Baseball-Reference.com

Milwaukee Journal

Milwaukee Sentinel

New York Times

Retrosheet.org

SABR.org

Sporting Life

The Sporting News

NOTES

1   "Nemo Leibold, Former Brewer, Has One Fear—He's Afraid He Will Get Fat," *The Milwaukee Journal*, April 2, 1914, 13.

2   Ibid.

3   Ibid.

4   Ibid.

5   Manning Vaughn, "Nemo Passes From Big Show," *Milwaukee Journal*, January 31, 1926, 2.

6   All minor- and major-league statistics have been verified on Baseball-Reference.com.

7   *Sporting Life*, June 22, 1912, 17.

8   *Sporting Life*, November 23, 1912, 8.

9   *Sporting Life*, March 22, 1913, 11.

10 *Sporting Life*, October 10, 1913, 15.

11 Ancestry.com; interview with Richard Leibold, April 22, 2013.

12 *Milwaukee Sentinel*, March 12, 1915, 6.

13 "Leibold Will Get a Chance," *Pittsburgh Press*, December 23, 1916, 1.

14 "Griffith Says Sox Should Win the Series," *Easton* (Pennsylvania) *Daily Free Press*, September 9, 1919, 11.

15 *The Sporting News*, December 27, 1961, 37.

16 *The Sporting News*, December 27, 1961, 37.

17 *The Sporting News*, October 7, 1920, 2.

18 *The Sporting News*, December 27, 1961, 37.

19 *The Sporting News*, March 10, 1921, 3.

20 *The Sporting News*, September 25, 1924, 3.

21 Sam Levy, "Nemo Leibold Helped Nats, Says Griffith," *Milwaukee Journal*, September 26, 1924, 52.

22 *The Sporting News*, November 13, 1924, 3.

23 *The Sporting News*, March 12, 1932, 5.

24 Lloyd Johnson and Miles Wolff, eds., *Encyclopedia of Minor League Baseball* (Durham, North Carolina: Baseball America, 1997). The championship years were 1935, 1939, 1942, 1944, 1945, and 1946. (Leibold was replaced in the 1946 season by Fred Walters.)

25 Ibid.

26 *The Sporting News*, November 8, 1934, 6.

27 *The Sporting News*, July 14, 1938, 3.

28   *The Sporting News*, July 24, 1946, 9.

29   Eddie Jones, "Leibold 'Definite Candidate' for Hens' Manager After Quitting at Louisville," *Toledo Blade*, September 3, 1948.

30   Interview with Richard Leibold.

31   *The Sporting News*, April 25, 1951.

32   Interview with Richard Leibold.

33   Sam Levy, "Nemo Leibold Suggests Changes as he Quits Post at Louisville," *Milwaukee Journal*, September 3, 1948, 9.

34   Interview with Richard Leibold.

GROVER LOWDERMILK

By James E. Elfers

NAMED AFTER ONE PRESIDENT and toiling in the shadow of another pitcher named after the same president, Grover Cleveland "Slim" Lowdermilk had a career that spanned the second half of the Deadball Era. From 1909 to 1920 Lowdermilk was an adequate pitcher with occasional flashes of steadiness for six different teams. He closed out his major-league career as one of the "clean" Chicago White Sox players who weren't involved with the tainted 1919 World Series.

Lowdermilk's wildness kept him from being a more successful pitcher. In 590⅓ major-league innings, he surrendered 376 walks against 296 strikeouts, and he hit 37 batters. He finished with a won-lost record of just 23-39 in the majors, but his lack of control wasn't as much of a hindrance in the minors, where he won 181 games in 12 seasons. Still, Lowdermilk frustrated managers and teammates who expected more from a pitcher whose fastball was often compared with Walter Johnson's.

Hall of Fame umpire Billy Evans once wrote, "Lowdermilk ought to be one of the greatest pitchers in the business. [He] has a world of speed, a fast breaking curve, a peculiar windup that has the ball on the batsman very quickly, in fact every asset of a great pitcher except control. Inability to get the ball over the plate has been Lowdermilk's fatal fault."[1]

The Lowdermilk family's presence in the United States is older than the nation itself. Their patriarch, Jacob Lautermilch, Sr.—the spelling means "clear milk" in German—was born in Baden, Germany, in 1716 and emigrated to the American colonies sometime before 1750.[2] After settling in Maryland, he was a distinguished soldier in the Revolutionary War, a second lieutenant in the Continental Army.[3] His descendants spread westward with the new nation and the family name became Americanized thereafter.

Grover Cleveland Lowdermilk was born on January 15, 1885, in Sandborn, Indiana. In a fashion that was not uncommon at the time, he was christened with the name of the current president, Grover Cleveland. Four years later, Grover's parents, William and Mary Lowdermilk, moved the family several hundred miles south to Marion County, Illinois, where they operated a grocery store in the town of Odin. Odin soon became a coal-mining boom town. By 1902 the Odin Coal Company was running at full capacity and the Lowdermilk family prospered. Even during his baseball career, Grover often returned to Odin in the offseason to work in the mines.

Grown tall and lean, which earned him the nickname Slim, Grover stood 6-feet-4 and weighed 190 pounds. Before long, he and his younger brother, Lou, a left-handed pitcher, were starring on the local sandlots. Both would make it to the majors; Lou made 20 appearances with the St. Louis Cardinals in 1911-12.

Grover signed his first professional contract with the Decatur Commodores of the Three-I League at the age of 22 in 1907, but after just one lackluster appearance, he was farmed out to the Mattoon Giants of the low-level Eastern Illinois League. He was the ace of the Giants' pennant-winning staff, winning 33 games and losing 10 with a stellar ERA of 0.93. He also struck out a whopping 458 batters in 388 innings, including 17 in one game,[4] and his speed clearly made him the class of the league.

During that season, he also married Honora "Nora" Soulon, the daughter of a French-born blacksmith who had settled in Odin. They had two daughters, Ruth (born 1908) and Irma (1911.)

Recalled to the Commodores in 1908, Lowdermilk went 12-10 but also began to exhibit the wildness that plagued him for the rest of his career. In 217 innings, he walked 124 batters. Although few could hit his fastball, professional batters learned to be patient and wait for him to throw one across the plate. In 1909 he tossed a no-hitter against Peoria, but he allowed two runs in the third inning when he walked two batters and hit another.[5] The St. Louis Cardinals were intrigued enough by Lowdermilk's potential to purchase his contract for $2,500 in July.[6]

Lowdermilk made an inauspicious major-league debut for the Cardinals, on July 3 in the second game of a doubleheader against the Cincinnati Reds, walking four batters and recording a wild pitch in 2⅓ innings. In seven appearances for St. Louis, he finished with an 0-2 record, a 6.21 ERA, and 30 walks in 29 innings. After he had a poor spring training with the Cardinals in 1910, manager Roger Bresnahan sent him to the Springfield (Illinois) Senators of the Three-I League.

Under manager Dick Smith, Slim responded with a superb season for the pennant-winning Senators, winning 25 games and losing 9. He logged 334 innings and managed to walk just 3.8 batters per nine innings, an improvement that earned him a promotion back to the Cardinals in 1911.

Used almost exclusively in relief by St. Louis, Lowdermilk rode the bench most of the summer and appeared in just 11 games. He did throw one shutout but was mostly unimpressive (0-1, 7.29 ERA), and lack of control as usual was his downfall (33 walks in 33⅓ innings). After the season, the disgruntled Lowdermilk demanded a trade[7] and Bresnahan sold his contract to the Louisville Colonels of the American Association, where he found steady work as a starter over the next three seasons, winning an average of 18 games a year from 1912 through 1914.

The Chicago Cubs, in the heat of a pennant race and desperate for pitching, gave Lowdermilk a brief opportunity to return to the majors in August 1912. But he struggled in his only two games (0-1, 9.69 ERA). The Cubs finished in third place, 11½ games behind the New York Giants. In December the Cubs included the lanky right-hander in an eight-player deal that

sent future Hall of Fame shortstop Joe Tinker to the Cincinnati Reds. But weeks later, the Reds sent Lowdermilk back to where he started the season, Louisville, in order to acquire another former Cubs great, Mordecai "Three Finger" Brown.

While Lowdermilk found steady work with the Louisville Colonels, his control never really improved—one newspaper called him "the wildest bird in big league captivity." Nonetheless his velocity and eye-popping strikeout numbers (254 Ks in 284 IP in 1914) continued to win him new chances to succeed in the majors.[8]

In 1915 St. Louis Browns manager Branch Rickey became the latest to try to tame the "wild bird." Rickey gave the 30-year-old Lowdermilk his first extended opportunity to make good in the majors, and Lowdermilk responded well to a consistent workload, recording a solid 3.12 ERA and 14 complete games over 29 starts. A typical Lowdermilk start came in his second appearance, on April 19 against the Cleveland Indians: He struck out seven and allowed just two hits in a complete-game 7-2 win, but he also walked five and hit three batters. The Browns' mediocre offense usually didn't offer much support, and Lowdermilk won just nine games to 17 losses. In September the Detroit Tigers picked him up for the stretch run and they won all five of his starts that month. But Detroit finished 2½ games behind the Boston Red Sox for first place in the American League.

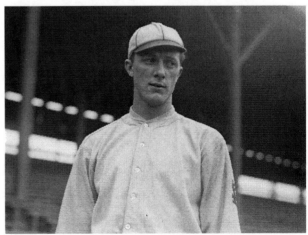

Grover Lowdermilk with the St. Louis Cardinals, circa 1911 (Bain Collection, Library of Congress, Prints and Photographs Division)

The Tigers brought in personal coaches in 1916 to help Lowdermilk gain better control of his fastball[9], but nothing seemed to work. In midseason, Detroit traded him to Cleveland but he made just 10 appearances with the Indians before he was sent down to the Pacific Coast League's Portland Beavers. Grover disliked playing on the West Coast and quit the team after going 1-4 in seven games; he went home to Odin before the season ended.[10]

Once again the hard-throwing pitcher was given another chance. His old teammate Joe Tinker, now managing the American Association's Columbus Senators, persuaded Lowdermilk to return to baseball in 1917. At the age of 32, he put up his best full season since his days in the low-level Eastern Illinois League: 25-14, a 1.70 ERA, and 250 strikeouts in 355 innings pitched. He also allowed just 128 walks, or 3.2 per nine innings.

In September the St. Louis Browns re-acquired Lowdermilk on waivers from Cleveland and in his first start back in the American League, he pitched a four-hit shutout against the New York Yankees—without issuing a single walk. In the post-season City Series[11] between the Browns and Cardinals, Lowdermilk had his greatest day in baseball on October 7, when he pitched both ends of a double-header and didn't allow a single run. In the opener, which was Game Five of the City Series, Lowdermilk shut out the Cardinals 2-0 on seven hits. Then he held them scoreless again through nine innings in Game Six until it was called for darkness in a 0-0 tie. Lowdermilk pitched all 18 innings and walked only two batters. But despite Lowdermilk's heroics, the Cardinals clinched the City Series in Game Seven the next day at Sportsman's Park.

Umpire Billy Evans credited Lowdermilk's success to better control of his emotions on the mound: "My pet name for Lowdermilk has always been 'Three and Two' … he doesn't groove very many, but he is always just over the inside or outside corner or just missing it…. Since he is never very wild, Lowdermilk has always had the idea the umpires were missing them on him, and thus were really responsible for his so-called wildness. I have always argued to the contrary with Grover and assured him that he would be far more successful if he just forgot there was ever such a person as the umpire."[12]

Expectations were high entering 1918, but after battling injuries in spring training, Lowdermilk couldn't hold onto the form he had shown the previous season. He went 2-6 in just 13 appearances with an ERA of 3.15 and by midseason at least one newspaper writer complained that he was "as wild as ever" and "a sorry failure" in the American League.[13]

Still, that live arm enticed interest from other teams and on May 18, 1919, the Chicago White Sox, short on pitching depth, purchased Lowdermilk's contract from the Browns and added him to their starting rotation. He pitched solidly for the White Sox, finishing 5-5 with a 2.79 ERA in 20 appearances. Despite the excitement of playing for a championship team in a pennant race, Grover was unhappy in Chicago and in July announced he was going home.[14] But the feeling quickly faded and a week later he was back with the White Sox. However, manager Kid Gleason gave him only one start in the final six weeks as the White Sox went on a tear and cruised to the AL pennant.

The White Sox were favored to win the World Series against the Cincinnati Reds, and with Eddie Cicotte and Lefty Williams anchoring the rotation, Lowdermilk didn't figure to see much playing time in October. But in Game One, Cicotte was knocked out early after allowing five runs in the fourth inning and Lowdermilk was sent in for mop-up duty at the end. He allowed an RBI triple to pitcher Dutch Ruether, and walked a man and hit another in the eighth inning as the Reds won 9-1.

Although Cicotte and Williams struggled to pitch effectively throughout the Series, Gleason never turned to Lowdermilk again. A year later, it was revealed that Cicotte, Williams, and six other White Sox teammates had conspired to throw the World Series to the Reds. They were all banned for life from baseball.

Later, Lowdermilk said he often wished he could forget the whole Series. "I don't think we could have beaten Cincinnati anyway," he said. "The Reds had a great ball club."[15]

Lowdermilk didn't see much playing time with the White Sox in 1920, either. He made three relief appearances — his final games in the big leagues — and didn't appear to be in Gleason's pitching plans in the immediate future. In mid-May, the White Sox reportedly turned down a $5,000 offer for Lowdermilk from Joe Tinker's Columbus Senators, but a week later they released him to the Minneapolis Millers of the same league.[16]

He spent the next two seasons with the Millers, winning 14 games in 1920 and 11 more in 1921 before calling it a career at the age of 37 after a short stint with his old team in Columbus in 1922. Between the majors and minors, Lowdermilk won 204 games but his true legacy was, of course, his lack of control. Decades later, baseball historian Paul Dickson noted that "Lowdermilk" had entered the lexicon to describe a pitcher given to acute wildness.[17] He would never be confused with Grover Cleveland Alexander, the Hall of Fame pitcher and contemporary who shared his given names.

Grover and his wife, Nora, returned to Odin, where he continued to find work in the coal mines. He lived in retirement on his pension as a miner.[18] He died at 83 on March 31, 1968, and is buried at Odin's Peaceful Valley Cemetery.

Both Grover and his brother Lou Lowdermilk's names reappeared in the news during the baseball card boom of the late 20th century. Grover's 1910 Broadleaf Tobacco Co. card has been valued at several hundred dollars and only about 100 are said to exist.[19] Meanwhile, Lou's T207 tobacco card from 1912 is one of the rarest in the world and sold for more than $3,800 in a 2014 online auction.[20]

NOTES

1   *The Sporting News*, April 18, 1918.

2   Robert Gene Tucker application for Sons of the American Revolution, July 8, 1960, accessed at Ancestry.com.

3   Ibid.

4   Henry Chadwick, ed., *1908 Spalding's Official Base Ball Guide* (American Sports Publishing Co., 1908), accessed online on October 10, 2014, at Archive.org.

5   *Chicago Inter Ocean*, August 15, 1908.

6   *Decatur* (Illinois) *Daily Review*, April 21, 1910.

7   *Decatur* (Illinois) *Daily Review*, December 5, 1911.

8   *Decatur* (Illinois) *Daily Review*, March 17, 1915.

9   *Reading* (Pennsylvania) *Times*, March 27, 1916.

10 *Washington Herald*, January 11, 1917.

11 The City Series were officially sanctioned postseason series held in the first half of the 20th century between two rival teams in the same city. The City Series in Chicago between the White Sox and Cubs was extremely popular and lasted until World War II. Other two-team cities attempted to capitalize on the idea with limited success. The St. Louis teams held only one City Series, in 1917. See retrosheet.org/Regional%20Series.

12 *The Sporting News*, April 18, 1918.

13 *Decatur* (Illinois) *Daily Review*, August 1, 1918.

14 *Chicago Tribune*, July 18, 1919.

15 *The Sporting News*, April 13, 1968.

16 *Chicago Tribune*, May 18, 1920.

17 Paul Dickson, *The Dickson Baseball Dictionary* (New York: Facts on File, 1989), 252.

18 *The Sporting News*, April 13, 1968.

19 *Colorado Springs Gazette Telegraph*, March 26, 1978; *New York Times*, January 24, 1988.

20 Robert Edward Auctions, LLC; Spring 2014, Lot #469. Accessed online on October 10, 2014, at robertedwardauctions.com/auction/2014_spring/469.html.

BYRD LYNN

By Russell Arent

GIVEN FUTURE HALL OF Famer Ray Schalk's mastery of the catcher's position with the Chicago White Sox for nearly two decades, Byrd Lynn had little chance to land the starting job during his short major-league career. His prospects likely became even slimmer once the 1919 Black Sox Scandal episode went public.

Although no evidence has yet emerged that links Lynn's name to any possible wrongdoing in the fix, his close associations with Joe Jackson and Claude "Lefty" Williams might have sealed his fate with the White Sox.[1] In the winter of 1921, only months before the Black Sox criminal trial began in Chicago, he was shipped off to the Salt Lake City Bees and never played another game in the major leagues.

Byrd Lynn was born in Unionville, Illinois, on March 13, 1889. (Some contemporary sources say it was 1890.)[2] His father, William, was at different times a farmer and a grocer.[3] After William married Esther Dye in 1874, six children ensured that the household would not remain calm for long. Byrd was third in line, with two older brothers, Anson and Clarence, and three younger sisters, True, Grace, and Kate.[4] Young Byrd and his brothers helped out with their father's grocery business.[5]

Around 1908 or 1909, Byrd Lynn relocated to the West Coast and met Ethel Powell. The teenage couple both worked as attendants at the Western Washington Insane Hospital in Tacoma, Washington, and were wed at the First Presbyterian Church in that city on October 12, 1910.[6] They had three children together: Vernon, Byrd Jr., and Dorothy.

Lynn signed his first contract in professional baseball with the San Jose Bears of the low-level California State League in 1913.[7] The 24-year-old Lynn appeared in 71 games and batted .294 in 235 at-bats under manager Walter "Judge" Nagle. The performance

earned him a promotion to the Sacramento Sacts of the Pacific Coast League. He struggled at first, hitting .188 in 11 games. In 1914 his hitting improved to .292 in limited action, but his fielding was a concern.[8] Among Lynn's teammates with Sacramento was 21-year-old Lefty Williams.

In the offseason, while the Sacts were being sold to a Salt Lake City businessman who moved the team to Utah, Lynn played for Van Nuys (California) in a winter league and honed his batting skills in the cleanup slot.[9]

The Chicago White Sox got their first glimpse of the 5-foot-11-inch, 165-pound Salt Lake City Bees catcher[10] in an exhibition game under adverse playing conditions on February 28, 1915: "Everybody is talking about Byrd Lynn.… The way he shoots the ball around the bases is something good to see. In practice he had all the basemen begging for mercy."[11]

A couple of weeks later, Lynn arranged for a special exhibition game between the Bees and staff and patients from Agnews State Hospital for the Insane[12] in Santa Clara, where he worked in the offseason:

[Bees manager Cliff] Blankenship tonight accepted an invitation to play the ball club of the Agnew state hospital for the insane. Afterward the Salt Lake players will be the guests of the hospital staff at luncheon. They will remain over during the evening for a dance to be given by the hospital staff. The Agnew hospital is one of the show institutions of California. The invitation was extended to the training squad through the instrumentality of Byrd Lynn, who is an attendant in one of the hospital wards. The hospital team is made up of attendants and some of the patients who are only mildly deranged mentally.[13]

Lynn no doubt saw the transformative power of the game on some of the patients and staff that he and Ethel had come to know personally.

In May 1915 Lynn was released by the Bees and signed by the Phoenix Senators of the Rio Grande Association. In a June 20 game at Albuquerque, Lynn broke umpire Harry Kane's toe with his bat and earned a suspension—and even a few hours in the city jail after the game.[14] Less than two weeks later, the league folded for lack of financial support, and Lynn returned to Salt Lake City.[15]

Lynn finished the 1915 season at Salt Lake with one of his best offensive performances, a .311 average in 55 games. It earned him an invitation to spring training with the White Sox, who purchased his contract from the Bees for $2,500.[16] In the offseason Lynn returned to California to resume his work at the Agnews State Hospital.[17]

In spring training at Mineral Wells, Texas, Lynn made a positive impression: "The veteran pitchers on the club say that Lynn is almost sure of becoming a regular."[18] But with Ray Schalk entrenched behind the plate, there was no spot in the lineup for Lynn. He played in 31 games as a rookie and batted .225 in 40 at-bats. In 1917 his results were similar: he hit .222 in 72 at-bats (35 games). In the World Series against the New York Giants, Lynn struck out in one pinch-hit appearance. The White Sox were victorious in six games.

After playing in only five games in 1918, Lynn responded to the US government's "work or fight" order by going to work in the shipyards with his teammates and friends Lefty Williams and Joe Jackson. White Sox officials found this decision to be insufficiently patriotic:

Williams and Lynn informed Manager [Pants] Rowland they would stick around awhile to help him out if he needed them, but they admitted they were headed soon for the ship yards.... Rowland told the boys he didn't want to see them around the park any longer. They were ordered to hand in their uniforms and told to leave, and the quicker the better.... [Owner Charles Comiskey said] "There is no room on my ball club for players who wish to evade the Army draft by entering the employ of ship concerns."[19]

In reality, Lynn's situation was more complicated, as *The Sporting News* explained:

Lynn undoubtedly had a real grievance. He had been placed in Class Two-A ... despite the fact he has two children and a wife.... Friends of Lynn had taken it up with legal talent of his home county and an appeal in the case was under consideration. Lynn said the day of his departure from the Sox that he expected to succeed in his appeal and be reclassified, but sooner or later he would be called and he might as well start work in the shipyards at once.[20]

The stance of the White Sox was typical during the World War I era. Lynn's decision to work in the shipyards instead of enlisting in the military was also quite common for professional ballplayers. Whether his case merited reclassification is a detail that has often been overlooked. The moment he headed to the shipyards, that point became forever moot.

Choosing profit over his thoughts regarding their patriotism, Comiskey allowed Lynn, Williams, and Jackson to return to the team in 1919. Lynn's fielding improved with a .982 fielding percentage in 28 games, but his batting was still subpar (.227 in 66 at-bats.) Lynn's only appearance in the tainted World Series against the Cincinnati Reds was in Game Five, after Schalk was ejected for arguing a play at home plate. Lynn caught the final three innings and flied out in his only at-bat as the White Sox lost, 5–0.

In 1920, with a livelier ball and offense up across the major leagues, Lynn recorded a .320 batting average in only 25 at-bats (16 games) and did not make an error in the field. When the Black Sox scandal exploded near the end of the season, Lynn went on record with charges that some of his teammates had thrown regular-season games on purpose:

"We soon noticed how carefully they studied the scoreboard—more than even the average player does in a pennant race—and that they always made errors when Cleveland and New York were losing. If Cleveland won—we won. If Cleveland lost—we lost.

Byrd Lynn, circa 1919 (Bain Collection, Library of Congress, Prints and Photographs Division)

The idea was to keep up the betting odds, but not let us win the pennant."[21]

The next day, Lynn was one of 10 players who signed a public thank-you note to owner Comiskey, who had sent each of the "clean Sox" a $1,500 check to make up the difference between the winning and losing players' shares from the 1919 World Series.[22]

It was the final paycheck Lynn received from the White Sox. He was sent back to Salt Lake City, along with Ted Jourdan, in exchange for promising first baseman Earl Sheely. As Chicago newspaperman Harry Neily explained, "Lynn certainly was out of luck when he was drafted on a ball club that has a complete catching staff consisting of one man [Schalk]."[23] Lynn's major-league career ended with a .237 batting average in 116 games over five seasons.

After returning to the Bees in 1921, Lynn played in 91 games and batted .247 with 23 doubles and four home runs.[24] On July 15 he suffered a dislocated shoulder in a collision with Los Angeles Angels catcher Earl Baldwin that sidelined him for six weeks.[25] When he returned, his effectiveness apparently was diminished: "He is back in the game now, but his throwing is yet nothing like a catcher's should be or as Lynn's was before his injury."[26]

In the days before specialized sports medicine, a player had to choose between sitting out, typically without pay, or playing through the pain. Lynn initially chose the latter but he apparently changed his mind, since there is no record of him playing professional ball in 1922 (presumably to rest his shoulder).

By 1923 Salt Lake was unwilling to keep Lynn on the roster. The club attempted to sell him to the Reading (Pennsylvania) Keystones in May to replace Frank Kohlbecker, who had been optioned to Memphis from the St. Louis Cardinals. Since Kohlbecker was subject to recall by the Cardinals and Reading could not honor such a provision according to International League guidelines, Lynn was sent instead to the Memphis Chickasaws of the Southern Association.[27]

After 17 games, in which Lynn hit poorly (.235) but fielded well (.988), Reading worked out a new deal to obtain his services. He played well in the International League, hitting .306 in 373 at-bats, the most plate appearances he would get in any professional season.[28]

In 1924 Lynn's batting average plummeted to .222 and the following year Reading traded him to the Newark Bears, who moved to Providence in midseason then sent him back to Reading. In 1926 Lynn was named interim manager of Reading for one month, but the team continued to struggle and he was replaced by former New York Giants star Hooks Wiltse. Lynn closed his 13-year professional career with a disappointing .217 average in 345 at-bats.[29]

Lynn stayed involved with the sport after his days in Organized Baseball were over.

In January 1927 he answered Commissioner Kenesaw Mountain Landis's call to come to Chicago and tell what he knew about charges by Chick Gandil and Swede Risberg that a 1917 regular-season series between the Detroit Tigers and Chicago White Sox had been fixed for the Tigers to win. Lynn, like most of the players from both teams, didn't corroborate Gandil and Risberg's accusations, testifying that he didn't think the games were fixed. Judge Landis agreed and dismissed the charges.[30]

In 1927 and 1928 Lynn managed an amateur team at Dam 52 on the Ohio River near Brookport, Illinois,[31] possibly to be closer to his father, William. In 1932, after resettling in Northern California, he tried his hand at scouting by referring a San Jose player to the El Paso Texans club.[32]

Lynn never strayed too far from the diamond, making appearances in an old-timer's game (as a representative of the 1913 Sacramento team) in 1935 at San Francisco's Seals Stadium[33] and as an umpire in Napa a few years later.[34]

Throughout his adult life, Lynn worked as a hospital attendant at various state hospitals for the mentally ill in Northern California and Washington state. The first documented instance of this work is at the Western Washington Hospital for the Insane in 1911. During the same decade, he also worked at Agnews State Hospital for the Insane in Santa Clara and continued there off and on until 1936, when he moved north to Imola in Napa County. In 1937 he worked at Napa State Hospital,[35] where he was employed until his death.

Lynn's wife, Ethel, died in 1934. He died on February 5, 1940, in Napa, California. His ashes were interred next to Ethel at Mission City Memorial Park in Santa Clara.

NOTES

1   During the Cook County grand jury proceedings in 1920, Jackson was asked, "Who was your best chum on the team, who did you go with on the club?" and his answer was, "Williams and Lind. I hardly ever pal with any of them there except those two." It is clear that the court stenographer made a mistake when spelling Lynn's name. (There was no one on the team named Lind or anything close to that.) Lynn also formed a friendship with Williams while they were teammates at Sacramento in the Pacific Coast League in 1913 and 1914 and at Salt Lake in 1915. Eliot Asinof's *Eight Men Out* (pages 77-78) describes Lynn and Williams as longtime roommates who knew each other well and rarely talked, with a more pronounced silence occurring after the Black Sox Scandal broke publicly. Asinof also writes (page 188) that Williams ran into Lynn right after testifying before the grand jury. "In an emotional encounter," Asinof writes, "the two shook hands without uttering any words and then never saw each other again." The Joe Jackson biography, *Shoeless*, by David Fleitz, the claim is made (pages 170 and 214) that Lynn's best friend on the White Sox, Williams, succeeded in hiding all the details of the 1919 World Series fix from Lynn by freezing him out of conversations with Williams and Jackson. The exact sources for Asinof's and Fleitz's intriguing observations are unknown.

2   While Lynn's tombstone and most baseball reference sources list his birth year as 1889, his World War I draft registration card and the 1900 US Census both list 1890.

3   William was listed as a farmer on the death certificate from April 1938, but he was described as a grocer in the 1900 US Census.

4   1900 United States Census, accessed online at Ancestry.com.

5   Ibid.

6   Washington Marriage Records 1865-2004, accessed online at Ancestry.com; 1911 Tacoma City Directory by R.L. Polk and Company.

7   *Reading Times*, March 7, 1921.

8   He reportedly compiled a .950 fielding percentage in 1914; *Salt Lake Tribune*, March 14, 1915.

9   *Van Nuys News*: October 23, 1914; November 6, 1914; November 13, 1914; and November 20, 1914.

10   *Salt Lake Tribune*, March 14, 1915.

11   The source of the quote is Salt Lake Bees business manager Bill O'Connor. *Salt Lake Tribune*, March 3, 1915.

12   The official name was Agnews State Hospital for the Insane, though it was commonly referred to as Agnew State Hospital.

13   *Salt Lake Tribune*, March 11, 1915.

14   *El Paso Herald*, June 21, 1915; *Arizona Republican*, June 21, 1915. Lynn was jailed for the rest of the afternoon on an assault charge, but was released on his own recognizance.

15   *Santa Fe New Mexican*, July 6, 1915.

16   *Arizona Republican*, November 10, 1915.

17   *Arizona Republican*, September 27, 1915; *Salt Lake Tribune*, November 1, 1915.

18   *Decatur Review*, March 27, 1916.

19   *The Sporting News*, June 20, 1918.

20   Ibid.

21   *New York Times*, October 4, 1920.

22   *Chicago Tribune*, October 5, 1920.

23   *Washington Times*, December 17, 1920.

24   1922 *Reach Official American League Baseball Guide*, 294, 296.

25   *Salt Lake Tribune*, July 16, 1921; *Reno Evening Gazette*, July 18, 1921.

26   *Salt Lake Tribune*, September 11, 1921.

27   *The Sporting News*, May 17 and May 24, 1923.

28   1923 stats are from *1924 Reach Official American League Baseball Guide*.

29   *The Evening Independent* (St. Petersburg, Florida), October 16, 1926; *Syracuse Herald*, February 13, 1927.

30   *Salt Lake Tribune*, January 8, 1927.

31   *Decatur Review*, April 8, 1928; *Southern Illinoisan* (Carbondale, Illinois), August 22, 1971.

32   *El Paso Herald Post*, May 31, 1932.

33   *Oakland Tribune*, July 28, 1935.

34   *Oakland Tribune*, June 21, 1935.

35   A note in *The Sporting News* on June 15, 1933 reports that Byrd was working at Napa State Hospital. Byrd was listed in the directory for Agnews State Hospital that year (where voter records also place him in 1932 and 1934). If Byrd was actually at Napa State Hospital in 1933, then he might have had a more complex employment arrangement than originally thought, possibly shuttling back and forth between the different hospitals in the region.)

ERSKINE MAYER

By Lyle Spatz

ERSKINE MAYER HAD A MOST interesting background, one that was very different from that of most players of the early 20th century. Mayer's paternal grandparents were Jews who came from Germany. His great-grandfather (his grandmother's father) had been a buyer for Otto von Bismarck, the Prussian statesman who unified Germany. He disappeared one day, and it wasn't until years later that his body was discovered buried in a stable. Both of his grandparents were musicians, a talent they passed on to Erskine's father, Isaac, who composed an opera written in Hebrew.

That lineage was poles apart from Mayer's family on his mother's side. His mother, born Henrietta Frankel, traced her ancestry back to the Mayflower. Her family owned tracts of land in what was then Virginia Territory and today is the state of Kentucky. His maternal grandmother's brother, James Allen, captained a riverboat that ran from Hannibal, Missouri, to New Orleans. It was from marking twain on Captain Allen's boat that young Samuel Clemens chose the nom de plume of Mark Twain. Mayer's maternal grandmother had converted to Judaism, and both his parents were raised in the Jewish religion.

Mayer's father continued the family's musical tradition,[1] working as both a concert pianist and music teacher in Ohio and then Georgia, where Erskine (his birth name was Jacob Erskine) was born in Atlanta on January 16, 1889. Evidently not concerned about his son's injuring his hands, Mayer's father, who enjoyed baseball, would often play catch with Erskine and his two brothers. One of the brothers, Sam, played in 11 games for the 1915 Washington Senators and for 16 seasons in the minors.

Mayer graduated from the Georgia Military Academy (today's Woodward Academy) and entered Georgia Tech in the fall of 1907. Though Mayer made the varsity baseball squad the following spring, Tech's Coach John Heisman (of Heisman Trophy fame) displayed a reluctance to use Mayer early in the season, putting him in only four games as Tech stumbled to a 5-8 start. Mayer started four of Tech's final eight games, posting a 3-1 mark and finishing 5-2 on Tech's first losing team since 1903. In Mayer's second campaign at Tech, he posted a 7-3 mark in 10 starts on a team that finished 13-8.

In February 1910, Mayer was dismissed for poor grades.[2] A few days later the *Atlanta Constitution* reported that he had signed a contract with the Atlanta Crackers, whose team president, John Heisman, coincidentally served as Tech's baseball coach.[3] Mayer's professional debut came on April 24 in Memphis, a game in which he was freely hit, surrendering three triples, a home run, and a double among 13 hits while losing 7-2.

Ultimately, after he ran his record to 4-4, the Crackers sent Mayer to the Fayetteville Highlanders in the Class D Eastern Carolina League. In reporting on his being sent down, the *Atlanta Constitution* wrote, "Mayer is considered a good prospect, but not fast enough for the Southern League."[4] Mayer would post a 15-2 mark, and his .882 winning percentage helped Fayetteville win the pennant.

In 1911 Mayer left spring training with the Crackers again, but after three appearances Atlanta sent him to the Albany Babies in the Class C South Atlantic League where he posted a 14-13 mark. The spring of 1912 found Mayer training with the Crackers once again. Without making any regular-season appearances, he was assigned to Portsmouth of the Virginia League.

Mayer starred in the Virginia League, posting a 12-2 mark by late June, when the Atlanta papers reported that he would be returning to Atlanta.[5] Within a couple of days it was apparent that Portsmouth had balked at returning its star pitcher to Atlanta; the *Atlanta Constitution* reported the matter was before the National Commission.[6] Three days later Secretary John Farrell of the National Commission advised Atlanta's management that Portsmouth had been told to pay for the players taken from the Crackers or forfeit the franchise. Despite these warnings, Mayer did not return to Atlanta and in early August reports surfaced that he would join the team after it finished its road swing around the league.[7]

A week later Atlanta papers reported that the Philadelphia Phillies had outbid the Pirates for Mayer, paying Atlanta $2,500.[8] Mayer reported to the Phillies after the Virginia League season ended, having posted a 24-8-1 mark with eight shutouts and 18 one-run games, according to the *Atlanta Journal*,[9] for a Portsmouth team that posted a .508 winning percentage. His final Portsmouth record ended at 26-9.

He debuted for the Philadelphia Phillies on September 4, 1912, pitching two scoreless innings in a 5-2 loss to the pennant-bound New York Giants. *Philadelphia Inquirer* reporter Edgar Wolfe, who wrote under the pseudonym Jim Nasium, had this to say about Mayer's debut: "He looked more like regular pitching material than anything we have lamped [seen] breaking in for some time."[10]

Mayer appeared in seven games over the final month of the 1912 season, making one start and losing his only decision. In 1913, his first full year as a major leaguer, he had a 9-9 record as the Phillies, behind the pitching of Tom Seaton and Pete Alexander, finished second. Mayer set a major-league record (since broken) on August 18 of that season, a record he surely would have preferred not to have. Called in to face the Chicago Cubs in the ninth inning of a 4-4 game, Mayer retired the first batter he faced and then yielded a record-breaking nine consecutive hits.

Philadelphia's second-place finish in 1913 was its best showing since 1901, but in 1914 the ballclub was victimized by the formation of the Federal League. The Phillies lost Seaton, a 27-game winner, and their double-play combination of Mickey Doolan and Otto

Knabe to the new league and dropped all the way to sixth place. Alexander and Mayer accounted for 48 of the team's 74 victories. Alexander won 27, while Mayer went 21-19, with an excellent 2.58 ERA. The highlight of his season came in the second game of a doubleheader against St. Louis on July 27. Mayer defeated the Cardinals, 2-0, allowing just two hits,. Earlier in the season, on June 9 at Baker Bowl, Mayer gave up a ninth-inning double to Honus Wagner, the great Pittsburgh star's 3,000th hit.

After the 1914 season, owner William Baker changed managers, replacing Red Dooin with Pat Moran. He also executed a series of trades, including one that sent the great Sherry Magee to the Boston Braves and another that sent standout third baseman Hans Lobert to the Giants. Yet despite the loss of these two stars, the 1915 Phillies, led by the pitching of Alexander and Mayer, the slugging of Gavy Cravath, and the fine all-around play of rookie shortstop Dave Bancroft, won their first-ever National League pennant.

Mayer had his best season as a big leaguer in 1915. He again won 21 games (21-15), and lowered his ERA to 2.36. Always a fine hitter, he batted .239 (in a season when the Philadelphia team as a whole had a batting average of .247), with four extra-base hits (one a homer). But once again Mayer was overshadowed by his pitching partner and roommate, Alexander, who led the league in wins (31-10), ERA (1.22), and several other pitching categories. "Every time I pitched well, Alexander topped me," Mayer later remembered.[11]

Philadelphia won the coin toss with the American League champions, the Boston Red Sox, and chose to play the first two games of the World Series at home. Alexander got the Phillies off to a great start, defeating the Red Sox, 3-1, in the opener. In Game Two Mayer allowed Boston just two runs, but lost when Rube Foster held the Phillies to three hits and a single run. The Red Sox got the game-winner in the ninth inning on a two-out single by Foster.

Although the pitching on both sides was outstanding, the game is probably best remembered as the first World Series game to host the president of the United

States. Woodrow Wilson and his fiancé and future wife, Edith Bolling Galt, were among the spectators at Philadelphia's Baker Bowl on October 9, and Wilson even threw out the ceremonial first ball.

Boston won the next three games, 2-1, 2-1 (beating Alexander), and 5-4 (all four of their wins were by one run) to take the Series in five games. Down three games to one, Moran planned to give Alexander a third start in Game Five, but Alex's arm was hurting, so he turned to Mayer. Once again facing Foster, Mayer allowed two first-inning runs and left after 2⅓ innings, but was not charged with the defeat.

The Phillies slipped to second in 1916, 2½ games behind Brooklyn, due in part to an off year by Mayer, who won only seven (7-7). He was 11-6 with a 2.76 ERA in 1917 and had a 7-4 record in 1918 when on July 1 Philadelphia traded him to Pittsburgh for another right-handed pitcher, Elmer Jacobs.

Exactly one month later, on August 1, Mayer was a major participant in one of the greatest pitching duels in big-league history. Pitching against the Braves at Boston, he and Braves starter Art Nehf pitched scoreless baseball for 15 innings. Wilbur Cooper finally relieved Mayer with one out in the 16th inning, and Cooper got the win when the Pirates pushed across two runs against Nehf in the 21st inning.

In all, Mayer won nine games for Pittsburgh while losing only three to finish the 1918 season with a 16-7 record, 18 complete games, and an ERA of 2.65. He was 5-3 for the Pirates in 1919 when on August 6 they put him on waivers. No team in the National League claimed him, but the Chicago White Sox picked Mayer up for the $2,500 waiver price. The White Sox were in the thick of the American League pennant race and were glad to add an experienced pitcher. Mayer was not much help to the White Sox. He appeared in six games, two of which were starts, and had a 1-3 record and an 8.37 earned-run average.

The White Sox won the pennant anyway, but lost the best-of-nine World Series in eight games to Cincinnati.

Mayer pitched one inning in a mop-up role in Game Five, allowing one unearned run. He was totally unaware that several of his teammates had accepted money in a conspiracy to lose the Series. It was his final big-league appearance. He ended his career with 91 wins, 70 losses, and an excellent 2.96 earned-run average.

Mayer's revulsion when the details of the Black Sox Scandal surfaced probably contributed to his decision to retire. "Erk loved baseball for the true sport it afforded," Mayer's wife, Grace, said, "and he felt if a game had been thrown he was through with baseball."[12] (He did return briefly in 1923 as an umpire in the South Georgia League.)

At 6 feet tall and weighing less than 170 pounds, Mayer was not overpowering on the mound. He had good speed, but relied more on good control and an excellent side-arm curveball, a pitch that led Brooklyn manager Wilbert Robinson to call Mayer "Eelskine" because the pitch was "so slippery." It was also Robinson who said that you could upset the Atlanta-born Mayer by

Erskine Mayer with the Philadelphia Phillies, circa 1913 (Bain Collection, Library of Congress, Prints and Photographs Division)

whistling "Marching Through Georgia" or riding him about the South.[13]

Mayer was operating a cigar store in downtown Los Angeles when he died in that city of a heart attack on March 10, 1957. He was buried in Forest Lawn Memorial Park Cemetery in nearby Glendale.

SOURCES

Erskine Mayer file, National Baseball Library, Cooperstown, New York

Ribalow, Harold Z. and Meir U., *Jewish Baseball Stars* (New York: Hippocrene Books, 1984)

Mason, Ward, "Alexander's Right Hand Man," *Baseball Magazine*, November 1915

The Sporting News

Philadelphia Inquirer

Pittsburgh Post

Chicago Tribune

NOTES

1   *Hartford Courant*, May 16, 1926.

2   Committee on Deficiencies Report, February 1910, Georgia School of Technology, archives Georgia Institute of Technology.

3   *Atlanta Constitution*, February 26, 1910.

4   *Atlanta Constitution*, June 11, 1910.

5   *Atlanta Constitution*, June 22, 1912.

6   *Atlanta Constitution*, June 26, 1912.

7   *Atlanta Constitution*, August 10, 1912.

8   *Atlanta Constitution*, August 18, 1912.

9   *Atlanta Journal*, September 2, 1912.

10 *Philadelphia Inquirer*, September 5, 1912.

11 Harold Z. Ribalow and Meir U. Ribalow, *Jewish Baseball Stars* (New York: Hippocrene Books, 1984), 22.

12 *Jewish Baseball Stars*, 25.

13 *The Sporting News*, March 20, 1957.

HERVEY MCCLELLAN

By Jack Morris

"**H**ARVEY" MCCLELLAN didn't get much respect—especially from the press. Often characterized as a good-field, no-hit infielder, he managed to last six seasons with the Chicago White Sox despite often being derided in the press. Worse, Harvey wasn't his first name or even his nickname. It was a simple misspelling by the press. Because of that, for many decades he has been listed in the baseball record books under his misspelled name.[1]

McClellan, often called "Little Mac," was a 5-foot-9, 143-pound utility infielder who batted and threw right-handed. What kept him in the majors was a combination of superb fielding and a bit of luck. He was lucky enough to have been a utility infielder who could play both shortstop and third base when the White Sox had both their third baseman and shortstop banished from baseball following the Black Sox Scandal. But his luck ended tragically in 1925 when, in the prime of his baseball career, he was struck down by cancer.

Hervey McDowell McClellan was born on December 22, 1894, in Cynthiana, Kentucky. He was the youngest of three sons of Hugh McClellan, a harness manufacturer, and Mattie (McClure) McClellan. Hugh, whose family emigrated from Ireland to Canada when he was 9 years old, had moved to Cynthiana when he was 21. It was in Cynthiana, a town halfway between Lexington, Kentucky, and Cincinnati, where he had met his future wife Mattie, a native Kentuckian.[2]

From an early age, McClellan was active in sports. At Cynthiana High School he played forward on the basketball team and was shortstop on the baseball team.[3]

It was in 1913, as an 18-year-old playing for the semipro Cynthiana town team, that he signed with the Lexington Colts of the Class D Ohio State League

for the 1914 season. He appeared in 51 games, batting only .190, before leaving the team to start his senior year of high school.[4]

But Lexington officials must have seen something in the youngster because they re-signed him for the 1915 season. He had a fine spring training, earning the starting shortstop job while batting second in the lineup on Opening Day.

Playing every day didn't improve McClellan's hitting; in fact, he batted a paltry .157 in 102 games. But his fielding was so spectacular that he was able to keep himself in the lineup. The *Lexington Herald* wrote that McClellan "would grace any short field in the circuit, and some higher up."[5]

One of McClellan's teammates was fellow Cynthiana townsman and pitcher Charlie Rorer. The Lexington management was so appreciative of the duo's efforts that on September 1, "Cynthiana Day" was declared for Lexington's game with Ironton. Both Hugh McClellan and Charles Rorer, Sr. were invited to Lexington and watched Lexington defeat Ironton, 8-3. McClellan had an excellent day, going 2-for-4 with two runs scored.

McClellan finished second in fielding percentage among shortstops and led the league in sacrifices. Lexington again re-signed him for the 1916 season.[6]

Finally, in 1916, McClellan found his hitting stroke. But the Colts folded on July 16, the third team in the six-team league to disband within a few days, and the entire league followed suit. Reports had McClellan being sold to the Asheville Tourists of the Class D North Carolina State League. It's unclear if he actually played any games with the Tourists, but by August he had moved to St. Joseph of the Class A Western League.[7] The big jump in classification didn't bother McClellan. Moved to third base, he hit .291 in 62 games for the Drummers.

St. Joseph liked what they saw out of McClellan and signed him for 1917. Midway through the season, the St. Joseph franchise moved to Hutchinson, Kansas. In 131 games he batted .275 and finished with a .936 fielding percentage at third base. So impressive was McClellan's fielding that, on August 27, Hutchinson owner Jack Holland sold him to the Chicago White Sox for $5,500. He was ordered to report for spring training in 1918.[8]

In the offseason, and for every offseason until his death, McClellan worked for the Liggett & Myers Tobacco Company as a bookkeeper.[9]

McClellan had two strikes against him trying to make the White Sox roster during 1918 spring training at Mineral Wells, Texas. First, the left side of the White Sox infield was deep with Buck Weaver, Swede Risberg, and Fred McMullin on the roster. Moreover, McClellan had been assigned to Class I by his hometown draft board, which meant he was subject to being called up for duty in World War I sometime in 1918.[10]

Once it was clear that McClellan was Class I, the White Sox released him back to Hutchinson. But before he left the team, veteran Shano Collins gave him some encouraging words: "Dig in boy, you'll sure be up with us next year."[11]

Collins's prediction came true, but not before McClellan experienced a whirlwind year in 1918. He started the season in Hutchinson and then moved with the franchise to Oklahoma City in June. On June 20 he married Laura Grace Milam, a native of Hutchinson whom he had met during the 1917 season. Grace had been a bank teller at the First National Bank of Hutchinson.[12] Then on July 6, McClellan was drafted into the U.S. Army. On July 15, he left for Fort Thomas in Kentucky, where he spent the rest of the war.[13]

In February 1919 McClellan was again sold to the White Sox. This time he stuck with the club. In spring training there were rumors that the Cincinnati Reds were interested in McClellan. But Comiskey held on to the youngster. "The fighting, peppery infielder"

became one of only two rookies (with Dickey Kerr) to make the White Sox out of training camp.[14]

But though McClellan was with the team the entire season, he played sparingly. He made it into only seven games, none as a starter. Four of the seven games were the last four of the season after the White Sox clinched the American League pennant. One newspaper wag wrote that McClellan "has been wearing out the seats of several uniforms on the bench during the season."[15]

As a result, McClellan's first major-league hit didn't come until September 25. In a 3-1 loss to the St. Louis Browns, he pounded out a single off Elam Vangilder. It was Vangilder's first game as a starter in the majors. Needless to say, McClellan did not play in the World Series against the Cincinnati Reds, which the tainted White Sox lost five games to three.

Despite McClellan's lack of playing time, the White Sox retained his services in 1920. There were rumors that the Washington Senators coveted McClellan, but he was kept almost exclusively on the White Sox bench. He played in only ten games in 1920—including the final three games after seven of the Black Sox players were suspended from the team in late September.[16]

On the last day of the season, October 3, McClellan and backup catcher Byrd Lynn told reporters that they believed their teammates had thrown three games in Boston at the end of August. But he added that he "could obtain no tangible evidence to support their hunches."[17]

Back at home in Cynthiana after the season, McClellan was feted with a "McClellan Day" on October 11 to celebrate the town's major leaguer. The highlight was a game between the Cynthiana town team, which McClellan played for, against the Louisville Colonels. McClellan knocked in the only run for Cynthiana with a solo home run in a 9-1 loss.[18]

In January 1921 McClellan's only son, Hervey Jr., was born. McClellan most certainly left weeks later for spring training in Waxahachie, Texas, on a high—in addition to his growing family, he would have a shot to earn a starting position with the White Sox for the first time in his career.[19] With Buck Weaver and Swede Risberg still suspended, both the third base and short-stop positions were wide open.

Though he was without two star players on the left side of the infield, Comiskey insisted that the team would be fine with the players now in spring training. "This young Harvey McClellan has been with us a long while now, has always responded when called on to cover short or third base, and he will easily fill the bill at third," Comiskey said.[20]

But Eddie Mulligan beat out McClellan for the job at third base, and McClellan found himself on the bench for most of the year. He did get into 63 games, rotating among second base, third base, shortstop, and right field. On July 30 he cracked his first major-league home run, into the left-field stands at Shibe Park off Bob Hasty of the Philadelphia Athletics in a 9-1 win.[21]

In late July, a few days before he hit that first major-league home run, McClellan was subpoenaed by defense attorneys in the Black Sox criminal trial, though he was never called to testify.[22]

McClellan hit .179 in 63 games in 1921. Yet when spring training rolled around, he found himself battling for the starting third-base job again. And this time he won it — at least for the first month or so of the 1922 season.[23]

McClellan was supposed to be battling Eddie Mulligan again for a starting position. But Mulligan held out in spring training and when he finally settled with Comiskey, he came down with an illness and missed a chunk of camp.[24] Manager Kid Gleason and coach Johnny Evers worked with McClellan on his batting all spring. The result was that he was given the starting third-base job out of spring training.[25] But the hitting lessons didn't help McClellan. By May 28 he was batting .173 and lost his job to Mulligan.

Before he lost his starting position, McClellan was part of history on April 30 in Detroit. Playing third base behind starting pitcher Charlie Robertson, McClellan helped the rookie right-hander record the

TCMA photo of Hervey McClellan (Courtesy of Michael Aronstein / TCMA Ltd.)

fifth perfect game in major-league history. McClellan had one of his better hitting days, going 1-for-3 in the 2-0 White Sox victory over the Tigers.

After his benching, McClellan rebounded with the bat and finished the season hitting .226 in 91 games. He swatted two more home runs. When the season ended, rumors swirled that McClellan would be sent to San Francisco as part of the franchise's record-high payment for star prospect Willie Kamm. Instead, the White Sox sent Eddie Mulligan.[26]

As spring training began in 1923, some newspapers reported that McClellan would battle Kamm for the starting job at third base. But the White Sox had paid a steep price for Kamm and he wasn't going to sit on the bench when the season started. McClellan found himself in a utility role once again.[27] Then on April 28 McClellan took over for the struggling Ernie Johnson at shortstop. This time, McClellan held on to the position for the entire season. *The Sporting News* noticed his improved play: McClellan "is continuing to play sensationally at short. He is fielding better than Ernie Johnson ever did and is going well with the stick." In fact, McClellan began a career-high 11-game hitting streak in late May.[28]

Even future Hall of Famer Eddie Collins took notice: "He is going to prove a most valuable man for the Sox after being buffeted around for five years as a man without a job."[29]

In all, McClellan played in 141 games in 1923, batting .235. He was second among American League starting shortstops in fielding percentage and was one of the AL leaders in sacrifices.

It appeared the shortstop position was McClellan's to lose in 1924 as the White Sox headed into spring training. *The Sporting News* wrote that the "weakest spot in the Sox attack is shortstop where Harvey McClellan probably will hold forth because of his excellent fielding."[30]

McClellan started the season as the starting shortstop but lost his job on April 24, when he was replaced by Ray French, a 29-year-old journeyman with his third team. A few days later, while in Detroit, McClellan nearly passed out with what at the time was thought to be acute indigestion.[31]

On May 1 it was reported that McClellan had "stomach problems" that would force him to miss a series against the Cleveland Indians. Then on May 5, he was operated on for a "stomach ailment" that turned out to be cancer.[32] According to his obituary in *The Sporting News*, McClellan was never told of the cancer.[33]

Remarkably, McClellan was back in uniform by June 23. But he was extremely weak. He was used as a pinch-hitter on July 6 and again on July 10, replacing Kamm at third base in a lopsided loss to the New York Yankees.[34]

McClellan even earned his starting job back on July 22, when starter Bill Barrett "turned up with an ailment." *The Sporting News* wrote, "The invalid is such

an improvement over Barrett as a fielder that he has been retained for regular duty."[35]

But it was obvious that McClellan wasn't well. Manager Johnny Evers was forced to pull him out of each game after six or seven innings. "Because of his condition, (McClellan) can't do much with the bat," *The Sporting News* reported.[36]

McClellan started 12 of the White Sox' 14 games between July 22 and August 3. The workload took its toll. After sporadic appearances in September, he managed to play in the team's final five games. His last major-league game was September 29, 1924, against the Detroit Tigers in a 16-5 win. He finished the season hitting .159 in 32 games.[37]

In the offseason McClellan traveled with his family and several White Sox teammates to California, intending to convalesce in the warm weather. He managed to find the time and energy to play baseball on Halloween, when he participated in a charity game in Brea with Babe Ruth and Walter Johnson, an exhibition that became famous for Ruth hitting two home runs off Johnson.[38]

McClellan went to spring training in 1925 looking to win his starting shortstop job back. The *Brooklyn Eagle* wrote that McClellan "looks about the best candidate for the job this year" and that it "appears as if his health has returned."[39]

But on Opening Day, McClellan wasn't in the lineup and he never did take the field in 1925. Seeing that his infielder was in a weakened condition, Eddie Collins, now the manager, had tried to work him as little as he could in spring training. But, as *The Sporting News* noted, "by the time the season was ready to start, (McClellan) began to fade physically."[40] On June 6 he was reported to be "dangerously ill" at Mercy Hospital in Chicago and had undergone another operation for gallstones."[41]

McClellan lived exactly five more months. After being discharged from Mercy Hospital in mid-July, he went home to Cynthiana.[42] In October his failing health took a turn for the worse and on November 6, just six weeks shy of his 31st birthday, McClellan died at Harrison Memorial Hospital in his hometown. The official cause of death was liver cancer, though his earlier problems were likely caused by stomach cancer. He left behind his wife, Grace, and his 4-year-old son, Hervey. He was buried in Battle Grove Cemetery in Cynthiana.[43]

"There probably hasn't been a man on a Chicago ball team in many, many seasons who was as popular as 'Little Mac,'" sports writer Irving Vaughan wrote after McClellan's death. "He was one of those sunny little fellows, always smiling and willing to take the good with the bad."[44]

NOTES

1   Correspondence between Grace McClellan and Cliff Kachline in Hervey McClellan's Hall of Fame file. In response to Kachline's question as to what McClellan's real first name was, his widow, Grace, wrote, "I am 80 years of age, same as Hervey's age…. 'Little Mac' was his nick-name and the sport writers nearly always spelled it Harvey."

2   Grace McClellan-Cliff Kachline correspondence.

3   *Lexington Herald*, February 28, 1914, and May 12, 1914.

4   *Lexington Herald*, July 28, 1913, and September 15, 1914; undated biography in Hervey McClellan's Hall of Fame file.

5   *Lexington Herald*, February 21, 1915; May 1, 1915; May 11, 1915; and September 3, 1915.

6   *Lexington Herald*, August 27, 1915; August 31, 1915; September 3, 1915; and October 26, 1915.

7   *Lexington Herald*, July 16, 1916, and July 20, 1916; *Portsmouth Daily News*, July 17, 1916; *Sporting Life*, August 26, 1916.

8   *Lexington Herald*, September 4, 1917, and February 20, 1918; *Hutchinson* (Kansas) *News*, August 28, 1917.

9   *Hutchinson News*, October 29, 1917; Grace McClellan-Cliff Kachline correspondence.

10 *Hutchinson News*, February 13, 1918, and April 15, 1918; *Bridgeport* (Connecticut) *Telegram*, April 9, 1918.

11 *Hutchinson News*, April 15, 1918.

12 *Hutchinson News*, May 1, 1918, and June 20, 1918.

13 *Lexington* (Kentucky) *Herald*, July 7, 1918.

14 *Des Moines News*, February 15, 1919; *Rockford* (Illinois) *Morning Star*, April 17, 1919; *Washington Times*, April 16, 1919; *Seattle Daily Times*, April 17, 1919.

15 *Muscatine* (Iowa) *Journal and News-Tribune*, September 26, 1919.

16 *Harrisburg Patriot*, October 1, 1920; *Schenectady Gazette*, September 29, 1920.

17 *Seattle Daily Times*, October 4, 1920.

18 *Lexington Herald*, October 7, 1920, and October 12, 1920.

19 Grace McClellan-Cliff Kachline correspondence. *Kalamazoo Gazette*, March 16, 1921; *Binghamton Press*, January 28, 1921.

20 *Duluth News-Tribune*, December 1, 1920.

21 *Trenton Evening Times*, March 7, 1921; Bob McConnell and David Vincent, eds. *SABR Presents The Home Run Encyclopedia* (New York: Macmillan, 1996), 843; *Philadelphia Inquirer*, July 31, 1921.

22 *Chicago Tribune*, July 28, 1921.

23 *Buffalo Express*, March 7, 1922.

24 *Rochester Democrat and Chronicle*, March 18, 1922; *Utica Herald-Dispatch*, April 1, 1922.

25 *Albuquerque Journal*, March 31, 1922.

26 *The Sporting News*, October 19, 1922.

27 *Binghamton Press*, April 7, 1923.

28 *The Sporting News*, June 14, 1923.

29 *Canton Evening Repository*, September 12, 1923.

30 *The Sporting News*, January 3, 1924.

31 *The Sporting News*, November 12, 1925.

32 *Appleton Post-Crescent*, May 1, 1924, and May 6, 1924.

33 *The Sporting News*, November 12, 1925.

34 *Rockford Register-Gazette*, June 24, 1924.

35 *The Sporting News*, July 31, 1924.

36 *The Sporting News*, July 31, 1924.

37 McClellan's official record lists his 1924 batting average as .176, but Retrosheet volunteers (retrosheet.org) discovered a mistake in the July 27 game; McClellan was given a hit when, he had none. Thus the .159 batting average.

38 *The Sporting News*, November 12, 1925; Grace McClellan-Cliff Kachline correspondence. *Bakersfield Californian*, November 1, 1924.

39 *New York Times*, March 12, 1925; *Brooklyn Daily Eagle*, March 11, 1925.

40 *The Sporting News*, November 12, 1925.

41 *La Crosse Tribune and Leader-Press*, June 12, 1925; *Oelwein* (Iowa) *Daily Register*, June 16, 1925; *Hutchinson News*, July 25, 1925.

42 *Brooklyn Daily Eagle*, July 7, 1925; *Oakland Tribune*, July 20, 1925; *Hutchinson News*, July 25, 1925.

43 *Port Arthur* (Texas) *News*, October 11, 1925; *Springfield* (Massachusetts) *Daily Republican*, November 9, 1925; author's correspondence with Dr. Stephen Boren.

44 *The Sporting News*, November 12, 1925.

TOM MCGUIRE

By Jack Morris

TOM MCGUIRE MUST HAVE found it odd to be on the mound for the first-place Chicago White Sox on August 9, 1919, at Griffith Stadium in Washington, D.C. The spitballing McGuire had never made an appearance in Organized Baseball. His professional baseball career had been played entirely in independent, "outlaw" leagues like the United States League and the Federal League. He had last thrown a professional pitch in 1914.

Unfortunately for McGuire, there was no Hollywood ending to the story. McGuire was hit hard in his three innings of work that day. He never played another game in the major leagues. The White Sox went on to play in the World Series without him, losing a tainted fall classic against the Cincinnati Reds that culminated in the Black Sox scandal.

Thomas Patrick McGuire was born on February 1, 1892, in Chicago, the first of five children of John and Nora (Cline) McGuire. John and Nora were born in Ireland and had emigrated to the United States in the 1880s. They were married in 1891. John was a Chicago policeman for most of his life.[1]

Young Tom took to sports and by the time he reached high school, he was a star athlete at Chicago's De La Salle Institute.[2] He played for several semipro teams in Chicago before he signed as a pitcher with the Chicago Green Sox of the "outlaw" United States League in 1912.[3] The United States League intended to compete with the established major leagues, but folded in mid-June because of lack of capital, rainouts, and poor attendance.[4] The right-handed McGuire compiled a 5-4 record in 12 games, and led the league with 38 walks given up. He played in the outfield on occasion, batting .213 with two home runs in 17 games.[5]

In 1913 McGuire joined another outlaw league team, the Federal League's Chicago Keeleys, nicknamed for

manager Burt Keeley. McGuire led the league in most pitching categories, including wins (18), games pitched (36), complete games (27), innings pitched (272), and strikeouts (170). He also led in runs allowed (118), walks (84), and hits allowed (264).[6]

McGuire pitched so well that he garnered the attention of the St. Louis Cardinals. In mid-June, published reports claimed that McGuire had signed with the Cardinals and that teammate Charlie "Silk" Kavanagh had signed with the Chicago Cubs. After the June 20 game against the Indianapolis Hoosiers, the *Indianapolis Star* wrote that the game "will probably go on record as (McGuire's) last game in the league."[7]

But Federal League President John T. Powers fought back. He announced that if McGuire and Kavanagh were signed by the National League teams, the Federal League would go after Roger Bresnahan (then playing for the Chicago Cubs). McGuire and Kavanagh finished the season in the Federal League.[8]

As the Federal League declared war on the major leagues during the winter of 1913-14, McGuire re-signed with Chicago and headed to Shreveport, Louisiana, for spring training. Manager Joe Tinker—the Federal League's first big-name signing—liked what he saw of McGuire, placing him on the Chi-Feds roster for the regular season. McGuire wasn't the only former Chicago semipro player to make the Chi-Feds squad. Pitchers Erv Lange and Max Fiske also went north with the club. In the first few months of the season, McGuire picked up where he left off in 1913, with a winning record on the mound and a .340 batting average into late July.[9]

He hit so well that when outfielder Max Flack left the team in early August because of illness in his family, McGuire played left field. His only major-league home run came during this stretch, when he took George Suggs of the Baltimore Terrapins deep on August 6. But by late August McGuire had begun began to struggle. Tinker offered McGuire and two other pitchers to the St. Louis Terriers for star pitcher Mordecai "Three Finger" Brown. Instead, St. Louis sent Brown to Brooklyn. Tinker eventually acquired Brown for the 1915 season and won the Federal League championship with him.[10] McGuire finished 5-6 with a 3.70 ERA in 24 games.

Tinker chose not to re-sign McGuire in 1915; *Sporting Life* reported that "he did not develop as Tinker expected." In February Burt Keeley came to McGuire's rescue and signed him to play on the William Hale Thompson-backed indoor team of the Woodlawn baseball league in Chicago. Cap Anson also played in the league, which used regulation balls and bats but had just five players in the field.[11]

McGuire's indoor play didn't lead to any offers from professional outdoor teams. There was a rumor that the Newark Pepper of the Federal League were interested in him but nothing came of it. In April conflicting reports came out about his whereabouts. One said he was working at Buck Weaver's billiard room in Chicago; the other claimed he had taken a job as a sportswriter in Prince George, British Columbia.[12]

While McGuire's exact occupation is unknown, it's clear he wasn't playing in Organized Baseball. In late September 1916, a report in *Sporting Life* said McGuire was preparing to join the Los Angeles Angels of the Pacific Coast League. If he did, he never played in a game.[13]

It wasn't until 1918 that McGuire's name started to appear in sports pages again. In the midst of World War I, he joined the US Army and was assigned to Camp Grant in Rockford, Illinois. He was attached to the 86th Infantry Division (known as the Black Hawk Division) as a sergeant major in charge of troop transportation, and pitched on the division's baseball team, which also included former major leaguers Ed "Jeff" Sweeney, William Marriott, Adam DeBus, and Austin Walsh.[14]

In July McGuire was sent to France with the Black Hawk Division.[15] He never saw combat and returned to the United States in January 1919. He began pitching for a Chicago semipro team called the J.P. Sheehans. On April 16, before 1,500 fans, McGuire pitched his team to a victory over the Jimmy Hutton All-Stars.[16]

Sometime that summer, McGuire's performance caught the eye of White Sox manager Kid Gleason. McGuire worked out for Gleason in late July and, amazingly, was offered a contract in professional baseball, five years after his last go-round in the Federal League.[17]

On August 9, 1919, McGuire made his first and last appearance in Organized Baseball. Another recently acquired veteran, Erskine Mayer, was tasked to start against the lowly Washington Senators. It didn't go well. Mayer lasted five innings before yielding to McGuire in the sixth. McGuire pitched three innings, allowing five hits, four runs, and three walks, before he was pulled. The White Sox lost, 11-6. Gleason had seen enough.[18]

Tom McGuire, circa 1913 (Chicago History Museum, SDN-058507, Chicago Daily News negatives collection)

Gleason was criticized the next day for his curious choice of pitchers for the first-place White Sox. Hampered all year by a lack of pitching depth, Gleason likely was looking for healthy arms down the stretch. It's unclear how long McGuire stayed on the roster, but he was not on the bench during the World Series and did not receive even a partial share of the championship money.[19]

McGuire may have continued to play semipro baseball after his stint with the White Sox but he later became a grain broker on the Chicago Board of Trade. He held that job for 37 years.[20]

In 1923 McGuire married Kathleen J. Freeman. They first lived in Oak Park, Illinois, but eventually settled in nearby River Forest. The couple had three children: daughter Margaret Mary and sons Thomas Patrick Jr. and John Joseph.

On December 8, 1959, at the age of 67, McGuire died at St. Joseph's Hospital in Phoenix, Arizona, while recuperating from surgery. The cause of death was acute renal insufficiency. His kidneys may have failed because of medication following his surgery. He was survived by his wife, Kathleen, and their three children. He was buried in Holy Sepulchre Cemetery in Worth, Illinois.[21]

NOTES

1   1900-1930 United States Censuses.

2   *The Sporting News*, December 16, 1959.

3   Ibid.; *Sporting Life*, May 11, 1912.   .

4   Rudolf K. Haerle, "The United States Baseball League of 1912: A Case Study of Organizational Failure," *North American Society for Sport History, Proceedings and Newsletter*, 1976, 36-37.

5   *Sporting Life*, May 11, 1912. McGuire's obituary in *The Sporting News* mentioned that he was signed by the 1912 Des Moines Boosters of the Western League. However, there is no evidence that he played for them. Statistics for 1912 were compiled by minor-league historian Ray Nemec.

6   Statistics for 1913 were compiled by minor-league historian Ray Nemec.

7   *Sporting Life*, June 21, 1913; *Indianapolis Star*, June 21, 1913.

8   *Sporting Life*, June 21, 1913.

9   *Miami Herald*, July 15, 1914; *Flint Daily Journal*, July 8, 1914; *Ann Arbor Daily Times News*, July 25, 1914.

10   *Sporting Life*, August 21 and 29, 1914; Bob McConnell and David Vincent, eds., *SABR Presents the Home Run Encyclopedia* (New York: Macmillan, 1996), 853.

11   *Sporting Life*, February 20, 1915; *Racine* (Wisconsin) *Journal-News*, February 9, 1915.

12   *Racine* (Wisconsin) *Journal-News*, April 19, 1915; *La Crosse* (Wisconsin) *Tribune*, April 17, 1915; *Sporting Life*, April 24, 1915.

13   *Sporting Life*, September 30, 1916.

14   *Grand Rapids* (Michigan) *Tribune*, March 7, 1918; *Rockford* (Illinois) *Morning Star*, April 18, 1918.

15   *Waterloo* (Iowa) *Times*, May 31, 1918; *Rockford* (Illinois) *Register-Gazette*, May 31, 1918, and January 15, 1919; Robert Charles Cottrell, *The Best Pitcher in Baseball: The Life of Rube Foster, Negro League Giant* (New York: NYU Press, 2004), 114-115.

16   *Grand Forks* (North Dakota) *Herald*, January 15, 1919; *Columbus* (Ohio) *Daily Express*, August 22, 1919; *Englewood* (Colorado) *Economist*, April 16, 1919.

17   *Rockford* (Illinois) *Morning Star*, July 24, 1919.

18   *Washington Post*, August 10, 1919.

19   "Black Sox Scandal (1914-69)," American League records, National Baseball Hall of Fame Library.

20   Bill Lee, *The Baseball Necrology* (Jefferson, North Carolina: McFarland, 2004), 264.

21   *The Sporting News*, December 16, 1959; Thomas McGuire, Arizona Certificate of Death from his Baseball Hall of Fame player file; Lee, *The Baseball Necrology*, 264. Thanks to SABR member Dr. Stephen Boren for help in interpreting McGuire's death certificate.

SEASON TIMELINE: JUNE 1919

White Sox record: 11-16 (.407)
Runs scored: 86 | Runs allowed: 94

AL standings
June 30, 1919

Team	W	L	PCT	GB
NYY	35	18	.660	—
CHW	35	23	.603	2½
CLE	33	24	.579	4
DET	30	26	.536	6½
SLB	27	28	.491	9
BOS	24	31	.436	12
WSH	24	33	.421	13
PHA	14	39	.264	21

PLAYER OF THE MONTH

	G	PA	AB	R	H	2B	3B	HR	RBI	SB	BB	SO	BA	OBP	SLG	OPS
Eddie Collins	27	119	100	12	32	3	1	1	14	4	9	3	.320	.376	.400	.776

A midseason slump dropped Collins's batting average to a season-low .250 on June 17, but he turned it on near the end of the month. In the final week of June, he had six multi-hit games to raise his average back to .301 by the morning of July 1. Collins's hot hitting would continue in July as the Sox began running away with the pennant.

PITCHER OF THE MONTH

	W	L	ERA	G	GS	CG	SHO	IP	H	R	ER	BB	SO	WHIP
Lefty Williams	4	3	1.98	7	7	5	1	59	38	13	13	14	25	0.881

Williams's 3-0 shutout of the defending World Series champion Boston Red Sox on June 11 began a dominant stretch in which he won eight of his next 10 games. Williams and Eddie Cicotte were manager Kid Gleason's only reliable starters for most of the season. The left-hander struck out a season-high seven Washington Senators on June 20, and allowed two runs or fewer in six of his seven June starts.

DAY BY DAY RECAP

Sunday, June 1
Comiskey Park, Chicago
"Bagby Gets Revenge on Sox, Indians Winning Game, 5-3" — *Chicago Tribune*

Indians (19-11)   100   001   300 — 5 14 3
White Sox (24-8)   101   100   000 — 3 7 2
WP: Jim Bagby (4-2). LP: Dave Danforth (0-2).

Dickey Kerr: 6 IP, 10 H, 2 R, 2 ER, 1 BB, 2 K.
Happy Felsch: 2-4, 3B, R. Buck Weaver: 2-4, R, SB.

Monday, June 2
Navin Field, Detroit
"Sox Donate Opener to Detroit, 5-3, Then Lose Second Also, 2-1" — *Chicago Tribune*

White Sox (24-9)   000   101   100—3 8 2
Tigers (15-16)   000   301   10x—5 6 3
WP: Howard Ehmke (5-4). LP: Red Faber (5-2).
Red Faber: 6 IP, 4 H, 4 R, 2 ER, 4 BB, 1 K.
Nemo Leibold: 3-4. Eddie Collins: 0-2, 2 BB, R, SB. Happy Felsch: 1-3, 3B, R, RBI.

White Sox (24-10)   000   000   010—1 6 0
Tigers (16-16)   001   000   10x—2 5 4
WP: Bernie Boland (2-4). LP: Lefty Williams (7-3).
Lefty Williams: 7 IP, 4 H, 2 R, 2 ER, 2 BB, 3 K.
Buck Weaver: 3-3, 2B, BB. Nemo Leibold: 2-4, R.

Tuesday, June 3
Navin Field, Detroit
"Gap at First Base Costs Sox Another, Tigers Winning, 7-3" — *Chicago Tribune*

White Sox (24-11)   020   000   001—3 11 2
Tigers (17-16)   104   000   02x—7 10 1
WP: Hooks Dauss (4-3). LP: Grover Lowdermilk (0-1).
Grover Lowdermilk: 3 IP, 4 H, 5 R, 1 ER, 2 BB, 2 K.
Nemo Leibold: 2-4, BB, RBI. Swede Risberg: 1-4, 2B, R. Grover Lowdermilk: 1-1, SB, RBI.

Wednesday, June 4
Scheduled day off
"Sox Spend Off Day Peeking at Giants; Look Ahead to Fall" — *Chicago Tribune*

Thursday, June 5
Polo Grounds, New York
"Eddie Collins' Homer With Bases Full Beats Yanks, 5-1" — *Chicago Tribune*

White Sox (25-11)   010   000   040—5 7 0
Yankees (19-12)   100   000   000—1 8 1
WP: Eddie Cicotte (10-1). LP: Ernie Shore (1-2).
Eddie Cicotte: 9 IP, 8 H, 1 R, 1 ER, 0 BB, 3 K.
Eddie Collins: 2-4, HR, R, 5 RBI. Happy Felsch: 0-3, R, 2 SB. Ray Schalk: 1-3, R.

THE 1919 CHICAGO WHITE SOX

Friday, June 6
Postponed, rain
"Rain Prevents Duel of Sox and Yanks; Gandil Back Today" — *Chicago Tribune*

Saturday, June 7
Polo Grounds, New York
"Quinn Subdues Gleason's Tribe as Yankees Win" — *Chicago Tribune*

White Sox (25-12) 000   110   011 — 4 6 1
Yankees (20-12)   010   003   02x — 6 10 1
WP: Jack Quinn (5-2). LP: Lefty Williams (7-4).
Lefty Williams: 7 IP, 8 R, 4 R, 4 ER, 3 BB, 3 K.
Buck Weaver: 1-4, HR, RBI. Ray Schalk: 1-3, BB, R, RBI. Eddie Collins: 1-3, 2B, BB, R.

Sunday, June 8
Polo Grounds, New York
"Shawkey of Yanks Gives Sox One Hit and Cops 4-0 Game" — *Chicago Tribune*

White Sox (25-13) 000   000   000 — 0 1 1
Yankees (21-12)   003   100   00x — 4 12 1
WP: Bob Shawkey (8-4). LP: Red Faber (5-3).
Red Faber: 3⅓ IP, 9 H, 4 R, 4 ER, 1 BB, 0 K.
Red Faber: 1-1. Happy Felsch: 0-2, BB, SB.

Monday, June 9
Postponed, rain
"Rain Stops Last of Sox Series at New York" — *Chicago Tribune*

Tuesday, June 10
Fenway Park, Boston
"Cicotte and Mates Heap Defeat Upon Red Sox Gang, 5-3" — *Chicago Tribune*

White Sox (26-13) 011   000   120 — 5 7 1
Red Sox (16-18)   100   000   200 — 3 7 4
WP: Eddie Cicotte (11-1). LP: Babe Ruth (5-1).
Eddie Cicotte: 9 IP, 7 H, 3 R, 2 ER, 5 BB, 4 K.
Buck Weaver: 2-5, 2 2B, R. Swede Risberg: 1-4, 3B, R, 2 RBI. Chick Gandil: 1-3, BB, 2 R.

Wednesday, June 11
Fenway Park, Boston
"Williams Feeds Goose Egg to Boston's World Champs" — *Chicago Tribune*

White Sox (27-13) 200   000   010 — 3 7 0
Red Sox (16-19)   000   000   000 — 0 6 3
WP: Lefty Williams (8-4). LP: Carl Mays (3-7).
Lefty Williams: 9 IP, 6 H, 0 R, 0 ER, 2 BB, 4 K.
Nemo Leibold: 2-2, 2 BB, SB, R. Eddie Collins: 2-3, R. Joe Jackson: 2-4, RBI.

Thursday, June 12
Fenway Park, Boston
"Ex-Gob Takes Game, First Place From White Hose, 4 to 0" — *Chicago Tribune*

White Sox (27-14)   000   000   000 — 0 3 2
Red Sox (17-19)   000   004   00x — 4 8 0
WP: Herb Pennock (2-1). LP: Red Faber (5-4).
Red Faber: 6 IP, 7 H, 4 R, 4 ER, 2 BB, 1 K.
Shano Collins: 2-3. Happy Felsch: 1-3.

Friday, June 13
Fenway Park, Boston
"Red Sox Whale Chicago, 6-1; Rout Shellenback, Russell" — *Chicago Tribune*

White Sox (27-15)   100   000   000 — 1 5 2
Red Sox (18-19)   010   050   00x — 6 7 0
WP: Sam Jones (3-4). LP: Frank Shellenback (1-2).
Frank Shellenback: 4⅔ IP, 6 H, 6 R, 5 ER, 6 BB, 2 K.
Nemo Leibold: 2-4, R. Buck Weaver: 1-4, RBI.

Saturday, June 14
Shibe Park, Philadelphia
"Triumph No. 12 for Ed Cicotte; Goes 14 Rounds" — *Chicago Tribune*

White Sox (28-15)   000   002   001   000   03 — 6 14 0
Athletics (9-30)   102   000   000   000   00 — 3 14 3
WP: Eddie Cicotte (12-1). LP: Tom Rogers (1-8).
Eddie Cicotte: 14 IP, 14 H, 3 R, 3 ER, 5 BB, 7 K.
Chick Gandil: 4-6, R. Happy Felsch: 2-6, HR, SB, 2 RBI. Ray Schalk: 3-6, 2B, 2 R. Eddie Cicotte: 3-5, R.

Sunday, June 15
Scheduled day off
"Gleasons Droop When Big 4 Lose Slugging Power" — *Chicago Tribune*

Monday, June 16
Shibe Park, Philadelphia
"Those White Sox Again Paint Philly Blue; Beat Macks, 5-1" — *Chicago Tribune*

White Sox (29-15)   100   103   000 — 5 13 1
Athletics (9-31)   000   010   000 — 1 6 1
WP: Lefty Williams (9-4). LP: Socks Seibold (2-3).
Lefty Williams: 9 IP, 6 H, 1 R, 1 ER, 1 BB, 3 K.
Joe Jackson: 3-4, HR, SB, 2 RBI. Buck Weaver: 2-4, 3B, R. Happy Felsch: 2-3, HR, BB, RBI. Ray Schalk: 1-4, 2 RBI.

Tuesday, June 17
Shibe Park, Philadelphia
"Sox Pluck Victory Out of a Jumble of Base Hits, 7 to 6" — *Chicago Tribune*

White Sox (30-15)   010   021   030 — 7 10 2
Athletics (9-32)   004   002   000 — 6 15 1
WP: Dickey Kerr (3-0). LP: Jing Johnson (2-6).
Red Faber: 5⅓ IP, 12 H, 6 R, 6 ER, 0 BB, 2 K.
Swede Risberg: 2-3, HR, SB, 2 RBI. Happy Felsch: 1-4, 3B, R, 2 RBI. Chick Gandil: 2-3, HBP, 2 R.

Wednesday, June 18
Griffith Stadium, Washington
"Cicotte's String of Wins Snapped By Senators, 2-0" — *Chicago Tribune*

White Sox (30-16)   000   000   000 — 0 8 1
Senators (17-27)   010   001   00x — 2 5 2
WP: Jim Shaw (7-5). LP: Eddie Cicotte (12-2).
Eddie Cicotte: 8 IP, 5 H, 2 R, 2 ER, 1 BB, 4 K.
Eddie Collins: 2-3. Chick Gandil: 2-4. Swede Risberg: 1-4, SB.

Thursday, June 19
Griffith Stadium, Washington
"Lowdermilk Goes Route for Gleason; Whips Griffs, 5 to 4" — *Chicago Tribune*

White Sox (31-16)   101   120   000 — 5 13 3
Senators (17-28)   000   002   002 — 4 8 2
WP: Grover Lowdermilk (1-1). LP: Charlie Whitehouse (0-1).
Grover Lowdermilk: 9 IP, 8 H, 4 R, 1 ER, 3 BB, 2 K.
Shano Collins: 3-5, 2 R. Eddie Collins: 3-3, BB, R. Joe Jackson: 1-3, BB, 2 RBI. Swede Risberg: 2-4, 3B, R.

Friday, June 20
Griffith Stadium, Washington
"White Sox Dance on Griffs, 5-2, to Williams' Music" — *Chicago Tribune*

White Sox (32-16)   001   012   100 — 5 10 0
Senators (17-29)   000   010   001 — 2 4 2
WP: Lefty Williams (10-4). LP: Harry Harper (3-7).
Lefty Williams: 9 IP, 4 H, 2 R, 2 ER, 2 BB, 7 K.
Buck Weaver: 1-4, HR, 2 RBI. Shano Collins: 1-3, HR, RBI. Lefty Williams: 1-3, 3B, RBI. Ray Schalk: 1-4, SB, 2 R.

Saturday, June 21
Griffith Stadium, Washington
"Sox Blow Up As Schalk and Lynn Are Injured, 6-3" — *Chicago Tribune*

White Sox (32-17)   000   120   000 — 3 10 3
Senators (18-29)   200   022   00x — 6 7 4
WP: Walter Johnson (8-7). LP: Red Faber (5-5).

Red Faber: 4⅓ IP, 6 H, 4 R, 4 ER, 2 BB, 1 K.
Joe Jackson: 3-4, 2B. Buck Weaver: 2-4, R, 2 RBI. Nemo Leibold: 2-5. Eddie Collins: 1-4, 2B, BB, R.

Sunday, June 22
Navin Field, Detroit
"Prodigal Hose Hand Out 5-4 Tilt to Tigers" — *Chicago Tribune*

White Sox (32-18)   100   002   001 — 4 9 3
Tigers (23-26)   103   000   01x — 5 8 1
WP: Hooks Dauss (6-4). LP: Frank Shellenback (1-3).
Frank Shellenback: 8 IP, 8 H, 5 R, 3 ER, 4 BB, 2 K.
Happy Felsch: 1-4, HR, 2 RBI. Joe Jackson: 2-4, 2B, RBI. Swede Risberg: 1-4, 2B, R.

Monday, June 23
Comiskey Park, Chicago
"Indians Kill Runs at Plate and Drop Sox to Third Place" — *Chicago Tribune*

Indians (32-18)   100   000   020 — 3 5 1
White Sox (32-19)   001   000   001 — 2 8 0
WP: Jim Bagby (8-3). LP: Eddie Cicotte (12-3).
Eddie Cicotte: 8 IP, 5 H, 3 R, 3 ER, 2 BB, 3 K.
Nemo Leibold: 1-3, 2B, SB, BB, RBI. Buck Weaver: 2-4, 3B, R. Happy Felsch: 2-4, 3B.

Tuesday, June 24
Comiskey Park, Chicago
"Sox, Shy on the 'Punch,' Lose to Indians, 2 to 0" — *Chicago Tribune*

Indians (33-18)   100   000   100 — 2 5 3
White Sox (32-20)   000   000   000 — 0 6 1
WP: Stan Coveleski (9-3). LP: Lefty Williams (10-5).
Lefty Williams: 9 IP, 5 H, 2 R, 2 ER, 2 BB, 1 K.
Buck Weaver: 2-4, 2B. Happy Felsch: 1-4, 2 SB. Eddie Collins: 2-4.

Wednesday, June 25
Comiskey Park, Chicago
"Indians Get 12 Hits Off Lowdermilk, But Sox Win" — *Chicago Tribune*

Indians (33-19)   001   000   000 — 1 11 2
White Sox (33-20)   202   201   00x — 7 10 1
WP: Grover Lowdermilk (2-1). LP: Guy Morton (6-5).
Grover Lowdermilk: 9 IP, 11 H, 1 R, 0 ER, 4 BB, 3 K.
Ray Schalk: 3-4, SB, 2 R. Eddie Collins: 2-3, 2 R, 2 RBI. Buck Weaver: 1-2, 3B, HBP, R, RBI. Joe Jackson: 1-4, 2 RBI.

Thursday, June 26
Sportsman's Park, St. Louis
"Bit O' Luck Gives Browns 13 Inning Win Over Sox, 3 to 2" — *Chicago Tribune*

White Sox (33-21)	000	010	001	000	0—2 8 0
Browns (25-26)	000	101	000	000	1—3 15 0

WP: Allan Sothoron (6-4). LP: Dickey Kerr (3-1).
Dickey Kerr: 12⅔ IP, 15 H, 3 R, 3 ER, 1 BB, 3 K.
Joe Jackson: 2-5, 3B, R, RBI. Eddie Collins: 2-5, 3B, R. Swede Risberg: 1-4, SB, BB.

Friday, June 27
Sportsman's Park, St. Louis
"Errors By Risberg Toss Off Cicotte's Third Loss in Row" — *Chicago Tribune*

White Sox (33-22)	010	000	000—1 9 3
Browns (26-26)	100	200	10x—4 9 1

WP: Carl Weilman (4-5). LP: Eddie Cicotte (12-4).
Eddie Cicotte: 8 IP, 9 H, 4 R, 2 ER, 0 BB, 4 K.
Happy Felsch: 2-4, 2B. Joe Jackson: 2-4, R. Chick Gandil: 2-3, HBP.

Saturday, June 28
Sportsman's Park, St. Louis
"Williams Stops Browns in Tight Battle, 3 to 2" — *Chicago Tribune*

White Sox (34-22)	000	002	100—3 6 1
Browns (26-27)	010	000	100—2 5 1

WP: Lefty Williams (11-5). LP: Urban Shocker (6-5).
Lefty Williams: 9 IP, 5 H, 2 R, 2 ER, 2 BB, 4 K.
Joe Jackson: 1-2, 2 RBI, 2 BB. Eddie Collins: 2-3, 2B, R, RBI, BB. Fred McMullin: 2-4.

Sunday, June 29
Sportsman's Park, St. Louis
"Five Hurlers Have Wild Session When Browns Wallop Sox" — *Chicago Tribune*

White Sox (34-23)	000	002	100—3 6 2
Browns (27-27)	100	300	01x—5 8 2

WP: Bert Gallia (8-5). LP: Grover Lowdermilk (2-2). SV: Allan Sothoron (2).
Grover Lowdermilk: 5 IP, 6 H, 4 R, 3 ER, 1 BB, 1 K.
Eddie Collins: 3-4, R, RBI. Joe Jackson: 0-0, 4 BB. Buck Weaver: 1-4, RBI.

Monday, June 30
Dunn Field, Cleveland
"Riot Call for Cops as Sox Take Stormy Game at Cleveland" — *Chicago Tribune*

White Sox (35-23)	010	111	100—5 14 1
Indians (33-24)	000	101	000—2 7 4

WP: Eddie Cicotte (13-4). LP: Jim Bagby (8-5).
Eddie Cicotte: 9 IP, 7 H, 2 R, 2 ER, 1 BB, 1 K.
Eddie Murphy: 4-4, 2B, R, RBI, BB. Eddie Collins: 3-5, RBI. Ray Schalk: 2-3, 2B, R, 2 BB. Chick Gandil: 2-5, R, RBI, SB.

JUNE HIGHLIGHTS

Road Warriors: In stark contrast to last month's schedule, the White Sox played 23 of 27 games away from Comiskey Park, including 18 consecutive road games from June 2 to June 22. This wasn't unusual in the American League — the Browns had a stretch of 26 road games in a row in 1919, while the Senators had one of 23, the Yankees 20, and the Red Sox 19, so all teams were used to dealing with the hardships of an extended trip. But that didn't make it any easier. Chicago stumbled to its worst monthly record at 11-16, suffering two different four-game losing streaks (a season high), and fell out of first place for the first time on June 23.

The Perils of Train Travel: After 20 consecutive days away from home, the White Sox wrapped up a series with Washington and then had to make one final detour to Detroit on June 22 to make up a game against the Tigers, who were heading home after a series in Philadelphia. The two teams took the same train west to Michigan. It wasn't a pleasant trip, as the *Chicago Tribune* explained: "All the players of both teams were [rousted] at 6:30 this morning to change from sleepers to parlor cars. They hung around a station platform for over thirty minutes waiting for the parlor cars, only to find they were the same sleepers they had crawled out of. The waiting killed the chance for breakfast at the station and on the crowded train it was 10 o'clock before some of the fellows could get in the dining car. An hour before that all the eggs had been eaten." The train arrived at Navin Field just a half-hour before the game was scheduled to begin.

Looking Ahead to October: Despite their struggles, the first-place White Sox couldn't help but turn their attention to October when they arrived in New York City on the morning of June 4. With a rare scheduled off-day, about half the team went to the Polo Grounds to "spy on the Giants" in their game against the Philadelphia Phillies. As the *Chicago Tribune's* James Crusinberry reported, "The boys on [Kid] Gleason's team have a sort of hunch they may play against [John] McGraw's National Leaguers" in the World Series. "They took a keen interest in all doings of McGraw's men, sizing them up in comparison to the Giants they beat in the fall of 1917." The Giants were leading the NL standings by 4½ games over the Reds, but Cincinnati played at a .724 clip the rest of the way to cruise to the pennant by nine games.

Hitting the Links: After leaving New York, the White Sox headed to Boston — and continued their sports sight-seeing on June 12. The *Chicago Tribune* explained: "Almost half the White Sox crew, including Boss Gleason, were out to Brae Burn this morning and saw Walter Hagen beat Mike Brady for the [U.S. Open] golf championship. There were about 3,000 other folks following the golfers around." Seeing Hagen's dramatic victory in an 18-hole playoff didn't help Chicago against the Red Sox that afternoon, as Boston's Herb Pennock faced the minimum 27 batters in a 4-0 shutout.

The Saga of Jack Quinn: In the middle of the war-shortened 1918 season, the White Sox signed right-handed spitballer Jack Quinn out of the Pacific Coast League. From August 1 until the end of the season, Quinn went 5-1 for the White Sox and owner Charles Comiskey expected to re-sign him to bolster Chicago's thin pitching rotation. But Quinn's old PCL club, the Vernon Tigers, had sold his rights to the New York Yankees and when the Yankees tried to claim Quinn in the offseason, American League president Ban Johnson awarded him to New York. The controversial decision infuriated Comiskey, who had been feuding with Johnson for years. Quinn pitched another 15 seasons in the American League, but never for the White Sox. Chicago continued to struggle with pitching depth in 1919, but they had success against their former teammate, winning five of the seven games Quinn pitched against them.

Happy Hauls 'Em In: On June 23, White Sox center fielder Happy Felsch set what was thought to be a modern major-league record with 11 putouts behind Eddie Cicotte against the Cleveland Indians. He also contributed one assist, and made a highlight-reel running catch when he took an extra-base hit away from Doc Johnston in right-center in the fifth inning, but his effort wasn't enough in a 3-2 loss that dropped the White Sox into third place. Felsch's mark was broken in the National League by the Boston Braves' Earl Clark in 1929, but no American League outfielder would record 12 putouts until the Minnesota Twins' Lyman Bostock turned the trick in 1977.

Calling the Cops: The White Sox and Indians got chippy again at the end of the month. Chicago's 5-2 win on June 30 was marred by a bench-clearing incident in the sixth inning that drew the attention of "a wagonload of cops" in Cleveland. The Indians were staging a two-out rally after an Elmer Smith RBI triple, but Eddie Cicotte picked off Smith from third base to end the inning. "The entire Cleveland club rushed upon the field calling balk," wrote the *Chicago Tribune's* James Crusinberry. "There wasn't a chance for it to be a balk, but the Cleveland players stormed and stamped and carried on … and not a man was put out [ejected.] The crowd took it up and for nearly ten minutes the game was delayed…. They called the Sox a lot of shipbuilders and slackers, and rode the visiting players and umpires from start to finish." Sensing the "riotous mood of the crowd," Indians official Walter McNichols called a nearby police station and "a dozen bluecoats" escorted umpire George Hildebrand to his dressing room after the game.

FRED MCMULLIN

By Jacob Pomrenke

UNTIL HIS FATEFUL INVOLVE-
ment in the plot to fix a World Series, Fred
McMullin was known as the Chicago White
Sox' "lucky man."[1] His addition to the starting lineup
coincided with late-season surges to win the American
League pennant in 1917 and 1919.

Today he is mostly thought of as the "forgotten
man"—in a scandal often called baseball's darkest
hour. Fred McMullin was the Eighth Man Out, the
most obscure of the White Sox players who agreed
to throw the 1919 World Series to the Cincinnati Reds.
He was banned from Organized Baseball by
Commissioner Kenesaw Mountain Landis and was
blackballed in semipro games near his home in
Los Angeles.[2]

Fred McMullin's story is a series of contrasts. A man
once commended for chasing gamblers off a field in
Boston was suspended permanently because he accepted a $5,000 bribe to help his team lose. He was
indicted by a Chicago grand jury in a story that made
headlines across the nation, yet he spent the final
decade of his life as a respected lawman in California.

Frederick Drury McMullin was born on October 13,
1891, in Scammon, Kansas. He was the first of nine
children born to Robert D. and Minnie Rea (Davis)
McMullin. Robert McMullin was born in Johnson
County, Indiana, and moved to Kansas after marrying
Minnie in 1890. Robert worked a stint as a railroad
laborer before turning to carpentry, a trade he continued for most of his life. Minnie—who would
outlive her son Fred by 11 years—was the only child
of Antrim and Louisa (Rea) Davis.[3]

After Robert and Minnie's sixth child, Dale, was born
in 1905, the family packed up and moved to Southern
California. They lived on Elmyra Street in the Lincoln
Heights neighborhood, a few miles northeast of
downtown Los Angeles, and Fred soon enrolled at
nearby Los Angeles High School. The school's baseball
team was a strong one: Fred Snodgrass, a recent
alumnus, had signed with the New York Giants, while
McMullin was a teammate of Johnny Rawlings, who
would also play in the major leagues.[4]

In 1910, at the age of 20, McMullin joined the Long
Beach Sand Crabs of the newly formed Trolley Car
League, so named because the teams in Pasadena,
Redondo Beach, and other towns were all linked by
the transit system of that era. The teams were subsi-
dized by the Pacific Coast League, but under-financed,
and many players did not get paid. The league folded
after a few weeks.[5]

McMullin took a job as a blacksmith apprentice that
summer and continued to play ball around Los
Angeles. In September he had a tryout with Sacramento
of the PCL, and made one appearance for them, in a
game against the hometown Los Angeles Angels. The
next year, he played in the Southern State League, for
teams in Long Beach and San Bernardino.[6]

In 1912 McMullin headed north to play for the powerhouse Seattle Giants of the Northwestern League.
The Northwestern League was considered "one of the
best of the smaller leagues for the development of
players,"[7] and included such helping hands as former
White Sox manager Fielder Jones and New York
Giants great Joe "Iron Man" McGinnity to coach the
young prospects. The Seattle Giants had little use for
a green youngster like McMullin. As Seattle fell into
last place two months into the season, Fred was sold
to the Tacoma Tigers.[8]

The move paid off for both. The Giants surged to win
27 of their final 31 games and take the pennant, while
McMullin finished the year strongly and began to feel
at home with Tacoma. Mac, as he was often called,
ended his first full professional season with a .250

average, including 21 doubles and 6 home runs, in 141 games.

Tacoma was a nurturing environment for the 22-year-old McMullin. He hit only .236 in 1913 and showed little patience at the plate. But he continued to stir praise with his play in the field, and won a starting job at third base, appearing in 172 games. His appetite for baseball didn't wane during the offseason, as he again played for various winter-league teams back home in California before reporting to Tacoma in the spring of 1914.[9]

Expectations were higher for McMullin after he had a year of experience. Manager Joe McGinnity placed his young second baseman in the cleanup spot to open the season, giving McMullin a great boost of confidence. Mac made enough of an impression that McGinnity released captain Bill Yohe on June 15 and installed McMullin at third base.[10] Mac began to set himself apart in the field, and he was frequently cited in newspaper reports for his heady play.

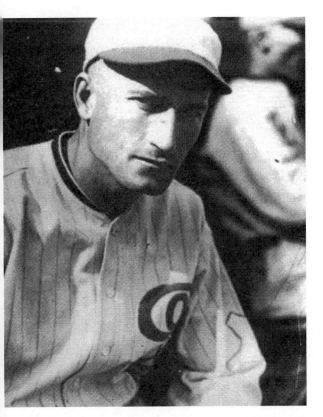

Fred McMullin (Courtesy of Michael Aronstein / TCMA Ltd.)

As the calendar rolled to July, Mac's play began to earn notice in Detroit. The major-league Tigers had an option to purchase players from the minor-league Tigers. The *Tacoma Daily News* profiled McMullin on July 23, stating that "his batting is much better than heretofore and as this was the only thing that kept him from the 'big noise' the past two years, he is almost sure to get his chance." The next day, he had two more hits, scored two more runs, and "played like a major leaguer.... No player who has worked on the local field this year could hold a candle to McMullin the way he has been going the past two weeks."[11]

The Detroit Tigers asked for Mac to report "at once."[12] McMullin's contract was sold for $2,000 on August 13, and he left to join the Tigers in Cleveland. But with Donie Bush firmly in place at shortstop, and George Moriarty and Ossie Vitt holding down the fort at third base, the Tigers didn't have much room in the infield for a rookie.

Mac rode the bench for nearly two weeks without once appearing in the lineup for Hall of Fame manager Hughie Jennings. Watching greats like Ty Cobb and Sam Crawford must have been exciting for McMullin, who had never attended a major-league game. But he longed to get on the field. He did—just once. His major-league debut came on August 27, 1914, and it was the only appearance Mac made with the Tigers.

Late in a blowout loss to the Boston Red Sox, manager Jennings decided to empty his bench, sending up rookie Harry Heilmann to pinch-hit in the eighth inning. After the future Hall of Famer drove in a run with a fly ball to center field, McMullin (playing his first game) was called upon to hit for reliever Ed McCreery (playing his last). Against the left-hander Ray Collins, who won 20 games that season, the 22-year-old McMullin was overmatched, striking out weakly. Taking the field for the bottom of the eighth, Mac recorded a hat trick of sorts: a putout, an assist, and an error.[13]

McMullin's one inning at Fenway Park was the last of his 1914 season. He spent the next month sitting beside Jennings in the dugout for the Tigers. There seemed to be no room for Mac in the Tigers' infield, and Tacoma exercised its option to re-sign him in January.[14]

During the 1914-15 offseason, McMullin played for an Imperial Valley winter-league team in El Centro, California, near the Mexican border; his teammates included major leaguers Dave Bancroft, Slim Love, and Emil "Irish" Meusel.[15] Although McMullin struggled at the plate, he still attracted the attention of Frank Dillon, manager of the Pacific Coast League's Los Angeles Angels, and signed with the Angels on February 11.[16]

McMullin was expected to fight for the third-base job with veteran George Metzger, a career minor leaguer. Surprisingly, it was Mac's hitting that was thought to give him an edge. His .293 average at Tacoma in 1914 was nearly 60 points higher than Metzger's, although Harry A. Williams of the *Los Angeles Times* cautioned that Mac "may encounter considerable difficulty in establishing business relations with the Coast League hurlers."[17]

Williams's words were on the mark, as McMullin started slowly at the plate while facing faster company. But his play at second base was solid, and he rivaled future major leaguer Joe Gedeon—who would play an indirect role in the Black Sox Scandal a few years later—among the PCL's top middle infielders. McMullin's average began to creep toward .300 by midseason. When the *Los Angeles Times* picked its PCL all-star team, Mac was chosen at third base, along with Gedeon and—coincidentally—two of Fred's future White Sox teammates, Swede Risberg of Vernon and Lefty Williams of Salt Lake City.[18]

McMullin sustained his first serious injury on July 23, when San Francisco's Biff Schaller spiked him in the leg in the first inning. Mac was carried off the field and taken to a local hospital. He was sidelined for nearly three weeks.[19] During the layoff, McMullin got married. He and his bride, 23-year-old Delia A. Barnabe, were wed on August 5 by a justice of the peace at the Orange County Courthouse in Santa Ana, California.[20]

Delia was the daughter of an Austrian immigrant who had moved west with her family around the same time as the McMullins a decade earlier; they had also settled in Lincoln Heights near downtown Los Angeles. Born in 1892 in Fort Lee, New Jersey, Delia was the oldest of Louis and Margaret (Kotze) Barnabe's three children. Their youngest son, Charles Barnabe, played 16 seasons in professional baseball, including 29 appearances for the White Sox in 1927-28.

In the meantime, the Chicago White Sox and New York Yankees were engaged in a fierce battle for McMullin's services.

George Davis, a Hall of Fame shortstop for the Giants and White Sox, was now a Yankees scout and he had been watching McMullin and infielder Zeb Terry for weeks. After the Angels returned home from a road trip to San Francisco on August 26, Davis went to Los Angeles vice president T.J. Darmody eager to sign the young pair to contracts. The White Sox had an agreement with the Angels to purchase any player on their roster, but the deadline for that option was August 15. When White Sox owner Charles Comiskey sent word that he wouldn't take any Angels—despite reports that one or both might be included in a trade for Cleveland Indians star Joe Jackson—Terry and McMullin became fair game for the Yankees.[21]

However, according to *Los Angeles Times* writer Harry A. Williams, an urgent telegram from Comiskey arrived in Darmody's office 10 minutes before Davis showed up—closing the deal with Chicago. Reported Williams: "Davis was visibly disappointed.... The sale of Terry and Mac to the White Sox was outright and for cash, delivery to be made next spring.... Fast and brainy, Terry and McMullen [sic] not only form the youngest keystone combination in the league, but one of the best in its history.... It was only by a small fraction of time that Terry and McMullen failed to land with New York instead of Chicago." The two players were sold for $7,000 each and finished out the season with the Angels.[22] McMullin hit at a solid .279 clip, with 25 doubles and 33 stolen bases (eighth in the league). He was also the PCL's top sacrifice bunter, with 49.

Chicago's infield, like the Tigers' a year earlier, was crowded. Mac had an idea how tough it would be to break into the Sox lineup: "The only chance I would have against [Eddie] Collins at second base would be for Eddie to drop dead."[23] Zeb Terry, not McMullin, won the shortstop's job in spring training, while Buck Weaver began the season at third base. Mac would have to wait to get a chance in the big leagues.

Even his first appearance with the White Sox was not an appearance at all—on April 16 against the Browns, McMullin was sent up to pinch-hit for pitcher Mellie Wolfgang in the seventh inning. St. Louis then substituted Dave Davenport for starter Carl Weilman, who had walked the bases loaded. So Chicago manager Pants Rowland replaced McMullin with lefty-hitting Jack Lapp to face the right-handed Davenport. Lapp walked to force in a run, but the White Sox still lost the game, 6-5.

Mac got his first major-league hit a week later at Cleveland, a single off left-hander Fritz Coumbe, after subbing for Terry at shortstop again. The White Sox, with a 6-8 start, had fallen to seventh place and Rowland was looking to shake things up. On April 27 he benched Terry and inserted McMullin into the starting lineup, moving Weaver back to shortstop.[24]

The moves paid immediate dividends, as the White Sox' three-game losing streak ended with a 5-3 win. Rowland stuck with the revamped lineup the next day, and Mac singled to drive in his first major-league run, the Sox' only run in a 2-1 loss to Cleveland, on April 28. Chicago ran off three straight wins after the shakeup, but then lost nine of 11 to fall into last place.

A bad break cost McMullin the best chance he would have to hold onto a regular spot. On June 2 he sustained an injury in pregame practice at Detroit. It was originally diagnosed as a badly sprained foot, thought to put him out for a couple of weeks. It turned out to be a bone fracture, and it sidelined McMullin for more than a month. He was hitting .295, 10th best in the American League, but Chicago was still only in sixth place.[25]

McMullin returned to the starting lineup on July 10, going hitless in seven at-bats in a doubleheader against the Red Sox. The time off had disrupted his hitting stroke. He began a 2-for-25 slump, and his average fell to .257 by the end of the season. Chicago moved into a tie for first in early August, but the White Sox' run atop the American League lasted less than a week and Boston won its second consecutive pennant.

For his part, McMullin hit .257 in 68 games as a rookie, although he scored just eight runs. He went home to California pleased with his performance and optimistic about 1917. In November he helped the Angels celebrate a "day" for ex-Cubs star Frank Chance. The "Peerless Leader" had managed Los Angeles to the PCL championship, and McMullin and Zeb Terry returned to play against the Angels as part of an all-star team formed for the occasion.[26]

Later that month, on November 23, Fred's wife, Delia, delivered a son, William, at home in Los Angeles. Mac was overjoyed—even going so far as to publicly request a trade back to the Coast League so he could be closer to his family.[27] McMullin's "holdout" didn't last long; he signed another one-year deal with Chicago on February 27 and prepared for training camp at Mineral Wells, Texas.[28] Thirty-year-old veteran Chick Gandil had been purchased from Cleveland for $3,500 to shore up first base. With Eddie Collins and Buck Weaver still around, shortstop was the only open position—and four players were fighting for it.

Risberg won the shortstop job to open the season and the White Sox started on fire, winning five of their first six games and nine of their first eleven. Pitcher Eddie Cicotte, on his way to a league-leading 28 wins and 1.53 ERA, no-hit the St. Louis Browns in his first start, on April 14.

By the end of the month, the White Sox were tied for first place and their lineup was set—and healthy. As a result, McMullin and four other reserves remained in Chicago as the team left for a road trip to Cleveland and St. Louis. Mac had made only two pinch-hit appearances, grounding out both times.

It wasn't until May 20 that Mac got any extended time in place of Risberg—even then, it took an injury to Swede, and a pinch-hitter for Zeb Terry, whom McMullin replaced in the sixth inning, for Fred to get into the game. His first start in 1917 did not even count as an official game: it was an in-season exhibition on May 28 in Waterloo, Iowa, although he made the most of his action, getting two hits and scoring twice. Mac got another start—and two more hits—in a June 4 exhibition at Newark, New Jersey.[29]

On June 16 McMullin's name appeared in the same sentence with gamblers for the first time. This time, he was hailed as a hero (at least in Chicago).

The White Sox had come to Fenway Park for four games with the second-place Red Sox. After Lefty Williams blanked Boston 8-0 on Friday, June 15, Eddie Cicotte and Babe Ruth hooked up in a pitcher's duel the next afternoon, when threatening clouds appeared in the sky. With the White Sox ahead 2-0 in the fifth inning, rain began to fall. Some fans behind first base, disappointed at the score, began cries of "call the game!"—ostensibly to save the rain checks on their tickets. But newspapers in both Chicago and Boston reported the real reason: to keep their bets on the home team from being lost.[30]

The Red Sox management had staffed the game with only two policemen for security, far too few to prevent an uprising in the stands. With two outs in the fifth—one more out and the game would become official—"some tall man in a long rain coat took command. Waving to his comrades to follow, he boldly leaped out upon the field. In ten seconds, he must have had 500 followers." On the surface, they appeared to be heading for the covered pavilion to escape the rain. But this also was the part of the park "where the so-called sporting men congregate daily," and it was there that "the first cries of 'call the game' were heard, and it spread like wildfire." Once on the field, the "rain-check athletes" milled around until officers from the nearby Boylston Street police station arrived and shooed them into the grandstands. It took 45 minutes to clear the field.[31]

Near the Chicago dugout, where the fans were being herded off the field, the White Sox players desperately tried to make their way under the stands and out of harm's way. In the commotion, McMullin and Buck Weaver got into an altercation with a fan, who later identified himself as Augustine J. McNally, of Norwood, Massachusetts. The *Chicago Tribune* reported: "During the fussing, [McNally] is supposed to have bumped McMullin's fist with his eye. Also he is supposed to have had his fingers on the railing just when Weaver let his bat fall."[32]

Eventually, the dust settled and play resumed in the fifth. Weaver became one of the first few players to hit a home run over the left-field wall at Fenway Park (not yet painted green, or known as "The Monster"), and the White Sox beat the Red Sox, 7-2.

The trouble lingered for McMullin and Weaver, who were served with arrest warrants—McNally had filed assault charges in Roxbury District Court—the following Monday. But after losing a Bunker Hill Day doubleheader, the White Sox immediately left for Chicago, and the case was defaulted until the players could return to Boston later that summer. The trial was delayed again on July 31, and the charges were dropped by the time the White Sox finished their final road trip to Fenway Park in late September.[33]

Ban Johnson raised a ruckus after hearing of the riot in Boston. The founder of the American League "declared war on gamblers," who he admitted had instigated the riot. "Gambling has never been tolerated by our league," Johnson said. "This spring, [Red Sox owner Harry] Frazee advised me he had installed special police in the pavilion where the gamblers congregate. They were put there solely to break up the practice."[34] The gamblers, of course, continued to congregate—at Fenway Park, and across the major leagues.

In early September the White Sox went on a tear. A four-game sweep of the Tigers on Labor Day weekend—an infamous series that would be recalled 10 years later, as Swede Risberg and Chick Gandil accused Detroit of laying down—was the start of a nine-game winning streak for Chicago. With Weaver out because of a broken hand, Mac was in the thick of it all. On September 5 he led a game-winning rally in the 11th inning to beat St. Louis, 4-1. Four days later he initiated a clash with Cleveland's Jack Graney that resulted in a riot, and the game was forfeited to the White Sox. Chicago opened up a six-game lead on Boston to coast to the pennant.

With the World Series in sight, manager Pants Rowland began to set his lineup for the National League champion New York Giants. Weaver's return in mid-September created a clutter in the infield, and this time Risberg was the odd man out. The *Chicago Tribune* reported: "McMullin has been hitting and fielding so well that Manager Rowland hates to remove him now that Weaver has recovered."[35]

McMullin's unexpected performance while filling in during Weaver's absence brought comparisons to another "super-sub" in Chicago's past — former infielder George Rohe, who took over for injured Hall of Fame shortstop George Davis (the same Davis who had tried to sign McMullin for the Yankees two years back) during the White Sox' first championship season, in 1906. Rohe was also one of the stars in the World Series victory over the Cubs.[36]

McMullin had a similar influence in Game One against the Giants. He was hailed as "Chicago's hero" after driving in the first run of the fall classic. His third-inning double eluded New York center fielder Benny Kauff and scored Shano Collins to give the White Sox a 1-0 lead. One inning later, Happy Felsch homered to provide the decisive margin in a 2-1 victory behind Eddie Cicotte. Mac finished 1-for-3 and made two spectacular plays in the field.

In Game Two, McMullin's RBI single to center knocked out losing pitcher Fred Anderson in the fourth inning as the White Sox scored five times and breezed to a 7-2 win. He again handled three chances in the field flawlessly.

Mac's bat went cold thereafter, as he finished the Series with one hit in his last 16 at-bats. But he remained "a

tower of strength defensively" at third base, starting two key double plays in Game Five and not committing an error.[37]

The White Sox won their second championship with a 4-2 victory in Game Six — made famous by Eddie Collins' "mad dash" across an unguarded home plate as New York's Heinie Zimmerman gave chase. (The day after the Series ended, McMullin and baseball clown Germany Schaefer re-enacted the play to great acclaim in an exhibition game for soldiers at Camp Mills, New York.)[38]

The White Sox partied hard on the train back to Chicago, where the players received their World Series bonus checks of $3,669.32. McMullin spent most of his on a small bungalow in Lincoln Heights, less than two miles from where he had grown up and a few blocks from where Delia's parents lived. He lived in that house on Baldwin Street for the rest of his life.[39]

McMullin began the 1918 season as a strong favorite to remain as a regular at third base. The press called the White Sox infield "the best in the country," and it was said "there is no chance that Mac will have to adorn the bench this year."[40] Risberg's spring performance turned heads, however, and by the end of spring training Pants Rowland was still deciding whether to remain with the lineup that won him the World Series. It was Risberg who opened the season at third base, but McMullin took over in the fourth game. The Sox promptly won four straight.[41]

Mac took advantage of the opportunity and, by May 8, he was hitting an even .400 — second only to Boston's Babe Ruth (.407) in the American League, and ahead of Tris Speaker (.393) and teammate Joe Jackson (.379). But a 4-for-27 slump over the next seven games dropped McMullin's average and, a week later, he was down to .299.

His productive season came to a halt on May 30, when he was spiked by Cleveland's Ray Chapman in the first inning of the nightcap and carried off the field with a deep gash just above his knee. He missed nearly three weeks and was only rushed back then because

Weaver was out with a strained groin and Risberg was bruised up, as well. At the time of his injury, McMullin was hitting .312.

By then the defending champion White Sox were floundering just barely above .500, in fourth place. They were without the services of Joe Jackson, who had taken a job in the shipyards. In late June Chick Gandil left a game in the seventh inning to make an appearance before his draft board on his plea for deferment.[42] World War I cast a great shadow over baseball in 1918, and every team was affected.

On July 1 the US government's "work or fight" order went into effect—and draft-eligible players had to join the military or find "essential" wartime jobs. McMullin played on for another five weeks—and reached a milestone in the process, hitting his only major-league home run, an inside-the-parker, on August 1 against Washington's Ed Matteson at Comiskey Park.[43]

Two days later McMullin had his sixth three-hit game of the season, this one against Philadelphia, in front of a tiny crowd of less than 1,000. On August 7 he and Risberg decided to enlist—Swede headed to an Army base in the Bay Area, while Mac joined the Navy and was placed at a submarine base in San Pedro, outside Los Angeles. There, he joined a servicemen's league that included future Hall of Famers Harry Heilmann and Sam Crawford, as well as major leaguers Irish and Bob Meusel, Howard Ehmke, and Red Killefer, among others.[44]

Mac's best season in the big leagues ended with a .277 average, one home run, 16 RBIs, and 32 runs scored in 70 games. When the war ended in November, he and the White Sox looked forward to another run at a championship. Worries about postwar attendance caused owners to shorten the 1919 season to 140 games and cut players' salaries. McMullin signed for $2,750 after staging a holdout through late March. The *Los Angeles Times* reported that he again was seeking a trade back to the Pacific Coast League, but White Sox owner Charles Comiskey seemed to ignore his demands again.[45]

While the holdout likely didn't play a role, Mac found himself opening the season on the bench as Risberg beat him out for a starting spot in the infield. After a solid year in 1918 and a contributing role in the 1917 championship stretch, McMullin's lack of playing time drew the attention of *The Sporting News*: "Can you beat it the way managers are letting this fellow hang around the Sox bench when one of them could grab him off—a player good enough to help win the league and flag and clinch a world's pennant, and at the height of his game in the big leagues!"[46]

But the White Sox, on the backs of pitchers Eddie Cicotte and Lefty Williams, soared to a 24-7 start to take a five-game lead on Cleveland. McMullin received scant playing time in the first three months. His longest stretch was in replacement of an injured Eddie Collins at second base for a few games in late May. But as the Sox slumped in June, falling out of the league lead for the first time on June 23, new manager Kid Gleason—a longtime White Sox coach who had taken over for Pants Rowland—decided to shake up his lineup.

For the second time in three seasons, McMullin was brought in to provide a spark. Just as in 1917, Buck Weaver moved back to shortstop and Mac took over at third base. "This arrangement, the same that was used in humbling the New York Giants ... proved a lucky one in the first game after it was made. The Sox defeated the Browns, and McMullin made two hits. Whether it makes a turning point in the club's fortunes remains to be seen," *The Sporting News* reported.[47]

It did. Just as in 1917, the White Sox immediately got hot. After leaving St. Louis, Chicago took three of four from Cleveland and came home to win four of five against Detroit to storm back atop the standings. McMullin's best effort was a 4-for-5, two-triple performance on July 13, his single-game high for hits. He finished the season with career-best totals in batting (.294), doubles (8), and RBIs (19) in 60 appearances.

By the end of August, Chicago's lead was up to six games, and the pennant was "a foregone conclusion." *The Atlanta Constitution* reported that the White Sox were a 7-to-10 betting favorite over the National League champion Cincinnati Reds. The odds dropped to 5 to 6 by late September, and late betting before the Series began made the Reds a 7-to-10 favorite in some places. The reason for the shift in odds would soon become clear.[48]

Joe Jackson clinched the pennant for good on September 24 with a ninth-inning walkoff single in a 6-5 victory over the St. Louis Browns. For the final week of the season, McMullin was assigned to travel to Cincinnati to scout the Reds in their last series, against the Chicago Cubs.[49]

Whether Mac followed manager Kid Gleason's orders and returned with accurate scouting reports remains up for debate nearly a century later.[50] What is known is that sometime that fall, McMullin found himself involved in what historians Harold and Dorothy Seymour called "baseball's darkest hour": the fixing of the 1919 World Series.[51]

Most sources, possibly following the lead of Eliot Asinof's *Eight Men Out*, seem to agree that McMullin's involvement in the plot happened by chance.[52] He overheard a conversation with good friend Swede Risberg, in a locker room or a bathroom or a hotel room, and asked to share in the profits. Some have claimed that McMullin, along with first baseman Chick Gandil, was one of the instigators of the fix.[53] (In fact, Eddie Cicotte was among them — the White Sox pitcher later testified that "the idea of the fix had originated in a conversation with Gandil and McMullin.")[54] The truth might be somewhere in between. Mac certainly was present for most of the meetings before the Series discussing the fix. He also roomed with pitcher Lefty Williams, a co-conspirator, at the Hotel Sinton in Cincinnati, and he was rarely seen without Swede Risberg, his fellow Californian, by his side throughout the Series.[55]

What compelled McMullin to risk his career for a promised payoff of $20,000? Perhaps he was frustrated over his lack of playing time — he had certainly played well enough to warrant a starting job in the major leagues, and the White Sox had never seemed to give

him a fair chance at that. Or maybe he was bitter at Comiskey's dismissal of his desire to be closer to Los Angeles, near his family. His preseason holdouts usually had been accompanied by demands for a trade. And while Comiskey's reputation as a penny-pinching magnate has lived on despite the fact that his payroll was near the top of the American League,[56] McMullin's salary of $2,750 was among the lowest on the team. A nearly 1,000 percent raise for a week's worth of work would go a long way.

Perhaps the answer is more basic: It looked like an easy score. Indeed, gambling had been a part of baseball since the sport became popular and rumors of fixed games, even in the World Series, had been rampant since the first one in 1903.[57] Money often changed hands from player to gambler and from player to player. Back in 1917, it was well known that the White Sox players had collected a pool of $45 apiece to pay off the Detroit Tigers — ostensibly as a "reward" for beating the rival Boston Red Sox in a crucial series down the stretch, but more likely it was to "thank" them for laying down in those infamous Labor Day doubleheaders which Chicago had swept.[58]

McMullin certainly knew the story of Hal Chase, formerly a teammate of some of his White Sox pals and widely suspected to be the most corrupt player in baseball. Chase had been accused numerous times of taking bribes and had openly tried to entice other players to do the same. After one such incident in Cincinnati, Chase was suspended by Reds manager Christy Mathewson, who reported it to National League President John Heydler. Instead, Chase was acquitted. Mathewson, infuriated, ran him off the team. It made no difference to Chase; he was soon picked up by John McGraw's New York Giants, and continued fixing games without repercussions. Chase — who like Gandil, Risberg, and McMullin had California connections — also became involved in the World Series fix, reportedly as a middleman for gamblers Bill Burns and Abe Attell.[59]

Whatever his motivation actually was, McMullin didn't receive many opportunities — at least on the field — to "earn" the $5,000 he reportedly received for agreeing to help throw the World Series. He singled in a pinch-hit appearance off Reds starter Dutch Ruether in the eighth inning of Game One, and grounded out against Cincinnati's Slim Sallee to end Game Two. Both were White Sox losses. Chicago went on to lose the best-of-nine Series in eight games.

Despite his lack of playing time, Mac's name quickly surfaced behind the scenes as rumors swirled that the World Series was not on the level. It was a charge that McMullin vehemently denied, threatening to "punch anybody in the nose who dared suggest he was in on any wrongdoing."[60] But St. Louis gambler Harry Redmon allegedly tipped off manager Kid Gleason to McMullin's involvement, and when White Sox owner Charles Comiskey sent a private detective, John Hunter, to California to investigate talk of a fix, McMullin was one of the players he tried to interview.[61]

For a few weeks Comiskey withheld World Series bonuses—the losers' share came out to $3,254.36 that year—for the eight players rumored to be involved. But McMullin and two other players complained to American League President Ban Johnson, and the checks were soon on their way.[62]

The Los Angeles Times reported that McMullin returned home "all upholstered like a davenport, … [with] a sufficient sum to make him fair picking for the profiteers this winter." It was an ominous note.[63]

McMullin played winter ball for a team called Killefer's All-Stars, headlined by Chicago Cubs catcher Bill Killefer and including stars such as Gavvy Cravath, Sam Crawford, and Jimmy Austin. Buck Weaver also headlined a team, Weaver's All-Stars, whose main attraction was newly crowned home run king Babe Ruth.[64]

Talk of the fixed World Series died down as the 1920 season began. Comiskey, eager to put all the rumors to rest, offered Mac a substantial raise, from $2,750 to $3,600, for his fifth season in Chicago. Unlike in years past, McMullin quickly sent back his signed contract and reported for spring training in Waco, Texas, where he took over at third base while Weaver moved to shortstop. Risberg staged a holdout until early April.[65]

On the field, Mac's season was forgettable: He posted career lows in every statistical category, batting just .197 in 46 games. Off the field there were persistent doubts about his activities—he was said to be the "point man" for gamblers in games that the White Sox were supposed to have thrown, a rumor that was even brought up by American League President Ban Johnson.[66]

If any games were lost purposely by the White Sox that year, there is no firsthand documentation of which ones they were, and McMullin's involvement never has been clarified. In Eight Men Out, Eliot Asinof specifically lists an April 27 loss to Cleveland as being one of them. On May 9 the "careless Sox" dropped another suspicious game to the Indians. There were reports that Mac offered Buck Weaver $500 to help throw a midseason game, which Weaver "angrily" declined.[67]

The pattern continued throughout the summer. Chicago stayed within range of the American League lead—but was in first place for only eight days after May 7. Ban Johnson had claimed he heard that "the Sox would not dare win the pennant" because of their ties to gamblers.[68]

By September the talk of corruption in baseball was too loud to ignore. A grand jury was convened in Chicago, and McMullin was implicated along with Buck Weaver, Chick Gandil, Swede Risberg, Joe Jackson, Eddie Cicotte, Lefty Williams, and Happy Felsch for fixing the 1919 World Series.

During the season's final week, the rumors made Mac a target for opposing fans—and ballplayers. Tris Speaker, the Cleveland manager, scuffled with McMullin before a game at League Park, snapping, "When you birds get back to Chicago and you feel like talking, you can do a lot of it before the grand jury, and your role won't be that of a witness, either!"[69]

McMullin was a major focus in one of the last stories before Cicotte made his confession to the grand jury.

On September 25 the *Chicago Tribune* wrote about a "mystery package … in the shape of currency" that Mac had reportedly delivered to Buck Weaver's home during the Series. The *Tribune* claimed it was the first evidence that the players had been paid to throw games the previous fall, and that new witnesses would be called to verify it. Mac immediately denied the charges that he had paid Weaver, and few sources since have claimed that Weaver ever received money. The story is mostly forgotten now.[70]

After Cicotte's confession on September 28, owner Charles Comiskey immediately suspended McMullin and the other six players. (Chick Gandil had held out in a contract dispute for the entire season.) They were indicted a few weeks later for the vague charge of "conspiracy to commit an illegal act." McMullin traveled to Illinois at his own expense and, accompanied by Buck Weaver and attorney Thomas Nash, paid a $10,000 bond on November 5. McMullin went back home to California and took a job as a carpenter as he awaited trial.[71]

While in Los Angeles, McMullin worked for the Universal film studio and accepted an invitation to play in a winter league for that company's team (which included his brother-in-law, Charlie Barnabe). Investigator Harry Neily, in a letter to AL President Ban Johnson, wrote that McMullin "enjoys a very good reputation out here and the natives were reluctant to believe that he was guilty of misconduct."[72]

Still, there was some grumbling about his presence until the local Manager's Association—which controlled dozens of independent and semipro teams in Southern California—passed a "vote of confidence" in January, allowing Mac to play. One week later, Philadelphia Phillies owner William F. Baker levied a $100 fine against outfielder Emil "Irish" Meusel for playing in a game with the disgraced "Black Sox" infielder, and other teams in Organized Baseball threatened to do the same. It was understood, *The Sporting News* reported, that McMullin was persona non grata on the same field with "honest" ballplayers. So Mac resigned from the team on January 12, reportedly "because of the embarrassment which it was causing some of the other players." He kept his job at the film studio, however.[73]

Even out of uniform, McMullin wasn't welcome around baseball. In May he paid his way into Washington Park to visit with former White Sox teammates Byrd Lynn, Ted Jourdan, and Joe Jenkins, who were playing for the Salt Lake club in the Pacific Coast League. But there developed "a situation so tense as to be almost painful," as manager Gavvy Cravath "turned his back" on McMullin and gave him "a stony stare" when he approached the bench. The *Los Angeles Times* opined that "Mac would save himself, the management and his friends … a lot of embarrassment if he would absent himself, or at least keep in the background." McMullin called the treatment a "persecution."[74]

Meanwhile, in Chicago, the conspiracy trial was no closer to opening and indictments were returned for a second time in the spring of 1921. McMullin was "in hard luck" financially and could not afford to travel back to Illinois. He sent word that the state would have to pay his way for him to be able to stand trial, but his requests—and, indeed, the charges against him—were ignored by all parties. He declined to pay his new bail of $7,500, and a warrant was issued for his arrest. But the state of California refused to extradite him. (It also had refused to extradite Hal Chase, on the grounds that a proper warrant for his arrest had not been issued.) By the time McMullin raised enough money to travel to Chicago on his own, the trial had already begun without him.[75]

The trial was beset by prosecutorial clumsiness and most observers considered it to be a farce. Before the jury began deliberation on August 2, Judge Hugo Friend stated that he would overturn guilty verdicts against Happy Felsch and Buck Weaver because so little evidence had been presented against them.[76]

So McMullin watched from afar as a jury failed to convict his seven former teammates, returning their verdict at 11:22 P.M. But whatever hope he had of returning to the White Sox was short-lived, as Judge

Landis famously banned them all the next day. McMullin's professional career was over.

Like many players of that era, McMullin kept quiet about the scandal in the decades afterward. How did he feel about losing his livelihood and being banished from the game at 29 years old? Only he knew. Unlike Buck Weaver, he never applied for reinstatement to the major leagues. Unlike Joe Jackson, he never proclaimed his innocence publicly. He did not give interviews, and if anyone asked him about it, what he revealed in those conversations is probably lost to history.[77]

The common perception is that McMullin disappeared after the trial. The phrases "dropped out of sight," "quietly vanished," and "mysterious" were all used to describe his life after baseball by writers who brought up the Black Sox. Eliot Asinof, in *Eight Men Out*, did not even mention his whereabouts.[78]

But he never really went anywhere. His sister, Faye, moved in with Fred and Delia for a year before moving back home to Inglewood, where she later married the city's first elected mayor, Hugh Lawrence. Meanwhile, Fred continued to work as a carpenter around Los Angeles through 1922, when a second child, Ionia, was born. (Another daughter, also named Delia, was born in 1923.) Fred took various office jobs until the end of the decade. In 1928 he signed on as a traffic manager with the Thomas Haverty Co., where his brother Dale worked as a salesman. But they both lost their jobs a few years later when the Great Depression hit home.[79]

Both son William and daughter Ionia exhibited their father's skill on the diamond, playing ball for their high-school teams in the mid-1930s. Fred attended their games regularly, and was also seen at various semipro games in Lincoln Heights and at Brookside Park in nearby Pasadena.[80] Ionia later earned a degree from UCLA, as did her younger sister, Delia.

In 1941 Fred began a new career, in law enforcement, that would last the rest of his life. He took a job as a Los Angeles County deputy marshal, where his duties included acting as a bailiff for the Municipal Court, enforcing repossessions and serving arrest warrants and eviction notices—incidents that sometimes required the same quick and brave reactions he used when he played third base in the major leagues.[81] McMullin showed a sense of compassion on the job, once delaying an eviction order against a blind woman after watching her struggle to pack up her four kids' belongings in her upstairs flat.[82] After four years, he earned a promotion to senior court officer (he was among the highest in his class in a written examination, although he finished last in the interview portion), and in 1947 moved up another rank, to captain, where he supervised a division of marshals. Even then, his salary was just $417 per month—less than what some of his White Sox teammates had been making in 1919.[83]

When the marshal department and municipal courts were reorganized by the Civil Service Commission in 1950-51, McMullin and another captain, Harry G. Hurley, who had joined the marshals around the same time as McMullin, were reassigned and lost their rank. They sued the commission in March 1952 and Superior Court Judge Frank Swain ordered the county marshal to restore their ranks and salary, also awarding them back pay of $286.50 apiece.[84]

McMullin would not live to benefit from the judgment for very long. In his final years, he suffered from arteriosclerosis, a heart ailment. On November 19, 1952, just over a month after his 61st birthday, he had a stroke that caused hemorrhaging in the brain; he died a day later, at 4:40 P.M. on November 20. He was buried at Inglewood Park Cemetery.[85]

ACKNOWLEDGEMENTS

Special thanks to the following for their generous assistance: Mark Armour, Carlos Bauer, Marc Blau, Gene Carney, Sesar Carreno, Judy Cash, Timothy Gay, Shav Glick, Tracy Greer, Bob Hoie, Rick Huhn, Bill James, Brian Kamens, Mike Kopf, Bill Lamb, Len Levin, Jim McConnell, Ray Nemec, Rod Nelson, Rob Neyer, Mike Nola, Bill Nowlin, Gabriel Schechter, Ron Selter, Bob Timmermann, David Turk, Dr. Ben Wedro, Paul Wendt, and the staff at the public libraries in Los Angeles, San Bernardino, and San Diego, California; Tacoma, Washington; and the National Baseball Hall of Fame Library in Cooperstown, New York.

NOTES

1   "The White Sox Lucky Man," *Chicago Tribune*, July 15, 1919, 16.

2   Paul Green, "After the Scandal: The Later Lives of the Banished Sox," *Sports Collectors Digest*, April 22, 1988, 198.

3   Information from United States Census via Ancestry.com and RootsWeb.com, accessed online January 24, 2007. Two of the nine McMullin children died in infancy.

4   Christopher Bell, *Scapegoats: Baseballers Whose Careers Are Marked By One Fateful Play* (Jefferson, North Carolina: McFarland & Co., 2002), 21; *Los Angeles Times*, December 28, 1930; March 25, 1936; May 5, 1940.

5   Jim McConnell, "Football Wasn't Pasadena's Only Game in Town," *Pasadena Star-News*, March 25, 2002; Jay Berman, "A Streetcar Named Obscurity," *The National Pastime*, Society for American Baseball Research, 2000, 58-60.

6   *Los Angeles Examiner*, September 26, 1910; *The Sporting News*, October 6, 1910, 8; "Fred McMullin." SABR Minor Leagues Database, accessed online at Baseball-Reference.com.

7   "Northwestern League." *Spalding's Official Base Ball Guide, 1915* (New York: A.G. Spalding & Bros.), 225, accessed online on July 16, 2008, at memory.loc.gov/ammem/spaldinghtml/spaldinghome.html.

8   Russ Dille, "When Giants Walked Seattle," The Online Encyclopedia of Washington State History, accessed online July 15, 2008, at historylink.org/essays/output.cfm?file_id=7124. Curated by David S. Eskenazi.

9   *Tacoma Daily News*, March 23, 1914.

10 *Tacoma Daily News*, June 16, 1914.

11 *Tacoma Daily News*, July 24, 1914; *Tacoma Daily News*, July 25, 1914.

12 *Tacoma Daily News*, August 12, 1914; *Tacoma Daily News*, August 14, 1914.

13 *Boston Globe*, August 28, 1914; *The Sporting News*, August 27, 1914; *The Sporting News*, August 20, 1914.

14 *Racine Journal-News*, January 7, 1915; *The Sporting News*, September 10, 1914; *The Sporting News*, September 10, 1914.

15 William F. McNeil, *The California Winter League: America's First Integrated Professional Baseball League* (Jefferson, North Carolina: McFarland & Co., 2002), 47-49.

16 *Los Angeles Times*, August 18, 1915.

17 *Los Angeles Times*, February 12, 1915.

18 *Los Angeles Times*, August 25, 1915.

19 *Los Angeles Times*, July 23, 1915; *Los Angeles Examiner*, August 4, 1915.

20 Marriage license for Fred McMullin and Delia Barnabe, Registration No. 1915400776, Orange County Clerk-Recorder's Office, Santa Ana, California.

21 *Washington Post*, August 6, 1915; *Los Angeles Examiner*, August 17, 1915; *Los Angeles Examiner*, August 20, 1915; *Los Angeles Examiner*, August 21, 1915; *The Sporting News*, August 26, 1915; *Reno Evening Gazette*, September 8, 1915.

22 *Los Angeles Times*, August 27, 1915; *Chicago Tribune*, August 27, 1915; *Chicago Tribune*, January 27, 1939.

23 *Los Angeles Times*, October 15, 1915.

24 *Chicago Tribune*, April 28, 1916.

25 *Chicago Tribune*, June 3, 1916; *Washington Post*, June 4, 1916; *Atlanta Constitution*, June 18, 1916.

26 *Los Angeles Times*, November 6, 1916.

27 *Los Angeles Times*, January 25, 1917.

28 Ancestry.com, *California Birth Index, 1905-1995*, *Chicago Tribune*, February 28, 1917; *Los Angeles Times*, February 28, 1917.

29 *Chicago Tribune*, May 21, 1917; *Chicago Tribune*, May 29, 1917; *Chicago Tribune*, June 4, 1917.

30 *Boston Globe*, June 17, 1917; *Chicago Tribune*, June 17, 1917.

31 Ibid.

32 *Chicago Tribune*, June 19, 1917.

33 *Chicago Tribune*, August 1, 1917; *Chicago Tribune*, June 18, 1917; Richard Lindberg, *Who's On Third: The Chicago White Sox Story* (South Bend, Indiana: Icarus Press, 1983), 39-40.

34 *Chicago Tribune*, June 18, 1917.

35 *Chicago Tribune*, September 19, 1917.

36 *Sheboygan Press*, August 20, 1917; *Warren* (Pennsylvania) *Evening Times*, October 2, 1917.

37 *Chicago Tribune*, October 14, 1917.

38 *New York Times*, October 17, 1917; *Washington Post*, October 16, 1917.

39 *Chicago Tribune*, October 18, 1917; "World Series Gate Receipts and Player Shares," Baseball-Almanac.com; accessed online June 22, 2008, at baseball-almanac.com/ws/wsshares.shtml; Los Angeles city directories, 1918-42.

40 *Washington Post*, March 26, 1918; *Chicago Tribune*, March 28, 1918.

41 *Chicago Tribune*, April 26, 1916.

42 *Chicago Tribune*, June 25, 1918.

43 *Chicago Tribune*, August 2, 1918; *Chicago Tribune*, August 2, 1918; *Washington Post*, August 2, 1918.

44 *Chicago Tribune*, August 8, 1918, 14; *Los Angeles Times*, August 9, 1918.

45 *Los Angeles Times*, February 15, 1919; *Chicago Tribune*, February 19, 1919; *Chicago Tribune*, April 2, 1919.

46 *The Sporting News*, June 19, 1919.

47 *The Sporting News*, July 3, 1919.

48 *Atlanta Constitution*, August 31, 1919; *Chicago Tribune*, October 2, 1919.

49 *Washington Post*, September 25, 1919; Gene Carney, *Burying the Black Sox: How Baseball's Cover-Up of the 1919 World Series Fix Almost Succeeded* (Washington, DC: Potomac Books, 2006), 168, 215-17.

50 Mike Kopf, "Advance Scouting … Black Sox-Style." From Rob Neyer, *Rob Neyer's Big Book of Baseball Blunders* (New York: Simon & Schuster, 2006). In the article and in several personal emails with the author on July 17, 2008, Kopf suggests that McMullin's scouting reports might have contributed to the so-called "Clean Sox," including Eddie Collins, Nemo Leibold and Shano Collins, each having a subpar Series against Cincinnati pitching. "Could McMullin have told them to watch for curve-balls when they should have been bracing for heat?" he asks. "Now more than ever I think that Fred McMullin was indeed an underrated crook."

51 Harold and Dorothy Seymour, *Baseball: The Golden Age* (New York: Oxford University Press, 1989).

52 Eliot Asinof, *Eight Men Out* (New York: Henry Holt and Co., 1963), 17.

53 David Pietrusza, *Rothstein: The Life, Times and Murder of the Criminal Genius Who Fixed the 1919 World Series* (New York: Carroll and Graf Publishers, 2003), 150. Pietrusza reports that Cubs owner Charles Weeghman recalled a meeting with gambler Mont Tennes at the Saratoga horse-racing track in New York in August 1919, and "as Weeghman remembered it," Gandil and McMullin were "the players involved" in the fix. In *Eight Men Out*, Eliot Asinof relates Eddie Cicotte's grand jury testimony: "Then Gandil and McMullin took us all, one by one, away from the others and we talked turkey."

54 Gene Carney, "New Light on an Old Scandal," *The Baseball Research Journal*, Society for American Baseball Research, 2007, 74-81. Parts of Cicotte's grand jury testimony from 1920 were read back to him when he was deposed four years later in Milwaukee. Happy Felsch, Swede Risberg, and Joe Jackson had each sued the White Sox for back pay due to them. Juries awarded them a pittance of what they seeked.

55 Asinof, *Eight Men Out*, 17, 91. "Black Sox Scandal (American League records)," National Baseball Hall of Fame Library archives via the SABR Baseball Research Center, San Diego Central Library.

56 For an overview of the White Sox' salaries in 1919, which weren't as low as commonly believed, see Bob Hoie, "1919 Baseball Salaries and the Mythically Underpaid Chicago White Sox," *Base Ball: A Journal of the Early Game*, Spring 2012, McFarland & Co.

57 Carney, *Burying the Black Sox*, 44.

58 No players were punished by Commissioner Landis as a result of this "bribe," which Swede Risberg and Chick Gandil brought to light in 1927. Landis called for hearings to discuss the matter at his Chicago office, but dismissed the accusations for lack of evi-dence. The only consequence of this series was that the practice of "rewarding" opposing players, which was common in those days, was formally banned.

59 Asinof, *Eight Men Out*, 14; Carney, *Burying the Black Sox*, 250; Martin Donell Kohout, *Hal Chase: The Defiant Life and Turbulent Times of Baseball's Biggest Crook* (New York: McFarland and Co., 2001), 244-46.

60 Warren Brown, *The Chicago White Sox* (New York: G.P. Putnam's Sons, 1952) 99.

61 Carney, *Burying the Black Sox*, 50, 55; Asinof, *Eight Men Out*, 131.

62 *Chicago Tribune*, September 24, 1920; Irving Stein, *The Ginger Kid: The Buck Weaver Story* (Dubuque, Iowa: Elysian Fields Press, 1992), 224; "Black Sox Scandal (American League records)," San Diego Central Library.

63 *Los Angeles Times*, October 14, 1919.

64 McNeil, *The California Winter League*, 63-65.

65 Carney, *Burying the Black Sox*, 15; Asinof, *Eight Men Out*, 141.

66 *Chicago Tribune*, September 24, 1920; Asinof, *Eight Men Out*, 145. Carney, *Burying the Black Sox*, 212.

67 Stein, *The Ginger Kid*, 216; Bill Veeck with Ed Linn, *The Hustler's Handbook* (New York: G.P. Putnam's Sons, 1965), 284; Pietrusza, *Rothstein*, 409; *Chicago Tribune*, May 10, 1920.

68 Stein, *The Ginger Kid*, 224.

69 *Van Nuys News*, November 25, 1920.

70 *Chicago Tribune*, September 26, 1920; *New York Times*, September 26, 1920; *Boston Globe*, September 27, 1920; Asinof, *Eight Men Out*, 167.

71 *Boston Globe*, September 29, 1920; *Atlanta Constitution*, October 30, 1920; *Atlanta Constitution*, November 6, 1920; *Chicago Tribune*, November 6, 1920; Carney, *Burying the Black Sox*, 215-17; Asinof, *Eight Men Out*, 138-42.

72 "Black Sox Scandal (American League records)," San Diego Central Library.

73 *The Sporting News*, January 20, 1921; *Los Angeles Times*, January 12, 1921; *Los Angeles Times*, January 13, 1921; *The Sporting News*, January 20, 1921, 8; *The Sporting News*, January 27, 1921; "Black Sox Scandal (American League records)," San Diego Central Library.

74 *Los Angeles Times*, May 9, 1921.

75 McMullin reportedly arrived in Chicago one day after the trial began. Because he was still under indictment, prosecutors could have chosen to bring a new trial against him even after his seven teammates were declared not guilty on August 2. But State's Attorney Robert Crowe announced after the trial that "as far as I am concerned, the case is a closed book" and the charges were eventually dropped. See: *Chicago Tribune*, March 2, 1921; *Fort Wayne News-Sentinel*. August 3, 1921; Carney, *Burying the Black Sox*, 215-17; Kohout, *Hal Chase*, 246; "State Searching For Lost Papers," *Washington Post*, August 4, 1921; Bill Lamb,

Black Sox in the Courtroom: The Grand Jury, Criminal Trial, and Civil Litigation (Jefferson, North Carolina: McFarland & Co., 2013), 106-109.

76 Carney, *Burying the Black Sox,* 142-44, 147.

77 Green, "After the Scandal," 197-98.

78 In order, those phrases were used in the following articles: Bob Considine, "On the Line," *Waterloo* (Iowa) *Sunday Courier,* January 12, 1947; John Lardner, "Remember the Black Sox," *The Saturday Evening Post,* April 30, 1938; "Concessions, Denials, Obscurity," *Sports Illustrated,* September 17, 1956.

79 Los Angeles city directories, 1921-31; *Los Angeles Times,* February 5, 1931; *California Voter Registrations, 1900-1968,* accessed online at Ancestry.com, July 20, 2008.

80 *Los Angeles Times,* May 24, 1936; Los Angeles City Directory, 1938; Shav Glick, "He's A Rose by Any Other Name," *Los Angeles Times,* January 21, 2004; Shav Glick, email correspondence with author, July 14, 2005.

81 Los Angeles city directories, 1941-42; *Los Angeles Times,* April 1, 1949; *Harry G. Hurley and Fred D. McMullin v. Roy W. Carter, et al,* Case No. 597431, Los Angeles County Superior Court, filed March 27, 1952.

82 *Los Angeles Times,* March 24, 1948.

83 *Hurley v. Carter,* 1952.

84 *Hurley v. Carter,* 1952; *Los Angeles Times,* May 20, 1952.

85 *Los Angeles Mirror,* November 21, 1952; *Los Angeles Examiner,* November 22, 1952; *Los Angeles Times,* November 22, 1952; *Los Angeles Herald and Express,* November 22, 1952; *The Sporting News,* December 3, 1952; "Certificate of Death: Fred D. McMullin." Filed November 21, 1952. State of California, Department of Public Health, Reg. Dist. 1901, File No. 19321.

EDDIE MURPHY

By John Heeg

ANCOCK, NEW YORK, HAS made numerous contributions to baseball history. A mill operated there by the Hillerich & Bradsby Co. for more than eight decades provided Louisville Slugger bats to Babe Ruth, Ty Cobb, Joe DiMaggio, Ted Williams, and other hitting stars.[1] Hancock was also the hometown of John "Honest Eddie" Murphy.

Murphy was a member of two of the greatest teams of the Deadball Era, Connie Mack's Philadelphia A's and the scandal-ridden Chicago White Sox, where he earned his nickname and a reputation for integrity after eight of his teammates were accused of throwing the 1919 World Series.

Decades later, in an interview with Chic Feldman of the *Scrantonian* newspaper in Pennsylvania, Murphy said, "We might have started the dynasty that was the (New York) Yankees' good fortune. But our best players … sold their honor and souls to the gamblers and a pennant purgatory came upon the White Sox."[2]

The youngest of Charles and Theresa Murphy's six children, John Edward Murphy was born on October 2, 1891. Hancock abuts the state line with Pennsylvania. His parents later relocated the family, including siblings Frank, Charlie, Helen, Anna, and Marie, from Hancock to nearby White Mills, Pennsylvania, where Charles worked as a hotel manager along the railroad that ran from Honesdale, Pennsylvania, to Lackawaxen, New York.

Charles had a college education, which kept him out of the coal mines that dominated the northeastern Pennsylvania landscape around the turn of the 20th century. The coal industry provided plentiful job opportunities, but those opportunities came at a price. The work itself was dangerous; death, dismemberment, and the dreaded black-lung disease were constant clouds over all workers. Miners and their families also lived in poorly built company housing, purchased their goods from company-owned stores, and paid wages arbitrarily calculated by the ton of coal they loaded. The average annual salary was $375.[3]

In the early 1900s, coal companies encouraged their employees to play baseball and often hired talented players for their services on the diamond.[4] Young Eddie Murphy earned money during the summer playing with Honesdale, Pennsylvania, in the semipro Anthracite League. One day he filled in when Honesdale's starting catcher did not show up. Pitcher Big Bill Steele took one look at the 5-foot-9, 155-pound Murphy and told the manager, "This kid will never hold me!" Murphy held his own. When the game was over, Steele said to Murphy: "See you in the big leagues, kid!" By 1912 Steele was pitching for the St. Louis Cardinals when Murphy made his debut in the American League with the Philadelphia Athletics.[5]

Murphy impressed observers with his consistent ability to reach base and his speed. Manager John Dorflinger of the White Mills team in the Anthracite League was able to arrange for Murphy to attend Villanova College on a scholarship.[6] He starred at nearly every position in 1911, and after the college season that spring, he signed with the Scranton Miners at the age of 19.[7] Murphy played in 91 games. In 323 at-bats, the left-handed-hitting Murphy batted .300 with 11 doubles, 6 triples, and 1 home run.

In 1912 Murphy was acquired by the Baltimore Orioles of the International League and his play was even better at a higher level of the minors. In 122 games he hit a league-best .361 with 14 doubles, 15 triples, and 7 home runs. His performance attracted the attention of Athletics manager Connie Mack, who traded for him in the midst of a pennant race with the Boston Red Sox. Murphy made his major-league debut with the two-time defending World Series champions on August 26, 1912. In 33 games he batted .317 and scored

24 runs but the Athletics could not catch up with the Red Sox for the AL pennant.

In 1913 Murphy won a starting outfield job, replacing the aging and injured veteran Danny Murphy in right field. "People were always getting us mixed up," Eddie later said.[8] But Eddie made a name for himself in his first full season. As the A's primary leadoff hitter, he batted .295, stole 21 bases, and scored 105 runs (fourth best in the AL) as Philadelphia returned to the World Series to face the New York Giants for the third time. Behind Christy Mathewson's record-setting three shutouts, the Giants had dominated the A's in the 1905 fall classic, but the A's, powered by the heroics of Home Run Baker, had gained a measure of revenge in 1911.

Murphy mostly struggled against the Giants in the 1913 Series, hitting .227, but he did reach base three times against Mathewson in the decisive Game Five as the A's closed out the Series. In the ninth inning, Larry Doyle's flyout to end the game settled in Murphy's glove in right field and the A's were once again champions of baseball.

Murphy's old semipro manager, John Dorflinger, whose father was president of the C. Dorflinger & Sons Glass Company in White Mills, honored the hometown hero with a special glass baseball bat that

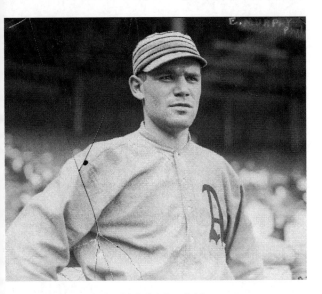

Eddie Murphy with the Philadelphia Athletics, circa 1913 (Bain Collection, Library of Congress, Prints and Photographs Division)

was hand-blown at the company's glass plant. Murphy was presented with the bat before Game Two of the World Series and it went on display at the John Wanamaker & Co. department store in Philadelphia for nearly a year before it was returned to Murphy.[9]

The 1914 season proved to be another banner year for Murphy. Playing in a career-high 148 games, he once again scored more than 100 runs and batted .272 with 36 stolen bases. His on-base percentage of .379 ranked seventh in the American League, giving sluggers like Home Run Baker, Stuffy McInnis, and Eddie Collins ample opportunities to drive him in.[10]

The A's captured their second consecutive pennant and fourth in five years, moving on to face the Boston Braves in the 1914 World Series. The Braves were heavy underdogs, but shocked the baseball world by sweeping the A's in four games, the first time that feat had been accomplished. Murphy batted just .188 with three hits in four games.

In disgust, Connie Mack broke up his A's dynasty in the offseason. He released pitchers Chief Bender, Eddie Plank, and Jack Coombs, and sold future Hall of Fame second baseman Eddie Collins to the Chicago White Sox. The depleted A's quickly became the worst team in the league and one of the worst in baseball history. By July 1 Philadelphia was in last place, 22 games behind the Red Sox, when Mack began another round of his unusual "fire sale." Young pitcher Bob Shawkey was sold to the New York Yankees, where he would become a star for the next decade, and shortstop Jack Barry was sold to the Red Sox. On July 15 Eddie Murphy joined the exodus, too. He was reunited with Collins on the White Sox, who bought him for $11,500.[11]

Murphy recalled the deal decades later: "We were in Chicago that day. Mr. Mack came to me on the field before the game and said, 'I'd like you to meet Clarence Rowland.' We went under the stands, and when I shook hands with Rowland, who was manager of the White Sox, he said, 'You ought to know I just bought you.' So, I just changed suits."[12]

Before the deal Murphy batted .231 with 13 stolen bases and 37 runs scored in 260 at-bats for the A's. His season turned around with his move to Chicago. He hit .315 over the rest of the year as the White Sox, led by Collins and the newly acquired Shoeless Joe Jackson, surged to win more than 90 games for the first time in a decade, finishing in third place.

As the White Sox' fortunes improved, however, Murphy found his playing time diminishing in the outfield. Left fielder Jackson was one of the American League's top stars, and rookie Happy Felsch promised to be a standout in center field for years to come. In right field, manager Rowland preferred to employ a platoon of Nemo Leibold and Shano Collins.

Beginning in 1916, Murphy was used primarily as a pinch-hitter in his seven-year tenure with the White Sox. After initially struggling in the role, he began to flourish and recorded batting averages of .314, .297, .486, and .339 from 1917 to 1920, averaging just 140 plate appearances a season during that span.

The White Sox finished atop the American League standings in 1917, Murphy's third pennant winner in his first five major-league seasons. But he was left off the postseason roster and did not appear in the World Series against the New York Giants, which the White Sox won in six games.

With World War I looming over the major leagues in 1918, Murphy briefly gained a starting position in the White Sox outfield after Joe Jackson and Happy Felsch left the team in midseason for war-essential work as shipbuilders. He hit .297 in 91 games, but the White Sox, missing many of their star players, tumbled to sixth place.

In 1919 Jackson, Felsch, and the others returned, and Murphy's playing time was cut back under new manager Kid Gleason. He appeared in just 30 games, but he hit .486 with 17 hits in 35 at-bats for a dissension-riddled White Sox team that beat out the Cleveland Indians for their second pennant in three years. His eight pinch hits led the American League.

Murphy later recalled that the White Sox, while "gifted" in talent, had "cliques within cliques" in the clubhouse: "The eight who were thrown out always hung out together, even at the batting cage.... (Buck) Weaver and Happy Felsch were very close, and Felsch would do anything Weaver wanted. Eddie Cicotte and Lefty Williams were close, and so were their wives." Murphy also praised Chick Gandil ("a good clutch hitter"), Joe Jackson (he "could murder the ball"), and Swede Risberg (who was "just coming into his own when the thing happened.")[13]

The "thing" Murphy referred to was the throwing of the 1919 World Series to the Cincinnati Reds. Those seven players plus utility infielder Fred McMullin were eventually banished from Organized Baseball for their roles in what became known as the Black Sox Scandal.

Murphy made just three pinch-hitting appearances in the World Series against the Reds and he was not involved in the scandal. But as he later recalled, it was hard for anyone on the team to ignore. Murphy later claimed that manager Gleason held a team meeting after Game Three and challenged the players to win the Series. According to Murphy, Gleason said, "I hear that $100,000 is to change hands if we lose." Murphy believed that "Gleason told the story to (owner Charles) Comiskey and almost anyone who would listen."[14]

But few in baseball were listening as the 1920 season began, and the White Sox returned most of their pennant-winning team for another year. Murphy was again used mostly as a pinch-hitter, batting .339 in 58 games, and the White Sox contended with the Cleveland Indians and New York Yankees for first place. As rumors of the World Series fix grew, and some observers suspected that the White Sox were throwing games in 1920 as well, tension began to mount. Murphy recalled: "We knew something was wrong for a long time, but we felt we had to keep silent because we were fighting for a pennant. We went along and gritted our teeth and played ball. It was tough."[15]

On September 28, 1920, Eddie Cicotte and Joe Jackson testified to a grand jury in Chicago about the World Series fix. All seven players implicated — Chick Gandil had retired in the offseason after a salary dispute — were immediately suspended before the final regular-season series against the St. Louis Browns. With the White Sox roster depleted, Murphy replaced Buck Weaver at third base for the final three games. He recorded four hits in the series and made one error as the White Sox were eliminated from contention and finished two games behind the Indians for the pennant.

Murphy and the other "clean Sox" not involved in the fix were hailed as heroes by the public and by team owner Charles Comiskey, who made a magnanimous gesture after the season by sending them checks for $1,500 — the difference between the winners' and losers' share of the 1919 World Series gate receipts. Comiskey's letter read, in part: "As one of the honest ball players of the Chicago White Sox team of 1919, I feel that you were deprived of the winner's share of the worlds series receipts through no fault of your own."[16]

Murphy's reputation for integrity would follow him for the rest of his life, and even into the 21st century, his nickname of Honest Eddie remains well known. A sports bar in his hometown of Hancock, New York, was named Honest Eddie's Tap Room.

Murphy returned to the White Sox in 1921, but made just six appearances before he was released on waivers to the Cleveland Indians, who reassigned him to the Columbus Senators of the American Association. As a full-time starter in the outfield again, he spent five productive years with Columbus, serving a stint as team captain and even winning a batting title at age 33 with a .397 average in 1925.[17]

Traded to Rochester (New York) of the International League after the 1925 season, Murphy was having another superb season when his contract was purchased by Pittsburgh Pirates owner Barney Dreyfuss in mid-August 1926.[18] Murphy injured his knee soon after he joined the Pirates and did not have much impact on the three-way National League pennant race.[19] He

hit just .118 in 22 plate appearances for the Pirates, who finished in third place, 4½ games behind the St. Louis Cardinals. Murphy finished his 11-season major-league career with a .287 average and 680 hits in 761 games.

In the winter of 1926-27, Murphy was called to Chicago to testify before Commissioner Kenesaw Mountain Landis about a disputed Chicago White Sox-Detroit Tigers series from a decade earlier. Murphy's disgraced former teammates Chick Gandil and Swede Risberg claimed the Tigers threw a four-game series to the White Sox in early September 1917, and that the White Sox players had paid them off to do so. Although many members of the White Sox, including Eddie Collins, admitted contributing money to the Tigers pool, they claimed it was to reward the Tigers for beating the rival Boston Red Sox instead. For his part, Murphy said he was never asked to contribute and wasn't aware of a plot.[20] Landis eventually dismissed Gandil and Risberg's claims, although he did put a stop to the once-common practice of "rewarding" opposing teams.

Murphy returned to the minor leagues for two final seasons, playing for Rochester in 1927 and splitting time in 1928 with the Montreal Royals and Jersey City Skeeters. When Jersey City sold him to the Reading Keystones, Murphy refused to report and abruptly ended his playing career.[21]

In retirement, Eddie and his wife raised two sons and lived in Dunmore, Pennsylvania, for the rest of their lives. He stayed involved with baseball, managing a semipro team in Stroudsburg and for a time operating an instructional school in Scranton.[22] Later, he worked as a supervisor of recreation for the Works Progress Administration in Lackawanna County and helped arrange exhibition baseball games for visiting troops at a USO club during World War II.[23]

Murphy died at the age of 77 on February 21, 1969, at his home in Dunmore. He was buried at Queen of Peace Cemetery in Hawley, Pennsylvania.

NOTES

1 Bob Hill, *Crack of the Bat: The Louisville Slugger Story* (New York: Sports Publishing, 2002).

2 *The Scrantonian* (Pennsylvania), September 13, 1959.

3 William C. Kashatus, *Diamonds in the Coalfields: 21 Remarkable Baseball Players, Managers, and Umpires From Northeastern Pennsylvania* (Jefferson, North Carolina: McFarland & Co., 2002).

4 Ibid.

5 Kashatus, 31.

6 Kashatus, 19.

7 Mark Simonsen, "Hancock native escaped 'Black Sox' scandal of 1919," *Oneonta* (New York) *Daily Star*, June 19, 2010.

8 *The Sporting News*, September 21, 1968.

9 Bob Warrington, "Eddie Murphy's Glass Bat," Philadelphia Athletics Historical Society, accessed online at philadelphiaathletics.org/event/glassbat.htm on October 10, 2013. In recent years, the bat has been displayed at the Corning Glass Museum in Corning, New York.

10 William Connelly, "Great Run-Getters Past and Present," *Baseball Magazine*, August 1915, 37-40. Accessed online at LA84.org on September 1, 2014.

11 Retrosheet.org lists Murphy's sale to the White Sox at $11,500, but several contemporary sources state that the deal was for $13,000.

12 *The Sporting News*, September 21, 1968.

13 Ibid.

14 *The Scrantonian*, September 13, 1959. For more discussion of Gleason's team meeting, see Gene Carney, *Burying the Black Sox: How Baseball's Cover-Up of the 1919 World Series Fix Almost Succeeded* (Washington, D.C.: Potomac Books, 2006), 46-47.

15 Kashatus, 93.

16 Charles Comiskey letter to Eddie Murphy, October 2, 1920. A copy of the letter can be found at honesteddiemurphy.com. Checks were also sent to Ray Schalk, Red Faber, Eddie Collins, Shano Collins, Nemo Leibold, Dickey Kerr, Roy Wilkinson, Hervey McClellan, and Byrd Lynn. See *Chicago Tribune*, October 5, 1920.

17 *Hamilton* (Ohio) *Journal News*, September 26, 1925.

18 *Franklin* (Pennsylvania) *News-Herald*, August 13, 1925.

19 *Scranton Republican*, September 16, 1926.

20 *Chicago Tribune*, January 4, 1927.

21 *Reading* (Pennsylvania) *Times*, June 13, 1928.

22 *Scranton Republican*, April 6, 1935.

23 *Scranton Republican*, July 3, 1936; Mount *Carmel* (Pennsylvania) *Item*, May 3, 1945.

WIN NOYES

By Bruce Allardice

WIN NOYES WAS ONE OF several ballplayers for whom service in World War I interrupted a promising big-league career. His brief stint with the 1919 White Sox was merely a footnote in a long, if not especially distinguished, baseball career.

Various baseball references say Winfield Charles Noyes was born on June 16, 1889, in Pleasanton, Nebraska. However, on his 1942 World War II draft registration, he gave his date of birth as June 10, 1892, Social Security records say June 10, 1891, and his tombstone gives a June 10, 1889, date of birth. On the 1900 Census, his parents reported that he was born in June 1889, so the weight of evidence suggests the tombstone date is the correct one.

Noyes's parents, Illinois-born Enoch W. Noyes (1860-1931) and Rose Mary Rubart Noyes (1862-1947), farmed in Pleasanton. Enoch's father, Evan H. Noyes (1833-89), a farmer in Adams County, Illinois, served in the Civil War. Win and his three siblings grew up on a prosperous Midwest farm.[1]

Win attended Nebraska Wesleyan University. He studied dentistry while there, and he starred for the college's baseball team. He pitched for the local Pleasanton team in 1909, frequently striking out 15 or more batters a game and leading Pleasanton on a 22-game winning streak.

Noyes entered Organized Baseball in 1910, at the age of 21. He starred for his hometown Kearney Kapitalists, posting a 24-12 record for the third-place team in the Nebraska State League.[2] He led the league in wins and strikeouts (323), earned 24 of the team's 60 wins, and tossed a no-hitter. When not pitching, Noyes worked as a salesman in a local drugstore, presaging his post-baseball career.

This stellar 1910 season led to an unsuccessful tryout the next spring with the St. Louis Browns.[3] Noyes showed enough to land a job with a better Class D league, the Central Association. Pitching for the Ottumwa (Iowa) Speedboys, he won 12 games through July 1911, helping lead Ottumwa to first place in the league. On August 1 Ottumwa sold Noyes to the San Francisco Seals of the Pacific Coast League. Noyes got into nine games with the Seals, with an 0-1 record. In his August 11 debut, understandably nervous, he showed "a lot of speed, but he was wild," giving up two runs and one hit in 2⅓ innings.[4] After that, Noyes pitched strictly mop-up duty. He didn't make much of an impression, with one newspaper lamenting that Noyes and another player "are both in bad with the local management. Neither have been putting in enough interest or energy in their work to please manager Long."[5]

Noyes began the 1912 season with the Seals. Much was hoped from the "angular, raw-boned"[6] 6-foot, 189-pound right-hander who was thought a "bloomer."[7] His seven-inning preseason shutout of Soledad, with 10 strikeouts, caused sportswriters to gush on how "splendid" he looked. But at the end of that game Noyes got "knocked unconscious … by one of Favell's speeders. The sound of the contact could be heard in every part of the bleachers."[8] Either because of that injury or inexperience, it soon became evident that Noyes had been promoted to the PCL too soon. The *Oakland Tribune* opined that he and others "have much to learn ere they will be big league timber."[9]

After appearing in only eight games, with an 0-2 record, Noyes was traded by the Seals with two other players to Spokane for Johnny Wuffli, an infielder who had torn up the Class D Northwestern League. Going back to Class D, Noyes (nicknamed Quiet Noyes by his punning San Francisco teammates) found his groove.[10] He finished with a sparkling 26-8 record for the Indians. At one point he won 12 straight games.

In September Spokane owner John Cehn sold Noyes to the Boston Nationals for $1,000.

Noyes signed with Boston in February 1913. At the time he was studying pharmacy at Northwestern University.[11] He cut short his studies to join the Braves prior to the season, but his absence from spring training evidently didn't find favor with Boston's management. Manager George Stallings relegated Noyes to mop-up roles. His major-league debut was typical of his appearances that season: relieving Lefty Tyler on May 19 in a 9-8 loss.

Stallings didn't see enough promise in Noyes to keep him for 1914. Faced with a surplus of pitchers, he farmed Noyes to Rochester of the International League. Rochester manager John Ganzel started Noyes in several spring-training games, and Noyes was bombed in each, losing one game 19-0 to Birmingham. He was shuttled around to Montreal of the IL and then to Jersey City. Noyes' debut with Jersey City set the tone for this disappointing year: He was knocked out in the third inning. Jersey City went on the finish in the cellar with a dismal 48-106 record. But Noyes was long gone by season's end. In June, his old Spokane team purchased his contract. Back in the Northwest, Noyes fashioned a 14-9 record for Spokane, with Noyes laboring 219 innings in what was essentially half a season.

In 1915 Noyes once again spearheaded the Spokane staff.[12] His 22-14 record essentially duplicated his 1912 season with the same team, and once again he pitched 310 innings. The highlight of his season came on July 9, when Noyes no-hit the Vancouver Canucks.[13]

Near the end of the Northwest League season, the Portland Beavers of the PCL purchased Noyes, who proclaimed himself in "good shape" for the Beavers' stretch run, though his arm was "a little tired."[14] He started four games for Portland, and compiled a 1-1 record with a 1.66 ERA. Proclaimed one newspaper, "When Noyes was [last] in the Coast league he was lacking in experience. It is believed that he is seasoned now and in his prime. Should he show as well as Coveleski [Stan Coveleski led the PCL in games

pitched that year], that is all the local owners will expect."[15]

In the winter of 1915-16 Portland's veteran manager, Walt McCreadie, helped turn Noyes' career around by teaching him the spitball. As with Stan Coveleski, the new pitch turned a good minor-league pitcher into a major-league prospect. "When he first joined the Beaver club … he depended upon only a fast one and a curve ball to win big games. The result was that he was batted out of the box frequently. McCreadie realized that Noyes should be taught the spit ball and since he has learned it, he has won game after game." McCreadie boasted that "Noyes, since he has mastered the spit ball, is now as good a pitcher as any in the league and I expect … that he will surely be grabbed by a major league club." Cleveland, with whom Portland had a working relationship, had already "expressed an interest."[16]

One incident much written about at the time featured Noyes beaning the popular Jack Coffey of the Seals. What bothered fans was not so much the beaning (Noyes' spitter had gotten away from him) but the impression that Noyes didn't come in from the mound to see how Coffey was doing. The unconscious Coffey recovered and walked away from the field, but local sportswriters labeled Noyes "cold blooded" for his alleged lack of concern.[17]

While mastering the spitball gave Noyes' career new life, the pitch came with its own unique problems. After the Los Angeles Angels walloped Noyes and Portland in a 15-2 loss, "Noyes complained to one and all that 'the Angels had sabotaged his spitter by putting alum in the water bucket.' This might have been true, for it was frequently done to overcome spitballers, and when Noyes puckered up after a drink he found he couldn't spit and the Angels took full advantage of the dry spell."[18]

A sportswriter looking at PCL players who might be drafted by the big leagues wrote in September that "Noyes will be the one selected [from Portland]. Noyes has been pitching consistent ball the greater part of the year, leads the Portland pitchers in percentage of victories, and is a different pitcher than he was when he was given a trial by the Boston Braves several years ago. Now he has acquired a spitter which makes him much more efficient."[19]

Noyes finished with a so-so 21-19 record with a 3.14 ERA for a mediocre Portland team. Another 341-inning season showed that he possessed a rubber arm. Manager Connie Mack of the Philadelphia Athletics was once again beating the bushes for talent to revive the glories of the 1910-14 A's, and on the recommendation of scout Ira Thomas, a friend of McCreadie's, purchased Noyes. Noyes enjoyed by far his best big-league season in 1917. Labeled Philadelphia's "star recruit pitcher,"[20] he started 22 games, going 10-10 for Mack's last-place team. His 2.95 ERA was better than the team ERA of 3.27 but higher than the league average.

It appeared that Noyes had finally established himself. Said one newspaper, "Where is the manager who wouldn't like to have … Noyes pitching for him?"[21] In

Win Noyes with the PCL's Portland Beavers, circa 1916 (Published in the Oregon Daily Journal and accessed via Newspapers.com)

August he beat the league-leading White Sox, impressing the Sox with his "speed" and his "puzzle on the pill."[22] Perhaps Noyes' best outing was a game in August in which he pitched a no-hitter for seven innings, and lost a shutout only when it became too dark for his fielders to follow the baseball.

In September the draft board called up Noyes and teammate Ray Bates. Although the call-ups wrecked Mack's plans to rebuild the A's (or at least this is what observers believed), Mack himself offered no complaints, observing, "Our country always comes first."[23] Noyes served with the 342nd Field Artillery, making it over to France in 1918, and rising to the rank of sergeant major. While in uniform he played a lot of baseball, pitching for his Camp Funston, Kansas, team, and with a service team in France that featured such major-league stars as Grover Cleveland Alexander.

Noyes returned to the Athletics in August 1919. In his debut, on August 9, he pitched four hitless innings against the league-leading White Sox. "His spitter had the Sox as helpless as newborn kittens," gushed the *Philadelphia Inquirer*, reawakening hopes that he could recover the 1917 form that made him "one of the best pitchers on the Athletics payroll."[24] But it soon became apparent that Noyes had lost something while in the Army. He pitched in ten games with the A's, starting six, but in contrast to 1917 compiled a 5.69 ERA and a 1-5 record. About his only noteworthy outing occurred when he gave up Babe Ruth's 25th homer of the season, tying what was then thought to be the major-league record set by Buck Freeman in 1899.

On September 19 the White Sox claimed Noyes on waivers. The White Sox had about clinched the pennant by then, but the team had pitching problems. One of their star pitchers, Red Faber, was lost for the season due to lingering influenza, complicated by arm injuries, which forced manager Kid Gleason to overwork his remaining two veteran starters, Eddie Cicotte and Lefty Williams. As the season wound down, rumors surfaced that Cicotte had a tired arm.

In any event, Gleason saw that the White Sox needed what would today be termed innings-eaters—rubber-armed pitchers who could soak up innings and give his stars a rest. Connie Mack, Gleason's close friend, may have recommended one-time prospect Noyes as both a September fill-in and someone with the potential to start in 1920. He had recently (September 12 and 15) pitched in relief against the White Sox, posting four scoreless innings in all, and perhaps impressing Gleason.

Noyes started one game for the White Sox—a meaningless game against Detroit on September 27. Pitching six innings, he gave up five runs and ten hits in a game that Detroit won in extra innings, 7-5.

Having been acquired so late in the season, Noyes was not eligible for the White Sox' World Series roster. As such, the gamblers never thought of recruiting him (or any of the other spare pitchers.) The question remains: Did Noyes know of the "fix"? He was new to the team, and most of the White Sox players who had been his teammates in the past—notably Grover Lowdermilk and Big Bill James—were part of the "Clean Sox" faction. However, Buck Weaver and Joe Gedeon had briefly been his teammates on the Seals, and it isn't beyond imagination that Noyes heard something. The fact that Noyes refused to report next year, and followed Black Sox fixer-in-chief Chick Gandil to an outlaw league in Idaho, may just be a coincidence, or it may suggest guilty knowledge.[25] In later years Noyes proclaimed to one-and-all that the " 'skinflint'" Comiskeys who owned the Black Sox—and not Shoeless Joe Jackson—should have been banned from baseball.[26]

The White Sox hoped that Noyes could recover his prewar form and contribute in 1920. Doubts about Red Faber's recovery from his 1919 injuries, along with Cicotte's advancing age, caused dopesters to look to Noyes and others to fill out the rotation. One newspaper reported that Noyes was "out to be one of the Kid's regulars, but can't be figured as a brilliant hurler."[27] Another writer thought Noyes "is as good a prospect as any of the others" behind Cicotte, Williams, and Kerr.[28]

But Noyes had other ideas. Dissatisfied with the money offered him, he refused to report, and dropped out of Organized Baseball for good. Another factor may have played a part—the banning of the spitball. During the winter of 1919-20, the league banned spitball throwing, except for two pitchers designated by each team, who were grandfathered in. The White Sox grandfathered in star pitchers Cicotte and Faber, so while Noyes already had lost some effectiveness, the banning of his "money" pitch signaled the end of any major-league career.

Former Black Sox first baseman Chick Gandil, like Noyes, refused to report in 1920, and managed in the Snake River League. Noyes bought into a drugstore business in Pocatello, and while not working he pitched and managed the Pocatello team in that league. In November he married Elsie MacKay, the daughter of Mr. and Mrs. Daniel MacKay of Salt Lake City, Utah, in a Mormon church ceremony. The couple divorced in the 1920s. When the Pocatello season ended in August, Noyes signed with Sterling, Colorado, in the Midwest League. In 1921 he hurled for Sterling again, but the one-time star was hit hard.

In 1922 Noyes approached Salt Lake City of the PCL for a tryout, but no job came of this.[29] He returned to the Midwest to join the Pontiac (Illinois) Standards and (by July 22) Beloit in the Midwest (semipro) League. The Beloit Fairies (the nickname refers to the Fairchild-Morse Engine Company, which sponsored the team) was run by former Chicago City leaguer Al Chubb, who used his Windy City contacts to sign ballplayers. Much stronger than most clubs in the division, it featured ex-major leaguers Hippo Jim Vaughn, Dave Davenport, Herb Kemman, and Zip Zabel.

Noyes' eligibility to pitch for Beloit was challenged by charges that he'd signed with the Chicago Pyotts instead, and charges that Beloit had stolen Noyes from the Pontiac team. The chairman of the league ruled that he was Pontiac's property, and he was held out of the Beloit rotation until his eligibility to pitch for the Fairies was confirmed. Beloit won the pennant anyway. Later in the year, Noyes pitched for independent teams in downstate Illinois.

The next season proved to be Noyes' last year pitching. Although Beloit finished second in the league, Noyes' 4-7 record indicates that the old fastball simply wasn't there anymore. After 1923 he gave up baseball for good.

Noyes began working full-time as a druggist in Arizona, moving soon to Prairie City, Oregon, but by 1929 he had returned to the state of Washington, familiar from his days as a ballplayer. By 1930 he was operating a pharmacy in Sumas, a small town adjacent to the British Columbia border, living with his second wife, Elizabeth (Reul) Noyes (1897-1984), and young daughter Elizabeth. He ran his drugstore there for many years.

Noyes died on April 8, 1969, in Chelan, Washington. He is buried beside his second wife in the City Cemetery in Cashmere, Washington, in the central part of the state, with a "veteran's" stone marking his final resting place.[30]

SOURCES

Hogg, Clyde, *Spitting on Diamonds: A Spitball Pitcher's Journey to the Major Leagues, 1911-1919* (Columbia, Missouri: University of Missouri Press, 2005).

Other newspapers: *Chicago Tribune, New Oxford* (Pennsylvania) *Item, New Castle* (Pennsylvania) *News, Philadelphia Inquirer, Rockford* (Illinois) *Morning Star, Rockford Daily Register, Canton* (Ohio) *Repository, Idaho Statesman* (Boise), *Denver Post, Salt Lake City Telegram, Illinois Republic* (Geneseo, Illinos), *Omaha World Herald, San Francisco Chronicle, Cleveland Gazette, Boston Journal, The Oregonian* (Portland), *Seattle Daily Times, Wilkes-Barre Times, New Orleans Picayune, Jersey Journal* (Jersey City), *Springfield* (Massachusetts) *Republican, South Carolina State* (Columbia, South Carolina), *New York Times, Watertown* (New York) *Daily Times, Grand Forks* (North Dakota) *Herald, Muscatine* (Iowa) *Journal, Waterloo* (Iowa) *Evening Courier, Indianapolis Star, Salt Lake City Tribune, Oakland Tribune, Ogden* (Utah) *Standard, Beatrice* (Nebraska) *Daily Sun, Chicago Examiner, San Diego Union, San Jose Mercury News, California Evening News* (San Jose), *California Evening Tribune* (San Diego), *Sandusky* (Ohio) *Register, Washington Post, Trenton* (New Jersey) *Evening Times, Grand Rapids Press, Riverside* (California) *Daily Press, Spokane Daily Chronicle, Lincoln* (Nebraska) *Daily Star, Cedar Rapids* (Iowa) *Evening Gazette*

1929 *Journal of the American Pharmaceutical Assn.*

Sporting Life

The Sporting News

Ancestry.com

Find-a-Grave.com

1880-1930 US Censuses

World War I and World War II draft registration records

Social Security records

Baseball-Almanac.com

Baseball-Reference.com

Nebraska State League website, nebaseballhistory.com

Player card, courtesy Ray Nemec

Northwestern University records

Utah Death Certificate, Mrs. Elsie Noyes

NOTES

1   While his given name was properly Winfield, Noyes was seldom called by that name. Contemporary newspaper accounts call him Win, Winn, Winnie, Wynne, and Wynn.

2   The Kapitalists were also known as the Buffaloes and the Cotton Pickers.

3   "Sportlets," *Cedar Rapids Evening Gazette*, July 27, 1912.

4   "Baseball Notes," *San Francisco Call*, August 12, 1911.

5   F.A. Purner, "Manager Long Will Begin Weeding Out Superfluous Seals This Week," *San Francisco Chronicle*, March 19, 1912.

6   "Pitching Honors Belong to Noyes," *Portland Oregonian*, August 11, 1912.

7   "Ewing's Bunch Looks Good, If Records Count," *Oakland Tribune*, February 11, 1912.

8   "Wynn Is Injured," *San Francisco Call*, April 1, 1912. See also "Noyes Is Beaned," *San Francisco Chronicle*, April 1, 1912.

9   "Additional Sports," *Oakland Tribune*, May 6, 1912.

10 "Seals Have Great Assortment of Nicknames," *San Francisco Chronicle*, March 31, 1912.

11 Northwestern University records show Noyes earned his degree in pharmacy in June 1913. He had been attending Northwestern in his offseason.

12 In February 1915, Spokane dealt Noyes to Omaha for first baseman Earl Chase. However, the deal fell through.

13 "Noyes Does Not Allow Beavers a Single Safety," *Seattle Daily Times*, July 10, 1915. In the 11-1 win, Noyes gave up four walks (and struck out only two); the run came after three passed balls. See also "No Hits Given to Vancouver Team," *Spokane Daily Chronicle*, July 10, 1915.

14 "Noyes Reports to Portland Beavers," *Salt Lake Tribune*, September 28, 1915.

15 "McCreadie Lives in Hopes of Climbing," *Salt Lake Tribune*, August 24, 1915.

16 "Wynn Noyes May Also Go to Majors," *Salt Lake City Telegram*, July 18, 1916.

17 "Seals and Saints Open Series Today," *Salt Lake Tribune*, July 11, 1916, citing the *Oakland Tribune*. See also "Wynn Noyes Is Sorry," *Portland Oregonian*, July 7, 1916.

18 Clyde Hogg, *Spitting on Diamonds*, 175. The game referred to was an October 19 loss to Los Angeles, with Noyes lasting only 1⅓ innings.

19 "Drafting Seasons Will Open Here Next Friday," *Oakland Tribune*, September 13, 1916.

20 "Nebraskans Will Play Ball," *Omaha World Herald*, September 9, 1917.

21 H.C. Hamilton, "Fans Respect Mack's Players," *Riverside Daily Press*, July 20, 1917.

22 "Noyes Makes His List of Victories Seven Straight," *Salt Lake Tribune*, June 24, 1916.

23 "Ray Bates Quits Mack for Uncle Sam," *Riverside Daily Press*, August 9, 1917.

24 "Macks Again Share Bill with Leaders," *Philadelphia Inquirer*, August 9, 1917.

25 Since the gamblers would bet only on a sure thing, and since the only players on the Sox who could (more or less) guarantee a loss in a specified game were the starting pitchers, the only Sox the gamblers really needed to bribe were Cicotte and Williams—in particular, Cicotte. The participation of the other "eight men out" was merely window dressing. Since bullpen pitchers might not even pitch in the Series, bribing them wasn't necessary either.

26 Bruce Brown, *Dr. Whacko's Guide to Slow-Pitch* Softball (New York: Collier Books, 1991). Accessed online at astonisher.com/archives/drwhacko/drwhacko_intro.html.

27 Norman E. Brown, "Gleason Has Bad Wreck This Year," *San Diego Evening Tribune*, April 15, 1920.

28 James Crusinberry, "Gleason Faces Toughest Task in Big Leagues," *Chicago Tribune*, March 23, 1920.

29 L.H. Gregory, "Many New Faces to be Seen in Coast Pitching Circles," *Portland Oregonian*, February 6, 1922.

30 His second wife, Elizabeth Reul, is buried beside him in Cashmere Cemetery. Daughter Betty (1928-2002) married local newspaper owner Bruce Van Klinken and had four children. Noyes' first wife, Elsie (1895-1951), divorced Noyes around 1925.

PAT RAGAN

By Andy Sturgill

LONG BEFORE FREE AGENCY and specialization promoted frequent player movement between teams, the journeyman tag was most aptly applied to men like Pat Ragan. Ragan played for seven major-league clubs between 1909 and 1923, and as of the end of the 1920s was one of only seven men to play for six or more major-league teams.[1]

Don Carlos Patrick Ragan was born on November 15, 1885, in Blanchard, Iowa. His official name and even his year of birth are the subject of some debate. Ragan's World War I draft card is signed "Patrick Don Carlos Ragan," and the California Death Index labels him "Donn Patrick Ragan."

Additionally, Ragan's birth year is listed as 1880 on his draft card, but this is almost certainly a misprint. Ragan's hometown of Blanchard, in the southwest corner of Iowa, had a population of around 400 at the time he was born, but in the 2010 Census indicated a population of just 32. He was born to C.B. and Luisie Ragan, both natives of Illinois. C.B. worked as a day laborer and Luisie's profession was indicated as "keeping house." Whether this meant she was a home-maker or worked as a housekeeper outside the home is unknown.

Ragan attended two private colleges in Iowa, Simpson and Cornell,[2] and broke into professional baseball by going 1-1 with the Terre Haute Hottentots of the Central League as a 19-year-old in 1905. His obituary states that he played for Manchester in the New England League in 1906, but only incomplete statistics for that team have survived.[3] After Terre Haute, Ragan played for Omaha of the Western League in 1907 and 1908.

After his two seasons with Omaha, Ragan joined the Cincinnati Reds in 1909, and made his debut on April 21. He pitched in two games for the Reds before he was sold to the Chicago Cubs in late May. He also pitched twice for the Cubs and spent the rest of 1909 and all of 1910 in the Eastern League with Rochester, where in almost two seasons he went 22-13 in more than 360 innings pitched.

Joining Brooklyn of the National League in 1911, Ragan received his first consistent time in the major leagues. He appeared in 22 games, going 4-3 with a 2.11 ERA. From 1912 to 1914, Ragan was a mainstay in the Brooklyn rotation, stellar but unremarkable for Brooklyn's consistently poor outfit. He allowed more hits than innings pitched, struck out few, walked too many and posted an ERA worse than the league average. Over the three seasons he posted a record of 32-51, with a 7-18 mark in 1912.

But Ragan showed enough promise to stay in the rotation; he made at least 25 starts and pitched in at least 200 innings each season from 1912 through 1914. He won nine games in a row in 1913, and after the season was Brooklyn's best pitcher as the club barn-stormed in Cuba.[4]

After the 1913 season, Ragan was one of many major leaguers targeted by the upstart Federal League. "(The Federal League) made me a handsome offer," he told the *New York Times*. "They offered me a two years' contract at a much better salary than the Brooklyn Club has paid me. While I much prefer to remain in Organized Baseball, sentiment is small consideration, and like every other ballplayer, I am prepared to take advantage of any proposition that carries a satisfactory financial agreement. I have not come to any terms thus far with the Brooklyn management, and shall wait for future developments before I do so."[5]

Several other Brooklyn players were recruited by the Federals, including Zack Wheat and Nap Rucker. In response, owner Charles Ebbets signed the recruited players, including Ragan, to multiyear deals at friendly salaries. Ragan received a three-year deal. Of locking up his players Ebbets said, "The Federal League wanted my stars—well, so did I."[6]

Ragan was regarded around the National League as a pitcher who relied upon his curveball to be effective. Contemporary accounts also describe him in terms such as "stout" and "burly."[7] Baseball-reference lists the right-hander at 5-feet-10 and 185 pounds.

Ragan gained a reputation as a Giant-killer because of the success he had against John McGraw's club.[8] A highlight for Ragan that was not against the Giants came on October 5, 1914, when he struck out three Braves on only nine pitches. Ragan's immaculate inning was the only one turned against the Braves for almost 100 years, until Juan Perez of the Phillies accomplished it in 2011.

Ragan spent four-plus seasons with Brooklyn before he was purchased on waivers by the Boston Braves in April 1915. Brooklyn had initially intended for Ragan to move to Cleveland in the American League, but the Braves claimed him before Cleveland had the opportunity to do so.[9]

While Ragan showed flashes of excellence in Brooklyn, he became a good starting pitcher on a good team with the Braves, joining Boston the year after they had swept the Philadelphia Athletics in the World Series. Whether he grew into the role or benefited from playing with a better team is a matter of debate.

With Ragan's reputation as a Giant-killer, Boston management believed he was worth his salary solely for his expected performance against New York.[10] Ragan took on the men of McGraw for the first time with his new team on June 1, 1915, and outpitched Christy Mathewson in a 7-0 Braves victory. He allowed only two hits, struck out four, had a hit, and scored a run.

On June 23, only eight weeks after Brooklyn let him go, Ragan took the hill against his former Robins teammates. Ragan got the last laugh that day, scattering seven hits and driving in Boston's first two runs in a 3-2 victory.

At season's end, the Braves finished 83-69, good for second place in the National League, seven games behind the pennant-winning Philadelphia Phillies. After coming to Boston, Ragan was the Braves' second-best starter, going 16-12 with a 2.46 ERA in 26 starts. He appeared in 33 games overall, pitched 227 innings and tied for second on the club with three shutouts.

In 1916 the Braves dropped to third place. Ragan went 9-9 with a 2.08 ERA in 23 starts and 182 innings pitched. He posted a 2-to-1 strikeout-to-walk ratio and allowed nearly 40 fewer hits than innings pitched. He went on to post similar numbers for the Braves in 1917 (6-9, 2.93 ERA, 13 starts) before falling to 8-17 with a 3.23 ERA for the 1918 squad, which finished in seventh place.

With World War I raging in Europe, and a work-or-fight order looming for major-leaguers, Ragan appeared before his draft board in Boston's Brighton neighborhood in July 1918.[11] With a wife and 2-year-old

TCMA photo of Pat Ragan (Courtesy of Michael Aronstein / TCMA Ltd.)

son to support, he was not called for duty before the war's end.

In May 1919 Ragan made four appearances for the Braves before being sent to the Giants to complete a trade that sent Jim Thorpe to Boston nine days earlier. Ragan stuck with the Giants for only four games before they placed him on waivers and he was claimed by the White Sox.

While the 1919 White Sox were a great club, they had concerns with pitching depth. Future Hall of Famer Red Faber missed large chunks of the season because of arm trouble and illness, and 25-year-old Dickie Kerr was a rookie. Seeking reinforcements for a starting staff that was thin behind aces Eddie Cicotte and Lefty Williams, the White Sox also acquired former 20-game-winner Erskine Mayer (who recorded an 8.37 ERA in six appearances) and tried to acquire Carl Mays from the Red Sox.[12] Mays was ultimately sent to the Yankees. When the White Sox were unable to acquire Mays, they signed Ragan, just a day after the Giants cut him loose.

Ragan appeared in only one game for the White Sox, pitching one inning in a 6-5 loss to the Yankees on August 25. Chicago went on to capture the American League pennant, but lost the best-of-nine World Series to the Cincinnati Reds in the fall classic marked by the Black Sox scandal.

After 1919, Ragan and Mayer combined to make only one more appearance in the major leagues, while Carl Mays won 127 games and pitched in two World Series. What would have happened in the infamous World Series had the White Sox acquired Mays instead of Mayer/Ragan? Would a fix have been averted because of Mays's ability? Would Mays have become a part of the conspiracy to dump the Series? It's another layer of mystery on top of the entire scandal.

In 1920 Ragan reported to the US Census bureau that he was living in Omaha as a farmer with his wife, Mae, and their 4-year-old son, Patrick, with Ragan's in-laws, J.A. and Anna (Hokensen) Noble.[13]

While he didn't appear in the major leagues in 1920, Ragan did pitch in 22 games for Omaha of the Western League and Oakland of the Pacific Coast League. He spent 1921 as a scout for the Boston Braves and in 1922 he managed Waterloo (Iowa) in the Mississippi Valley League.[14]

In 1923 the Philadelphia Phillies hired Ragan as a coach to work with the team's pitching staff. With the team stuck in last place by early July, Ragan made one last appearance in the majors on July 5, 1923, nearly four years after his last major-league outing. He went three innings, allowing six hits and two runs in a 16-12 loss to the St. Louis Cardinals.[15]

Ragan returned to the coaching ranks with the Phillies in 1924 under manager Art Fletcher, his former teammate with the Giants. Ragan managed the next two seasons in the low minors, spending 1925 with the Martinsburg Blue Sox of the Class D Blue Ridge League and 1926 with the Cumberland Colts of the Class C Middle Atlantic League.

In his later years, Ragan worked as a security guard for an aircraft company.[16] He and his family moved west to California, where he died from kidney cancer on September 4, 1956, at 70. He was survived by his wife, Mae, and son, Pat Jr., and was buried at Forest Lawn Memorial Park in Glendale, California.

NOTES

1   "Bobby Roth of Burlington Holds Record in Majors," *Milwaukee Sentinel*, December 15, 1929, 14.

2   *The Sporting News*, September 12, 1956.

3   Ibid.

4   Roberto Gonzalez Echevarria, *The Pride of Havana* (New York: Oxford University Press USA, 2001), 164.

5   "Pat Ragan Considering Offer," *New York Times*, December 29, 1913.

6   Robert Creamer, *Stengel: His Life and Times* (New York: Simon & Schuster, 1984), 76.

7   *New York Times*, September 16, 1917.

8   Rob Neyer and Bill James, *The Neyer/James Guide to Pitchers* (New York: Touchstone, 2004), 351.

9   "Brooklyn Brief," *Sporting Life*, May 8, 1915.

10   *New York Times*, September 16, 1917.

11   *Boston Daily Globe*, July 5, 1918.

12   *Toronto World*, July 31, 1919.

13   1920 US Census; California Death Index 1940-97, Ancestry.com.

14   "Pat Ragan Signs to Pilot Waterloo," *Cedar Rapids* (Iowa) *Republican and Times*, March 16, 1922.

15   "Hornsby Hits Brace of Homers as Cards Win," *Boston Globe*, July 6, 1923.

16   Bill Lee, *The Baseball Necrology* (Jefferson, North Carolina: McFarland & Co., 2003).

SWEDE RISBERG

By Kelly Boyer Sagert and Rod Nelson

ALIGHT-HITTING, RIFLE-armed shortstop who played a key role in baseball's biggest scandal, Swede Risberg was a rising young player in the American League when he was banned from the game at age 25. The youngest member of the Black Sox, he always found his home state of California and the Pacific Coast League preferable to the harsh spotlight of the majors. "He would gleefully toss up his chances for fame and lucre," a reporter wrote in 1917, "and take the first train back to the Pacific Coast, where he knows everybody and is known by everybody."[1] Risberg managed to survive in Chicago by adopting a tough veneer that led to frequent fisticuffs and a reputation for toughness, excitability, and standoffishness. That reputation was enhanced by the events of 1919, when he helped orchestrate the Series-fixing plot that resulted in his banishment from baseball and the wrecking of the White Sox franchise.

Charles August Risberg was born on October 13, 1894, in San Francisco, the youngest of three children of a Swedish-born longshoreman, Charles Peter, and his Danish wife, Trisini. Risberg was raised in the North Beach section of San Francisco and survived the great earthquake in 1906. Although he liked to say in later years that he had dropped out of school by the third grade because he had "refused to shave,"[2] Risberg's formal education extended to at least the eighth grade at Hancock Grammar School.[3] By the time he was 14 he was a star pitcher for the school team, and he soon won wide acclaim as a semipro pitcher in the Bay Area.

In 1912 the 17-year-old Risberg won a tryout in spring training with the Vernon Tigers of the Pacific Coast League. The *Los Angeles Times* reported that "the youngster looks like a fixture," but Risberg managed to pitch in only two games for the Tigers that year.[4] In 1913 he spent the year in the low minor leagues, struggling in 11 appearances for Spokane (Washington) of the Northwestern League before moving on to Ogden (Utah) of the Union Association, where he was converted to shortstop. He hit well (.284 with 30 extra-base hits) but made a whopping 68 errors in 82 games. Returning to Ogden in 1914, the 19-year-old continued to improve as a position player, batting .366 and earning another chance with the PCL Tigers at season's end.

He soon became a full-time utilityman for the Tigers, playing 175 games in 1915 and 185 in 1916 despite indifferent hitting performances, and spending time at first base, second base, shortstop, the outfield, and, occasionally, the pitcher's mound. During one game, Risberg reportedly "left his place at second base, took the mound and not only staved off a rally, but pitched his team to a victory."[5]

Risberg's strong arm was both an asset and a liability; his throwing ability garnered praise, but once, in a fit of anger, Risberg punched an umpire who called a third strike on him. In another incident, he got into a fistfight with Salt Lake player Tommy Quinlan, who had flattened Risberg with a takeout slide at second base.[6]

Risberg's manager at Vernon, former Chicago White Sox pitcher Doc White, gushed about his young star, calling him "the best utility man in these United States," and adding, "The big leagues haven't his equal.… I have never seen anything quite like him."[7] White recommended Risberg to Charles Comiskey, who had the right of first refusal on all Tiger players. In March 1915 Comiskey got a firsthand look at Risberg when the White Sox faced the Tigers in four spring exhibition games; Swede helped win one of the contests with a home run.[8] The next year, during Risberg's fifth minor-league season, Comiskey purchased his contract for $4,000.[9] Risberg, who at 6 feet tall and 175 pounds was one of the largest shortstops to play in the majors before World War II, replaced 129-pound Zeb Terry on the 1917 Sox roster.

Risberg's transition to the major leagues wasn't smooth. A newspaper article written in June 1917 revealed that he suffered from "the worst case of homesickness in the history of the Sox aggregation," adding that "he misses the soft blue skies of California. He wants to be back where the sun shines and his wife can cheer him on from the grand stand."[10] Risberg—a right-handed "marvel at shortstop"—even asked that Comiskey send him home, but the request was denied.

Risberg's 1917 batting average of .203 was abominable, but because of his defensive skills he played in 149 games that year for the White Sox. Still, Risberg maddened Chicagoans with his inconsistency. "He is liable to be a sensation one minute and a crape hanger the next, for he can throw them away as far and as hard as anyone," Hugh Fullerton wrote. "The boy is high strung, nervous, and inclined to panic.... His fault is that he seems striving constantly to conceal his nervousness under a veneer of pretended careless-ness and coolness."[11] Late in the season, Risberg went into a slump and as the White Sox fought for the American League pennant, manager Pants Rowland benched him. Buck Weaver shifted to his old position at shortstop and Fred McMullin took over at third base. Risberg only pinch-hit twice as the White Sox beat the New York Giants in the 1917 World Series. Heading into the 1918 season, Rowland told Risberg he would have to hit better if he wanted to keep his job.

The year 1918 was chaotic for professional baseball, as the "work or fight" order prevented players from being exempted from war duties. Though he batted an im-proved .256, Risberg appeared in just 82 games before leaving the team on August 8 and heading home to San Francisco. He had told Comiskey and the press that he would enlist in the Army upon his arrival, but instead he found work in an Alameda, California, shipyard owned by Bethlehem Steel. Although Risberg's job was termed essential and enabled him to avoid the draft, it consisted largely of playing base-ball, as he batted .308 for the shipyard team. Risberg had made his contribution to the war effort in May,

however, when he had to skip town to avoid arrest after punching a man at the White Sox' team hotel in New York for complaining about the Red Cross's persistent fundraising efforts.[12]

In 1919 Risberg signed a two-year contract worth $3,250 a season, making him one of the lowest-paid White Sox starters but commensurate with the 24-year-old's erratic performance thus far in his career.[13] He again hit .256, but recorded a career-high 19 stolen bases in 119 games as the White Sox returned to the World Series for the second time in three years.

But Risberg's season was a rocky one. As Chicago slumped in June and fell out of first place for the first time, new manager Kid Gleason turned to the tried-and-true lineup of Buck Weaver at shortstop and Fred McMullin at third, bumping Risberg from a starting job. The White Sox immediately got hot and built a 6½-game lead by the end of July. Risberg had returned to the lineup by then and played well enough to remain as the starting shortstop for the World Series against the Cincinnati Reds.

In September Risberg received good press in the *Atlanta Constitution*, which labeled him a "miracle man (who had) blossomed out as a wonder." More than one big leaguer, according to this article, claimed that Risberg possessed the "greatest throwing arm of any infielder in the big show," boasting "almost un-believable speed."[14] Manager Gleason offered his own assessment in the *New York Times* that month, stating with as-yet-unknown irony that Risberg might end up being the "star of the show" in the coming World Series.[15]

Darker undertones, however, stalked Risberg and the White Sox during the 1919 season. The team was split into two factions—the more educated players, led by second baseman and team captain Eddie Collins; and the more rough-and-tumble group, led by former boxer and current first baseman Arnold "Chick" Gandil. Risberg, who belonged to the second group, agreed to throw the 1919 World Series in exchange for payoffs from gamblers. In addition, he assisted Gandil in organizing the scheme, collecting money from the gamblers, delivering it to teammates, and helping to persuade Joe Jackson to participate. Jackson later said in a deposition that when he didn't receive his promised money, he had threatened to expose the plot. Risberg threatened to kill Jackson if he blabbed, and was convincing. "Swede," Jackson said, "is a hard guy."[16]

Risberg took home a reported $10,000 to $15,000 for his role in the conspiracy.[17] He also sent a telegram before the Series to his friend, St. Louis Browns infielder Joe Gedeon, informing Gedeon that the Series was fixed and advising him to bet on Cincinnati.[18] A year later Gedeon informed on Risberg to the White Sox, hoping to collect a $20,000 reward offered by Charles Comiskey for information on the fix. Gedeon didn't get the reward, but he was later banned from baseball for his prior knowledge.

Risberg played horribly in the Series, hitting only .080 (2-for-25) and making four errors. His involvement in the fix was solidified in Game One, when he failed to complete a critical double play in the fourth inning and the Reds went on to score five runs off White Sox ace Eddie Cicotte.[19] In Game Six Risberg almost single-handedly eliminated his team from the World Series. He lined into two double plays (both times with a runner in scoring position), booted a grounder, and made an errant throw to allow a run to score. But his fellow conspirator Chick Gandil singled in the winning run in the 10th inning to keep the White Sox alive. Perhaps to cover up for the reasons behind his poor performance, Risberg claimed to have a cold during the Series. In the 1921 criminal trial, a team trainer testified that he had indeed given Risberg cold medicine before Game One.[20]

Risberg and the other suspected players (except Gandil, who had retired in a contract dispute) returned to the White Sox in 1920. Despite persistent rumors that the White Sox were continuing to throw games during the pennant race, Swede had his best season yet, batting .266 and setting career highs with 21 doubles, 10 triples, and 65 RBIs. He missed some time with a spike wound in May and then abruptly left the team in June, going home to San Francisco for two weeks, reportedly

because his toddler son, Lawrence, was ill.[21] Down the stretch, with dark clouds swirling over the White Sox, Risberg had some of the best performances of his career. He hit .380 in his final 13 games, including consecutive four-hit games on September 20-21 against the Philadelphia A's as the White Sox tried to keep pace with the Cleveland Indians for the AL lead.

But one week later, Eddie Cicotte appeared before a Chicago grand jury and confessed to throwing the World Series. He was immediately suspended by owner Charles Comiskey, and so were Risberg, Gandil, Joe Jackson, Happy Felsch, Fred McMullin, Lefty Williams, and Buck Weaver. They were later acquitted in court, but none of them ever played in Organized Baseball again. A day after the jury's verdict came back, Baseball Commissioner Kenesaw Mountain Landis banned them all for life.

That didn't mean Risberg—the youngest of the expelled Black Sox at 26—stopped playing ball. Throughout the following decade, he traveled around the country and even into Canada, making a living in "outlaw" and semipro leagues, sometimes with his old teammates. Risberg did comparatively well playing outlaw ball; his son Robert later claimed that his father earned more money playing in outlaw leagues than he ever had playing for Comiskey.

His wife of nearly a decade, the former Agnes Garibaldi, who hailed from the same San Francisco neighborhood as the Risbergs, wanted no part of his nomadic lifestyle; in 1922 she filed for divorce, citing cruelty and neglect. In court Agnes stated that the couple had been happy when Risberg was playing in the Pacific Coast League, but not during his major-league career. As for the game-fixing scandal, Agnes said that Risberg grew fond of saying, "Why work when you can fool the public?"[22] The divorce was granted in December 1922 and Agnes received custody of their two children, Charles and Lawrence. Her request for alimony was denied, however, because Swede had fled the jurisdiction of the court.

During that same summer of 1922, Risberg joined Cicotte, Williams, Weaver, and Felsch on a traveling team known as the "Ex-Major League Stars." They scheduled a series of games against teams from northern Minnesota's Iron Range, but lackadaisical play and poor management meant the players left with only a few hundred dollars afterward. Cicotte left the team in mid-June after an argument with Risberg over money—the hard-nosed Swede reportedly responded by punching him in the mouth.[23]

Risberg moved on to Minnesota, where he married a woman from Rochester, Mary Frances Purcell, with whom he had two sons, Robert and Gerald. In between his travels with the independent Rochester Aces team, Swede also operated a small farm for several years, selling eggs and other wares to the nearby Mayo Clinic to supplement his baseball income. With the Aces, Risberg used his strong right arm to return to his roots as a pitcher and he dominated the regional semipro competition. In 1923 he threw a no-hitter against a team of Minnesota collegians and struck out 21 batters in a game against a town team from Rice Lake, Wisconsin.[24] Semipro pitchers were able to command higher salaries and under-the-table bonuses for high strikeout totals, so Risberg took the mound as often as his arm would allow for the rest of his "outlaw" career.

In 1926, Judge Landis contacted Risberg to garner testimony about a gambling scandal involving Ty Cobb and Tris Speaker. Although he had nothing to add to that case, Risberg (with the help of Chick Gandil) made national headlines by suggesting that in September 1917 the Detroit Tigers deliberately lost four games to the White Sox, helping Chicago capture the pennant. Two weeks later, Risberg added, he and Gandil collected $45 each from White Sox players, and forwarded the money to players in Detroit. Landis called dozens of players from both teams to his Chicago office to testify about the "new" baseball scandal. All of the other former White Sox and Tigers players contradicted their story, claiming that the money was paid out to Detroit players as a reward for winning late-season games against the Boston Red Sox, Chicago's chief rival for the pennant. The practice of "rewarding" opponents was common during the Deadball Era, but Landis quietly banned it and cleared

Swede Risberg, circa 1919 (Bain Collection, Library of Congress, Prints and Photographs Division)

the Tigers of any wrongdoing. Will Rogers attended Risberg's hearing and, in his view, "It was just that bottled up hate against everything that made [Risberg] think he hadn't had a square deal in the game, and he exaggerated the incident."[25]

Risberg stayed out of the spotlight afterward, but continued to play ball until the mid-1930s. He and Happy Felsch spent a summer playing for a mining company team in Scobey, Montana, and then toured western Canada together for a while, playing games against all challengers in Saskatchewan and Manitoba. During the Great Depression, he played for teams in Jamestown, North Dakota, and Sioux Falls, South Dakota, and also tried his hand at many other businesses (among them a car dealership, a hotel, and a miniature-golf course) as his ability to make a living in "outlaw" baseball subsided. Struggling to make ends meet, Risberg decided to move back home to Northern California, eventually settling in a town called Weed near the Oregon border. After finally retiring from baseball, he operated a successful tavern there for almost two decades.

Author Eliot Asinof, working on the book that became the classic *Eight Men Out*, visited Risberg at his tavern in the early 1960s. He described the nearly 70-year-old ballplayer as "balding and gray, his pale face relatively free of creases." When approached, Risberg "seemed pleasant enough, although uninterested, as if sensing there was nothing in it for him." Once Risberg realized Asinof's intent to interview him, though, "His look was so cutting, so full of suspicion," and Risberg claimed not to remember anything about the infamous events that had transpired so long ago.[26]

In his later years, Risberg's health suffered as he developed osteomyelitis in his knee. The condition, which was supposedly caused by an old spike wound and possibly exacerbated by a bad car accident in Jamestown, forced Risberg to walk with a pronounced limp. The leg eventually became infected and had to be amputated. By this time, his wife, Mary, had died and Swede had moved in with his son Robert and family in Red Bluff, California, where he spent the final years of his life. In 1970 the local newspaper asked him to analyze the coming World Series between the Baltimore Orioles and Cincinnati Reds. He picked the Reds to win.[27] (The Orioles won in five games.)

Risberg died on his 81st birthday, October 13, 1975, in a convalescent home in Red Bluff; he was the last of the "Eight Men Out" to die. He was buried next to Mary in Mount Shasta, California.

SOURCES

Asinof, Eliot. *Bleeding Between the Lines* (New York: Holt, Rinehart, and Winston, 1979).

Cottrell, Robert C. *Blackball, the Black Sox and the Babe: Baseball's Crucial 1920 Season.* (Jefferson, North Carolina: McFarland, 2002).

Muchlinski, Alan. *After the Black Sox: The Swede Risberg Story* (Authorhouse, 2005).

Seymour, Harold. *Baseball: The Golden Age* (New York: Oxford University Press, 2002).

Atlanta Constitution

Baseball Magazine

Chicago Tribune

Los Angeles Times

New York Times

Red Bluff (California) *Daily News*

The Sporting News

Washington Post

NOTES

1 *Los Angeles Times*, June 1, 1917.

2 *Red Bluff* (California) *Daily News*, October 9, 1970.

3 See the SABR Black Sox Scandal Research Committee newsletter for June 2012 at SABR.org. Historian Bob Hoie also noted that Swede had fine penmanship, a sign that "he was taught, and taught well."

4 *Los Angeles Times*, March 29, 1912.

5 *Atlanta Constitution*, September 14, 1919.

6 *Los Angeles Times*, May 7, 1916.

7 *Los Angeles Times*, June 25, 1915.

8 *Los Angeles Times*, March 11, 1915.

9 *Los Angeles Times*, August 6, 1916.

10 *Los Angeles Times*, June 1, 1917.

11 *Washington Times*, September 27, 1917.

12 *Chicago Tribune*, May 23, 1918.

13 Bob Hoie, "1919 Baseball Salaries and the Mythically Underpaid Chicago White Sox," *Base Ball: A Journal of the Early Game* (Jefferson, North Carolina: McFarland & Co., Spring 2012).

14 *Atlanta Constitution*, September 14, 1919.

15 *New York Times*, September 28, 1920.

16 *Chicago Tribune*, September 29, 1920.

17 Ibid.

18 Tipped off by Risberg about the fix, Joe Gedeon reportedly won $600 betting on the World Series through St. Louis gamblers Carl Zork and Ben Franklin. See *Washington Post*, October 27, 1920.

19 The botched double-play ball, hit by the Reds' Larry Kopf and fielded by pitcher Eddie Cicotte, remains one of the most disputed plays in the 1919 World Series. Some writers suggested that Cicotte's throw to Risberg at second base was too low or too slow, while others thought Risberg delayed his throw to first, enabling Kopf to beat it out. The *Chicago Tribune* called it the "break of the game," as the double play would have ended the inning and kept the game scoreless. A rare newsreel film discovered decades later and made public by the Library and Archives Canada in 2014 actually shows footage of the controversial play. See Jacob Pomrenke, "Rare Footage of 1919 World Series Discovered in Canadian Archive," SABR.org, May 2, 2014, sabr.org/latest/rare-footage-1919-world-series-action-discovered-canadian-archive.

20 *New York Times*, July 29, 1921.

21 *Chicago Tribune*, June 14, 1920.

22   *Duluth* (Minnesota) *News Tribune,* August 28, 1922.

23   *Chicago Tribune,* June 25, 1922.

24   Stew Thornley, *Baseball in Minnesota: A Definitive History* (St. Paul, Minnesota: Minnesota Historical Society Press, 2006).

25   *Indianapolis News,* January 22, 1927.

26   Eliot Asinof, *Bleeding Between the Lines* (New York: Holt, Rinehart, and Winston, 1979), 92.

27   *Red Bluff* (California) *Daily News,* October 9, 1970.

CHARLIE ROBERTSON

By Jacob Pomrenke

IF THERE WAS ONE THING THE Detroit Tigers could do under player-manager Ty Cobb, it was hit. They set an American League record with a .316 team batting average in 1921, and six of their eight starters in 1922 finished over .300. Even four of their backups hit over .300 that year. They were strong up and down the lineup.

So when the 25,000 fans at Navin Field in Detroit rose for the seventh-inning stretch on Sunday, April 30, 1922, and word spread throughout the overflow crowd that the Tigers still had not recorded a single hit, they turned their attention to the opposing pitcher: 26-year-old Chicago White Sox rookie Charlie Robertson.

Robertson was the last pitcher anyone—least of all the Detroit faithful—expected to be shutting out the mighty Tigers offense. He was a journeyman with an unremarkable résumé who had recorded his first major-league victory just four days earlier. But here was Robertson following up future Hall of Famer Red Faber's shutout the day before with one of his own.

So in the seventh inning, the Navin Field fans let him have it, in one final effort to unsettle the rookie right-hander.[1] Nursing a 2-0 lead, Robertson was unfazed. In the seventh he set down Lu Blue, George Cutshaw, and Ty Cobb—the latter on a called strike three. Cobb was furious and loudly accused Robertson of doctoring the ball. Umpire Dick Nallin didn't take the bait. In the eighth Bobby Veach took Robertson to a full count but anxiously chased a pitch out of the strike zone and flied out. Harry Heilmann and Bob Jones also went down in order. By the ninth, the crowd's mood had changed. History was being made, and now they were rooting for Robertson to finish the job.

Cobb sent Dan Clark to pinch-hit for rookie Topper Rigney. Clark struck out for the first out. Clyde Manion lifted an easy pop fly to second base for the second out. Only pinch-hitter Johnny Bassler, the regular starting catcher, stood in Robertson's way now. Robertson called timeout and walked behind the mound to prepare himself. Shortstop Eddie Mulligan was startled to hear Robertson talking to him: "Do you realize that little fat man up there is the only thing between me and a perfect game?"[2] Mulligan was too stunned to reply. He pushed Robertson back toward the mound.

Robertson wound up and delivered a fastball to Bassler, who looped it into short left field. Johnny Mostil squeezed the ball in his glove for the 27th out. Charlie Robertson's perfect game—perhaps the most unlikely perfect game in major-league history—was officially in the books.

After Robertson's second major-league victory, there was nowhere to go but down.

Charles Culbertson Robertson, who pitched in one game for the 1919 White Sox, was born on January 31, 1896, in Dexter, Texas, on the Red River in the north-eastern part of the state. He was the eighth of nine children born to Mathias and Nancy Robertson, farmers from Tennessee who moved to Texas around 1890 and eventually settled in Montague County.[3] Not much is known of Charlie's early life, but he was well educated for his time. He graduated from Nocona High School in 1915 and began studying for the ministry at Austin College in Sherman, Texas. According to his file at the National Baseball Hall of Fame Library, he played baseball, football, and basketball at Austin College and graduated around 1918.[4]

While in college, Robertson was signed by the Sherman team of the low-level Western Association in 1917 and developed a reputation as a "shine ball expert."[5] He reportedly pitched shutouts in both games of a doubleheader against Ardmore, and won 23 out of 27 starts.[6] This drew the attention of the Chicago White Sox and Robertson was invited to spring training with the major-league club in 1918 at Mineral Wells, Texas. Manager Pants Rowland and coach Kid Gleason "thought he was not quite ready" and sent him to the Minneapolis Millers of the American Association.[7] He went 2-7 with a 1.94 ERA in nine games for the Millers before enlisting in the U.S. Army Air Service as baseball players and other nonessential employees were ordered to "work or fight" during World War I. He saw no combat and returned to Minnesota after the war ended.

In early 1919 Robertson was called up to the White Sox for the first time. With a critical series against the defending World Series champion Boston Red Sox approaching in mid-May, Gleason—who had replaced Rowland as White Sox manager—gave his rookie pitchers a chance to show off their abilities against the lowly St. Louis Browns at Comiskey Park. Robertson made his major-league debut on May 13 against the Browns. He lasted just two innings, allowing five hits and two runs, and was replaced by fellow rookie Dickey Kerr, who pitched seven shutout innings in a 2-1 loss.[8] Kerr stayed with the White Sox and became a relief ace of sorts for Gleason as Chicago went on to win the American League pennant. The two innings were all Robertson pitched in the majors until 1922. Robertson was sent back to the Minneapolis Millers and struggled to an 11-13 record and a 3.10 ERA in the minor leagues.

Robertson watched from afar as the White Sox lost the tainted 1919 World Series to the Cincinnati Reds—and later as eight of his former teammates were implicated in throwing the Series for a promised $100,000 bribe from gamblers in what became known as the Black Sox Scandal. The eight Black Sox implicated in the fix were banned from Organized Baseball for life following the 1920 season.

As the scandal unfolded in Chicago, Robertson spent two more years with the Minneapolis Millers. He was a solid but unspectacular prospect, logging more than 300 innings apiece in 1920 and 1921 and compiling 35 wins to 31 losses. In the offseason he went home to

TCMA photo of Charlie Robertson (Courtesy of Michael Aronstein / TCMA Ltd.)

Nocona, Texas, and worked as a salesman at a rubber company.[9]

In 1922, with the depleted White Sox searching for dependable pitchers, the 26-year-old Robertson finally earned a spot in Kid Gleason's starting rotation. His early-season performances gave no indication that he was about to make history. He pitched two innings of mop-up relief in a 14-0 loss to the Browns on April 15 and was pulled after six innings in a 10-5 win at St. Louis on April 21. Five days later Robertson hurled his first complete game, pitching in and out of trouble in a 7-3 win at Cleveland. It was his first major-league victory. No one could have predicted the historic nature of his second.

Robertson's perfect game on April 30 against the Tigers was the third in American League history, after those of Cy Young in 1904 and Addie Joss in 1908. With a lineup powered by Hall of Famers Ty Cobb and Harry Heilmann and the great Bobby Veach,

Detroit was an unlikely no-hit victim. Robertson's feat included an added degree of difficulty because of the overflow crowd at Navin Field. With spectators on the field, ground rules dictated that any ball hit into the crowd would be ruled a double. Only one ball came close. In the second inning Bobby Veach lined a sharp drive toward the roped-off boundary in left field. But as Johnny Mostil backed up, the crowd parted, allowing him to make the catch with ease. In the same inning Harry Hooper made a splendid running catch of a hard-hit ball by Bob Jones.[10] The Tigers hit only five balls out of the infield and struck out six times.

Led by manager Cobb, a master of gamesmanship, the Tigers seemed to spend more time worrying about the legality of Robertson's pitches than in actually trying to hit them. Cobb stopped the game on several occasions to complain to umpire Nallin, accusing Robertson of using oil or grease to make the ball jump noticeably, a charge the White Sox mocked afterward. The next day Nallin dutifully took two game balls to American League President Ban Johnson's office in Chicago. Johnson quickly denied the Tigers' protest, stating, "I consider Robertson one of the cleanest pitchers in organized baseball today."[11]

April 30 wasn't the only shining moment in Robertson's rookie season. On June 13 he took a no-hitter into the eighth inning against the Red Sox, settling for a two-hit shutout. His third shutout of the year was a rain-shortened, five-inning affair against the Indians on September 1. He would record just three more shutouts in his major-league career. For the most part, Robertson rarely found the magic touch he possessed that Sunday afternoon in Chicago. His 1922 season could best be described as erratic; he allowed at least 10 hits in 11 of his 34 starts and finished with a 14-15 record and a 3.64 ERA in 272 innings. The Tigers, in particular, took pleasure in beating up on the right-hander, who struggled to a 5.58 ERA in 17 appearances against Detroit after the perfect game, his worst against any American League club.[12]

Some reporters and teammates said the early success went to Robertson's head, because in 1923 he staged a lengthy holdout during spring training and threatened to jump to a semipro team in Chicago, as teammate Dickey Kerr had done.[13] *The Sporting News* reported that the White Sox' offer to Robertson was just $100 more than what he had been making ($3,750) in 1922; he figured his performance entitled him to a raise of about ten times higher than that.[14] He got what he was asking for and signed a contract worth $5,000, but didn't get over the slight quickly.

In late June of 1923, White Sox manager Kid Gleason suspended a petulant Robertson after a poor start against the Tigers in Detroit. Gleason claimed his pitcher was "not trying"—an accusation now taken extremely seriously by the White Sox since the World Series scandal—by pitching side-arm and walking three batters in the first inning. Robertson was sent home to Chicago and did not make another appearance for two weeks.[15]

Despite pitching well after his return, Robertson was put on the trading block in the offseason. The Sox and Yankees nearly agreed to a blockbuster deal sending future Hall of Famer Eddie Collins and Bibb Falk to New York for Bob Meusel, Aaron Ward, and Waite Hoyt (another future Hall of Famer), but the Yankees demanded an extra pitcher from the White Sox and were not willing to accept Robertson. Gleason "insisted that if one (pitcher) had to go Robertson would have to be the man."[16] The talks ended without a deal and Collins—and Robertson—stayed in Chicago for the time being.

An elbow injury limited Robertson to 97⅓ innings in his third full season with the White Sox, 1924. He walked nearly twice as many batters as he struck out and finished 4-10 with a 4.99 ERA.[17] He had surgery to remove bone chips that fall, and felt well enough to join some of his White Sox teammates on an around-the-world tour organized by White Sox owner Charles Comiskey and Giants manager John McGraw. It was a reprise of their successful tour held during the offseason of 1913-14. Stars like Red Faber, Willie Kamm, Stuffy McInnis, Sam Rice, Johnny Evers, Heinie Groh, Frank Frisch, Ross Youngs, and Casey Stengel participated. Games were scheduled in

England, Ireland, France, Japan, Hong Kong, the Philippines, and Australia, but poor weather and even worse crowds—fewer than 20 people showed up for an exhibition in Dublin—abruptly ended the tour overseas after seven games. The group sailed back to New York in late November.[18]

Healthy again, Robertson showed a brief resurgence early in 1925, recording two shutouts. But he went 1-6 in his final nine appearances for the White Sox and was claimed off waivers by the St. Louis Browns in the offseason.

Robertson's first appearance for the Browns in 1926 was against his old teammates at Comiskey Park; he lasted just two innings against the White Sox. In June, with Robertson sporting an atrocious 8.36 ERA, the Browns sent him down to the minor leagues for the first time in five years. He pitched well for the Milwaukee Brewers of the American Association, and the Boston Braves took a flyer on him in the Rule 5 draft that fall. But Robertson had nothing left. He went 7-17 for the Braves in 1927 and 2-5 in 1928 before the Braves sold his contract. He lost 34 games in two forgettable seasons with the Brewers in 1929 and '30, then hung up his spikes for good.

Robertson's eight-year major-league career ended with a 49-80 record, the worst winning percentage (.380) by any pitcher who has thrown a perfect game. His crowning achievement was one of the White Sox' lone bright spots in the decade after the World Series scandal, but he didn't have the ability or temperament to succeed consistently in the majors.

He retired to his native Texas with his wife, the former Fay Redus, whose ancestors were early settlers in Palo Pinto County, where Robertson had first been invited to spring training with the White Sox at Mineral Wells. Robertson became a prosperous pecan broker in Fort Worth and ignored the baseball world until 1956, when Don Larsen of the New York Yankees threw the major leagues' first perfect game—in the World Series, no less—since Robertson had done it 34 years before. Reporters across the country sought

out Robertson for interviews and he reluctantly appeared on the CBS television show *What's My Line?*[19]

Robertson told *The Sporting News* he was glad to be out of the limelight:

"[If I] had known then what I know now, I wouldn't have been in baseball," he said. "It isn't sour grapes. Baseball didn't give me a particularly bad break, but I went through it and found out that it's ridiculous for any young man with qualifications to make good in another profession to waste time in professional athletics.... When they get through with an athlete, he has to start over and at an age when it's the wrong time to be starting.... Just forget my name. It was long ago."[20]

But Charlie Robertson is still remembered, then and now. His name resurfaces on the rare occasion when a major-league pitcher throws a perfect game. When he died at age 88 on August 23, 1984, at a Fort Worth nursing home, his niece Nancy Ward said he "still gets fan mail from all over the world. He got three letters last week."[21] Baseballs, photos, and other mementos often show up at his gravesite in Palo Pinto Cemetery.

Robertson's one shining moment was just that: a moment. For one afternoon, as unlikely as it was, he could say he was perfect.

SOURCES

Special thanks to the National Baseball Hall of Fame Library in Cooperstown, New York, for making Robertson's player file available. Other sources, in addition to those cited in the endnotes, include Baseball-Reference.com, Retrosheet.org, Ancestry.com, the *Chicago Tribune*, and *The Sporting News*.

NOTES

1   Edward Prell, "Thirty Years Ago Today: Sox Pitcher Was Perfect," *Chicago Tribune*, April 30, 1952, B2.

2   Norman Kronstadt, "The Perfect Game," Undated article in Charlie Robertson player file, National Baseball Hall of Fame Library, Cooperstown, New York.

3   1900 United States Census, accessed at Ancestry.com; McDaniel, Robert Wayne. "Dexter, TX," Handbook of Texas Online, Published by the Texas State Historical Association.

4   An uncredited May 2, 1922, article in Robertson's Hall of Fame player file said he graduated in January 1918. A January 30, 1981, letter from Mike Barry, director of alumni relations at Austin College, to SABR founding member Joe Simenic, available in Robertson's Hall of Fame player file, stated that "Mr. Robertson graduated in 1920."

5   *Paris* (Texas) *News*, August 30, 1917. Charlie Robertson player file, National Baseball Hall of Fame Library, Cooperstown, New York.

6   Uncredited article from July 26, 1917, Charlie Robertson player file, National Baseball Hall of Fame Library, Cooperstown, New York.

7   "Robertson No Juvenile Wonder," uncredited article from May 2, 1922, Charlie Robertson player file, National Baseball Hall of Fame Library, Cooperstown, New York. This article and another by Edward Prell of the *Chicago Tribune* said the White Sox paid $250 to the Sherman (Texas) team in 1918 for Robertson's contract, with an additional $1,750 to be paid if they kept him. When the White Sox sent him to Minneapolis for seasoning, they got no response from Sherman and the additional money was never paid. In 1922, after Robertson's perfect game, the Sherman club suddenly "came to life and demanded the payment." On advice from Commissioner Kenesaw Mountain Landis, the White Sox settled with Sherman rather than fight the case.

8   Irving Sanborn, "Old Man Horseshoes Helps Browns Lick White Sox, 2-1," *Chicago Tribune*, May 14, 1919, 19.

9   Baseball-Reference.com; 1920 United States Census, Ancestry.com.

10 "Sox Close First Series Here With Monday Game," uncredited article from May 1, 1922, Charlie Robertson player file, National Baseball Hall of Fame Library, Cooperstown, New York.

11 "Absolves Pitcher of All Suspicion." *Spartanburg* (South Carolina) *Herald*, May 3, 1922.

12 Charlie Robertson pitching splits, Retrosheet.org, accessed online on February 20, 2012.

13 "'No-Hit Bobby' Holdout As Sox Arrive In Camp," *Chicago Tribune*, March 1, 1923. Dickey Kerr, the 1919 World Series hero, spent two seasons out of major-league baseball pitching for a Chicago semipro team, was suspended for the entire 1924 season, and made an aborted comeback in 1925.

14 "'Reward' For Perfect Game," *The Sporting News*, February 8, 1923; salary data from SABR member Michael Haupert's study of the National Baseball Hall of Fame Library contract cards.

15 "Disciplined," *Chicago Tribune*, June 25, 1923.

16 "Big Deal Depends on One Player," *New York Times*, December 19, 1922; "Yankees and White Sox End All Negotiations for Big Trade Involving Collins," *Providence News*, February 20, 1923.

17 Irving Vaughan, "Crooked Arm Lays Up Robertson, Sox Ace," *Chicago Tribune*, May 1, 1924.

18 Ancestry.com; "Players Named For Tour," *The Sporting News*, October 9, 1924, 1; John Mullin, "Comiskey Rewarded Pals With Sox-Giants World Tours," *Chicago Tribune*, March 30, 1998.

19 "Robertson on 'What's My Line?'" *The Sporting News*, October 24, 1956, 28. "Introduced only as C.C. Robertson of Fort Worth, Texas, his identity was guessed immediately by panelist Bennett Cerf but the panel nearly ran out of time before guessing his present occupation as a pecan broker."

20 "Robertson Would Turn Down Game If He Had New Chance," *The Sporting News*, October 17, 1956, 7.

21 "Enduring Popularity," uncredited article dated August 26, 1984, Charlie Robertson player file, National Baseball Hall of Fame Library, Cooperstown, New York.

SEASON TIMELINE: JULY 1919

White Sox record: 22-10 (.688)
Runs scored: 178 | Runs allowed: 151

AL standings
July 31, 1919

Team	W	L	Pct	GB
CHW	57	33	.633	—
DET	50	39	.562	6½
CLE	50	39	.562	6½
NYY	48	39	.552	7½
SLB	47	40	.540	8½
BOS	39	48	.448	16½
WSH	38	53	.418	19½
PHA	24	62	.279	31

PLAYER OF THE MONTH

	G	PA	AB	R	H	2B	3B	HR	RBI	SB	BB	SO	BA	OBP	SLG	OPS
Chick Gandil	18	73	66	13	30	5	4	0	12	3	3	3	.455	.486	.652	1.137

Gandil was having one of the best months of his career when he hurt his knee on July 17. He hit safely in 16 of 18 games, including a 4-for-4 performance in a 17-1 rout of the Cleveland Indians on July 3. He also drove in four runs and scored two more as the White Sox beat the Red Sox 14-9 on July 13. Gandil's 10 multi-hit games were the most in July by any player on the team.

PITCHER OF THE MONTH

	W	L	ERA	G	GS	CG	SHO	IP	H	R	ER	BB	SO	WHIP
Eddie Cicotte	6	1	1.86	8	7	6	1	63	56	15	13	8	18	1.016

The White Sox' reputation as a two-man pitching staff was almost cut in half in July. Cicotte did his part, winning six of his seven starts, including a 10-inning shutout of the St. Louis Browns on July 24 that improved his record to 19-4 (and a superb 1.28 ERA) with two months left in the season. But co-ace Lefty Williams didn't register a win over the final two weeks and then was beaned by a line drive to the head, forcing manager Kid Gleason to scramble for healthy pitchers to fill in the gaps.

DAY BY DAY RECAP

Tuesday, July 1
Dunn Field, Cleveland
"Indians Bat Sox All Over Lots, Win 14-9; Three Hurt" — *Chicago Tribune*

White Sox (35-24)	003	101	103 — 9 15 6
Indians (34-24)	703	210	10x — 14 16 1

WP: Hi Jasper (1-1). LP: Lefty Williams (11-6).

Lefty Williams: ⅓ IP, 4 H, 6 R, 5 ER, 0 BB, 0 K.
Fred McMullin: 2-4, 2B, 3B, 2 R. Buck Weaver: 3-5, 3 R.

Wednesday, July 2
Dunn Field, Cleveland
"Sox Whip Indians in Another Scrappy Affair; Score, 6 to 4" — *Chicago Tribune*

White Sox (36-24)	310	000	002 — 6 9 0
Indians (34-25)	000	001	210 — 4 11 0

WP: Dave Danforth (1-2). LP: George Uhle (3-5).
Dickey Kerr: 6⅔ IP, 8 H, 3 R, 3 ER, 3 BB, 2 K.
Joe Jackson: 2-4, 2B, 2 R. Dickey Kerr: 1-3, 2B, R.

Thursday, July 3
Dunn Field, Cleveland
"Sox Trim Cleveland; Indians Knocked For Count of 10 in Fourth Inning" — *Chicago Tribune*

White Sox (37-24)	010	(10)33	000 — 17 15 2
Indians (34-26)	100	000	000 — 1 5 4

WP: Lefty Williams (12-6). LP: Guy Morton (6-7).
Lefty Williams: 9 IP, 5 H, 1 R, 1 ER, 2 BB, 0 K.
Chick Gandil: 4-4, 3B, R. Joe Jackson: 3-6, 2 2B, 2 R. Eddie Collins: 2-4, 2B, R.

Friday, July 4
Comiskey Park, Chicago
"Sox Delight 35,000 Fans By Taking a Pair from Detroit" — *Chicago Tribune*

Tigers (31-29)	100	000	000 — 1 8 1
White Sox (38-24)	005	000	30x — 8 11 1

WP: Eddie Cicotte (14-4). LP: Bernie Boland (6-7).
Eddie Cicotte: 9 IP, 8 H, 1 R, 1 ER, 2 BB, 3 K.
Fred McMullin: 2-3, 2 2B, 2 R. Chick Gandil: 3-3, 2 R. Ray Schalk: 2-3, 3B.

Tigers (31-30)	100	000	000 — 1 7 0
White Sox (39-24)	000	001	001 — 2 6 0

WP: Dickey Kerr (4-1). LP: Slim Love (2-2).
Dickey Kerr: 9 IP, 7 H, 1 R, 1 ER, 1 BB, 2 K.
Joe Jackson: 2-3, 2B, R, RBI. Buck Weaver: 1-3, 2B, R.

Saturday, July 5
Comiskey Park, Chicago
"Tigers Profit by Sox Errors and Win, 6 to 3" — *Chicago Tribune*

Tigers (32-30)	100	400	100 — 6 9 1
White Sox (39-25)	000	200	010 — 3 8 3

WP: Hooks Dauss (8-5). LP: Red Faber (5-6).
Red Faber: 8 IP, 8 H, 6 R, 1 ER, 2 BB, 2 K.
Joe Jackson: 2-4, 2 RBI. Buck Weaver: 2-4, 2B, R.

Sunday, July 6
Comiskey Park, Chicago
"White Sox Near Top Place by Defeating Tigers, 4 to 1" — *Chicago Tribune*

Tigers (32-31)   000   000   001 — 1 9 2
White Sox (40-25)   010   110   01x — 4 8 1
WP: Lefty Williams (13-6). LP: Dutch Leonard (4-6).
Lefty Williams: 9 IP, 9 H, 1 R, 1 ER, 2 BB, 3 K.
Joe Jackson: 2-4, 2B, 2 RBI. Eddie Collins: 2-4, R, RBI. Chick Gandil: 1-3, 3B, RBI.

Monday, July 7
Comiskey Park, Chicago
"Hose Stick on Yanks' Heels by Whipping Tigers, 8 to 3" — *Chicago Tribune*

Tigers (32-32)   000   120   000 — 3 10 1
White Sox (41-25)   023   200   01x — 8 15 2
WP: Eddie Cicotte (15-4). LP: Howard Ehmke (9-7).
Eddie Cicotte: 9 IP, 10 H, 3 R, 1 ER, 3 BB, 1 K.
Chick Gandil: 2-3, 2 2B, HBP, R, 2 RBI. Happy Felsch: 2-5, SB, 2 R, RBI. Eddie Cicotte: 2-4, 2 RBI.

Tuesday, July 8
Scheduled day off
"Beloit Fairies Trim White Sox in Exhibit, 4 to 2" — *Chicago Tribune*

Wednesday, July 9
Comiskey Park, Chicago
"Sox Beat Macks Twice and Trail First Place by an Atom" — *Chicago Tribune*

Athletics (17-46)   400   010   002 — 7 10 0
White Sox (42-25)   000   200   33x — 8 11 1
WP: Red Faber (6-6). LP: Tom Rogers (3-10).
Dave Danforth: 3 IP, 0 H, 0 R, 0 ER, 0 BB, 2 K.
Happy Felsch: 3-4, 2 2B, 2 R, RBI. Joe Jackson: 2-4, 3B, 2 R. Fred McMullin: 1-3, HBP, 2 R.

Athletics (17-47)   000   001   001 — 2 6 2
White Sox (43-25)   022   000   20x — 6 12 1
WP: Red Faber (7-6). LP: Jing Johnson (4-9).
Red Faber: 9 IP, 6 H, 2 R, 1 ER, 2 BB, 1 K.
Joe Jackson: 3-3. Buck Weaver: 2-4, 2B, R. Red Faber: 1-2, R, 2 BB.

Thursday, July 10
Comiskey Park, Chicago
"Sox Use Macks as Stepping Stone to First Place, 9 to 2" — *Chicago Tribune*

Athletics (17-48)   000   000   011 — 2 8 3
White Sox (44-25)   102   004   11x — 9 10 2
WP: Lefty Williams (14-6). LP: Rollie Naylor (1-7).

Lefty Williams: 9 IP, 8 H, 2 R, 1 ER, 1 BB, 2 K.

Nemo Leibold: 2-3, 3 R, 2B, SB, BB. Chick Gandil: 2-3, 3B, R, 2 RBI. Joe Jackson: 2-3, 3B, R, RBI.

Friday, July 11
Comiskey Park, Chicago
"Macks Home Guards Bow to White Sox Again, 7 to 1" — *Chicago Tribune*

Athletics (17-49)	001	000	000—1 9 3
White Sox (45-25)	030	030	01x—7 12 0

WP: Eddie Cicotte (16-4). LP: Scott Perry (2-11).

Eddie Cicotte: 9 IP, 9 H, 1 R, 1 ER, 2 BB, 3 K.

Nemo Leibold: 3-4, BB, R, RBI. Joe Jackson: 2-3, 2B, BB, 2 R, RBI. Chick Gandil: 2-4, SB, R, RBI.

Saturday, July 12
Comiskey Park, Chicago
"Sox Are Given Terrific Mauling by Boston, 12 to 4" — *Chicago Tribune*

Red Sox (31-37)	014	202	003—12 17 1
White Sox (45-26)	210	000	001—4 10 0

WP: Herb Pennock (5-4). LP: Dickey Kerr (4-2).

Dickey Kerr: 2⅓ IP, 5 H, 3 R, 3 ER, 1 BB, 0 K.

Fred McMullin: 2-4, 2 SB, R, RBI. Chick Gandil: 1-4, 2B, SB, R.

Sunday, July 13
Comiskey Park, Chicago
"Sox Crush Red Hose in Old-Fashioned Swat Battle" — *Chicago Tribune*

Red Sox (31-38)	000	003	600—9 15 2
White Sox (46-26)	401	141	03x—14 17 2

WP: Red Faber (8-6). LP: Carl Mays (5-11). SV: Eddie Cicotte (1).

Red Faber: 6⅓ IP, 13 H, 9 R, 8 ER, 3 BB, 4 K.

Fred McMullin: 4-5, 2 3B, R, 4 RBI. Chick Gandil: 3-5, 2B, 2 R, 4 RBI. Buck Weaver: 2-4, R, 4 RBI. Joe Jackson: 3-5, 2 3B, 2 R.

Monday, July 14
Comiskey Park, Chicago
"Sox Cop Another, 9 to 3, and Increase Lead in Flag Race" — *Chicago Tribune*

Red Sox (31-39)	100	000	101—3 8 1
White Sox (47-26)	100	500	21x—9 11 0

WP: Lefty Williams (15-6). LP: Sam Jones (7-9).

Lefty Williams: 9 IP, 8 H, 3 R, 3 ER, 1 BB, 3 K.

Eddie Collins: 3-5, HR, 2 R, 3 RBI. Happy Felsch: 3-4, 2 2B, 2 RBI. Ray Schalk: 2-3, 2 R, 2 RBI.

Tuesday, July 15
Comiskey Park, Chicago
"Sox Rally in Seventh Again Beats Champions, 3 to 1" — *Chicago Tribune*

Red Sox (31-40)   100   000   000 — 1 5 0
White Sox (48-26)   000   000   30x — 3 8 1
WP: Eddie Cicotte (17-4). LP: Bill James (3-5).
Eddie Cicotte: 9 IP, 5 H, 1 R, 1 ER, 0 BB, 2 K.
Chick Gandil: 2-4, RBI. Joe Jackson: 1-4, 2B, R, RBI. Happy Felsch: 1-4, SB, R, RBI.

Wednesday, July 16
Comiskey Park, Chicago
"Sox Take a Real Drubbing From Senators; Score, 11 to 1" — *Chicago Tribune*

Senators (33-43)   001   225   010 — 11 15 1
White Sox (48-27)   100   000   000 — 1 4 3
WP: Eric Erickson (3-4). LP: Grover Lowdermilk (2-3).
Grover Lowdermilk: 5 IP, 7 H, 5 R, 4 ER, 2 BB, 5 K.
Eddie Collins: 1-4, R. Joe Jackson: 1-4, RBI. Fred McMullin: 1-3, 2B.

Thursday, July 17
Comiskey Park, Chicago
"Senators Hold Reunion at Plate, Beating Sox, 9 to 4" — *Chicago Tribune*

Senators (34-43)   210   010   212 — 9 17 0
White Sox (48-28)   100   021   000 — 4 9 1
WP: Jim Shaw (13-7). LP: Red Faber (8-7).
Red Faber: 9 IP, 17 H, 9 R, 6 ER, 2 BB, 3 K.
Eddie Collins: 4-5, R. Joe Jackson: 1-4, 3B, 2 RBI. Nemo Leibold: 1-3, 2 BB, 2 R.

Friday, July 18
Comiskey Park, Chicago
"Williams' Hurling Leads Sox to Win Over Senators" — *Chicago Tribune*

Senators (34-44)   000   000   000 — 0 4 1
White Sox (49-28)   001   200   00x — 3 11 1
WP: Lefty Williams (16-6). LP: Harry Harper (5-12).
Lefty Williams: 9 IP, 4 H, 0 R, 0 ER, 0 BB, 3 K.
Eddie Collins: 2-4, SB, R. Swede Risberg: 2-2, 2 BB. Lefty Williams: 1-3, R.

Saturday, July 19
Comiskey Park, Chicago
"Sox Battle Eleven Rounds to Beat Johnson, 6 to 5" — *Chicago Tribune*

Senators (34-45)   202   010   000   00 — 5 10 1
White Sox (50-28)   004   100   000   01 — 6 13 2
WP: Dickey Kerr (5-2). LP: Walter Johnson (13-9).
Dickey Kerr: 8 IP, 6 H, 1 R, 0 ER, 1 BB, 4 K.
Buck Weaver: 2-4, SB, BB, R, 2 RBI. Eddie Collins: 2-4, BB, R, 2 RBI. Ray Schalk: 2-3, R, BB.

Sunday, July 20
Comiskey Park, Chicago
"Jackson's Homer Beats Yanks, 2 to 1, Before 30,000 Fans" — *Chicago Tribune*

Yankees (44-32)	000	000	100	0—1	3	1
White Sox (51-28)	000	001	000	1—2	6	0

WP: Eddie Cicotte (18-4). LP: Ernie Shore (4-6).
Eddie Cicotte: 10 IP, 3 H, 1 R, 1 ER, 0 BB, 3 K.
Joe Jackson: 2-5, HR, 3B, R, RBI. Happy Felsch: 1-3, 3B, SB, R. Swede Risberg: 1-2, SB, BB, RBI.

Monday, July 21
Comiskey Park, Chicago
"Sox Trounce Yanks Twice; Lead Flag Race By Six Laps" — *Chicago Tribune*

Yankees (44-33)	000	000	321—6	14	2
White Sox (52-28)	000	004	021—7	11	2

WP: Dickey Kerr (6-2). LP: Jack Quinn (11-6).
Lefty Williams: 8⅔ IP, 14 H, 6 R, 6 ER, 2 BB, 5 K.
Buck Weaver: 4-5, 2 R, RBI. Swede Risberg: 2-4, 3B, 3 RBI. Eddie Collins: 1-3, 2B, 2 BB, SB, R, RBI.

Yankees (44-34)	000	002	020	0—4	9	0
White Sox (53-28)	220	000	000	1—5	6	0

WP: Dickey Kerr (7-2). LP: Hank Thormahlen (7-5).
Red Faber: 8 IP, 9 H, 4 R, 4 ER, 4 BB, 2 K.
Ray Schalk: 2-3, 2B, SB, BB, 2 R. Shano Collins: 2-5, 2B, 2 RBI. Happy Felsch: 1-4, 2B, 2 RBI.

Tuesday, July 22
Comiskey Park, Chicago
"Sox Pitcher That Was-To-Be Serves 'Em 6 to 1 Defeat" — *Chicago Tribune*

Yankees (45-34)	100	012	002—6	13	1
White Sox (53-29)	000	000	001—1	7	0

WP: Jack Quinn (12-6). LP: Dickey Kerr (7-3).
Dickey Kerr: 9 IP, 13 H, 6 R, 6 ER, 4 BB, 5 K.
Nemo Leibold: 1-4, SB, R. Buck Weaver: 2-4. Swede Risberg: 2-3.

Wednesday, July 23
Scheduled day off
"Sox Enjoy a Rest; Resume Today with Cicotte vs. Browns" — *Chicago Tribune*

Thursday, July 24
Comiskey Park, Chicago
"'Skin Ball' is Baffling, But Sox Skin Browns by 1 to 0" — *Chicago Tribune*

Browns (43-38)	000	000	000	0—0	8	4
White Sox (54-29)	000	000	000	1—1	8	0

WP: Eddie Cicotte (19-4). LP: Allan Sothoron (12-5).

Eddie Cicotte: 10 IP, 8 H, 0 R, 0 ER, 0 BB, 3 K.
Nemo Leibold: 2-5, R. Happy Felsch: 1-5, RBI. Joe Jackson: 0-2, 3 BB.

Friday, July 25
Comiskey Park, Chicago
"Everything Goes Wrong, But Sox Win Just the Same, 6-4" — *Chicago Tribune*

Browns (43-39)   011   020   000 — 4 10 0
White Sox (55-29)   002   100   03x — 6 7 3
WP: Dickey Kerr (8-3). LP: Bert Gallia (9-9).
Dickey Kerr: 7⅓ IP, 7 H, 3 R, 3 ER, 4 BB, 4 K.
Dickey Kerr: 2-2, 3B, BB, RBI. Fred McMullin: 1-2, 2B, 2 R, 2 BB, RBI. Ray Schalk: 2-3, BB, R.

Saturday, July 26
Comiskey Park, Chicago
"Browns Pound Faber to Trim White Sox by 5 to 2 Count" — *Chicago Tribune*

Browns (44-39)   000   101   120 — 5 12 0
White Sox (55-30)   010   100   000 — 2 7 2
WP: Urban Shocker (9-6). LP: Red Faber (8-8).
Red Faber: 9 IP, 12 H, 5 R, 4 ER, 1 BB, 1 K.
Happy Felsch: 2-4, 2B, 2 R. Eddie Collins: 2-4. Byrd Lynn: 0-3, 2 RBI.

Sunday, July 27
Comiskey Park, Chicago
"Browns Slam Four Sox Pitchers for 11 to 5 Victory" — *Chicago Tribune*

Browns (45-39)   202   150   010 — 11 14 0
White Sox (55-31)   001   400   000 — 5 9 2
WP: Allan Sothoron (13-5). LP: Grover Lowdermilk (2-4).
Lefty Williams: 3 IP, 6 H, 4 R, 3 ER, 1 BB, 2 K.
Shano Collins: 2-4, 2B, 3B, BB, 2 R, RBI. Buck Weaver: 3-5, SB, RBI. Byrd Lynn: 2-3, 2B, BB, R, 2 RBI.

Monday, July 28
Scheduled day off
"White Sox Hospital Train Arrives on Eastern Front" — *Chicago Tribune*

Tuesday, July 29
Polo Grounds, New York
"White Sox Casuals Fall Before Yankee Artillery, 10-1" — *Chicago Tribune*

White Sox (55-32)   001   000   000 — 1 6 1
Yankees (47-37)   220   040   02x — 10 16 2
WP: Hank Thormahlen (8-5). LP: Eddie Cicotte (19-5).
Eddie Cicotte: 5 IP, 12 H, 8 R, 8 ER, 1 BB, 1 K.
Swede Risberg: 1-4, 2B. Eddie Cicotte: 1-1, RBI. Fred McMullin: 0-4, R.

Wednesday, July 30
Polo Grounds, New York
"Faber Finally Gets Started and Earns Sox an Even Break" — *Chicago Tribune*

White Sox (55-33) 000 013 010 0 — 5 8 3
Yankees (48-37) 130 001 000 1 — 6 11 0
WP: Bob Shawkey (14-8). LP: Grover Lowdermilk (2-5).
Lefty Williams: 2 IP, 4 H, 4 R, 4 ER, 3 BB, 0 K.
Buck Weaver: 2-5, 2B, R, 2 RBI. Fred McMullin: 1-3, 2B, RBI.
White Sox (56-33) 100 002 000 2 — 5 13 2
Yankees (48-38) 011 000 001 0 — 3 6 0
WP: Red Faber (9-8). LP: Jack Quinn (12-7).
Red Faber: 10 IP, 6 H, 3 R, 1 ER, 1 BB, 3 K.
Joe Jackson: 3-4, 2B, BB, R, RBI. Buck Weaver: 2-5, 2B, R, RBI. Shano Collins: 2-5, 3B, R, 2 RBI.

Thursday, July 31
Polo Grounds, New York
"Dick Kerr a Great Success as Tamer of Yanks, 7 to 2" — *Chicago Tribune*

White Sox (57-33) 220 100 110 — 7 13 1
Yankees (48-39) 200 000 000 — 2 5 1
WP: Dickey Kerr (9-3). LP: Ernie Shore (4-7).
Dickey Kerr: 9 IP, 5 H, 2 R, 2 ER, 4 BB, 4 K.
Eddie Collins: 4-5, R, 2 RBI. Happy Felsch: 2-5, 2 RBI. Joe Jackson: 1-2, 3B, 3 BB, R.

JULY HIGHLIGHTS

Faber's Doubleheader Sweep: On July 9 Red Faber was credited with wins in both ends of a doubleheader against the lowly Philadelphia A's, and the White Sox moved atop the AL standings for good. The Sox rallied from a four-run deficit to win the opener, 8-7; Faber, who pitched two innings in relief, also contributed at the plate with a bases-loaded single to drive in two runs in the eighth. In the second game, Faber "hurled in old time style," scattering six hits in a complete-game 6-2 victory. By the end of the weekend, Chicago led the Yankees by three games. By the end of July, the White Sox had doubled their lead to 6½ games, and they encountered little trouble on their way to the pennant.

McMullin Is the Lucky Charm: After the White Sox fell into third place on June 27, manager Kid Gleason decided to shake up the lineup by inserting Fred McMullin at third base and moving Buck Weaver back to his old position at shortstop, replacing Swede Risberg. The White Sox responded by winning 22 of their next 29 games and regaining the top spot in the AL standings. That prompted the *Chicago Tribune* to exclaim, "Either Fred McMullin has a lot of ability or else a lot of luck.… The Sox have battled their way back to first place and McMullin's defensive as well as his offensive playing has had much to do with it." Back in 1917, former manager Pants Rowland had made the same lineup change after Weaver returned from a broken finger and the White Sox went on to capture the pennant. For the month of July, McMullin hit .303 with nine extra-base hits and 21 runs scored in 32 games.

Shoeless Joe Sends 'Em Home Happy: In one of the most dramatic finishes of the season, Joe Jackson gave a big thrill to 30,000 fans — "the biggest crowd of the year" — on Sunday, July 20, at Comiskey Park. His game-ending, 10th-inning home run off New York's Ernie Shore landed in the right-field bleachers and set off a wild celebration, as James Crusinberry of the *Chicago Tribune* described: "The tall and swarthy hero jogged in with a broad smile on his face and when he stepped on home plate his mates hugged him. Frantic fans who had leaped over from the boxes rushed over and slapped him on the back, and husky athletes hoisted him to their shoulders and bore him off triumphant.… The demonstration given Joe Jackson after the game was the greatest seen at the Sox park in ten years. A crowd was waiting for him to come out of the clubhouse and if it hadn't been for two husky policemen, he would have been carried out of the ballpark. As it was, he barely saved his straw hat."

The Injury Bug Bites: The disabled list didn't exist in 1919, but the White Sox would have filled it up in July. First baseman Chick Gandil was out of action for three weeks after spraining his knee on July 17, and while recovering, he also suffered a bout of appendicitis (for which he would have surgery after the World Series). Catcher Ray Schalk and center fielder Happy Felsch also missed time with leg injuries, and left fielder Joe Jackson was left hobbling for a few days after being hit by a pitch on the toe. The scariest injury of all happened to pitcher Lefty Williams, who was beaned in the head by a line drive off the bat of the Browns' Hank Severeid on July 25. Williams walked off the field under his own power, and gamely made another start against St. Louis two days later, but he lasted only three innings and was yanked after two innings in his following start against the Yankees. Humorist Ring Lardner, in his unique storytelling style, recounted the White Sox's struggles this way in a *Saturday Evening Post* column (published October 18, 1919): "Don't nobody on this ball club feel gay and no wonder. In the 1st. place to look at our club you would think we had just come back from the Marne as Gandil was left home in a hospital with appendix and Felsch is so lame that he can't cover no more ground than where his dogs is parked and Cracker Schalk has to be wheeled up to the plate and back you might say and to cap off the climax I got stomach trouble from something I eat or something and wile I don't pitch with my stomach a man can't do themself justice when the old feed bag acts up."

Triumph and Tragedy: Jackson's homer was the second in a spectacular run of four straight walk-off victories by the White Sox from July 19-21. On Friday the 19th, Dickey Kerr pitched eight strong innings of one-run relief and then scored the winning run himself on Eddie Collins's 11th-inning single off Washington Senators ace Walter Johnson to win, 6-5. In a Monday doubleheader on the 21st, Kerr duplicated Red Faber's feat from earlier in the month by winning two games in one day against the Yankees. The rookie left-hander was needed for only 2⅓ innings this time, relieving Lefty Williams for the final out of the ninth inning in the first game before Buck Weaver broke a 6-6 tie with a two-out RBI single to score Nemo Leibold. In the second game, Kerr took over for Faber after the eighth and held the Yankees hitless until Shano Collins drove in Ray Schalk with a game-winning single in the 10th to win 5-4. Late in the second game, fans at Comiskey Park were horrified to witness the tragedy of the Wingfoot Air Express, a dirigible that caught fire while flying over downtown Chicago and crashed into the Illinois Trust and Savings Building. Thirteen people were killed and dozens injured after the Goodyear Tire Company-owned blimp's gas tanks exploded and sent flaming debris through the bank's glass roof. The whole scene was visible from the ballpark and the game was stopped "as nearly everyone at the Sox park … watched the catastrophe," the *Tribune* reported. "After that, there wasn't much enjoyment felt over the ball games."

The White Sox and the Race Riot: As the first-place White Sox wrapped up a four-game series with the St. Louis Browns on Sunday, July 27, at Comiskey Park, one of the largest race riots in American history erupted just two miles away at the 29th Street Beach on the South Side. A black teenager, Eugene Williams, was swimming with friends when he supposedly drifted across the invisible line in Lake Michigan separating the whites-only beach from the blacks. White bathers began throwing rocks at Williams from the shore; the teenager was hit in the head, fell into the water, and drowned, setting off five days of violence that terrorized the city. Thirty-eight people died during the rioting, which extended across the city's Black Belt neighborhoods and into the downtown Loop. It's impossible to say what effect the Chicago race riot had on the White Sox' season; the team left for New York on Monday, July 28, for an extended two-week road trip against the Yankees, Red Sox, Athletics, and Senators. But the White Sox players lived and worked on the South Side, where most of the violence took place, and so did some of their families. During the worst of the rioting, armed militia regiments drilled in the parking lot adjacent to Comiskey Park, waiting for a call to action from Chicago Mayor William Hale "Big Bill" Thompson or Illinois Governor Frank Lowden. The Washington Park neighborhood, where Buck Weaver and Joe Jackson both owned businesses, "became a hotbed of racial tension" during the riot, according to the Chicago Historical Society. The riot is almost never mentioned in articles or books about the Black Sox Scandal, but no one living in Chicago during the summer of 1919 could escape the citywide tension.

REB RUSSELL

By Richard Smiley

WITH SUPERB CONTROL AND a rising fastball, left-hander Reb Russell rose to stardom with one of the best rookie pitching performances of the Deadball Era, notching 22 victories and tossing eight shutouts for the Chicago White Sox in 1913. A typical Russell start featured few walks, few strikeouts, few runs, and many balls hit in the air as popups to the infielders or soft flies to the outfielders. "Russell gets out of a lot of tight places on his nerve," White Sox manager Jimmy Callahan said. "Three men on the bases, with none out, is a situation that fails to shake him. In fact, it is in the pinches that he shows to advantage."[1]

After an arm injury cut short his pitching career, Russell returned to the big leagues in 1922 as a slugging outfielder with the Pittsburgh Pirates in another impressive "debut" season. Although he was a bit naïve when he entered the big leagues, Russell's eagerness to learn and his calm demeanor helped him to polish his rough edges both on and off the field. By 1915 the pitcher who had once been a major source of inspiration for Ring Lardner's self-centered pitcher Jack Keefe of *You Know Me, Al* fame had become a mainstay of high society, discussing music, literature, and psychology.

Ewell Albert Russell was born on March 12, 1889, on a farm near Albany, Mississippi, the second of three children of Tobias and Naomi Russell. When he was one year old, his family moved to Texas and eventually settled on a 100-acre farm eight miles outside Bonham, an agricultural center of 5,000 people in north Texas and a key stop on the Texas and Pacific Railroad. Although Russell attended primary school and helped his father on the farm, he developed a passionate love of baseball and could often be found ignoring his chores while playing ball on a crude diamond in the nearby town of Telephone. When he was 15 he left

the farm for good and got a job driving teams for the railroad.

In May 1912 Russell signed to pitch for Bonham of the Texas-Oklahoma League at a salary of $75 a month. Despite using "nothing but curves," he impressed scouts by striking out many while walking few.[2] After his success in Bonham, Russell's contract was purchased by the Fort Worth Panthers of the Texas League. At Fort Worth a line drive off his thumb removed the curveball from his arsenal and he had to rely on his fastball and changeup. While posting a 4-4 record in 13 games for the seventh-place Panthers, Russell was spotted by White Sox scout and former major-league pitcher Harry Howell, who liked what he saw and recommended the young pitcher to owner Charles Comiskey. After the 1912 season, the White Sox drafted Russell for $1,200.

The 5-foot-11, 185-pound Russell arrived at camp in the spring of 1913 with great speed, exceptional control, confidence, coolness under pressure, and a willingness to learn. He also arrived with barely any money in his pocket and little knowledge of major-league hitters. Although he had success early in camp based strictly on his fastball, coach Kid Gleason helped him to return the curveball to his arsenal by showing him a new grip, which generated a sharp break. The White Sox initially intended to farm Russell out to the Pacific Coast League for more seasoning, but Gleason successfully argued against it and, to the surprise of many, Russell made the club.[3]

On April 18, 1913, Russell made his major-league debut and justified Gleason's confidence in dazzling style. With the White Sox trailing Cleveland 4-0, Russell was inserted in the seventh inning and proceeded to retire nine of the 10 batters he faced, including five strikeouts. His fine performance earned him a spot in the starting rotation, where he quickly blossomed into one of the league's best pitchers. "That boy has everything," Callahan marveled. "He has speed, he has curves, he has control, he has nerve, he has strength. What more could I ask for?"[4]

Reb Russell with the Pittsburgh Pirates, circa 1923 (Bain Collection, Library of Congress, Prints and Photographs Division)

Russell, now called Reb or Tex by the papers, finished the season with 22 wins, a 1.90 ERA, and a league-leading 52 games pitched. He ranked second in the American League with 316⅔ innings pitched, and his eight shutouts tied the major-league rookie record established by Russ Ford three years earlier. Demonstrating a knack for winning close games, Russell won five by the score of 1-0. Displaying the first glimpse of his hitting skills, Russell also connected for three triples during the season, and hit his first major-league home run on June 16, against the Washington Senators.

After the season, on October 14, Russell married Charlotte Benz, a cousin of his White Sox roommate Joe Benz, and relocated to her hometown of Indianapolis. He did not join his White Sox teammates on the world tour organized by Charles Comiskey and John McGraw, but he did participate in an exhibition game with them in Bonham, Texas, in which he was presented with a gold watch and got a rousing ovation.[5]

On May 26, 1914, Russell was in the midst of a shutout when he collided with Yankee first baseman Les Nunamaker while attempting to get on base. The collision resulted in injuries to his left ankle and hip and kept him out of action for three days. Upon his return to the mound, Russell was no longer effective and was hit hard. The combination of the injury and an increase in his weight led to a loss of velocity on his fastball and a loss of break on his curve. By the end of the season, in which his ERA rose a full run to 2.90, doubts arose as to whether Russell would ever be effective again.

Russell reported to spring training in 1915 grossly overweight and new White Sox manager Pants Rowland threatened to cut him from the team. Under Rowland's direction, Reb underwent an intensive program of hot mud baths and extensive workouts in an attempt to reduce weight. He also immediately went on a diet consisting solely of lettuce with French dressing, side orders of lemon ice, and pickles.[6] By early March he had dropped nearly 40 pounds and was back near his playing weight. By mid-March, he had regained his form and Sam Weller reported in the *Chicago Tribune* that "Russell let loose more speed than he has shown in a year and his curve ball, which disappeared so mysteriously last season, was seen to crack sharply across the plate several times."[7] His job was safe. Splitting his duties between the starting rotation and the bullpen, Reb turned in a fine season, winning 11 games and pitching three shutouts.

In 1916 Reb reported to camp already in shape and so impressed Rowland that he was chosen as the club's Opening Day starter against Detroit. After getting shelled by the Tigers, he was relegated to relief duties, where he regained his manager's confidence by contributing a number of solid outings. He spent the rest of the season shuffling between the rotation and bullpen, and was the workhorse of the staff, leading the team in innings pitched (264⅓) and victories (18) while posting a 2.42 ERA. Russell also led the league with the fewest walks per nine innings pitched, as he allowed just 42 free passes. A turbulent four years into his big-league career, many observers still considered Russell to be the best left-handed pitcher in baseball next to Babe Ruth.

Such comparisons did not stand up for long. Russell's first attempts to throw a curveball in the spring of 1917 left him unable to straighten his left arm. X-rays revealed the presence of "two fibrous growths in Reb's left arm just above the elbow."[8] To combat this malady, the doctor prescribed "exercise and heavy lifting."

Once again Russell spent the year going back and forth between the bullpen and the starting rotation. With the White Sox in the midst of a tight pennant race against defending champion Boston, Reb pitched some of the best games of his career. In August he won several important games for Chicago, including two shutouts against the Red Sox. He finished the year with a 15-5 record and a sparkling 1.95 ERA and once again led the league with the fewest walks per innings pitched. Nevertheless, the arm injury took its toll and the White Sox could never be sure about whether he'd be able to pitch on a given day. Russell's one start in that year's World Series was a disaster; he failed to get a single out before being removed from the game. "Opposing batters haven't the least respect for a man with a bum arm," he wrote afterward in a column for *Baseball Magazine*. "Still … it is something to be a member of the greatest club in the world, even if you couldn't contribute your share to that end."[9]

Russell didn't sign his 1918 contract until early April, and was used sparingly during the first two months of the season. Back in the starting rotation by mid-June, he was not as effective as he had been in previous years, displaying uncharacteristic wildness and often losing his effectiveness late in games. Starting 15 games, he finished the year 7-5 with a 2.60 ERA.

In 1919 Russell was not impressive in spring training and barely made the team. After facing two Red Sox batters and not recording an out in his only outing, on June 13, Reb was removed for good. Released to Minneapolis of the American Association, he finished the year playing center field, and hit nine home runs, more than twice as many as anyone else on the team. He was not with the White Sox during the tainted World Series against the Cincinnati Reds.

In 1920 Russell attempted one last comeback as a pitcher with the White Sox but could not make the team. He returned home to Indianapolis, where he found work in a garage as an auto assembler. Later that season the Minneapolis Millers traveled to Indianapolis and were in emergency need of an outfielder. Reb agreed to fill in and he came through with a couple of hits in the game. The Millers signed him and he went on to have a great season at the plate, hitting .339 with six home runs and 41 RBIs in 85 games. He did even better in 1921, leading the Millers in batting (.368), home runs (33), and RBIs (132), while also posting a 1.64 ERA in five games on the mound.[10]

After clouting 17 homers for the Millers in his first 77 games of 1922, Russell was picked up by the Pittsburgh Pirates in July 1922. As part of a right-field platoon with Clyde Barnhart, he rapidly became one of the most feared hitters in the National League and finished the season with 12 home runs, 75 RBIs, and a .368 average in 60 games. The next year he failed to follow up on his sensational 1922 campaign, but still turned in a solid hitting performance, batting .289 with 9 home runs and 58 RBIs in 94 games. Given his limited defensive abilities, this performance was not enough to hold his spot in the starting lineup, and by the end of July Russell was benched. He finished the season with the team, but received scant playing time in the last two months.

After being released by the Pirates, Russell returned to the American Association, where he emerged as one of the league's best hitters. With Columbus in 1924 and '25, he smashed 55 home runs and drove in 247 runs while splitting time between the outfield and first base. From 1926 to 1929 he played for Indianapolis, winning a batting title in 1927 at .385. Released by Indianapolis in 1929, Russell finished out his minor-league career with Quincy (Illinois) of the Three-I League, and Mobile and Chattanooga of the Southern League. His lifetime minor-league batting average was .323.

When his minor-league career ended, Reb got a job as a security guard at the Kingan and Company meat-acking plant in Indianapolis and worked there until he retired in 1959. During that time he played for a number of local semipro teams including the Sterling Beers, which were managed by Clyde Hoffa, a relative of labor leader Jimmy Hoffa.

Russell died at the age of 84 on September 30, 1973, two weeks short of his 60th wedding anniversary, in an Indianapolis nursing home, and was buried in St. Joseph Cemetery in Indianapolis. He was survived by his wife and two children.

SOURCES

Chicago Tribune

Indianapolis Star

New York Times

Baseball Magazine

Hilton, George W., ed., *The Annotated Baseball Stories of Ring W. Lardner 1914-1919* (Palo Alto, California: Stanford University Press, 1995).

Debano, Paul, *The Indianapolis ABCs: History of a Premier Team in the Negro Leagues* (Jefferson, North Carolina, McFarland & Co., 1997).

Davids, L. Robert, ed., *Minor League Baseball Stars, Volume III* (Cleveland: Society for American Baseball Research, 1992).

Census of the United States, 1900, United States Bureau of the Census.

Census of the United States, 1920, United States Bureau of the Census.

Responses to Questionnaire from Hall of Fame by Ewell Albert Russell.

Retrosheet.org.

January 15, 1965, letter to Lee Allen from Ewell Albert Russell.

NOTES

1   *Washington Post*, July 8, 1913.

2   *Chicago Tribune*, June 1, 1913.

3   Ibid.

4   *Washington Post*, July 8, 1913.

5   Frank McGlynn, "Striking Scenes From the Tour Around the World," *Baseball Magazine*, August 1914.

6   *Chicago Tribune*, March 14, 1915.

7   *Chicago Tribune*, March 18, 1915.

8   *Chicago Tribune*, March 27, 1917.

9   Reb Russell, "How I Got My Chance," *Baseball Magazine*, December 1917.

10 *The Sporting News*, January 5, 1922.

RAY SCHALK

By Brian Stevens

IN AN ERA WHEN THE COMMON impression of a baseball catcher was a sturdy player with bulging shoulders, a husky framework, and brute strength, the 5-foot-7 (many sources say 5-foot-9), 155-pound Ray Schalk did not convey an imposing figure behind the dish. But as John C. Ward wrote in *Baseball Magazine* in 1920, "Schalk is unquestionably the hardest working catcher in baseball as he is doubtless also the brainiest, the nerviest, the most competent. He presents the unique distinction of performing more work than any other catcher and at the same time performing it better. Both in quantity and in quality of service Ray Schalk is unquestionably the premier backstop in baseball."[1]

Raymond William Schalk was born in Harvel, a small village in central Illinois, on August 12, 1892, the fifth of six children of Herman and Sophia Schalk, German immigrants who had arrived in the United States in 1875. Herman supported his family as a day laborer in Litchfield, 20 miles away, where his children, including Ray, attended public school. As a youngster Schalk worked as a newsboy and carried the *Chicago Tribune* and weekly *Litchfield News*. Ray was captain of the Litchfield basketball team, but left high school at the end of his second year to learn the printer's trade. Two years later he traveled to Brooklyn, New York, to study how to operate the Linotype machine. In 1910, after mastering the intricacies of this noble mechanism, Schalk returned home, but found his desire to progress in his chosen field was not matched by career advancement. Rather, it was Schalk's participation in local baseball games that soon earned him the promotion he was looking for.

First a member of the town team, he soon moved up to semipro ball for the sum of $2 a game. From there he quickly progressed to Taylorville (Illinois) in the Class D Illinois-Missouri League, where he caught 64 games, batted .387, and earned $65 a month. Later in the 1911 season, the 18-year-old moved up to the Milwaukee Brewers of the American Association, and appeared in 31 games. Returning to Milwaukee for the 1912 campaign, he batted .271 in 80 contests, attracting so much attention for his aggressive approach to the catching position and his feisty on-field leadership that he was purchased by the Chicago White Sox for $10,000 and two players.

On August 11, 1912, the day before his 20th birthday, Ray Schalk saw his first major-league game—and he was the starting catcher in it. Arriving by streetcar minutes before the first game of a doubleheader against the Philadelphia Athletics, the rookie was told by manager Jimmy Callahan, "Young man, here's your pitcher, Doc White. You're the catcher."[2] In his first at-bat, Schalk grounded out to Frank Baker but did manage to get a hit later in the game against Chief Bender. Reflecting back on the experience nearly 50 years later, Schalk reminisced, "You think of no-hit games and playing in the World Series, but that first game was my greatest day."[3]

Schalk played in 23 games for the White Sox in 1912, batting a respectable .286. But it was his energy, willingness to learn, and outright desire that made the biggest impression on his coaches and teammates. The electric Schalk soon became the favorite of White Sox coach Kid Gleason, who helped the young backstop hone his skills. "We'd start a game at 3:00 P.M., but he'd have me out practicing at 9:30 in the morning. We'd work on catching the double steal, he had me chasing from behind the plate to field bunts, and running under pop flies. He taught me to crouch over and make myself a target on the throws from the outfield. He taught me to give, or yield with the catch, to never hold the ball high when making a throw—to cock my hand by my ear. He was a tireless worker."[4] And Schalk was undoubtedly an indefatigable student.

The diminutive Schalk, weighing a scant 148 pounds in his first season, was thought at first too small to catch Chicago ace Ed Walsh's sharply breaking spitball. But with the help of Gleason, he was soon handling Walsh better than Billy Sullivan, Bruno Block, or Red Kuhn did. Even more difficult than catching Walsh was backstopping Ed Cicotte, who had more pitches than a carnival barker. Said Schalk about Cicotte, "He had command of every type of pitch. That includes

Ray Schalk, circa 1919 (Bain Collection, Library of Congress, Prints and Photographs Division)

the knuckler, the fadeaway, the slider, the screwball, the spitter, and emery ball."[5]

But more important than handling the ball was Schalk's ability to handle his pitchers. John Sheridan of *The Sporting News* wrote in 1923, "… Schalk at all times insists that his pitcher shall have and use his stuff, that he shall be able to control it, and that he should use it whenever the catcher calls for it. The manner in which Schalk handles his pitchers must be of inestimable value to his team. He, more than any

catcher that I can remember, makes a pitcher work up to the mark all the time. No catcher that I have known made or makes the pitcher work right, stand right on the rubber and use a correct motion, hold runners close to base, better than said Schalk. As a manager of young pitchers, Schalk stands head and shoulders above the others of all time."[6]

Though it may be inferred that Schalk earned his nickname, "Cracker," because he cracked the whip over his White Sox hurlers, the moniker may have been hung on him by White Sox outfielder Shano Collins. Apparently Collins saw a resemblance between Schalk's physique when viewed from behind and a cracker box. Another version holds that it was probably someone in the White Sox clubhouse who spied Schalk on his first day with the team and asked, "Who's the little cracker pants?" The nickname stayed with the popular Schalk long after his playing days ended.

Schalk was revered by his teammates for his intelligent, nervy play and aggressive style on the diamond. His easy disposition made him a favorite off the field as well, and his youthful looks made for some interesting horseplay. One rainy day in 1915 in Washington, Cicotte, Walsh, and Shano Collins were enjoying their favorite beverages in a tavern when Schalk entered the bar wearing a cap and raincoat. He sidled up to the trio, but before he could order his own beer the bartender growled, "We don't allow no school kids in this joint." Schalk suggested to his teammates that they identify him, but they gave no hint of recognition and instead congratulated the bartender for enforcing the policy that barred little boys from pestering men at their amber.[7]

Another off-field adventure drew the ire of owner Comiskey. Looking to use the Chicago skyline's newly constructed Tribune Tower for a promotional stunt, a movie company came upon the idea of using Schalk to catch a ball dropped from the top of the Tower—a height of 463 feet. Smiling for the cameras, Cracker caught the third ball tossed. "Didn't sting me any more than one of those high fouls Ruth used to hit," he later said.[8] But Comiskey caught wind of the stunt and was irate when Schalk arrived at the ballpark later that day. Comiskey chided Schalk over the consequences had his star catcher misjudged the ball. Schalk's unadorned response—"But I didn't misjudge it"—did not placate the Old Roman.

Schalk played the catching position like a fifth infielder. He was one of the first catchers to regularly back up infield throws to first base and outfield throws to third.[9] His speed, alertness, and prowess led to his claim of being the only major-league catcher to make a putout at every base. His first putout at second base occurred in 1918 against St. Louis in Chicago. On a hit-and-run, the Browns' Ray Demmitt sped past second as Joe Jackson made a great catch in deep left off the bat of Joe Gedeon. Schalk, in the middle of the diamond, ran to second to take the relay from White Sox shortstop Swede Risberg and slapped the tag on Demmitt.[10] Putouts at first were more common because Schalk would often follow runners to first on hits to right field. Chick Gandil, the first baseman, would then decoy himself away from the bag, drawing the runner into a wide turn at first. Right fielder Eddie Murphy would then peg the ball back to Schalk at first to tag out the unsuspecting runner.

Over his 18-year career (1,757 games with the White Sox and five with the New York Giants in 1929), Schalk participated in more double plays (222) than any other backstop in history, and his lifetime total of 1,811 assists ranks second all-time behind 19th-century backstop Deacon McGuire. Schalk led the American League in fielding percentage five times and in putouts nine times, the latter still a major-league record entering the 2015 season. He also arguably shares the record[11] for career no-hitters caught with four (historians have since dismissed Jim Scott's May 14, 1914, gem, as he lost his no-hitter in a losing effort in the 10th inning).

In 1916 Schalk established the single-season stolen-base record for catchers with 30, a mark not broken until 1982, when John Wathan swiped 36 bags. Though his lifetime batting average was just .253, the lowest of anyone elected to the Hall of Fame as a position player, Schalk was considered an excellent bunter, both for the base hit and the sacrifice. Cracker was a frequent selection to *Baseball Magazine's* All-Star

American League Team, and was named by both Ty Cobb and Babe Ruth to their own personal all-time all-star teams.

Schalk won his only World Series with the White Sox in 1917, a year in which he hit .226 with fewer than 20 extra-base hits in 140 games. But he caught all six games in the World Series and the New York Giants, who led the National League in stolen bases, attempted just six steals during the fall classic, getting caught twice. In the White Sox' dramatic Game Five comeback, Schalk's own skill on the basepaths paid off. In the seventh inning he drew a throw from his Giants counterpart, Bill Rariden, on the front end of a double steal with Chick Gandil that scored the tying run before the White Sox rallied for three runs in the bottom of the eighth to win, 8-5. They went on to capture the championship two days later in New York.

From 1913 to 1926, Schalk caught nearly 80 percent of the White Sox' contests. His durability was legendary—broken fingers, deep spike lacerations, and sprained ankles did not sideline him. During one game against the Tigers in 1922, Schalk was knocked unconscious by a foul tip. Trainer William "Doc" Buckner of the White Sox resorted to artificial respiration and use of oxygen to revive him. Recounted Buckner, "As soon as he got his breath and collected his senses, he immediately wanted to get back behind the plate."[12]

In 1920 Cracker backstopped 151 of the 154 games for the second-place White Sox. He maintained he would have caught the full 154 but for an extremely hot sun on a no-Sunday-baseball offday in Philadelphia. Related Schalk, "I went over to Atlantic City that Sabbath and frisked on the sand too much and too long. When I got back to Philly that night, I looked more like a boiled lobster than any human I ever saw."[13] The sunburn, not cracked knuckles, charley horses or aching dogs, kept Schalk from catching every game in 1920.

Schalk's best season was probably 1922, when he batted .281, one point below his career best of .282 (in 1919). In that 1922 campaign Schalk hit four of his 11 career home runs, stole 12 bases in 16 attempts, hit for the cycle on June 27 (the next White Soxer to do so was Jack Brohamer in 1977), and drove in 60 runs. He led the league in putouts and assists, while committing only eight errors, tying the American League record for fielding percentage at .989. He finished third in voting for the 1922 American League Most Valuable Player Award.

Ray Schalk's silence regarding the Black Sox Scandal of 1919 and his status as one of the honest men of the Series (in which he batted .304) is well known. Schalk knew something was amiss when both Cicotte and Lefty Williams continually crossed him up on pitches. Regarding the penalties doled out to the conspirators, Schalk did not disagree with the banishment, but later portrayals of the eight as vicious criminals bothered him.

In a discussion with Ed Burns of the *Chicago Tribune* in 1940, Schalk conveyed his compassion: "As long as I live, I'll never forget the day Charles A. Comiskey come into the clubhouse and told eight [sic] of the boys they had been exposed and were through forever. It was a shocking scene and my mixed emotions never have been straightened out since I watched several of the ruined athletes break down and cry like babies. I never have worried about the guys who were hard-boiled, but those tears got me."[14]

Pennant purgatory followed the White Sox after the revelation of the Series fix in late 1920. The dismissal of seven players (Gandil had retired after the 1919 fiasco) wore a large hole in the team that left the lineup talent-threadbare for years. But Schalk's keen efforts on and off the diamond helped bring respectability to the club. In addition to his MVP-caliber year in 1922, Schalk was responsible for discovering future Hall of Famer Ted Lyons in March 1923 at Baylor College in Waco, Texas. Lyons joined the club later that year in St. Louis, and would collect a franchise-record 260 victories for the White Sox.

The respect and regard for Schalk's knowledge of the game led him to succeed his friend Eddie Collins as White Sox player-manager in November 1926. But Schalk's lenient style led to his forced resignation in July 1928. Expecting to retain his contract as a catcher at an estimated $15,000 (his managerial salary had been $25,000), Schalk—who had only one plate appearance that year—was distressed when Comiskey cut his pay to $6,000. Schalk considered litigation, but a lawsuit was never filed.

Instead, Schalk joined the New York Giants coaching staff with John McGraw in 1929, appearing as a player in five games that year. He became a coach for the crosstown Chicago Cubs in 1930 and 1931, managed the Buffalo Bisons in the International League from 1932 to 1937, and then returned to Milwaukee of the American Association later in 1940, 28 years after he had last played for the club.

It was in these later years that Schalk operated a popular bowling and pool hall establishment in Evergreen Park, a Chicago suburb. Ray was also one of the founders of Baseball Anonymous, an organization whose charge was to assist indigent ballplayers. In 1965, after working as assistant baseball coach at Purdue University for 18 years, Ray Schalk finally retired from baseball at the age of 72. Interestingly, throughout all his years following the game of baseball, Schalk would never fail to call and congratulate the catcher of a no-hitter. Schalk always remained popular with Chicagoans, and was invited to catch the first ball of the 1959 World Series, thrown out by Red Faber.

In 1955 Schalk was named to the Baseball Hall of Fame by the Veterans Committee. Fittingly, he was inducted to the Hall on the same day as Ted Lyons, the man he "discovered" 32 years earlier. At the ceremony, Schalk thanked his strongest supporter, his wife, the former Lavinia Graham, saying, "Whatever I've accomplished, I owe to Mrs. Schalk."[15] The Schalks later celebrated their 50th wedding anniversary on October 25, 1966. The couple had two children and several grandchildren. When Ray Schalk died of cancer at 77 on May 19, 1970, the White Sox and California Angels observed a moment of silence prior to their contest in memory of the Hall of Famer. He was buried at Evergreen Cemetery in Evergreen Park.

SOURCES

Ray Schalk's Hall of Fame player file

Baseball Magazine

Baseball Weekly

The Sporting News

Chicago Tribune

Washington Post

New York Times

Author's personal collection

Assistance and contributions from Brian Cooper, author of *Ray Schalk: A Baseball Biography* (Jefferson, North Carolina: McFarland & Co., 2009)

NOTES

1 *Baseball Magazine*, October 1920.

2 *Chicago Tribune*, February 1, 1955.

3 Ibid.

4 *The Sporting News*, March 28, 1962.

5 *The Sporting News*, May 24, 1969.

6 *The Sporting News*, August 30, 1923.

7 *The Sporting News*, November 28, 1940.

8 *Chicago Tribune*, February 8, 1955.

9 Schalk biographer Brian Cooper notes, "Some sources credit Schalk with being the first catcher to back up plays in this manner, but Harry Smith was doing it for the Philadelphia Athletics as early as 1901, nearly a dozen years before Schalk joined the majors." See Cooper, *Ray Schalk: A Baseball Biography* (Jefferson, North Carolina: McFarland & Co., 2009), 126.

10 *Chicago Daily News*, June 29, 1918.

11 In 2008, Jason Varitek of the Boston Red Sox caught his fourth official no-hitter to set a major-league record that Schalk had proudly claimed to hold throughout his lifetime. Schalk's Hall of Fame plaque says he caught four no-hitters, but only three of them are now considered to be official no-hitters, thanks to a 1991 ruling by baseball's committee on statistical accuracy that eliminated any no-hitter lost in extra innings. In addition to the "lost" Jim Scott no-hitter in 1914, Schalk also caught no-hitters by Joe Benz (1914) and Eddie Cicotte (1917), and a perfect game by Charlie Robertson in 1922.

12 *Chicago Tribune*, September 8, 1922.

13 *The Sporting News*, November 21, 1940.

14 *Chicago Tribune*, May 21, 1970.

15 *Chicago Tribune*, July 26, 1955.

FRANK SHELLENBACK

By Brian McKenna

MANY BELIEVE THAT SPIT-baller Frank Shellenback had his major-league career stolen from him when his key pitch was outlawed. In 1920 the National Commission did away with trick deliveries, including the spitball—and Shellenback's team, the Chicago White Sox, for whom he had pitched in 1918 and 1919, didn't list his name among those grandfathered to legally throw the pitch in the majors because he was then in the American Association. "That oversight prevented my ever getting another chance in the big leagues," he later remarked.[1]

For the very reason that Shellenback was an effective pitcher, he wasn't welcomed back. But the Pacific Coast League allowed Shelly, as he was known in the clubhouse, to utilize his complete arsenal. He lasted another 19 years in the PCL and amassed 300 or more career victories in the minors. When he retired as a player after the 1938 season, he was the last legal spitball pitcher in Organized Baseball. (Burleigh Grimes was the last in the major leagues.)

There's another side of the story. Shellenback grew up in Los Angeles and preferred the fine weather and leisurely pace of the West Coast to the predominantly Eastern major leagues. In fact, he asked the White Sox to trade him to a Pacific Coast League club even before the spitball was banned. He was also more than happy to stay close to his family. As Shellenback later professed, "I enjoyed my stay at Hollywood, was well paid and didn't have to worry about moving my wife and six children from one city to another."[2]

Yet while Frank was torn about his exclusion from the majors—he noted, "In a way that was a good break for me but in another way it wasn't so good"—it was fortuitous that he parted ways with the White Sox when he did.[3] At the age of 19, Shellenback played most of the 1918 season in Chicago, as pitchers Red Faber and Lefty Williams lost much of the year to

World War I. Young Frank was friendly with and played beside Chick Gandil and Fred McMullin over the winter of 1918-19 in California. He was also well acquainted with fellow West Coast players Williams, Buck Weaver, and Swede Risberg. Had Shellenback stayed with the White Sox at the end of 1919, it's conceivable that these associations might have led him down the path to expulsion from Organized Baseball in the wake of the tainted World Series.

Frank Victor Shellenback was born on December 16, 1898, in Joplin, Missouri. He was the youngest of five children born to John Albert Shellenback and Caroline A. Nolte. John had been born in Ohio in 1860 to parents from France. Baptismal records indicate that John's surname was originally Schellenbach, which suggests a German heritage. This may be, since the family hailed from Alsace-Lorraine, a border region that often changed hands via war between France and Germany. John initially supported the family as a machinist but later found steady employment as an automotive mechanic. Caroline, or Carrie, was born in Illinois in 1867 to German-born parents.

By the time Frank was 10 years old the family had moved to Los Angeles. He attended Hollywood High School, where he played baseball, football, basketball, and rugby. The 1915 Hollywood High baseball squad, featuring Frank and his brother Paul, won the Southern California championship. That season Frank tossed a no-hitter against Los Angeles High. During the summer, the 16-year-old Shellenback started playing semipro baseball. He already stood out on the ball field with his baby face, blond hair, and stature (6-feet-2 and 189 pounds).

In the fall of 1915 Frank attended Santa Clara University, playing rugby and basketball for the school. Early the next year, however, he decided to enroll at Hollywood Junior College. He was immediately offered the position of assistant baseball coach. In March he was invited to spring training by Frank Chance, manager of the PCL's Los Angeles Angels. He failed to make the team; instead, he ended up pitching in a mining league for a club near Ely, Nevada, where he also worked as an ore assayer. By July he had joined the Ruth, Nevada, club in a copper league, rolling off eight straight victories for that team.

At 18, Shellenback joined the White Sox for spring training in March 1917 in Mineral Wells, Texas. It was his first of three springs with the club. He claimed he learned the spitball from the White Sox pitchers. He recalled, "I just had to learn spitball pitching while I was with the White Sox because most of the club's twirlers used the moist ball. Besides (Eddie) Cicotte, there were Red Faber and Joe Benz on the club using spitters."[4]

In another version of his story, Shellenback said he asked Cicotte to teach him the pitch but was repeatedly rebuffed. So on the sly he examined the balls Cicotte used while warming up to study just what he did to them. On his own, he then tried to emulate Cicotte's style. At first he threw the spitter with the full force of a fastball but the pitch never really broke; eventually, he learned to finesse the delivery to gain the maximum break. To add a little something to the pitch, Shellenback sucked on slippery-elm tablets and spat on the balls. However he learned the spitter, the fact is that he was throwing it before he joined the White Sox that first spring. Thus, he didn't learn the pitch from Cicotte or any other Chicago pitcher.

White Sox coach Kid Gleason, a retired pitcher, didn't care for the idea of such a young pitcher relying on the spitball. I.E. Sanborn wrote in the *Chicago Tribune* on March 24, 1917, "Gleason is working on Schellenbach [sic], the Los Angeles semi-pro, to convert him from a spitball to curve pitcher. The youngster is tall and has long arms able to pitch overhand, so that it looks to the batsmen as if the ball were coming off a hill top. Gleason figures he will be mighty effective with a curve, and it is seldom a pitcher can develop both a good spitter and a good curveball."

Frank Shellenback, circa 1918 (Chicago History Museum, SDN-061538, Chicago Daily News negatives collection)

In the end Gleason and manager Pants Rowland felt their rotation was solid enough, which it was. They sent the young Shellenback to Providence in the International League on April 15. In 24 games with Providence, he posted a 9-6 record. On August 16 the White Sox moved him to Milwaukee in the American Association; in eight games he won three and lost three. Over the winter he attended and played sports for Santa Clara.

On February 6, 1918, Shellenback re-signed with Chicago and joined the team for spring training. On April 28 the White Sox optioned him to Minneapolis. In three games there he notched a 1-2 record. A little more than a week later, he was recalled and made his major-league debut on May 8, in relief. He was wild that day, ceding five hits, two runs, and three bases on balls in four innings, but walked away with a 9-5 victory over Cleveland.

Chicago had won the World Series in 1917 with a solid rotation of Cicotte, Faber, Lefty Williams, and Reb

Russell. They needed help in 1918, though; Faber was in the Navy and Williams was working in a Delaware shipyard. Owner Charles Comiskey sniped that Williams was a draft dodger, but Shellenback had no such worry. At 19, he was one of 63 major leaguers ineligible for the draft because of his age. The White Sox were happy to plug him into the rotation. In 28 games for the team he posted a 9-12 record with a solid 2.66 ERA, a mark lower than the league and White Sox' average.

At the end of October, Shellenback enlisted in the aviation branch of the Army, passed all the required tests, and was assigned to the aviation school at Berkeley, California. He never got the chance to attend because the war ended in November. Instead, he spent the winter playing semipro ball for an oil company on the West Coast with Chick Gandil, Fred McMullin, Ivy Olsen, and Truck Hannah. Also playing in California that winter were three more White Sox teammates, Buck Weaver, Lefty Williams, and Swede Risberg. For years, Shellenback continued to play over the winter in and around Los Angeles. Often, he joined squads that played with and against major leaguers who drifted west after the season.

In March 1919, Shellenback, Gandil, and McMullin hopped a train for Mineral Wells and the White Sox's spring camp. Kid Gleason was now manager. With the return of Faber and Williams, Shellenback was the odd man out, starting only four games through June 22. Four days later, Gleason inserted Dickie Kerr into the rotation. The White Sox were set for another pennant run—without Frank. On July 5 he made his final major-league appearance, pitching a scoreless inning in a 6-3 loss to Detroit. At 20, his big-league career was over, with 10 wins and 15 losses in 36 appearances. Shellenback was shipped from Chicago to Minneapolis on July 9 and in 20 games for Minneapolis he won seven games and lost three.

In January 1920, Shellenback informed the White Sox that he preferred to remain in California, close to home. He asked to be traded to the Vernon club of the Pacific Coast League. Instead, the White Sox sold him to Oakland on January 28. Shelly wasn't happy about being peddled to Oakland because he wanted to play in the Los Angeles area. In March 1920 Oakland acquiesced, trading him to Vernon. In 35 starts there he posted an 18-12 record and 2.71 ERA, helping the club win the pennant.

On February 9, 1920, the major leagues formally banned pitchers from putting foreign substances on the baseball. No longer would they be allowed to apply saliva, rosin, talcum powder, paraffin, or any other substance before pitching. They were further prohibited from spitting on the ball or in their glove and from rubbing the ball on their person or in their glove. As conciliation to the game's veterans, each club was permitted to name two men who could legally throw such pitches through the 1920 season. The White Sox naturally chose proven starters Eddie Cicotte and Red Faber as their designated two.

As it turned out, the majors ruled in December 1920 that 18 men would be granted dispensation to throw the spitball until their careers ended. Cicotte didn't make that list; he was given his pink slip in the Black Sox affair. Shellenback didn't either; he had been out of the majors for a year and a half and was no longer the property of a major-league club. Fortunately for Shellenback, the Pacific Coast League grandfathered him. He had to register every year with the league office, but would be permitted to throw the spitball in the minors. (A list of other PCL spitballers included Ray Keating, Al Gould, Buzz Arlett, Doc Crandall, Harry Krause, and Vean Gregg.)

If non-grandfathered spitball pitchers wanted to crack "The Show," they had to revamp their game, as Heinie Meine and Hal Carlson did. Shellenback couldn't or wouldn't reinvent himself; thus, his return to the majors was effectively barred. Minor-league officials were a little more liberal. They permitted legally designated spitballers to change leagues. Also, quite a few of the 18 designated by the majors later pitched legal spitballs in the minors, among them Keating, Doc Ayers, Ray Caldwell, Dana Fillingim, Marv Goodwin, Burleigh Grimes, Clarence Mitchell, Jack Quinn, Allen Russell, and Allen Sothoron.

Over the winter and well into 1921, Shellenback played in the integrated California Winter League for Bob Fisher's All-Stars, which included a slew of past or future major leaguers. They played black clubs like the Lincoln Giants and the Los Angeles White Sox, a club that featured Bullet Joe Rogan, Dobie Moore, Lem Hawkins, and others.

Shellenback went 18-10 for Vernon in 1921. As the season wore on he developed a bone chip in his elbow. Near the end of the season he had "a large piece of solid bone removed from his pitching arm."[5] After that, he had a tough time rounding his arm into shape every spring.

On January 17, 1922, Shellenback married Elizabeth H. Taylor, a District of Columbia native two years his junior. (They had six children beginning in 1925.) Shellenback's arm still hadn't recovered when spring training came in 1922. He appeared in only five games for Vernon before the club released him in early May. Shellenback ended up pitching for Fresno in the semipro San Joaquin Valley League. In late October, however, he was re-signed by Vernon.

Shellenback posted a 33-26 record for Vernon in 1923 and 1924, tailing off at the end of 1924. He started only 23 games that year because of injury. Robert E. Ray of the *Los Angeles Times* commented, "Shellenback went good at the start but was useless the last part of the year with a bad arm." By October he was pitching for the semipro Hollywood Merchants. He also pitched for Hammond in the California Winter League. On December 3, Vernon traded Shellenback to Sacramento.

Shellenback turned in a mediocre 14-17 record for his new club in 1925. On October 18, Tony Lazzeri of the Salt Lake City Bees set a new mark in Organized Baseball with his 60th home run, an inside-the-parker off Shellenback in the seventh inning. Lazzeri did benefit from the pleasant Western weather, which permitted him to play in 197 league games that year.

Over the winter, Salt Lake City relocated to Hollywood, playing home games at the Los Angeles Angels' park.

Shellenback, a Los Angeles native, held out at the beginning of the year and asked to be traded to the relocated franchise after a season away from his hometown. On February 17, 1926, Sacramento relented and shipped him to Hollywood for pitcher Rudy Kallio, who (like Shellenback) amassed more than 500 decisions in the minors. Shellenback reached his tenth pro season in 1926, but he was still only 27 years old. He posted a 16-12 record in 29 starts. Over the next two seasons he added 42 more victories to his career total.

In 1929 Shellenback led the PCL in wins with a 26-12 record, even though his ERA rose to 3.98. He also chipped in a .322 batting average in 152 at-bats, with 12 home runs. During much of his PCL career, Shellenback was considered one of the best-hitting pitchers in the league, if not the best. For his career, he hit .269 in more than 1,800 minor-league at-bats, with 73 home runs. He won quite a few games with his bat; game recaps are strewn with his hitting contributions. He was often used as a pinch-hitter. After one game in 1933, the *Modesto News-Herald* exclaimed that Shellenback "proved again he is one of the league's best pinch-hitters by hitting for the circuit with the bases loaded to score four of the Hollywood runs."[6] The postseason of 1929 was a prime example of Frank's all-around efforts. As Hollywood defeated the San Francisco Missions in the playoffs, Shellenback won two playoff games and knocked three home runs, helping his club win the series in seven games.

In the early spring of 1930 Shellenback coached baseball at Loyola College in Los Angeles. Hollywood won the pennant again that season and defeated Los Angeles in the playoffs. Shellenback chipped in 19 wins. He had a tough time prepping for the season in 1931 because his arm wasn't rounding into shape. He sought the advice and manipulating skills of bonesetter Doc Spencer. For the next several seasons, the pitcher spent part of his spring working with Spencer. In 1931 Shellenback won a career-high 27 games in 46 appearances, with a 2.85 ERA. He lost on May 3, ending a 16-game winning streak that had begun the previous season. He then immediately kicked off another 15-game streak.

In August 1931 Connie Mack of the Philadelphia A's showed interest in acquiring Shellenback (the St. Louis Browns had also previously shown an interest). Mack contacted Hollywood owner Bill Lane, who was amenable. Mack then inquired with Commissioner Kenesaw Mountain Landis concerning the pitcher's eligibility under the spitball regulations. Landis probably could have easily granted a special exception, but instead ruled that his authority didn't extend to decisions made before his hiring. Any lingering hopes Shellenback may have had about resuming a major-league career were quashed. Lane later declared that he could have gotten as much as $50,000 to $100,000 for the spitballer if Landis had ruled otherwise. (New York Giants manager Bill Terry also made a plea on Shellenback's behalf in 1933.)

Shellenback held out for more money in 1932. The club was coming off back-to-back playoff appearances and he was luring the biggest crowds for the days he pitched. He and the Stars came to terms and Shellenback again led the league in victories (26, against 10 losses) and complete games (35). He won 21 games in 1933, bringing his total from 1928 through 1933 to 142 victories. That was his last 20-win season, though, and his ERA climbed to 4.53.

Shellenback's glaring weakness was beginning to show. As one sportswriter noted, "His best offering is his spitter and when that is working he never has any trouble on the mound. But let his saliva slant go back on him and Frank is sunk. That's why the Angels bumped him so vigorously the other day. His spitter wasn't breaking and that settled matters then and there."[7]

Shellenback won 14 games for Hollywood in 1934, topping Spider Baum as the all-time PCL victory leader. In the spring of that year, neuritis started to bother him. Shellenback was named manager of Hollywood in 1935, replacing longtime skipper Oscar Vitt. Although Frank was still capable of 14 wins, the team finished in last place. (That year he also appeared

as a pitcher in the screwball comedy movie *Alibi Ike*, which was filmed at Wrigley Field in Los Angeles.)

In 1936 the Stars relocated to San Diego and were called the Padres. By the end of the previous season, the neuritis and persistent back pain had prevented Shellenback from taking his regular turn in the rotation. As the Padres' player-manager from 1936 to 1938, he appeared in 15, six, and three games respectively. The club jumped to second place in '36, missing the pennant by a game and a half. That club boasted Bobby Doerr, Vince DiMaggio, and rookie Ted Williams.

Williams was especially fond of Shellenback, declaring in his autobiography *My Turn At Bat*, "He was a wonderful, wonderful man, a man I respected as much as any I've known in baseball."[8] Doerr also benefited from his manager's skill with young players — though he had to be careful about his throws to first when Frank was pitching. He would sometimes grab the slick spot on the ball after fielding a grounder.

San Diego finished in third in 1937, but proceeded to win the PCL championship in the playoffs. However, the club fell off to fifth place in '38. On October 2, Shellenback was unceremoniously fired. Bill Lane, who had been his employer since 1926, sent assistant Spider Baum with a pink slip that tersely read, "Frank Shellenback released unconditionally, W.H. Lane."[9]

Shellenback also retired as a player. He appeared in 640 minor-league games, amassing a 316-191 record, approximately 360 complete games, and 4,500 innings pitched. His 296 wins in the Pacific Coast League are the most by any pitcher in one minor league; he was one of the first five PCL players elected to the league's Hall of Fame in 1943. Of minor note, he used only one glove during his entire PCL career.[10]

A month after his release, Shellenback returned to the majors at long last, signing with the St. Louis Browns as a pitching coach for 1939. After the season he asked out of his contract with St. Louis to become the pitching coach for the Boston Red Sox, reuniting with quite a few of his minor-league charges. The Shellenback family left Los Angeles and settled in the Boston area, where they remained. Shellenback coached for the Red Sox from 1940 through 1944 and then joined the Detroit Tigers as a New England scout for 1945. In 1946 he became the Tigers' pitching coach, lasting for two seasons. Each year he oversaw the team during manager Steve O'Neill's brief hospital stints.

In 1948 Shellenback became manager of the Minneapolis Millers in the New York Giants' organization. He managed the club to a 31-33 record before turning it over to Babe Herman because of health issues; his doctor insisted that he take time away from the game. Shellenback returned in 1949 as a roving pitching coach for the Giants, impressing manager Leo Durocher. After the season Durocher added him to his major-league staff. Durocher held Shellenback in high regard, once commenting, "I take Shelly's word on anything about pitching. If he says a fellow is ready, he's ready. He's the best. He has a genius for spotting when a pitcher is doing something wrong. I may sense it. But Shelly sees it immediately—and has the answers."[11]

Shellenback remained in this capacity through 1955, including World Series appearances in 1951 and 1954, until Durocher left the organization. At least once Frank filled in for the manager while Durocher was visiting his sick mother in September 1953. Shellenback was one of the leading authorities in the game when it came to the spitball. He was often quoted as describing its effectiveness and discussing its proper use. Throughout Shellenback's stint with the Giants, opponents accused the club of being one of the foremost abusers of doctoring baseballs.

Shellenback continued in the Giants organization as supervisor of minor-league personnel from 1956 to 1959 and as a part-time Eastern scout and traveling coach from 1960 to 1969. During this time, the spitball was a hot topic in the press, in the clubhouse, and on the field. Shellenback fueled the debate by helping Bob Shaw and Gaylord Perry develop and gain control of the wet one. Accusations flew in 1965 as the Giants challenged for the pennant, though the Dodgers edged them by two games.

On August 17, 1969, Shellenback died at his home in Newton, Massachusetts, at the age of 70. He had been ill off and on, but death came unexpectedly. He was interred at Newton Cemetery. His nephew Jim Shellenback pitched for four teams in the majors from 1966 to 1977.

Baseball analyst Bill James said, "Frank Shellenback may have been the best pitcher in the history of the minor leagues." Other pitchers have posted more victories—but none did it at the same level as Shellenback. Aside from his 36 games in the majors, his entire career in Organized Baseball was spent at the top tier of the minors. The last legal spitballer in Organized Baseball attributed his success to his bread-and-butter pitch, declaring, "I wouldn't have lasted as long as I did if it weren't for the spitter."[12]

SOURCES

Beverage, Richard, *The Hollywood Stars* (Mount Pleasant, South Carolina: Arcadia Publishing, 2005).

Halberstam, David, *The Teammates* (New York: Hyperion, 2004).

James, Bill, *The New Bill James Historical Baseball Abstract* (New York: Simon & Schuster, 2003).

McNeil, William, *The California Winter League: America's First Integrated Professional Baseball League* (Jefferson, North Carolina: McFarland, 2002).

Porter, David L., *Biographical Dictionary of American Sports: Baseball* (New York: Greenwood Press, 1987).

Szalontai, James, *Close Shave: The Life and Times of Baseball's Sal Maglie* (Jefferson, North Carolina: McFarland, 2002).

Williams, Ted, and John Underwood, *My Turn at Bat: The Story of My Life* (New York: Simon and Schuster, 1988).

Zingg, Paul J., and Mark D. Medeiros, *Runs, Hits, and an Era: The Pacific Coast League, 1903-58* (Champaign, Illinois: University of Illinois Press, 1994).

Newspapers: *Atlanta Daily World, Chicago Tribune, Christian Science Monitor,*

Jefferson City (Missouri) *Daily Capital News, Fairbanks* (Alaska) *Daily News-Miner,*

Fitchburg (Massachusetts) *Sentinel, Fort Wayne* (Indiana) *Journal-Gazette, Galveston* (Texas) *Daily News, Hartford Courant, Indiana* (Pennsylvania) *Evening Gazette, Iowa City Citizen, Le Grand* (Iowa) *Reporter, Lima* (Ohio) *Daily News, Logansport* (Indiana) *Pharos-Reporter, Los Angeles Times, Modesto* (California) *News-Herald, Benton Harbor* (Michigan) *News-Palladium, The New York Times, Ogden* (Utah) *Standard-Examiner, Racine* (Wisconsin) *Journal News,*

Salt Lake Tribune, San Mateo (California) *Times, Valparaiso* (Indiana) *Vidette-Messenger, Waterloo* (Iowa) *Times-Tribune.*

Ancestry.com

Baseballlibrary.com

Baseball-reference.com

NOTES

1   *Los Angeles Times,* November 4, 1934.

2   *Atlanta Daily World,* July 26, 1960.

3   *Los Angeles Times,* November 4, 1934.

4   *Los Angeles Times,* August 17, 1930.

5   *Chicago Tribune,* October 10, 1921.

6   *Modesto News-Herald,* July 21, 1933.

7   *Los Angeles Times,* April 15, 1933.

8   Ted Williams and John Underwood, *My Turn at Bat: The Story of My Life* (New York: Simon and Schuster, 1988), 39.

9   *Los Angeles Times,* October 3, 1938.

10 See, for instance, the *Benton Harbor* (Michigan) *News-Palladium,* May 20, 1936.

11 *New York Times,* May 21, 1954.

12 *Atlanta Daily World,* July 26, 1960.

JOHN "LEFTY" SULLIVAN

By Jacob Pomrenke

LEFTY SULLIVAN HAD EVERY-thing a pitcher could want: a blazing fastball, a knee-buckling curve, a disappearing spitball, and pinpoint control. The one thing he couldn't do was field.

Because he felt dizzy every time he picked up a bunt—a lifelong heart condition cut off the flow of oxygen to his brain when he bent over too far—Sullivan's considerable talent was overshadowed by the one weakness that major-league hitters could exploit. He pitched in just four games for the Chicago White Sox in 1919, making three errors in five chances, then sat on the bench during the fateful World Series that fall.

After refusing a minor-league assignment and engaging in a spat with owner Charles Comiskey, he quit the White Sox in 1920 and returned to the semipro ranks on Chicago's South Side. The broad-shouldered, gregarious left-hander became a fan favorite in his hometown—Sullivan was considered the strikeout king of the city leagues for nearly two decades. His duels with ex-Cubs star Jim "Hippo" Vaughn were legendary, often drawing more than 5,000 fans to neighborhood diamonds on Sunday afternoons.

John Jeremiah Sullivan was born on May 31, 1894, to Jeremiah and Anna (Meany) O'Sullivan. The Irish-born Jeremiah O'Sullivan, according to family lore, had killed an English police officer in retaliation for a relative's death and fled to Canada.[1] He was repeatedly questioned by authorities there and soon relocated to Chicago, where he met his wife and found steady work at a bank; his name was anglicized along the way.

John, one of six siblings, excelled at athletics despite the disapproval of his harsh father, who was a stickler for education. Even in an era of "no Irish need apply," living wherever they could on the South Side, his parents were able to send him to the private Catholic high school St. Rita, where he starred in baseball and football.[2] After working and playing in a Chicago industrial league for a few years, he attracted enough attention to sign with Wichita of the Western League in 1915. The 21-year-old Sullivan went 2-5 with a mediocre 3.72 ERA in 22 games. His fielding statistics there are unknown.[3]

He moved back home after the season to start a family with his new bride, Anna Conick, the strong-willed daughter of a Chicago police detective. Their grandson, James P. Sullivan Jr., said Anna's father was a "lace-curtain Irishman ... who was suspicious of everybody. But Lefty swept her off her feet. She just loved him.... She always called him Sully, which I thought was the coolest thing I ever heard of. Except when she got mad—then she called him John."[4]

In Chicago Lefty rejoined the industrial leagues and began to make a name for himself as a pitcher. He worked odd jobs during the week and often earned a little extra cash by playing pool. He enlisted in the US Army in 1918 and became a star for the 86th Division team, based at Camp Grant, Illinois. During one mid-May game against a team from the nearby Great Lakes Naval Station, Sullivan outpitched future Hall of Famer Red Faber in front of a reported 12,000 fans.[5] That caught the attention of Faber's employer, the Chicago White Sox. When Sullivan returned from a quick deployment to France in the last throes of World War I, he was invited to spring training with the major-league squad.

At 25 years old in 1919, Sullivan was not considered to be a top prospect because of his advanced age for a rookie and limited professional experience. But his talent, while raw, was hard to deny.

More than 50 years after last facing Sullivan, Negro Leagues star Willie Powell remembered him well in an interview with author John Holway: "He'd beat any team in the world, pretty near, if he could field bunts. We'd keep bunting it down the third base line most of the time…. But you didn't hit him too often. I never got a hit off him—I never got one hit off Lefty Sullivan…. God, he was something!"[6]

White Sox manager Kid Gleason liked the charismatic left-hander immediately—and the feeling was mutual. Gleason spent time teaching Sullivan a curveball and attempting to cure his long-standing fielding woes. When the season began, the pitching-rich White Sox opted to send him down to Louisville in the American Association for more seasoning. The headstrong Sullivan refused the assignment,[7] in part because the American Association had just banned his best pitch, the controversial spitball, from being used. (The major leagues followed suit a year later.)

Instead, Lefty signed with a semipro team on the West Side of Chicago and dominated that circuit for most of the summer, racking up huge strikeout totals every week. In the few games he lost, it was said that batters "bunted him to death."[8]

On July 17, 1919, journeyman pitcher Grover Lowdermilk suddenly quit the White Sox and went home to Olin, Illinois. Sullivan "was immediately

Lefty Sullivan, circa 1919 (Chicago History Museum, SDN-061828, Chicago Daily News negatives collection)

located," signed, and given an old uniform. He warmed up that day at Comiskey Park against the Washington Senators, but didn't get in the game.[9]

Two days later, on July 19, he made his major-league debut—in a surprise start opposing future Hall of Famer Walter Johnson. Sullivan's fielding reputation preceded him; major-league hitters wasted little time in exploiting it. In the second inning, Sam Rice tapped a bunt back to the mound and Sullivan proceeded to throw it to the farthest corner of right field, allowing two runs to score. In the fourth, Washington's Howie Shanks laid down a bunt and, as the *Chicago Tribune* reported it, "though [Sullivan] had oceans of time to fire to first and retire his man, he simply held the ball in his hand and carried it back to the slab."[10] That was all for Lefty that day, as Gleason immediately yanked him. The White Sox, on their way to a second American League pennant in three years, rallied to win in 11 innings.

The pattern continued each time Sullivan pitched. For example, on August 14, he pitched two scoreless innings against the Red Sox at the end of a 15-6 loss. In his one attempt to field a ball, he threw it straight into the ground, nowhere close to first baseman Chick Gandil. No one—not even Sullivan, at the time—had heard of such a problem, let alone understood it. The press seemed mostly amused by his affliction, and always made sure to mention it when he pitched. After the White Sox clinched the pennant, Sullivan was given a start on September 26 against the Detroit Tigers, who bunted on him twice in the first two innings, then decided to "play it straight" after that.[11] Sullivan made one error and was hit hard in a 10-7 loss.

He never made another appearance in the major leagues.

Sullivan watched from the bench as eight of his teammates were implicated in throwing the 1919 World Series to the Cincinnati Reds, in what became known as the Black Sox scandal. Although Sullivan wasn't a part of the fix, his grandson said, "He must have known what was going on. But he never said one word about it…. All he would say is that whatever happened to Comiskey, Comiskey deserved."[12]

Sullivan's loyalties, like those of most players of that era, did not extend to the front office. And while he made friendships with pitchers Red Faber and Eddie Cicotte and catcher Ray Schalk that lasted the rest of his life, his rift with owner Charles Comiskey continued to grow in 1920. Sullivan was left behind on an Eastern road trip, having not pitched all season, and jumped the team in May.[13] He later believed, according to his family, that the White Sox owner tried to "blackball" him from Organized Baseball, in part because of his loyalty to the disgraced Cicotte, whose involvement in the Black Sox scandal was never questioned. In truth, players had little leverage against management in those days—especially with the reserve clause in effect, which permanently bound a player to the team that owned his contract. After Sullivan jumped the team, there was nowhere else in Organized Baseball for him to go.

Sullivan carried that resentment with him—his grandson said the lifelong South Side resident "would rather go to Cubs games, when he was an old man, than give Comiskey a dollar. It was pure hate.… And Lefty was not that kind of a guy."[14]

At any rate, Sullivan was more than happy to play baseball anywhere. He took a job with Fairbanks-Morse, a prominent auto manufacturer in nearby Beloit, Wisconsin, and pitched for the highly competitive company team during the summers of 1920 and '21. He and his wife, Anna, were still struggling to begin their family, having lost their first four children in infancy to lung and heart problems.[15] The couple were heartbroken, but their devout Catholic faith helped them persevere. In 1922 a healthy son was finally born, named James Patrick. Three more kids followed—Anna Rita, Robert, and Margaret. The daughters were both lifelong Dominican nuns, later working as activists in Washington, D.C., to help Salvadoran refugees, and Robert became a priest for nearly a decade until he requested dispensation from the Vatican in order to marry.[16]

Meanwhile, working as a salesman in his brother's insurance company, Lefty continued to play baseball on Sundays for nearly 20 more years. The semipro

leagues in Chicago were filled with major-league talent—in 1922, for example, Sullivan split two match-ups against his old White Sox teammate, Dick Kerr, who was in the midst of a holdout against Comiskey, and won two out of three games against ex-Cubs southpaw Jim "Hippo" Vaughn, famous for his participation in the only "double no-hitter" in big-league history back five years earlier.[17]

Vaughn and Sullivan hooked up for many duels during that decade and the next, both of them bouncing around various teams sponsored by local philanthropists and politicians. Because of his crowd-pleasing strikeout totals, which were almost always in double digits, and his propensity to create drama when balls were hit back to him, Sullivan was arguably the most memorable character in his league. It was reported that fans "actually [went] out to games to see Lefty throw the ball away."[18]

Sullivan never did shake his inability to field, but few semipro lineups were able to take advantage of his weakness. His stuff was simply too overpowering; many batters struck out just trying to lay down a bunt against him. In an era when few pitchers strove for strikeouts, Lefty soon realized how much he could benefit from them, regularly demanding a bonus from his team's financial backers for each "K" he notched. And in the less regulated environment of the semipro game, which wasn't under the same ethical constraints on gambling as Organized Baseball, Sullivan sometimes would place a $10 wager with an opposing fan if he happened to strike out 10 or more hitters—and he usually did.[19] It was quite a lucrative career for Lefty, and he made more money there than he did while playing professionally.

By the mid-1930s, Lefty was the undeniable ace of the Chicago semipro leagues. His starts were often guaranteed by team management, especially when established major leaguers came around during off-season barnstorming tours. When Hall of Famer Dizzy Dean and his brother Paul brought their exhibition tour to the West Side after the 1934 World Series, it was Sullivan who relieved them on the mound in the middle innings, after the crowd had gotten a taste of the colorful Gas House Gang pitchers in action.[20] Months later, Lefty was the starting pitcher against the vaunted Tokyo Giants and star pitcher Eiji Sawamura when Japan's premier team stopped in Chicago during a US tour.[21]

Off the field, Sullivan decided—"on a wild hair"—that he wanted to make a run at politics. As his grandson explained, "He wanted to participate as an author, not a consumer, of the American dream…. And also, he was a little resentful of his immigrant father's ignorance."[22] While Sullivan was well known throughout the city, his connections to the dominant Democratic Party machine in Chicago were limited; without its full support, he lost a race for alderman and was also unsuccessful in a bid for the state Senate. He later worked a number of politically affiliated jobs in Cook County, including a stint on the Traffic Safety Commission.[23] While Lefty's own political dreams were never realized, another grandson, John V. Sullivan, became chief parliamentarian of the US House of Representatives in 2004.

Lefty Sullivan finally stopped pitching competitively in 1938, though he could always be enticed to show up for Old Timers Games, high-school fundraisers, or any other event related to the sport he loved. He joined a group called Baseball Anonymous, co-founded by his old White Sox teammate Red Faber, which assisted down-on-their-luck ballplayers with living expenses and other necessities. He kept in touch with many of his old baseball buddies, including Faber, Vaughn, Buck Weaver, and Ray Schalk, who all remained in Chicago after their careers were over.

In 1945, his son James—a former football player at Marquette University who later married his college sweetheart, Mary Claire, and became a steelworker—was shot down over Germany on a bombing mission while serving in the 8th Air Force during World War II. He was liberated from a prisoner-of-war camp after several months.[24]

The Sullivans celebrated the arrivals of 19 grandchildren and 48 great-grandchildren, though Lefty wouldn't live to see them all. He enjoyed his last years,

teaching his oldest grandsons (and anyone else in their Rainbow Beach neighborhood of Chicago) to play baseball, eating vanilla ice cream every night, and snacking on his beloved beef fat. But "he never drank a drop," his grandson said, a product of watching his own father, Jeremiah, suffer from violent episodes of alcoholism for years.[25] Lefty's nutritional vices undoubtedly worsened his lifelong health problems—he suffered no fewer than *six* heart attacks, the last one proving to be fatal on July 7, 1958. He was buried at St. Mary Cemetery in Evergreen Park, Illinois.

SOURCES

Adrian Dominican Sisters, Adrian, Michigan.

Ancestry.com.

Appleton (Wisconsin) *Post Crescent*, 1925-32.

Baseball-Reference.com.

Chicago Daily News, 1919-1958.

Chicago Defender, 1918-1935.

Chicago Tribune, 1915-1958.

Farrell, James T., *Dreaming Baseball* (Kent, Ohio: Kent State University Press, 2007).

Hammond (Indiana) *Times*, 1930-39.

Holway, John, *Black Diamonds: Life in the Negro Leagues From the Men Who Lived It* (Westport, Connecticut: Meckler Publishing, 1989).

Interview with James P. Sullivan Jr., November 7, 2010.

Interview with John V. Sullivan, November 8, 2010.

Retrosheet.org.

Sheboygan (Wisconsin) *Press*, 1926-38.

Southtown Economist, 1931-1958.

The Sporting News, 1919-1958.

NOTES

1 Interview with James P. Sullivan Jr., November 7, 2010 (Hereafter James Sullivan Jr. interview).

2 Ibid.

3 Baseball-Reference.com.

4 James Sullivan Jr. interview.

5 *Chicago Tribune*, June 21, 1918.

6 John Holway, *Black Diamonds: Life in the Negro Leagues From the Men Who Lived It* (Westport, Connecticut: Meckler Publishing, 1989), 50.

7   *Chicago Tribune*, April 24, 1919.

8   *Chicago Daily News*, July 7, 1958.

9   *Chicago Tribune*, July 18, 1919. Manager Kid Gleason, desperate for pitching depth, persuaded Lowdermilk to return to the White Sox one week later.

10 *Chicago Tribune*, July 20, 1919.

11 *Chicago Tribune*, September 27, 1919.

12 James Sullivan Jr. interview.

13 *Chicago Tribune*, May 13, 1920.

14 James Sullivan Jr. interview.

15 Ibid.

16 *Chicago Daily News*, July 7, 1958; interviews with James P. Sullivan Jr. and John V. Sullivan, November 2010.

17 On May 2, 1917, Jim "Hippo" Vaughn of the Cubs and Fred Toney of the Reds both threw no-hitters through nine innings, the only "double no-hitter" in major-league history. Vaughn allowed a hit in the 10th inning and lost the game, 1-0.

18 *Appleton* (Wisconsin) *Post Crescent*, June 24, 1925.

19 *Sheboygan* (Wisconsin) *Press*, April 23, 1932.

20 *Chicago Tribune*, October 14, 1934.

21 *Chicago Tribune*, June 9, 1935.

22 James Sullivan Jr. interview.

23 *Chicago Daily News*, July 7, 1958.

24 *Wisconsin Rapids* (Wisconsin) *Daily Tribune*, October 16, 1945.

25 James Sullivan Jr. interview.

BUCK WEAVER

By David Fletcher

BEST KNOWN AS THE THIRD baseman banned from Organized Baseball for his knowledge of the 1919 World Series fix in which he did not participate, Buck Weaver spent most of his nine-year major-league career as a shortstop, only converting full time to the third sack in 1917. Initially a right-handed batter, Weaver learned to switch-hit after a poor rookie season, and from there he made his mark as one of the American League's most resourceful players, twice leading the circuit in sacrifices, and using his excellent range to reach balls that escaped most of his peers.

Nelson Algren once described Weaver as a "territorial animal ... who guarded the spiked sand around third like his life."[1] Despite his competitiveness, the infectious Weaver, nicknamed the Ginger Kid,[2] was also one of the most popular players of his day, known for his ever-smiling, jug-eared face that mimicked a Halloween Jack. Throughout the Deadball Era, Weaver steadily improved his game, enjoying his best season in 1920, just before he was permanently banished from the game he loved. An optimist by nature, Weaver spent the rest of his life fighting to restore his name.

George Daniel Weaver was born on August 18, 1890, in Pottstown, Pennsylvania, the fourth of five children of Daniel and Sarah Weaver. Located 41 miles northwest of Philadelphia, Pottstown had become one of the centers for the state's emerging iron industry, and Daniel Weaver supported his family by working in one of the area's iron furnaces.[3] By late 19th century standards, the heavily unionized iron industry paid good wages, and George Weaver's childhood was a contented one. Not very interested in school, Weaver turned his attention to baseball, where his energy and natural athletic talent were noticed at an early age by fellow players, coaches and scouts. A veteran ballplayer, Curt McGann, was so fascinated by Weaver's passionate style of play and his upbeat, positive attitude

that he nicknamed him Buck, a name in Chicago that would soon be synonymous for sympathy.[4]

Buck began his professional career in 1908 with Mount Carmel (Pennsylvania) of the outlaw Atlantic League, batting approximately .243 (the stats are incomplete) and splitting his time between shortstop and second base. After a year of semipro ball, in 1910 Weaver joined Northampton (Massachusetts) of the Connecticut State League, where he caught the eye of Philadelphia Phillies manager Red Dooin, who signed Buck to a $175-a-month contract and farmed him out to York (Pennsylvania) of the Tri-State League.[5] He hit .289 in 78 games for York and in the fall of 1910, superscout Ted Sullivan of the Chicago White Sox bought Buck's contract for $750 and assigned him to the San Francisco Seals of the Pacific Coast League.[6]

Separated from home for the first time, Weaver enjoyed an excellent season with the Seals in 1911, batting .282 in 182 games and drawing praise for his defensive skills. The performance was good enough to elicit an invitation to spring training with the Chicago White Sox in 1912, but just as Buck made his way to the White Sox camp in Waco, Texas, tragedy struck: His mother succumbed to illness. It was then that Buck faced a tough personal choice: Attend his mother's funeral or attend spring training. A telegram from his father persuaded Buck to go to camp instead of returning for the funeral.[7]

Upon his arrival in Waco, Weaver initially told no one of his mother's passing. When the *Chicago Tribune* learned what had happened, the newspaper published a feature article on the young recruit, applauding his grit. "Not a man on the squad displayed as much enthusiasm," *Tribune* reporter Sam Weller observed. "He has confessed that later when he was alone in his room he couldn't help but weep over the matter. However, he knew he could do no good by going home and he was determined to make good as a ball player and couldn't afford to quit the training squad."[8]

Despite the pain engendered by his mother's death, Weaver impressed the White Sox with a superlative camp, winning the starting shortstop job out of spring training. Irv Sanborn dubbed Weaver the Ginger Kid after Buck gamely played with an injured left hand wrapped in bandages. "Buck hasn't a thing against him but his age," Weller observed. "He is only twenty years old now and lacks only in experience. In his fielding he looks every bit as fast as [Donie] Bush of Detroit."[9]

In fact, as Weaver's performance during the 1912 season demonstrated, Buck wasn't as ready for the big leagues as the White Sox hoped or the beat writers imagined. Playing in 147 games, Weaver batted just .224 with nine walks, and led the league with 71 errors at short-stop. Knowing his position on the Chicago White Sox roster was not secure, he spent the entire offseason learning how to become a switch-hitter.[10] Heading into the 1913 season with new ammunition, Buck was able to raise his batting average from .247 to .272 in the last month of the season. Despite his excellent range, Weaver's defense remained problematic, as he again led the league with 70 errors, though he also led the circuit in putouts and double plays.

After the 1913 season Buck joined the world tour organized by Charles Comiskey and John McGraw, one of only a few White Sox players to make the trip. The touring party traveled 38,000 miles over a span of 17 weeks, not returning to Chicago until the following March. The lengthy trip may have sapped Buck's strength for the 1914 season, as his batting average dipped to .246, with a .279 on-base percentage. Despite this poor showing, Buck had become the leader of the White Sox and was appointed team captain after Harry Lord jumped to the Federal League.[11]

In a 1915 poll of White Sox fans, Weaver was voted the most popular member of the team, but the next two seasons would be rough ones for him.[12] After spending most of the spring of 1915 recovering from surgery to remove his adenoids and tonsils, Weaver

batted .268 and scored 83 runs. The following season, however, his batting average dipped to an abysmal .227, and Weaver began splitting his time in the field between shortstop and third base. At the end of the season, Buck filed for bankruptcy when his Chicago billiard-hall operation went broke. At the time, the newspapers reported that he had no other assets.[13] His salary was reportedly $6,000 a year, above average for the era.[14] Weaver prided himself on being a shrewd negotiator.

Nonetheless, after the 1916 season Weaver, along with teammates Eddie Collins and Joe Jackson, publicly promised owner Charles Comiskey they would capture the 1917 American League pennant.[15] This they did, thanks in large part to a superlative season from Weaver, one of the best of his career. He hit .284, the best average of his career to that point, despite missing time with a broken finger down the stretch. Switched to third base to make room for rookie shortstop Swede Risberg, Weaver proved an instant sensation at his new position, displaying excellent range, an adeptness at scooping up bunts down the third-base line, and leading the league in fielding percentage. "In stopping men coming around the bases, going after a fly ball, and digging in for hard chances Buck has few equals

Buck Weaver swinging, circa 1913 (Harris & Ewing Collection, Library of Congress, Prints and Photographs Division)

in the major leagues," *Baseball Magazine* observed near the end of the season.[16]

In the 1917 World Series, Weaver batted an impressive .333, though he made four errors at shortstop after manager Pants Rowland benched Risberg for Fred McMullin and moved Weaver back to his old position. In the postgame celebration that followed Chicago's championship-clinching victory in Game Six, Buck "danced around in a manner which indicated he had completely lost himself," the *Chicago Tribune* reported. "He tossed his cap into the air and followed with his sweater and a dozen bats and three or four hats that belonged to the spectators, and if there had been anything within reach it, too, would have gone into the air."[17]

The war-shortened 1918 season was a successful one for Buck, as he returned to shortstop and batted an even .300, the first time he reached that threshold in his major-league career. At season's end Weaver went to Beloit, Wisconsin, where he worked as a mechanic in the Fairbanks-Morse manufacturing plant and played for the company's semipro baseball team.[18] As the 1919 season approached, Buck demanded a raise from Comiskey, and negotiated a rare three-year contract worth $7,250 per season—the second-highest salary on the White Sox but still less than half of what second baseman Eddie Collins was making.[19]

For the 1919 season, Weaver returned to third base and enjoyed another outstanding season, smashing a career-high 45 extra-base hits and batting .296. As the White Sox surged toward the pennant, some of Buck's teammates, disgruntled over the shabby treatment they had received at the hands of Comiskey and looking for a big payday, began conspiring to throw the World Series. That September, Weaver attended two meetings regarding the proposed fix. Buck was skeptical that the scheme could work, telling his teammates and the gamblers present that throwing the World Series "couldn't be done."[20]

Weaver approached the World Series unsure of his teammates' intentions. Rumors were rampant that the fix was on but, by all accounts, Buck wanted no part of it. Declining the advances of his crooked teammates, Weaver played his best in the Series, batting .324 with four doubles and four runs scored in Chicago's eight-game loss to the Cincinnati Reds. In the wake of the White Sox' stunning defeat, sportswriters suspicious of the outcome alluded to the role of the seven conspirators, but often went out of their way to praise Weaver's efforts. "Though they are hopeless and heartless, the White Sox have a hero," the *Cincinnati Post* declared.[21] "He is George Weaver, who plays and fights at third base. Day after day Weaver has done his work and smiled. In spite of the certain fate that closed about the hopes of the Sox, Weaver smiled and scrapped. One by one his mates gave up. Weaver continued to grin and fight harder."

Weaver's 1920 season, which would prove to be his last in the major leagues, was also his finest. In 151 games, Buck posted career highs in batting average (.331), on-base percentage (.365), slugging percentage (.420), runs (102), hits (208), and doubles (34). Still only 29 years old and a nine-year veteran, Weaver was at the top of his game, leading Chicago in its fight for a second consecutive pennant. But it all came crashing down on September 28, when gambler Billy Maharg alleged in the press that eight members of the White Sox had thrown the Series.[22] Immediately after Maharg's allegations were published, Comiskey had suspension letters hand-delivered to Weaver and the other accused players.[23]

When Weaver was served his suspension letter by White Sox employee Norris "Tip" O'Neill, he instantly marched to Comiskey's office and declared his innocence. He was the only player of the eight accused to do so. *Collyer's Eye*, a weekly periodical focused mostly on sports and gambling, later reported that Comiskey promised Weaver—separate from the other seven players—that he would be reinstated to baseball if he was acquitted in the Cook County trial.[24]

Though Buck requested a separate trial from the other seven players, he was forced to sit with his Black Sox teammates during the proceedings. Judge Hugo Friend, presiding over the trial, all but declared Buck innocent by saying he wouldn't allow a conviction to stand against him if the jury ruled that way. Three hours of deliberation on August 2, 1921, returned a verdict of not guilty for all players accused. The next day the new commissioner of baseball, Kenesaw Mountain Landis, released his famous statement banning all eight of the accused for life. One clause in the statement was specifically targeted at Weaver: "… no player who sits in conference with a bunch of crooked players and gamblers where the ways and means of throwing games are discussed and does not promptly tell his club about it will ever play professional baseball."[25]

Unlike the other seven Black Sox, Weaver had not accepted any money to throw the Series, and there is no doubt that he played the games to win. His "crime" was simply his silence, and in this respect there was little to distinguish Weaver's actions from those of others who had also known about the fix and yet had done nothing to stop it.

But there was a method to Landis's harshness. By making an example of Weaver, Landis sent a message to the rest of Organized Baseball that any player who learned of a fix was guilty in the eyes of baseball unless he immediately reported it. The effect of this policy is readily apparent: Prior to Weaver's banishment, baseball authorities usually only discovered game-fixing schemes after they had already occurred. After Weaver's suspension, some attempted conspiracies were brought to light before they ever unfolded on the field, thanks to the honesty of players frightened by the Weaver precedent.

For instance, in 1922 New York Giants pitcher Phil Douglas was banned for life after Cardinals outfielder Les Mann reported Douglas's efforts to extract money from the Cardinals in exchange for Douglas abandoning the Giants. In 1924 Jimmy O'Connell and Cozy Dolan, two other members of the Giants, were banned for life after they tried to give Phillies shortstop Heinie Sand $500 to throw a game. Sand immediately reported the bribe offer. In this light, Weaver's suspension, and the object lesson it imparted to the rest of Organized Baseball for years to come, was one of Landis's most successful moves as commissioner.

All of this was small consolation to Weaver, his family, and the legion of Chicago fans who wanted to see him reinstated. Within one year of the 1921 verdict banning Buck from baseball for life, he submitted the first of many petitions to Commissioner Landis. Weaver was turned away every time. He collected the signatures of 14,000 fans, hired a New York City attorney, and tried to get the courts to intervene.[26] It was all to no avail.

After his banishment, Buck remained in Chicago, where he lived with his wife, the former Helen Cook. Buck took a job with the city as a day painter and also tried his hand in the drugstore business. With his pharmacist brother-in-law William Scanlon, he opened six drugstores on Chicago's South Side. Noticing Buck's business sense, Charles Walgreen, whose drugstore empire was about to skyrocket, asked Scanlon and Weaver to join him as junior partners. They declined the invitation. Then the Great Depression hit and Scanlon and Weaver were forced to close their stores.

In the meantime, Weaver continued to play ball on the semipro and outlaw circuits, sometimes playing with his former Black Sox teammates. In 1922, he joined Swede Risberg, Happy Felsch, and Lefty Williams on a tour of northern Minnesota for a series of games with local teams. In 1925, he traveled west to Arizona to form a star infield with Chick Gandil and manager Hal Chase for the Douglas team in the Copper League, which included teams in El Paso, Texas; Santa Rita/Fort Bayard, New Mexico; and across the U.S.-Mexico border in Ciudad Juarez. They were joined the following year by Williams, who joined the Douglas team before jumping to Fort Bayard.[27] Weaver played in the Copper League for two summers and was immensely popular among fans throughout the league.

He returned to Chicago in 1927 and made a personal plea to Judge Landis to clear his name, which the commissioner again denied. In March of that year, Weaver agreed to play semipro ball in Chicago and it was hailed by the press as a triumphant return for the former White Sox star.[28] He was frequently honored with "Buck Weaver Days" by adoring fans, and continued to play and manage for South Side teams into the early 1930s.

Into his old age, Weaver continued to pursue every avenue to return to the good graces of Organized Baseball. His final petition came in 1953, when he again requested reinstatement from Commissioner Ford Frick. In the letter, which is held by the Baseball Hall of Fame, Buck pleaded, "You know ... the only thing we have left in this world is our judge and the 12 jurors and they found me not guilty. They do some funny things in baseball."[29] Weaver received no response.

Shortly before his death, Buck was interviewed by author James T. Farrell about his banishment. The good-natured man who had once exuded joy and optimism in all he did had clearly been embittered by his ordeal. "A murderer even serves his sentence and is let out," Buck observed. "I got life."[30] On January 31, 1956, Weaver died of a heart attack at the age of 65; his body was found on West 71st Street by a Chicago policeman. Survived by his wife, Weaver was buried in Chicago's Mt. Hope Cemetery.

Nearly a century after he last played for the White Sox, Weaver continued to enjoy strong support in the ongoing effort to clear his name. His nieces and surrogate daughters, Patricia Anderson and Bette Scanlon[31], made public appearances on behalf of their uncle, including at the 2003 All-Star Game at U.S. Cellular Field and at the Society for American Baseball Research's 2013 national convention in Philadelphia, as part of the ClearBuck.com campaign.[32] Back in 1920, *The Sporting News* reported on Weaver's faithful supporters with the headline "Chicago Fans Grieve Most for Weaver and Still Hope for Him." In some quarters, that sentiment remains strong.

SOURCES

Farrell, James T., *My Baseball Diary*. (New York: A.S. Barnes & Co., 1957).

Stein, Irving M., *The Ginger Kid: The Buck Weaver Story*. (Dubuque, Iowa: Elysian Fields Press, 1992).

Farrell, James T., "Did Buck Weaver Get a Raw Deal?" *Baseball Digest*, August 1957.

Klein, Frank O., "Buck Weaver Back With the White Sox?" *Collyer's Eye*, December 14, 1920.

Reichow, Oscar C., "Chicago Fans Grieve Most for Weaver and Still Hope for Him." *The Sporting News*, October 14, 1920.

Tenney, Ross, "Weaver Dies, As Reds Roll On," *Cincinnati Post*, October 10, 1919.

Weller, Sam, "Sox Recruit of 20 Shows Real Grit, Hiding Sorrow to Fight for Berth." *Chicago Tribune*, March 15, 1912.

George D. Weaver v. American League Baseball Club of Chicago in the United States District Court, Northern District of Illinois, Filed 11/26/1921. Case No. 33870.

George D. Weaver v. American League Baseball Club of Chicago in the Municipal Court of Chicago. Case No. 855871.

NOTES

1   Nelson Algren, "So Long, Swede Risberg," *Chicago* (Vol. 30, No. 7, July 1981).

2   *Chicago Tribune*, May 10, 1912.

3   1900 US Census, Ancestry.com.

4   Irving M. Stein, *The Ginger Kid: The Buck Weaver Story* (Dubuque, Iowa: Elysian Fields Press, 1992), 3.

5   SABR Minor League Database, Baseball-Reference.com; Stein, 5.

6   Stein, 6.

7   *Chicago Tribune*, March 15, 1912.

8   Ibid.

9   *Chicago Tribune*, May 10, 1912.

10   *Chicago Tribune*, February 28, 1913.

11   *Chicago Tribune*, May 14, 1914.

12   *Chicago Tribune*, May 2, 1915.

13   *Chicago Tribune*, September 14, 1916.

14   Baseball-Reference.com.

15   *Chicago Tribune*, December 27, 1916.

16   John J. Ward, "Who's Who on the Diamond," *Baseball Magazine*, September 1917.

17   *Chicago Tribune*, October 16, 1917.

18   Stein, 121-22.

19   Bob Hoie, "1919 Baseball Salaries and the Mythically Underpaid Chicago White Sox," *Base Ball: A Journal of the Early Game*, Volume 6, No. 1 (Jefferson, North Carolina: McFarland & Co., Spring 2012).

20   Stein, 155.

21   *Cincinnati Post*, October 10, 1919.

22   *Philadelphia North American*, September 28, 1920.

23   Chick Gandil was the only one of the Black Sox who did not receive a suspension letter, as he sat out the 1920 season in a contract dispute with Charles Comiskey.

24   *Collyer's Eye*, December 14, 1920.

25   *New York Times*, August 4, 1921.

26   *New York Tribune*, January 14, 1922.

27   Lynn F. Bevill, "Outlaw Baseball Players in the Copper League: 1925-1927." Master's thesis, Western New Mexico University, 1988.

28   *Chicago Tribune*, March 13, 1927.

29   *Kansas City Star*, December 27, 1953.

30   James T. Farrell, *My Baseball Diary* (New York: A.S. Barnes & Co., 1957), 179.

31   Buck and Helen Weaver raised her sister's children for 16 years after William Scanlon's death in 1931. Helen Weaver and Marie Scanlon were very close and were buried next to each other at Mt. Hope Cemetery in Chicago.

32   At the 2003 All-Star Game, Patricia Anderson was joined by another Weaver niece, Marjorie Follett, to help launch ClearBuck.com with this author in Chicago.

ROY WILKINSON

By William F. Lamb

RIGHT-HANDED PITCHER ROY Wilkinson reached the pinnacle of his modest baseball career in only his second major-league game. A capable seven-year minor-league veteran, Wilkinson had been acquired by the Chicago White Sox late in the 1919 pennant chase to provide some respite for a strained pitching corps. Given a September start against the Philadelphia A's, Roy responded with a five-hit shutout. But from that auspicious beginning, his big-league career soon went into decline.

Wilkinson was a nonfactor in the notorious 1919 World Series, providing mop-up relief in two lopsided Chicago losses. In 1920 he underperformed when placed in the White Sox rotation, posting victories in only two of his 12 starting assignments (although he pitched competent long relief.)

After the late-1920 season banishment of Black Sox Eddie Cicotte and Lefty Williams, Wilkinson was designated as the No. 3 Chicago starter for the ensuing campaign—and flopped miserably, going 4-20 in 1921. Early the following year, Chicago gave up on Wilkinson and released him to the minors. Back at lesser altitude, Wilkinson reverted to earlier form, hurling 11 more years of solid minor-league ball. In the final analysis, it appears that Wilkinson was among that legion of able minor-league pitchers whose stuff simply was not good enough to handle major-league opposition.

Roy Hamilton Wilkinson was born in Canandaigua, New York, on May 8, 1893.[1] He was the fourth of seven sons born to coachman Edward C. Wilkinson (1855-1921) and his wife, the former Mary Bond (1856-1938).[2] Little is known of Roy's early life or schooling. He first came to attention pitching for amateur and semipro teams in and around his hometown. Eye-catching performances against overmatched locals—Wilkinson reportedly struck out 44 batters and allowed but three hits over a three-game stretch while pitching for a Canandaigua nine—brought him to the notice of pro scouts.[3] According to one account, Wilkinson entered the professional ranks in 1913, signing with the Waterbury Contenders of the Class B Eastern Association.[4] In late July his services were acquired by the Cleveland Naps, but Wilkinson saw no American League action during his brief stay with the club. The Naps then farmed Wilkinson to the St. Thomas Saints of the Class C Canadian League, where he posted a sparkling 7-1 record in nine late-season outings.

The year 1914 was an eventful one for 21-year-old Roy Wilkinson. On the domestic front, he tied the knot with hometown girl Melissa Elizabeth Beers.[5] Meanwhile, a squabble had broken out regarding the baseball rights to Wilkinson. "The St. Thomas club has refused to sell Roy Wilkinson to the Cleveland American League club, which club loaned the player to St. Thomas last August," reported *Sporting Life*.[6] Eventually the Saints prevailed in the rights dispute but Wilkinson had a disappointing sophomore campaign in the Canadian League, going 10-12 in 30 appearances.

He returned to St. Thomas for a third season in 1915. Baseball-Reference.com provides no stats for Wilkinson that season but he must have impressed, for the next year he jumped all the way up to the Newark Indians of the Double-A International League. Pitching for a last-place (52-87) Newark club, Wilkinson struggled, posting a lackluster 4-12 log in 18 appearances. He bounced back in 1917, going 12-6 with a fine 2.39 ERA in 222 innings pitched. Following this creditable season, Wilkinson was reportedly drafted by the National League's Philadelphia Phillies.[7] But his major-league debut would be made elsewhere, when the Philadelphia draft was canceled and Newark sold his contract to the American League's Cleveland Indians.[8]

On April 29, 1918, the Indians sent Wilkinson to the mound to pitch the ninth inning of a game irretrievably lost to Chicago. He pitched a perfect frame but never received another chance with Cleveland. Wilkinson spent the remainder of the 1918 season with the Rochester Hustlers of the International League. For reasons unknown, he pitched only 55 innings for Rochester, going 3-2, with a 1.64 ERA.

No record of World War I military service has been found for Wilkinson, but he did lose his wife that year. Melissa Beers Wilkinson was only 22 when she died sometime in 1918. Thereafter, Roy remarried quickly, taking 25-year-old Jessie Josephine Rosenbloom of nearby Monroe, New York, as his second wife on March 24, 1919.

Wilkinson went to 1919 spring training with Cleveland but was squeezed off the Opening Day squad by returning military veterans. He responded to the demotion by having an outstanding year for the Columbus Senators of the Double-A American Association. By early September his record stood at 17-15, with a league-leading 2.08 ERA in 298 innings pitched. At that point, the Chicago White Sox obtained Wilkinson from Columbus in exchange for veteran left-hander Dave Danforth. Roy was now joining a major-league outfit overloaded with playing talent but divided by clubhouse dissension. One faction was headed by Ivy League-educated Eddie Collins, the star second baseman and team captain. The other, a more hard-scrabble group, was led by first baseman/tough guy Chick Gandil. New arrival Wilkinson, no more than a late-season extra arm for a pitching staff thinned by the shutdown of ailing and injured Red Faber, was not a member of either side.

On September 12, 1919, Wilkinson provided the pitching help that manager Kid Gleason had been seeking, shutting out the Philadelphia A's 7-0 in his first appearance in a Chicago uniform. He then backed up his sterling debut with scoreless relief appearances against the New York Yankees and Boston Red Sox. The only blemish on his log came on the season's final day, a seven-inning relief loss in a meaningless game against Detroit. In his brief time with the White Sox,

Wilkinson had made a good impression, going 1-1 with a fine 2.05 ERA in 22 innings pitched.

But with the pennant-winning Sox entrusting World Series starting assignments to staff mainstays Eddie Cicotte (29-7), Lefty Williams (23-11), and rookie Dickie Kerr (13-7), Wilkinson was not expected to see any postseason action against the NL champion Cincinnati Reds. That all changed in Game One, when Cicotte suddenly collapsed in the fourth inning. With the White Sox trailing 6-1, manager Gleason turned to his second-line hurlers, beginning with Wilkinson. Roy pitched decently through the seventh (five hits, one earned run), all to no avail. The Reds posted a decisive, one-sided 10-1 victory.

Wilkinson also saw action in Game Eight, holding the Reds in check over the final four frames (four hits, no earned runs), as the Sox tried to rally from the insurmountable early deficit left by the strangely ineffective Lefty Williams. Again, Wilkinson's good work was for naught. The Reds captured the contest 10-5, completing the Series upset of the once-heavily-favored White Sox.

Despite the disappointing World Series outcome, the White Sox remained a powerhouse. Stars like Eddie Collins, Shoeless Joe Jackson, Buck Weaver, and Happy Felsch posted gaudy offensive stats in the high-octane AL of 1920. And the recovery of health and form by Red Faber gave the team a formidable pitching staff. By season's end, Faber, Eddie Cicotte, Lefty Williams, and Dickie Kerr were all members of the 20-win club.

The depth of the White Sox rotation provided little starting opportunity for Roy Wilkinson. And when starting assignments were presented, he pitched poorly. In 12 randomly-spaced starts, Wilkinson went 2-8 with a high ERA. He held his place on the club with competent relief work (5-1, with two saves), suggesting that his effectiveness often depended on how many times the day's batting order faced him.

Meanwhile, in the midst of this up-and-down campaign, a personal highlight occurred for Roy. Early on the morning of July 1, 1920, daughter June Mary

TCMA photo of Roy Wilkinson (Courtesy of Michael Aronstein / TCMA Ltd.)

Wilkinson was born.[9] Hours later, the new father marked the occasion by tossing eight innings of score-less relief against the St. Louis Browns.

By late September the White Sox, Cleveland, and New York were locked in a three-way pennant dog-fight. Then long-murmured allegations about the integrity of Chicago's play in the 1919 World Series exploded in the press. With little more than a week left in the regular season, Cicotte, Williams, Jackson, Weaver, Felsch, and other Chicago stalwarts were placed on suspension, pending the disposition of a grand-jury probe.

With that, White Sox pennant hopes expired. Pitching for a 96-58 second-place club, Wilkinson had been substandard, posting a 7-9 record with a 4.03 ERA. In 145 innings pitched, Roy surrendered 162 hits and walked 48 while striking out only 30 batters. But with White Sox pitching ranks depleted by the Cicotte

and Williams suspensions, Wilkinson still figured prominently in Chicago's plans for 1921.

Wilkinson tried to work the situation to his financial advantage, holding out when the White Sox opened 1921 spring training. He was also among the "honest White Sox" who voted to deny their suspended team-mates a share of the 1920 second-place money.[10] Once signed, the "tall and willowy [6-foot-1, 170-pound] pitcher" was designated a key component in the re-building of the Sox rotation.[11]

But the 1921 season proved to be a disaster for Wilkinson. Slotted behind Red Faber and Dickie Kerr in the rotation, he dropped his first ten decisions and did not post a victory until July 20. Although the White Sox were not the same club that had been an American League juggernaut, the 1921 lineup still featured future Hall of Famers Eddie Collins, Ray Schalk, and now Harry Hooper, plus new talents like Bibb Falk, Earl Sheely, and Johnny Mostil. That a White Sox hurler could succeed with this cast behind him is reflected in the records of Faber (25-13) and Kerr (19-17). But not No. 3 starter Roy Wilkinson, who lost with numbing regularity. Press accounts of Wilkinson's defeats followed a monotonous outline, usually reporting that he had pitched well the first couple of times through the opposition lineup, only to be hit hard in the later innings. An undeserved (three earned runs in one inning's work) relief win over Cleveland on October 2 elevated the final Wilkinson log to an abysmal 4-20, with a 5.13 ERA. In 198⅔ innings pitched, he had been racked for 259 hits and surrendered 78 walks, while striking out only 50.

Notwithstanding Wilkinson's 1921 record, *The Sporting News* maintained that "critics were favorably impressed and speak encouragingly of his prospects."[12] But Wilkinson was not long for the majors. Following a bad start (0-1, 8.74 ERA on 24 hits/6 walks in 14⅓ innings pitched), the White Sox sent Wilkinson and ineffective left-hander John Russell to the Kansas City Blues of the American Association in exchange for veteran pitcher Ferdie Schupp.[13] Although he continued pitching professionally for another decade, Roy Wilkinson's major-league career was over. In parts of five seasons, he compiled a 12-31 (.279) record with a 4.66 ERA in 380⅔ innings pitched.

As he had earlier, Wilkinson pitched capably once he returned to the minors. His time with Kansas City was highlighted by an 18-6 record for the American Association champions of 1923. After a mid-1925 transfer to the Louisville Colonels, Wilkinson continued to work effectively, going 17-11 in 1930 and remaining with Louisville until he called it quits at the conclusion of the 1932 season. In 18 minor-league seasons, Wilkinson's cumulative record was a respectable 166-152 (.522), with a 3.04 ERA in more than 2,700 innings pitched.

Once his playing career was over, Wilkinson receded into obscurity. In January 1932 it was reported that second wife Jessie had filed for divorce and custody of their now 11-year-old daughter, June.[14] But the 1933 Louisville City Directory listed Roy and Jessie Wilkinson as living together at a local address. The 1941 Louisville Directory, however, has Roy and an unknown Catherine Wilkinson living in rooms on South Second Street, not far from the Seagram's Distillery, where Roy had found work.[15] Wilkinson then disappears from the directory rolls until June 1956, when he was admitted to Louisville General Hospital suffering from lung cancer. He died there on July 2, 1956, aged 63.[16] No obituary was published in Louisville newspapers, and Wilkinson's survivors and his place of burial are unknown.[17]

NOTES

1   Some sources, including Baseball-Reference.com, give 1894 as the year of Roy Wilkinson's birth. But his death certificate and most contemporaneous accounts of his playing career list May 8, 1893, as the date of his birth.

2   Sources for the biographical information presented herein include the Roy Wilkinson file at the Giamatti Research Center, National Baseball Hall of Fame and Museum, Cooperstown, New York; US Census data, and certain of the newspaper articles cited below. Roy's brothers were twins Edward N. (1882-1957) and Frank (1882-1931), Bert (born 1886), Hugh (1888), Merton (1896), and Henry (1897-1957). Statistics cited in the text have been taken from Baseball-Reference.com.

3   As reported in the *Concord Junction* (Concord, Massachusetts) *News,* preserved in *Our Paper,* the journal of the Massachusetts Reformatory, Vol. 29, August 2, 1913. Another report stated that professional interest in Wilkinson was an "outgrowth of a record of two no-hit games and the unusual achievement of fifty-five strikeouts in his last four contests." *Louisville Courier-Journal,* July 31, 1913.

4   Unidentified circa 1919 news clipping in the Roy Wilkinson file at the Giamatti Research Center. Baseball-Reference.com has no record of Wilkinson pitching for Waterbury in 1913.

5   *Sporting Life,* May 9, 1914.

6   *Sporting Life,* April 25, 1914.

7   Tom Munn and Matt Vitticore, *Ontario County: The Golden Age of Railroads and Baseball* (Charleston, South Carolina: Arcadia Publishing, 1999), 78.

8   Unidentified circa 1919 news clipping in the Roy Wilkinson file at the Giamatti Research Center.

9   *Chicago Tribune,* July 2, 1920.

10   As reported by the Associated Press. See e.g., *Louisville Courier-Journal,* November 20, 1920. Ironically, Wilkinson and four other "Clean Sox" would later appear as quasi-alibi defense witnesses at the July 1921 criminal trial of these same suspended teammates.

11   I.E. Sanborn, *Chicago Tribune,* March 12, 1921.

12   *The Sporting News,* November 24, 1921.

13   *Chicago Tribune/Louisville Courier Journal,* May 16, 1922, and elsewhere.

14   Unidentified January 7, 1932 news clipping in the Roy Wilkinson file at the Giamatti Research Center.

15   Wilkinson's whereabouts while living in Louisville are traced through 1941 in a letter of Mark Harris of the Louisville Free Public Library, dated January 25, 1980, a copy of which is in the Wilkinson file in Cooperstown.

16   Roy Wilkinson death certificate, obtained from the Kentucky Division of Vital Statistics.

17   In 2010, the Ontario County Historical Museum in Canandaigua, New York, hosted a yearlong exhibit on local baseball that included photos and family reminiscence about Roy Wilkinson. See *Henrietta* (New York) *Post,* June 14, 2010. Regrettably, repeated attempts by the writer to contact the Wilkinson great-grandson featured in the *Henrietta Post* article were unsuccessful.

A notation on the Wilkinson death certificate indicates that the place of burial was probably the Manslick Road Pauper Cemetery in Louisville. But gaps in burial records maintained by the City of Louisville in the 1950s preclude confirmation. The writer is indebted to Joe Hardesty of the Louisville Free Public Library and staff archaeologist Philip DiBlasi of the University of Louisville for their assistance in trying to track down the final resting place of Roy Wilkinson.

SEASON TIMELINE: AUGUST 1919

White Sox record: 18-9 (.667)
Runs scored: 140 | Runs allowed: 110

AL standings
August 31, 1919

Team	W	L	Pct	GB
CHW	75	42	.641	—
CLE	68	47	.591	6
DET	68	48	.586	6½
NYY	64	51	.557	10
SLB	60	56	.517	14½
BOS	53	62	.461	21
WSH	44	72	.379	30½
PHA	30	84	.263	43½

PLAYER OF THE MONTH

	G	PA	AB	R	H	2B	3B	HR	RBI	SB	BB	SO	BA	OBP	SLG	OPS
Joe Jackson	27	122	100	15	37	8	1	1	21	2	16	2	.370	.462	.500	.962

Jackson's batting eye was consistent and spectacular during the second half of the season, as he batted .375 in July, .370 in August, and .373 in September with just seven strikeouts in 255 plate appearances. He played a big role in the White Sox' 10-game winning streak in August with 16 hits, 10 RBIs, and 6 runs scored during that span. Jackson began his own 13-game hitting streak on August 17 and his two-run go-ahead single two days later helped the White Sox overcome a 7-2 deficit against the Philadelphia A's.

PITCHER OF THE MONTH

	W	L	ERA	G	GS	CG	SHO	IP	H	R	ER	BB	SO	WHIP
Eddie Cicotte	7	2	2.61	9	7	6	1	62	58	21	18	11	21	1.113

Looking ahead to the World Series, manager Kid Gleason remained on the hunt for another dependable starter, giving four starts in August to Grover Lowdermilk, two to Big Bill James, and one to Erskine Mayer, all midseason pickups. Meanwhile, Eddie Cicotte kept taking his regular turn. With the rotation in flux, Cicotte made three starts in August on two days' rest, and he won all of those games, including a 12-inning, six-hit shutout of the Washington Senators on August 10. He ended the month with a 26-7 record and was in the middle of an eight-game winning streak as September began.

DAY BY DAY RECAP

Friday, August 1
Postponed, rain
"Sox Fray Called Off in Sunshine" — *Chicago Herald and Examiner*

Saturday, August 2
Fenway Park, Boston
"Sox Slaughter Ball, 10-1, After Losing 5-3 Tilt" — *Chicago Tribune*

| White Sox (57-34) | 210 | 000 | 000 — 3 10 1 |
| Red Sox (40-48) | 100 | 020 | 20x — 5 11 0 |

WP: Allen Russell (6-5). LP: Eddie Cicotte (19-6).
Eddie Cicotte: 8 IP, 11 H, 5 R, 4 ER, 3 BB, 3 K.
Nemo Leibold: 4-5, R, RBI. Buck Weaver: 1-3, 3B, R, RBI. Swede Risberg: 2-4, R.

| White Sox (58-34) | 000 | 000 | 181 — 10 14 2 |
| Red Sox (40-49) | 000 | 100 | 000 — 1 7 1 |

WP: Lefty Williams (17-6). LP: Herb Pennock (8-6).
Lefty Williams: 9 IP, 7 H, 1 R, 0 ER, 1 BB, 5 K.
Happy Felsch: 2-4, 2B, R, 3 RBI. Lefty Williams: 1-4, 2B, R, 2 RBI. Buck Weaver: 3-5, 2B, 2 R, RBI.

Sunday, August 3
Scheduled day off
"Day of Rest is Boon to Ailing Sox" — *Chicago Tribune*

Monday, August 4
Fenway Park, Boston
"Sox Lack Punch; Faber is Wild, so Red Hose Cop Victory, 2-1" — *Chicago Tribune*

| White Sox (58-35) | 000 | 000 | 010 — 1 8 2 |
| Red Sox (41-49) | 100 | 010 | 00x — 2 11 1 |

WP: Sam Jones (9-12). LP: Red Faber (9-9).
Red Faber: 7 IP, 11 H, 2 R, 1 ER, 5 BB, 2 K.
Happy Felsch: 3-4. Shano Collins: 1-1, 3B, R. Nemo Leibold: 1-4, 2B, RBI.

Tuesday, August 5
Postponed, rain
"Sox Sentenced to Double Bill in Philly Today" — *Chicago Tribune*

Wednesday, August 6
Postponed, rain
"Sunshine Hides On Sox, Piling Up Doubleheaders" — *Chicago Tribune*

THE 1919 CHICAGO WHITE SOX

Thursday, August 7
Shibe Park, Philadelphia
"Sox Don't Laugh at Macks Who Get Even Break, 2-1, 3-2" — *Chicago Tribune*

White Sox (59-35)　000　000　101 — 2 4 2
Athletics (25-65)　　000　000　001 — 1 8 0
WP: Eddie Cicotte (20-6). LP: Scott Perry (4-16).
Eddie Cicotte: 9 IP, 8 H, 1 R, 0 ER, 0 BB, 5 K.
Happy Felsch: 1-4, HR, R, RBI. Swede Risberg: 1-4, 3B, R. Nemo Leibold: 1-3, 2B, BB.

White Sox (59-36)　001　010　000 — 2 13 2
Athletics (26-65)　　110　100　00x — 3 9 0
WP: Rollie Naylor (2-12). LP: Lefty Williams (17-7).
Lefty Williams: 8 IP, 9 H, 3 R, 3 ER, 3 BB, 2 K.
Buck Weaver: 2-4, 2B, 2 RBI. Joe Jackson: 2-3, HBP. Swede Risberg: 2-4, 2B.

Friday, August 8
Shibe Park, Philadelphia
"Mack Uses Kid to Defeat Sox; Divide 2 Games" — *Chicago Tribune*

White Sox (59-37)　001　200　100　000　0 — 4 8 2
Athletics (27-65)　　001　000　300　000　1 — 5 14 1
WP: Walt Kinney (6-9). LP: Dickey Kerr (9-4).
Dickey Kerr: 6⅓ IP, 5 H, 1 R, 1 ER, 3 BB, 1 K.
Ray Schalk: 3-5, 2B, R, RBI. Joe Jackson: 1-5, HR, 2 RBI. Shano Collins: 2-5, 2B, BB, RBI.

White Sox (60-37)　212　010　000 — 6 9 0
Athletics (27-66)　　001　000　010 — 2 8 3
WP: Grover Lowdermilk (3-5). LP: Tom Rogers (4-13).
Grover Lowdermilk: 9 IP, 8 H, 2 R, 2 ER, 0 BB, 6 K.
Fred McMullin: 2-4, R, 2 RBI. Joe Jackson: 2-4, SB, R, RBI. Nemo Leibold: 1-1, 2B, BB, 2 R.

Saturday, August 9
Griffith Stadium, Washington
"Woeful Baptism of New Hurlers Beats Sox, 11-6" — *Chicago Tribune*

White Sox (60-38)　001　000　023 — 6 11 3
Senators (40-58)　　220　030　13x — 11 12 4
WP: Walter Johnson (15-12). LP: Erskine Mayer (5-4).
Erskine Mayer: 5 IP, 7 H, 7 R, 7 ER, 3 BB, 1 K.
Joe Jackson: 2-5, 3 RBI. Nemo Leibold: 2-5, 2 R. Buck Weaver: 2-5, R, RBI.

Sunday, August 10
Griffith Stadium, Washington
"Foster's Heave in Twelfth Gives Cicotte Victory, 1-0" — *Chicago Tribune*

White Sox (61-38)   000   000   000   001 — 1 6 1
Senators (40-59)   000   000   000   000 — 0 6 2
WP: Eddie Cicotte (21-6). LP: Jim Shaw (15-10).
Eddie Cicotte: 12 IP, 6 H, 0 R, 0 ER, 2 BB, 4 K.
Buck Weaver: 1-5, R. Nemo Leibold: 1-4, BB. Joe Jackson: 1-5.

Monday, August 11
Griffith Stadium, Washington
"Sox Hop Senators For 5 in First, Win 7-4, And Start Home" — *Chicago Tribune*

White Sox (62-38)   501   010   000 — 7 14 0
Senators (40-60)   000   001   003 — 4 8 4
WP: Lefty Williams (18-7). LP: Harry Harper (6-16).
Lefty Williams: 9 IP, 8 H, 4 R, 4 ER, 2 BB, 5 K.
Shano Collins: 4-5, R, SB. Chick Gandil: 3-5, 2B, 2 R, 2 RBI. Lefty Williams: 0-3, 2 RBI.

Tuesday, August 12
Scheduled day off
"Sox Reach Crest of Strength for Year; Slab Problem Solved" — *Chicago Tribune*

Wednesday, August 13
Scheduled day off
"Gleason's Sox Open Long At Home Stay Today With Boston" — *Chicago Tribune*

Thursday, August 14
Comiskey Park, Chicago
"With Ruth as Head Villain, Bostons Butcher Sox, 15-6" — *Chicago Tribune*

Red Sox (46-52)   027   001   500 — 15 20 1
White Sox (62-39)   000   021   003 — 6 10 2
WP: Allen Russell (7-6). LP: Eddie Cicotte (21-7).
Eddie Cicotte: 2⅓ IP, 8 H, 8 R, 7 ER, 2 BB, 0 K.
Buck Weaver: 3-5, SB, R. Joe Jackson: 2-4, 2 2B. Chick Gandil: 2-5, 2B, R.

Friday, August 15
Comiskey Park, Chicago
"John Collins Gets Into Game in Time to Aid in Win, 6 to 5" — *Chicago Tribune*

Red Sox (46-53)   100   100   300   00 — 5 11 1
White Sox (63-39)   001   000   031   01 — 6 11 2
WP: Eddie Cicotte (22-7). LP: Sam Jones (9-14).
Lefty Williams: 8 IP, 8 H, 5 R, 3 ER, 1 BB, 4 K.

Nemo Leibold: 4-5, 2B, R, RBI. Eddie Collins: 1-5, 2B, R, 2 RBI. Swede Risberg: 1-4, 3B, RBI. Shano Collins: 0-0, 2 R.

Saturday, August 16
Comiskey Park, Chicago
"Ruth Cracks Record Homer, But White Sox Win, 7 to 6" — *Chicago Tribune*

Red Sox (46-54)   011   020   200 — 6 8 0
White Sox (64-39)   110   030   011 — 7 12 0
WP: Red Faber (10-9). LP: Sam Jones (9-15).
Erskine Mayer: 7 IP, 7 H, 5 R, 5 ER, 2 BB, 2 K.
Ray Schalk: 3-5, 3B, 2 R. Happy Felsch: 3-4, HBP, R. Nemo Leibold: 1-2, 2 BB, 2 R. Eddie Collins: 2-4, 3B, R, BB.

Sunday, August 17
Comiskey Park, Chicago
"Hustling Sox Grab Game Before Weather Man Spoils It" — *Chicago Tribune*

Athletics (28-72)   001   000 — 1 5 2
White Sox (65-39)   201   00x — 3 5 0
WP: Grover Lowdermilk (4-5). LP: Rollie Naylor (2-15).
Grover Lowdermilk: 6 IP, 5 H, 1 R, 1 ER, 0 BB, 3 K.
Joe Jackson: 2-2, 2B, 2 RBI. Buck Weaver: 1-2, R, RBI. Nemo Leibold: 1-3, 3B, R.

Monday, August 18
Comiskey Park, Chicago
"Sox Display Fancy Frills, Beating Athletics, 11 to 6" — *Chicago Tribune*

Athletics (28-73)   000   100   032 — 6 9 4
White Sox (66-39)   131   210   12x — 11 17 4
WP: Dickey Kerr (10-4). LP: Win Noyes (0-1).
Dickey Kerr: 9 IP, 9 H, 6 R, 3 ER, 5 BB, 6 K.
Chick Gandil: 4-4, 3 2B, 3 R, RBI. Dickey Kerr: 2-4, 2B, 2 R, RBI. Joe Jackson: 3-5, 2B, R, 2 RBI.

Tuesday, August 19
Comiskey Park, Chicago
"Sox Sweep From 5 Runs Behind and Trim Athletics, 8-7" — *Chicago Tribune*

Athletics (28-74)   001   031   200 — 7 13 3
White Sox (67-39)   101   000   42x — 8 14 1
WP: Erskine Mayer (6-4). LP: Walt Kinney (7-10). SV: Lefty Williams (1).
Grover Lowdermilk: 5 IP, 7 H, 4 R, 4 ER, 4 BB, 1 K.
Buck Weaver: 4-5, 2 R. Nemo Leibold: 2-3, 3 R. Joe Jackson: 1-3, 2 BB, R.

Wednesday, August 20
Comiskey Park, Chicago
"Thirteen Sox Wallops Enough to Trim Senators, 10 to 3" — *Chicago Tribune*

Senators (42-64)   010   002   000 — 3 9 0
White Sox (68-39)   003   003   31x — 10 13 0
WP: Eddie Cicotte (23-7). LP: Eric Erickson (4-10).
Eddie Cicotte: 9 IP, 9 H, 3 R, 3 ER, 2 BB, 4 K.
Eddie Collins: 3-4, 2B, SB, HBP, R, 3 RBI. Buck Weaver: 2-4, SB, R, 2 RBI. Eddie Cicotte: 1-3, 3B, BB, 2 R, RBI.

Thursday, August 21
Comiskey Park, Chicago
"Bungling Senators Allow Sox to Hold Stride, 11 to 4" — *Chicago Tribune*

Senators (42-65)   210   010   000 — 4 10 6
White Sox (69-39)   500   221   01x — 11 12 0
WP: Lefty Williams (19-7). LP: Tom Zachary (0-2).
Lefty Williams: 9 IP, 10 H, 4 R, 4 ER, 2 BB, 2 K.
Happy Felsch: 3-4, 2B, BB, 3 RBI. Joe Jackson: 3-5, R, 3 RBI. Lefty Williams: 2-4, R, BB, RBI.

Friday, August 22
Comiskey Park, Chicago
"James, in Debut, Pitches 3-0 Win for Pacemakers" — *Chicago Tribune*

Senators (42-66)   000   000   000 — 0 5 1
White Sox (70-39)   001   010   01x — 3 7 1
WP: Bill James (5-5). LP: Jim Shaw (15-12).
Bill James: 9 IP, 5 H, 0 R, 0 ER, 3 BB, 4 K.
Eddie Collins: 2-4, SB, R. Happy Felsch: 0-2, BB, 2 RBI. Joe Jackson: 1-2, 2 BB, R.

Saturday, August 23
Comiskey Park, Chicago
"Sox on Rampage Swat New York in 10 to 2 Game" — *Chicago Tribune*

Yankees (57-50)   000   000   200 — 2 6 2
White Sox (71-39)   400   041   10x — 10 14 1
WP: Eddie Cicotte (24-7). LP: Bob Shawkey (15-11).

Eddie Cicotte: 9 IP, 6 H, 2 R, 2 ER, 0 BB, 2 K.
Chick Gandil: 3-4, 2B, 2 R, 3 RBI. Joe Jackson: 3-5, 2B, R, 2 RBI. Eddie Collins: 2-3, 2B, 2 BB, 2 R.

Sunday, August 24
Comiskey Park, Chicago
"Daring Base Running by Sox Features 4-1 Win Over Yanks" — *Chicago Tribune*

Yankees (57-51)   001   000   000 — 1 7 0
White Sox (72-39)   110   001   01x — 4 7 2
WP: Lefty Williams (20-7). LP: Jack Quinn (12-11).

Lefty Williams: 9 IP, 7 H, 1 R, 0 ER, 4 BB, 3 K.
Joe Jackson: 2-2, 2B, 2 BB, R, RBI. Eddie Collins: 1-2, 3B, SB, BB, 2 R. Happy Felsch: 1-3, RBI.

Monday, August 25
Comiskey Park, Chicago
"White Sox Winning Gait is Halted at Ten Straight, 6 to 5" — *Chicago Tribune*

Yankees (58-51)	000	141	000 — 6	13	0
White Sox (72-40)	000	200	021 — 5	11	0

WP: Hank Thormahlen (10-6). LP: Bill James (5-6).
Bill James: 5⅓ IP, 11 H, 6 R, 6 ER, 1 BB, 1 K.
Chick Gandil: 2-4, 2B, BB, 2 R. Swede Risberg: 2-4, 2 RBI. Joe Jackson: 2-4, BB, 2 R.

Tuesday, August 26
Sportsman's Park, St. Louis
"Eddie Collins' Homer Beats Browns in 10th Inning, 4 to 3" — *Chicago Tribune*

White Sox (73-40)	300	000	000	1 — 4	9	0
Browns (59-52)	000	002	010	0 — 3	9	3

WP: Eddie Cicotte (25-7). LP: Allan Sothoron (16-9).
Dickey Kerr: 8 IP, 8 H, 3 R, 3 ER, 1 BB, 1 K.
Eddie Collins: 1-5, HR, RBI. Chick Gandil: 3-4, 2 RBI. Joe Jackson: 2-4, SB, R, BB.

Wednesday, August 27
Sportsman's Park, St. Louis
"Felsch's Homer With Two On Puts Sox Closer to Flag, 6-5" — *Chicago Tribune*

White Sox (74-40)	030	000	300 — 6	9	2
Browns (59-53)	010	013	000 — 5	7	0

WP: Lefty Williams (21-7). LP: Bert Gallia (12-11).
Lefty Williams: 9 IP, 7 H, 5 R, 4 ER, 3 BB, 2 K.
Happy Felsch: 2-3, HR, BB, 2 R, 3 RBI. Swede Risberg: 2-4, 2B, RBI. Joe Jackson: 1-3, BB, 2 R.

Thursday, August 28
Scheduled day off

Friday, August 29
Dunn Field, Cleveland
"Sox Cop, 3 to 2, And Now Lead Flag Race by Eight Games" — *Chicago Tribune*

White Sox (75-40)	000	000	021 — 3	9	0
Indians (66-47)	100	010	000 — 2	8	0

WP: Eddie Cicotte (26-7). LP: Ray Caldwell (8-5).
Eddie Cicotte: 9 IP, 8 H, 2 R, 2 ER, 1 BB, 3 K.
Joe Jackson: 2-4, 2B, R, RBI. Happy Felsch: 2-3, 2B, BB, RBI. Eddie Collins: 2-4, R, BB.

Saturday, August 30
Dunn Field, Cleveland
"Indians Gain in Flag Race by Whipping Sox, 4 to 0" — *Chicago Tribune*

White Sox (75-41) 000 000 000 — 0 5 2
Indians (67-47)   002 001 10x — 4 10 1
WP: Elmer Myers (5-5). LP: Bill James (5-7).
Bill James: 7 IP, 9 H, 4 R, 4 ER, 4 BB, 3 K.
Joe Jackson: 1-3, 2B, BB. Nemo Leibold: 1-4, 2B. Swede Risberg: 1-2, HBP.

Sunday, August 31
Dunn Field, Cleveland
"Cleveland Cuts White Sox Pennant Lead to Six Games" — *Chicago Tribune*

White Sox (75-42) 000 001 000 — 1 6 1
Indians (68-47)   401 010 00x — 6 11 2
WP: Stan Coveleski (21-9). LP: Lefty Williams (21-8).
Lefty Williams: ⅓ IP, 3 H, 4 R, 4 ER, 1 BB, 0 K.
Nemo Leibold: 2-4, BB, R. Swede Risberg: 2-4, 2B. Joe Jackson: 0-3, RBI.

AUGUST HIGHLIGHTS

Turning Their Attention to Cincinnati: For most of the season, the first-place White Sox looked ahead to a possible World Series rematch with the New York Giants. But the Cincinnati Reds took over the National League lead on the final day of July, then beat the Giants in six of nine games in August to coast to the pennant. The White Sox were paying attention, as reported in the *Chicago Tribune* on August 6: "Until the last few days one heard them discussing the merits of Fred Toney and Jess Barnes as pitchers likely to be met in the big show this fall.… During the last week the talk has switched to the athletes performing for Pat Moran in Cincinnati. The Sox are wondering how the gate receipts of a series between Chicago and Cincinnati would compare with the receipts between Chicago and New York. A number of the Sox have asked in the last few days the seating capacity of the ball park in Cincinnati. Also they want to know just how great a hitter this fellow Roush is, and if it's really true that Hod Eller has a new kind of hop on a fastball, and if this big Dutch Ruether is as great as he's pitched."

Felsch Ties Assists Mark: On August 14, White Sox center fielder Happy Felsch tied a major-league record by throwing out four Red Sox baserunners in one game, three at home plate and one at third base. Two of his assists completed double plays. The record for outfield assists was first set by the White Sox' James "Ducky" Holmes in 1903 and has been tied several times since. Despite Felsch's effort, Boston handed Chicago a 15-6 defeat and Babe Ruth set a new American League single-season record with his 17th home run off Dickey Kerr in the seventh inning.

Schalk's Endurance Record: On August 20, in a 10-3 win over the Washington Senators, Ray Schalk played his 100th game behind the plate — for the seventh consecutive season. No other catcher before him had even played 100 games in a season seven times, let alone consecutively. The White Sox' indomitable "Cracker" went on to surpass the 100-game mark in 11 consecutive seasons, from 1913 to 1923, setting a record that wouldn't be broken until Bill Dickey in 1940. Dickey added one more in 1941 to his streak of 13 consecutive seasons with

100-plus games at catcher, which is still the major-league record entering the 2015 season, matched only by Johnny Bench (1968-80), Brad Ausmus (1995-2007), and A.J. Pierzynski (2001-13).

White Sox Get Hot, But The Heat Stays On: The White Sox began a season-high 10-game winning streak on August 15, but weren't much closer to clinching the AL pennant at the end of it than they were at the start. Chicago's win over the Red Sox on August 15 put the White Sox ahead by four games over the Detroit Tigers. After sweeping the A's and Senators, then beating the Yankees twice, the White Sox were still just six games up on Detroit after winning their 10th straight on August 24. It took them until September 24 to finally clinch the pennant.

Late-Game Dominance: According to Retrosheet's Tom Ruane, the 1919 White Sox blew the fewest late leads (3) of any team in major-league history over the last 95 years (entering the 2015 season). They also had a knack for rallying from a deficit after the seventh inning, doing so 14 times in 1919. Six of those wins came in August, including on back-to-back afternoons against Boston on August 15-16 at Comiskey Park. Why were the White Sox so good late in games — a team relatively thin on pitching in an era before bullpen specialization and a low-scoring Deadball environment that discouraged late rallies? Timely hitting and a "wee" reliever. Manager Kid Gleason didn't rely on his bullpen much, but he did have one unlikely reliever to call on in a pinch: Dickey Kerr. The 5-foot-7 left-hander was a rookie in 1919, too unproven to join the regular rotation at first. But he flourished in his role as a reliever, posting a 7-1 record and a 1.78 ERA in 22 appearances out of the bullpen.

Devil Dogs Have Their Day: The specter of World War I continued to loom over baseball in 1919. On Saturday, August 23, Chicago Mayor William Hale "Big Bill" Thompson honored the US Marine Corps with a citywide celebration for their service in the war. More than 2,500 Marines who fought in battles like Chateau Thierry, Belleau Wood, and Saint-Mihiel were recognized with a downtown parade, a luncheon at the Hotel La Salle, and a pregame ceremony at Comiskey Park. During the festivities, a group of Marines leaped over the outfield fence, ran to the dugout, and "captured" their former teammate, White Sox second baseman Eddie Collins, who had enlisted in the Marines in August 1918 and served during the war at the Philadelphia Naval Yard. Collins was hoisted onto their shoulders and carried back to the grandstand as a "prisoner." He was released before the game and had a fine day at the plate, reaching base four times and scoring two runs in a 10-2 win over the Yankees.

LEFTY WILLIAMS

By Jacob Pomrenke

IN 1915, AMERICA'S LEADING syndicated sportswriter, Hugh Fullerton, published a forgettable baseball novel in which a star left-handed pitcher named Williams is bribed and threatened by gamblers to lose the pennant for his team.[1]

Fullerton, who dedicated the novel to his friend and mentor, Chicago White Sox owner Charles Comiskey, had been writing about the menace of gambling in professional baseball for more than a decade. Little did he know how prescient his story would turn out to be.

Just a few years later, Fullerton had a front-row seat in the press box as one of the Chicago White Sox' star pitchers, Claude "Lefty" Williams, became embroiled in the most devastating game-fixing scandal baseball had ever seen, the throwing of the 1919 World Series. Williams and seven of his teammates were expelled from Organized Baseball for their roles in losing the tainted World Series to the Cincinnati Reds. Williams set a World Series record with three losses all by himself, including a disastrous one-inning appearance in the Series' final game that left no doubt as to his involvement in the Black Sox Scandal.

Considered one of the most promising left-handers in baseball, Williams recorded back-to-back 20-win seasons with the White Sox in 1919 and '20, and he was being groomed to replace Eddie Cicotte as the staff ace. But he threw away his career for a $5,000 reward from gamblers, ending the White Sox' potential championship dynasty before it ever really began. More than any other player involved in the 1919 World Series fix, Williams struggled to make peace with his fateful decision to accept the bribe; only with the unconditional support of his strong-willed wife, Lyria, did he turn around his life after he was kicked out of baseball prematurely.

Claude Preston Williams was born on March 9, 1893, in Aurora, Missouri, the second child in a rural farming family that originally hailed from Crawford County, Arkansas. When Claude was about 8 years old, his father, William H. Williams, died and his mother, Mary "Addie" Seratt, soon married Robert A. Grimes, a railroad worker for the St. Louis-San Francisco Railway in nearby Springfield.[2] Claude and his older brother, Jessie, welcomed a half-brother, Lawrence, in 1904.[3]

Claude Williams attended one year of high school[4] before taking a job in town as a grocery clerk. Like many boys his age, he was more interested in athletics than academics. In 1910 he paid 50 cents to join the O'Leary's Athletic Club gymnasium with his friend, Luther McCarty, a promising boxer.[5] Williams was "fairly handy with his dukes" and sparred regularly at the gym, but he rebuffed his friends' pleas to take boxing more seriously. His future was in baseball.[6]

In 1911 the 18-year-old Williams signed a contract to play with Springfield in the independent Kansas-Missouri League.[7] Despite a "peculiar" motion, in which he released the ball low from a side-arm position but kept his torso upright,[8] his strong pitching caught the attention of the Nashville Vols of the Southern Association. But "wildness kept him from making good" in a tryout and the Vols farmed him out to Morristown, Tennessee, of the Appalachian League for the 1912 season.[9]

Williams, who filled out to be a slim 5-feet-9 and 160 pounds, dominated the Appalachian League in 1912, finishing 18-11 with a 1.92 ERA for Morristown. His control also improved greatly, as he walked just 46 batters in 253 innings pitched. In August Nashville sold his contract to the Brooklyn Dodgers, but manager Bill Dahlen decided not to recall Williams and several other prospects during the season's final month. Before the 1913 season began, Williams was optioned back to Nashville.[10]

Williams's second stint in Tennessee was much more productive. He was the youngest member on the Vols roster at age 20, called "The Kid" by fans in Nashville that year.[11] He led the Vols in wins (18), ERA (2.30), and WHIP (1.078.) In August Williams was sold to the Detroit Tigers for $3,500.[12] This time, he was sent up to the majors.

Ty Cobb helped Lefty Williams win his major-league debut for the Tigers, on September 17, 1913. In the second game of a doubleheader at Washington, Cobb hit a first-inning grand slam and Williams scattered eight hits in a 4-2 complete-game victory.[13] In his next start, against the Philadelphia A's, he didn't fare so well—he allowed ten hits and ten runs in a single inning against the eventual World Series champs.[14] Williams made three other appearances for Detroit, but lost two of them.

The Tigers kept Williams around to begin the 1914 season, but he made just one start—another blowout loss to the A's on May 22 in which future Hall of Fame outfielder Harry Heilmann made three errors in the first inning. Two weeks later, Detroit sold a frustrated Williams to the Sacramento Wolves of the Pacific Coast League. His PCL debut, on June 7, was a sign of things to come as he struck out 12 Portland Beavers batters, setting a new career high. Despite joining the

Lefty Williams, circa 1917 (Bain Collection, Library of Congress, Prints and Photographs Division)

Wolves in June, two months after the PCL season began, Williams finished fifth in the league in strike-outs with 171.[15]

Williams's season of turmoil continued all summer as he suffered a string of hard-luck losses, finishing with just a 13-20 record. The Sacramento Wolves were also in financial turmoil; in September, they abandoned California's capital city and played the rest of their home games in San Francisco's Mission district.[16]

In 1915 the financially strapped Wolves transferred operations to Utah and found a permanent home as the Salt Lake Bees. There, Lefty Williams, now 22, found his greatest success on the field and enduring love off the field in Lyria Leila Wilson, the charismatic, independent daughter of Mormon pioneers.

Lyria, the youngest of 15 children to Calvin and Emeline (Miller) Wilson, was three years older than Lefty and had been living on her own since at least 1909.[17] Her grandfather, Whitford Gill Wilson, had moved his family to the Mormon-established town of Nauvoo, Illinois, in the late 1830s before migrating to Ogden, Utah, as part of the forced exodus of Mormon settlers from the Midwest.[18]

By 1915, Lyria was working as a waitress at a Salt Lake City hotel frequented by Coast League ballplayers. No player that year was more dominant than Lefty Williams. Before the season, the *Salt Lake Telegram* reported, "Everybody on the coast predicts a great year for [Williams.] In fact, some of them feel that he will be a Coast League sensation."[19] After several outstanding performances in California during the winter-league season, Williams turned heads in a late February exhibition game against the Chicago White Sox in San Jose.[20]

Perhaps the excitement of his courtship with Lyria, or the close rapport he established with Bees catcher Byrd Lynn, helped raise Lefty's game to new heights. Whatever the reason, Williams far outclassed the rest of the PCL in 1915, finishing with a stellar 33-12 record, a 2.84 ERA, 36 complete games, and a league-leading 294 strikeouts in 418⅔ innings pitched for Salt Lake

City. The league's runner-up in strikeouts, Bill Prough of Oakland, finished nearly 100 behind Williams.[21] Williams struck out 12 San Francisco Seals on May 2 and set a season high by fanning 13 Vernon Tigers on September 8.[22] It was one of the best PCL pitching performances of the decade, earning Williams a call-up to the Chicago White Sox in 1916.

Williams was one of five Coast League recruits purchased by Charles Comiskey's White Sox that off-season, including his Salt Lake batterymate Byrd Lynn. The 23-year-old left-hander made the White Sox roster out of spring training and quickly established himself as one of the top strikeout pitchers in the American League in 1916.

The rookie left-hander saved his best performances for the stretch run, compiling a 5-1 record in September with four complete games in seven starts. But the defending champion Boston Red Sox outlasted the young White Sox and won the pennant by two games over Chicago. Williams finished 13-7 with a 2.89 ERA in 224⅓ innings, and his rate of 5.5 strikeouts per nine innings was second-best in the American League to only Hall of Famer Walter Johnson.[23]

Off the field, Lefty and Lyria decided that a long-distance relationship wasn't suitable for them. So a few weeks into the season, Lyria packed up and traveled by train from Salt Lake City to Chicago, where the couple was married on June 6, 1916. No one on the White Sox except catcher Byrd Lynn, Lefty's roommate at the Warner Hotel, knew about the nuptials before they took place.[24]

Perhaps happiness at home helped lead to a spectacular start for Williams at the ballpark in 1917. Despite not lasting past the first inning on Opening Day against the St. Louis Browns, Williams won his first nine decisions and didn't suffer his first loss until June 28 in a relief appearance against the Detroit Tigers.[25] By then the White Sox were in first place with the best-scoring offense and stingiest pitching in the American League.

But Williams's stellar won-loss record (he finished 17-8) was mostly the product of strong run support, and his frequent bouts of wildness caused manager Pants Rowland to skip his turn in the rotation sometimes.[26] His ERA hovered over 3.00 for most of the season, above the league average, and his 85 strikeouts were far off the pace he had set as a rookie.

In the World Series against the New York Giants, the struggling Williams was passed over for a Game Five start in favor of Reb Russell, who didn't record a single out before he was replaced by Eddie Cicotte in the first inning. With the White Sox down 4-2, Williams relieved Cicotte in the seventh, allowing one run and striking out three in his only inning of the Series. The White Sox rallied to win, 8-5. Two days later, Williams watched from the dugout at the Polo Grounds as Chicago clinched its second World Series championship.

The White Sox' championship lineup remained intact to start the 1918 season under manager Pants Rowland. But as local draft boards all over the United States began selecting able-bodied adult men for military service in World War I, the White Sox were depleted by the sudden loss of star outfielder Shoeless Joe Jackson in mid-May. With enlistment in the armed forces a near-certainty due to a change in his draft status, Jackson chose to take a war-essential job with the Harlan & Hollingsworth shipbuilding company in Wilmington, Delaware.[27]

As *The Sporting News* later observed with tongue only partially in cheek, "Where Jackson goes, Williams follows."[28] Williams, who like Jackson was married and at age 25 was five years younger, was considered exempt from active military service (since his wife, Lyria, depended on his income).[29] But all professional ballplayers knew they would soon have to find another line of work, as the US government issued a "work or fight" order in July that prematurely ended the 1918 baseball season.[30]

Four weeks after Jackson went to Delaware, Williams and catcher Byrd Lynn abruptly left the White Sox and joined Jackson at the Harlan & Hollingsworth plant. Owner Charles Comiskey responded by suspending the three players indefinitely and stripping them of their uniforms. "I don't consider them fit to play on my ballclub," he said.[31] Comiskey also refused to issue Williams his final paycheck, a grand total of $183.16 for the 11 days he spent with the team in June.[32]

In the typical wartime frenzy of patriotism, many baseball fans and members of the press took Comiskey's side; the White Sox players were considered to be "slackers" and "cowards" for avoiding military service.[33] "Nothing was too mean to call them," said one American League ballplayer.[34]

Williams spent the duration of the war pitching for Harlan's company team in the prestigious Delaware River Shipbuilding League, one of many industrial leagues that employed major-league players. In September Williams pitched a 4-0 shutout and Jackson hit two home runs to help Harlan clinch the championship of Atlantic Coast shipyards against Standard Shipbuilding of Staten Island, New York, in a game played before 4,000 fans at the Baker Bowl, the Philadelphia Phillies' home ballpark.[35]

Despite Comiskey's bluster in the press, he allowed all of his "unpatriotic" shipyard players to return to the White Sox in 1919 under new manager Kid Gleason.[36] Williams signed a contract for $2,625, with a $375 bonus if he won 15 games and an additional $500 bonus if he won 20 games.[37] With teammate Red Faber under the weather due to influenza, Williams was counted on to pick up the slack and the little left-hander responded with a stellar season.

Williams led the American League in 1919 by making 40 starts, including ten alone in July when the White Sox surged to the top of the standings for good. He also ranked second with 27 complete games and five shutouts, and third with 125 strikeouts. In September, he tossed two shutouts to finish 23-11 with a 2.64 ERA as Chicago won its second pennant in three seasons.

Williams also gained a reputation as a great control pitcher, ranking fourth in the AL in walks per nine innings. Before the World Series, manager Gleason

exclaimed in a syndicated column, "It isn't often that a batter gets a ball in the groove when Williams is pitching. He's always on the edge of the plate … where they've got to swing and where they can't often get a good hold of the ball."[38]

But Williams didn't intend to live up to his reputation in the 1919 World Series. On the White Sox' final Eastern road trip in late September, he was approached by first baseman Chick Gandil outside the Ansonia Hotel in New York. Gandil said a group of teammates were planning to throw the World Series to the Cincinnati Reds. Lefty agreed to participate, for a promised payoff of $10,000. He told Gandil that "anything they did would be agreeable to me, if it was going to happen anyway.… I had no money and I might as well get what I could."[39]

Although most of the White Sox players were well paid compared with their peers,[40] Williams's $500-a-month salary was half of what his good friend Joe Jackson was making. Williams was also still bitter that Comiskey hadn't paid him the salary he felt he was owed after he went to work in the shipyards the previous June.[41]

Picked to start Game Two of the World Series, Williams immediately raised suspicions with an uncharacteristically wild performance. After facing the minimum nine batters through three scoreless innings, he abruptly lost his command in the fourth inning. He walked three Reds batters and allowed an RBI single to Edd Roush and a two-run triple to light-hitting Larry Kopf. Williams allowed only four hits but walked six (tying a career high) in the 4-2 loss.

Irving Sanborn of the *Chicago Tribune* wrote that Williams's pitching was "almost criminally wild,"[42] although umpire Billy Evans, who was behind home plate that day, later said he "regarded the loss of that game at the time as one of the hardest bits of luck I ever saw."[43] All of the fourth-inning walks were on full counts[44] and "not one of them was over six inches inside or outside," Evans recalled. But White Sox catcher Ray Schalk suspected something was off. He reportedly confronted Williams after the game about his lack of control, and may have even physically assaulted him.[45] It was a sign of the rising tensions in the White Sox clubhouse.

Williams expected to get paid by the gamblers for his losing effort, but when the money didn't show up after Game Two or Three, he began to suspect a double-cross. Finally, after Game Four—with the White Sox now down three games to one—Williams collected $10,000 from Chick Gandil, who instructed him to give half of the cash to Joe Jackson.[46] Lefty gave the money to Jackson in a dirty envelope, sealing both of their fates. Lefty's wife, Lyria, was furious when she found out. "You have done it," she told him after seeing the cash. "What can I say now? Let it go and just get the best of it."[47]

Flush with cash, Williams pitched poorly enough to earn his payoff in his next start, in Game Five against the Reds. Once again one disastrous inning was his downfall. After allowing just one hit through five innings, Williams gave up four runs in the sixth. Cincinnati's rally began with a double by the pitcher, Hod Eller. The White Sox lost, 5-0. Williams later admitted that he was nervous because the fix was on his mind. "I was sorry," he said. "I wanted to be out of it and not mixed up in it at all."[48]

If the World Series had been played under its traditional best-of-seven format, the Reds would have clinched the championship after Williams's loss in Game Five. But baseball owners had expanded the fall classic to a best-of-nine series[49] and Williams took the mound for one more start after the resurgent White Sox, on the verge of elimination, won Games Six and Seven. By then the fixers hadn't received any more of their promised payoff from gamblers and were seemingly playing to win. Before Game Eight, Williams told Joe Jackson on the way to Comiskey Park, "If we have been double-crossed, I am going to pitch to win this game if I can possibly win it."[50]

Instead, Williams had the worst performance of his life. He lasted all of five batters in Game Eight as the Reds battered him for four hits and four runs before manager Kid Gleason yanked him in the first inning.

The White Sox were never in the game and the Reds won, 10-5, to clinch their first World Series championship.

It is widely believed that a threat was made against Williams's life before the game, but the evidence to substantiate that claim is thin.[51] Lyria Williams reportedly said years later that Lefty was fearful of retaliation if he didn't lose Game Eight quickly and decisively.[52] "It'll be the biggest first inning you ever saw," one gambler predicted to sportswriter Hugh Fullerton before the game, perhaps insinuating that Williams was warned to put the game out of reach before three outs were made.[53] But Williams testified later that he pitched to win in Game Eight; he also told Cicotte during the Series "that he was out to win because he had been double-crossed."[54]

Regardless of whether a real threat was made, Williams got the message all right. His 0-3 record in the World Series set a record that still stood as of 2014 and undoubtedly helped the gamblers turn a tidy profit betting on the Reds. Williams, like Joe Jackson, earned just $5,000 for throwing the Series—about $200 less than each player on the Reds received for actually winning the Series.[55]

Although owner Charles Comiskey, manager Kid Gleason and other team officials were aware of the fix, they were intent on sweeping it under the rug and keeping their championship team intact in 1920.[56] The White Sox offered generous contracts to seven of the eight White Sox conspirators in the offseason. Williams signed for $6,000, more than he had received for fixing the World Series the previous fall.[57]

With a black cloud hanging over baseball because of the fix rumors, Williams had a turbulent season in 1920. His won-loss record was again superb at 22-14, and he finished second in the AL in games started (38) and strikeouts (128). But in the first year of the live-ball era, Williams's longtime tendency to be a fly-ball pitcher caused him to lead the league in home runs allowed (15), and his 3.91 ERA was again above the league average.[58]

In September a grand jury was empaneled in Chicago to investigate gambling in baseball. The grand jury soon turned its focus to the 1919 World Series, and pressure mounted on the White Sox players to come clean. On September 28 pitcher Eddie Cicotte cracked first, testifying about his involvement in throwing the Series to the Reds and igniting a scandal that made headlines all across the country.

Later that afternoon, Joe Jackson followed Cicotte to the witness stand and told the grand jury that he had received $5,000 from Williams after Game Four.[59] Once again, Williams found himself suspended by Charles Comiskey, along with the other seven White Sox players named as fixers: Cicotte, Jackson, Swede Risberg, Chick Gandil, Happy Felsch, Fred McMullin, and Buck Weaver.

The next day, September 29, Williams paid a visit to the office of Alfred Austrian, the White Sox' team counsel, where he gave a sworn statement admitting his involvement in the World Series fix. He then went to the Cook County Criminal Court Building and testified in front of the grand jury, shedding new light on the multiple groups of gamblers involved in fixing the World Series.[60] Williams's testimony was the third and final confession that the grand jury heard. It was more than enough evidence to return indictments against all eight players, along with a handful of gamblers. The White Sox, without their suspended stars, played out the final weekend with a makeshift roster and finished in second place, two games behind the Cleveland Indians.

In the summer of 1921, Williams and his seven former teammates went on trial in Chicago for fixing the World Series. The proceedings were farcical from the start, characterized by an inept, clumsy prosecution and a star-struck jury. On the evening of August 2, the first verdict was announced: "We, the jury, find the defendant Claude Williams … not guilty."[61] A loud cheer broke out in the courtroom and jurors celebrated by asking for the players' autographs.

But hours later, baseball's new commissioner, Judge Kenesaw Mountain Landis, delivered a different verdict: The Black Sox were permanently banned from playing in Organized Baseball. At age 27, Lefty Williams's major-league career was over just as he was coming into his prime. Nearly a century later, no other American League pitcher had recorded more wins in his final active season than Williams's 22 in 1920.[62] In seven seasons, he finished with 82 wins against just 48 defeats, a .631 winning percentage that ranked in the top 25 all-time among American League pitchers in the 20th century (with a minimum 100 decisions.)[63]

Life after baseball was a constant struggle for Lefty Williams. Like many players of his era, he had few other marketable skills outside of his ability to play baseball. After struggling to run a pool hall on Chicago's South Side that Joe Jackson sold to him for $1, Williams took odd jobs as a painter, a department store floorman, and a tile-fitter to make ends meet.[64] He began drinking more and his marriage suffered. In 1923 he reportedly suffered a serious bout of pneumonia that landed him in the hospital and nearly killed him.[65] The following year, with Lefty still drinking heavily, Lyria kicked him out of the house and the couple separated.[66] So Lefty turned back to baseball, the only job he knew.

After the Black Sox were banned in 1921, they mostly went their separate ways. But none of them stayed away from a baseball field for long. And in the 1920s, semipro baseball could be a lucrative career for a former professional of Williams's caliber. In the summer of 1922, he joined Swede Risberg, Buck Weaver, and Happy Felsch on a team promoted as the "Ex-Major League Stars," which toured the Midwest playing town teams in Illinois, Wisconsin, and Minnesota. Fans grew disillusioned by their lackluster play, however, and the "Ex-Stars" earned just a few hundred dollars for their efforts.[67]

Williams continued pitching for hire and, in 1926, after his separation from Lyria, Buck Weaver persuaded him to move west for the summer. Weaver, Chick Gandil, and the notorious game-fixer Hal Chase were members of an outlaw league near the US-Mexico border called the Copper League. The Copper

League could employ the Black Sox players and others who had been banned by Judge Landis because it was unaffiliated with Organized Baseball. Weaver, the popular manager of the Douglas (Arizona) Blues, signed Williams to a salary of about $160 per month.[68]

Money woes plagued Douglas throughout its tenure in the Copper League and by mid-June, Williams had jumped to the Fort Bayard (New Mexico) Veterans for more money and a steady job in the motor-vehicle division of the military hospital there.[69] With Fort Bayard, Williams and Jimmie O'Connell—a former New York Giants outfielder who was kicked out of baseball for allegedly offering a bribe to an opponent[70]—quickly became the cream of the outlaw crop. Williams threw the season's only no-hitter, on August 8 against Buck Weaver's Douglas Blues.[71] O'Connell hit .546 and led the Copper League in home runs as the Veterans won the championship. After the season, Williams joined an all-star team that toured Mexico City, Chihuahua, and other Mexican cities in the fall.

Williams stayed in Fort Bayard for the winter, working contentedly at the hospital and spending most days drinking and playing cards.[72] In 1927 he and O'Connell led the Veterans to first place once again and the powerhouse team became known locally as the "Bayard Express."[73] But they lost the championship series to the Chick Gandil-managed Chino Twins, from nearby Santa Rita, New Mexico.[74] Williams's time in rural New Mexico was the last significant baseball experience of his life, a far cry from the bright lights of the major leagues he had enjoyed just seven years earlier. The Copper League, which was hanging on by a thread financially, disbanded after the 1927 season when Judge Landis promised to give minor-league teams to the league's cities if they stopped using banned players.

By the early 1930s, Lefty Williams was back in Chicago, living in a small basement apartment in Rogers Park on the North Side of town, and he had begun patching up his relationship with Lyria, who continued to work as a cashier.[75] They stayed in Illinois until 1937, when Lyria's increasing involvement with the Christian Science church compelled them to move west again, this time together. They were among the more than 1

million Americans who migrated to California, the land of opportunity, during the Great Depression.[76]

The Williamses settled first in Burbank, where Lyria's brother, Lawrence Wilson, likely helped Lefty get a job as a truck driver.[77] Lyria, no longer working outside the home, put her boundless mental energy to other uses. Over the years she developed a reputation as a civic gadfly and a community activist; she often appeared at city council meetings questioning zoning changes, street pavings, and other neighborhood proposals.[78] Lefty and Lyria also maintained their close friendship with Joe and Katie Jackson over the years and visited each other occasionally. When Shoeless Joe died in 1951, the Williamses wired their condolences to his widow.[79]

During World War II, Lefty and Lyria relocated for a few years—although it's unclear exactly why—to Pearblossom, a remote area in the Antelope Valley north of Los Angeles.[80] Lefty worked as a carpenter and he also tried his hand at gardening at their modest property off Pearblossom Highway. They lived a few miles from the ranch of eccentric author Aldous Huxley, who had moved to California's High Desert for the cleaner air.[81] After the war ended, the Williamses moved back to the San Fernando Valley, where they bought a house in Northridge.[82]

In 1954 Lefty made the final move of his nomadic life, about 80 miles south to Laguna Beach, where he opened nursery business.[83] He and Lyria bought a hillside beach cottage in the historic Coast Royal neighborhood of South Laguna, with a view of the Pacific Ocean—and, on clear days, Catalina Island—from their front window.[84]

Lefty's last years were plagued by the effects of Hodgkin's disease, and by 1959, when the White Sox won their first pennant since the Black Sox Scandal, their former star pitcher was on his deathbed. A *Santa Ana Register* columnist wrote, "Under normal circumstances, this would have been a happy year for Williams. He would have been sounded out for stories of the old days, interviewed, maybe given a chance to throw out a first ball at the World Series. Instead he was tired and aging and ill and sick at heart.… I should say that if ever men paid for their sins, these did."[85]

At age 66, Claude "Lefty" Williams died at home on November 4, 1959, less than a month after the White Sox lost to the Los Angeles Dodgers in the World Series. A Christian Science funeral was held and his ashes were interred in an unmarked location at Melrose Abbey Memorial Park in Anaheim, California.[86]

Like most of his old White Sox teammates, Williams rarely spoke publicly about the Black Sox Scandal or his role in the World Series fix. Always a quiet, thoughtful type, he and Lyria stayed out of the spotlight and didn't respond to any known interview requests.[87] *Eight Men Out* author Eliot Asinof suggested that the shame of the scandal left a lasting impression. "There's a lingering impact on all of baseball," Asinof said decades later. "You don't talk about this thing.… Even sympathetic ballplayers who did not involve themselves in the fix refused to talk."[88]

But as one childhood friend reminisced after Williams's death, "he couldn't help but have done a lot of reflecting" over the years.[89] Lefty Williams might have been remembered as one of the top left-handed pitchers in the American League during the 1920s — if not for the scandal. He and future Hall of Famer Red Faber might have led a White Sox team that challenged the famous Murderers' Row dynasty of Babe Ruth, Lou Gehrig, and the New York Yankees. Instead, without their banished stars, the White Sox sank in the doldrums and didn't win another World Series for the rest of the 20th century. Williams's record of three losses in a single World Series, which still stood in 2014, might never be broken.[90]

NOTES

1   Hugh S. Fullerton, *Jimmy Kirkland and the Plot for a Pennant* (Philadelphia: The John C. Winston Co., 1915).

2   1900–1910 United States censuses and Arkansas County Marriages Index, 1837-1957, accessed at Ancestry.com.

3   "The Frisco" was the major employer in the area; both Robert and Lawrence Grimes worked at the railroad's Springfield operational center for many years. "The Frisco: A Look Back at the St. Louis-San Francisco Railway," Springfield-Greene County Library District. Accessed online at thelibrary.org/lochist/frisco/about.cfm on October 9, 2013.

4   1940 United States census, accessed online at Ancestry.com. Contrary to most reports, the banned Black Sox ballplayers were more educated than they sometimes let on. Fred McMullin and Chick Gandil both told census takers in 1940 that they had attended four years of high school, while Buck Weaver said he had completed at least two years. Swede Risberg stayed in school through the eighth grade and pitched for his school's baseball team. Eddie Cicotte and Happy Felsch both completed five or six years of grammar school. Only Joe Jackson was truly uneducated; the famously illiterate ballplayer dropped out after the third grade.

5   "Claude Williams and Lute McCarty Started Athletic Careers Together," *Gulfport Daily Herald*, March 7, 1914.

6   "Luther McCarty," BoxRec Boxing Encyclopedia. Accessed online at boxrec.com/list_bouts.php?human_id=039623&cat=boxer on January 11, 2014. McCarty made his pro debut in 1911 and quickly built a national reputation as the top "white hope" challenger to the black heavyweight champion Jack Johnson. But in May 1913, the 21-year-old McCarty collapsed during a fight in Calgary and died of a brain hemorrhage.

7   "Who's Who in the World's Series," *Salt Lake Telegram*, October 1, 1917.

8   "American League News," *Sporting Life*, July 8, 1916, 8. Video of Williams pitching from the 1919 World Series can also be found online at BlackBetsy.com.

9   Lefty Williams player file, National Baseball Hall of Fame Library, Cooperstown, New York; "Who's Who in the World Series," *Salt Lake Telegram*, October 1, 1917.

10 "Cubs Buy Recruit From Brooklyn," *Washington Post*, August 22, 1912, 8; "Buy Players' Releases," *New York Times*, August 29, 1912, 7.

11 *Nashville Banner*, April 18, 1919.

12 Williams player file, Hall of Fame Library.

13 Stanley T. Milliken, "Tigers Win Two Games By Having Big Innings," *Washington Post*, September 18, 1913, 8.

14 "Athletics Score 10 Runs in One Inning," *Hartford Courant*, September 24, 1913, 16.

15 "Ed Klepfer Is Strikeout King," *Los Angeles Times*, November 17, 1914.

16 "Strict Censorship On Coast's Plans," *The Sporting News*, October 1, 1914, 3.

17 1910 US census, accessed online at Ancestry.com.

18 Florence C. Youngberg, *Conquerors of the West: Stalwart Mormon Pioneers* (Salt Lake City: Agreka Books, 1999); Mormon Pioneer Overland Travel Database, accessed online at history.lds.org/overlandtravels on April 11, 2014.

19 "Blankenship Signs Southpaw Williams," *Salt Lake Telegram*, February 17, 1915.

20 "Big Leaguers Beat Mormons," *The Oregonian*, March 1, 1915.

21 "Claude Williams the Whole Show in League," *Los Angeles Times*, October 28, 1915.

22 Ibid.; *Salt Lake Telegram*, September 9, 1915.

23 Baseball-Reference.com.

24 "Lefty Gets a June Bride," *Los Angeles Times*, June 7, 1916; "Diamond Dust," *Salt Lake Telegram*, June 7, 1916; Cook County Marriages Index, 1871-1920, accessed at Ancestry.com.

25 Baseball-Reference.com game logs.

26 Despite a reputation for good control, Williams in 1917 walked five batters in three different starts, and walked four batters apiece in six starts. All statistics are from Williams's Baseball-Reference.com game logs.

27 "Sox Manager Sends Joe Jackson Away With Best Wishes," *Chicago Tribune*, May 14, 1918, 15; "Comiskey Wipes 2 Shipbuilders Off Roster," *Chicago Tribune*, June 12, 1918, 11. Jackson's local draft board in Greenville, South Carolina, reclassified him as 1A, the most likely to be called up, despite the fact that he was married. Williams and most of the other married ballplayers were classified 2A and unlikely to be called up to the service.

28 "Where Jackson Goes, Williams Follows," *The Sporting News*, March 3, 1919, 3.

29 Ibid.

30 "Baseball Season Will Close Sept. 1," *New York Times*, August 3, 1918.

31 "Comiskey Wipes 2 Shipbuilders Off Roster," *Chicago Tribune*, June 12, 1918, 11. Happy Felsch also quit the team later in the season to go work in a shipyard.

32 Bob Hoie, "1919 Baseball Salaries and the Mythically Underpaid Chicago White Sox," *Base Ball: A Journal of the Early Game*, Vol. 6, No. 1 (Spring 2012), Jefferson, North Carolina: McFarland & Co., 30-31. According to Hoie, "Williams later told Kid Gleason that he would never rejoin the White Sox until they paid him the $183.16 that was owed to him … a claim rebuffed by the National Commission." It's unknown whether the White Sox ever did pay him.

33 Jim Leeke, "The Delaware River Shipbuilding League, 1918." *The National Pastime: From Swampoodle to South Philly*, SABR, 2013.

34 Ibid.

35 Ibid.

36 James Crusinberry, "Gleason Dispels Doubt Regarding Players' Return," *Chicago Tribune*, February 21, 1919, 11.

37 Hoie, 31.

38 William Gleason, "James and Kerr Will Be Able to Back Up Cicotte and Williams Successfully, If Necessary, Their Pilot Writes." *Washington Post*, September 28, 1919, 22.

39 "Got $5,000 After Fourth Game, Says Williams," *Boston Globe*, September 29, 1920, 16.

40 Black Sox historian Bob Hoie provides evidence in his *Base Ball* article, based on American League contract cards now available at the Baseball Hall of Fame, that the White Sox had the third-highest Opening Day payroll among American League teams and the highest total salary payout in 1919—a far cry from the myth of Charles Comiskey's miserliness that has endured over the years. For a detailed explanation of the issue, read Hoie's "1919 Baseball Salaries and the Mythically Underpaid Chicago White Sox."

41 Hoie, 30-31.

42 I.E. Sanborn, "White Sox Crushed Again, 4 to 2," *Chicago Tribune*, October 3, 1919, 21.

43 Billy Evans, "Umpire Fooled by Chicago's Work," *Evansville Courier*, December 19, 1920.

44 "Story of Second Game by Innings," *New York Times*, October 3, 1919, 11.

45 Gene Carney, *Burying the Black Sox: How Baseball's Cover-Up of the 1919 World Series Fix Almost Succeeded* (Dulles, Virginia: Potomac Books, 2006), 202-03.

46 *Boston Globe*, September 29, 1920.

47 Quotation from Lefty Williams grand-jury testimony cited in Bill Lamb, *Black Sox in the Courtroom: The Grand Jury, Criminal Trial and Civil Litigation* (Jefferson, North Carolina: McFarland & Co., 2013), 58. There were also reports, before Lefty Williams gave his grand-jury testimony in September 1920, that Lyria had placed bets against the White Sox during the Series. It's unclear when she first learned of the fix.

48 Carney, 203.

49 The best-of-nine experiment lasted only until 1921.

50 Lamb, 59.

51 Carney, 199-205.

52 J.M. Flagler, "Requiem for a Southpaw," *The New Yorker*, December 5, 1959. Some sources claim the threat was made against Lyria's life instead. We do know one thing for sure: The character "Harry F.," who supposedly made the threat against Williams's life in Eliot Asinof's *Eight Men Out*, was invented by the author. Asinof told Gene Carney in an interview for *Burying the Black Sox* that he created "Harry F." for legal reasons, in order to protect his work against copyright theft. See Carney, 204-05.

53 Hugh Fullerton, "Is Big League Baseball Being Run for Gamblers, With Players in the Deal?" *New York Evening World*, December 15, 1919.

54 Carney, 203. Williams was deposed twice, in May 1923 and January 1924, for Joe Jackson's lawsuit against the White Sox

seeking back pay owed to him. In the latter deposition, Williams was inconsistent about many aspects of the World Series scandal, including when he received the payoff from Chick Gandil and Jackson's role in the fix. But his testimony is more credible than a second-hand anecdote about Lyria told 40 years after the Series ended, which seems to be the strongest independent evidence that any threats were made against Lefty and/or Lyria. Although it's impossible to know how truthful they were, Williams, Cicotte, Jackson, and Felsch all made public statements about feeling double-crossed during the Series and that they began playing to win. See, e.g., *The Sporting News,* October 7, 1920, 2: "Williams and Cicotte said that after the awful howl was raised they decided they had better pitch real ball in the closing games of the Series, but by that time things were so upset on the team because of accusations, threats, etc., that it didn't make much difference whether the conspirators tried to play ball or not."

55 "World Series Gate Receipts and World Series Player Shares," Baseball-Almanac.com. Accessed online at baseball-almanac. com/ws/wsshares.shtml on August 11, 2010.

56 For an analysis of baseball's institutional cover-up of the 1919 World Series fix, read Gene Carney's *Burying the Black Sox.*

57 Hoie, 30-31.

58 Baseball-Reference.com.

59 A copy of Shoeless Joe Jackson's grand-jury testimony transcript is available online at BlackBetsy.com.

60 Lamb, 57-59. Williams's grand-jury testimony was not made available to the public until 2007 by the Chicago History Museum.

61 Lamb, 141.

62 Baseball-Reference.com Play Index.

63 Ibid.

64 The bill of sale between Jackson and Williams was filed on October 6, 1921, in Chicago; a copy is now held by the National Pastime Museum.

65 "Near Death," *Chicago Tribune,* March 30, 1923, 26. The *Tribune* reported that Williams lapsed into a coma at Columbus Hospital in Chicago, but he came out of it a day later.

66 A February 19, 1924, report filed by a private investigator hired by White Sox counsel Alfred Austrian stated that Lyria had not seen her husband in three weeks. She was working as a waitress at the Seafoam Restaurant at 22nd Street and Michigan Avenue, while he had reportedly traveled to Milwaukee to attend Joe Jackson's back-pay trial against the White Sox. This letter is now housed in the Chicago History Museum.

67 Louis Gollop, "Black Sox Invade Duluth-Range Ball League," *Duluth News Tribune,* June 23, 1922; "Black Sox Close Northern Invasion With Duluth Game," *Duluth News Tribune,* July 6, 1922; "Black Sox-Hibbing Teams Clash at Athletic Park," *Duluth News Tribune,* July 16, 1922. The "Ex-Stars" went just 4-8 on their 12-game tour of the Mesabi Iron Range in northern Minnesota.

68 Lynn E. Bevill, "Outlaw Baseball Players in the Copper League: 1925-1927," Master's thesis, Western New Mexico University, 1988. Accessed online at bevillsadvocate.com on April 5, 2010.

69 Ibid.

70 Lowell Blaisdell, "Mystery and Tragedy: The O'Connell-Dolan Scandal," *Baseball Research Journal No. 11,* Society for American Baseball Research, 1982.

71 *El Paso Times,* August 9, 1926. Williams hit the first batter, threw him out at second base when he tried to advance, and then retired the next 20 in a row.

72 Bevill, "Outlaw Baseball Players in the Copper League: 1925-1927."

73 Ibid.

74 Gandil abruptly quit the Chino Twins right before the postseason began. Despite two wins by Williams, Chino won the series four games to three.

75 1930 United States Census, accessed online at Ancestry. com. Chicago Telephone Directories, 1931-36, Chicago History Museum.

76 "State Leads in Increase of Population," *Los Angeles Times,* December 4, 1937. Charles C. Cohan, "Steady Gain in Population," *Los Angeles Times,* December 4, 1938. Lorania K. Francis, "California Now Fifth State in Population," *Los Angeles Times,* September 14, 1940. "Southland Important Hub of World Affairs," *Los Angeles Times,* January 2, 1941.

77 Index to Register of Voters, Los Angeles County, California, 1938-42, accessed online at Ancestry.com. Burbank City Directories, 1937-42, Burbank Central Library. Lyria's brother, Lawrence Wilson, a widower, had been living in Burbank since at least 1928 and one of his sons, Louis, was also listed as a truck driver in the Los Angeles County voter rolls.

78 Email to the author from Bob Hoie, August 21, 2010. See also: "Owners File Paving Plea For Lindley Ave.," *Los Angeles Times,* November 2, 1953.

79 A copy of the telegram can be found at BlackBetsy.com.

80 Index to Register of Voters, Los Angeles County, California, 1944-46, accessed online at Ancestry.com.

81 David Dunaway, *Aldous Huxley Recollected: An Oral History* (Walnut Creek, California: AltaMira Press, 1999).

82 Index to Register of Voters, Los Angeles County, California, 1948-54, accessed online at Ancestry.com.

83 Index to Great Register, Orange County, California, 1954-64, accessed online at Ancestry.com; Eddie West, "West Winds," *Santa Ana Register,* November 8, 1959.

84 1959 Laguna Beach Criss Cross City Directory, Orange County Public Library; Laguna Beach Historic Survey, Vol. 4, California Department of Parks and Recreation, 1981.

85 West, "West Winds."

86 "Claude (Lefty) Williams of Sox Fame Dies at South Laguna," *Santa Ana Register*, November 6, 1959, B-2; "Certificate of Death: Claude Preston Williams," filed November 9, 1959, State of California, Department of Public Health. Numerous inquiries by researchers and journalists with Melrose Abbey have failed to uncover the specific location of Williams's ashes.

87 After Chick Gandil was interviewed by *Sports Illustrated* in September 1956, Lyria wrote a letter to Katie Jackson on October 16 in which she commented, "I am glad they do not know where we live. We sure would send them chasing if they came here." This handwritten letter was sold by Christie's Auctions in 1998.

88 Paul Green, "The Later Lives of the Banished Sox," *Sports Collectors Digest*, April 22, 1988, 196-97.

89 Flagler, "Requiem for a Southpaw." In the same article, Lyria gave additional credence to the idea that they had not forgotten the gamblers' ominous message: "He was wrong, I guess," she said, "but he was only a youngster when it happened. All those others were doing it, and he didn't understand what it really meant and, besides, he was threatened."

90 In 1981 the Yankees' George Frazier tied Williams's record with three World Series losses against the Los Angeles Dodgers. But no one suggested that he had thrown the Series.

CHARLES COMISKEY

By Irv Goldfarb

ONE OF THE MOST INFLUEN-
tial figures in the history of the sport, Charles Comiskey had a 55-year odyssey through professional baseball that ran the gamut: captain of one of the greatest teams of the nineteenth century; league-jumper during the 1890 players' rebellion; one of the chief architects of the American League's emergence in 1901 as a major league; long-time owner of one of the league's most successful franchises, the Chicago White Sox; and a central figure in the 1919 Black Sox Scandal.

During his long association with the game, Comiskey was at various points regarded as a labor radical, a visionary executive, and a domineering patriarch who lavished money on his ballpark and the press while at the same time being accused of underpaying his best players. Baseball, Comiskey once wrote, "is the only game that is complicated enough to be always interesting and yet simple enough to be always understood."[1] Ultimately, the same can be said of the Old Roman himself.

Charles Albert Comiskey was born in Chicago on August 15, 1859, at the corner of Union and Maxwell Streets, one of seven children of John Comiskey, an Irish immigrant, and his wife, Mary, a native New Yorker. John served at various times as county board clerk, assistant county treasurer, and representative on the Chicago City Council (including as its first president),[2] a résumé that may have given young Charlie valuable experience in the ways of backdoor local politics, which he would later put to use in the halls of the American League's offices.

It wasn't long before Charlie discovered baseball, spending as much time as he could on the old Garden City grounds on the west side of Chicago, enjoying the fledgling game with his neighborhood friends. James T. Hart recalled just before the 1917 World Series how his boyhood pal was already the unspoken leader

during their sandlot days in Chicago. He "… seldom went to school more than two months a year," Hart recalled. "He was the captain of our team. He played all positions, and when any of us were sick, or our parents kept us at home to do the chores, Charlie was ready at a moment's notice to serve as utility man."[3]

Hart also remembered how difficult it was for the team to obtain bats and balls, often using the broken castoffs of older players. "When our team played we would compete on the proposition that the losing team would forfeit a bat…. (W)hen we … were threatened with a loss, Comiskey would start a row with the umpire or the opposing players and break up the game before we lost our bats. He was the foxiest kid in Chicago."

From Father O'Neill's Holy Family parochial school, through religious colleges in Chicago and Kansas, Comiskey never let his studies interfere with his principal outdoor recreation. He developed into a fairly skilled hurler, but the elder Comiskey objected to his son's obsession with baseball, and quickly signed him up as an apprentice to a local plumber. Arguments ensued and in 1876, at the age of 17, Comiskey left home to play third base for an independent team in Milwaukee at $50 per month. His manager, Ted Sullivan, became a scout for Comiskey in later years.[4]

The following season, Comiskey moved on to pitch for Elgin, Illinois. A right-handed thrower and hitter who stood approximately 6 feet tall, Comiskey included in his repertoire a solid fastball and an assortment of curves. Elgin didn't lose one of his starts all season, despite facing fairly tough competition from around the Chicago area.[5] From there, Comiskey shifted to the Dubuque (Iowa) Red Stockings, where he was reunited with Sullivan. Once again a utilityman, he played first base, second base, and the outfield, and pitched. Possibly more importantly, Sullivan also employed Comiskey as a representative of his successful news agency, where Charlie's 20 percent commission dwarfed his baseball salary. Comiskey stayed with Sullivan's Dubuque club for four seasons,[6] helping the team win the Northwest League pennant in 1879.

With future Hall of Famer Charles "Old Hoss" Radbourn and Laurie Reis on the same pitching staff, Comiskey turned full-time to first base, where, as legend has it, he revolutionized the position. According to most accounts, Comiskey did not "hug the bag," as was the habit of contemporary first basemen; instead, Charlie positioned himself closer to second, enabling him to cut off grounders hit toward right field.[7] He practiced with his pitchers in the morning, making sure they became adept at covering first base whenever he snagged a groundball. Some recent historians have claimed that this approach was already in practice well before Comiskey employed it with Dubuque.[8] Even if he was not the first, the story is an early indication of Comiskey's keen baseball instincts and his penchant for leadership.

The big leagues finally beckoned after an exhibition game in St. Louis in 1882, when Chris Von der Ahe, owner of the St. Louis Browns of the new American Association, offered Comiskey a contract. Though Von der Ahe originally suggested that Comiskey not ask for too much money as part of his terms, Charlie found that by his second paycheck his salary was a lot higher than what he had signed for. Comiskey never forgot the gesture, and was said to be one of the old man's benefactors when Von der Ahe lost his fortune later in life.[9]

When Von der Ahe and his manager, Comiskey's old friend Ted Sullivan, had a dispute late in the 1883 season, the Browns owner chose Commy as his new skipper. Charlie responded by piloting his team to four straight American Association pennants, and won the world's championship in 1886, beating Cap Anson's Chicago White Stockings of the National League in six games. Although he carried a reputation as an excellent team leader and solid defensive player, Comiskey was not a great hitter. For his career he batted .264 with 28 home runs and 416 stolen bases. Perhaps his best season came in 1887, when he batted

.335, scored 139 runs, drove in 103, and stole 117 bases. Far more typical, however, was his showing the previous year, when he batted .254 with 95 runs scored, 76 RBIs, and 41 stolen bases.

In 1890, in a bold move, Comiskey jumped to the Chicago club of the maverick Players League, only to return to the Browns at the end of the season when the PL disbanded and peace was declared. The first baseman's desertion caused friction between him and Von der Ahe, however, and in 1892 Comiskey signed with the Cincinnati Reds of the National League, where he spent the next three seasons as the club's manager. Though his annual salary was $7,500, his promised share of the club's profits never materialized, as there were none to be had.[10]

Prior to the 1894 season, his last as an active major-league player, the 34-year-old Comiskey was advised by his doctors that he was "threatened with tuberculosis."[11] To aid his health, Comiskey headed for the warmer climes of the South, scouting for new players along the way. Reportedly it was on this trip that Commy hit upon the idea of a new league featuring clubs from the Western states. Upon his return Comiskey contacted Ban Johnson, the sports editor of the *Cincinnati Commercial-Tribune*, asking if he would be interested in helping to lead this new venture.

Johnson was already embroiled in a feud with Comiskey's boss, John T. Brush, but Charlie's well-honed powers of persuasion helped convince Brush to campaign for Johnson to become the first president of the new Western League. The plan worked, and Johnson took control, quickly transforming it into one of the best circuits in the country.

Comiskey, meanwhile, spent the 1894 season with Cincinnati, fulfilling his obligations to Brush. After the season, Comiskey purchased the new league's Sioux City Cornhuskers and moved the team to St. Paul. There he built his first ballpark, at a cost of $12,000.[12] After five seasons in Minnesota as both owner and manager, Comiskey was granted permission by the National League to relocate his franchise to Chicago, on the condition that he could not use the name "Chicago" for his relocated ballclub. Therefore, recalling perhaps his finest moments as a player, Comiskey decided on "White Sox," honoring the team his Browns had beaten for the 1886 championship.[13]

Meanwhile, Johnson and Comiskey positioned the Western League to challenge the monopoly of the established NL. In October 1899 it changed its name to the American League. Before the 1901 season, with franchises now placed in Washington, Baltimore, Philadelphia, Boston, Cleveland, Detroit, Chicago, and Milwaukee, the circuit declared major-league status. Quickly gaining credibility with the public, the AL was heralded by *The Sporting News* as being devoid of the "... cowardly truckling, alien ownership, syndicalism ... jealousies, arrogance ... mercenary spirit, and disregard of public demands" that the National League had become infamous for.[14] Comiskey and Johnson were making a favorable impression with baseball fans, and the NL knew it. The ugly war between the leagues, rife with player-jumping, franchise-shifting, and acrimony on both sides, finally concluded with the establishment of the National Agreement in 1903.

During the first years of the new century, Comiskey built his club into one of the best in the country. The White Sox captured the 1901 American League pennant behind the strong pitching of manager Clark Griffith and an offense powered by outfielders Fielder Jones and Dummy Hoy. After falling to seventh place in 1903, Comiskey's White Sox gravitated toward the top of the standings again, with strong finishes in 1904 and 1905 and a second pennant in 1906. Led by pitchers Ed Walsh, Nick Altrock, Doc White, and Frank Owen, and the potent (despite its name) Hitless Wonders offense featuring Frank Isbell, George Davis, and Jones, now the club's player-manager, the White Sox upset the crosstown Chicago Cubs, winners of a record 116 games, in the 1906 World Series.

Though the team did not win another pennant and World Series title for 11 years, Comiskey built his franchise into one of the most financially successful in the country. At the end of the century's first decade,

the White Sox showed a 10-year profit of $700,000, highest among recorded earnings during that time.[15] He turned some of those profits into the World Tour, taken with the New York Giants after the 1913 season.

From the beginning of his tenure, Comiskey established a reputation as an owner passionately involved in the day-to-day affairs of his club. Comiskey was never afraid to express his opinions about the game from his private box. Reporters shared numerous stories of Comiskey railing at his team over bonehead plays or games tossed away. "Sitting next to him at a game, one is likely to be nudged in the ribs, or have his toes stepped on as Comiskey 'pulls' on a close play," stated *Baseball Magazine*.[16]

Nor was Comiskey afraid to spend money on his team or his ballpark. By the time of its opening on July 1, 1910, the cost of Comiskey Park and its grounds totaled $750,000, a remarkable amount for the time. Additional seating in subsequent seasons raised the cost to over a million dollars. Commy was also the only owner at this time to own his entire club, the grounds, and all the equipment.[17]

And though he did everything he could to hold down his players' salaries, Comiskey spent large sums of money putting together his second great team of the Deadball Era. In December 1914 he purchased second baseman Eddie Collins from the Philadelphia Athletics for a reported $50,000. Less than a year later, he acquired Cleveland Indians slugger Joe Jackson for three players and $31,500.

Throughout his reign, Comiskey polished his reputation as a benevolent monarch. Beginning in 1900, he handed out free grandstand tickets to 75,000 schoolboys each season. He constantly professed love for the fans and when it rained at his ballpark, the occupants of the bleachers were permitted to enter the higher-priced sheltered sections without extra charge. "Those bleacherites made this big new plant possible," announced Comiskey. "The fellow who can pay only twenty-five cents to see a ball game always will be just as welcome at Comiskey Park as the box seat holder."[18]

He later claimed to have given away a quarter of a million tickets to servicemen, and followed that by donating a reported 10 percent of his 1917 home gate receipts to the Red Cross, an amount totaling about $17,000.[19] Comiskey regularly allowed the city of Chicago to use his park for special events, often free of charge. The owner's benevolence also extended to the press, whom he regularly feted with roasts and free drinks.

Comiskey had no qualms when it came to spending money on his ballpark, his city, and his fans. But with his players, those stories are few and far between. Like almost every owner of the time, he held a hard line on player salaries, although recent research has revealed that the White Sox had one of the highest team payrolls in the majors. As historian Bob Hoie has written, the "depiction of Chicago players as woefully underpaid by a tightwad boss" does not stand up to scrutiny.[20] Likewise the legend often repeated about Comiskey's team being known as the "Black Sox" long before the scandal due to their dirty uniforms, a result of their owner's efforts to cut down on laundry bills; though an amusing anecdote, no evidence has yet been found to confirm that this story is true. Another apocryphal tale has Comiskey benching his star pitcher Eddie Cicotte to keep him from winning his 30th game and collecting on a promised $10,000 bonus. In reality, Cicotte did have a chance to win No. 30—and clinch the American League pennant—in late September 1919, but he didn't pitch well and was pulled before the White Sox rallied to win the game.[21]

During the course of the Deadball Era, Comiskey's amicable relationship with Ban Johnson disintegrated into open warfare. According to legend, the discord erupted in 1905, when Johnson sent Comiskey a load of fresh fish on the same day that he suspended out-fielder Ducky Holmes for an altercation with an umpire the day before. Comiskey, who had already given his extra outfielder, Jimmy Callahan, the day off, was irate. "What does he want me to do?" he bellowed. "Put one of these bass out in the left field?"[22] (Versions of this story abound: Some sources say the incident occurred in 1907, and involved Fielder Jones,

Charles Comiskey, circa 1914 (Bain Collection, Library of Congress, Prints and Photographs Division)

not Holmes.) A further series of disagreements set the stage for 1919, when two scandals rocked the league and irrevocably split Comiskey and Johnson.

In July 1919 Boston pitcher Carl Mays abandoned the Red Sox and demanded a trade. Johnson ruled that the temperamental pitcher could not be traded until disciplinary action was taken, but Boston owner Harry Frazee ignored the edict and dealt Mays to the Yankees, only to see Johnson suspend Mays. The Yankee owners responded by securing an injunction allowing Mays to play.

League owners immediately took sides: Frazee, Yankee owners Jacob Ruppert and Tillinghast Huston, and Comiskey were labeled "The Insurrectionists," while most of the remaining AL moguls sided with Johnson.

Comiskey even pursued a proposal to have his club join the National League; that plan never got off the ground after an uneasy truce between the parties was brokered the following winter.[23]

By then the Black Sox Scandal hung like a dark cloud over the sport. There is some evidence that Comiskey was aware of the plot to throw the World Series as early as Game One and did nothing to stop it.[24] Johnson helped fuel these accusations, while Comiskey threw the burden of the scandal back on Johnson. "I blame Ban Johnson for allowing the Series to continue," he announced. "If ever a league president blundered in a crisis, Ban did."[25]

But Comiskey certainly knew of the fix after the Series ended. One of his players, Joe Jackson, reportedly tried to return his share of the payoff only to be turned away by team executive Harry Grabiner.[26] As rumors of the fix spread throughout the sport, Comiskey responded by publicly offering $20,000 to anyone with knowledge of the fix. The announcement was no doubt a public-relations move, intended to make Comiskey appear nobly dedicated to uncovering the truth, no matter the cost. When St. Louis Browns infielder Joe Gedeon did come forward with information, Comiskey rebuffed him and never paid the reward.[27]

By the end of the 1920 season, details of the plot began to emerge, as several conspirators confessed to their involvement. Even though the eight accused Black Sox were ultimately acquitted of the conspiracy charges filed against them, the scandal devastated Comiskey's franchise. The eight accused players were banned from the game for life, and after 1920 the White Sox never again finished in the first division during Comiskey's lifetime.

Charles Comiskey died of heart complications at his lakeside estate in Eagle River, Wisconsin, on October 26, 1931, at the age of 72, and was buried in Calvary Catholic Cemetery in Evanston, Illinois. He was survived by a son. His wife, Nan Kelly, whom he had married in 1882, preceded him in death in 1922. The Comiskey family continued to control the White Sox

until 1959, when they were bought out by a consortium led by Bill Veeck Jr.

SOURCES

For this biography, the author used a number of contemporary sources, especially those found in the subject's file at the National Baseball Hall of Fame Library.

NOTES

1   *San Francisco Chronicle*, September 30, 1917.

2   M.L. Ahern, *The Political History of Chicago* (Chicago: Michael Loftus Ahern, 1886), 145-46.

3   *Los Angeles Times*, October 12, 1917.

4   David L. Fleitz, *The Irish in Baseball: An Early History* (Jefferson, North Carolina: McFarland & Co., 2009), 43-45.

5   *New York Times*, October 26, 1931.

6   Hugh C. Weir, "The Real Comiskey," *Baseball Magazine*, February 1914. Accessed online at LA84.org.

7   Ibid.

8   Peter Morris, *A Game of Inches: The Stories Behind the Innovations that Shaped Baseball* (Chicago: Ivan R. Dee, 2006), 149.

9   Richard Egenriether, "Chris Von der Ahe: Baseball's Pioneering Huckster," *The Baseball Research Journal #18* (Kansas City, Missouri: SABR, 1989.)

10 Weir, "The Real Comiskey."

11 Ibid.

12 Ibid.

13 Ibid.

14 Harold and Dorothy Seymour, *Baseball: The Early Years* (New York: Oxford University Press, 1960), 309.

15 Harold and Dorothy Seymour, *Baseball: The Golden Age* (New York: Oxford University Press, 1971), 71.

16 Weir, "The Real Comiskey."

17 Ibid.

18 Ibid.

19 *New York Times*, October 26, 1931.

20 Bob Hoie, "1919 Baseball Salaries and the Mythically Underpaid Chicago White Sox." *Base Ball: A Journal of the Early Game* (Jefferson, North Carolina: McFarland & Co., Spring 2012).

21 *Chicago Tribune*, September 25, 1919.

22 *Reading Times*, October 27, 1931.

23 *Washington Post*, December 11, 1919.

24 For a detailed analysis, see Gene Carney, *Burying the Black Sox: How Baseball's Cover-up of the 1919 World Series Fix Almost Succeeded* (Washington, D.C.: Potomac Books, 2006), 26-60.

25 David Pietrusza, Matthew Silverman, and Michael Gershman, *Baseball: The Biographical Encyclopedia* (New York: Total Sports, 2000).

26 Carney, *Burying the Black Sox*, 69-71.

27 *Chicago Tribune*, October 27, 1920.

KID GLEASON

By Dan Lindner

HE IS REMEMBERED AS THE manager of the most infamous baseball team ever, but less well known as a versatile and gutsy ballplayer of the 19th century. His counseling and humor became crucial to the success of many big leaguers in the years between the World Wars. He was the Kid from the coal country who rose above his humble beginnings to become a much-loved figure in the national pastime.

William J. Gleason was born on October 26, 1866, in Camden, New Jersey, across the river from Philadelphia. His family moved to the coal regions of Pennsylvania's Pocono Mountains, and Gleason grew up in the hard life of a "coalcracker" family. As with many boys of the era, he played games with his five brothers and one sister. His recreational interests turned to baseball; indeed, younger brother Harry played five years at third base in the American League with Boston and St. Louis. Gleason skipped college to become a professional ballplayer, displaying both a potent bat and strong pitching arm (he batted and threw right-handed). He was not a large man, growing to 5-feet-7 and weighing just under 160 pounds as an adult, and was therefore labeled with the everlasting nickname "Kid."

Gleason played two seasons in the minor leagues of northern Pennsylvania. In 1886 at Williamsport of the Pennsylvania State Association, he batted .355 and stole 20 bases in 36 games.[1] In 1887, again at Williamsport, he posted a 9-11 record with a glittering 1.97 earned-run average as a pitcher, and batted .348 as a change player — today known as a utility player — at both second base and the outfield. His obvious talent landed him a spot with the nearby Scranton team of the International League, then as now a top minor league. Though his pitching record was abysmal (1-12, 3.67 ERA), his all-around talents shone through as he batted .313 as an outfielder when not pitching.

Harry Wright, manager of the Philadelphia National League entry (then known as the Quakers, but later as the Phillies), heard about the prowess of young Gleason and invited him to try out with the team in the spring of 1888. He made the team largely on the basis of his performance in a March 31 exhibition game against the University of Pennsylvania varsity, when he struck out 12 batters and yielded no earned runs.

From the day of Gleason's major-league debut on April 20, his 1888 season was largely limited to the pitcher's mound, even though Philadelphia's batting lineup that season was relatively anemic. Gleason started 23 games for the Phillies in his inaugural season, winning seven, though his 2.84 ERA closely tracked with the league average. His follow-up season in 1889 was significantly less successful as his ERA ballooned to over five runs per game.

As 1890 arrived, the rival Players League was formed and Gleason had the opportunity to jump the team. Instead he displayed a rather unusual (for his time) level of loyalty for his manager and decided to stay with the Phillies, saying, "Harry Wright gave me my chance two years ago when I was just a fresh kid playing coal towns, and I'm not running out on him now."[2] As a result, Gleason was one of several prominent players expelled from the Brotherhood of Base Ball Players for refusing to jump to the new Players League.

The outcome of his decision was a coming of age for Gleason's pitching abilities. His 38 victories and .691 winning percentage ranked second in the National League for 1890. Gleason displayed workhorse abilities by hurling 506 innings and completing 54 games (all but one of his starts), both ranking third in the league.

His follow-up season of 1891, significantly more challenging after the absorption of Players League returnees, still produced 24 victories, tops on the team.

Gleason was sold to St. Louis before the 1892 season and assumed a position in the starting rotation for the next two seasons, winning 20 or more games both seasons while playing more games as a spare fielder. He started 45 games each season, completing all but two in 1892 while hurling 400 innings (he added 380⅓ in 1893). Though not among the league leaders, he nonetheless made solid contributions.

It should not be surprising that Gleason, like any spirited St. Louis player of the day, ran afoul of team owner Chris Von der Ahe. One day, the owner imposed a fine on Gleason by withholding $100 from his pay envelope. Kid marched into Von der Ahe's office and yelled, "Look here, you big, fat Dutch slob. If you don't open that safe and get me the $100 you fined me, I'm going to knock your block off." Gleason got his refund immediately.[3]

Gleason got off to a poor start in 1894, losing six out of eight starts, and was sold to Baltimore for $2,400 in late June. According to David Ball's research, Gleason did not report until July 17 because of a money dispute resulting from either back pay or a desire to obtain a share of the sale price (a common practice of the day).[4] Once he arrived in Baltimore and received the tutelage of Ned Hanlon, Gleason rebounded with another successful season, winning 15 out of 20 starts and averaging only 2.3 walks per game, third best in the league. His contribution helped lead Baltimore to a pennant, something Gleason had yet to encounter in his career. More importantly, however, Gleason's batting skills increased dramatically, as he averaged .349 in 86 at-bats.

Hanlon noted this quality as the 1895 season dawned. Due to strong pitching and uncertainty in his infield, Hanlon decided to remove Gleason from the mound after only five starts and position him at second base. Gleason earned some $2,000 for the season, among the best salaries in the league.[5] Gleason responded with a .309 average, though his fielding percentage was below .900, abysmal even in those days. Despite winning another pennant, Hanlon decided that he could develop a better defense with a healthy John McGraw at third base and Henry Reitz back at second. He traded Gleason in the offseason to the New York Giants in exchange for slugging first baseman Jack Doyle.

Gleason closed his pitching career with 138 victories, a lifetime winning record, and a 3.79 ERA. In a 1931 interview with the *Philadelphia Inquirer*, Gleason reflected on his demise as a pitcher: "When I won 38 games for the Phillies (1890) I pitched every other day—had to, we had only 15 men. The reason the hurlers can't work so often now is because of the increased pitching distance."[6]

His pitching days behind him, Gleason settled into second base in New York over the next five years. He developed into one of the better second basemen of the time, leading the league twice in assists and once in putouts. His batting peaked at .317 with 106 RBIs in 1897 before a steady decline, though not enough to get him out of the lineup.

Gleason also served as team captain, and was credited by *Baseball Magazine* with inventing that most curious of baseball stratagems, the intentional walk.[7] In a high-scoring contest against Chicago, the bases loaded with Colts in the eighth inning with two outs, and the Giants nursing a fragile 9-6 lead, Gleason strolled to the mound and proceeded to confer with pitcher Jouett Meekin and catcher Parke Wilson. Coming up to bat was Jimmy Ryan, one of the most feared Colts, but Gleason noted that the less intimidating hitter George Decker was on deck. All players returned to their position, and Meekin proceeded to toss four pitches wide of the plate. Ryan dutifully, though somewhat astonished, took his free pass and a run was forced in. Meekin then proceeded to fan Decker, and the Giants went on to win the game.

Gleason reached heroic status in New York City, though not only for his on-field abilities. He was going to the Polo Grounds on April 26, 1900, with teammates George Davis and Mike Grady when the ballplayers noticed smoke from an apartment house. Rushing to the scene, Davis climbed a fireman's ladder to rescue a fainted woman, then Gleason joined him to lead another woman and a child down the fire escape. The fire left 45 families homeless but alive, thanks to the quick thinking of the Giants players.[8]

Baseball players have long been accused of gullibility, and Gleason was no exception. Upon completion of the 1900 season, a number of players assembled to play a series of exhibition games in Cuba. Some unnamed prankster convinced Gleason and Pirates outfielder Tom O'Brien that drinking an excessive amount of seawater would ultimately cure seasickness, though with some immediate illness. Both men fell for the trick and became violently ill. Gleason recovered, but O'Brien suffered internal damage and, tragically, later died from the prank.[9]

Gleason was a hard worker and believed in preseason conditioning long before the popularity of spring training. Residing in Trenton, upriver from Philadelphia on the New Jersey side, he paid a daily visit to the gymnasium and worked out for a few hours each day. The results became more critical as he was now in his mid-30s, past his physical prime.

The temptation of a rival league arose again with the advent of the American League raids in 1901. This

Kid Gleason, circa 1919 (National Photo Company Collection, Library of Congress, Prints and Photographs Division)

time however, Gleason owed no allegiance to his manager and signed on with the new Detroit franchise, which featured two Kids up the middle—Gleason at second base and Elberfeld at shortstop. Gleason's next two years in Detroit saw continued success in the field with significant putouts and assists, though he committed more errors both seasons than the rest of the league's second basemen.

When peace arrived between the warring leagues in time for the 1903 season, Gleason was part of the interleague player-swapping, reuniting with the Phillies. For the next four seasons, he held forth at second base, leading the league in putouts at that position in 1905. His batting also showed a resurgence in both 1904 and 1905 while back in his adopted home town; he paced the 1904 team in games played, at-bats, hits, and total bases. In 1905 he tied for the team lead in games played and was the leader in at-bats.

During the 1906 season, Gleason's everyday playing skills were diminishing, but not his spirit. On June 20 he spiked Pittsburgh's Honus Wagner, who had just drilled a hit deep into the outfield, causing Wagner to stop at third base with a painful limp and miss three games. By 1907, at the age of 40, Gleason had become a utility player. Two brief but hitless appearances in 1908 completed his major-league playing career (other than one brief appearance at second base four years later). He ended his nearly 2,000-game career with more than 1,000 runs, averaging about a hit per game, accumulating a .261 batting average, 329 stolen bases, and 501 bases on balls.

The next three seasons saw Gleason move progressively down the minor leagues, with stops at Jersey City (International), Harrisburg (Tri-State), and Utica-Binghamton (New York State).[10] Twenty years later, in the *Philadelphia Inquirer* interview, he reflected on the style of play at second base: "They can't bring back the old kind of game, not the way we played it.… I'd let them slide onto the bag, then kick them off the bag. That's the way we put them out." As for playing off the pitching mound, "Any time a man tried to steal I'd run over in front of him and slow him up."[11]

Gleason returned to the major leagues in 1912 as a coach, when former teammate Jimmy Callahan became manager of the Chicago White Sox. He also played a game at second base, obtaining his final major-league hit despite his advanced age of 45. But his prime contribution was as team sparkplug. The Kid's favorite trick was to sneak into Eddie Collins's room during road trips and tie him to the bed with a razor strop.

Cleveland hurler Cy Falkenberg once told *Baseball Magazine* of his ability to stymie Gleason with his emery ball: " 'Kid' Gleason used to watch me like a hawk, whenever I pitched against the White Sox. He would say to me, 'I know you are doing something to that ball. You must be doing something to get it to break in that way.' And then he would pick up the ball I had used and examine it carefully. But he could never detect the slight and almost invisible roughening of a small spot on the side. He kept at me continually, but I would jolly him along and he never got on to the secret."[12]

Promoted to manager before the 1919 season, Gleason led the White Sox to the pennant with a record of 88-52. The White Sox led the league in runs scored, batting average, and stolen bases, showing the same spark at bat and in the field that Gleason had shown in his playing career. He called them the "best baseball team in the world," a club he claimed had no weaknesses.[13]

One longstanding mystery of Gleason's team in 1919 is why he held out his star pitcher, Eddie Cicotte, at the end of the regular season. Although the pennant race was locked up, Cicotte was the only major-league pitcher that season with a fair chance to win 30 games, a mark of pitching mastery in the 20th century. Yet he started only three games after September 5; he won his 29th game on September 19 and failed to win his 30th five days later. Speculation has long circulated that team owner Charles Comiskey refused to pay Cicotte a bonus that he would have earned had he won 30 games, so he is accused of ordering Gleason not to pitch Cicotte until the World Series.

The trouble with this theory is its lack of verification by the principals involved. Neither Cicotte nor Gleason ever raised the issue in any interview. Lowell D. Blaisdell has an excellent analysis of this dilemma, reaching a different conclusion.[14] He notes that Gleason faced some serious concerns over the Series. First, pitcher Red Faber developed a sore arm and was inactive for the Series. Gleason now had only two reliable starters, Cicotte and Claude Williams, and the untested potential of Dickey Kerr. Moreover, the Series that year had the trial idea of a best-of-nine series, requiring the winner to post five victories before clinching the Series. Finally, the close proximity of the competing cities (Chicago and Cincinnati) led the leagues to decide on nine consecutive days of play, without travel days. How could Gleason hope to win such a Series with only two proven starters? His only chance was to alternate Cicotte and Williams on only two days' rest, at most. Therefore, it seems plausible that Gleason merely held Cicotte out of the regular season to save him for the Series. This theory is bolstered by the *New York Times* report of September 21, 1919: "Gleason is not worrying much about his individual record. He is looking ahead and is loathe *(sic)* to take any chances with his star." The news account added that Gleason "is figuring on using his star in three games of the series ..."

History records the deeds of that team during the World Series, earning the sobriquet of Black Sox. When the gambling story finally broke the next year and came to trial, Gleason was the first witness for the defense, challenging an alleged meeting between players and gamblers at the very time they were holding a team practice in Chicago. Not only was Gleason not involved in the gambling, but he probably knew from the first game what was happening (prominent journalists Ring Lardner and Hugh Fullerton held similar suspicions). Author Gene Carney found some evidence that Gleason confronted his team about the fix during the World Series, but his efforts didn't stop the White Sox from losing to the Reds in eight games. Gleason told a reporter afterward, "Something was wrong. I didn't like the betting odds. I wish no one had ever bet a dollar on the team."[15]

Though Gleason was found to be uninvolved in the scandal, he was personally affected by it for the rest of his life. His team finished a close second the following season, 1920, but failed to post a winning record in the three remaining years of his tenure. He ended his managerial career in 1923 with a record of 392-364.

Gleason returned to live in retirement in Philadelphia, but after two years the baseball bug bit him again. Now, it was Athletics manager Connie Mack who invited him to return to the coaching ranks. Gleason played a pivotal role in building an obscure franchise into a three-time world championship team through his clubhouse antics and seasoned advice. Gleason became known as the unofficial greeter at spring training with his winning smile and iron-tight handshake.

Gleason retired for the last time after the 1931 season, at the height of the Athletics' success. He suffered from a heart ailment and became bedridden about the time of the 1932 World Series, the first one in four years without his beloved A's. As Connie Mack was dismantling his team of stars, Gleason himself began slipping away from the scene. Living in the Philadelphia home of his daughter, Mamie Robb, Gleason died on January 2, 1933. Though his wife had died five years earlier, all of his siblings were still alive at the time, according to the *New York Times* obituary.

Gleason's funeral reflected his popularity. The *Philadelphia Inquirer* estimated that more than 5,000 people attended, including longtime Giants manager and former teammate John McGraw; Mack; and Commissioner Kenesaw Mountain Landis. To accommodate the crowd that could never fit into the funeral parlor, amplifiers were set up on the sidewalk for people to hear the service. Gleason was then buried in Northwood Cemetery in north Philadelphia.

Kid Gleason was much beloved by the baseball community. Upon hearing of his death, McGraw was quoted by the *Philadelphia Inquirer* as saying: "He was, without doubt, the gamest and most spirited ball player I ever saw and that doesn't except Ty Cobb. He was a great influence for good on any ball club, making

up for his lack of stature, by his spirit and fight. He could lick his weight in wildcats and would prove it at the drop of a hat."[16] McGraw was right: The spirit and guidance of the Kid from the coal fields was felt by his contemporaries and his players for years to come.

SOURCES

Ball, David, "Nineteenth Century Transactions Register," version 2 (Cincinnati: David Ball, 2003).

Blaisdell, Lowell D, "Legends as an Expression of Baseball Memory," *Journal of Sport History*, Vol. 19, No. 3, 1992, 227-43.

Erardi, John, "A Series That Will Live in Infamy," *Cincinnati Enquirer*, June 12, 1997.

Kelleher, Garrett J., "More Than a Kid: The Story of Kid Gleason." *Baseball Research Journal*, No. 17 (Kansas City, Missouri: Society for American Baseball Research, 1988).

Kofoed, J.C., "A Twenty-Five Year Record," *Baseball Magazine*, April 1916.

Lane, F.C., "The Emery Ball: Strangest of Freak Deliveries." *Baseball Magazine*, July 1915.

Linder, Douglas, "The Black Sox Trial: An Account," accessed online at law.umkc.edu/faculty/projects/ftrials/blacksox/blacksoxaccount.html.

Lindner, Dan, "William J. Gleason (Kid)," in Ivor-Campbell, Frederick; Tiemann, Robert L.; and Rucker, Mark, eds. *Baseball's First Stars* (Cleveland: Society for American Baseball Research, 1996).

New York Times

Philadelphia Inquirer

Thorn, John, and Pete Palmer, eds. *Total Baseball* (New York City: Warner Books, Inc., 2002).

NOTES

1   J.C. Kofoed, "A Twenty-Five Year Record," *Baseball Magazine*, April 1916.

2   *Philadelphia Inquirer*, March 16, 1890.

3   Kofoed.

4   David Ball. "Nineteenth Century Transactions Register," version 2 (Cincinnati: David Ball, 2003).

5   Garrett J. Kelleher, "More Than a Kid: The Story of Kid Gleason." *Baseball Research Journal*, No. 17 (Kansas City, Missouri: Society for American Baseball Research, 1988).

6   Ibid.

7   Kofoed. Subsequent research by author Peter Morris has shown that the intentional walk goes back at least to the 1870s.

8   *Chicago Tribune*, April 27, 1900.

9   *New Castle* (Pennsylvania) *News*, February 13, 1901.

10   Kofoed.

11   Kelleher.

12   F.C. Lane, "The Emery Ball: Strangest of Freak Deliveries." *Baseball Magazine*, July 1915.

13   *Washington Post*, September 28, 1919.

14   Lowell D. Blaisdell, "Legends as an Expression of Baseball Memory," *Journal of Sport History*, Vol. 19, No. 3, 1992, 227-43.

15   *Chicago Tribune*, October 10, 1919. More analysis of Gleason's efforts can be found in Gene Carney, *Burying the Black Sox: How Baseball's Cover-Up of the 1919 World Series Fix Almost Succeeded* (Washington, DC: Potomac Books, 2006), 46-47.

16   Kelleher.

HARRY GRABINER

By Steve Cardullo

DURING HARRY GRABINER'S four-decade-long tenure as a front-office official with the Chicago White Sox, he saw the team experience its highest highs and lowest lows. Beginning his career as a scorecard salesman in 1905 and serving for many years as the team's secretary and vice president, Grabiner was involved with the White Sox' first two World Series championships, in 1906 and 1917, and the construction of Comiskey Park. He also helped with the planning and logistics of Charles Comiskey and John McGraw's successful world baseball tour in 1913-14, and played a key role in the building of the White Sox' great teams in the latter half of that decade. That team would shock the baseball world with the exposure of the Black Sox Scandal after the 1919 World Series, but Grabiner would stick around through three generations of the Comiskey family to run the White Sox' front office. After a brief retirement, he re-emerged in Cleveland as a partner of Bill Veeck in the building of a championship contender in the 1940s.

Harry Mitchell Grabiner was born on December 26, 1890, in Chicago. He and his brother, Solomon (called Joseph), and two sisters, Sophie and Fannie, were raised by their Polish-born parents, Samuel and Hannah, just outside of the Loop. Samuel, a hardware store salesman, had emigrated in 1883 and sent for his wife and family a year later.[1]

In 1905 Harry met White Sox owner Charles Comiskey when he wandered into South Side Park after a rainstorm and found Comiskey working on the field to get it ready for that afternoon's game against the Detroit Tigers. The 15-year-old Grabiner asked if he could help and Comiskey put him to work.[2] Grabiner remained an employee of the White Sox for the next 40 years.

Grabiner began his long tenure with the White Sox as a scorecard salesman on a salary of $50 a month. Soon he added groundskeeping, ticket sales, and finances to his responsibilities. He had a keen eye for numbers and was quick to add up daily receipts, often in his head. That skill brought him to the attention of club secretary Charles Fredericks, Comiskey's nephew, who mentored him in the business of baseball.[3] Fredericks died in 1916 after a long illness and Grabiner, who had served as acting secretary along with Joseph O'Neill, took over the job full time at the age of 25.[4] The secretary's role was in many ways equivalent to that of a modern-day general manager. Author Gene Carney noted that "although Grabiner may have been stingier than Comiskey in negotiating contracts and running the club, it is Comiskey who has been portrayed by some as a Scrooge."[5]

Grabiner was with the White Sox for their greatest triumphs in Comiskey's reign: World Series championships in 1906 and 1917, and the opening of Comiskey Park in 1910. He recalled that despite the team finishing out of the first division that year, the new ballpark kept everyone busy. "Its initial capacity was 26,000," he said, "and while it was being built, many scoffed at the idea of constructing a ballpark so large. In that first year, there were many days when the new park wasn't large enough."[6]

Grabiner also played an instrumental role in the 1913-14 world baseball tour led by Comiskey and New York Giants manager John McGraw with a select group of major-league players. Although he did not accompany the teams overseas, Grabiner and his new bride, Dorothy, enjoyed a trip to San Francisco and up the West Coast to Vancouver, British Columbia, as he helped make final preparations for the teams to set sail across the Pacific in the fall of 1913.[7] The tour, during which games were played in Asia, Australia,

India, Africa, and Europe, captured the imagination of many fans across the globe.

Dorothy Grabiner, born Sophia Maistrovich to Austrian parents who immigrated to America around 1895,[8] became friends with many Chicago socialites, including Eleanor Twitchell, who later married Lou Gehrig. Eleanor drove Dorothy and her sister Mary—married to Harry's brother, Joe (known to be a prominent gangster in Chicago)—around town on sightseeing and shopping trips or to attend a game at Comiskey Park.[9]

Harry and Dorothy's daughter, June, was born in 1914. Through the help of comedian Joe E. Brown, she signed a film contract with Paramount Pictures in 1935 and enjoyed a brief but memorable career as a Hollywood actress under the stage name June Travis.[10] Brown's son, Joe L. Brown, later got his start in baseball through Harry Grabiner and served as general manager of the Pittsburgh Pirates for more than 20 seasons, leading the team to two World Series championships.

By 1916, with the addition of stars like Shoeless Joe Jackson and Eddie Collins, Comiskey and Grabiner had put together a White Sox team that could compete with any in the American League. The White Sox finished in second place, two games behind the Boston Red Sox, for the American League pennant but they came out on top the next year and defeated John McGraw's New York Giants in six games to win their second World Series.

After a forgettable war-shortened season in 1918, the White Sox seemed poised to return to glory in 1919 and for years to come. The Black Sox Scandal put an end to those thoughts. While the story of the fixing of the 1919 World Series has been told many times, Harry Grabiner's role in the story remains a bit of a mystery.

After the White Sox lost the World Series in eight games to the Cincinnati Reds, rumors swirled that the Series had not been played on the level. Comiskey launched a private investigation of the suspected players (Eddie Cicotte, Lefty Williams, Joe Jackson,

Harry Grabiner (National Baseball Hall of Fame Library, Cooperstown, N.Y.)

Happy Felsch, Chick Gandil, Swede Risberg, Buck Weaver, and Fred McMullin) during the offseason. Publicly, Comiskey offered a $10,000 reward for evidence that the Series had been fixed.[11] In the meantime, he directed Grabiner to offer contracts to the returning players for the 1920 season.

Grabiner kept a private journal with notes on the investigation and on the status of contract negotiations with the players.[12] During the offseason, he traveled to Savannah, Georgia, the winter home of Joe Jackson, to sign the star outfielder. This trip would later become a focal point during Jackson's back-pay lawsuit against the White Sox after he was banned from baseball. Jackson claimed that he attempted to contact Comiskey after the World Series in order to return the $5,000 he had received from gamblers, but that Grabiner told him to keep the money.[13] Comiskey and Grabiner both denied having any knowledge of the World Series fix. Whatever conversation Jackson and Grabiner had in Savannah about the tainted World Series will probably never be known. In any case, Grabiner offered Jackson a three-year contract for $8,000 per season, a 33 percent raise over what he had been making in 1919.[14] Some of the other Black Sox players got raises, too, and the pennant-winning team returned mostly intact for the 1920 season.

While the Black Sox Scandal was still unknown to the public, baseball's top officials, including Comiskey and Grabiner, were working hard behind the scenes to influence the game's structure of power. The three-man National Commission, led by American League President Ban Johnson, had become ineffective, and a plan was hatched to hire a single commissioner to rule over the sport. Johnson and Comiskey, once close friends, were now feuding and Grabiner tried to help ensure that Johnson did not get the job as commissioner. Instead, it went to federal judge Kenesaw Mountain Landis.

Comiskey's support, however, did not stop Landis from breaking up his great team when the dust settled in the Black Sox Scandal. Although the eight Chicago players were acquitted in a jury trial that most observers considered to be a farce, Landis banned them all for life in August 1921. Without Jackson, Cicotte, and the others, the White Sox fell to seventh place. They remained in the second division for nearly two decades and, by all accounts, Comiskey remained devastated by the scandal for the rest of his life.

Charles Comiskey died in 1931 and his son, J. Louis Comiskey, inherited the team. Lou was not a baseball man as his father had been, and he relied heavily on Grabiner to run the overall operation, both on the baseball side and the business side. Grabiner had overseen the renovation of Comiskey Park into a double-decker stadium in 1927 and, while the team was still struggling overall, he had acquired stars like Ted Lyons, Luke Appling, Zeke Bonura, and Jimmy Dykes. But long-suffering White Sox fans began to criticize Grabiner as the losses mounted. As *Baseball Digest* later reported, "Grabiner was blasphemed by the fans and players, criticized by the press, and gener-ally blamed for inefficacies which were not of his own doing. Yet he struggled doggedly against the great odds until he fled the scene."[15]

When Lou Comiskey, who was in poor health for most of his life, died in 1939, he instructed in his will that Grabiner remain in charge of the team with a 10-year guaranteed contract at a minimum salary of $25,000 a year.[16] Grabiner did not stick around that long, resigning after the 1945 season because of his own poor health. His tenure with the White Sox lasted 41 years, spanning three generations of the Comiskey family.

Harry was not comfortable in retirement. In early 1946 he got a call from his friend Bill Veeck, the former Chicago Cubs executive and marketing wizard who was itching to get back into the game. The two had worked together to schedule exhibition games between the White Sox and Cubs, and like Charles Fredericks many decades before, Veeck was amazed at Grabiner's business acumen.[17] Veeck selected Grabiner to be his vice president when he bought the Cleveland Indians in June 1946, calling him "the smartest man I ever met in baseball."[18] Although many of baseball's old guard hoped Grabiner's conservative nature would help curtail some of Veeck's crazier stunts, the two got along supremely well. Grabiner later said, "Every day of my association with him in the operation of the Cleveland club has been a thrilling experience.... And what a joke has been turned on those who said I was in the setup to throw ice water on Bill's exuberance."[19]

Grabiner served as a valuable resource in the Indians front office. He had a hand in the bold July 1947 signing of Negro Leagues star Larry Doby, breaking the color line in the American League just three months after Jackie Robinson made his debut for the Brooklyn Dodgers in the National League. The following year, the Indians signed the most famous and talented African-American pitcher in the country, Satchel Paige, on their way to the AL pennant — their first since 1920, when the exposure of the Black Sox Scandal kept Grabiner's White Sox from winning again.

Before the Indians clinched the 1948 pennant, however, Grabiner suffered a serious stroke, collapsing in his office at Cleveland's Municipal Stadium. He was taken to his summer home in Allegan, Michigan, to recover but he never came out of a coma. Less than two weeks after the Indians defeated the Boston Braves to win the World Series, and two days after undergoing an operation to relieve pressure on his brain, the 57-year-old Grabiner died on October 24, 1948.

Grabiner is buried in Chicago's Rosehill Cemetery. At the time of his death, he ranked third in seniority among executives in the American League behind Connie Mack of the Philadelphia Athletics and Clark Griffith of the Washington Senators. His funeral was attended by dozens of baseball leading officials and former players, including Commissioner A.B. "Happy" Chandler, league presidents William Harridge and Ford Frick, and Charles A. Comiskey II, the White Sox secretary and the grandson of his old boss and friend.

NOTES

1   1910 US Census, accessed online at Ancestry.com.

2   *The Sporting News*, February 15, 1945.

3   Ibid.

4   *Chicago Tribune*, January 12, 1916.

5   Gene Carney, *Burying the Black Sox: How Baseball's Cover-Up of the 1919 World Series Fix Almost Succeeded* (Washington, D.C.: Potomac Books, 2006), 342.

6   *The Sporting News*, February 15, 1945.

7   For a comprehensive account of the world tour, see James E. Elfers, *The Tour to End All Tours: The Story of Major League*

Baseball's 1913-1914 World Tour (Lincoln, Nebraska: University of Nebraska Press, 2003).

8   *Chicago Tribune*, February 21, 1913; 1910-40 US Censuses.

9   Ray Robinson, *Iron Horse: Lou Gehrig in His Time* (New York: W.W. Norton & Co., 1990), 179.

10   *Los Angeles Times*, April 15, 1935.

11   Gene Carney, "Comiskey's Detectives," *Baseball Research Journal*, Society for American Baseball Research, Fall 2009.

12   Few knew of the Harry Grabiner diary's existence until it was discovered by Bill Veeck's nephew Fred Krehbiel, a White Sox employee, in the cellar of Comiskey Park in 1963. Veeck, who owned the White Sox from 1958 to 1961, revealed some of the diary's contents in his 1965 book with Ed Linn, *The Hustler's Handbook*. According to Veeck, the Grabiner diary—actually, a collection of two ledger and legal pads—included chronological notations about the investigation initiated by Charles Comiskey into the fixing of the 1919 World Series. The diary also included a list of team salaries in 1918 and 1920 (the 1919 list was missing), the 1890 Players League Constitution and By-Laws, and other notes. It is one of the few firsthand accounts of the Black Sox Scandal from an insider's perspective. Veeck wrote that he turned the ledger books over to the Grabiner family in the early 1960s. Over the years individual pages have surfaced and been posted on the Internet, but the entire diary has not been seen since. For more on Krehbiel's discovery, see "Harry's Diary: The Elusive Missing Link," by Dr. David Fletcher and Paul Duffy in the SABR Black Sox Scandal Research Committee's June 2013 newsletter at SABR.org.

13   Carney, *Burying the Black Sox*, 2-15.

14   Carney, *Burying the Black Sox*, 11.

15   John C. Hoffman, "The Black Curse of the White Sox," *Baseball Digest*, October 1950, 53.

16   *The Sporting News*, November 3, 1948.

17   Paul Dickson, *Bill Veeck: Baseball's Greatest Maverick* (New York: Walker Publishing Co., 2012), 108.

18   *The Sporting News*, November 3, 1948.

19   Ibid.

NORRIS "TIP" O'NEILL

By Brian McKenna

NORRIS O'NEILL, ONE OF THREE nineteenth-century baseball figures nicknamed Tip, made a name for himself on the West Coast, where he captained the Oakland squad for several years. He played and/or managed in the minors from 1885 to 1899. In his youth, O'Neill was an acclaimed catcher, but after turning pro he tired of the demands of the position and switched to the infield, where he was far less effective, making many fielding and throwing errors. O'Neill had a contentious personality and numerous run-ins with the media, fans, opponents, and even his own teammates. Many believed, though, that as a team leader and captain few were his superior.

After hanging up his spikes, O'Neill became president of the Western League, serving for more than a decade beginning in 1905 while constantly antagonizing team owners, not least for maintaining league headquarters in Chicago, far from any league city. O'Neill became one of White Sox owner Charles Comiskey's top advisers and intimate friends. He played a minor role in the aftermath of the Black Sox affair. Outside of baseball, he became wealthy in the oil-drilling business.

Norris Lawrence O'Neill was born on February 1, 1867, in Rouseville, Pennsylvania, to Irish-born parents Dennis and Ellen O'Neill. He was the sixth of seven children. His parents had immigrated to the United States in 1855, first settling in South Paterson, New Jersey. They moved to Pennsylvania in the mid-1860s just before Norris's birth, settling in Rouseville and then Cornplanter, both in Venango County, in the oil region of northwestern Pennsylvania. Dennis supported the family as a night watchman. Ellen was listed as an invalid in the 1870 US Census, just a few years after giving birth to Norris.

After his father died, Norris went to work at the age of 15 to help support his mother. He was hard-working and frugal. By the age of 22, when he moved to

California, O'Neill had $4,000 in the bank and owned his own house, all the while continuing to send money to his mother. He found time to play ball, first as an amateur and then as a semipro player in and around Venango County. He was a strongly-built 5-foot-9-inch-tall catcher. He attended and played ball at Hamilton College in Clinton, New York, in the mid-1880s. Two decades later, he was still recognized as the finest catcher in the school's history. One of his favorite tricks was to throw pebbles at the umpire to distract him during certain plays and to buy time for a tired pitcher.

O'Neill, a right-hander, entered professional baseball in 1885. He played eight games for Waterbury (Connecticut) of the Southern New England League, seven games for Wilmington-Atlantic City in the Eastern League, and five games for Columbus (Georgia) in the Southern League. In 1886 he caught for the Bradford (Pennsylvania) semipro club much of the year. He also played three games behind the plate that season for Charleston in the Southern League. In 1887 he played in 27 games for Allentown in the Pennsylvania State Association, hitting .374. He also appeared in 35 games for Shamokin in the Central Pennsylvania League, batting .356. That was the season O'Neill started to move away from catching, filling in at second base and third base, and in the outfield.

In 1888 he caught, captained, and managed the Kalamazoo (Michigan) squad in the Tri-State League. In 86 games, O'Neill batted .328 and smacked 24 doubles. O'Neill then returned to the Allentown lineup with the club now in the Central League. He appeared in 24 games at shortstop and in the outfield. By this time, he was nicknamed Tip, presumably after James "Tip" O'Neill, the hard-hitting outfielder for the major-league St. Louis Browns. (The third Tip O'Neill of that era was Fred, who played in six games for the

New York Metropolitans of the American Association in 1887.)

O'Neill followed a friend, Charlie Dooley, a former Bradford teammate with family ties to Paterson, to California in 1889. They joined the Oakland Colonels of the California League. O'Neill became the shortstop for a $1,000 salary, permanently leaving his catching days behind. Oakland was owned and managed by Colonel Tom Robinson. O'Neill and Robinson became close friends, and Robinson named O'Neill the team captain. Baseball team captains in those days had important roles, making many of the decisions a manager or a general manager does today. The manager performed mostly business functions.

O'Neill had a contentious time throughout his stay on the West Coast. First, he didn't transition well from catcher to middle infielder. His fielding was poor. Second, he didn't hit well. For his part, O'Neill was quick to anger and was combative by nature. He had a poor relationship with sportswriters and fans. The *Oakland Tribune* wrote of him, "O'Neill is considered by some to be the poorest player in the league. As a shortstop he is a dismal failure but as a coacher he is somewhat of a success."[1] Another press report called him the "man with the large mouth."[2] He was roundly hissed by fans in Stockton and Sacramento. The San Francisco newspapers oozed contempt for O'Neill. He even had run-ins with teammates, who by the end of the year threatened mass desertion if he was retained for 1890. He was; Robinson held O'Neill in high regard for his on-the-field presence and his absolute loyalty.

One thing everyone agreed on was that O'Neill was a leader. The *Oakland Tribune* said, "O'Neill is without doubt the best captain in the California League. His method of handling his men, both on and off the field, is superior to any ever seen in the coast. Not only does he pay close attention to the baseball work of the players, but they are obliged to indulge in such athletic exercises as will keep them in proper trim. In fact, one cause of his frequent errors is his neglect of his own practice in order that he may devote more time to superintending his subordinates."[3] Oakland won the pennant that year, and O'Neill got much of the credit,

even though his players led the league in nearly all the major batting and pitching categories. It was a close race, with Oakland topping San Francisco by a mere game. Toward the end of the season, O'Neill picked up San Francisco catcher Pop Swett's signs. That may have swung the pennant race.

The field was new in Oakland in 1889 and hadn't settled. As a result, groundballs bounced to and fro. More than once O'Neill took a ball to the face. He eventually donned a mask that season while in the field to protect his features. During the season, O'Neill switched from shortstop to third base for a few weeks after Will Smalley was injured. One newspaper sarcastically noted that third base offered fewer opportunities to boot the ball. The *Oakland Tribune* jeered, "Tip O'Neill never did know how to play shortstop."[4] Downstate, the *Los Angeles Times* claimed, "O'Neill has the reputation of being the best catcher in the state, as well as one of the heaviest hitters."[5] It must have been on reputation only, as O'Neill virtually quit catching before joining Oakland. In 93 games on the left side of the infield in 1889, he hit .257.

O'Neill returned to Oakland from his Pennsylvania home on March 11, 1890. He quickly renewed his up-and-down relationship with teammates and fans. On May 4 he was taunted by the Sacramento crowd for unleashing an errant throw to first base. O'Neill fired obscenities back at the crowd; all could hear such banter in this era of cozy ballparks. Umpire Clay Chipman fined him $5. Later in the game, O'Neill interfered with a ball in play while he was coaching at third base. Chipman fined him another $5, which sparked an argument that ended with a punch to the umpire's face. O'Neill was arrested. The Sacramento manager asked the league to permanently ban the Oakland captain. San Francisco manager Mike Finn, a staunch O'Neill basher, fired off similar sentiments.

O'Neill continued to spar with opponents and even the local press and his teammates. He lived in a hotel apart from the rest of the club, one of only two men on the club who didn't share one rented house. In November Sacramento's management gave O'Neill $50 as a reward for Oakland's efforts against certain

Sacramento rivals. The rest of the Oakland roster felt the money was a gift to the entire squad; Tip didn't see it that way and pocketed the money. Perhaps his teammates also didn't like the fact that O'Neill wore a $250 ring, an extravagance that probably none of them could afford. In August he was blasted by the press and teammates for falling out of shape. He left the club and worked himself back into condition at Byron Hot Springs in nearby Contra Costa County, a retreat that would become famous in the twentieth century for its clientele, movie stars and athletes.

If anything, O'Neill sparked polarizing opinions. In June the *Oakland Tribune* commented, "Norris O'Neill played the game of his life last Sunday and won over many of his enemies. Tip can play ball when he gets right down to business and forgets the grand stand."[6] Later, the *Tribune* writer noted, "When he makes a clever play, and Tip does make a clever play once in a while, I venture to say that O'Neill is the speediest man in the league in making the double play, and always knows just where to throw the ball without stopping to debate on the subject."[7] He even received his share of applause on the road in 1890. In October O'Neill topped the list for most popular player on the club in an *Oakland Tribune* poll, with David Levy finishing a distant second. As always, O'Neill had the backing of Tom Robinson, who told *Sporting Life* that

Tip O'Neill, circa 1911 (Chicago History Museum, SDN-057137, Chicago Daily News negatives collection)

O'Neill "suits me exactly. He handles my business and my team better than any other man I could employ. I do not consider him the best ballplayer in the world, but he is a man who is always working in the interest of his team, never shirks responsibility, is possessed with fine executive ability in the ball field."[8]

In October 1890 O'Neill and teammate Joe Cantillon were suspended by league directors for rough play. O'Neill had purposely tripped a runner. Robinson fought hard and had them reinstated. In early December Tip tangled with teammate Kid Carsey. They started arguing in the clubhouse after the game, trekked onto the field, and went at it. They battled to an acknowledged draw. The next day Carsey was seen about town with two black eyes and a swollen face. O'Neill didn't emerge from his hotel room for three days.

In 97 games with Oakland in 1890, O'Neill batted a miserable .183. The following year was hardly better, as he posted a .212 average in 139 games. On April 30, 1891, Oakland lost 8-3 to San Jose. The *San Francisco Daily Evening Bulletin* said, "The baseball general O'Neill lost his head and contributed five of the errors himself and only extraordinary playing on the part of the infielders prevented him from having four more on skyrocket throws."[9] The paper added a few additional shots that season, writing, for instance, that Tip "has a reputation of playing better ball with his mouth than with his hands" and "Noisy O'Neil (*sic*) is going to the spring as he is out of condition. The question arises is he ever in condition to play ball?"[10]

On June 22, 1891, Robinson released O'Neill amid pressure from fans, the press, and teammates. But he brought O'Neill back a week later, maintaining that he had been inundated with pleas by the fans to reinstate the team captain. O'Neill soon left the club again. Robinson gave him a management position in one of his warehouses in San Francisco. O'Neill worked there throughout the winter. Robinson couldn't do without O'Neill on his club, though. He brought him back as a ticket taker in April 1892. O'Neill then acted as the club's road manager en route to Los Angeles.[11] On May 8 O'Neill returned to the field and was soon reinstated as captain, replacing Fred Carroll. That team included quite a few who made their mark in the majors, including Joe Cantillon, Charlie Irwin, Bill Lange, Charlie Sweeney, and George Van Haltren. In September O'Neill was officially given the title of field manager.[12] In 135 games for the club he hit a so-so .233.

In 1893 the California League suffered financial difficulties from the start. On May 2 the Oakland players, now including the forceful personality of Clark Griffith, rebelled over lack of pay. They refused to board a train for Los Angeles. Robinson quickly came up with some cash and the players headed out the following day. The players spoke up again on May 18; they were not being paid again. The next day, Robinson sold out. The new owners released O'Neill. Stockton owner Mike Finn wanted to make O'Neill captain of his team, but the players would have none of it, perfectly happy with the popular Kid Peeples as head of the club. The players vowed to rebel, and Finn threatened to fine them $100 each if they followed through. Finn said O'Neill "may not be the most desirable man to work under but his ability as a captain is unquestioned."[13] Unhappy in the league anyway, Finn soon departed and the club relocated to Sacramento without him; he had been a member of the California League since its inception in 1886. The league itself soon collapsed, failing to operate from 1894 through 1897. O'Neill never did join Stockton. Instead, he went east and joined New Orleans in the Southern League for 28 games.

O'Neill slipped out of Organized Baseball in 1894. The following year he joined Montgomery in the Southern League to kick off the season, as the club's new second baseman and captain. He took the field in 49 games for the club, hitting .269. The Montgomery roster included longtime baseball men Fritz Clausen, Tacks Latimer, Kid Peeples, and Tully Sparks. After the season O'Neill captained a barnstorming team that traveled through the South and West. It included George Harper, Billy Hulen, Billy Nash, and Jack McCarthy. Many assumed O'Neill was Montgomery's manager, but in January 1896 the ownership formally announced that he was not. Some of the players ap-

parently carried a beef against him. In February O'Neill was announced as the new captain of San Antonio. The *Galveston Daily News* wrote, "Having been captain of every team he ever played with, he has the competitive spirit, quick wit and generalship that goes to make up an able commander. He is a great coacher and one of the most original 'heady' players in the business today."[14] O'Neill headed to San Antonio in April but it's unclear if he appeared in a regular-season game with the club. Instead, he left Texas and joined Oakland in two leagues, a new California League for four games, and in the San Francisco City League. He also played in two games for Victoria (British Columbia) in the New Pacific League.

In 1897 O'Neill tried his hand at umpiring on the West Coast. The next season he joined the renewed California League, once again landing with Oakland for seven games in April and May. Oakland switched to the Pacific Coast League, where O'Neill hit .185 in 40 games. In 1899 he played second base for San Francisco in the California League, appearing in 55 games and batting .213. In 1900 O'Neill was listed in the US Census as living in Oakland and working as a watchman. In 1902 he umpired in the American Association.

On January 13, 1905, O'Neill was elected president of the five-year-old Class A Western League, and ran the league for the next decade. He immediately established his office in Chicago, which wasn't a member of the league, in fact was far from any league city. He struck up a strong friendship with White Sox owner Charles Comiskey, eventually moving the league office into Comiskey Park. League owners tolerated the situation until 1914, when they pressured O'Neill to relocate. Defiant, O'Neill declared, "I shall live any place I damn please." He carried his defiance even further by driving to Des Moines, a league city, and purchasing a mailbox at the corner of Seventh and Locust Streets. Very publicly, he gathered up the city's mayor, police chief, and several politicians and walked them to his new purchase, where he announced, "I want you to bear witness, gentlemen, that I, as president of the Western League, am establishing my office in this mailbox. However, I shall live in Chicago or any other place I please. I have no desire to live in the league."[15] Perhaps this was the last straw; the league owners fired O'Neill at the end of 1915.[16]

The frugal O'Neill never married and guarded his money carefully. In November 1901 he purchased an established oil field in Bradford, Pennsylvania, with his brother Charles and oilman D.W. Daley for $20,000. At the time, the six wells, spread over 37 acres, were producing 14 barrels a day. The men added more wells, which provided them with a steady stream of income. In September 1917 they sold the oil field for a reported $100,000 to $200,000. O'Neill also went into business with Joe Cantillon and Clark Griffith in late 1907 to raise sheep in Montana. O'Neill accepted responsibility for overseeing the venture while the other two tended to their teams during the baseball season.

O'Neill and Charles Comiskey developed a close relationship. Working at Comiskey Park, O'Neill became an adviser and business manager for the White Sox owner. O'Neill often oversaw spring training, traveling with the White Sox to training camps, arranging transportation and exhibition contests, entertaining reporters, and performing other duties in Comiskey's stead, especially when the White Sox owner was ill or out of town. He also did the same for the Boston Red Sox in 1911 as they rode to California, near owner John I. Taylor's winter home in Redondo Beach, and for the Cubs in 1917. For Comiskey, O'Neill was the business manager for the White Sox' international barnstorming tours in 1913 and 1924. It was said that no one was closer to Comiskey, especially after the Black Sox mess. O'Neill was one of his most sympathetic advisers as the White Sox franchise fought off collapse. He maintained an office at Comiskey Park for three decades, trekking to work every day even after Comiskey died in 1931.

In wake of the Black Sox Scandal, O'Neill handled several duties for the White Sox boss. According to Comiskey's testimony in the 1924 Milwaukee trial, he received a call from Chicago gambler Mont Tennes the day after Game One of the 1919 World Series.

Tennes claimed to have information about the fix. Comiskey sent O'Neill to meet Tennes. O'Neill obtained the information and reported back. He then alerted National League President John Heydler about the concerns. Heydler later told the *Washington Post*, "Tip O'Neill, former Western League president, came to me after the first World Series game last fall and told me Comiskey and Gleason (Kid Gleason, field manager) felt that something was wrong, but that they did not want to go to Ban Johnson because of the bad feeling between him and Comiskey at the time. I considered the matter preposterous at first, but after Gleason and I had analyzed the games, I went to Johnson."[17] O'Neill testified at the initial grand-jury hearings on October 5, 1920, concerning the fix.

O'Neill retired in the early 1930s, not long after Comiskey's death. O'Neill himself died of heart trouble in Alexian Brothers Hospital in Chicago on November 16, 1937, after a long illness. He was 70 years old and had been a patient at the hospital the last couple of years of his life. He was buried in Paterson, New Jersey, near his mother. Among the kind words, one of his obituaries noted, "He was a gabby, witty Irishman with a gracious smile and natty attire, always ready to talk baseball as long as anybody would listen."[18]

SOURCES

Special thanks to Ray Nemec for providing O'Neill's statistics and other essential information.

Ancestry.com

Atlanta Constitution

Carney, Gene, Notes From the Shadows of Cooperstown blog

Cedar Rapids Evening Gazette

Chicago Tribune

Christian Science Monitor

Daily Era (Bradford, Pennsylvania)

Daily Evening Bulletin (San Francisco)

Daily News (Galveston, Texas)

Hartford Courant

Lange, Fred W. *History of Baseball in California and Pacific Coast Leagues* (Oakland: Fred Lange, 1938).

Daily Star (Lincoln, Nebraska)

Los Angeles Times

Morris, Peter. *A Game of Inches: The Stories Behind the Innovations That Shaped Baseball, The Game on the Field* (Chicago: Ivan R. Dee, 2006).

New York Times

Oakland Tribune

SABR.org

San Antonio Gazette

Spalding, John E. *Always on Sunday: The California Baseball League, 1886 to 1915* (Manhattan, Kansas: Ag Press, 1992).

Sporting Life

Titusville (Pennsylvania) Herald

Washington Post

NOTES

1   *Oakland Tribune*, July 3, 1889.

2   Ibid.

3   Ibid.

4   *Oakland Tribune*, July 16, 1890.

5   *Los Angeles Times*, March 12, 1890.

6   *Oakland Tribune*, June 18, 1890.

7   Ibid.

8   *Sporting Life*, April 18, 1891.

9   *San Francisco Daily Evening Bulletin*, May 1, 1891.

10   *San Francisco Daily Evening Bulletin*, 1891.

11   *Oakland Tribune*, May 4, 1892.

12   *Oakland Tribune*, September 28, 1892.

13   *Sporting Life*, June 10, 1893.

14   *Galveston Daily News*, February 2, 1896.

15   *Hartford Courant*, November 17, 1937.

16   *Lincoln Star*, November 14, 1915.

17   *Washington Post*, September 27, 1920.

18   *Boston Globe*, November 17, 1937.

EDDIE BENNETT

By Peter Morris

ANY OBJECTIVE SUMMARY OF Eddie Bennett's contributions to baseball makes him seem at best a minor figure in the game's history. Yet during the 1920s and early 1930s, his evident devotion for the game made him a powerful symbol to many fans. Although his time in the limelight was brief, there are signs that he has not been entirely forgotten.

Eddie was born in Flatbush section of Brooklyn in 1903; any chance at a career in baseball appeared over after an accident during infancy left him with a serious spinal injury. The life of the handicapped youngster was further blighted when both of his parents died in the 1918 influenza epidemic.

In 1919 Bennett's fortunes took a dramatic turn for the better when he attended a Yankees game at the Polo Grounds. Happy Felsch, center fielder of the visiting White Sox, noticed Eddie's smile and, sharing the superstitions of many ballplayers of the era, told teammates that "a hunchback should be lucky for him."[1] When Felsch did indeed have a good day, he and Eddie Cicotte persuaded manager Kid Gleason to hire Eddie as a batboy and unofficial mascot.

It seems most likely that these events occurred during a July 30 doubleheader, if we are to believe later accounts that the White Sox lost the first game but then rebounded in the second game. But the details don't match exactly and there is no contemporary documentation, so Bennett's first appearance in a major-league dugout may well have taken place on a different date.

It's equally unclear how long he remained with the White Sox. Sportswriter Westbrook Pegler reported in 1926 that the White Sox collected $200 for Bennett at the end of the 1919 Black Sox World Series.[2] But SABR researchers Jack Kavanagh and Norman Macht have noted that he does not appear in any team photos or in photos of the World Series, and suggested that Bennett probably remained with the club for only a couple of 1919 regular-season series.[3]

After the White Sox lost that fall's World Series, and Felsch and Cicotte were subsequently banned for life for their role in the resulting scandal, it seemed natural to assume that Eddie Bennett's stint in baseball had ended almost before it had begun. Instead, Bennett began to frequent Ebbets Field in 1920, and one of the Brooklyn Robins players decided that he would be a good-luck charm.

The Robins won that year's pennant and faced Cleveland in a best-of-nine World Series. The first three games were played at Ebbets Field, and the Robins pulled out two of them. But then the series moved to Cleveland for four games, and Eddie Bennett was left behind in Brooklyn. After the Indians won four straight games to capture the championship, fingers were pointed. Bennett, it was said, had been distraught over being left behind and had put a curse on the Robins, resulting in the team's collapse.[4]

This version of events may have helped Bennett gain employment as the Yankees' mascot and batboy in 1921. While mascots and batboys had been part of baseball since the 1880s, including such notable ones as Charles "Victory" Faust, there had never been one quite like Eddie. He remained in that dual role for almost 12 years and saw the Yankees capture seven pennants and four World Series titles.

During that time, Bennett became perhaps the best-known batboy in baseball history. As Joseph Herzberg later wrote, he "was No. 1 man, the envy of the kids, who wondered why Eddie got paid for what they considered a rare and wondrous privilege, not only of seeing a ball game free every day but of sitting on the same bench and rubbing shoulders with Ruth, Gehrig

... and all the rest of the mighty men of Yankee Stadium."[5]

Yet although he was the envy of many, it was impossible to begrudge Bennett his good fortune. This was not only because of his handicap, but also because he immersed himself in his duties with such single-mindedness. Bennett, as Westbrook Pegler explained, "raised the job of bat boy from a summer pastime to a solemn and responsible business."[6]

Perhaps it was precisely because Eddie Bennett had no thought of hogging the limelight that he became a minor celebrity in his own right. Westbook Pegler noted in 1932: "Eddie's picture has shown in all the papers at one time or another in the last 13 years and stories have been written around and about him on many a rainy day."[7]

In almost 12 years as Yankees batboy, during which he aged from a teenager to a man of nearly 30, he never showed any sign that he viewed his job with any less reverence than the young fans who envied him. He lived with evident joy and with his heart on his sleeve, just as they would have done in his place. And, as Pegler observed, he never for a moment lost sight of the reality that the players were the show, and that his was a supporting role: "There are about 100 bats to be kept straight and counted and watched in Eddie's job, and of course he isn't required to carry this cord of wood onto the field and off, but only to mind his business, keep out of gossip and arguments, and mind the clubs."[8]

Eddie was always the first to shake the hand of a Yankees slugger after a home run and he became integral to the rituals of many players. Ace relief pitcher Wilcy Moore insisted that Bennett catch his first warm-up toss, and many of the players allowed nobody else to handle their bats, even after Eddie was given an assistant.

One of Bennett's closest relationships was with Babe Ruth. According to Herzberg, "Ruth used to make laughs for early comers at the Stadium by having a game of catch with Eddie. They would start ten feet

Batboy Eddie Bennett with the New York Yankees, circa 1921 (Bain Collection, Library of Congress, Prints and Photographs Division)

or so apart, tossing the ball to each other. Ruth then would throw it about a foot above the reach of the stumpy mascot. Eddie would dutifully chase the ball, and Ruth would heave it again just high enough to elude Eddie's fingers. Eddie would jabber angrily at the Babe, who would stare back in wide-eyed innocence, only to throw the ball over Eddie's head once more and keep throwing it over his head until Eddie was backed up against the screen behind home plate."[9]

This seems cruel to modern sensibilities, but the affection between the two men was mutual and genuine. Bennett doted on the Babe and knelt alongside him in the on-deck circle before each at-bat. He never missed an opportunity to run an errand for Ruth, such as bringing the great slugger regular dollops of bicarbonate of soda.

Ruth seems to have been just as fond of Eddie Bennett. After first meeting his future wife, Claire, it was Bennett whom he entrusted to deliver an admiring note. One of the batboy's most treasured possessions was a baseball that had been signed by Ruth, upon which Eddie had inscribed, "This was the last ball pitched in the 1921 World Series."

They were, Westbrook Pegler noted, "the two orphans on the Yankee ball club who made the baseball bat their weapon in life and achieved a lot of glory, each in his own way"[10] And as their rapport in the on-deck circle suggested, the two men also seemed to share a deeper bond: both retained a childlike ability to openly show their emotions. Many men wished to be Babe Ruth, but Bennett was one of the few who felt no self-consciousness about his admiration for the Babe. And perhaps Ruth saw Bennett and realized that, had fate treated him differently, he might well be in the batboy's shoes.

Another kindred spirit was pitcher Urban Shocker. When Shocker returned to the Yankees in 1925, he was unable to sleep lying down because of a serious mitral valve disorder. But the pitcher was unwilling to let any of his teammates know about his condition, so he roomed on the road with Eddie Bennett. No doubt the two men felt a special bond as a result of their respective disabilities.

Shocker died in 1928 and the next year Bennett lost another valued compatriot with the passing of long-time Yankee skipper Miller Huggins. Bennett's emotional attachment to the Yankees was nowhere better symbolized than by Huggins' death. While few members of the team were grief-stricken by the passing of the crusty manager, Bennett wept unashamedly throughout the evening after learning the news.

Perhaps with the passing of two close associates, Eddie Bennett sensed that his glorious run was drawing to a close. On May 19, 1932, he was hit by a taxicab and suffered a broken leg. The injury healed slowly, and he had to watch the World Series on crutches. By the following spring it was clear that he would not recover fully, and so he relinquished the job that he had loved so dearly. Yankee owner Jacob Ruppert continued to support Bennett financially, but Eddie was unable to find anything to take the place of his beloved role at Yankee Stadium.

He began drinking heavily to ease the pain from his injuries and, after a three-week bout of especially heavy drinking, died of alcoholism in his rented room on January 16, 1935. He was surrounded by memories of his glory days: "[T]he walls were covered with

autographed pictures of ballplayers. Piled everywhere were gloves, bats, score cards, clippings of stories of ball games. He had a drawer full of signed baseballs."[11] Two of the centerpieces were the Ruth baseball and a team photo of the 1928 world champions with Eddie front and center.

Eddie had no known relatives, so the Yankees paid for his funeral and his burial at St. John's Cemetery in Queens. Ruth was still abroad on a tour that had begun in Japan and unable to attend, nor did any other ballplayers. But the entire Yankees office staff, including Paul Krichell, Mark Roth, George Perry, Gene McCann, and Charlie McManus, was on hand to pay final respects to the team's loyal mascot and batboy.

The decades since Eddie Bennett's passing have naturally dimmed memories of him, but there are those who still remember him and they do so with genuine fondness. Legendary investor Warren Buffett used three paragraphs of his 2002 annual report to stockholders to explain why Eddie Bennett was his "managerial model." After recapping Bennett's career, Buffett concluded, "What does this have to do with management? It's simple—to be a winner, work with winners. In 1927, for example, Eddie received $700 for the one-eighth World Series share voted him by the legendary Yankee team of Ruth and Gehrig. This sum, which Eddie earned by working only four days (because New York swept the Series) was roughly equal to the full-year pay then earned by batboys who worked with regular associates."[12]

The message, Buffett explained, was as simple and straightforward as the unassuming way in which Bennett went about his business: "Eddie understood that how he lugged bats was unimportant; what counted instead was hooking up with the cream of those on the playing field. I've learned from Eddie. At Berkshire [Hathaway], I regularly hand bats to many of the heaviest hitters in American business."[13]

Westbrook Pegler may have given the best concise summary of Eddie Bennett's appeal when he wrote: "Eddie Just Minds Bats and His Own Business." Who better than Warren Buffett to grasp that this was

Eddie Bennett's essence and use it as a model for his own approach?

SOURCES

Berkshire Hathaway Inc., 2002 Annual Report.

Creamer, Robert W., *Babe* (New York: Simon & Schuster, 1974).

"Funeral Services for Eddie Bennett," *New York Times*, January 20, 1935, 32.

Herzberg, Joseph, "Eddie Bennett, 31, Passes in His Room From Alcoholism; His Luck Credited for Championships as Much as Ruth's Hits; Envy of Boy Fans," *New York Herald Tribune*, January 18, 1935.

Kavanagh, Jack, and Norman Macht, *Uncle Robbie* (Cleveland: SABR, 1999).

Pegler, Westbrook, "Nobody's Business," *Chicago Tribune*, February 28, 1932.

Pegler, Westbrook, "The Sporting Goods," *Chicago Tribune*, January 10, 1926.

Schechter, Gabriel, *Victory Faust* (New York: Charles April, 2000).

Smelser, Marshall, *The Life That Ruth Built* (New York: Quadrangle, 1975)

Steinberg, Steve, personal communications.

NOTES

1   *New York Herald Tribune*, January 18, 1935.

2   *Chicago Tribune*, January 10, 1926.

3   Jack Kavanagh and Norman Macht, *Uncle Robbie* (Cleveland: SABR, 1999).

4   *Chicago Tribune*, January 10, 1926.

5   *New York Herald Tribune*, January 18, 1935.

6   *Chicago Tribune*, January 10, 1926.

7   *Chicago Tribune*, February 28, 1932.

8   Ibid.

9   *New York Herald Tribune*, January 18, 1935.

10   *Chicago Tribune*, February 28, 1932.

11   *New York Times*, January 20, 1935.

12   Berkshire Hathaway Inc., 2002 Annual Report.

13   Ibid.

SEASON TIMELINE: SEPTEMBER 1919

White Sox record: 13-10 (.565)
Runs scored: 124 | Runs allowed: 90

AL standings
September 30, 1919

Team	W	L	Pct	GB
CHW	88	52	.629	—
CLE	84	55	.604	3½
NYY	80	59	.576	7½
DET	80	60	.571	8
BOS	66	71	.482	20½
SLB	67	72	.482	20½
WSH	56	84	.400	32
PHA	36	104	.257	52

PLAYER OF THE MONTH

	G	PA	AB	R	H	2B	3B	HR	RBI	SB	BB	SO	BA	OBP	SLG	OPS
Happy Felsch	21	92	86	12	33	8	3	2	12	2	4	6	.384	.411	.616	1.027

After a rough first half, the 28-year-old center fielder was red-hot in September, reaching base at least once in every game he played. He hit .413 during a 12-game, four-city road trip in the middle of the month, highlighted by a 4-for-5, 3-RBI performance in the second game of a doubleheader sweep of the Yankees on September 17 at the Polo Grounds.

PITCHER OF THE MONTH

	W	L	ERA	G	GS	CG	SHO	IP	H	R	ER	BB	SO	WHIP
Dickey Kerr	3	3	2.23	6	5	4	1	48⅓	47	16	12	11	16	1.200

The rookie left-hander from Texas made his case for a prominent spot in the White Sox' World Series plans with a solid showing in September. He shut out the New York Yankees on seven hits on September 17 and then, one week later, held the St. Louis Browns at bay with two shutout innings in relief of Eddie Cicotte as the White Sox clinched the American League pennant on Shoeless Joe Jackson's walk-off single at Comiskey Park. Kerr also was valuable as an innings-eater for manager Kid Gleason, who was trying to rest his stars, Cicotte and Lefty Williams, for the World Series.

DAY BY DAY RECAP

Monday, September 1
Navin Field, Detroit
"Sox Beat Tigers Twice, and Can Hear That Pennant Flap" — *Chicago Tribune*

White Sox (76-42)   000   200   211—6 14 1
Tigers (68-49)   000   000   000—0 8 0
WP: Lefty Williams (22-8). LP: Hooks Dauss (19-7).
Lefty Williams: 9 IP, 8 H, 0 R, 0 ER, 0 BB, 4 K.
Nemo Leibold: 3-4, 2 2B, R. Happy Felsch: 2-4, 2B, 2 RBI. Buck Weaver: 2-3, 2 R, RBI.

White Sox (77-42)   000   003   110—5 9 3
Tigers (68-50)   100   000   000—1 4 0
WP: Eddie Cicotte (27-7). LP: Bernie Boland (13-12).
Eddie Cicotte: 9 IP, 4 H, 1 R, 0 ER, 1 BB, 6 K.
Joe Jackson: 2-4, HR, 2 R, 2 RBI. Swede Risberg: 1-4, 2B, 2 RBI. Eddie Collins: 2-4, RBI.

Tuesday, September 2
Navin Field, Detroit
"Tigers Take Hectic 16 Inning Battle From White Sox, 4-3" — *Chicago Tribune*

White Sox (77-43)   000   012   000   000   000   0—3 17 1
Tigers (69-50)   021   000   000   000   000   1—4 14 4
WP: Howard Ehmke (15-9). LP: Dickey Kerr (10-5).
Dickey Kerr: 15⅓ IP, 14 H, 4 R, 3 ER, 4 BB, 4 K.
Happy Felsch: 3-8, 2B, 3B. Eddie Collins: 2-6, 2 BB. Dickey Kerr: 3-7, R, RBI.

Wednesday, September 3
Scheduled day off
"Reds Beat Alex, 6-1; White Sox Watching Future Foes" — *Chicago Tribune*

Thursday, September 4
Scheduled day off
"Sox and Indians Start Crucial Series Today" — *Chicago Tribune*

Friday, September 5
Comiskey Park, Chicago
"White Sox Defeat Cleveland, 9-1, Before 25,000 Crowd" — *Chicago Tribune*

Indians (70-50)   000   000   100—1 6 3
White Sox (78-43) 130   020   03x—9 13 1
WP: Eddie Cicotte (28-7). LP: Elmer Myers (5-6).
Eddie Cicotte: 9 IP, 6 H, 1 R, 0 ER, 6 BB, 4 K.
Buck Weaver: 3-4, 2B, 2 R. Swede Risberg: 2-3, 2B, 2 R, BB. Eddie Cicotte: 2-3, R, BB.

Saturday, September 6
Comiskey Park, Chicago
"Swats, Boots and Walks Give Indians Win Over Sox, 11 to 2" — *Chicago Tribune*

Indians (71-50)   110   242   001 — 11 11 1
White Sox (78-44)   000   001   001 — 2 14 2
WP: Jim Bagby (16-9). LP: Lefty Williams (22-9).
Lefty Williams: 4 IP, 6 H, 4 R, 3 ER, 1 BB, 2 K.
Eddie Collins: 2-4, BB. Buck Weaver: 1-4, R, 3 SB. Joe Jackson: 2-5, R.

Sunday, September 7
Comiskey Park, Chicago
"White Sox Bump Fading Pennant Hopes of Indians, 8-3" — *Chicago Tribune*

Indians (71-51)   200   000   100 — 3 7 0
White Sox (79-44)   140   003   00x — 8 12 0
WP: Dickey Kerr (11-5). LP: Stan Coveleski (21-11).
Dickey Kerr: 9 IP, 7 H, 3 R, 3 ER, 2 BB, 3 K.
Joe Jackson: 3-4, 2B, RBI. Eddie Collins: 1-3, 2B, R, 2 RBI. Ray Schalk: 2-2, 2 R, 2 RBI, 2 BB.

Monday, September 8
Scheduled day off
"Sox to Battle Senators Today in Hot Capital" — *Chicago Tribune*

Tuesday, September 9
Griffith Stadium, Washington
"Bill James Beats Johnson, Sox Copping Victory, 2-0" — *Chicago Tribune*

White Sox (80-44)   000   000   020 — 2 6 0
Senators (47-78)   000   000   000 — 0 5 0
WP: Bill James (6-7). LP: Walter Johnson (19-14).
Bill James: 9 IP, 5 H, 0 R, 0 ER, 4 BB, 2 K.
Nemo Leibold: 2-3, BB, SB, RBI. Ray Schalk: 1-3, R. Eddie Collins: 0-2, BB, RBI.

Wednesday, September 10
Postponed, rain
"Sox Game Postponed by Damp Grass, Then Pilots Fuss" — *Chicago Tribune*

Thursday, September 11
Griffith Stadium, Washington
"Sox and Griffs Divide Their Final Show of Year, 4-3; 5-0" — *Chicago Tribune*

White Sox (80-45)   003   000   000 — 3 4 0
Senators (48-78)   310   000   00x — 4 9 1
WP: Jim Shaw (17-15). LP: Dickey Kerr (11-6).
Dickey Kerr: 8 IP, 9 H, 4 R, 4 ER, 0 BB, 5 K.
Joe Jackson: 1-4, R, RBI. Dickey Kerr: 1-3, R. Happy Felsch: 1-3, BB, RBI.

White Sox (81-45)   010   000   211 — 5 8 0
Senators (48-79)   000   000   000 — 0 2 2
WP: Lefty Williams (23-9). LP: Tom Zachary (1-3).
Lefty Williams: 9 IP, 2 H, 0 R, 0 ER, 3 BB, 6 K.
Swede Risberg: 3-4, SB, R, RBI. Eddie Collins: 2-4, 2B, SB, BB, RBI. Happy Felsch: 1-3, 3B, BB, R, RBI.

Friday, September 12
Shibe Park, Philadelphia
"Gleason Springs Kid Hurler to Trim Mack's Youngsters, 7-0" — *Chicago Tribune*

White Sox (82-45)   600   010   000 — 7 11 0
Athletics (34-92)   000   000   000 — 0 5 2
WP: Roy Wilkinson (1-0). LP: Lefty York (0-1).
Roy Wilkinson: 9 IP, 5 H, 0 R, 0 ER, 6 BB, 1 K.
Eddie Collins: 2-4, 3B, 2 R. Swede Risberg: 2-4, 2B, R. Roy Wilkinson: 2-3, 2B, BB.

Saturday, September 13
Shibe Park, Philadelphia
"Sox Advance Pennantward by Whaling Macks, 8 to 2" — *Chicago Tribune*

White Sox (83-45)   003   102   200 — 8 9 2
Athletics (34-93)   110   000   000 — 2 6 3
WP: Grover Lowdermilk (5-5). LP: Jimmy Zinn (1-2).
Grover Lowdermilk: 9 IP, 6 H, 2 R, 2 ER, 3 BB, 3 K.
Swede Risberg: 3-4, 2B, 2 R. Happy Felsch: 2-4, 3B, R. Nemo Leibold: 2-4, 2 R, BB.

Sunday, September 14
Scheduled day off
"Sox May Play Boston Games in Brooklyn Park" — *Chicago Tribune*

(Note: The Boston police strike and subsequent riots concerned manager Kid Gleason, but the situation had quieted by the time the White Sox arrived in Boston on September 19.)

Monday, September 15
Shibe Park, Philadelphia
"Faber Hurls Sox to Victory, Macks' Rally Failing, 11-10" — *Chicago Tribune*

White Sox (84-45)   330   100   301 — 11 13 2
Athletics (34-94)   003   000   016 — 10 13 2
WP: Red Faber (11-9). LP: Lefty York (0-2).
Red Faber: 9 IP, 13 H, 10 R, 8 ER, 2 BB, 4 K.
Happy Felsch: 2-4, 2B, HR, 2 R, 4 RBI. Joe Jackson: 2-3, 2B, 3B, 3 R, 2 RBI. Eddie Collins: 1-3, 2 SB, 2 BB, 2 R, RBI.

Tuesday, September 16
Postponed, rain
"Eddie Collins Idle as He Passes 13th Milestone as Major" — *Chicago Tribune*

Wednesday, September 17
Polo Grounds, New York
"White Sox Cop Pair and the Flag Race is About Over" — *Chicago Tribune*

White Sox (85-45) 000   001   001 — 2 7 1
Yankees (70-57)   000   000   000 — 0 7 1
WP: Dickey Kerr (12-6). LP: Jack Quinn (14-13).
Dickey Kerr: 9 IP, 7 H, 0 R, 0 ER, 1 BB, 3 K.
Buck Weaver: 2-3, HR, R, 2 RBI. Dickey Kerr: 1-3, R. Chick Gandil: 1-3.

White Sox (86-45) 211   023   200 — 11 19 2
Yankees (70-58)   000   001   010 — 2 9 2
WP: Bill James (7-7). LP: Hank Thormahlen (11-8).
Bill James: 9 IP, 9 H, 2 R, 1 ER, 2 BB, 1 K.
Eddie Collins: 5-6, 2B, 3 SB, 3 R. Happy Felsch: 4-5, 2B, SB, 3 RBI. Nemo Leibold: 3-5, 2B, 3 RBI.

Thursday, September 18
Polo Grounds, New York
"Sox Lose to Yanks and Delay Clinching of Flag" — *Chicago Tribune*

White Sox (86-46) 200   001   010 — 4 9 1
Yankees (71-58)   006   000   00x — 6 13 2
WP: Carl Mays (12-14). LP: Erskine Mayer (6-5).
Erskine Mayer: 3 IP, 8 H, 6 R, 6 ER, 2 BB, 1 K.
Joe Jackson: 3-5, 2B, R, 2 RBI. Ray Schalk: 2-4, 2B, RBI. Eddie Collins: 0-3, R, SB, 2 BB.

Friday, September 19
Fenway Park, Boston
"Cicotte Puts Sox Within One Game of Clinching the Flag" — *Chicago Tribune*

White Sox (87-46) 020   000   010 — 3 10 3
Red Sox (63-67)   101   000   000 — 2 7 1
WP: Eddie Cicotte (29-7). LP: Waite Hoyt (4-5).
Eddie Cicotte: 9 IP, 7 H, 2 R, 1 ER, 0 BB, 3 K.
Ray Schalk: 3-4, RBI. Chick Gandil: 1-3, 2B, R. Swede Risberg: 1-4, R, RBI.

Saturday, September 20
Fenway Park, Boston
"Boston Impedes Sox Dash to Flag by Winning Pair" — *Chicago Tribune*

White Sox (87-47) 000   201   000 — 3 9 0
Red Sox (64-67)   300   000   001 — 4 5 1
WP: Allen Russell (15-7). LP: Lefty Williams (23-10).

Lefty Williams: 8⅓ IP, 5 H, 4 R, 4 ER, 2 BB, 5 K.
Buck Weaver: 2-4, 2 2B, 2 R. Joe Jackson: 2-4, R, RBI. Happy Felsch: 2-4, 2B, RBI.

White Sox (87-48)   000   130   000 — 4 14 3
Red Sox (65-67)   002   210   00x — 5 10 0
WP: Herb Pennock (16-8). LP: Dickey Kerr (12-7). SV: Allen Russell (5).
Dickey Kerr: 5 IP, 8 H, 5 R, 2 ER, 4 BB, 0 K.
Buck Weaver: 2-5, 2 2B, 2 R, RBI. Eddie Collins: 2-5, 2B, R, RBI. Chick Gandil: 2-4, 2B, RBI.

Sunday, September 21
Scheduled day off
"Victories of Sox and Reds Upset Major League Dope" — *Chicago Tribune*

Monday, September 22
Scheduled day off
"Forget That Worry About Sox Hurlers, Says Kid Gleason" — *Chicago Tribune*

Tuesday, September 23
Scheduled day off
"Cicotte Will Pitch and Sox Expect to Clinch Flag Today" — *Chicago Tribune*

Wednesday, September 24
Comiskey Park, Chicago
"White Sox Crown Themselves American League Champs" — *Chicago Tribune*

Browns (65-71)   301   000   100 — 5 13 1
White Sox (88-48) 000   020   202 — 6 14 0
WP: Dickey Kerr (13-7). LP: Allan Sothoron (20-12).
Eddie Cicotte: 7 IP, 11 H, 5 R, 5 ER, 1 BB, 4 K.
Joe Jackson: 2-5, GW RBI. Nemo Leibold: 3-5, 2B, 2 R. Ray Schalk: 2-3, R, BB.

Thursday, September 25
Comiskey Park, Chicago
"White Sox Ease Up a Bit and Lose to Browns, 3 to 1" — *Chicago Tribune*

Browns (66-71)   010   000   020 — 3 9 4
White Sox (88-49) 010   000   000 — 1 8 0
WP: Elam Vangilder (1-0). LP: Lefty Williams (23-11).
Lefty Williams: 9 IP, 9 H, 3 R, 3 ER, 0 BB, 3 K.
Eddie Collins: 3-4. Shano Collins: 1-4, R. Swede Risberg: 1-4, RBI.

Friday, September 26
Comiskey Park, Chicago
"Tigers Pound Ball for Sixteen Swats, Beating Champs, 10-7" — *Chicago Tribune*

Tigers (78-60)   001   134   010 — 10 19 8

White Sox (88-50)   000   203   002 — 7 13 4
WP: Hooks Dauss (21-9). LP: John Sullivan (0-1).
John Sullivan: 9 IP, 19 H, 10 R, 5 ER, 5 BB, 6 K.
Nemo Leibold: 2-4, BB, 2 R. Eddie Murphy: 2-3, 2B, R. Hervey McClellan: 2-3, R.

Saturday, September 27
Comiskey Park, Chicago
"Sox Drop Scrap to Detroit, 7-5, in Tenth Round" — *Chicago Tribune*

Tigers (79-60)   101   003   000   2 — 7 14 1
White Sox (88-51) 031   100   000   0 — 5 13 0
WP: Slim Love (5-4). LP: Erskine Mayer (6-6).
Win Noyes: 6 IP, 10 H, 5 R, 5 ER, 0 BB, 4 K.
Swede Risberg: 2-4, HR. Happy Felsch: 1-4, HR. Fred McMullin: 1-4, 3B, R.

Sunday, September 28
Comiskey Park, Chicago
"Gleasons Give Last Game to Tigers, 10-9; Cicotte in Workout" — *Chicago Tribune*

Tigers (80-60)   102   400   030 — 10 13 4
White Sox (88-52) 201   101   211 — 9 19 3
WP: Slim Love (6-4). LP: Roy Wilkinson (1-1).
Eddie Cicotte: 2 IP, 3 H, 1 R, 1 ER, 0 BB, 1 K.
Buck Weaver: 3-4, 2 3B, SB, R. Chick Gandil: 3-4, 2B. Happy Felsch: 2-4, 2 R.

SEPTEMBER HIGHLIGHTS

Sox Clinch Pennant on Jackson's Walk-off Single: It took longer than expected, but the White Sox clinched their second AL pennant in three years on September 24 against the St. Louis Browns. After ace Eddie Cicotte faltered by allowing five runs and 11 hits in seven innings, the White Sox rallied to score two runs in the seventh and then tied the game on a Buck Weaver sacrifice fly with the bases loaded in the ninth. Up stepped Shoeless Joe Jackson with a chance to make history. He took a "vicious swat" at Allan Sothoron's pitch and lined it to deep right-center field. The *Chicago Tribune* reported the hit would have gone "for two or three bases under ordinary circumstances," but the White Sox mobbed Jackson after Nemo Leibold strolled across home plate with the winning run in a 6-5 White Sox victory. No American League team had ever clinched a pennant with a walk-off victory and the feat wouldn't be accomplished again for a quarter-century.

The Infamous Cicotte 30-Win Bonus: It has long been thought that one of the reasons Eddie Cicotte entered into the World Series fix was that he was angry at White Sox owner Charles Comiskey for promising him a $10,000 bonus if he won 30 games — and then benching him for two weeks in September. But there's simply no evidence to substantiate the theory. It's true that Cicotte, whose salary in 1919 was $5,000, did not make any appearances down the stretch between September 6-18. But after Cicotte uncharacteristically walked six Indians batters on September 5, the *Chicago Tribune* and *Cleveland Plain Dealer* reported that he was suffering from a sore arm and Cicotte himself admitted to the *New York Times* that he needed a rest. (On the other hand, manager Kid Gleason strongly *denied* that Cicotte's arm was tired, insisting the long layoff was just to keep his ace fresh for the best-of-nine World Series in which he hoped to use Cicotte at least three times.) Following Cicotte's victorious return on September 19 against the Red Sox, *The Sporting News* reported that his arm had "responded to rest and treatment the last two weeks." Afterward, the pitcher reportedly was allowed to leave the team to go visit his family in Detroit. In any case, Cicotte did have a chance to win his 30th game—and clinch the AL pennant—in his next start, on September 24 against the Browns. But he allowed five runs and 11 hits in seven innings and was relieved by Dickey Kerr before the White Sox rallied to win 6-5. As for the bonus, recent research by historian Bob Hoie has shown that Cicotte and Comiskey did agree to a "substantial" off-contract bonus in 1918, which Cicotte failed to earn in a subpar, war-shortened season. But after Cicotte rebounded to go 29-7 in 1919, Comiskey paid a $3,000 bonus to his star pitcher after the season. Hoie speculates that the bonus was likely a carryover from the 1918 agreement. Including bonuses, Cicotte was the second-highest-compensated pitcher in baseball, behind future Hall of Famer Walter Johnson.

World Series Lengthened to Nine Games: Entering September, Charles Comiskey didn't know that the White Sox might have to win five games in a span of nine days to win the World Series. But on September 2, Cincinnati Reds owner Garry Herrmann, who also served as chairman of the National Commission, proposed extending the World Series to a best-of-nine affair in order to accommodate the massive demand for tickets among fans in his city. Herrmann surely knew—and so did Comiskey—that the Reds had a much deeper pitching staff than the White Sox and would benefit from a longer schedule. Comiskey opposed the plan, saying, "We have got along all right for nearly fifteen years (with a best-of-seven series) and everybody has been satisfied.… Lengthening the series by one or two games will not help solve [the] problem, because everybody will want to see all the games played in Cincinnati, all the same … as I have learned by experience." On September 11, Herrmann announced that the nine-game plan had been approved by a majority of league owners. But the idea only lasted three seasons, from 1919 to 1921, before the World Series returned to a best-of-seven format.

Turmoil at the Top: While Charles Comiskey's team was on its way to a pennant in the fall of 1919, the White Sox owner was involved in a fierce fight to oust American League President Ban Johnson as the de facto head of baseball's governing body, the National Commission. In July Johnson suspended pitcher Carl Mays after the Boston Red Sox traded the disgruntled star to the New York Yankees, in a unilateral attempt to void the deal. The decision ignited a civil war between the AL owners that would ultimately result in the hiring of federal judge Kenesaw Mountain Landis as baseball's first commissioner in 1920. But in September 1919, Comiskey, Red Sox owner Harry Frazee, and Yankees co-owner Jacob Ruppert held a series of high-profile meetings in Chicago to investigate Johnson's actions and censure their former ally. After the three "Insurrectionist" owners threatened to join with the National League to form a new 12-team circuit, Johnson backed down and Mays went on to pitch five seasons for the Yankees. But the feud between Johnson and Comiskey continued, and when the AL president saw an opportunity to hurt Comiskey by investigating rumors that White Sox players had thrown the 1919 World Series, he put the full resources of the American League to use, tracking down key witnesses and digging up dirt on the accused players before their criminal trial.

Early Betting Odds Favor Chicago: With the White Sox looking like a sure bet to win the pennant, wagers on the World Series began long before they actually clinched. Betting on baseball was big business in 1919, with the *New York Times* estimating that more than $2 million changed hands during the World Series at betting establishments within the city. And while many baseball experts thought the Reds had a realistic chance to beat the White Sox on the level—pitching depth was the factor most commonly cited as the difference-maker—bettors around the country considered the Sox to be heavy favorites, enabling high-rolling gamblers like Arnold Rothstein to make a considerable profit if they got their bets down early. In the week leading up to Game One on October 1, bookies in Chicago and New York were taking 10-to-7 odds on the White Sox to win it all. The *Chicago Tribune* reported, "Even in Redland, the bettors, after a patriotic flash of even money, are now asking odds of 6 to 5 for wagers of any considerable amount." On the final day of the season, the *Cincinnati Enquirer* noted, "So far very little betting has been done on the Series. There is plenty of White Sox money in town, but it is being offered at evens or 6 to 5 at the best, and the local speculators are holding out for better odds." That would all change by the conclusion of Game One, when the Reds pounded Eddie Cicotte and the White Sox, 9-1, and changed the fate of the World Series.

WALKING OFF TO THE WORLD SERIES

By Jacob Pomrenke

ON SEPTEMBER 24, 1919, Shoeless Joe Jackson stepped up to the plate at Comiskey Park in the bottom of the ninth inning with a chance to make history for the Chicago White Sox.

The score stood at 5-5 with one out. The winning run — the American League *pennant-clinching* run — stood on third base in the form of Nemo Leibold. Jackson stepped in to face 20-game winner Allan Sothoron, on the mound for the St. Louis Browns. The right-handed spitballer was enjoying his finest season, but he was undoubtedly tiring in this ninth-inning jam after having allowed 13 hits to the White Sox. Jackson, Chicago's powerful cleanup hitter boasting a .349 average, was the last man in the lineup Sothoron wanted to see right now.

The Browns had taken a 5-2 lead off White Sox ace Eddie Cicotte after 6½ innings, but the first-place White Sox were the toughest team in the major leagues to put away. On 13 previous occasions they had rallied from a deficit after the seventh inning to win; their propensity to score runs late made them dangerous in any situation.

The Sox had almost tied the game in the seventh, but Eddie Collins, Chicago's team captain and a future Hall of Famer, was thrown out at the plate on an "extremely close" play. Collins protested the decision so vigorously that he was ejected from the game by umpire George Hildebrand (or as the *Chicago Tribune* reported it: "banished from the scrap by a peevish umpire for kicking over a hairline decision.")

Cicotte, seeking his 30th victory, had been battered around by the Browns for five runs and he was removed for a pinch-hitter in the bottom of the seventh. The 35-year-old veteran with an intoxicating "shine ball" had won six straight starts and even picked up two wins in relief since August 15.

A side note deserves mention here: One of the most compelling scenes in the 1988 film *Eight Men Out* shows Eddie Cicotte (played by David Strathairn) arguing with owner Charles Comiskey (played by Clifton James) about a promised bonus for winning 30 games. Comiskey's miserliness is given as a reason why Cicotte joined the World Series fix, but later research has shown that this bonus was never promised. In fact, Cicotte did have his chances to win 30 games in 1919, including on this Wednesday afternoon in late September at Comiskey Park. But with the White Sox needing a win to secure their berth in the World Series and with his ace pitcher struggling, manager Kid Gleason decided to replace Cicotte, down by three runs in the seventh.

Gleason selected rookie left-hander Dickey Kerr to come on in relief of Cicotte. In the Deadball Era, long before bullpen specialization, Kerr was something of a relief specialist for the White Sox. In 1919 and '20, he compiled an 11-2 record with a 2.80 ERA out of the bullpen. As the White Sox rallied against the St. Louis Browns on September 24, Kerr held his opponents at bay with two scoreless innings.

Meanwhile, the White Sox scored twice against Sothoron in the seventh, cutting the Browns' lead to 5-4. In the ninth Kerr led off with a single and moved to third on Nemo Leibold's base hit. Utility infielder Fred McMullin, who had taken Eddie Collins's place in the lineup, worked Sothoron for a walk to load the bases. Then Buck Weaver slammed a long sacrifice fly to center field, which scored Kerr to tie the game and moved Leibold to third base. He was 90 feet away from clinching the pennant, with Shoeless Joe Jackson due up next.

The White Sox had been alone in first place since July 9, when Jackson had scored the go-ahead run in another patented late-inning rally to beat Connie Mack's Philadelphia Athletics. On September 24 the

Sox held a four-game lead over the Cleveland Indians with five left to play. Telegraph reports had already come in to Comiskey Park that the Indians had lost in Detroit, ensuring Chicago at least a share of its second AL pennant in three seasons. A win would send the White Sox to Cincinnati for a World Series matchup with the National League champion Reds.

Jackson came through with a flourish. He took a "vicious swat" at a Sothoron pitch and lined it to deep right-center field—the *Chicago Tribune* reported the hit would have gone "for two or three bases under ordinary circumstances"—but the White Sox mobbed Jackson after Leibold strolled across home plate with the winning run and a 6-5 White Sox victory.

Never before had an American League team clinched a pennant with a walk-off victory. The feat would not happen again for nearly a quarter-century.

In fact, a walk-off victory to clinch a World Series berth has happened only 20 times in baseball history (entering the 2015 season). In addition to Shoeless Joe Jackson in 1919, here are the others:

- **1903:** Claude Ritchey doubled to score Honus Wagner in the ninth as the Pittsburgh Pirates captured the first NL pennant in the World Series era with a 7-6 walk-off victory over the Boston Beaneaters on September 18.

- **1914:** George "Possum" Whitted drove in Johnny Evers with a game-winning double in the ninth to clinch the NL pennant for the "Miracle" Boston Braves with a 3-2 win over the Chicago Cubs on September 29.

- **1922:** George "High Pockets" Kelly singled in Frankie Frisch with the winning run in the 10th inning as the New York Giants won their second of four consecutive NL pennants with a 5-4 win over the St. Louis Cardinals on September 25.

- **1943:** Lou Klein beat out a potential inning-ending double play in the ninth and Ray Sanders scored the winning run from third base as the St. Louis

Cardinals clinched the pennant with a 2-1 victory over the Chicago Cubs on September 18.

- **1943:** One week later, Bill Dickey clinched the AL pennant for the New York Yankees with a 14th-inning single over second base to score Billy Johnson from second base and give the Yankees a 2-1 win over the St. Louis Browns on September 25.

- **1951:** Bobby Thomson's famous ninth-inning home run off Brooklyn's Ralph Branca sent the New York Giants to the World Series with a 5-4 win in the third and decisive game of an NL playoff tiebreaker.

- **1957:** Henry Aaron of the Milwaukee Braves lined an 11th-inning home run against the St. Louis Cardinals to clinch the NL pennant on September 23, the only other time besides Thomson that a walk-off home run won a pennant in the pre-divisional era.

Shoeless Joe Jackson's walk-off single to beat the St. Louis Browns on September 24, 1919, was the first time any American League team had clinched a pennant in such dramatic fashion. (Library of Congress, Prints and Photographs Division)

- **1959:** Carl Furillo hit an infield single in the 12th inning and Gil Hodges scored from second base on an errant throw by Felix Mantilla as the Los Angeles Dodgers beat the Milwaukee Braves 6-5 in Game Two of the NL playoff tiebreaker.

- **1968:** Don Wert of the Detroit Tigers hit a ninth-inning RBI single off Lindy McDaniel of the New York Yankees to clinch the AL pennant on September 17.

- **1972:** George Foster of the Cincinnati Reds scored on a ninth-inning wild pitch by Pittsburgh's Bob Moose to end Game Five of the NL Championship Series and send the Reds to the World Series.

- **1976:** Ken Griffey of the Cincinnati Reds hit an infield single to first base with the bases loaded to score Dave Concepcion in the ninth inning of Game Three of the NL Championship Series, breaking a 6-6 tie with the Philadelphia Phillies.

- **1976:** Chris Chambliss of the New York Yankees knocked out the Kansas City Royals with a ninth-inning homer in Game Five of the AL Championship Series.

- **1978:** Bill Russell of the Los Angeles Dodgers knocked out the Philadelphia Phillies with a 10th-inning single to score Ron Cey in Game Four of the NL Championship Series.

- **1992:** Francisco Cabrera of the Atlanta Braves drove in David Justice and Sid Bream with a two-run single in the ninth inning to down the Pittsburgh Pirates in Game Seven of the NL Championship Series.

- **1999:** Andruw Jones of the Atlanta Braves drew an 11th-inning bases-loaded walk from Kenny Rogers of the New York Mets to end Game Six of the NL Championship Series.

- **2002:** Kenny Lofton of the San Francisco Giants hit a single to right field, scoring David Bell from second base to beat the St. Louis Cardinals 2-1 and end Game Five of the NL Championship Series.

- **2003:** Aaron Boone's 11th-inning home run off Tim Wakefield of the Boston Red Sox ended Game Seven of the AL Championship Series, sending the New York Yankees to the Fall Classic.

- **2006:** Magglio Ordonez of the Detroit Tigers finished a sweep of the Oakland A's with a three-run home run in the ninth inning in Game Four of the AL Championship Series.

- **2014:** Travis Ishikawa of the San Francisco Giants hit a three-run home run in the ninth inning off Michael Wacha of the St. Louis Cardinals to end Game Five of the NL Championship Series.

The day after Jackson's game-ending blow, the *Chicago Tribune* feted the White Sox for their second pennant in three years. The headlines read "Gleasons' Fight Among Hardest in Flag Annals" and "Eddie Collins of White Sox Great Money Player in Game." But next to the game story on page 23 of the *Tribune* was a more ominous headline, previewing a World Series that would become the most notorious in baseball history:

"Bookies favor Sox."

Note: A version of this article first appeared at TheNationalPastimeMuseum.com. It is used with permission.

THE 1919 WORLD SERIES: A RECAP

By Rick Huhn

A GREAT DEAL HAS BEEN written about the faceoff between the Chicago White Sox and the Cincinnati Reds in the best-of-nine 1919 World Series. Probably no other baseball World Series has drawn more attention from commentators and historians. However, the vast majority of words written about the Series relate to what has become commonly known as the Black Sox Scandal. In that regard, discussion has centered on a few plays regarded as proving or, in some cases, disproving that certain players on the White Sox team conspired to throw the World Series at the behest of a group or groups of professional gamblers and for their own monetary gain.

Nonetheless, an eight-game series was played in which suspicion is cast on only a few key plays. There is even general agreement among knowledgeable observers that several of the games were played entirely on the up-and-up. What follows is a game-by-game description of this Series with minimal attention to the controversial plays. While some of the more obvious ones will be pointed out, the whys and wherefores will be left for others to study and write about here and elsewhere.

The Teams

The 1919 edition of Charles Comiskey's Chicago White Sox entered their second World Series in three seasons with an American League record of 88-52. They led the Cleveland Indians by 3½ games at season's end. Chicago hit .287 as a team and scored 668 runs, ranking the team number one in each category among AL teams. They had a team ERA of 3.04 (fourth in the AL) and allowed 534 runs (second). Their manager, William J. "Kid" Gleason, was in his first year in that position.

The Cincinnati Reds were owned by August "Garry" Herrmann and managed by Pat Moran, a veteran of four previous campaigns at the helm of the Philadelphia Phillies. The Reds' record of 96-44 was nine games better than the New York Giants in the National League pennant race. The Reds hit .263 as a team and scored 578 runs, both second-best figures among NL teams (to the Giants). They had a team ERA of 2.23 (second-best) and allowed an NL-low 401 runs. This was Cincinnati's first World Series appearance.

——————— **Game One** ———————

Wednesday, October 1
Redland Field, Cincinnati

"White Sox Lose in Opener, 9 to 1" —
Chicago Tribune
"Chicago, Outclassed, Loses First Game 9 to 1; Reds Quickly Hammer Eddie Cicotte From Box" — *Cincinnati Enquirer*

White Sox	010	000	000—1 6 1
Reds	100	500	21x—9 14 1

WP: Dutch Ruether (1-0).
LP: Eddie Cicotte (0-1).
Dutch Ruether: 9 IP, 6 H, 1 R, 0 ER, 1 BB, 1 K.
Eddie Cicotte: 3⅔ IP, 7 H, 6 R, 6 ER, 2 BB, 1 K.
Dutch Ruether: 3-3, 2 3B, BB, R, 3 RBI. Greasy Neale: 3-4, 2 R. Jake Daubert: 3-4, 3B, R, RBI. Chick Gandil: 2-4, RBI. Joe Jackson: 0-4, R. Buck Weaver: 1-4. Eddie Collins: 1-4, CS.
Attendance: 30,511. Time: 1:42.

The starting pitchers for Game One were lefty Dutch Ruether (19-6 W-L, 1.82 ERA regular season) for the Reds and right-hander Eddie Cicotte (29-7, 1.82) for the White Sox. The Reds initiated the scoring with a run in the bottom of the first inning. Their leadoff batter was second baseman Morrie Rath. Cicotte's second pitch struck him in the back. The pitch is one of the most analyzed in World Series history; many believing the pitch was a signal from Cicotte to bettors that the fix was in. The next batter up, first baseman Jake Daubert, singled Rath to third. Third baseman Heinie Groh's sacrifice fly to deep left field sent Rath home with the first run of the Series.

In the top of the second, the White Sox struck back. Left fielder Joe Jackson led off the inning by reaching second base on a bad throw by shortstop Larry Kopf. Jackson reached third on a sacrifice bunt by center fielder Happy Felsch, then scored when first baseman Chick Gandil's short fly to left dropped in for a hit. The inning ended with the score tied at 1 apiece.

The score remained tied until the Reds' half of the fourth inning. Joe Jackson's counterpart in left, Pat Duncan, started the ball rolling with a one-out single to right. Duncan was forced at second by Kopf for out number two. Eyebrows were raised by some who thought Cicotte hesitated before tossing the ball to shortstop Swede Risberg covering second. Others noted that Risberg seemed to stumble over the bag as he attempted unsuccessfully to double Kopf to end the inning. This proved costly as Reds right fielder Greasy Neale scratched out an infield single. That brought up catcher Ivey Wingo, who sent Kopf home with a single for what proved to be the winning run. The score jumped to 4-1 when pitcher Ruether tripled to deep left-center to drive Neale and Wingo across. The offensive show continued with Rath's double scoring Ruether. The scoring for the inning ended with the Reds up 6-1 when Daubert's single drove

home Rath. At that point Kid Gleason removed Cicotte and replaced him with Roy Wilkinson. The right-hander ended the inning by retiring Groh on a fly ball to center.

Staked to a 6-1 lead, Ruether limited the White Sox to four hits, all singles, and no runs the rest of the way. In the meantime the Reds increased their lead with a pair of runs in the seventh as Groh followed a Daubert triple with a single and later scored on a force play. The Reds' final run scored in their half of the eighth when Ruether stroked his second triple of the afternoon to score Neale, who had begun the inning with a single. Ruether then proceeded to complete his day's work and secure the first-ever World Series win for the Reds by retiring Jackson, Felsch, and Gandil in order to end the game. The final score was 9-1.

—————— Game Two ——————

Thursday, October 2
Redland Field, Cincinnati

"White Sox Crushed Again, 4 to 2" —
Chicago Tribune
"White Sox Sluggers Helpless With Men on Bases; Reds Defeat Kid Gleason's Second Ace 4 to 2" — *Cincinnati Enquirer*

White Sox	000	000	200—2 10 1
Reds	000	301	00x—4 4 3

WP: Slim Sallee (1-0). LP: Lefty Williams (0-1). Slim Sallee: 9 IP, 10 H, 2 R, 0 ER, 1 BB, 2 K. Lefty Williams: 8 IP, 4 H, 4 R, 4 ER, 6 BB, 1 K. Larry Kopf: 1-3, 3B, 2 RBI. Edd Roush: 1-2, R, 2 BB, RBI. Greasy Neale: 1-3, RBI. Joe Jackson: 3-4, 2B, K. Ray Schalk: 2-4, R. Buck Weaver: 2-4, 2B. Attendance: 29,698. Time: 1:42.

The White Sox sent Claude "Lefty" Williams (23-11, 2.64) to the mound for Game Two. The Reds countered with another lefty, Slim Sallee (21-7, 2.06). Both pitchers started off strong. It was the bottom of the fourth

Unused ticket to Game One of 1919 World Series at Redland Field in Cincinnati (Courtesy of Mike Nola / BlackBetsy.com)

inning when the Reds broke the ice in a big way. It all started when Williams walked leadoff batter Rath, who reached second via a sacrifice and then watched as Groh was walked. A single by center fielder Edd Roush, the Reds' best hitter, drove home Rath with the first run for the National Leaguers. After Roush was thrown out at second on an attempted steal, Williams issued yet another walk, to Duncan. This was Lefty's third walk of the inning and fourth of a game that would see him pass six Reds in eight innings pitched. Skeptics of Williams's efforts that day, and in the Series as a whole, could point to the left-hander's reputation as one of the game's premier control pitchers. In 1919, for example, he had issued 58 walks in 297 innings pitched. His career totals were 347 walks in 1,186 innings. Kopf made sure the last two fourth-inning walks were costly by tripling to left to score Groh and Duncan. The inning ended with the Reds ahead by three.

The White Sox did not score until the top of the seventh inning, breaking a string of 13 scoreless frames. By then the Reds had increased their lead to 4-0 when Williams began the bottom of the sixth inning by walking Roush. It was the third inning of six in which Williams had issued a free pass to the Reds' leadoff batter. Twice the leadoff walk yielded a run, this time when Roush reached second on a sacrifice bunt by Duncan and scored on a single by Neale. When the White Sox finally scored, it was a pair of unearned runs. Their only runs of the afternoon came in the seventh when Risberg singled with one out. Catcher Ray Schalk followed with a single. Risberg scored on the play as a result of an errant throw to second by Reds right fielder Neale. Schalk scored as well when third baseman Groh threw wildly to home plate. That was the end of the scoring as a White Sox rally in the ninth fell short. The 4-2 victory, secured despite the fact that the White Sox had 10 hits—three by Jackson, two each by Schalk and Buck Weaver—to the winner's four, put the Reds ahead in the Series by two games.

Game Three

Friday, October 3
Comiskey Park, Chicago

"Kerr Hurls Sox to Victory, 3 to 0"—
Chicago Tribune
"Kerr Stops Reds, Registering Shut-Out;
Fisher's Wild Throw Gives Sox Two Runs"—
Cincinnati Enquirer

Reds	000	000	000—0 3 1	
White Sox	020	100	00x—3 7 0	

WP: Dickey Kerr (1-0). LP: Ray Fisher (0-1).
Dickey Kerr: 9 IP, 3 H, 0 R, 0 ER, 1 BB, 4 K.
Ray Fisher: 7 IP, 7 H, 3 R, 2 ER, 2 BB, 1 K.
Joe Jackson: 2-3, R. Chick Gandil: 1-3, K, 2 RBI.
Swede Risberg: 1-2, 3B, BB, R. Ray
Schalk: 1-3, RBI.
Attendance: 29,126. Time: 1:30.

Manager Kid Gleason's choice to pitch his club back into the Series was Dickey Kerr (13-7, 2.88). The rookie left-hander was pressed into front-line duty due to the absence of Red Faber. The future Hall of Fame pitcher was battling illness and injury. The choice of Pat Moran to secure yet another Reds win was expected to be Hod Eller. Instead, right-handed veteran Ray Fisher (14-5, 2.17) received the starting nod.

In the bottom of the second inning the White Sox, playing for the first time at home, scored twice. Jackson led off with a single and reached third base when Fisher fielded Felsch's attempt at a sacrifice and threw wildly to second attempting a force out. Felsch continued on to second on the miscue. The next batter, Gandil, drove in both baserunners with a single to right, Gandil ending up at second. Although Risberg walked, no further damage was done as the next three White Sox batters made outs. The first of those batters, Schalk, attempted to move Gandil and Risberg up with a sacrifice bunt, but Fisher's throw to third forced Gandil. Some have argued that Gandil could have beaten the throw with a better effort.

The two-run lead held for the White Sox until the bottom of the fourth, when they scored their third and final run. A one-out triple by Risberg followed by a Schalk single did the trick. White Sox hitters had produced three runs in four innings. Kerr did the rest, twirling a three-hit shutout while retiring the last 15 Reds batters. Kerr's magnificent performance—he struck out four and walked only one—was in stark contrast to the performances of his more heralded pitching colleagues, Cicotte and Williams.

—————— Game Four ——————

Saturday, October 4
Comiskey Park, Chicago

"Sox Humbled in Fourth Game, 2-0"—
Chicago Tribune
"Ring Whitewashes Sox, Giving Reds 3-to-1
Lead; Cicotte Suffers His Second Defeat of
Series"—*Cincinnati Enquirer*

Reds	000	020	000—2	5 2
White Sox	000	000	000—0	3 2

WP: Jimmy Ring (1-0). LP: Eddie Cicotte (0-2).
Jimmy Ring: 9 IP, 3 H, 0 R, 0 ER, 3 BB, 2 K.
Eddie Cicotte: 9 IP, 5 H, 2 R, 0 ER, 0 BB, 2 K.
Ivey Wingo: 2-3. Greasy Neale: 1-3, 2B, RBI.
Larry Kopf: 1-3, R, RBI.
Joe Jackson: 1-4, 2B, K. Happy Felsch: 1-3, SH.
Chick Gandil: 1-4, K.
Attendance: 34,363. Time: 1:37.

The largest crowd to date in the Series saw Cicotte take his second turn on the mound for the White Sox. Yet another top-flight hurler, righty Jimmy Ring (10-9, 2.26), was the Reds' choice to oppose him. The game was scoreless into the top of the fifth inning, when the Reds scored the game's only runs. It all started out quite harmlessly as Roush was thrown out at first by catcher Schalk. The second out seemed assured when the next Reds batter, left fielder Duncan, hit the ball right back to Cicotte. However, the Sox pitcher bobbled the ball, then threw wildly to first, allowing Duncan to reach second. Kopf promptly singled to

left. The ball was fielded by Joe Jackson. He threw toward home plate to hold Duncan at third. While the ball was in flight, Cicotte reached up and deflected it. The ball rolled toward the stands as Duncan headed home with the game's first run and Kopf took second base. Cicotte's error, his second of the inning, ignited another wave of speculation that some of the White Sox were not in the Series to win. This was only emphasized further when the next man up, Neale, doubled to left to drive in Kopf. When the inning ended the score was 2-0, and there it stayed as the Reds took a three-games-to-one lead in the Series. Until that "fateful fifth," Cicotte had given up only two harmless singles. In all he gave up five hits—only one single after the fifth—and walked none. In shutting down the White Sox, Ring gave up a mere three hits while issuing three walks.

—————— Game Five ——————

Monday, October 6
Comiskey Park, Chicago

"Sox Crumble Before Eller, 5 to 0"—
Chicago Tribune
"Eller Humbles White Sox, Pitching Shut-
Out, Practically Clinching Big Series For
Cincinnati"—*Cincinnati Enquirer*

Reds	000	004	001—5	4 0
White Sox	000	000	000—0	3 3

WP: Hod Eller (1-0). LP: Lefty Williams (0-2).
Hod Eller: 9 IP, 3 H, 0 R, 0 ER, 1 BB, 9 K.
Lefty Williams: 8 IP, 4 H, 4 R, 4 ER, 2 BB, 3 K.
Edd Roush: 1-4, 3B, SB, 2 R, 2 RBI. Hod Eller:
1-3, 2B, R. Morrie Rath: 1-3, R, BB, RBI.
Buck Weaver: 2-4, 3B. Ray Schalk: 1-2, K. Nemo
Leibold: 0-3, BB, K.
Attendance: 34,379. Time: 1:45.

Delayed one day by rain, the fifth game of the Series saw the Reds trot out their fifth different starter and third straight right-hander in Hod Eller (19-9, 2.39). Kid Gleason showed his continued faith in Williams, giving him the ball for the second time. The two starters gave evidence early on that this would be a classic pitchers' duel. In the second and third innings Eller struck out six White Sox batters in a row, four on called third strikes. Williams was seemingly equal to the task, hurling hitless ball through four innings. The game was scoreless when the Reds came to bat in the top of the sixth. Then they hit pay dirt. Pitcher Eller led off the inning with a double to center, only the second Reds hit. He took third on the play when center fielder Felsch uncorked a bad throw. It was the second of three White Sox fielding errors in the game. Rath wasted no time in singling Eller home with the game's first run. After Daubert was out sacrificing Rath to second, Williams walked Groh. Then Roush struck the game's big blow, a triple to center, scoring both Rath and Groh. Some questioned Felsch's positioning on the play as Roush's drive went over his head. Schalk, who had protested vehemently when Groh was called safe at home, was ejected from the game for bumping and shoving home-plate umpire Cy Rigler. Duncan then drove Roush home with a sacrifice fly. The inning ended with the Reds in command at 4–0.

They scored an additional unearned run in the ninth off reliever Erskine Mayer. The final score was 5–0. Reds pitchers, fresh off a second straight three-hit gem, had now held the White Sox scoreless for 22 consecutive innings. Heading to Cincinnati, the AL champions were on the brink of elimination.

Ticket to Game Five of 1919 World Series at Comiskey Park (the ticket says "3" because it was the third home game in Chicago) (Courtesy of Mike Nola / BlackBetsy.com)

Game Six

Tuesday, October 7
Redland Field, Cincinnati

"Sox Fight to Victory in Tenth, 5-4"—
Chicago Tribune
"Carelessness by Reds Gives Sox Game, Cincinnati 'Blowing' Four-Run Lead"—
Cincinnati Enquirer

White Sox	000	013	0001—5 10 3
Reds	002	200	0000—4 11 0

WP: Dickey Kerr (2-0). LP: Jimmy Ring (1-1). Dickey Kerr: 10 IP, 11 H, 4 R, 3 ER, 2 BB, 2 K. Jimmy Ring: 5 IP, 4 H, 1 R, 1 ER, 3 BB, 2 K. Buck Weaver: 3-5, 2 2B, 2 R. Joe Jackson: 2-4, BB, R, RBI. Happy Felsch: 2-5, 2B, R, RBI. Greasy Neale: 3-4, 3B, R. Pat Duncan: 1-5, 2B, 2 RBI. Jake Daubert: 2-4, SB, R. Dutch Ruether: 1-2, 2B, R, RBI.
Attendance: 32,006. Time: 2:06.

For what they hoped would be the final game of the Series, the Reds sent a well-rested Ruether, the winning pitcher in Game One, to the mound. Kid Gleason countered by calling on Game Three winner Kerr for more heroics. Initially it did not appear to be such a good move. The Reds ended Kerr's scoreless inning string at 11 by scoring a pair of runs in both the third and fourth innings to take a 4-0 lead. The Reds' runs in the third came after one was out. Daubert singled and stole second as Groh struck out. Kerr then filled the vacancy at first base by hitting Roush, and Duncan followed with a double to drive home both Daubert and Roush. The Reds built upon their lead in the fourth. Neale led off the inning with a triple to deep right field. Neale remained at third as the next batter, catcher Bill Rariden, grounded out. Ruether, one of the hitting stars of Game One, then helped out his cause again; this time he doubled to left to score Neale. Rath was up next. He was safe at first when White Sox shortstop Risberg fielded his grounder cleanly but committed his second error of the game—fourth of the Series—trying to cut down Ruether at third. An unearned run scored as a result of the bad throw. The score jumped to 4-0 and could have been worse as Rath, who had taken second on Risberg's miscue, promptly stole third. There was still only one out when Daubert lifted a fly ball to Jackson in left. After Jackson made the catch, Rath attempted to score. Jackson's throw doubled him at home to end the inning. There were some who credited Jackson with a strong, accurate throw, while others claimed the throw was wide and the run saved when catcher Schalk lunged across to block the plate.

Now the White Sox trailed the Reds by four runs, a seemingly insurmountable lead to overcome for a team held scoreless for the previous 26 innings. In the top of the fifth, the Sox finally broke through, albeit for only a single run. Ruether, dominating to that point, suddenly lost his control, issuing leadoff walks to Risberg and Schalk. Kerr scratched out a single to load the bases. No one was able to move up as Shano Collins flied out to short center. Eddie Collins then lifted a fly ball to center field. It was deep enough to score Risberg with the first White Sox run, but Schalk remained at second. Kerr did not notice. He advanced to second and was tagged out. An error by Felsch in the bottom of the fifth did no damage. The score at the end of five was 4-1 in favor of the Reds.

The White Sox half of the sixth proved to be their best to date. Weaver started with a double to shallow left. He scored as Jackson singled and in turn scored on a double to left-center by Felsch. The Sox now trailed by only one. Pat Moran had seen enough. He replaced Ruether with Game Four winner Ring. He retired Gandil and Risberg, but Schalk tied the game with a single that scored Felsch, who had advanced to third.

The game remained tied through regulation. In the top of the 10th, the White Sox broke through against Ring. Again, Weaver led off the inning with a double. A successful Jackson bunt single placed runners at the corners with no one out. Felsch struck out, but then Gandil broke the deadlock with a groundball single to center that scored Weaver. Risberg ended the inning

by lining into a double play. Nonetheless, Kerr secured his second win of the Series with a one-two-three 10th. There was talk of sloppy fielding and sloppy baserunning—in addition to Kerr's gaffe, Jackson was also thrown out on the bases twice—but the bottom line was the White Sox win had extended the Series to a seventh game.

Game Seven

Wednesday, October 8
Redland Field, Cincinnati

"Sox Battle to Third Victory, 4-1"—*Chicago Tribune*
"Cicotte Keeps Sox in Series, Trimming Cincinnati 4 to 1"—*Cincinnati Enquirer*

White Sox	101	020	000—4 10 1
Reds	000	001	000—1 7 4

WP: Eddie Cicotte (1-2). LP: Slim Sallee (1-1).
Eddie Cicotte: 9 IP, 7 H, 1 R, 1 ER, 3 BB, 4 K.
Slim Sallee: 4⅓ IP, 9 H, 4 R, 2 ER, 0 BB, 0 K.
Shano Collins: 3-5, 2B, 2 R. Eddie Collins: 2-4, R. Joe Jackson: 2-4, 2 RBI. Happy Felsch: 2-4, 2 RBI.
Heinie Groh: 1-4, 2B, R. Pat Duncan: 1-4, RBI.
Ivey Wingo: 1-1, 3 BB.
Attendance: 13,923. Time: 1:47.

Pat Moran selected Sallee, the winning pitcher in Game Two, as the Reds took their second shot at wrapping up the Series. Kid Gleason, hoping the third time was a charm, gave the ball to Cicotte. By far the smallest crowd to date was on hand at Redland Field, in part because the Reds front office mishandled the availability of tickets. Shano Collins, playing center field, started the game with a single. He was sacrificed to second by Eddie Collins. Then, after another out, Jackson singled to left. Shano Collins scored to put the Chicagoans on top. The White Sox added a second run in the top of the third when Jackson again singled to drive in Shano Collins, this time from third base. They struck again in the top half of the fifth. After

Shano Collins flied out, Eddie Collins singled to center. Weaver batted next, reaching first when Reds third baseman Groh misplayed his groundball. Yet another error on a grounder, this time by second baseman Rath, loaded the bases. Happy Felsch then singled, driving across both Eddie Collins and Weaver. Both runs were unearned.

The White Sox, behind much stronger pitching from Cicotte, held their 4-0 lead into the bottom of the sixth inning when a one-out ground-rule double to deep left by Groh and a two-out single by Duncan gave the Reds their only run of the afternoon. The final score was 4-1. Cicotte finally had a win. Sallee, who deserved better, took the loss. The Reds defense sprang a leak as they made four errors. The White Sox victory brought them to within a game of forcing the Series to its full nine games.

Game Eight

Thursday, October 9
Comiskey Park, Chicago

"Reds Are New World's Champions" — *Chicago Tribune*
"Reds End Series With Slaughter of Sox Pitchers, Winning Baseball Classic, Five Games to Three" — *Cincinnati Enquirer*

Reds	410	013	010—10 16 2
White Sox	001	000	040—5 10 1

WP: Hod Eller (2-0). LP: Lefty Williams (0-3). Hod Eller: 9 IP, 10 H, 5 R, 4 ER, 1 BB, 6 K. Lefty Williams: ⅓ IP, 4 H, 4 R, 4 ER, 0 BB, 0 K. Edd Roush: 3-5, 2 2B, 2 R, 4 RBI. Pat Duncan: 2-4, 2B, R, 3 RBI. Bill Rariden: 2-5, SB, 2 RBI. Morrie Rath: 2-4, SB, 2 BB, R. Joe Jackson: 2-5, 2B, HR, 2 R, 3 RBI. Eddie Collins: 3-5, 2B, SB, R. Buck Weaver: 2-5, 2B, R. Attendance: 32,930. Time: 2:27.

The eighth game of the Series presented each manager with an intriguing decision for his choice of a starting pitcher. Lefty Williams seemed a logical choice for Kid Gleason, but he had not performed well in two previous starts. The third time around had worked for Cicotte; Gleason decided to give Williams a third chance, too. Pat Moran had a number of seasoned starters to choose from to try to close out the Series. He went with Hod Eller, a shutout winner in Game Five. Williams quickly made Gleason regret his decision. After retiring the first batter on an infield pop fly, he gave up four straight hits. Jake Daubert opened the parade with a single to center and Heinie Groh followed suit with a single to right. A double by Edd Roush sent Daubert home and Groh to third. Pat Duncan's double knocked in Groh and Roush to give the Reds a 3-0 lead. Gleason pulled his left-hander and replaced him with Bill James. Williams's effort or lack thereof became the subject of endless discussion, including speculation that he pitched to lose due to threats of violence. James walked the first batter he

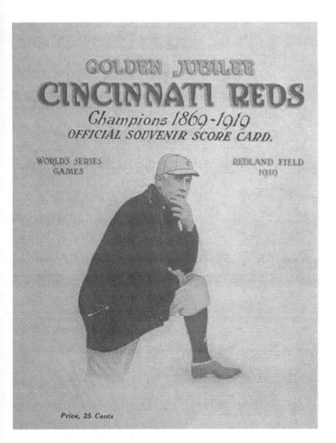

1919 World Series program (Courtesy of Mike Nola / BlackBetsy.com)

faced, but limited the Reds to just one more run, a two-out single by Bill Rariden that drove in Duncan.

In their half of the first, the White Sox started strong. Nemo Leibold, playing center field, opened with a single and went to third on a double by Eddie Collins. However, Eller proceeded to shut down the threat by retiring the side on a pair of strikeouts and an infield pop fly. The Reds then added another run in the second. After two were out Groh singled and scored on a double by Roush. When Roush tried to take third on the throw to the plate, he was thrown out. In the bottom of the third the White Sox broke the ice when Jackson homered to right. Any thoughts of a quick comeback were dashed, however, as the Reds scored a run in the fifth and three more in the sixth. The score in the fifth was produced by a two-out triple by Kopf and a single to left by Neale. James was still on the mound for the White Sox in the sixth, but after giving up an opening single to pitcher Eller and issuing a walk to Morrie Rath, he was replaced by Roy Wilkinson. The first batter he faced, Daubert, bunted and was safe on an errant throw to third by Ray Schalk. This loaded the bases. After Groh struck out, Roush singled home both Eller and Rath. When Duncan followed with a single to center scoring Daubert, the Reds had what would prove to be an insurmountable 9-1 lead.

The Reds scored their 10th and final run of the Series in the top of the eighth. Wilkinson hit Roush with a pitch. A sacrifice bunt by Duncan moved Roush to second, where he watched as Larry Kopf popped up and Greasy Neale walked. Roush then scored on a single by Rariden. The White Sox started out the bottom half of the eighth with a flyout. Then suddenly their bats came alive. An Eddie Collins single was followed by a pair of doubles. The first one, by Weaver, sent Collins to third. The second, by Jackson, drove home both Collins and Weaver. After Felsch popped up to the first baseman, Gandil tripled to right to score Jackson. When Risberg reached first on an error by Roush in center, Gandil scored the fourth run of the inning. The rally ended one batter later, however, when Schalk grounded to second. Entering the bottom of the ninth the White Sox trailed 10-5. Although

Eller hit one batter, pinch-hitter Eddie Murphy, and gave up a single to Eddie Collins, the game and the Series were over when Jackson's groundout to second gave Eller his second complete-game victory. The Cincinnati Reds were World Series champions for the first time in team history.

Series Summary

Normally once the final out of a World Series is made, the shouting quickly dies. But in the aftermath of the 1919 World Series, the shouting had just begun. Perhaps more would be written about this World Series than any other because of what would become known as the Black Sox Scandal. But just like any World Series, the on-the-field play would produce a cold, hard set of numbers. No recap would be complete without a recitation of some of the key figures.

In winning the World Series five games to three, the Reds outscored the White Sox 35-20. The Reds batted .255, while the Sox team average was .224. The Reds accumulated 17 extra-base hits, including seven triples. The White Sox followed closely with 14, equaling the Reds with their 10 doubles.

Individually for the Reds' regulars, Greasy Neale had the highest batting average at .357. Pat Duncan and Edd Roush knocked in eight and seven runners respectively. Pitcher Hod Eller won twice, while Dutch Ruether, Slim Sallee, and Jimmy Ring were credited with one win apiece. Joe Jackson topped White Sox batters with a .375 average and six RBIs. Chick Gandil had five RBIs. Other hitters topping .300 were Buck Weaver (.324) and Ray Schalk (.304). Future Hall of Famer Eddie Collins had only one extra-base hit and batted .226. Swede Risberg garnered but two hits in 25 at-bats and hit a woeful .080. Pitcher Dickey Kerr won twice for the White Sox and Eddie Cicotte once. Perhaps fittingly, the home run hit by Joe Jackson in the third inning of Game Eight was the only home run hit in the final World Series of the Deadball Era.

SOURCES

Information for this article was obtained from Retrosheet.org and Baseball-Reference.com.

1919 WHITE SOX: THE PITCHING DEPTH DILEMMA

By Jacob Pomrenke

AS SOON AS RED FABER reported for spring training, Kid Gleason knew he had a big problem.

Entering the 1919 season, the Chicago White Sox' first-year manager was counting on his workhorse aces Faber and Eddie Cicotte to lead his team back to the American League pennant they had won two years earlier. But Faber, the right-handed spitball specialist who had spent most of the 1918 season in the Navy during World War I, was weak from influenza and didn't look well in his early throwing sessions at Mineral Wells, Texas, where the White Sox were getting in shape for the campaign.

The White Sox were returning almost their entire championship team from 1917. (The 1918 season had been cut short by the war as players were forced to comply with the US government's "work or fight" order.) But some writers, like *Baseball Magazine's* W.A. Phelon, predicted they would finish no better than fourth in the AL standings, primarily due to their lack of pitching depth.

Kid Gleason quickly grew tired of the criticism, but he never stopped worrying about his pitchers. The White Sox' unreliable rotation proved to be a concern all season long and was a contributing factor in their World Series loss to the underdog Cincinnati Reds. In fact, some historians have argued that the White Sox might have lost to the pitching-rich Reds even if the Series had been played on the level.

Long before it became known that some White Sox players were intentionally throwing the Series, American League umpire Billy Evans was among the experts to cast doubt on Chicago as heavy favorites, writing in a syndicated column a day before Game One, "I am much in doubt as to Chicago's chances. It is a pretty big task to ask two pitchers, Eddie Cicotte and Lefty Williams, to carry the burden of a nine-game series."

Red Faber, the hero of the 1917 World Series and a future Hall of Famer, might have made the difference if he had been available. He tried for most of the year to assure Gleason that he was feeling fine, but the manager wasn't fooled — and neither were American League hitters. Faber, weakened by illness and then hampered by arm and ankle injuries, started just 20 games in 1919 and compiled an 11-9 record with a 3.83 ERA, far above the league average of 3.22.

Without Faber at full strength, the White Sox' pitching staff was extraordinarily thin, even by Deadball Era standards when complete games were common and bullpen specialization was a concept that was decades into the future. Faber's struggles forced Gleason to conduct an extensive (and mostly unsuccessful) search for other pitchers to provide support and much-needed rest for his two stars, Cicotte and Williams.

The 35-year-old Eddie Cicotte was the team's undisputed ace, using his dazzling array of trick pitches — including the knuckleball, the emery ball, and his patented "shine ball" — to dominate AL hitters. He finished 29-7 with a 1.82 ERA and five shutouts in a league-leading 306⅔ innings pitched. Near the end of the season, with the White Sox safely in first place, he took two weeks off to rest his tired arm in preparation for an extended best-of-nine World Series against the Reds. This layoff in early September, which was widely reported in the newspapers, has long fueled speculation that White Sox management benched its star pitcher to spoil Cicotte's chance at a 30th victory and deny him a promised $10,000 bonus. But there appears to be no truth to that story.

In any case, Cicotte *did* have a chance to win his 30th game and clinch the AL pennant, on September 24,

The White Sox used 17 different pitchers in 1919, but only rookie Dickey Kerr, center, provided effective support behind aces Eddie Cicotte and Lefty Williams. Pictured from left(Backup catcher Joe Jenkins, rookie pitcher Frank Shellenback, Kerr, pitcher Grover Lowdermilk, starting catcher Ray Schalk. (Courtesy of Michael Aronstein / TCMA Ltd.)

but he faltered in the seventh inning and was pulled before the White Sox rallied to dramatically beat the St. Louis Browns, 6-5. Cicotte pronounced himself ready for the Reds after making a final tune-up start four days later, but questions still lingered about his health up until Game One of the World Series.

Claude "Lefty" Williams had shown flashes of stardom as the White Sox won it all in 1917, but in spite of his 17 victories, his inconsistency caused then-manager Pants Rowland to use him for just a single inning of that year's World Series against the New York Giants. By 1919 Kid Gleason still wasn't convinced the slightly-built southpaw with the peculiar side-arm delivery could hold his own as a full-time starter. But the 26-year-old Williams proved he was up to the task and followed Cicotte's lead to go 23-11 with a 2.64 ERA and five shutouts in a team-high 41 games. Together, they combined for 52 of the White Sox' 88 wins and almost half of the team's 1,265⅔ innings pitched in the regular season.

To help take the load off Cicotte and Williams, manager Gleason and team owner Charles Comiskey made trades for other pitchers, called up minor leaguers and aging veterans, and even signed stars from the Chicago sandlots in the hopes that one or two of them might work out for the White Sox as a replacement for Red Faber.

Their biggest success story was a 25-year-old rookie named Dickey Kerr. The little left-hander, who stood just 5-feet-7, was a 20-game winner three times in the minor leagues before getting his chance in Chicago. In his first season with the White Sox, 1919, he went 13-7 with a 2.88 ERA in 39 games. But where he really shined was in his role as a bullpen ace, where he had a knack for holding opponents at bay as the White Sox' explosive offense rallied for a victory in the late innings. Kid Gleason called on Kerr 22 times in relief and he went 7-1 with a 1.78 ERA in those appearances.

In the World Series, Kerr's strong performances gave Chicago fans hope after Cicotte and Williams were trounced by the Reds. His three-hit shutout in Game Three and a 10-inning victory in Game Six helped keep the White Sox' chances alive. After Kerr's second win, Gleason was so frustrated by his team's uncharacteristic performance in the Series that he suggested he might start Kerr in every game the rest of the way. He didn't follow through on the threat, and the White Sox lost the World Series, but Kerr was a lone bright spot in the franchise's darkest hour.

Two other young pitchers who went on to greater acclaim but didn't contribute much for the White Sox in 1919 were Charlie Robertson and Frank Shellenback. Robertson made his major-league debut on May 13 against the St. Louis Browns but was clearly overmatched by big-league hitters; he lasted just two innings before he was relieved by Kerr. The White Sox sent Robertson down to the minors for more seasoning and he wouldn't return to Chicago for three more years. But in his fourth career start, on April 30, 1922, he threw a perfect game — just the fifth in major-league history — against Ty Cobb and the Detroit Tigers, a once-in-a-lifetime highlight in an otherwise mediocre career.

Shellenback, who possessed an outstanding spitball, had pitched decently for the White Sox as a 19-year-old rookie in 1918 and was expected to be a steady member of the rotation in 1919. But Shelly struggled to post a 1-3 record with a 5.14 ERA in eight games before he, too, was sent down to the minors in July. Those were his only career appearances in the major leagues; he never made it back because the National Commission banned his best pitch, the spitter, that offseason. Fortunately for him, he was allowed to continue throwing the wet one in the Pacific Coast League and he went on to enjoy a long, illustrious career with the Hollywood Stars, winning more than 300 games as one of the greatest minor-league pitchers ever.

The surprising thing about the White Sox' lack of pitching depth is that just a few years earlier, they actually had the deepest pitching staff in the major leagues. Chicago had led the AL in team ERA in 1913, 1916, and 1917, and finished runner-up in 1914. But two of their former mound stars, Joe Benz and Reb Russell, each pitched in just a single game in 1919. Benz, known as "Butcher Boy" because he spent his offseasons working in the family shop, had risen to fame in 1914 after pitching a no-hitter against the Cleveland Naps and taking another no-hitter into the ninth inning two starts later against the Washington Senators. He was a steady pitcher with the White Sox for several years afterward, but age and injuries hampered his effectiveness. His final big-league appearance was a two-inning relief stint on May 2, 1919, and he was released two weeks later.

The Mississippi-born Ewell "Reb" Russell had one of baseball's all-time best rookie seasons in 1913, winning 22 games and tossing eight shutouts. But he later suffered an elbow injury that left him unable to throw his curveball effectively, and he barely made the team out of spring training in 1919. In his only appearance, on June 13, he was yanked after two batters without recording an out. Russell was also given his release, and never pitched another game in the majors. But he resurfaced a few years later as an outfielder with the Pittsburgh Pirates, hitting .368 in 60 games as a platoon player in 1922.

None of them helped Kid Gleason solve his pitching dilemma, however. Cicotte and Williams helped lead the White Sox into first place on Opening Day and rarely looked back, but their manager kept looking for more pitching all season long.

In mid-May the White Sox acquired one of the fastest but wildest pitchers in the big leagues, Grover Lowdermilk, from the St. Louis Browns. On his sixth team in eight seasons—Chicago would be his last stop—Lowdermilk was given numerous chances to harness his talent. But the 6-foot-4 right-hander never overcame his lack of control. While he pitched well for the White Sox overall (5-5, 2.79 ERA in 20 games), Gleason didn't feel comfortable using him down the stretch in tight games. Lowdermilk made just one start after August 31 and pitched one mop-up inning in Game One of the World Series.

John "Lefty" Sullivan was another talented fireballer with one glaring shortcoming who was given a tryout by the White Sox that summer. Plucked off the Chicago sandlots when Lowdermilk abruptly quit the team in mid-July (he returned two weeks later), Sullivan made a big name for himself as the strikeout king of the city's semipro leagues. During World War I, while pitching for a military team based at Camp Grant, in Rockford, Illinois, he caught the White Sox' attention when he outpitched Red Faber in a service game in front of a reported 12,000 fans. Sullivan was invited to spring training in 1919 but didn't make the team, and then refused a minor-league assignment until the desperate Gleason called him back to make a surprise start against Walter Johnson and the Washington Senators on July 19. There was just one problem: Sullivan couldn't field his position because of a lifelong heart condition that caused him to feel dizzy whenever he bent over to pick up a ball. Major-league hitters had trouble with Sullivan's great stuff, but they could exploit his one weakness—and they bunted him right out of the league. He made just four appearances for the White Sox, finishing with an 0-1 career record and three errors in five fielding chances.

As the summer rolled on and the first-place White Sox began to look ahead to the World Series, a handful of other pitchers, with varying degrees of talent and experience, tried to earn a spot in the postseason rotation: Win Noyes, Tom McGuire, Roy Wilkinson, Erskine Mayer, Dave Danforth, Big Bill James, and the superbly named Don Carlos Patrick Ragan. None were successful enough to warrant a start against the Reds.

Before the World Series began, prominent pundits like syndicated columnist Hugh Fullerton gave Cincinnati the edge on pitching strength and warned that the White Sox would be weakened if they had to rely solely on their two aces: "Critics … have been arguing that the Reds have a chance to beat the American Leaguers because of their superior pitching strength.… If Gleason gets away to a good start he will not force Cicotte or Williams to the limit of endurance, but will take a chance with others. But if the Reds get the jump on the Sox, Gleason has little choice but to fall back upon the two men who have won the championship for him."

Cincinnati had five good starters—Dutch Ruether, Slim Sallee, Ray Fisher, Jimmy Ring, and Hod Eller—to Chicago's two great ones, but they were plenty good enough to win the NL pennant by nine games over the New York Giants. The Reds' 96-44 record was also eight games better than the White Sox' at 88-52, although most observers agreed that the American League was the stronger circuit, having won eight of the previous nine World Series. The White Sox were heavy betting favorites entering the Series, but that all depended on Cicotte and Williams giving their best efforts. As Hugh Fullerton predicted, once they faltered in the first two games, Gleason had no one else but Dickey Kerr to fall back on.

Hall of Fame catcher Ray Schalk maintained for the rest of his life that if the White Sox had a healthy Red Faber for the 1919 World Series, they would have won it all even with eight of their teammates conspiring to hand it to the Reds. Back in 1917, Faber had appeared in four of the six World Series games against the Giants, winning three of them. There's no telling how he would have fared against the Reds, but we can safely assume that he would have given the White Sox a better chance to win than the fixers Cicotte or Williams.

It's also worth wondering how the White Sox might have fared if Gleason had been able to call on Joe Benz or Reb Russell or Frank Shellenback, too. The first two were proven winners (and Shelly would go on to win more pro games than anyone on the staff) who might have put a quicker stop to the bleeding after Cicotte was blasted out of the box in Game One and Williams lost his control in Game Two. Or Gleason might have chosen to start one of them in place of Cicotte on two days' rest in Game Four or Williams in Game Five. (The tight World Series schedule, eight games played in nine days, also did the White Sox no favors.) Instead, the other pitchers Gleason did use—Roy Wilkinson, Grover Lowdermilk, Erskine Mayer, and Bill James—generally only made things worse when they took the mound. None of them were intentionally throwing games; the White Sox' pitching just wasn't all that strong outside of Cicotte and Williams.

Perhaps, then, we ought to give the Reds' pitching staff a little more credit for winning the World Series. The White Sox batted only .224 in the World Series, and it wasn't just the fixers who struggled. Leadoff man Nemo Leibold batted .056 (1-for-18) against Cincinnati pitching and future Hall of Famer Eddie Collins, who was considered one of the great "money" players in baseball by his contemporaries, hit .226 with just one RBI. Reds manager Pat Moran rotated his starting pitchers wisely, as he had been doing all season, and they responded well.

Kid Gleason didn't have nearly as many good options, and he knew it. He spent all season trying to overcome his team's one big weakness, and in the end it wasn't enough. The White Sox just didn't have enough pitching to beat the Reds.

SOURCES

All statistics were found using Baseball-Reference.com and Retrosheet.org. Biographical information was found in the players' SABR biographies and by accessing newspaper archives at ProQuest and Newspapers.com. In addition, the following articles were used as sources:

Evans, Billy. "Hard to Predict Winner of Series," *New York Times*, September 30, 1919.

Fullerton, Hugh. "Cincinnati Shows Superiority With Leading Twirlers," *Atlanta Constitution*, September 29, 1919.

Phelon, W.A. "Who Will Win the Big League Pennants?" *Baseball Magazine*, May 1919.

1919 AMERICAN LEAGUE SALARIES

By Jacob Pomrenke

IN *EIGHT MEN OUT,* **AUTHOR** Eliot Asinof wrote about the 1919 Chicago White Sox: "Many players of less status got almost twice as much on other teams.… (Charles Comiskey's) ballplayers were the best and were paid as poorly as the worst." This passage sums up the entire foundation of Asinof's thesis: Low salaries and poor treatment by management are now widely considered to be the driving forces behind the White Sox players' decision to fix the 1919 World Series. But the actual salary numbers tell a very different story. The White Sox were not among the worst-paid teams in baseball; in fact, they were one of the highest paid.

The National Baseball Hall of Fame Library in Cooperstown, New York, holds a collection of thousands of organizational contract cards that were provided to the Hall by Major League Baseball in 2002. As researcher Bob Hoie notes, these cards, which go back to the 1912 season, "contain salary, bonus payments, and any modifications to the standard contract covering each season (of a player's career)." Although many other numbers have been tossed around by historians in the past, we can now say with certainty how much the Black Sox players were paid—and how much their teammates and peers were paid, too. The comparison helps shed light on whether any of the Chicago players had a legitimate reason to grumble about their salaries, at least any more than other teams around the league.

Hoie, with the help of fellow researcher Mike Haupert, analyzed the contract cards for a landmark 2012 article in *Base Ball: A Journal of the Early Game* on major-league salaries in 1919. Hoie discovered that the 1919 White Sox had one of the highest team payrolls in the major leagues; at $88,461, it was more than $10,000 higher than that of the National League champion

Reds' $76,870, which would have ranked sixth in the American League.

As has been well documented, the White Sox team payroll was extremely top-heavy and the player with the biggest bankroll was future Hall of Fame second baseman Eddie Collins. Collins's $15,000 salary placed him number 2 among American League players behind only Ty Cobb at $20,000. The college-educated Collins, nicknamed "Cocky" and for good reason, wasn't well liked by some of his teammates. Perhaps this included a sense of jealousy at his high salary. Indeed, Collins's salary was nearly double that of anyone else on the team. But that wasn't unusual in 1919: In Detroit, Cobb was making *three times* as much as any other Tiger and Cleveland's Tris Speaker ($13,125) was also making twice as much as the next-highest-paid Indian.

But even if Collins's salary was out of line with those of the rest of the team, the other White Sox stars were paid comparatively well, according to the Hall of Fame contract cards. Four other Chicago players ranked among the top 20 highest-paid players in the American League, including World Series fixers Eddie Cicotte ($8,000, number 8 in the AL), Buck Weaver ($7,250, number 11), and Shoeless Joe Jackson ($6,000, number 15). Another future Hall of Famer, catcher Ray Schalk, was the 13th-highest-paid player in the league at $7,083.

Eddie Cicotte's salary deserves a closer look. The White Sox ace earned $8,000 in 1919—which included a $5,000 base salary and a $3,000 performance bonus that Hoie says was a carryover from his 1918 contract (but unrelated to the mythical bonus "promised" to Cicotte if he won 30 games; that story is discussed elsewhere in this book). That also doesn't include an additional $2,000 signing bonus paid to Cicotte before the start of the 1918 season, for a total compensation of $15,000 in 1918 and '19. When he signed his contract, Cicotte had only one truly outstanding season (1917) to his credit. But he was the second-highest-paid pitcher in baseball behind the Washington Senators' Walter Johnson, who had a much stronger track record. To put this in comparison, Eliot Asinof reported in *Eight Men Out* that Cincinnati Reds pitcher Dutch Ruether was "getting almost double (Cicotte's) figure." Ruether, whose sterling 1.82 ERA in 1919 matched Cicotte's regular-season figure, was actually making $2,340. Talk about underpaid!

The rest of the players who would later be banned in the Black Sox Scandal had little reason to squawk about salaries, either, at least compared with other players at their positions and experience level—and especially coming off a 1918 season in which the White Sox finished in sixth place. For instance, Chick Gandil's $3,500 salary was fifth-highest among AL first baseman, and the four players ahead of him were far superior in talent: George Sisler (Browns), Stuffy McInnis (Red Sox), Wally Pipp (Yankees), and Joe Judge (Senators). Happy Felsch, an emerging star center fielder, might have felt disgruntled that Cobb and Speaker were making so much more than his $3,750, but he had only four seasons under his belt entering 1919. The only other center fielders with higher salaries, Clyde Milan (Senators) and Amos Strunk (Red Sox), had been in the league since 1907 and '08, respectively.

Now that we have accurate salary information for all players in 1919, it's hard to make the case that the Chicago White Sox were underpaid. There were many reasons that the eight Black Sox might have agreed to fix the World Series, but it wasn't because they were being paid so much less than other major leaguers of equal or lesser talent.

Eliot Asinof, along with many writers before and after him, long insisted that the White Sox had the best talent and the worst payroll. But that claim just doesn't stand up to modern scrutiny. With few exceptions, owner Charles Comiskey—long portrayed as a greedy miser and a villain in the Black Sox story—paid salaries that were comparable, and in many cases even favorable, to the rest of the league. The numbers bear that out.

American League Opening Day team payrolls, 1919

Boston Red Sox, $93,475
New York Yankees, $91,330
Chicago White Sox, $88,461
Detroit Tigers, $81,433
Cleveland Indians, $78,913
St. Louis Browns, $63,000
Washington Senators, $63,000
Philadelphia A's, $42,000

(Note: These figures are Opening Day payrolls and do not include any performance bonuses paid later in the season. According to Hoie, if you include total salary payouts plus earned bonuses at the end of the season, the White Sox ended up with the top payroll in the major leagues for 1919, $10,000 more than the Red Sox, who began dumping salaries as soon as it became apparent they weren't going to repeat as AL champions.)

Top American League player salaries in 1919

Ty Cobb, DET, $20,000
Eddie Collins, CHW, $15,000
Tris Speaker, CLE, $13,125
Frank Baker*, NYY, $11,583
Babe Ruth, BOS, $10,000
Walter Johnson, WSH, $9,500
Harry Hooper, BOS, $9,000
Eddie Cicotte**, CHW, $8,000
Carl Mays, BOS/NYY, $8,000
Roger Peckinpaugh, NYY, $7,500
Buck Weaver, CHW, $7,250
George Sisler, SLB, $7,200
Ray Schalk, CHW, $7,083
Dutch Leonard, DET, $6,500
Del Pratt, NYY, $6,185
Joe Jackson***, CHW, $6,000
Bob Shawkey, NYY, $6,000
Ernie Shore, NYY, $6,000
Ray Chapman, CLE, $6,000
Donie Bush, DET, $5,500

American League player salaries in 1919, by position

First base
George Sisler, SLB, $7,200
Stuffy McInnis, BOS, $5,000
Wally Pipp, NYY, $5,000
Joe Judge, WSH, $3,675
Chick Gandil, CHW, $3,500
Harry Heilmann, DET, $3,500
George Burns, PHA, $2,625
Doc Johnston, CLE, $2,500

Second base
Eddie Collins, CHW, $15,000
Del Pratt, NYY, $6,185
Jack Barry, BOS, $4,500
Dave Shean, BOS, $4,000
Joe Gedeon, SLB, $3,675
Bill Wambsganss, CLE, $3,500
Ralph Young, DET, $3,500
Hal Janvrin, WSH, $2,625
Whitey Witt, PHA, $2,362

Shortstop
Roger Peckinpaugh, NYY, $7,500
Ray Chapman, CLE, $6,000
Donie Bush, DET, $5,500
Everett Scott, BOS, $5,000
Howie Shanks, WSH, $3,400
Swede Risberg, CHW, $3,250
Wally Gerber, SLB, $2,365
Joe Dugan, PHA, $2,100

Third base
Frank Baker, NYY, $11,583
Buck Weaver, CHW, $7,250
Larry Gardner, CLE, $5,000
Ossie Vitt, BOS, $4,500
Jimmy Austin, SLB, $3,675
Eddie Foster, WSH, $3,675
Fred McMullin, CHW, $2,750
Bob Jones, DET, $2,500
Fred Thomas, PHA, $2,100

Left field
Babe Ruth, BOS, $10,000
Joe Jackson, CHW, $6,000
Duffy Lewis, NYY, $5,500
Bobby Veach, DET, $5,000
Jack Graney, CLE, $4,000
Mike Menosky, WSH, $2,650
Jack Tobin, SLB, $2,500
Merlin Kopp, PHA, $2,400

Center field
Ty Cobb, DET, $20,000
Tris Speaker, CLE, $13,125
Clyde Milan, WSH, $5,000
Amos Strunk, BOS $4,800
Happy Felsch, CHW, $3,750
Tillie Walker, PHA, $3,750
Ping Bodie, NYY, $3,600
Baby Doll Jacobson, SLB, $1,969

Right field
Harry Hooper, BOS, $9,000
Joe Wood, CLE, $4,400
Braggo Roth, PHA/BOS, $4,200
Chick Shorten, DET, $3,200
Sam Rice, WSH, $3,150
Nemo Leibold, CHW, $2,650
Shano Collins, CHW, $2,625
Elmer Smith, CLE, $2,625
Ira Flagstead, DET, $2,500
Sammy Vick, NYY, $2,000
Earl Smith, SLB, $1,594

Catcher
Ray Schalk, CHW, $7,083
Steve O'Neill, CLE, $5,000
Oscar Stanage, DET, $4,500
Wally Schang, BOS, $4,500
Hank Severeid, SLB, $3,750
Sam Agnew, WSH, $3,675
Eddie Ainsmith, DET, $3,500
Truck Hannah, NYY, $3,000
Val Picinich, WSH, $2,750
Muddy Ruel, NYY, $2,700

Patsy Gharrity, WSH, $2,100
Cy Perkins, PHA, $1,890

Pitcher

Walter Johnson, WSH, $9,500
Eddie Cicotte, CHW, $8,000
Carl Mays, BOS/NYY, $8,000
Dutch Leonard, DET, $6,500
Bob Shawkey, NYY, $6,000
Ernie Shore, NYY, $6,000
Bullet Joe Bush, BOS, $5,700
Sam Jones, NYY, $5,000
Jim Shaw, WSH, $5,000
Jack Quinn, NYY, $4,850
Red Faber, CHW, $4,000
Stan Coveleski, CLE, $4,000
Ray Caldwell, BOS/CLE, $4,000
Pete Schneider, NYY, $4,000
Guy Morton, CLE, $4,000
George Mogridge, NYY, $3,800
Allan Sothoron, SLB, $3,625
Carl Weilman, SLB, $3,625
Hooks Dauss, DET, $3,600
Johnny Enzmann, CLE, $3,600
Jim Bagby, CLE, $3,600
Hooks Dauss, DET, $3,600
Lefty Williams****, CHW, $3,500

NOTES

* Frank Baker's salary includes a $1,000 performance bonus paid to him after the season.

** Eddie Cicotte's salary includes a $3,000 performance bonus paid to him after the season, a carryover agreement from his 1918 contract. According to Bob Hoie, "this was apparently a verbal agreement, but it shows up in the White Sox ledgers presented during the criminal trial in 1921."

*** Joe Jackson's salary includes a $750 bonus paid to him for being "a member in good standing" of the White Sox at the end of the season, undoubtedly due in part to his abrupt departure in 1918. His $1,000-per-month contract normally earned him $6,000, but because of the shortened season in 1919, he was only due to make $5,250 instead. Comiskey made it up to him with an extra $750 after the season.

**** Lefty Williams's salary includes a $375 performance bonus for winning 15 games and an additional $500 bonus for winning 20 games, both of which he earned in 1919.

SOURCES

Hoie, Bob, "1919 Baseball Salaries and the Mythically Underpaid Chicago White Sox," *Base Ball: A Journal of the Early Game*, Volume 6, No. 1 (Jefferson, North Carolina: McFarland & Co., Spring 2012), 17-34.

Michael Haupert Player Salary Database

THE BLACK SOX SCANDAL

By William F. Lamb

OVER THE DECADES, MAJOR-league baseball has produced a host of memorable teams, but only one infamous one — the 1919 Chicago White Sox. Almost a century after the fact, the exact details of the affair known in sports lore as the Black Sox Scandal remain murky and subject to debate. But one central and indisputable truth endures: Talented members of that White Sox club conspired with professional gamblers to rig the outcome of the 1919 World Series.

Another certainty attends the punishment imposed in the matter. The permanent banishment from the game of those players implicated in the conspiracy, while perhaps an excessive sanction in certain cases, achieved an overarching objective. Game-fixing virtually disappeared from the major-league landscape after that penalty was imposed on the Black Sox.

Something else is equally indisputable. The finality of the expulsion edict rendered by Commissioner Kenesaw Mountain Landis has not quelled the controversy surrounding the corruption of the 1919 Series. Nor has public fascination abated. To the contrary, interest in the scandal has only grown over the years, in time even spawning a publishing subgenre known as Black Sox literature. No essay-length narrative can hope to capture the entirety of events explored in the present Black Sox canon, or to address all the beliefs of individual Black Sox aficionados. The following, therefore, is no more than one man's rendition of the scandal.

The plot to transform the 1919 World Series into a gambling insiders' windfall did not occur in a vacuum. The long-standing, often toxic relationship between baseball and gambling dates from the sport's infancy, with game-fixing having been exposed as early as 1865. Postseason championship play was not immune to such corruption. The first modern World Series of 1903 was jeopardized by gambler attempts to bribe

Boston Americans catcher Lou Criger into throwing games. Never-substantiated rumors about the integrity of play dogged a number of ensuing fall classics.

The architects of the Black Sox Scandal have never been conclusively identified. Many subscribe to the notion that the plot was originally concocted by White Sox first baseman Chick Gandil and Boston bookmaker Joseph "Sport" Sullivan. Surviving grand-jury testimony portrays Gandil and White Sox pitching staff ace Eddie Cicotte as the primary instigators of the fix. In any event, the fix plot soon embraced many other actors, both in uniform and out. Indeed, dissection of the scandal has long been complicated by its scope, for there was not a lone plot to rig the Series, but actually two or more, each with its own peculiar cast of characters.

Since it was first deployed as a trial stratagem by Black Sox defense lawyers in June 1921, motivation for the Series fix has been ascribed to the miserliness of Chicago club owner Charles A. Comiskey. The assertion is specious. Comiskey paid his charges the going rate and then some. In fact, salary data recently made available establish that the 1919 Chicago White Sox had the second highest player payroll in the major leagues, with stalwarts like second baseman Eddie Collins, catcher Ray Schalk, third baseman Buck Weaver, and pitcher Cicotte being at or near the top of the pay scale for their positions.

But the White Sox clubhouse was an unhealthy place, with the team long riven by faction. One clique was headed by team captain Eddie Collins, Ivy League-educated and self-assured to the point of arrogance. Aligned with Cocky Collins were Schalk, spitballer Red Faber, and outfielders Shano Collins and Nemo Leibold. The other, a more hardscrabble group united in envy, if not outright hatred, of the socially superior Collins, was headed by tough guy Gandil and the more amiable Cicotte. Also in their corner were

Weaver, shortstop/fix enforcer Swede Risberg, outfielder Happy Felsch, and utilityman Fred McMullin.

According to the grand-jury testimony of Eddie Cicotte, his faction first began to discuss the feasibility of throwing the upcoming World Series during a train trip late in the regular season. Even before the White Sox clinched the 1919 pennant, Cicotte started to feel out Bill Burns, a former American League pitcher turned gambler, about financing a Series fix. Again according to Cicotte, the Sox were envious of the $10,000 payoffs rumored to have been paid certain members of the Chicago Cubs for dumping the 1918 Series against the Boston Red Sox. The lure of a similar score was enhanced by the low prospect of discovery or punishment.

Although they surfaced periodically, reports of player malfeasance were not taken seriously, routinely dismissed by the game's establishment and denigrated in the sporting press. And the imposition of sanctions arising from gambling-related activity seemed to have been all but abandoned. Even charges of player corruption lodged by as revered a figure as Christy Mathewson and corroborated by affidavit were deemed insufficient grounds for disciplinary action, as attested by the National League's recent exoneration of long-suspected game-fixer Hal Chase. By the fall of 1919, therefore, the fix of the World Series could reasonably be viewed from a player standpoint as a low risk/high reward proposition.

In mid-September the Gandil-Cicotte crew committed to the Series fix during a meeting at the Ansonia Hotel in New York. Likelihood of the scheme's success was bolstered by the recruitment of the White Sox' No. 2 starter, Lefty Williams, and the club's batting star, outfielder Joe Jackson. In follow-up conversation with Burns, the parties agreed that the World Series would be lost to the National League champion Cincinnati Reds in exchange for a $100,000 payoff.

Financing a payoff of that magnitude was beyond Burns's means, and efforts to secure backing from gambling elements in Philadelphia came up empty. Thereafter, Burns and sidekick Billy Maharg ap-

proached a potential fix underwriter of vast resource, New York City underworld financier Arnold Rothstein, known as the "Big Bankroll." In all probability, word of the Series plot had reached Rothstein well before Burns and Maharg made their play. According to all concerned (Burns, Maharg, and Rothstein), Rothstein flatly turned down the proposal that he finance the Series fix. And from there, the plot to corrupt the 1919 World Series thickened.

The prospect of fix financing was revived by Hal Chase who, by means unknown, had also gotten wind of the scheme. Chase put Burns in touch with one of sportdom's shadiest characters, former world featherweight boxing champ Abe Attell. A part-time Rothstein bodyguard and a full-time hustler, the Little Champ was constantly on the lookout for a score. Accompanied by an associate named "Bennett" (later identified as Des Moines gambler David Zelcer), Attell met with Burns and informed him that Rothstein had reconsidered the fix proposition and was now willing to finance it. The credulous Burns thereupon hastened to Cincinnati to rendezvous with the players on the eve of Game One.

In the meantime, the campaign to fix the Series had opened a second front. Shortly before the White Sox were scheduled to leave for Cincinnati, Gandil, Cicotte, Weaver, and other fix enlistees met privately at the Warner Hotel in Chicago. A mistrustful Cicotte demanded that his $10,000 fix share be paid in full before the team departed for Cincinnati. He then left the gathering to socialize elsewhere. The others remained to hear two men identified as "Sullivan" and

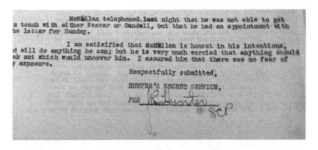

Private detective J.R. Hunter was hired by White Sox owner Charles Comiskey to spy on the suspected World Series fixers in the fall of 1919. He filed this report on Fred McMullin to the White Sox office on December 4, 1919. (Collection of Jacob Pomrenke)

"Brown" from New York. A confused Lefty Williams later testified that he was unsure if these men were the gamblers financing the fix or their representatives.

The first Warner Hotel fixer has always been identified as Gandil's Boston pal, Sport Sullivan, but the true identity of "Brown" would remain a mystery to fix investigators. Decades later, first Rothstein biographer Leo Katcher and thereafter Abe Attell asserted that "Brown" was actually Nat Evans, a capable Rothstein subordinate and Rothstein's junior partner in several gambling casino ventures. Whoever "Brown" was, $10,000 in cash had been placed under the bed pillow in Cicotte's hotel room before the evening was over. The Series fix was now on, in earnest.

The Warner Hotel conclave was unknown to Burns, then trying to finalize his own fix arrangement with the players. He, Attell, and Bennett/Zelcer met with all the corrupted players, save Joe Jackson, at the Sinton Hotel in Cincinnati sometime prior to the Series opener. After considerable wrangling, it was agreed that the players would be paid off in $20,000 installments following each White Sox loss in the best-five-of-nine Series.

Later that evening, Burns encountered an old acquaintance, Chicago sportswriter Hugh Fullerton. Like most experts, Fullerton had confidently predicted a White Sox triumph. But something in the tone of Burns's assurance that the Reds were a "sure thing" unsettled Fullerton. Burns made it sound as though the Series had already been decided. Almost simultaneously, betting odds on the Series shifted dramatically, with a last-minute surge of money transforming the once-underdog Reds into a slight Series favorite. To Fullerton and other baseball insiders, something ominous seemed to be afoot.

To those unaware of these developments, the Game One matchup typified the inequity between the two sides. On the mound for the White Sox was 29-game-winner Eddie Cicotte, a veteran member of Chicago's 1917 World Series champions and one of the game's finest pitchers. Starting for Cincinnati was left-hander

Dutch Ruether, who, prior to his 1919 season's 19-win breakout, had won exactly three major-league games.

Aside from control master Cicotte plunking Reds leadoff batter Morrie Rath with his second pitch, the match proceeded unremarkably in the early going. Then Cicotte suddenly fell apart in the fourth. By the time stunned Chicago manager Kid Gleason had taken him out, the White Sox were behind 6-1. The final score was a lopsided Cincinnati 9, Chicago 1. Following their delivery of the promised loss, the players were stiffed, fix paymaster Attell reneging on the $20,000 payment due.

The White Sox fulfilled their side of the fix agreement in Game Two, in which Lefty Williams's sudden bout of wildness in the fourth inning spelled the difference in a 4-2 Cincinnati victory. With the corrupted players now owed $40,000, Burns was hard-pressed to get even a fraction of that from Attell. Accusations of a double-cross greeted Burns's delivery of only $10,000 to the players after the Game Two defeat. Still, he and Maharg accepted Gandil's assurance that the Sox would lose Game Three. The two fix middlemen were then wiped out, losing their entire wagering stake when the White Sox posted a 3-0 victory behind the pitching of Dickey Kerr.

Whether the Series fix continued after Game Two is a matter of dispute. Joe Jackson would later inform the press that the Black Sox had tried to throw Game Three, only to be thwarted by Kerr's superb pitching performance. Those maintaining that the White Sox were now playing to win often cite the decisive two-RBI single of erstwhile fix ringleader Chick Gandil.

With the Series now standing two games to one in Cincinnati's favor, Cicotte retook the mound for Game Four, the most controversial of the Series. Locked in a pitching duel with Reds fireballer Jimmy Ring, Cicotte exhibited the pitching artistry that had been expected from him at the outset. His fielding, however, was another matter, with the game turning on two egregious defensive misplays by Cicotte in the Cincinnati fifth. Those miscues provided the margin in a 2-0 Cincinnati victory.

Cicotte later maintained that he had tried his utmost to win Game Four, but whether true or not, Eddie had received little offensive help from his teammates. The White Sox, both Clean and Black variety, were mired in a horrendous batting slump that would see the American League's most potent lineup go an astonishing 26 consecutive innings without scoring. Chicago bats were silent again in Game Five, managing but three hits in a 5-0 setback that pushed the Sox to the brink of Series elimination.

Meanwhile, uncertainty reigned in gambling quarters. After the unscripted White Sox victory in Game Three, Burns, reportedly acting at the behest of Abe Attell, approached Gandil about resuming the fix. Gandil spurned him. But whether that brought the curtain down on the debasement of the 1919 World Series is far from clear. The Burns/Attell/Zelcer combine was not the only gambler group that the White Sox had taken money from. Admissions later made by the corrupted players make it clear that far more than the $10,000 post-Game Two payoff was disbursed during the Series. But who made these payoffs; when/where/how they were made; how much fix money in total was paid out by gambler interests, and how much of that money Gandil kept for himself, remain matters of conjecture.

More well-settled is the fact that awareness of the corruption of the World Series was fairly widespread in professional gambling circles. After the post-Game Two player/gambler falling-out, a group of Midwestern gamblers convened in a Chicago hotel to discuss a fix revival. Spearheading this effort were St. Louis clothing manufacturer/gambler Carl Zork and an Omaha bookmaker improbably named Benjamin Franklin, both of whom were heavily invested in a Reds Series triumph. The action, if any, taken by these Midwesterners is another uncertain element in the fix saga.

Back on the diamond, the White Sox teetered on the brink of elimination, having won only one of the first five World Series games. Their outlook turned bleaker in Game Six when the Reds rushed to an early 4-0 lead behind Dutch Ruether. At that late moment, slumbering White Sox bats finally awoke. Capitalizing on timely base hits from the previously dormant middle of the batting order (Buck Weaver, Joe Jackson, and Happy Felsch), the White Sox rallied for a 5-4 triumph in 10 innings. The ensuing Game Seven was the type of affair that sporting pundits had anticipated at the Series outset: a comfortable 4-1 Chicago victory behind masterly pitching by Eddie Cicotte and RBI-base hits by Jackson and Felsch.

Now only one win away from evening up the Series, the hopes of the White Sox faithful were pinned on regular-season stalwart Lefty Williams. Williams had pitched decently in his two previous Series outings, only to see his starts come undone by a lone big inning in each game. In Game Eight, disaster struck early. Lefty did not make it out of the first inning, leaving the White Sox an insurmountable 4-0 deficit. The Reds continued to pour it on against second-line Chicago relievers. Only a forlorn White Sox rally late in the contest made the final score somewhat respectable: Cincinnati 10, Chicago 5.

The next morning, the sporting world's approbation of the Reds' World Series triumph was widespread, tempered only by a discordant note sounded by Hugh Fullerton. In a widely circulated column, Fullerton questioned the integrity of the White Sox' Series performance. He also made the startling assertion that at least seven White Sox players would not be wearing a Chicago uniform the next season. More explicit but little-noticed charges of player corruption quickly followed in *Collyer's Eye,* a horse-racing trade paper.

Although a few other intrepid baseball writers would later voice their own reservations about the Series bona fides, Fullerton's commentary was not well-received by most in the profession. A number of fellow sportswriters characterized the Fullerton assertions as no more than the sour grapes of an "expert" embarrassed by the misfire of his World Series prediction. In a prominent *New York Times* article, special World Series correspondent Christy Mathewson also dismissed the Fullerton suspicions, informing readers that a fix of the Series was virtually impossible.

Three of the accused Chicago players, Swede Risberg (far left), Buck Weaver (middle), and Happy Felsch (far right), sit on a bench with defense attorneys Michael Ahern (second from left) and Thomas Nash (second from right) during the Black Sox criminal trial in July 1921. (Courtesy of Mike Nola / BlackBetsy.com)

For its part, Organized Baseball mostly ignored Fullerton's charges, leaving denigration of Fullerton and his allies to friendly organs like *Baseball Magazine* and *The Sporting News*. In the short run, the strategy worked. Despite reiteration in follow-up columns, Fullerton's concerns gained little traction with baseball fans. By the start of the new season, the notion that the 1919 World Series had not been on the level was mostly forgotten—except at White Sox headquarters.

Unbeknownst to the sporting press or public, White Sox owner Charles Comiskey had not dismissed the allegations made against his team. While the 1919 Series was in progress, Comiskey had been disturbed by privately received reports that his team was going to throw the championship series. Shortly after the Series was over, club officials were dispatched to St. Louis to make discreet inquiry into fix rumors. Much to Comiskey's chagrin, disgruntled local gambling informants endorsed the charge that members of his team had thrown the Series in exchange for a promised $100,000 payoff. Lingering doubt on that score was subsequently erased when in-the-know gamblers Harry Redmon and Joe Pesch repeated the fix details to Comiskey and other club brass during a late December meeting in Chicago.

Of the courses available to him, Comiskey opted to pursue the one of self-interest. Rather than expose

the perfidy of his players and precipitate the breakup of a championship team, Comiskey kept his fix information quiet. Early in the new year, the corrupted players were re-signed for the 1920 season, with Joe Jackson, Happy Felsch, Swede Risberg, and Lefty Williams receiving substantial pay raises, to boot. Only fix ringleader Chick Gandil experienced any degree of Comiskey wrath; Gandil was tendered a contract for no more than his previous season's salary. When, as expected, Gandil rejected the pact, Comiskey took pleasure in placing him on the club's ineligible list. That suspension continued in force all season and effectively ended Chick Gandil's playing career. He never appeared in a major-league game after the 1919 World Series.

From a financial standpoint, Comiskey's silence paid off. Fueled by a return to pre-World War I "normalcy" and the unprecedented slugging exploits of a pitcher-turned-outfielder named Babe Ruth, major-league baseball underwent an explosion in popularity. With its defending AL champion team intact except for Gandil, the White Sox spent the 1920 season in the midst of an exciting three-way pennant battle with New York and Cleveland. With attendance at Comiskey Park soaring to new heights, club coffers overflowed with revenue. Then late in the 1920 season, it all began to unravel. The immediate cause was an unlikely one: the suspected fix of a meaningless late August game between the Chicago Cubs and Philadelphia Phillies.

At first the matter seemed no more than a distraction, the latest of the minor annoyances that bedeviled the game that season. That spring, baseball had been mildly discomforted by exposure of the game-fixing proclivities of Hal Chase, revealed during the trial of a breach-of-contract lawsuit instituted by black-sheep teammate Lee Magee. Then in early August, West Coast baseball followers were shaken by allegations that cast serious doubt upon the legitimacy of the 1919 Pacific Coast League crown won by the Vernon Tigers. In time, the PCL scandal would have momentous consequences, providing Commissioner Landis with instructive precedent for dealing with courtroom-acquitted Black

Sox defendants. In the near term, however, the significance of these matters resided mainly in their effect upon Cubs president William L. Veeck Sr. Unhappy connection to both the Magee affair and the PCL scandal—Veeck's boss, Cubs owner William Wrigley, was livid over the prospect that his Los Angeles Angels might have been cheated out of the PCL pennant—prompted Veeck to make public disclosure of the Cubs-Phillies fix reports and to pledge club cooperation with any investigative body wishing to delve into the matter.

Revelation that the outcome of the Cubs-Phillies game might have been rigged engaged the attention of two of the Black Sox Scandal's most formidable actors: Cook County Judge Charles A. McDonald and American League President Ban Johnson. Only recently installed as chief justice of Chicago's criminal courts and an avid baseball fan, McDonald promptly empaneled a grand jury to investigate the game fix reports.

But within days, influential sportswriter Joe Vila of the *New York Sun*, prominent Chicago businessman-baseball fan Fred Loomis, and others were pressing a more substantial target upon the grand jury: the 1919 World Series. Privately, Johnson, a longtime acquaintance of Judge McDonald, urged a similar course upon the jurist. Like Comiskey, Johnson had conducted his own confidential investigation into the outcome of the 1919 Series. And he too had uncovered evidence that the Series had been corrupted. McDonald was amenable to expansion of the grand jury's probe, and by the time the grand jury conducted its first substantive session on September 22, 1920, inquiry into the Cubs-Phillies game had been relegated to secondary status. The panel's attention would be focused on the 1919 World Series.

The ensuing proceedings were remarkable for many reasons, not the least of which was the wholesale disregard of the mandate of grand-jury secrecy. Violation of this black-letter precept of law was justified on the dubious premise that baseball would benefit from the airing of its dirty laundry, and soon newspapers nationwide were reporting the details, often verbatim, of grand-jury testimony.

This breach of law was accompanied by another extra-legal phenomenon: almost daily public commentary on the proceedings by the grand-jury foreman, the prosecuting attorney, and, on occasion, Judge McDonald himself. In a matter of days, the transparency of the proceedings permitted the *Chicago Tribune* to announce the impending indictment of eight White Sox players: Eddie Cicotte, Chick Gandil, Joe Jackson, Buck Weaver, Lefty Williams, Happy Felsch, Swede Risberg, and Fred McMullin—the men soon branded the Black Sox. For the time being, the charge against them was the generic conspiracy to commit an illegal act. The scandal spotlight then shifted briefly to Philadelphia, where a fix insider was giving the interview that would blow the scandal wide open.

In the September 27, 1920, edition of the *Philadelphia North American*, Billy Maharg declared that Games One, Two, and Eight of the 1919 World Series had been rigged. According to Maharg, the outcome of the first two games had been procured by the bribery of the White Sox players by the Burns/Attell/Bennett combine. The abysmal pitching performance that cost Chicago any chance of winning Game Eight was the product of intimidation of Lefty Williams by the Zork-Franklin forces, Maharg implied.

Wire service republication of the Maharg expose produced swift and stunning reaction. A day later, first Eddie Cicotte and then Joe Jackson admitted agreeing to accept a payoff to lose the Series when interviewed in the office of White Sox legal counsel Alfred Austrian. The two then repeated this admission under oath before the grand jury. Interestingly, neither Cicotte nor Jackson confessed to making a deliberate misplay during the Series. Press accounts that had Cicotte describing how he lobbed hittable pitches to the plate and/or had Jackson admitting to deliberate failure in the field or at bat were entirely bogus. According to the transcriptions of their testimony, the two had told the grand jury no such thing. While each had taken the gamblers' money, Cicotte and Jackson both insisted that they had played to win at all times against the Reds. The other player participants in the Series fix were identified by Cicotte and Jackson, but apart from laying blame on Gandil, neither man disclosed much knowledge of how the fix had been instigated or who had financed it.

This exercise repeated itself when Lefty Williams spoke the following day. Like Cicotte and Jackson, Lefty admitted joining the fix conspiracy and accepting gamblers' money, first confessing in the Austrian law office, and thereafter in testimony before the grand jury. But Williams also denied that he had done anything corrupt on the field to earn his payment. He said he had tried his best at all times, even during his dismal Game Eight start. For the grand-jury record, Lefty officially identified the fix participants as "Cicotte, Gandil, Weaver, Felsch, Risberg, McMullin, Jackson, and myself." Williams also put names on some of the gambler co-conspirators. At the Warner Hotel in Chicago, they had been named "Sullivan" and "Brown." At the Sinton Hotel in Cincinnati, the fix proponents had been Bill Burns, Abe Attell, and a third man named "Bennett."

A similar tack was taken by Happy Felsch when interviewed by a reporter for the *Chicago Evening American*. Like the others, Felsch admitted his complicity in the fix plot and his acceptance of gamblers' money. But his subpar Series performance, particularly in center field, had not been deliberate, he said. Lest the underworld get the wrong idea, Felsch hastened to add that he had been prepared to make a game-decisive misplay, but the opportunity to do so had not presented itself during the Series. Unlike the others, Happy confined admission of wrongdoing to himself, although he had come to admire the way that Cicotte had demanded his payoff money up-front. Felsch did not know who had financed the fix, but he was willing to subscribe to press reports that it had been Abe Attell.

A far different public stance was adopted by the other Black Sox. Chick Gandil, Swede Risberg, Fred McMullin, and Buck Weaver all protested their innocence, with Weaver in particular adamant about his intention to obtain legal counsel and fight any charges

preferred against him in court. Those charges would not be long in coming. On October 29, 1920, five counts of conspiracy to obtain money by false pretenses and/or via a confidence game were returned against the Black Sox by the grand jury. Gamblers Bill Burns, Hal Chase, Abe Attell, Sport Sullivan, and Rachael Brown were also charged in the indictments.

The stage thereupon shifted to the criminal courts for a whirl of legal events, few of which are accurately described or well understood in latter-day Black Sox literature.

The return of criminal charges in the Black Sox case coincided with the Republican Party's political landslide in the November 1920 elections. An entirely different administration soon took charge of the Cook County State's Attorney's Office, the prosecuting agency in the baseball scandal. When the regime of new State's Attorney Robert E. Crowe assumed office, it found the high-profile Black Sox case in disarray. The investigation underlying the indictments was incomplete. Evidence was missing from the prosecutors' vault, including transcriptions of the Cicotte, Jackson, and Williams grand-jury testimony.

Worse yet, it appeared that their predecessors in office had premised prosecution of the Black Sox case on cooperation anticipated from Cicotte, Jackson, and/or Williams, each of whom had admitted fix complicity before the grand jury. But now, the trio was standing firm with the other accused players, and seeking to have their grand-jury confessions suppressed by the court on legal grounds. This placed the new prosecuting attorneys in desperate need of time to rethink and then rebuild their case.

In March 1921, prosecutors' hopes for an adjournment were dashed by Judge William E. Dever, who set a quick peremptory trial date. This prompted a drastic response from prosecutor Crowe. Rather than try to pull the Black Sox case together on short notice, he administratively dismissed the charges. Crowe coupled public announcement of this stunning development with the promise that the Black Sox case would be presented to the grand jury again for new indictments.

Before the month was out, that promise was fulfilled. Expedited grand-jury proceedings yielded new indictments that essentially replicated the dismissed ones. All those previously charged were re-indicted, while the roster of gambler defendants was enlarged to include Carl Zork, Benjamin Franklin, David (Bennett) Zelcer, and brothers Ben and Lou Levi, reputedly related to Zelcer by marriage and long targeted for prosecution by AL President Ban Johnson.

With the legal proceedings now reverting to courtroom stage one, prosecutors had acquired the time necessary to get their case in better shape. That extra time was needed, as the prosecution remained besieged on many fronts. The State was deluged by defense motions to dismiss the charges, suppress evidence, limit testimony, and the like. Prosecutors were also having trouble getting the gambler defendants into court. Sport Sullivan and Rachael Brown remained somewhere at large. Hal Chase and Abe Attell successfully resisted extradition to Chicago, and Ben Franklin was excused from the proceedings on grounds of illness.

In the run-up to trial, however, prosecution prospects received one major boost. Retrieved from the Mexican border by his pal Billy Maharg (via a trip financed by Ban Johnson), Bill Burns had agreed to turn State's evidence in return for immunity. Now, prosecutors had the crucial fix insider that their case had been lacking.

Jury selection began on June 16, 1921, and dragged on for several weeks. Appearing as counsel on behalf of the accused were some of the Midwest's finest criminal defense lawyers: Thomas Nash and Michael Ahern (representing Weaver, Felsch, Risberg, and McMullin; McMullin did not arrive in Chicago until after jury selection had begun, and for this reason, the trial went on without him and the charges against him were later dismissed); Benedict Short and George Guenther (Jackson and Williams); James O'Brien and John Prystalski (Gandil); A. Morgan Frumberg and Henry Berger (Zork), and Max Luster and J.J. Cooke (Zelcer and the Levi brothers). Cicotte, meanwhile, was represented by his friend and personal attorney Daniel Cassidy, a civil lawyer from Detroit.

Although outnumbered, the prosecution was hardly outgunned, with its chairs filled by experienced trial lawyers: Assistant State's Attorneys George Gorman and John Tyrrell, and Special Prosecutor Edward Prindiville, with assistance from former Judge George Barrett representing the interests of the American League in court, and a cadre of attorneys in the employ of AL President Johnson working behind the scenes.

About the only unproven commodity in the courtroom was the newly assigned trial judge, Hugo Friend. Judge Friend would later go on to a distinguished 46-year career on Illinois trial and appellate benches. But at the time of the Black Sox trial, he was a judicial novice, presiding over his first significant case. Although his mettle would often be tested by a battalion of fractious barristers, Friend's intelligence and sense of fairness would stand him in good stead. The Black Sox case would be generally well tried, if not error-free.

In a sweltering midsummer courtroom, the prosecution commenced its case with the witnesses needed to establish factual minutiae—the scores of 1919 World Series games, the employment of the accused players by the Chicago White Sox, the winning and losing Series shares, etc.—that the defense, for tactical reasons, declined to stipulate. Then, chief prosecution witness Bill Burns assumed the stand. For the better part of three days, Burns recounted the events that had precipitated the corruption of the 1919 World Series. Those who had equated Burns with his "Sleepy Bill" nickname were in for a shock. Quick-witted and unflappable, Burns was more than a match for sneering defense lawyers, much to the astonishment, then delight, of the jaded Black Sox trial press corps. Newspaper reviews of Burns's testimony glowed and, by the time their star witness stepped down, prosecutors were near-jubilant. Thereafter, prosecution focus temporarily shifted to incriminating Zork and the other Midwestern gambler defendants.

Halfway through the State's case, the jury was excused while the court conducted an evidentiary hearing into the admissibility of the Cicotte, Jackson, and Williams grand-jury testimony. Modern accounts of the Black Sox saga often relate that the prosecution was grievously injured by the loss of grand-jury documents. That was hardly the case. When prosecutors discovered that the original grand-jury transcripts were missing, they merely had the grand-jury stenographers create new ones from their shorthand notes. These second-generation transcripts were available throughout the proceedings, and Black Sox defense lawyers did not contest their accuracy.

What was contested was whether, and to what extent, the trial jury should be made privy to what Cicotte, Jackson, and Williams had told the grand jurors. According to the defense, the Cicotte, Jackson, and Williams grand-jury testimony had been induced by broken off-the-record promises of immunity from prosecution. If this were true, the testimony would be deemed involuntary in the legal sense and inadmissible against the accused.

With testimony restricted exclusively to what had happened in and around the grand-jury room, the proceedings devolved into a swearing contest. Cicotte, Jackson, and Williams testified that they had been promised immunity. Lead grand-jury prosecutor Hartley Replogle and Judge McDonald denied it. During the hearing, grand-jury excerpts were read into the record at length. After hearing both sides, Judge Friend determined that the defendants had confessed freely, without any promise of leniency. Their grand-jury testimony would be admissible in evidence — but not before each grand-jury transcript had been edited to delete all reference to Chick Gandil, Buck Weaver, or anyone else mentioned in it, other than the speaker himself. Once this tedious task was accomplished, the redacted grand-jury testimony of Eddie Cicotte, Joe Jackson, and Lefty Williams was read to the jury, a prolonged and dry exercise that seemed to anesthetize most panel members.

The numbing effect that the transcript readings had on the jury was not lost on prosecutors. Wishing to close their case while it still enjoyed the momentum of the Burns testimony, prosecutors made a fateful strategic decision. They jettisoned the remainder of their scheduled witnesses (Ban Johnson, Joe Pesch, St. Louis Browns second baseman Joe Gedeon, et al.)

and wrapped up the State's case with another fix insider: unindicted co-conspirator Billy Maharg. The affable Maharg provided an account of the fix developments that he was witness to, providing firm and consistent corroboration of many fix details supplied by Bill Burns earlier.

Pleased with Maharg's performance, prosecutors rested their case. Now they would be obliged to accept the cost of short-circuiting their proofs. In response to defense motions, Judge Friend dismissed the charges against the Levi brothers for lack of evidence. He also signaled that he would be disposed to overturn any guilty verdict returned by the jury against Carl Zork, Buck Weaver, or Happy Felsch, given the thinness of the incriminating evidence presented against them. These rulings, however, did not visibly trouble the prosecutors, for they had plainly decided to concentrate their efforts on convicting defendants Gandil, Cicotte, Jackson, Williams, and the gambler David Zelcer.

The defense had long advertised that the Black Sox would be testifying in their own defense. But that would have to wait, as the gambler defendants would be going first. Once the Zelcer and Zork defenses had presented their cases, the Gandil defense took the floor, calling a series of witnesses mainly intended to make a liar out of Bill Burns.

Also presented was White Sox club secretary Harry Grabiner, whose testimony about soaring 1920 club revenues undermined the contention that team owner Comiskey or the White Sox corporation had been injured by the fix of the 1919 World Series. (Years later, jury foreman William Barry would tell Judge Friend that the Grabiner testimony had had more influence on the jury than that of any other witness.)

Then, with the stage finally set for Chick to take the stand, the Gandil defense abruptly rested. So did the other Black Sox. Little explanation for this change in defense plan was offered, apart from the comment that there was no need for the accused players to testify because the State had made no case against them. Caught off-guard by defense maneuvers, the prosecution scrambled to present rebuttal witnesses, most of whom were excluded from the testifying by Judge Friend. As little in the way of a defense had been mounted by the player defendants, there was no legal justification for admitting rebuttal.

The remainder of the trial was devoted to closing stemwinders by opposing counsel and the court's instructions on the law. Then the jury retired to deliberate. Less than three hours later, it reached a verdict. With the parties reassembled in a courtroom packed with defense partisans, the court clerk announced the outcome: Not Guilty, as to all defendants on all charges. A smiling Judge Friend concurred, pronouncing the jury's verdict a fair one.

With that, pandemonium erupted. Jurors shook hands and congratulated the men whom they had just acquitted. Some in the crowd even hoisted defendants onto their shoulders and paraded them around. Thereafter, defendants, defense lawyers, jurors, and defense followers gathered on the courthouse steps, where their mutual joy was captured in a photo published by the *Chicago Tribune*. Later, a post-verdict celebration brought the defendants and the jurors together once again at a nearby Italian restaurant. There, the revelry continued into the wee hours of the morning, closing with jurors and Black Sox singing "Hail, Hail, The Gang's All Here."

This extraordinary exhibition of camaraderie suggests that the verdict may have been a product of that courthouse phenomenon that all prosecutors dread: jury nullification. In a criminal case, jurors are carefully instructed to abjure passion, prejudice, sympathy, and other emotion in rendering judgment. They are to base their verdict entirely on the evidence presented and the law. But during deliberations in highly charged cases, this instruction is susceptible to being overridden by the jury's identification with the accused. Or by dislike of the victim. Or by the urge to send some sort of message to the community at large.

In the Black Sox case, defense counsel, notably Benedict Short and Henry Berger, worked assiduously to cultivate a bond between the working-class men on the jury and the blue-collar defendants. The de-

fense's closing arguments to the jury, particularly those of Short, Thomas Nash, A. Morgan Frumberg, and James O'Brien, stridently denounced the wealthy victim Comiskey and his corporation. The defense lawyers also raised the specter of another menace: AL President Ban Johnson, portrayed as a malevolent force working outside of jury view to ensure the unfair condemnation of the accused.

In the end, of course, the underlying basis for the jury's acquittal of the Black Sox is unknowable all these years later. Significantly, the fair-minded Judge Friend concurred in the outcome. Still, jury nullification remains a plausible explanation for the verdict, particularly when it came to jurors' resolution of the charges against defendants Cicotte, Jackson, and Williams, against whom the State had presented a facially strong case.

Few others shared the jurors' satisfaction in their verdict, with many baseball officials vowing never to grant employment to the acquitted players. That sentiment was quickly rendered academic. Commissioner Kenesaw Mountain Landis had taken note of the minor leagues' prompt expulsion of the Pacific Coast League players who had had their indictments dismissed by the judge in that game-fixing case. Landis,

A jubilant trio of former White Sox players — Buck Weaver (center, in suit), Eddie Cicotte (in bow tie), and Happy Felsch (far right) — shake hands with members of the jury and other courtroom spectators immediately after they were acquitted on charges related to the fixing of the 1919 World Series on August 2, 1921, in Chicago. (Courtesy of Mike Nola / BlackBetsy.com)

who had been hired as commissioner in November 1920, now utilized that action as precedent.

With a famous edict that began "Regardless of the verdict of juries …," Landis permanently barred the eight Black Sox players from participation in Organized Baseball. And with that, Joe Jackson, Eddie Cicotte, Buck Weaver, and the rest were consigned to the sporting wilderness. None would ever appear in another major-league game. The Black Sox saga, however, was not quite over.

In the aftermath of their official banishment from the game, Buck Weaver, Happy Felsch, Swede Risberg, and Joe Jackson instituted civil litigation against the White Sox, pursuing grievances grounded in breach of contract, defamation, and restraint on their professional livelihoods.

Outside of Milwaukee, where the Felsch/Risberg/Jackson suits were filed, little attention was paid to their complaints. Jackson's breach-of-contract suit was the only one that ever went to trial. It was founded on the three-year contract that Jackson had signed with the White Sox in late February 1920, months after the World Series. The club had unilaterally voided the pact when it released Jackson in March 1921, and he had gone unpaid for the 1921 and 1922 baseball seasons.

In a pretrial deposition, plaintiff Jackson disputed that his termination by the White Sox had been justified by his involvement in the Series fix. On that point, Jackson swore to a set of fix-related events dramatically at odds with his earlier grand-jury testimony. Jackson now maintained that he had had no connection to the conspiracy to rig the 1919 Series. He had not even known about it until after the Series was over, when a drunken Lefty Williams foisted a $5,000 fix share on Jackson, telling him that the Black Sox had used Jackson's name while trying to persuade gamblers to finance the fix scheme.

When the suit was tried in early 1924, its highlight was Jackson's cross-examination by White Sox attorney George Hudnall. Confronted with his grand-jury testimony of September 28, 1920, Jackson did not attempt to explain away the contradiction between his civil deposition assertions and his grand-jury testimony. Nor did he attempt to harmonize the two. Rather, Jackson maintained—more than 100 times—that he had never made the statements contained in the transcript of his grand-jury testimony.

An outraged Judge John J. Gregory subsequently cited Jackson for perjury and had him jailed overnight. The court vacated the jury's $16,711.04 award in Jackson favor, ruling that it was grounded in false testimony and jury nonfeasance. After the proceedings were over, civil jury foreman John E. Sanderson shed light on the jury's thinking. Sanderson informed the press that the jury had entirely disregarded Jackson's testimony about disputed events. The foreman also rejected the notion that the panel had exonerated Jackson of participation in the 1919 World Series fix.

Rather, the jury had premised its judgment for Jackson on the legal principle of condonation. As far as the jury was concerned, White Sox team brass had known of Jackson's World Series fix involvement well before the new three-year contract was tendered to him in February 1920. Having thus effectively condoned (or forgiven) Jackson's Series misconduct by re-signing him, the club was in no position to void that contract once the public found out what club management had known about Jackson all along. Jackson was, according to the Milwaukee jury, therefore entitled to his 1921 and 1922 pay.

In time, the four civil lawsuits, including that of Jackson, were settled out of court for modest sums. Little notice was taken, as the baseball press and public had long since moved on. In the ensuing years, the Black Sox Scandal receded in memory, recalled only in the random sports column, magazine article, or, starting with the death of Joe Jackson in December 1951, the obituary of a Black Sox player.

Revival of interest in the scandal commenced in the late 1950s, but did not attract widespread attention until the publication of Eliot Asinof's classic *Eight Men Out* in 1963. Regrettably, this spellbinding account of the scandal was marred by historically inaccurate detail, attributable presumably to the fact that much of the criminal case record had been unavailable to Asinof, having disappeared from court archives over the years. This had compelled Asinof to rely upon scandal survivors, particularly Abe Attell, an engaging but unreliable informant.

Asinof also exercised artistic license in his work, creating, apparently for copyright protection purposes, a fictitious villain named "Harry F." to intimidate Lefty Williams into his dreadful Game Eight pitching performance. Asinof likewise embellished his tale of the Jackson civil case, inserting melodramatic events, such as White Sox lawyer Hudnall pulling a supposedly lost Jackson grand-jury transcript out of his briefcase in midtrial, into *Eight Men Out* that are nowhere memorialized in the fully extant record of the civil proceedings.

Over the years, the embrace of such Asinof inventions, as well as the repetition of more ancient canards — the miserly wage that Comiskey supposedly paid the corrupted players, the notion that disappearing grand-jury testimony hamstrung the prosecution, and other fictions — has become a recurring feature of much Black Sox literature.

In 2002 scandal enthusiast Gene Carney commenced a near-obsessive re-examination of the Black Sox affair. First in weekly blog posts and later in his im-portant book *Burying the Black Sox: How Baseball's Cover-Up of the 1919 World Series Fix Almost Succeeded* (Potomac Books, 2006), Carney circulated his findings, which were often at variance with long-accepted scandal wisdom. Sadly, this work was cut short by Carney's untimely passing in July 2009. But the mission endures, carried on by others, including the membership of the SABR committee inspired by Carney's zeal.

That scandal revelations are still to be made is clear, manifested by events like the surfacing of a treasure trove of lost Black Sox documents acquired by the Chicago History Museum several years ago. As the playing of the 1919 World Series approaches its 100th anniversary, the investigation continues. And the final word on the Black Sox Scandal remains to be written.

SOURCES

This essay is drawn from a more comprehensive account of the Black Sox legal proceedings provided in the writer's *Black Sox in the Courtroom: The Grand Jury, Criminal Trial, and Civil Litigation* (McFarland & Co., 2013). Underlying sources include surviving fragments of the judicial record; the Black Sox Scandal collections maintained at the Chicago History Museum and the National Baseball Hall of Fame and Museum's Giamatti Research Center; the transcript of Joe Jackson's 1924 lawsuit against the Chicago White Sox held by the Chicago Baseball Museum; newspaper archives in Chicago and elsewhere; and contemporary Black Sox scholarship, particularly the work of Gene Carney, Bob Hoie, and Bruce Allardice.

EPILOGUE: OFFSEASON, 1919-20

By Jacob Pomrenke

ONE DAY AFTER THE 1919 World Series ended, Chicago White Sox owner Charles Comiskey responded publicly to rumors that his team had intentionally thrown games to the Cincinnati Reds. "I believe my boys fought the battles of the recent world's series on the level," he told the *Chicago Times*, and he even offered a $10,000 reward if anyone could provide him with credible evidence of a fix.

It was an empty promise, because Comiskey already had all the evidence he needed. According to reporter Hugh Fullerton, a friend and ally of the White Sox owner, Comiskey knew all about the fix before Game One — and he wasn't alone, for the World Series fix was the worst-kept secret in baseball.

Comiskey, American League President Ban Johnson, and other baseball officials spent the offseason of 1919-20 investigating the ugly rumors that had plagued the fall classic, but ultimately they chose to ignore the many red flags they discovered. The revelation of the World Series fix to the public at large came about only after nearly another full season had been played, and even then it may have never come to light if not for a long-standing feud between Comiskey and Johnson, who pushed Chicago civic leaders to empanel a grand jury and look into the World Series rumors. In addition to airing baseball's dirty laundry with the Black Sox Scandal, their feud led to the installation of Judge Kenesaw Mountain Landis as commissioner and changed the power structure of baseball forever.

The World Series fix came as no surprise to anyone knowledgeable about baseball or its intimate relationship with gambling. Historians Harold and Dorothy Seymour later wrote, "When the scandal of 1919 became public knowledge, the men who controlled Organized Baseball acted as though it were a freakish exception, a sort of unholy mutation.... The evidence is abundantly clear that the groundwork for the crooked 1919 World Series, like most striking events in history, was long prepared."

It took some time, however, for the dust to settle after the World Series ended. On October 10, the same day that Comiskey first defended his players publicly, Fullerton's syndicated newspaper column asserted that seven unnamed members of the White Sox would not be back with the club in 1920. Years later, Fullerton claimed that he got their names — which turned out to be the seven accused Black Sox, minus Buck Weaver, who by most accounts had played his best and had not received a dime from gamblers — from Comiskey himself. In a vivid (possibly apocryphal) description of their meeting written in 1935, Fullerton tells of "a broken and bitter" Comiskey banging a table with his fist and crying, "Keep after them, Hughie; they were crooked. Some day you and I will prove it."

Unbeknownst to Fullerton, Comiskey was already hard at work behind the scenes gathering more information about the fix. Three days after the World Series ended, on October 12, Comiskey sent White Sox manager Kid Gleason to St. Louis to meet with theater owner Harry Redmon, who claimed to have lost more than $5,000 betting on the World Series. Redmon, apparently seeking some of Comiskey's reward money to recoup his gambling losses, confirmed to Gleason the names of the eight ballplayers involved in the fix, including Weaver, who had attended multiple pre-Series meetings with the rest of the players.

Redmon had firsthand knowledge: After the White Sox had surprisingly won Game Three and it appeared as if the fix had been called off, Redmon was connected with a group of Midwestern gamblers who launched an attempt to raise more money to pay off the players and revive the fix. Redmon and fellow St. Louis gambler Joe Pesch repeated the fix details to Comiskey in a second meeting in late December at the White

Sox offices. Comiskey again ignored his pleas for the reward.

Near the end of October, White Sox team counsel Alfred Austrian met with the head of a private investigation firm, John R. Hunter of Hunter's Secret Service, and hired him to find out as much as possible about the suspected players: Eddie Cicotte, Happy Felsch, Chick Gandil, Joe Jackson, Fred McMullin, Swede Risberg, Buck Weaver, and Lefty Williams.

For the next three months, Hunter and his detectives trailed the White Sox players around the country, interviewing their families and checking their bank accounts. Hunter's first stop was California, where he met with McMullin, Gandil, Risberg, and Weaver, posing at one point as a real-estate salesman or as a reporter in an attempt to talk about the World Series with them. Hunter found nothing especially incriminating, but he filed regular reports back to Austrian and Comiskey throughout the offseason.

Another Hunter operative traveled to Milwaukee in November to check up on Happy Felsch, who was busy selling Christmas trees when he wasn't fishing and hunting. The detectives also befriended two female acquaintances of Swede Risberg's in Chicago to whom he had allegedly given money, but came back with no fruitful information. They were instructed, however, not to visit Eddie Cicotte at home in Detroit or Joe Jackson in Savannah, Georgia — the two players who would later crack open the case by testifying before a grand jury to their involvement.

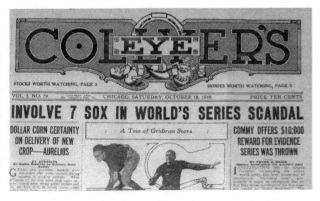

Collyer's Eye was the first publication to publicly name the suspected White Sox fixers — all seven Black Sox minus Buck Weaver — on October 18, 1919, just one week after the World Series ended. (Collection of Jacob Pomrenke)

The detectives' reports themselves were filed away by Comiskey and not publicly revealed until 2007, when the Chicago History Museum acquired them as part of a large collection of Black Sox-related legal documents. Historian Gene Carney, in his seminal book *Burying the Black Sox*, argued that "the investigating Comiskey did — through his employees, his reporter friends like Fullerton, and his paid detectives — was carried on to ensure that any hard evidence found would remain hidden from public view."

But too many people knew about the fix for it to remain hidden for long. In mid-November, reporter Frank O. Klein of a Canadian-based gambling publication called *Collyer's Eye* became the first to publicly name the suspected White Sox fixers. (Although here too, Buck Weaver was omitted from the list of the accused.) American League President Ban Johnson, whose feud with Comiskey caused him to dismiss any opportunities to learn more about the fix during the World Series and perhaps even put a stop to it then, also began his own private investigation. His efforts uncovered additional evidence of the plot and, more important, key witnesses — namely, the gamblers Sleepy Bill Burns and Billy Maharg — who would later be used against the White Sox players in their criminal trial.

Another group that knew about, or at least strongly suspected, the World Series fix started talking during the offseason, too: teammates of the fixers who later became known as the "clean Sox." Future Hall of Fame catcher Ray Schalk got into hot water when he bluntly told *Collyer's Eye* on December 13, 1919, that seven White Sox players would not return to the team in 1920. Unlike Hugh Fullerton months earlier, Schalk even named them. (As usual, Buck Weaver was not among them.)

Although Fullerton continued to write about the rumors, railing against the baseball establishment for not taking the fix seriously, no other whistle-blowers besides *Collyer's Eye* took up the cause that offseason. Fullerton's accusations were routinely dismissed and even mocked in *The Sporting News*, *Baseball Magazine*, and other publications considered friendly to

The careers of two of baseball's best players were headed in different directions in 1920. Chicago White Sox ace Eddie Cicotte, left, was suspended in September and later banned for his role in the 1919 World Series scandal. Babe Ruth, right, was sold by the Boston Red Sox to the New York Yankees before the season and broke his own single-season record with 54 home runs in his first season in the Big Apple. (Courtesy of Mike Nola / BlackBetsy.com)

Organized Baseball. "There is not a breath of suspicion attached to any player, nor a hint that any effort in any manner was made to influence a player's performance," editor J.G. Taylor Spink wrote in the October 9, 1919, issue of *The Sporting News.*

As the calendar flipped over to the new year, talk of the World Series died down and Charles Comiskey likely breathed a sigh of relief. His championship team would remain mostly intact for the 1920 season. He began sending out new contracts to his players — even some of the suspected fixers — and the terms tended to be more generous than usual. Pitcher Eddie Cicotte agreed to a doubling of his base salary, from $5,000 to $10,000 (the same amount he later admitted receiving from gamblers to fix the World Series). Joe Jackson, who had been making $6,000 since 1914, signed a three-year deal for $8,000 per season. On average, according to Black Sox researcher Bob Hoie, White Sox players "received raises of about 32 percent, with no significant difference between the suspected and the clean Sox." Although the White Sox already had one of the top payrolls in baseball, everyone in baseball was making more money.

Part of the reason for Comiskey's extra generosity was that baseball had enjoyed a tremendous resurgence in popularity after World War I, leading to record profits for owners. This would continue in the 1920s as baseball entered a new era defined by high-scoring offenses and home-run records by the likes of Babe Ruth, Lou Gehrig, and Rogers Hornsby.

Attendance had soared across the major leagues in 1919, with three teams (the Reds, Tigers, and Yankees) setting single-season records at their home ballparks. In 1920 seven more teams would set attendance records, including the White Sox who, despite the lingering rumors of corruption, drew more than 833,000 fans to Comiskey Park. The Yankees, thanks in large part to Ruth's record-setting 54 homers, became the first major-league team to surpass 1 million fans in a single season.

The offensive explosion that contributed greatly to baseball's expanded popularity was triggered by several new rules instituted in February 1920, including an attempt at banning intentional walks and the prohibition of the spitball and other "freak deliveries" like the emery ball and Eddie Cicotte's signature "shine ball." Only a handful of spitballers were allowed to continue throwing the wet one in the major leagues; teams were forced to designate two players from their active rosters who could use the pitch. The White Sox selected Cicotte and future Hall of Famer Red Faber, who continued to throw the spitter until he retired in 1933; the last legal spitball was thrown a year later, in 1934, by Burleigh Grimes, who had also been grandfathered in.

Many modern fans have been led to believe that these changes were put in place *as a result of* the Black Sox Scandal, as a concerted effort to excite fans and clean up the game from the corruption and pitching-dominant style of play that characterized the Deadball Era (commonly defined as 1901 through 1919). But the spitball ban was enacted seven months before Cicotte, Jackson, and Lefty Williams testified to a Chicago grand jury, confirming their involvement with the World Series fix. And by Opening Day 1920, Babe Ruth was already one of baseball's biggest stars, having broken the single-season home-run record with 29 homers for the Boston Red Sox the year before. His sale to the Yankees for the unprecedented price of $125,000 was the biggest story of that offseason, not the Black Sox Scandal.

One big change also being discussed in 1919-20 was an overhaul of baseball's governing body, the three-man National Commission, and this would have more far-reaching consequences. The Commission—consisting then of AL President Ban Johnson, NL President John Heydler, and chairman August "Garry" Herrmann, owner of the Cincinnati Reds—was considered by just about everyone in baseball to be ineffective, with Johnson's authoritarian ways alienating owners and players alike. Herrmann's term was also up and the NL owners refused to reappoint him. In February 1920 he resigned from the National Commission and his absence threw Organized Baseball into even more turmoil.

Baseball's inability to deal with its gambling problems was in no small measure due to the weakness of the National Commission, which had ignored most signs of game-fixing, betting on games by players or fans, and bribe offers. These transgressions generated a lot of smoke during the Deadball Era, and sometimes even fire. The poster child for this behavior was Hal Chase, a supremely talented but morally challenged first baseman who bounced from team to team fixing games for more than a decade. Even when he was caught red-handed by his manager, Christy Mathewson—the former New York Giants superstar whose credibility was as high as that of anyone else in the game—nothing had been done to stop Chase. Mathewson's suspension of his player in 1918 was overturned by the National Commission and Chase was allowed to move on to the New York Giants, Matty's old team. Chase promptly organized a new game-fixing ring with the Giants. When Mathewson learned about the World Series fix later, he reportedly told Hugh Fullerton, "Damn them, they [baseball officials] deserve it. I caught two crooks [Chase and Lee Magee] and they whitewashed them." It was an out-of-character outburst for Matty, but his sentiments

reflected baseball's widespread frustration with the National Commission.

By the time the Black Sox affair finally came to light in the fall of 1920, the (now two-man) National Commission was in its final days. In the midst of the biggest scandal in baseball history, three American League owners who had been fighting with Ban Johnson for years were now in full-scale revolt against their league president. This group of "Insurrectos," as they came to be called, included the White Sox' Charles Comiskey, the Red Sox' Harry Frazee, and Yankees co-owner Jacob Ruppert. The other five AL owners remained loyal to Johnson. This rift threatened to tear baseball apart and there was even talk of forming a new 12-team league with the eight NL teams, the three AL "Insurrectos," and whichever owner who was loyal to Johnson broke ranks first.

In November 1920 the baseball owners decided to break up the National Commission once and for all by hiring a new single authority figure, federal judge Kenesaw Mountain Landis, who would rule the game with an iron fist for the next 24 years. Landis single-handedly solved the game's gambling problem, too, with his decision in August 1921 to ban the eight White Sox World Series fixers for life. Not only did he punish acknowledged game-fixers and bribe-takers

Federal judge Kenesaw Mountain Landis was hired as baseball's first commissioner in November 1920, two months after the Black Sox Scandal became widely known (Bain Collection, Library of Congress, Prints and Photographs Division)

like Eddie Cicotte and Joe Jackson, but he also banished those with lesser degrees of guilt like Buck Weaver, who had only been accused of sitting in on meetings with gamblers. While the fairness of Landis's decision has been debated for nearly a century afterward, there can be no doubting its effectiveness. As Landis biographer David Pietrusza has written, banning the Eight Men Out "had a great chilling effect on dishonest play—and *talk* of dishonest play.... Once prospectively crooked players knew that honest players would no longer shield them, the scandals stopped." The commissioner's decision cleaned up the game for good, which the National Commission had never been able to do.

The scandal also put an end to Charles Comiskey's hopes for another championship. The White Sox were just a half-game behind the first-place Cleveland Indians on September 28, 1920—the day the Black Sox players were suspended after Cicotte, Jackson, and Williams testified before the grand jury. With a depleted lineup for the season-ending series against the St. Louis Browns, the White Sox finished two games back with a 96-58 record.

From 1916 to 1920, Chicago had won two AL pennants and barely missed two more in five seasons. And with just three of the White Sox' starting position players over the age of 30 in 1920—not to mention four 20-game winners on the pitching staff in Cicotte, Williams, Red Faber, and Dickey Kerr, a first in baseball history—they were poised to contend for many years to come. Chicago might have provided strong competition for the New York Yankees' emerging dynasty in the early 1920s. Even after the scandal broke up his team, Comiskey continued paying top dollar for new talent, bringing in the likes of infielders Luke Appling and Willie Kamm, outfielders Johnny Mostil and Bibb Falk, and pitcher Ted Lyons. Appling and Lyons were later inducted into the Baseball Hall of Fame, but they played almost their entire careers with the White Sox on second-division teams.

The scandal ended any chance of the White Sox establishing their own dynasty, and four decades passed before fans saw another World Series game on the South Side. That took place in 1959—one year after the Comiskey family heirs sold the team to an ownership group led by Bill Veeck. The team set another attendance record that year, drawing 1.4 million fans to Comiskey Park, once known as the "Baseball Palace of the World." The venerable ballpark was replaced in 1991 by a $167 million facility also named Comiskey Park at 35th Street and Shields Avenue. In 2005 that stadium, since renamed U.S. Cellular Field, finally celebrated the franchise's first World Series championship since the Black Sox Scandal.

SOURCES

Carney, Gene. *Burying the Black Sox: How Baseball's Cover-Up of the 1919 World Series Fix Almost Succeeded.* (Washington, D.C.: Potomac Books, 2006).

Carney, Gene. "Comiskey's Detectives," *Baseball Research Journal,* Volume 38, Issue 2 (Cleveland, Ohio: Society for American Baseball Research, Fall 2009).

Felber, Bill. *Under Pallor, Under Shadow: The 1920 American League Pennant Race That Rattled and Rebuilt Baseball* (Lincoln, Nebraska: University of Nebraska Press, 2011).

Fullerton, Hugh. "Fullerton Says Series Should Be Called Off," *Atlanta Constitution,* October 10, 1919.

Fullerton, Hugh. "I Recall." *The Sporting News,* October 17, 1935.

Klein, Frank O. "Catcher Ray Schalk in Huge White Sox Exposé." *Collyer's Eye,* December 13, 1919.

Klein, Frank O. "Discover 'Pay Off' Joint in White Sox Scandal?" *Collyer's Eye,* November 15, 1919.

Pietrusza, David. *Judge and Jury: The Life and Times of Judge Kenesaw Mountain Landis* (South Bend, Indiana: Diamond Communications, 1998).

Seymour, Harold, and Dorothy Z. Seymour. *Baseball: The Golden Age* (New York: Oxford University Press, 1971).

Spink, J.G. Taylor. "Concerning Bets and Bettors." *The Sporting News,* October 9, 1919.

"When Baseball Gets Before The Grand Jury." *The Sporting News,* October 7, 1920.

CONTRIBUTORS

Bruce Allardice is a Professor at South Suburban College, teaching Political Science and History. He has authored or co-authored six books and numerous articles on the American Civil War. His article on "The Spread of Baseball in the South Prior to 1870" received the McFarland-SABR Baseball Research Award in 2013.

Russell Arent is a freelance writer based in Maine who has been actively looking for Black Sox Scandal jigsaw pieces since picking up a copy of Gene Carney's book a few years ago. He was raised as a Twins fan, but has since learned to appreciate other team histories such as the Red Sox and White Sox.

Steve Cardullo is a retired civil servant and a lifelong New York Yankees fan. He lives in Northern California with his wife, Robin, and family.

Brian Cooper is the executive editor of the *Telegraph Herald* in Dubuque, Iowa. He is the author of full biographies of Red Faber (2007), Ray Schalk (2009) and college football star Jay Berwanger, winner of the first Heisman Trophy (2013).

James E. Elfers is a lifelong Phillies fan who has seen more than his share of bad baseball. He is a Library Analyst at the University of Delaware, his place of employment for the last 28 years. The author of *The Tour To End All Tours: The Story of Major League Baseball's 1913-1914 World Tour*, winner of the 2004 Larry Ritter Book Award from SABR's Deadball Era Research Committee, he is currently at work on various writing projects.

David Fleitz is a writer, baseball historian, and computer systems analyst from Pleasant Ridge, Michigan. Since 2001, he has written eight books on baseball history, including biographies of Shoeless Joe Jackson, Louis Sockalexis (the first Native American major league player), and 19th-century star Cap Anson. His latest work, *Napoleon Lajoie: King of Ballplayers*, was published by McFarland in 2013.

Dr. David Fletcher is founder and president of the Chicago Baseball Museum. A native Chicagoan, David is an occupational medicine specialist and co-founder of SafeWorks Illinois, a private medical practice which he operates in downstate Illinois. In 2005, he was the recipient of the Hilda Award from the Baseball Reliquary, honoring baseball fans and their importance to the game.

Daniel Ginsburg was the youngest founding member of SABR, joining the organization at the age of 15 in 1971. His expertise was in 19th-century baseball and baseball's gambling scandals, which culminated in the publication of his 1995 book *The Fix is In*. He died in 2009.

Irv Goldfarb has been a member of SABR since 1999. He first met the great Gene Carney at the 2004 SABR convention and a few years later was proudly invited to be a charter member of the Black Sox Scandal Research Committee, a group which has grown exponentially since its inception. Irv has contributed to numerous SABR publications and newsletters, and lives in Union City, New Jersey, with his wife, Mercedes, and cat, Consuelo. They are all lifelong Met fans.

John Heeg has been a social studies teacher for 14 years in Long Island, New York.

Rick Huhn is the author of full-length biographies of Hall of Famers Eddie Collins and George Sisler. His most recent book, *The Chalmers Race* (University of Nebraska Press, 2014), analyzes the controversial 1910 batting race. He is a founding member and co-coordinator of the Hank Gowdy Columbus (Ohio) Chapter of SABR.

William F. Lamb spent more than 30 years as a state/county prosecutor in New Jersey. In retirement, he lives in Meredith, New Hampshire, and serves as the editor of "The Inside Game," the quarterly newsletter of SABR's Deadball Era Research Committee. He has contributed more than 50 bios to the SABR BioProject.

Len Levin has been a SABR member since 1977. A retired newspaper editor in Providence, Rhode Island, he is the grammarian for the Rhode Island Supreme Court, editing the justice's written decisions. He is also the copy editor for many of the books produced by SABR members.

Dan Lindner, a SABR member since 1985, has contributed to numerous SABR publications, including the *Baseball Research Journal*, *The National Pastime*, *Nineteenth Century Stars*, and *Baseball's First Stars*. He also is a member of the Nineteenth Century and Negro Leagues committees.

Adrian Marcewicz is a Philadelphia native, born eight days before Chico Ruiz initiated one of the greatest collapses in sports history: the fall of the 1964 Phillies. He is a graduate of the since-closed Cardinal Dougherty High School (at one time the largest Catholic high school in the world) and earned a B.A. degree in English Literature from Bloomsburg University. He now lives in Warrington, Pennsylvania, with his wife, four cats, and the terminal cynicism only a born-and-bred Philadelphia fan could possibly understand.

Brian McKenna was born, raised, and lives in Baltimore County, not too far from the old Memorial Stadium. He has authored two books on baseball history, Early Exits: The Premature Endings of Baseball Careers and *Clark Griffith: Baseball's Statesman,* and contributed more than 50 articles for SABR publications and the Baseball Biography Project.

Steven G. McPherson grew up playing ball on the ballparks in and around San Francisco's South Peninsula where at age 15, during the late 1950s, he blossomed as a player-manager in John Noce's Belmont Bush League. A retired private insurance investigator, he now lives on the outskirts of Sherrill, New York. He has written two previous biographies for the SABR BioProject.

Paul Mittermeyer of East Rochester, New York, is at the cusp of formal retirement, anticipating bi-coastal life with his amazing spouse. He plans to enjoy reading, writing, philosophy, history, politics, art, horticulture, fermentation, distillation, travel, dining, volunteering, swimming, walking, entertaining, golfing, bridge, scrabble, and all the individual and joint interests for which there never seems to be enough time, enough days.

Jack Morris is a corporate librarian for a pharmaceutical company. He lives in East Coventry, Pennsylvania, with his wife and two daughters. His baseball biographies have appeared in six books, including *The Team That Forever Changed Baseball* and *America: The 1947 Brooklyn Dodgers* and *Bridging Two Dynasties: The 1947 New York Yankees*. He is not the Jack Morris of World Series fame but every once in a while wishes he was.

Peter Morris is the author of eight books, including *A Game of Inches* and *Baseball Fever*.

Rod Nelson is the former Research Services Manager for SABR and Managing Editor of *The Emerald Guide to Baseball*. He helped facilitate the 1919 Black Sox online discussion forum which led to the formation of the 1919 Black Sox Scandal Research Committee. As chairman of the SABR Scouts Committee, he developed the Who-Signed-Whom database and Historical Scouts Register which empower the Diamond Mines exhibit at the Baseball Hall of Fame in Cooperstown, New York.

James R. Nitz is a middle school business education teacher and high school softball coach in the Milwaukee suburb of Menomonee Falls. He is a Milwaukee native and Marquette University graduate who has researched and written other Milwaukee baseball topics including Ken Keltner, the 1944 AAGPBL Milwaukee Chicks (team and individual players), and Borchert Field. He is married to Wendee and they have two grown children, Jeff and Beth, both of whom were ballplayers in their high school and college days.

Bill Nowlin has been Vice President of SABR since 2004. He's written or edited nearly 50 books, mostly on baseball. A co-founder of Rounder Records and a former university professor, he enjoys travel in his spare time, adding Mongolia and Tajikistan in the last year of this book's gestation.

Jacob Pomrenke is SABR's Web Content Editor/ Producer. He has been a SABR member since 1998 and is the chairman and newsletter editor for the Black Sox Scandal Research Committee. He moderated panel discussions on Shoeless Joe Jackson at the 2010 SABR Convention and commemorating the 50th anniversary of *Eight Men Out* at the 2013 SABR Convention. Previously, he spent 10 years working as a reporter, page designer, and editor at the *North County Times* and *San Bernardino Sun* newspapers in California, and *The Times* in Gainesville, Georgia. He lives in Scottsdale, Arizona, with his wife, Tracy Greer, and their cats, Nixey Callahan and Bones Ely.

Kelly Boyer Sagert is a professional writer and editor with 25 years of experience. She is a member of the invitation-only American Society of Journalists and Authors and the Society of Professional Journalists, and she has traditionally published a dozen books (including *Joe Jackson: A Biography*) plus thousands of shorter pieces. Commissioned to write three full-length plays, one is being turned into a PBS documentary where Sagert will receive writing credits, and she appeared on an ESPN documentary titled *The Top Five Reasons You Can't Blame the Black Sox*.

Jim Sandoval devoted many years to chronicling the lives of baseball's unsung heroes: the scouts. His crowning achievement was the comprehensive book *Can He Play? A Look At Baseball Scouts And Their Profession*, published by SABR in 2011. He was the longtime co-chair of SABR's Scouts Committee, a regular presence at SABR conventions and regional meetings, and an expert on the 1919 Cincinnati Reds. He died in 2012.

Richard A. Smiley authored the biographies of Reb Russell and Matty McIntyre which appeared in SABR's *Deadball Stars of the American League* (Potomac Books, 2006). He also wrote the article "I'm a Faster Man Than You Are, Heinie Zim," which appeared in SABR's *The National Pastime*, Number 26 (2006) and

contributed the chapter "Diamond in the Rough: The Transformation of a Forgotten Area into a Home for Baseball" to the 2014 McFarland publication *Old Comiskey Park: Memories of the Historic Home of the Chicago White Sox, 1910–1991*.

Lyle Spatz has been a SABR member since 1973 and chairman of the Baseball Records Committee since 1991. He is the author and editor of numerous books on baseball history and the editor of two baseball record books. Two of his books, *Willie Keeler: From the Playgrounds of Brooklyn to the Hall of Fame*, and *The Colonel and Hug: The Partnership that Transformed the New York Yankees* (written with co-author Steve Steinberg) were published in the spring of 2015. His book, *1921: The Yankees, the Giants, and The Battle for Baseball Supremacy in New York*, also written with Steve Steinberg, won the Seymour Medal for the best book of baseball history or biography published in 2010. Lyle lives in Florida with his wife, Marilyn.

Steve Steinberg has collaborated with Lyle Spatz on *The Colonel and Hug: The Partnership that Transformed the Yankees*, about owner Jacob Ruppert and manager Miller Huggins, published by the University of Nebraska Press in the spring of 2015. Their earlier book, *1921: The Yankees, the Giants, and the Battle for Baseball Supremacy in New York*, was awarded the 2011 Seymour Medal. Steve is also co-editing a book on the Deadball Era World Series with Tom Simon. He has written *Baseball in St. Louis, 1900-1925*, and many articles revolving around early 20th-century baseball, including a dozen for SABR publications and a number of BioProject biographies.

Brian Stevens resides with his wife, Catherine, and their canine companions in Jericho, Vermont. He is a CPA, a 25-year Smugglers' Notch Resort employee, and as a consequence of perpetual residential remodeling projects, is well recognized in area hardware stores. His goal of visiting all major league ballparks joyfully continues.

Andy Sturgill has been fascinated by the Black Sox Scandal since first seeing the movie version of *Eight Men Out* as a child. A lifelong Phillies fan, he lives in suburban Philadelphia with his wife, Carrie. A college administrator by day, he enjoys reading and visiting ballparks in his free time.

Gregory H. Wolf, a lifelong Pirates fan, was born in Pittsburgh, but now resides in the Chicagoland area with his wife, Margaret, and daughter, Gabriela. A Professor of German and holder of the Dennis and Jean Bauman endowed chair of the Humanities at North Central College in Naperville, Illinois, he recently served as editor of the SABR books, *That's Joy in Braveland: The 1957 Milwaukee Braves* (2014) and *Winning on the North Side: The 1929 Chicago Cubs* (2015).

Join SABR today!

If you're interested in baseball — writing about it, reading about it, talking about it — there's a place for you in the Society for American Baseball Research.

ABR was formed in 1971 in Cooperstown, New York, with the mission of fostering the research and dissemination of the history and ecord of the game. Our members include everyone from academics to professional sportswriters to amateur historians and statisticians to students and casual fans who merely enjoy reading about baseball history and occasionally gathering with other members to talk baseball.

SABR members have a variety of interests, and this is reflected in the diversity of its research committees. There are more than two dozen groups devoted to the study of a specific area related to the game — from Baseball and the Arts to Statistical Analysis to the Deadball Era to Women in Baseball. In addition, many SABR members meet formally and informally in regional chapters throughout the year and hundreds come together for the annual national convention, the organization's premier event. These meetings often include panel discussions with former major league players and research presentations by members. Most of all, SABR members love talking baseball with like-minded friends. What unites them all is an interest in the game and joy in learning more about it.

Why join SABR? Here are some benefits of membership:

- Two issues (spring and fall) of the *Baseball Research Journal*, which includes articles on history, biography, statistics, ersonalities, book reviews, and other aspects of the game.
- One expanded e-book edition of *The National Pastime*, which focuses on baseball in the region where that year's SABR national convention is held (in 2015, it's Chicago)
- ✦ 8-10 new and classic e-books published each year by the SABR Digital Library, which are all free for members to download
- ✦ *This Week in SABR* newsletter in your e-mail every Friday, which highlights SABR members' research and latest news
- ✦ Regional chapter meetings, which can include guest speakers, presentations and trips to ballgames
- ✦ Online access to back issues of *The Sporting News* and other periodicals through Paper of Record
- ✦ Access to SABR's lending library and other research resources
- ✦ Online member directory to connect you with an international network of SABR baseball experts and fans
- Discounts on registration for our annual events, including SABR Analytics Conference & Jerry Malloy Negro League Conference
- Access to SABR-L, an e-mail discussion list of baseball questions & answers that many feel is worth the cost of membership itself
- The opportunity to be part of a passionate international community of baseball fans

R membership is on a "rolling" calendar system; that means your membership lasts 365 days no matter when you sign up! all the benefits of SABR membership by signing up today at SABR.org/join or by clipping out the form below and mailing it to R, Cronkite School at ASU, 555 N. Central Ave. #416, Phoenix, AZ 85004.

SABR MEMBERSHIP FORM

	Annual	3-year	Senior	3-yr Sr.	Under 30
	❑ $65	❑ $175	❑ $45	❑ $129	❑ $45
da/Mexico:	❑ $75	❑ $205	❑ $55	❑ $159	❑ $55
seas:	❑ $84	❑ $232	❑ $64	❑ $186	❑ $55

a Family Member: $15 for each family member at same address (list on back)
nior: 65 or older before 12/31/2015
ll dues amounts in U.S. dollars or equivalent

Participate in Our Donor Program!
I'd like to desginate my gift to be used toward:
❑General Fund ❑Endowment Fund ❑Research Resources ❑_____
❑ I want to maximize the impact of my gift; do not send any donor premiums
❑ I would like this gift to remain anonymous.
Note: Any donation not designated will be placed in the General Fund.
SABR is a 501 (c) (3) not-for-profit organization & donations are tax-deductible to the extent allowed by law.

me _____

dress _____

y _____ ST_____ ZIP_____

ne _____ Birthday _____

nail: _____
ur e-mail address on file ensures you will receive the most recent SABR news.)

Dues $_____

Donation $_____

Amount Enclosed $_____

Do you work for a matching grant corporation? Call (602) 496-1460 for details.

If you wish to pay by credit card, please contact the SABR office at (602) 496-1460 or visit the SABR Store online at SABR.org/join. We accept Visa, Mastercard & Discover.

Do you wish to receive the *Baseball Research Journal* electronically?: ❑ Yes   ❑ No
Our e-books are available in PDF, Kindle, or EPUB (iBooks, iPad, Nook) formats.

Mail to: SABR, Cronkite School at ASU, 555 N. Central Ave. #416, Phoenix, AZ 85004

04/15

Made in the USA
Charleston, SC
21 October 2016